DREAMWEAVER® MX: DESIGN AND TECHNIQUE™
ETHAN WATRALL
ISBN: 0-7821-4100-5   496 pages   US $35.00

Dreamweaver MX: Design and Technique teaches you how to make your web pages look their best and perform even better. Whether you've already dabbled in Dreamweaver or want to get up to date, Ethan Watrall offers insights and step-by-step instructions designed to help you build and sharpen your skills. You'll get the most out of Macromedia's dramatically expanded software, including tips on: creating your web page; working with basic layout and design; inserting and manipulating multimedia; saving time with templates; integrating interactive Dynamic HTML; creating basic database-driven sites; and collecting user data with forms.

MASTERING™ HTML AND XHTML
DEBORAH S. RAY AND ERIC J. RAY
ISBN: 0-7821-4141-2   1,136 pages   US $49.99

This book is for the millions of businesses and individuals that need to create or modify web and intranet pages. It's the most complete, up-to-date book on the core language of the Web. You'll learn everything you need to know about coding web pages in both HTML and XHTML, the latest, more powerful version of HTML. But it doesn't stop there. You also get practical instruction in complementary web technologies such as JavaScript, CSS, and Dynamic HTML, along with a Masters Reference that makes it easy to find the information you need, including HTML and XHTML tags, style sheets, JavaScript, HTML special characters, and XHTML color codes. Tying it all together is the authors' expert guidance on planning, developing, and maintaining effective, accessible websites.

XHTML COMPLETE
SYBEX INC.
ISBN: 0-7821-2822-X   1,056 pages

D1545627

XHTML Complete is a one-of-a-kind book—valuable both for its broad content and its low price. The book contains all the essentials of XHTML 1.0, from formatting fundamentals to forms, frames, tables, imagemaps, and integrating Java, JavaScript, ActiveX, and multimedia. It provides in-depth coverage of the hottest topics, including cascading style sheets, optimizing your pages for the latest browsers, developing forms, DHTML, Perl and CGI, JavaScript and Jscript, as well as an introduction to XML. There's also an essential XHTML reference to all XHTML tags (including the browser-specific tags).

HTML COMPLETE

HTML COMPLETE

THIRD EDITION

SYBEX®

SAN FRANCISCO ► LONDON

Associate Publisher: Dan Brodnitz

Acquisitions Editor: Mariann Barsolo

Compilation Editor: Lucinda Dykes

Development Editor: James A. Compton

Production Editor: Kylie Johnston

Technical Editor: Steve Potts

Copy Editor: Gene Redding

Book Designer: Maureen Forys, Happenstance Type-o-Rama

Compositor: Rozi Harris, Interactive Composition Corporation

Proofreaders: Emily Hsuan, Laurie O'Connell, Yariv Rabinovitch, Nancy Riddiough

Indexer: Nancy Guenther

Cover Designer: Design Site

Cover Illustrator/Designer: Design Site

Library of Congress Card Number: 2002116882

ISBN: 0-7821-4209-5

Acknowledgments

This book is the work of many, both inside and outside Sybex, including publishing team members Dan Brodnitz, Mariann Barsolo, and Jim Compton and the editorial/production team of Kylie Johnston, Gene Redding, Rozi Harris, Bill Clark, and Nancy Guenther.

Lucinda Dykes deserves particular thanks for making sure all of the material in this book was up to date and organized and flowed together in a cohesive manner. In verifying the accuracy of updated material, she was ably assisted by Steve Potts.

Finally, our thanks to those contributors who agreed to have their work excerpted into *HTML Complete*, Third Edition: Ethan Watrall; Deborah S. Ray and Eric J. Ray; E. Stephen Mack and Janan Scott Saylor; Molly E. Holzschlag; Chuck White, Liam Quinn, and Linda Burman; Martin C. Brown; and James Jaworski.

CONTENTS AT A GLANCE

CONTENTS

Appendix B ▫ Cascading Style Sheets Reference 863

General Information 864
Font Properties 872
Text Properties 879
Box Padding Properties 887
Box Border Properties 891
Box Margin Properties 898
Box Position Properties 901
Background and Color Properties 904
Positioning 910
Printed Media Style Sheets 915

Index *921*

INTRODUCTION

*H*TML Complete, Third Edition, is a one-of-a-kind computer book—valuable both for the breadth of its content and for its low price. This thousand-page compilation of information from some of Sybex's very best books provides comprehensive coverage of HTML and XHTML. This book, unique in the computer book world, was created with several goals in mind:

- ▶ To offer a thorough guide covering all the important features of HTML/XHTML at an affordable price.

- ▶ To acquaint you with some of our best authors, their writing styles and teaching skills, and the level of expertise they bring to their books—so that you can easily find a match for your interests and needs as you delve deeper into web design and development.

HTML Complete, Third Edition, is designed to provide you with all the essential information you'll need to get the most from the Hypertext Markup Language—the "universal language" for designing and developing web content. At the same time, the book will invite you to explore the even greater depths and wider coverage of material in the original books.

If you have read other computer "how to" books, you have seen that there are many possible approaches to using the technology effectively. The books from which this one was compiled represent a range of teaching approaches used by Sybex and Sybex authors. From the hands-on designer tips of *Dreamweaver MX: Design and Technique* to the hardcore coder's *XML Processing with Perl, Python, and PHP* style, you will be able to choose which approach and which level of expertise works best for you. You also will see what these books have in common: a commitment to clarity, accuracy, and practicality.

In these pages, you will find ample evidence of the high quality of Sybex's authors. Unlike publishers who produce "books by committee," Sybex authors are encouraged to write in their individual voices, voices that reflect their own experience with the software at hand and with the evolution of today's personal computers, so you know you are getting the benefit of their direct experience. Nearly every book represented here is the work of a single writer or a pair of close collaborators. Similarly, all of the chapters here are based on the individual experience of the authors, their first-hand testing of prerelease software, and their subsequent expertise with the final product.

In adapting the various source materials for inclusion in *HTML Complete*, Third Edition, the compilation editor preserved these individual voices and perspectives. Chapters were edited to minimize duplication, omit coverage of non-essential information, update technological issues, and cross-reference material so that you can easily follow a topic across chapters. Some sections may have been edited for length in order to include as much updated, relevant, and important information as possible.

Who Can Benefit from This Book?

HTML Complete, Third Edition, is designed to meet the needs of a wide range of web designers and web developers working with HTML and XHTML to produce web pages. It provides an extraordinarily rich environment, with some elements that everyone uses, as well as features that may be essential to some users but of no interest to others. Therefore, while you could read this book from beginning to end—from basic and advanced HTML and XHTML to Cascading Style Sheets, JavaScript, Dynamic HTML, and XML—all of you may not need to read every chapter. The contents and the index will guide you to the subjects you're looking for.

Beginners   Even if you have only a little familiarity with the World Wide Web and its basic terminology, this book will start you producing HTML and XHTML web pages. You'll find step-by-step instructions for all the operations involved in designing web pages, writing the HTML and XHTML code, and uploading your pages to a web server. You'll want to start at the very beginning of this book, Part I, which covers the basics.

Intermediate Users   Chances are you already know how to do routine tasks in HTML and have a head start when it comes to Cascading Style Sheets. You know your way around the web and web servers, use e-mail extensively, and have explored JavaScript. You also know that there always is more to learn about scripting, cross-browser design, and web standards, and you want to get up to speed on XHTML. Throughout this book, you'll find instructions for just about anything you want to do. Nearly every chapter has nuggets of knowledge from which you can benefit.

Power Users   Maybe you're a hardcore web multimedia fiend looking to take advantage of Flash and other streaming media; maybe you're the unofficial web standards guru of your web development group; maybe you're ready to explore XML. There's plenty for you here, too, particularly in the chapters from *Mastering HTML and XHTML* and from *XML Processing with Perl, Python, and PHP*.

This book is for people doing web design and web development in any environment. You may be a SOHO (small-office/home-office) user, working with a stand-alone computer or part of a large web development group. You'll find plenty of information about basic web design and page layout, HTML, XHTML, Cascading Style Sheets, and XML.

How This Book Is Organized

Here's a look at what *HTML Complete*, Third Edition, covers in each part:

Part I: Introducing HTML   In Part I, you're off to a running start—creating web pages and websites. The chapters in this section cover the basics of web design and provide an in-depth introduction to creating HTML and XHTML pages, publishing pages to a web server, and website planning and maintenance.

Part II: Planning and Designing Your Web Page   Planning a site is crucial to efficient and productive web design and development. In this section, you'll learn about layout technology, web graphics, tables, frames, and the essentials of web typography.

Part III: Advanced HTML   In this section, you'll take your skills in basic site design and development further as you learn to incorporate advanced features in your web pages such as Cascading Style Sheets, multimedia elements, and forms. You'll also learn about the latest versions of the Internet Explorer and Netscape Navigator browsers and how to optimize your web pages for a cross-browser environment.

Part IV: XML   This section includes further information on XHTML and introduces the fundamentals of XML, an important tool for modeling data in a structured way for portability between applications.

Part V: Appendices   The appendices—a comprehensive guide to HTML and XHTML elements and attributes, and a thorough Cascading Style Sheets reference—will prove invaluable as you venture further into site design and web development.

TIP

See the *HTML Complete* page on www.sybex.com for an extra chapter, "Introducing JavaScript and JScript," an extra appendix, "XHTML Basic Specification," and an expanded version of the "Cascading Style Sheets Reference" appendix.

A Few Typographic Conventions

Whenever you need to navigate through pages of a site, or an operation in a browser or development interface requires a series of choices from menus or dialog boxes, the ➤ symbol is used to guide you through the instructions, like this: "you'll find it under Web Development ➤ HTML and Dynamic HTML ➤ SDK Documentation ➤ Reference ➤ HTML Elements" or "choose File ➤ Save or File ➤ Save As." The items the ➤ symbol separates may be hyperlinks, menu names, toolbar icons, check boxes, or other elements of the interface—anyplace you can make a selection.

`This typeface` is used to identify Internet URLs and HTML code, and **boldface type** is used whenever you need to type something into a text box.

You'll find these types of special notes throughout the book:

TIP

You'll see a lot of these Tips—quicker and smarter ways to accomplish a task, which the authors have based on many hours spent testing and using HTML and its related tools.

NOTE

You'll see Notes, too. They usually represent alternate ways of accomplishing a task or some additional information that needs to be highlighted.

WARNING

In a few places, you'll see a Warning like this one. These alert you to possible pitfalls that can prevent your site or application from working the way you intend. When you see a Warning, pay attention to it.

YOU'LL ALSO SEE SIDEBAR BOXES LIKE THIS

These sections provide added explanations of special topics that are referred to in the surrounding discussions, but that you may want to explore separately in greater detail.

For More Information

See the Sybex website, www.sybex.com, to learn more about all the books that contributed to *HTML Complete*, Third Edition. On the site's Catalog page, you'll find links to any book you're interested in. Also, be sure to check out the Sybex site for late-breaking developments about HTML, XHTML, and web design.

We hope you enjoy this book and find it useful. Happy computing!

Part I
INTRODUCING HTML

Chapter 1

INTRODUCTION TO WEB DESIGN

Web designers and web developers today play many different roles, and need a tool kit with a wide variety of skills. Designing and creating a website includes both technical skills and design skills, as well as an overall knowledge of how the web and web technologies work. In this chapter, you will learn some fundamental principles of design and information architecture for the web and be introduced to the history of the web and the development of HTML.

If you were to venture to your local bookstore, you would find that web design books are for the most part split into two separate sections: tools/technology and design. Why is this? Aren't design issues important to those learning web design tools? Absolutely! Unfortunately, most tool-specific books on web design are just that: tool-specific. Readers buy them to learn about a specific program. Many people have difficulty seeing that

Adapted from *Dreamweaver® MX Design and Technique™* by Ethan Watrall
ISBN 0-7821-4100-5 $35

the tool itself is just the beginning of web design. It's something you use to realize the creations that, if you've done your job right, have already been completed in your head and on paper.

This paper and brain production (sometimes referred to as *predigital production*) is the web design topic that appears in those *other* books in the *other* part of your local bookstore's computer section. What's the big deal about big picture web design issues anyway? It is that your website will sink or swim based on its *design* (a general term that covers many different issues that will be discussed in this chapter). As a result, even if you are focusing on a specific tool, it's a good idea to at least have a primer in the basics of web design.

This chapter is an *introduction* to the big picture of web design issues; there is no way that I could cover everything you need to know in one chapter. However, this chapter, which is part web history lesson and part web design starter, should give you a basic introduction to web design, along with an idea of what you might want to explore further on your own. At the very least, it will introduce you to some of the most important design issues, so that you don't inadvertently make a major blunder when you are building your HTML creation.

How the Web Works

As early as the 1940s, computers were seen to be instruments to manage and distribute huge amounts of information. Douglas Engelbart, upon reading Vannevar Bush's famous 1945 *Atlantic Monthly* article "As We May Think," noted that "If these machines [could] show you information on printouts, they could show you that information on a screen." Further, he saw a link between the TV-like interface and the information processor as a medium for representing symbols. An individual could steer through different information spaces, viewing data and graphics in different ways. Most importantly, however, was the fact that Engelbart saw the expansion of the medium into a theater-like environment in which one could sit with colleagues and exchange information simultaneously on many levels. The realization of these ideas, however, did not come to fruition for some 44 years.

Why should a humble web designer or web developer care about the roots of the web? In order to better understand the medium in which you'll be working, it's helpful to have at least a cursory idea as to how it all came about. After all, most traditional artists (whether they are painters, printmakers, or sculptors) benefit from a solid understanding of the particular form in which they are working.

This section of the chapter will start off with a brief exploration of how the web got started. From there, we'll move on to how Hypertext Markup Language (HTML), the lifeblood of the web, works. Finally, we'll finish off this section with a brief look at the web as it exists today.

Not So Humble Beginnings

Originally developed as an initiative of the Defense Agency Research Projects Administration (DARPA) in partnership with several prestigious universities and research institutions, the Internet, which at that time was called ARPAnet, was a prototype communication system designed to withstand the inevitable electromagnetic pulse generated by a thermonuclear attack. It wasn't long before ARPAnet spawned a sister network for the research community, supported and funded by the National Science Foundation (NSF). Called the NSFnet, the network soon found its way into most universities around the world.

For all of its technological wonder, however, NSFnet was little more than an obscure scientific endeavor. NSFnet, which ultimately became known as the Internet, required adeptness at cryptic computer programs and obscure protocols. Even if one mastered the necessary skills to take advantage of the Internet, where to go and what to do was pretty puzzling, and it wasn't useful for much other than e-mailing.

At its height, NSFnet was a massive library of some of the most advanced information on the planet. The problem rested on the fact that it was extremely difficult to identify and locate a given source of information. It was akin to walking down each isle of an enormous library in the dark and scanning each book to figure out what was available. Once you found something relevant to your needs, you had to "read" (that is, download) the entire book rather than browse just the parts that were of interest to you. Worse still, once found, a piece of information often referred to another valuable source without providing the means to locate it.

In 1989, tired of the perpetual hunt and peck of the Internet, a researcher named Tim Berners-Lee at the CERN atomic research center in Switzerland proposed software and protocols that would enable computers to browse the information contained on the NSFnet. This one event irrevocably changed the nature of how this global computer network was used.

NOTE

CERN stands for Conseil Européen pour la Recherche Nucleaire.

Berners-Lee's software (dubbed a *browser*) and protocols created the ability to browse information easily and navigate not only different documents on the same computer, but documents on other computers. Key to the technology was the concept of *hyperlinks*, which were highlighted words or symbols the user could click and be transported to the next "page" in the sequence. Berners-Lee's Hypertext Markup Language (HTML) made hyperlinks possible.

Within months of the release of the early version of the web browser developed by Berners-Lee, web software spread throughout the research community like wildfire. By July 1993, more than 130 servers were web enabled.

Shortly thereafter, a small group of students at the University of Illinois, among them Marc Andreessen (who later founded Netscape), took it upon themselves to rectify many of the shortcomings of the very primitive prototype web browser available to the public. Most significant among their accomplishments was the addition of a graphical user interface (GUI) to what had been mostly text-based software and the adaptation of the browser, enabling it to function on the Windows operating system. Following this, there was an incredible jump in the number of websites—a phenomenon that can be directly correlated with the release of the first version of the University of Illinois NCSA (National Center for Supercomputing Applications) Mosaic web browser (see Figure 1.1).

The rest, as they say, is history. NCSA Mosaic changed everything. Not only did the web become graphical, but it became accessible way beyond the academic community. Not long after Mosaic's introduction, Andreessen, along with five others, left the University of Illinois to found the Mosaic Communications Corporation, which later became the Netscape Communications Corporation, one of the first truly commercial web software ventures. Before you could say "holy alleged antitrust, Batman," Microsoft got in on the action, and thus begun the browser wars. However, before we discuss these and other browser-related design issues, there is some additional ground that needs to be covered in this section.

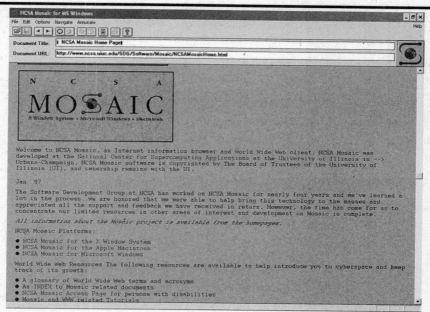

FIGURE 1.1:   Mosaic is crude by today's standards, but compared to what was available when it came out, it was an earth-shattering piece of software.

HTML: The Lifeblood of the Web

As mentioned earlier, Hypertext Markup Language (HTML) was one of the things that made the web possible. In reality, HTML is not a computer language such as C++ or Pascal; it is a system for describing documents. A plain text document is "marked up" using a series of commands called *tags* (see Figure 1.2). A browser interprets the HTML document and displays it.

The fact that an HTML document is plain text is significant for a couple of reasons. First, because plain text can be interpreted by any platform (IBM, Macintosh, and UNIX), HTML is truly cross platform and universal. Second, because HTML is plain text, it can be written using the simplest of programs (such as Windows' Notepad or Mac's SimpleText).

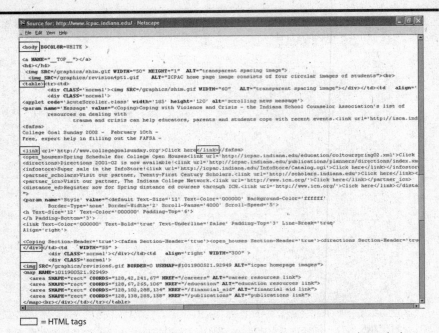

☐ = HTML tags

FIGURE 1.2:   A web page is composed of content given structure through the use of HTML tags.

The first incarnation of HTML (version 1) allowed very basic page layout, including font size, hyperlinks, and embedding of graphics. It is important to remember that HTML 1 was the standard only insofar as the first popular browser, Mosaic, was designed to interpret it. It wasn't until more browsers appeared on the market that a standard version of HTML was defined. As various versions of HTML were proposed and adopted by the World Wide Web Consortium (W3C, an organization that develops web standards), the language became more powerful. The inclusion of new layout features, such as frames and tables, allowed greater options for the development of web pages. In addition, image maps and new graphics formats increased the integration of images and basic interactivity.

The most recent version of HTML (version 4.01), which has been dubbed Dynamic HTML (DHTML), has some very exciting features that give web designers a lot more freedom than they previously experienced. Although each successive version of HTML offered unparalleled opportunities for publishing hypertext documents, the medium was not as malleable as many would have liked. HTML documents were far more difficult to lay out than traditional print documents. In HTML, text could be arranged only in a limited number of ways, making it hard to create a compelling visual experience. In addition, the way HTML treated graphics made it difficult to lay out a document. Finally, the interactivity in HTML documents was limited to the actual hypertext. It was not until the release of Dynamic HTML that many of these problems were solved.

Strictly speaking, Dynamic HTML is really just the most recent version of HTML. The difference, which is relatively substantial, comes from two primary new features: Cascading Style Sheets (CSS) and the capability to integrate scripting languages more efficiently with HTML.

NOTE

If you are particularly interested in learning how to create Dynamic HTML, see Chapter 18, "Bringing Pages to Life with DHTML and XHTML."

CSS lets the designer precisely define fonts, margins, line spacing, and other elements of an HTML document. Unlike HTML, in which fonts could be defined in only four sizes, DHTML allows type to be defined in point size. In addition, CSS allows designers to specify *x* and *y* coordinates to achieve exact positioning of elements within a document. Further, much like traditional print documents made with Adobe PageMaker or QuarkXPress, elements can be stacked one upon another by defining their position with *z* coordinates. Simply put, CSS gives designers the opportunity to lay out web pages with a greater degree of accuracy, enables much more control over how a document will appear in a browser, and provides for the stacking and composition of text and images.

NOTE

The word *element* has a specific meaning when we talk about markup languages such as HTML and XHTML. An element in HTML and XHTML is used to define a structure in a document, for example, p is an HTML/XHTML element that defines a paragraph structure. For more details on using elements in HTML and XHTML, see Chapters 2 and 3.

DHTML becomes even more powerful when you add in the greater integration of scripting languages. For some time now, designers have been using JavaScript to create simple effects and mouseover events. In most cases, however, the script controlling the event was just replacing one image with another, creating the effect of a dynamic change. With DHTML, JavaScript or Microsoft's VBScript can be used to achieve true dynamic control of page elements. For example, using conventional HTML and JavaScript, a designer can make a headline appear to change when the user runs his mouse over it. What really happens is that the script replaces the image of the headline with another image. With DHTML, the same effect can be accomplished using text and changing the font definition tag in runtime. This is extremely important because text is loaded far faster than images are. Figure 1.3 illustrates an HTML document in which JavaScript has been integrated.

JavaScript —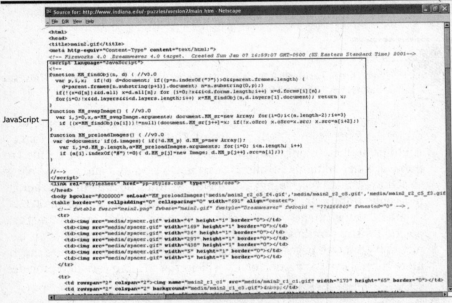

FIGURE 1.3: The integration of a scripting language such as JavaScript or VBScript lets designers add an incredible range of interactivity into the HTML document.

NOTE

Offered up by the W3C in January 2000, XHTML, a synthesis of HTML and XML, is the heir apparent to HTML. For more information on XHTML, go to www .oreillynet.com/pub/a/network/2000/04/28/feature/xhtml_rev.html.

Waiter, There's a Fly in My Soup

How does the web *work*? Without getting too crazy and technical, you can think of the web as a fancy restaurant.

Let's start off with a brief exploration, in very dry terms, of how the web works, and then we'll bring in the restaurant thing. It's important to know that the web works on what is called a client/server relationship. A client, the web browser in this case, is software that runs on a local computer that communicates with a server in another location. The other half of the equation is the server, which is a computer that performs tasks for other computers, such as sending out e-mail. When you type a URL into a browser (or click a hyperlink), two separate technologies (HTTP and TCP/IP) are used to send a request to a router. The router, which is a piece of hardware that sits between the user's computer and the web server, looks at the request and decides to which web server (there are hundreds of thousands, perhaps millions, in the world) it should be sent. The server examines it, decides (based on the URL itself) which document is being requested, locates and retrieves the document from somewhere within its directory structure, and sends it back along the route from which the request came. On the way back, the router makes sure the requested document is sent to the client that originally made the request. The last leg happens when the client (the web browser) receives the requested document and displays it for the user's reading (or viewing) pleasure. That's the basics of how the web works.

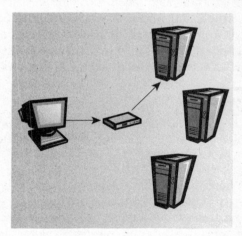

A little confused? Don't worry; even a description as stripped down as this can be a tad perplexing. This is where the restaurant analogy comes into the picture. Imagine if you were to walk into one of your favorite restaurants and were seated at your favorite table. You peruse the menu and decide upon a delectable soup to start your meal. You put down the menu and signal your waiter. When he comes to your table, you say,

"Good evening my good man, I would like to start off with a bowl of gazpacho, please." He nods his head, quickly moves to the kitchen and hands the order to the head chef, who gives the order to one of his newest chefs (it *is* only a bowl of soup). After a while, the soup is made. From there, it is handed back to the head chef, who hands it to the waiter, who takes it to your table, where you sit back and enjoy the beginning of a lovely meal.

Let's recap: You tell the waiter what you want to eat—that is, you type a URL into a browser. From there, the browser/waiter sends your request to the head waiter, who fulfills a task not unlike a router, making sure the request gets to the proper place. After your request/order has been passed on to the appropriate chef/server, it is fulfilled and handed back to the router/head chef, who then hands it back to the waiter/browser, who finally gives it to you for consumption. Make a little more sense?

BROWSER MADNESS

We left off in our history of the World Wide Web somewhere in 1994. Netscape Communications Corporation had just released the first version of Netscape, affectionately nicknamed Mozilla. Not long after that, wanting to get in on the action, Microsoft released Internet Explorer, which quickly became Netscape's primary competitor. In addition, around the same time, Sun Microsystems developed a browser called HotJava, and America Online (AOL) developed one called the AOL browser.

NOTE
There are a lot more browser alternatives out there than Netscape or Internet Explorer. For a full accounting, check out CNET's browser topic center at www.browsers.com.

It didn't take too long for things to get crazy—very crazy. The web was becoming the hottest thing since sliced bread, and everyone wanted their piece. In an attempt to establish total market domination, the two primary browsers (Netscape and Internet Explorer) adopted a policy under which new versions were released at very regular intervals. When a new version was released, it often had a spate of new features (such as the capability to display new HTML content). It seemed like a pretty good situation—new browsers, new features, better looking and more fully featured web pages. There was one slight hitch: For the most part, the new elements were unique and exclusive to the browser in which they were featured. As a result, there was tons of content floating out on the web that was accessible only with one browser or another. This constant attempt by Netscape and Microsoft to one-up each other is often referred to as the *browser wars* and was probably one of the most disastrous periods for web design.

Where does that leave us today? A couple of noteworthy things have happened. First, for all intents and purposes, Netscape lost (or, if you aren't keen on putting the last nail in the coffin just yet, is losing) the browser wars. While browser use statistics are extremely hard to generate (and are often somewhat misleading), it looks as if Internet Explorer (in its various versions and incarnations) commands between 78 percent and 93 percent of the market (perhaps even more, depending on the source of the statistics), and Netscape has about 4 percent to 12 percent. The remaining percentage points are the domain of a myriad of different browser alternatives that exist.

NOTE

For more information on browser use statistics, check out Browser News at www.upsdell.com/BrowserNews.

The second noteworthy thing is that the World Wide Web Consortium was founded. Established in 1994 by many of the individuals who "invented" the World Wide Web, the World Wide Web Consortium (W3C) was man-dated to develop standards that promote the web's evolution and ensure its interoperability.

In theory, the best way to prevent the sort of madness that resulted from competition between Netscape and Microsoft and to ensure that web pages will display consistently and legibly in *any* browser would be to develop standards to which everyone could stick. The primary problem is (and was at the time when the W3C started its undertaking) that no one owns the web. Instead, the web is made up of thousands of individual net-works and organizations, each of which is run and financed on its own. As a result, despite the fact that the W3C is a fairly powerful entity, it has no real way to enforce the web standards that it proposes. Ultimately, it's up to those companies that make the browsers to adopt the standards them-selves. The good thing is that, even before the browser wars were winding down, both Netscape and Microsoft were adopting many of the W3C proposed standards as baselines for their browsers. As a result, one could design with the most up-to-date W3C standard version of HTML and be relatively certain that it would work predictably on different browsers.

NOTE

The W3C is an interesting entity. Not only does it develop standards for HTML, but it also is constantly developing other cutting-edge technologies for the web in an effort to prevent any future browser wars. For more information about the W3C, go to www.w3c.org.

However, even today, you'll find that some features (especially those associated with Dynamic HTML (DHTML) display inconsistently from browser to browser.

Designing for Today's Web Browser (and Yesterday's, While You're at It)

What's the moral of this story? Despite the fact that Microsoft's Internet Explorer seems to be reigning supreme (at least for now), lots of people are using lots of different browsers and different versions of those browsers to surf the web. If you want to ensure that the maximum number of people can enjoy your website, you need to stick to the W3C's standards. It's important that you constantly and consistently test your HTML creation in all the browsers you foresee it being viewed with.

NOTE

For more information on features of the two major browsers, see Chapter 13, "Optimizing Your Pages for Internet Explorer," and Chapter 14, "Optimizing Your Pages for Netscape Navigator."

FUNDAMENTALS OF INTERACTIVE DESIGN

Strictly speaking, the issues you need to address when you're designing your website are relatively universal (at least when it comes to interactive design). Whether you are creating a CD-ROM, a DVD-ROM, a website, an interactive kiosk, or any information-driven application, you need to create something that fulfills the needs of your audience. From the designer's perspective, it would be great if everything created was intended solely for the consumption of the individual who created it—an audience of one, so to speak. However, that is far from the case. Even the most insignificant of interactive creations usually is intended for an audience other than just the designer. Because of this, you need to create something that is all things to all people. As such, there are some *extremely* important issues you should consider during the creative process. This section explores some of them.

It's important to remember that what is presented here is only an introduction to the fundamentals of interactive design. However, the discussion will provide you with the necessary foundations upon which to further your own exploration of the topic.

Information Design and Architecture

Information architecture has absolutely nothing to do with traditional architecture. In this section, you won't learn how to tell the difference between an Ionic and a Doric column. (This was a big disappointment to one of my Web Design students who thought she could indulge her passion for Renaissance architecture in my class!) Instead, you are going to get an introduction to the art and science of information design and architecture for the web.

Essentially, information architecture is the process by which a website's content is organized into easily accessible components that support a wide variety of user access techniques (casual browsing, direct searching, and so on). As you would expect, information architecture is intimately related to the navigational system of a site. As a result, you'd have a difficult time designing one without the other.

NOTE

This section of the chapter is designed to be a simple introduction to information architecture. Extra resources are a must. You might want to seek out Louis Rosenfeld and Peter Morville's *Information Architecture for the World Wide Web*, Second Edition (O'Reilly, 2002). If you are interested in extending your search to the web, check out the Argus Center for Information Architecture at www.argus-acia.com.

At its most basic, the process by which you develop a site's information architecture is usually a two-step affair. The first step involves organizing your site's information into a variety of categories. You'll need to decide how many sections, subsections, and categories you need, how your site's content will fit into those categories, and how the units of information (individual web pages) will relate to units of information within the same category and to units in other categories. This is arguably one of the most difficult things about designing a site. The way we human beings organize information is determined largely by our cultural context. As a result, what constitutes well-organized information is *extremely* subjective. You must contend with all manner of problems, such as linguistic ambiguity (a word or term may mean different things to different people) or different perspectives of how information should be organized.

As with many other issues in web design, the way you organize information will depend largely on your audience. You must put yourself in their shoes and predict the best way to develop an information architecture so that your users' needs are met. Developing a way to organize your content often can be a fairly painful process, but it is absolutely necessary in developing a functional and usable information architecture.

Once you've decided how to organize your information, you need to formalize that structure with something called an *information architecture diagram* (IA diagram). Designed to provide a visual representation of the information architecture of your site, an IA diagram can take many different forms (see Figure 1.4). Ultimately, the specific style is up to you.

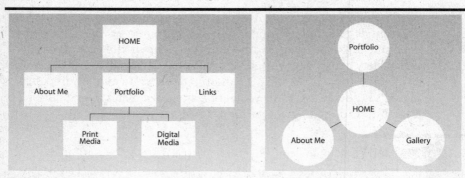

FIGURE 1.4:   There are many different ways to create an information architecture diagram. The example on the left is a reverse branching tree model; the example on the right is the spherical model.

An IA diagram isn't supposed to show the links between various pages within your site. Instead, it represents the hierarchical relationship between sections/subsections and individual pages.

NOTE
An IA diagram also is very useful for developing the structure of your site on the server (folders, subfolders, and so on).

Part I

Developing a Visual Metaphor

A visual metaphor is often a pretty slippery concept to put into words, but it can be easy to unconsciously interpret when it's used properly. Essentially, a visual metaphor, which is universally applied to an entire website, uses familiar visual elements such as images, interface elements, icons, colors, or fonts to reinforce the site's subject matter. The visual metaphor for a major Hollywood movie's promotional website will be completely different from that of an interactive design firm or an online merchant.

For example, in the screenshots depicted in Figure 1.5, the goal was to create a website for the Glenn A. Black Laboratory of Archaeology, a highly prestigious independent research unit at Indiana University, Bloomington, Indiana. Because of the archaeological theme, the website used an earthy palette of colors, consisting of shades of brown, gray, rust, dark green, and tan, combined with archaeologically oriented design elements to reinforce its content visually.

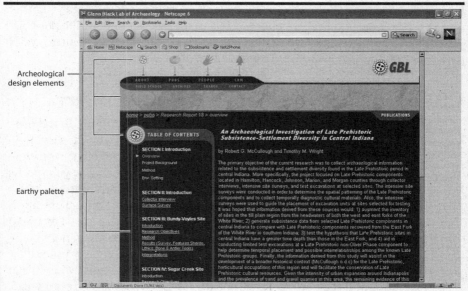

FIGURE 1.5:   The Glenn A. Black Laboratory of Archaeology's website employs earth tone colors and archaeologically oriented imagery to create a solid visual metaphor.

Creating an effective visual metaphor requires some serious brainstorming and inspired free association. You'll need to think about what kinds of colors, fonts, images, icons, and interface/layout elements unconsciously reinforce the site's content.

NOTE

Before you begin brainstorming for your visual metaphor, you need to be sure of your audience. You can't design an effective visual metaphor if you aren't exactly sure who'll be using the site.

For example, suppose you are creating a children's online community site geared towards ages seven to ten. You might think about using bold primary colors with cartoony interface elements and fonts. On the other hand, the website for a movie would draw its visual metaphor from the film's look and feel (check out the *Planet of the Apes* website at www.planetoftheapes.com for a great example).

There are no hard and fast rules for creating a visual metaphor. The only real guideline is that they should be used wisely: be subtle and don't overdo it. Always have your ideas checked by individuals not associated with the project; they often will have suggestions or comments you never thought of. Don't get too attached to a visual metaphor; it's quite possible that, given an outside opinion (perhaps one of a prospective user), you'll decide that it doesn't work for your site.

Creating Storyboards and Concept Art

One of the most important steps in the paper and brain predigital production process is creating storyboards or concept art, an idea swiped from the film industry. Generally one of the last steps before you go digital with your grand creation, storyboards are used to visualize your design as a complete entity. You get a chance, among other things, to see how colors interact with one another, how interface elements play off one another, how your navigational system is realized, how your visual metaphor plays out, and whether content is represented in the best way possible. Storyboards provide you with a painless way of catching any potential design problems before you get to the stage where you build your design in HTML and they become major obstacles. Storyboards also are a great way to play with design ideas and visually brainstorm.

As illustrated in Figure 1.6, there is no hard and fast rule as to how a storyboard should look. If you are brainstorming ideas, the back of a cocktail napkin is as good a medium as any. However, if you are preparing a pitch to a potential client, it's a good idea to come up with something more polished and formal. The bottom line is that storyboards, in whatever form they appear, should communicate your design ideas efficiently without too much ambiguity.

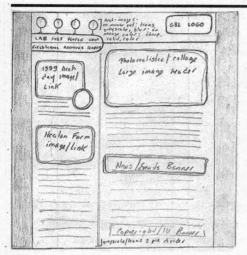

FIGURE 1.6: Storyboards can range from "quick and dirty" (left) to formal and polished (right). Whatever their level of quality, they should communicate your design ideas effectively.

You even may want to create your storyboards in a photocopy of an empty browser window. This is a great way to give your client the necessary context.

Getting from Here to There: Developing Intuitive Navigation

One could easily argue that designing an intuitive and usable system of navigation is one of—if not *the*—most important goals when it comes to web design. User experience on the web is all about moving in space from one location to another in search of *something*. Whether or not the user knows what he is looking for is moot. It's up to you to crawl inside the head of the user, figure out what he wants from your site, and then figure out the easiest way for him to get it. If you don't provide a system for your users to get from one point to another, they'll go elsewhere, and that is the last thing you want.

Don't be fooled into thinking that a navigation scheme is simply buttons and hyperlinks. The best-designed navigation is a highly artful mix of many different things: a pinch of interface design, a dash of information architecture, and a generous dollop of psychology.

As I've mentioned, there is no way that I could effectively condense all that you need to know about designing intuitive navigation into one section of one chapter of one book. However, there are certain general concepts that are both fundamentally important and self-contained enough that they can be discussed.

Keeping Things Consistent

One of the ways human beings define the world around them and how they interact with it is based on the consistency and predictability of events. When a navigational system works properly, people unconsciously come to rely upon it. For this to happen, the navigational system must be consistent. This means (as shown in Figure 1.7) that the menu must remain in the same location, it must retain the same appearance and contents, and the interface where the navigational elements reside must not change to any significant degree.

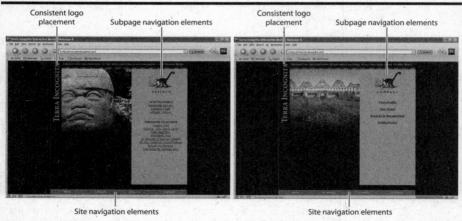

Consistent logo placement   Subpage navigation elements   Consistent logo placement   Subpage navigation elements

Site navigation elements   Site navigation elements

FIGURE 1.7:　These two screenshots are of two different pages within the same site. Note that the navigational elements remain exactly the same.

One of the obstacles to designing a consistent and predictable navigation system revolves around the interplay between navigational elements and interface design at deep levels within the website. Often, as you get deeper and deeper into a site, a certain point is reached at which the navigation scheme breaks down due to a lack of foresight. Designers tend to put most of their effort into developing a navigation scheme that will work best in the more consistently accessed areas of a site. As they move deeper and deeper into their site and the amount of information in any given screen increases, they spend less and less time ensuring that the navigation scheme they developed will function properly.

NOTE

The best-designed websites have a pyramid-shaped information distribution. The top levels of the site contain information that doesn't take up a great amount of screen real estate. As you move deeper into the site and into more specialized information, a larger amount of space is consumed by the website's content.

It's at this point that chaos often sets in, and the all important consistency and predictability go out the window. To cope with the additional information, designers will toss in additional navigational elements (menus, buttons, and so on) or even alter the existing navigational scheme that worked just fine in the upper levels of the site.

Instead of succumbing to bedlam and anarchy, make sure that when you create the navigational scheme, you think deep into your site's structure. It may seem time consuming, but it could save you valuable time later. Because your user will probably spend more time in the deeper sections of your site, ask yourself whether what you've designed will work just as well with the content in the upper sections of your site as with the content in the deeper sections of your site. If you can't answer with a resounding "yes," start again.

NOTE

Remember that the web is a nonlinear medium. Users don't always enter your site through the front door: they can just as easily enter through a side or back door into a section deep within your site's hierarchy. Because of this, you should make sure that your entire site maintains a consistent scheme of navigation.

Help Users Quickly Learn Your Navigation Scheme

When you create a website of any kind, you are providing something to your user. Whether it's a mega online bookstore like Amazon.com, a major educational institution like the University of Toronto, or your own personal corner of cyberspace, content is king. You don't want users to have to spend a huge amount of time learning how to find what they want. In other words, you don't want an overly complex navigational system to stand in the way.

The key to easily learned navigational systems lies in several different issues. First, as I just mentioned, your navigational system should be consistent. If you switch the way you require your users to move around the site, they'll have to start from scratch and relearn your navigational scheme—not good. Second, as will be covered shortly, make sure the way your user identifies navigational elements (labels, visual imagery, and so on) is straight to the point and not overly complex or confusing. There is nothing worse than a series of buttons whose labels make no sense. The general rule of thumb (and this is pretty general as rules go) is to create navigational schemes that are intuitive and thereby easy to learn.

Providing Clear and Obvious Visual Cues

Because the web is a visual medium, effective navigational schemes should provide clear visual messages. I'm not talking about just the buttons here. Integrating clear visual cues into a navigational scheme requires some very broad (and often subtle) thinking.

Color One of the best ways to provide your users with a quick and easy (and often unconscious) method of identifying exactly where they are located in your site is to use color. You may have noticed that many large sites use a consistent navigational system whose color changes slightly depending on the section or subsection where the user currently resides. This is a very effective technique that, when used properly, creates "signposts" for the user that are easily learned and recognized. When using color to increase the usability of your navigational system, you definitely have some options. Changing the background color of individual pages is one way, but you also can use color for subtle emphasis—highlighting certain navigational or interface elements such as buttons, banners, or header graphics.

However, there are some caveats to using color in this way. First, to avoid overwhelming the user with a new color for each subsection, pick a very limited palette and apply those colors to the top level sections of your site. For example, if you're designing your own personal website and you use a nice light rust color for the "About Me" section, you can avoid overwhelming the user by using the same color for the "My Favorite Movies," "My Family," and "My Favorite Music" sections, all of which are subsections of the "About Me" page. You also should choose a palette of colors that fits with your visual metaphor.

Branding   Consistent and clear branding also is a good way to provide your audience with visual cues. Given the nature of the web, people have a tendency to jump from site to site with mouse clicks. When your audience is cavorting around your site, you want them to know *exactly* where they are. This is best accomplished with clearly and consistently placed logos, as shown in Figure 1.8.

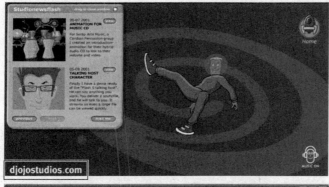

FIGURE 1.8:   Notice that in both websites, a logo is always prominently displayed to remind the audience exactly where they are.

Breadcrumb Trail   One of the biggest problems in particularly large, content-heavy websites is that people can easily get lost and end up with no clue where they are and no idea how to get back to where they were several clicks ago. One of the easiest and most elegant ways to work around this problem (and one of the most cost-effective in terms of effort and screen real estate consumed) is to create a simple navigational tool called a bread-crumb trail (Figure 1.9). Essentially, a breadcrumb trail (sometimes referred to as a link buildout) is a horizontal line of hyperlinked words indicating the location of the current page within the site's overall information architecture. An example of a breadcrumb trail is Home ≻ About Me ≻ Favorite Movies. Each item in the trail is a hyperlink to that specific section or subsection.

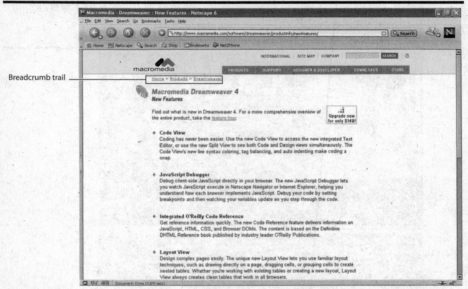

Breadcrumb trail

FIGURE 1.9:   A breadcrumb trail provides a clear indication of the position of the current page within the site's overall structure; it also provides an easy way of moving back up that particular section or subsection's hierarchy.

Labels   One of the most often overlooked methods to provide clear and concise visual cues to your audience is to use effective labels. For example, suppose a section of your site has images of all the photographs you've taken, all the paintings you've painted, and all the sculpture you've sculpted. Instead of having a link or a button that says "Everything I've ever created on film, with canvas, or with clay," you could simply use the word "Portfolio" or "Gallery."

TIP

It's important to remember that many of the conventional web labels used are culturally based. Although the average web user in North America wouldn't have any difficulty understanding your intentions, if you used the word "Home" in your navigational scheme, someone from Egypt, the Czech Republic, or Malaysia may have absolutely no clue to what you are referring.

When creating clear labels, you must avoid using what I call *geek speak*, or terminology familiar only to those individuals within a specific field. For example, as an archaeologist, I've created websites where the term "Gray Literature" is used. If you have no experience in the field of archaeology, you probably don't have a clue what gray literature is. However, there are individuals out there who, despite the fact that they aren't familiar with the strange terms we archaeologists use, would be interested in gray literature. (Gray literature refers to the excavation reports generated by federally mandated salvage archaeological excavations.) To avoid geek speak in this particular situation, I changed "Gray Literature" to "Excavation Reports," which is a lot more understandable to the general public.

Visual Vocabulary: Navigational Elements   Another good way to provide users with clear visual cues is by using consistent and universally understandable visual vocabulary. There are three general schools of thought when it comes to creating navigational elements (buttons, menus, and so on). The first one tends to emphasize the use of icons or imagery, while the second one emphasizes the use of purely text-based navigation. The third, which I think is the most rational, encourages the appropriate and contextually suitable use of both text and images as navigational elements.

If you've decided to use a purely visually based navigation system, you are in for some serious obstacles. Using icons or images in navigation is fine, but you must realize that the web itself has no real standardized conventions for visual vocabulary. For instance, if you've created a button on your main page that links to your "About Me" section, what icon do you use? The possibilities are literally endless. The problem pops up especially when you choose an icon that, although significant to you, means nothing to your audience. In this situation, your audience is faced with a series of unfamiliar (at least for them) icons with which they are expected to navigate your site. The only true universal solution for this problem is to create navigational elements that incorporate both text and images. If you include text that answers the user's "what the heck is this button for?" kinds of questions, you can use funky icons that fit into your visual metaphor.

Multiple Roads from Here to There

Lots of people do things in lots of different ways. People drive differently, have different tastes in movies and music, talk differently, eat differently, and most important to this discussion, use different methods to move about the web. Some like to wander aimlessly until they stumble across something interesting, and others want to locate specific information as quickly and efficiently as possible. Some people use the newest browser on a fast machine with a fast Internet connection; others have older browsers, slower machines, and slow Internet connections. Some people use text browsers or screen readers. Get the point? It's up to you to try to accommodate all of them so that you don't alienate possible visitors.

NOTE

A screen reader is software that "reads" the content of a website for those who are visually impaired or blind. For more information on web accessibility issues, see Chapter 6, "Planning for a Usable, Maintainable Website."

To ensure that your website is accessible to as wide an audience as possible, you have to create a navigational system that supports many different personal styles. For instance, provide a low bandwidth version for those whose Internet connection or computer is on the slower side. You also can employ a series of different tools, such as a search feature, a site map, and a traditional text and icon menu so that a user can choose how to move about your site.

Designing with Bandwidth in Mind

The way users connect to the Internet plays a major role in how websites should be designed. Remember that when you view a web page in your browser, you are downloading the HTML file, all the associated media (images, Flash movies, and so on), and all the associated style sheets and scripts onto the hard drive of your computer. As a result, the size of the file and the speed at which a web page downloads are directly proportional to the speed of the Internet connection the user is employing.

TIP

The current recommended figure for the total size of any individual web page is 30KB to 50KB. You can calculate the total file size for a web page and then estimate the download time for a user at a given connection speed. Add up the size of every file associated with a web page—this figure is in kilobytes. Multiply this figure by 8 to convert it to kilobits (modem speeds are measured in kilobits per second (Kbps)). Take your kilobits total and divide it by modem speed; the result is a "best guess" of how many seconds the page will require to download.

I'm sure you've heard your share of "bandwidth this" and "bandwidth that" in the media. What exactly is bandwidth, anyway? Essentially, it's a measure of the amount of data that can be sent across an Internet connection over a certain unit of time (per second, per minute, and so on).

NOTE

Most standard modems range from 14.4KBps to 56KBps, while high-speed connections (such as cable models, DSL, or T1 lines) range from 64KBps to 1500KBps (and even higher).

An Internet connection is the method by which you connect to the Internet itself and can range from a modem to a digital subscriber line (DSL). Each method has a different level of bandwidth, which can range from very low (downloads data from the web slowly) to very high (downloads from the web quickly). You can think of your Internet connection as a pipe through which the material you're downloading is shoved. A faster connection means a larger pipe, which means more stuff can be downloaded at a quicker rate. A slower connection, on the other hand, means a smaller pipe, which means things are downloaded at a far slower rate.

What does this mean to you as a designer? Like all other file types, HTML files consume a specific amount of computer memory. Granted, they are usually quite small because HTML files are plain text. However, when you start adding images and other multimedia (Flash and Shockwave movies, audio, or digital video, for example), a web page can get quite large. The larger a web page is, the longer it will take to download. As a result, particularly multimedia-rich websites often are time consuming to download for those users who don't have high speed connections. Would *you* want to hang around waiting to download a web page whose content is pretty much unknown? Probably not. That's why you should put a lot of thought into the size of the web pages you create.

NOTE

You might think that everyone has fast connections these days. Although the number of people connecting to the Internet with high-speed connections is growing by leaps and bounds, dial-up modems still reign supreme. Statistics show that in 2001, more than 17 million people in the United States were connected to the Internet with high-speed connections, while about 64 million were using 56K modems, 15 million were using either 28.8K or 33.6K modems, and about 3 million were using 14.4K modems. (These statistics are just for the United States. Statistics for Canada and Europe, which are more "wired" than the U.S., were not included. Also, don't forget the rest of the world!)

As a designer, you've got to make a decision about your audience. Do you want to include cool, bandwidth-consuming features such as Flash, Shockwave, or digital video and run the risk of alienating those people who have a slower connection? Do you want to curtail your multimedia leanings and design for the most common denominator (which, given the numbers, is probably a 56K modem)? Ultimately, it's all about balance: cool features for limited audience, or not-as-cool features for a wider audience.

If you plan to create a site that is more suitable for high-bandwidth connections, it is vital that you give your users some indication of this early on in their navigation of your site (usually on the top page). That way, those individuals with low-bandwidth connections don't unwittingly get stuck having to download a bandwidth-intensive site. One way to work around the problem of low-bandwidth users accessing a high-bandwidth site is to create two versions of your site: one for high bandwidth access and one for lower bandwidth access.

WHAT'S NEXT?

This chapter covered basic web design issues, and you learned the history of the web, browsers, and HTML. In the next chapter, you'll learn the basics of the HTML and XHTML languages and start developing the skills you need to create web pages.

Chapter 2

GETTING ACQUAINTED WITH HTML AND XHTML

In this chapter, we'll introduce you to HTML and XHTML, which, as you'll see, are markup languages you can use to develop documents for a variety of online uses. This chapter aims to help you build the vocabulary and basic understanding you'll need to *use* HTML and XHTML.

Adapted from *Mastering™ HTML and XHTML*,
by Deborah S. Ray and Eric J. Ray
ISBN 0-7821-4141-2 $49.99

Why Use HTML or XHTML?

HTML and XHTML are both markup languages. A *markup language* is a system of codes that identify parts and characteristics of documents published online. Before you say, "Yikes, that sounds techie," consider that you're probably already familiar with the most common application for HTML and XHTML—web pages. HTML and XHTML are not what you see on-screen as a web page; instead, they're the behind-the-scenes "code" that tells web browsers what to display.

Let's look at some possible uses for HTML and XHTML:

Developing Websites   Using HTML- or XHTML-developed web pages and sites, users can jump from topic to topic, view images, fill out forms, submit information, and search databases, among many other possibilities. These markup languages provide many of the capabilities and functionality you're accustomed to using when you visit websites.

Developing Intranet or Extranet Sites   HTML and XHTML are commonly used to develop intranet sites—websites accessed by people within a company or organization from one or more locations—or extranet sites, used by people from a specific group of companies or organizations that routinely share information among themselves.

Creating Help Files or Documentation   HTML and XHTML also can be used to develop online help files that are accessible on any platform. Online help files enable developers to produce documentation inexpensively.

Developing Network Applications   HTML and XHTML are used for developing applications, such as training programs or online classes, or for providing access to databases through web pages.

Developing Kiosk Applications   You also can use HTML and XHTML to help implement kiosk applications—those stand-alone computers with the neat touch-screen capabilities.

Delivering Information via Wireless Devices   HTML and XHTML can be used to display documents on a variety of wireless devices, including web-enabled phones, personal digital assistants, and handheld computers. It's expected that this will be an area of tremendous growth over the next few years.

WHAT'S THE DIFFERENCE BETWEEN HTML AND XHTML?

In general, you'll find that HTML and XHTML are very similar, and most web browsers handle both equally well. The main differences include the following:

XHTML Is Pickier About How You Type the Code (the Markup) into the Documents As you'll see later in this chapter, XHTML requires your documents and markup to follow very specific rules. For example, whereas HTML lets you use uppercase, lowercase, or a combination of the two when marking up your documents, XHTML requires that you use only lowercase letters. Similarly, although you can get away with using only an opening element in HTML—for instance, using just an opening paragraph element (<p>) to mark a paragraph—XHTML requires that you always use both opening and closing tags: <p>...</p>. These XHTML rules aren't hard to learn or follow, but you need to pay special attention as you develop XHTML documents and make sure all of the details are accurate and complete.

NOTE

If you're familiar with HTML, you're probably used to hearing the word *tag* to describe HTML markup. You might think of tags as being generally equivalent to "elements," with "tag" being the less formal term. Technically, the tag (or tag pair) refers to the elements and the surrounding <> and </> characters. Throughout this book, we'll generally use the term *element* to refer to both the more familiar "tag" and the more accurate "element," unless we particularly need to emphasize the components of a tag—as we will later in this chapter.

XHTML Can Provide More Capabilities and Flexibility Than HTML Does XHTML is based on a larger markup language called XML (Extensible Markup Language, which we'll cover in Chapter 20, "Introduction to XML," and Chapter 21, "Fundamentals of XML"), which provides developers with powerful capabilities and flexibility far beyond what HTML offers. For example, suppose you want to generate a table of contents for your website pages automatically. Because XHTML documents have more structure and are more predictable than HTML documents, you'll find that automatically extracting specific pieces of XHTML documents to generate the content is easier than extracting specific pieces of HTML. In general, XHTML gives you a bit more power and flexibility than you have with straight HTML, yet it doesn't have XML's steep learning curve.

XHTML Can Provide a Good Start if You or Your Company May Move to Using a More Structured Markup Language in the Future

Although XHTML doesn't have the depth of structure that XML or Standard Generalized Markup Language (SGML) offers, it does have basic document-level structure and regularity. Although transferring from using XHTML to one of those markup languages is a complex undertaking, XHTML will give you a far better start than HTML will.

Does this mean you should choose XHTML rather than HTML? The short answer is that there's no reason not to use XHTML. In fact, we encourage you (even if you're new to markup languages or new to developing documents for online uses) to use XHTML. It's not that much harder to learn and use than HTML, following the rules can provide you with some good planning and document-development skills, and it gives you future options and flexibility.

TIP

Web browsers handle HTML and XHTML equally well, and XHTML is not much more difficult to implement than HTML (and it's more flexible). Therefore, we recommend using XHTML in most cases.

The long answer is that you should first consider what your needs are. Are you developing a simple personal website? Documents for an intranet or extranet site where only HTML is being used? Documents that have to be developed as quickly as possible and will be discarded shortly thereafter? Documents that will need to be maintained by very untechnical folks? If so, then HTML might be the better choice for you.

However, if you are developing more than a minimal website, a site that will likely require some amount of maintenance or revision, or a site in which other parts are already using XHTML, then using XHTML is highly recommended. Similarly, if you're developing documents for online help, kiosks, or wireless devices, we'd highly recommend using XHTML simply because it's more flexible, forward looking, and compatible with XML (on which XHTML is based).

NOTE

Throughout this chapter, we'll be using primarily XHTML for examples of documents and code. Note that these examples will work equally well whether you're using HTML or XHTML.

WHERE DID HTML AND XHTML COME FROM?

HTML is based on a formal definition created using a powerful *meta-language* — a language used to create other languages — called the *Standard Generalized Markup Language* (SGML). SGML is an International Organization for Standardization (ISO) standard tool designed to create markup languages of many kinds.

The World Wide Web Consortium (W3C) has governed HTML and related markup language specifications since the early 1990s. Public release of HTML (and its companion protocol, the *Hypertext Transfer Protocol*, or HTTP, which is what browsers use to request web pages, and what web servers use to respond to such requests) launched the web revolution that has changed the face of computing and the Internet forever.

In the years since HTML became a public standard, HTML has been the focus of great interest, attention, and use. The original definition of HTML provided a way to identify and mark up *content* — specific information judged to be of sufficient importance to deliver online — without worrying too much about how that information looked or how it was presented and formatted on the user's computer display. As commercial interest in the Web exploded, graphic designers and typographers involved in web design found themselves wishing for the kind of presentation and layout controls that they received from software such as PageMaker and QuarkXPress. HTML was never designed as a full-fledged presentation tool, but it was being pulled strongly in that direction, often by browser vendors such as Microsoft and Netscape, who sought market share for their software by accommodating the desires of their audience.

Unfortunately, those browser-specific implementations resulted in variations in the HTML language definitions that weren't supported by all browsers and resulted in functionality that wasn't part of any official HTML language definition. Web designers found themselves in a pickle — forced either to build web pages for the lowest common denominator that all browsers could support or to build web pages that targeted specific browsers that not all users could necessarily view or appreciate.

XHTML was created as a means to address this discrepancy. XHTML provides a way to take advantage of a newer, more compact underlying meta-language called Extensible Markup Language (XML)

CONTINUED ➡

Part I

that is inherently extensible and, therefore, open ended. More importantly, XHTML helps rationalize and consolidate a web markup landscape that had become highly fragmented (a result of different and incompatible implementations of HTML). There are many other good reasons for using standard-compliant HTML or XHTML, and you'll learn more about them later in this chapter.

The HTML and XHTML specifications—all versions, revisions, and updates—are maintained by the W3C and can be found at www.w3.org. Taking a tour through the W3C web pages can be quite useful in terms of learning what issues are considered most pressing or least important to the people making the specifications. In addition, you can find out if your personal concerns are being addressed.

At the time this book was written, the primary issues being addressed by the HTML Working Group were final development of XHTML 2.0 (continuing in the direction of modularization of XHTML begun in XHTML 1.1) and use of XFrames, an XML application that replaces HTML and XHTML Frames. Both of these issues reflect the importance of moving HTML toward standards that are:

- ▶ Compatible with existing browsers and tools
- ▶ Flexible enough to accommodate non-traditional browsers, such as handheld computers and web-enabled cell phones
- ▶ Consistent and predictable enough to be readily parsed and processed by web servers and other programs to provide tailored content

That said, you do not need to worry about the future of HTML as you know it. No plans are under way to make any changes or improvements to HTML 4.01, and XHTML 1.0 is explicitly defined as being a "reformulation" of HTML 4.01 in XML; therefore, your investment of time and effort in learning HTML or XHTML won't be wasted. In our opinion, given the number of web pages out there, there's virtually no possibility that HTML 4.01 or XHTML will change substantially or cease to exist in the next several years—high-end websites and information delivery systems will evolve to take advantage of the new features that the W3C defines, but all the basics

CONTINUED ➡

Part I

(for example, everything in this book) will continue to work for the foreseeable future.

You'll find more history about markup languages in Chapter 20, which discusses XML in the context of how it fits into HTML and SGML.

NOTE

To view the current activities of the HTML Working Group, visit www.w3.org/MarkUp/Activity.

WHAT TOOLS DO YOU NEED?

Whether you're planning to develop HTML or XHTML documents, you'll need three basic tools:

- ▶ A plain-vanilla text editor, which you will use to create and save your documents. The "HTML and XHTML Editors" sidebar, later in this chapter, provides more information about some of the editors that are available; however, keep in mind that we highly recommend using a plain-text editor for developing HTML and XHTML documents—at least when you're learning to use those markup languages.

- ▶ A web browser, which you will use to view and test your documents. In fact, you should have multiple web browsers available so that you can see how your documents look when viewed in the different browsers.

- ▶ A validator, which you will use to verify that your HTML or XHTML documents are developed and coded correctly. We recommend using a validator if you're developing HTML documents; however, because browsers often can display HTML code that's a bit sloppy or not completely "standard," validating your HTML documents isn't an absolute must. If you're developing XHTML documents, however, you *must* use a validator as part of your document-development and publishing process.

The XHTML standard has specific rules to follow, and if you want to use XHTML, you must ensure that your XHTML code is applied correctly.

Let's take a more in-depth look at these tools.

Text Editors

Text editors force you to *hand-code,* meaning that you, not the software, enter the code. Hand-coding helps you learn HTML and XHTML elements, attributes, and structures, and it lets you see exactly where you've made mistakes. Also, with hand-coding, you can easily include the newest enhancements in your documents, whereas WYSIWYG (What You See Is What You Get) editors don't have those enhancements available until updated product versions are released.

Some basic text editors are these:

- ▶ Notepad for all Windows versions
- ▶ Vi or Pico (command line), or GEdit or Kate (GUI) for Linux/Unix
- ▶ TeachText or SimpleText for Macintosh

WARNING

Using a word processing program such as Word, StarOffice, or even WordPad to create HTML documents often inadvertently introduces unwanted formatting and control characters, which can cause problems. HTML and XHTML require plain text, so either make a special effort to save all documents as plain text within such applications or take our advice and use a text editor, instead.

HTML AND XHTML EDITORS

In general, editors fall into two categories:

- ▶ Text- or code-based editors, which show you the HTML or XHTML code as you're creating documents

A variety of code-based HTML and XHTML editors exist for Windows, Macintosh, and Linux/Unix, and most of them are fairly easy to use (and create HTML code just as you wrote it). That said, as we write this chapter, few editors are available that produce XHTML code (or rigorously standard-compliant HTML code, for that matter).

CONTINUED ➡

However, it's possible to use an HTML editor or a simple text editor to create an initial version of your XHTML documents and then to use a special-purpose tool such as HTML Tidy or HTML-Kit to transform your HTML into equivalent, properly formatted XHTML. Because this requires a bit more savvy than we assume from our general readership, this material is aimed only at those more experienced readers to whom this kind of approach makes sense.

▶ WYSIWYG (What You See Is What You Get) editors, which show the results of code, similar to the way it will appear in a browser, as you're formatting your document

Simple WYSIWYG editors such as Netscape Composer and Microsoft FrontPage Express are good for quickly generating HTML documents. These editors give you a close approximation of page layout, design, and colors and are good for viewing the general arrangement of features. However, they do not give you as much control over the final appearance of your document as code-based editors do. Additionally, although there have been improvements over the last couple of years, many WYSIWYG editors notoriously introduce unneeded elements, noncompliant code, and other characteristics that purists object to.

After you've developed a few HTML documents and understand basic HTML principles, you may choose to use both a WYSIWYG editor and a code-based editor. For example, you can get a good start on your document using a WYSIWYG HTML editor and then polish it (or fix it) using a code-based one. Others prefer web editing/publishing tools such as Dreamweaver, which offers a combined approach with both WYSIWYG and code-based modes.

For now, though, we recommend that you hand-code HTML and XHTML using a plain-text editor.

Web Browsers

The most common browsers are Microsoft Internet Explorer (IE) and Netscape Navigator; however, many other browsers also are available for virtually all computer platforms and online services. We're especially fond of Opera (available free at `www.opera.com`) and Amaya (available free at `www.w3.org/Amaya/`) because they often support advanced features and functions better and sooner than the more popular IE and Netscape browsers do.

As you're developing HTML or XHTML documents, keep in mind that exactly how your documents appear varies from browser to browser and from computer to computer. For example, most browsers in use today are *graphical browsers*: they can display elements other than text. A *text-only* browser can display—you guessed it—only text. How your documents appear in each of these types of browsers differs significantly, as shown in Figures 2.1 and 2.2.

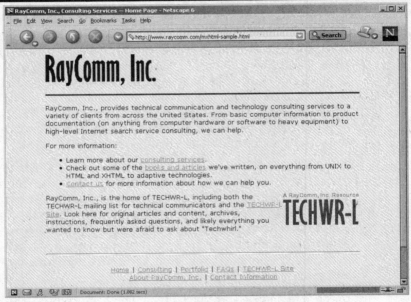

FIGURE 2.1: An HTML document displayed in Netscape Navigator

Even graphical browsers tend to display things a bit differently. For example, one browser might display a first-level heading as 15-point Times New Roman bold, whereas another might display the same heading as 14-point Arial italic. In both cases, the browser displays the heading bigger and more emphasized than regular text, but the specific text characteristics vary. Figures 2.3 and 2.4 show how two other browsers display the same XHTML document.

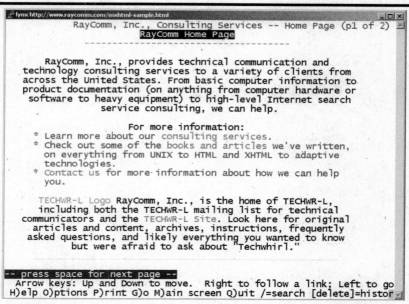

FIGURE 2.2:   The same HTML document viewed in Lynx, a text-only browser

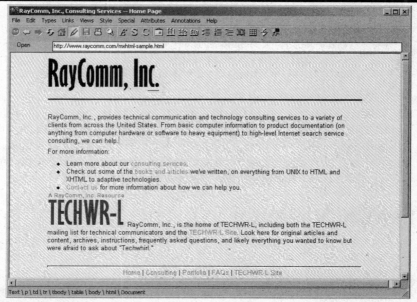

FIGURE 2.3:   The W3C Amaya browser has its own unique look and feel.

FIGURE 2.4:   The Opera browser shows the same document with slightly different formatting.

TIP

Finally, your user's computer settings also can make a big difference in how your HTML or XHTML documents appear. For example, the computer's resolution and specific browser settings can alter a document's appearance.

As you're developing and viewing your documents, remember that what you see may look a bit different to your users. Test your documents in as many different browsers as possible, at as many different resolutions and color settings as possible, on as many different computers as possible. You won't be able to test for all variations, but you should be able to get a good idea of what your users might see.

The W3C Validator

You also should use an HTML or XHTML *validator*, a tool that examines your documents and verifies that they follow the rules for applying code and document structure.

Although a number of validators exist, the W3C validator is the most definitive because it's developed by the same folks who developed the

HTML and XHTML specification. To use it, first open your browser. Then:

1. Go to `http://validator.w3.org/file-upload.html`.

2. Browse your local hard disk, and upload the file you want using the validator's interface.

If you're in luck, what you get back looks like what's shown in Figure 2.5. If you're not in luck, you will need to find out how to read and interpret the validator's sometimes-cryptic error messages.

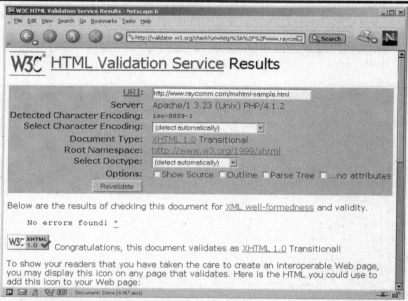

FIGURE 2.5:   When the W3C validator finds no errors, its output is both short and very sweet!

You should make validation part of your standard authoring process. That way, you'll get the best possible guarantee that most browsers will be able to view and display the contents of your documents.

TIP

Using a validator is helpful even if you're a beginner in HTML or XHTML. The validator will help you learn the rules of the languages and aid you in writing web standards–compliant code that appears as uniformly as possible in different browsers and on different platforms.

NOTE

Remember, validating your XHTML is necessary to ensure that it is compliant with the XHTML standards.

WHAT DOES HTML AND XHTML CODE LOOK LIKE?

As Figure 2.6 shows, HTML and XHTML documents are plain-text files. They contain no images, no sounds, no videos, and no animations. However, they can include *pointers*, or links, to those file types, which is how web pages end up looking as if they contain non-text elements.

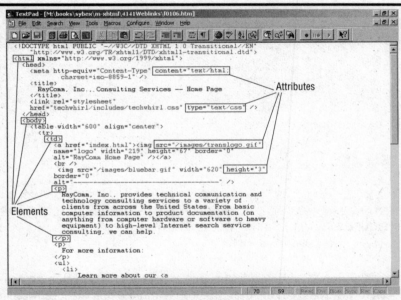

FIGURE 2.6:   HTML and XHTML documents are just text files containing the code and content you provide.

As you can see, HTML and XHTML documents look nothing like the web pages you view in your browser. Instead, documents are made up of *elements* and *attributes* that work together to identify document parts and tell browsers how to display them. Listing 2.1 shows the elements and attributes that create the web page shown in Figures 2.1 through 2.4.

Listing 2.1: HTML and XHTML Code Includes Context, Elements, Attributes, and Links That Form a Web Page

```
<!DOCTYPE html PUBLIC
"-//W3C//DTD XHTML 1.0 Transitional//EN"
  "http://www.w3.org/TR/xhtml1/DTD/xhtml1-transitional.dtd">
<html xmlns="http://www.w3.org/1999/xhtml">
  <head>
    <meta http-equiv="Content-Type" content="text/html;
          charset=iso-8859-1" />
    <title>
      RayComm, Inc., Consulting Services -- Home Page
    </title>
    <link rel="stylesheet"
    href="techwhirl/includes/techwhirl.css"
type="text/css" />
  </head>
  <body>
    <table width="600" align="center">
      <tr>
        <td>
          <a href="index.html">
        <img src="/images/translogo.gif"
          name="logo" width="219" height="67" border="0"
          alt="RayComm Home Page" /></a>
          <br />
          <img src="/images/bluebar.gif" width="620"
          height="3" border="0"
          alt="" />
          <p>

          RayComm, Inc., provides technical communication
          and technology consulting services to a variety
          of clients from across the United States. From
          basic computer information to product
          documentation (on anything from computer hardware
          or software to heavy equipment) to high-level
          Internet search service consulting, we can help.
          </p>
          <p>
            For more information:
          </p>
          <ul>
```

```
        <li>
            Learn more about our
            <a href="consulting.html">
consulting services</a>.
        </li>
        <li>
            Check out some of the <a href="books.html">
        books and articles</a>
        we've written, on everything
            from UNIX to HTML and XHTML to adaptive
            technologies.
        </li>
        <li>
            <a href="contact.html">Contact us</a>
          for more information about how we can help you.
        </li>
    </ul>
    <p>
    <img src="/techwhirl/images/techwhirllogo.gif"
    alt="TECHWR-L Logo" align="right" />

    RayComm, Inc., is the home of TECHWR-L, including
    both the TECHWR-L mailing list for technical
    communicators and the
    <a href="techwhirl/">TECHWR_L Site</a>.
    Look here for original articles and content,
    archives, instructions, frequently asked
    questions, and likely everything you wanted to
    know but were afraid to ask about "Techwhirl."
    </p>
    <br clear="all" />
    <hr />
    <p class="centered">
      <a href="index.html">Home</a> | <a
      href="consulting.html">Consulting</a> | <a
      href="portfolio.html">Portfolio</a> | <a
      href="faqs.html">FAQs</a> | <a
      href="/techwhirl/index.html">TECHWR-L Site</a>
      <br />
      <a href="aboutraycomm.html">
    About RayComm, Inc.</a>
      | <a href="contact.html">Contact Information</a>
    </p>
```

```
<p class="centered">
  Last modified on 1 April, 2002
  <br />
  Site contents Copyright &copy; 1997 - 2002
  RayComm, Inc.
  <br />
  Send comments to
  <a href="mailto:webmaster@raycomm.com">
  webmaster@raycomm.com</a>

  <br />
  </p>
  </td>
  </tr>
  </table>
  </body>
</html>
```

TIP

Throughout this chapter, we use the term *users* to describe the people who view and use the HTML and XHTML documents you develop.

Understanding Elements

HTML and XHTML elements serve two primary functions. First, they identify *logical document parts*—that is, major structural components in documents, such as headings (h1, a heading level 1, for example), numbered lists (ol, also called ordered lists), and paragraphs (p). For example, if you want to include a paragraph component in an HTML or XHTML document, you type the text and apply the appropriate elements (<p> to the beginning of the paragraph and </p> at the end) to that text, as this snippet from Listing 2.1 shows:

```
<p>
  RayComm, Inc., provides technical communication and
  technology consulting services to a variety of
  clients from across the United States. From basic
  computer information to product documentation (on
  anything from computer hardware or software to heavy
  equipment) to high-level Internet search service
  consulting, we can help.
</p>
```

And, voila, the paragraph element (<p>...</p>) marks that part of the document to be a paragraph.

Second, some elements refer to other things that are not included in the HTML or XHTML document itself. Whereas the <p> and <h1> elements just mentioned refer to paragraph and heading components within the document itself, elements also can mark *pointers*—essentially just links—to other documents, images, sound files, video files, multimedia applications, animations, applets, and so on. For example, if you want to include an image of your company's product in your document, rather than pasting an image directly into the document (as you might in a word processing file), you include an element that points to the file location of that image, as shown here:

```
<img src="logo.gif" alt="logo" />
```

In this example, the img (image) element points to a logo file (logo.gif) that the browser should display. This illustrates that browsers rely on information within the HTML or XHTML document to tell them what to display, as well as how to display it.

Understanding Attributes

Some HTML and XHTML elements take modifying values called *attributes*, which provide additional information about the elements, such as these:

- ▶ What other files should be accessed, such as an image file
- ▶ What alternative text should be associated with the element
- ▶ Which style classes should be used to format the element

Let's assume you want to center a heading level one in the browser window. You'd start with your heading and elements, like this:

```
<h1>A heading goes here</h1>
```

Next, you'd add the style and type attributes to the opening element, like this:

```
<h1 style="text-align:center">A centered heading goes
here</h1>
```

In this example, the heading level one element includes attributes that specify the style to be aligned in the center. As you can see, attributes normally have two parts: the attribute name (style=, in this example) and the value ("text-align:center"). The value *should* appear in quotes in HTML and *must* appear in quotes in XHTML.

ABOUT COMMON ATTRIBUTES

In HTML and XHTML, there are several attributes that can be applied to nearly all elements; these are known as the *common* attributes. They include the following:

`id="name"`   This assigns a unique name to an element within a document.

`style="style"`   This enables the author of the document to use Cascading Style Sheets (CSS) as attribute values or to define the presentation parameters for that specific element. You can use the `style` attribute with all elements except `html`, `head`, `title`, `meta`, `style`, `script`, `param`, `base`, and `basefont`.

`class="name"`   This assigns a class or a set of classes to an element. This attribute is frequently used with CSS to establish the display properties for a particular subset of elements.

`lang="language code"`   This specifies the language of the content contained by the element. For example, `lang="en"` declares that English is the language used.

`dir="ltr|rtl"`   This specifies the direction in which text should be displayed. This doesn't seem like an important attribute unless you remember that many of the world's languages are not read from left to right. `ltr` means left to right, and `rtl` means right to left.

`title="text"`   This functions in a manner similar to the `title` element but applies only to a specific element instead of an entire document. Caveat: The attribute's *behavior* is not defined by the HTML or XHTML specification. Instead, the way that behavior is rendered is left up to the browser, and the content is usually presented as a pop-up tooltip when the reader hovers the mouse pointer over the text. This attribute is currently most useful on sites or documents that the author knows will be viewed by users of Internet Explorer 5, Opera 6, or Netscape 6 (or later) browsers. The `title` attribute cannot be used with the following elements: `html`, `head`, `meta`, `title`, `script`, `param`, `base`, and `basefont`.

Typing Elements and Attributes Correctly

As our examples so far should illustrate, elements and attributes are reasonably intuitive. Although markup occasionally can be cryptic, you generally can get some idea of an element or attribute function from its name.

Before we get started on typing elements and attributes, be aware that entering elements and attributes varies *slightly* according to whether you're using HTML or XHTML. Remember that we mentioned XHTML is a bit pickier; entering XHTML markup is where that pickiness comes into play. Again, though, XHTML is not harder; you'll just have to pay a bit more attention as you're learning to use it. In the following sections, we'll do the following:

- ▶ Describe general guidelines for typing HTML and XHTML elements and attributes

- ▶ Show you how to *nest* elements (apply more than one element to a document part)

- ▶ Explain specific rules for typing XHTML elements and attributes

- ▶ Help you improve the readability of your HTML and XHTML documents

Typing Elements and Attributes in Either HTML or XHTML (General Information)

To begin, all elements are composed of *element names* that are contained within *angle brackets* (< >). The angle brackets simply tell browsers that the text between them represents HTML or XHTML markup rather than ordinary text content. Some sample elements look like these:

- ▶ <h2> (for a level 2 heading)

- ▶ <p> (for a document paragraph)

- ▶ <strong> (to emphasize a particular section of content)

TIP

You'll learn more about these elements and their uses in Chapter 3, "Creating Your First HTML or XHTML Document."

Second, most elements are designed to contain content; they use a pair of tags, where actual content is between the *opening tag* (for example, <h1>)

and the corresponding *closing tag* (</h1>). Both tags look alike, except the closing tag includes a forward slash (/) to denote the end of the element container. To apply tags to something in your document, place an opening tag before the content that should be associated with the element you want to use, and place the closing tag after it, as these examples show:

```
<h1>Information to which the tags apply</h1>
```
or
```
<title>Correctly Formed Title</title>
```

When typing elements, be particularly careful *not* to include extra spaces within the tag itself, as in this erroneous example:

```
< title >Incorrectly Formed Title< /title >
```

If you include spaces within the elements, browsers may not recognize the element and may not display the content correctly (or at all). Sometimes a browser will display the markup itself because it's unable to distinguish improperly formed markup from normal element content.

TIP

When creating HTML or XHTML markup by hand, enter both the opening and closing tags at the same time. That way, you won't forget the closing tag.

Keep in mind that you'll also use an occasional *empty element*, which does not include a closing tag. Some empty elements include the line break element (<br />) and the image element (<img />), which do not require the closing element but include a space and a forward slash (/) before the closing angle bracket. This example shows the break element (<br />), which puts a line break after each line:

```
<p>
   RayComm, Inc., provides technical communication and<br />
   technology consulting services to a variety of<br />
   clients from across the United States. From basic<br />
   computer information to product documentation (on<br />
   anything from computer hardware or software to heavy<br />
   equipment) to high-level Internet search service<br />
   consulting, we can help.
</p>
```

We'll point out empty elements throughout this book and show you how to use them correctly.

NOTE
Empty elements in HTML—as opposed to XHTML—do not require the closing /
character. However, the extra / causes no problems in HTML, so we customarily
use it in both HTML and XHTML.

As we discussed, elements don't usually appear by themselves; often
you'll also include attributes that provide supporting information about
the element. The `style=` attribute in this example indicates that the
level one heading should be centered:

```
<h1 style="text-align:center">
A centered heading goes here</h1>
```

As you enter attributes, remember these guidelines:

▶ Include the attribute within the element after the element name,
as in `<h1 style="text-align:center">`.

▶ Use spaces to separate attributes from other attributes and the element itself, as in `<h1 id="5325a" style="text-align:center">`.

▶ Enclose attribute values in quotes, as in `style="text-align
:center"`. The quotes are required in XHTML and part of devel-
oping "correct" HTML. Learning to include them now will help
you in the future, when newer specs are released that insist on
that convention.

Finally, be aware that:

▶ HTML allows you to type elements (and attributes) using uppercase,
lowercase, or a combination of both. It's not picky, and browsers
will display HTML code using whichever capitalization you use.

▶ XHTML requires that elements and attributes—with a few
exceptions—must be typed using all lowercase. We'll point
out exceptions throughout this book; however, we recommend that
you use lowercase for both HTML (for practice, should you ever
move to XHTML in the future) and XHTML (because lowercase is
required). The examples in this book all will be lowercase.

Applying More than One Element to a Document Component (Nesting Elements)

In the preceding examples, you saw how you apply elements around the
text to which they apply. Suppose, though, that you need to apply more

than one element to a document component. For example, say you have a paragraph that also includes a few words that you want to emphasize. To apply more than one element to a particular piece of content, you nest the tags. *Nesting* means placing one set of tags inside another set. For example, to apply strong emphasis to a word within a paragraph, you nest the `strong` element within the p (paragraph) element, as follows:

```
<p>The <strong>right</strong> way to use strong emphasis is
    to enclose only those words you want to emphasize inside
    a strong element.</p>
```

When you nest elements, the first opening tag must be matched by a corresponding closing tag at the end of the related block of content, and the second opening tag must be closed with a corresponding closing tag immediately after its related content block. XHTML is quite insistent that you nest tags in the right order. Therefore, a block of text like this:

```
<p>The last word gets strong <strong>emphasis.</p></strong>
```

is invalid because it closes the outside p element before closing the nested (inside) `strong` element. It's also technically incorrect for HTML, but such issues *usually* don't cause problems in HTML.

Typing XHTML Elements and Attributes

With the general information and guidelines for typing elements and attributes established, we'll now take a look at the specific rules you'll need to follow for developing XHTML documents. Although some of these XHTML rules seem pointless or arbitrary, keep in mind that the XHTML specification is based on the XML specification, and it applies some of the same constraints and conventions of that specification. Although you may not be interested in moving to XML, you still need to apply these rules to your XHTML documents.

Some of the following rules will look familiar; we mentioned them in the general guidelines for both HTML and XHTML documents.

All XHTML Elements Must Be Closed All XHTML elements must be balanced with an opening and a closing tag, which is referred to as making the document *well formed*:

```
HTML:  <p>This is a paragraph.
XHTML: <p>This is a paragraph.</p>
```

If you're already familiar with HTML, you're probably wondering what you do with the img and br elements in XHTML. These (and other) empty elements accept attributes but do not contain character data. Using HTML, these empty elements generally include just the opening tag, like this:

```
<img src="logo.gif" alt="Corporate Logo">
```

XHTML is a tad different in that you have to include markup to terminate the empty element, in one of two ways:

▶ Terminate the tag with a space and a slash, as follows:

```
<img src="logo.gif" alt="Corporate Logo" />
```

▶ Add a closing tag, as follows:

```
<img src="logo.gif" alt="Corporate Logo"></img>
```

The first option saves space and time, and logically it makes a little more sense. You can use either approach, but we suggest (and most developers use) the first option, rather than the latter.

WARNING

In XHTML, most white space within a tag is not significant. For example, `<img src="logo.gif" alt="Logo"/>` is the same as `<img src="logo.gif" alt="Logo" />`. In the second example, you should notice white space between the closing quotation mark (") *and the forward slash (/)*. However, older browsers have problems interpreting the first example because there is no white space separating those items. If you add a space before the /, you can ensure that most older browsers will interpret the empty element without any problems.

All Attributes Must Have Values   One of the trickier XHTML rules is that all attributes must have values. At first glance, this may seem to be an easy rule to grasp, but there's a trick or two you have to master when applying it to XHTML. For most attributes, it's fairly straightforward. For example:

```
<table align="center">
```

In this case, the align attribute has to have a value ("center") to tell the processor just how to align the table.

As you advance your skills, you'll encounter a few situations where including the value isn't as straightforward. For example, in Chapter 17, "Developing Forms," we discuss forms, which use the `<input>` element. This element accepts a *stand-alone value* (an attribute where the name and the value are the same thing) called `disabled`, which simply turns off the function. The element and attribute might look like this:

```
<input disabled>
```

If you added other attributes, the element would look something like the following:

```
<input disabled name="pet" value="cat">
```

Because this element is empty, we need to terminate it, like this:

```
<input disabled name="pet" value="cat" />
```

Although the preceding attribute is fine according to HTML, it's not well formed according to XHTML, because all attributes must have values. The problem is that these stand-alone attributes do not have any predefined values and, therefore, a value is not really needed. However, according to XHTML's rules, it must have a value, so a workaround was created. You set the attribute equal to itself:

```
<input disabled="disabled" name="pet" value="cat" />
```

All Attribute Values Must Be Enclosed in Quotes (" ")   Another XHTML rule is that all attribute values be delimited with quotation marks. HTML allows several attribute values to be defined without quotation marks—although the specification recommends that they always be used.

This rule is easy enough:

```
HTML:  <table align=center>
XHTML: <table align="center">
```

The HTML example does not contain quotation marks, and the XHTML example does.

TIP

In many HTML examples, you're likely to see the attribute value in uppercase (CENTER). Most attribute *values* are not case sensitive. In this book, we generally use lowercase to define attribute values, for readability.

XHTML Is Case Sensitive   As we mentioned, XHTML is case sensitive and requires—with few exceptions—that all elements and attributes be typed using lowercase letters. This may be a sticky point if you've been using HTML and are accustomed to using uppercase or a combination of upper- and lowercase. Nonetheless, using all lowercase letters just takes some getting used to:

```
HTML:   <TABLE>...</TABLE>
XHTML:  <table>...</table>
```

Elements Must Be Nested Correctly   In the previous section, we described the concept of nesting, where you apply one or more elements within another element. For example, the following markup defines a title element that is nested with the head element:

```
<head>
    <title>Document title</title>
</head>
```

This may seem straightforward; however, there are cases where people make mistakes. For example, can you spot the mistake in the following markup?

```
<p>You can bold a <b>word</p></b>
```

The problem is that the tags are overlapping; no one element is nested within the other. The golden rule is "what you open first, you close last." To correct this syntax, you would write:

```
<p>You can bold a <b>word</b></p>
```

Notice how the b element is nested completely within the p element.

TIP

When referring to an element that is nested within another element, we call the nested element a *child* of the container element; the container is the *parent* element. We refer to nested elements as "children of a parent element."

There are a few other XHTML-specific rules that apply to certain elements and attributes. We'll mention these as we come to them in this book. The XHTML rules described here are the ones you will need to know as you're getting started.

Improving Document Readability

Throughout this book, because of the width limits of the printed page, we wrap and indent code lines that are meant to be written all on one line.

This doesn't mean you have to wrap or indent the code you develop, but we do recommend using hard returns in your code to help make the lines a bit shorter and easier to read. Doing so does not affect how browsers display your documents (unless you inadvertently put in a space between an angle bracket and an element name); it just makes that document easier to read, for you and others who may have to maintain the code when you're editing its contents.

For example, take a look at this code:

```
<!DOCTYPE html PUBLIC
"-//W3C//DTD XHTML 1.0 Transitional//EN"
"http://www.w3.org/TR/xhtml1/DTD/xhtml1-transitional.dtd">
<html xmlns="http://www.w3.org/1999/xhtml"><head><title>
Mastering HTML Document Title</title></head><body>Mastering
HTML Document Body</body></html>
```

Although we've included line breaks so that the code won't run off the edge of the page, we could improve the readability by separating some of the code a bit, like this:

```
<!DOCTYPE html PUBLIC
"-//W3C//DTD XHTML 1.0 Transitional//EN"
  "http://www.w3.org/TR/xhtml1/DTD/xhtml1-transitional.dtd">
<html xmlns="http://www.w3.org/1999/xhtml">
    <head>
        <title>Mastering HTML Document Title</title>
    </head>
    <body>
        Mastering HTML Document Body
    </body>
</html>
```

No question which one's easier to read or follow, right?

WHAT OTHER RESOURCES CAN HELP?

In addition to this book, you can find information, resources, and specifications on the web. The W3C site in particular, as well as several product-specific websites, will help you learn, use, and keep up with changes in HTML (unlikely to change) and XHTML (likely to change).

Visit the W3C

The W3C was created in 1994 at the Massachusetts Institute of Technology (MIT) to oversee the development of web standards, eventually including the XHTML standard. This consortium defines and publishes HTML, XHTML, and numerous other web-related standards, along with information about the elements and attributes that may legally appear within HTML or XHTML documents. An excellent way to monitor changes is to visit the W3C site at www.w3.org/MarkUp. There you'll find new releases of XHTML standards and information about HTML standards.

For more information on proposed standards and other developments in web-related specifications, such as Cascading Style Sheets (CSS) and XML specifications, visit the W3C's home page at www.w3.org.

Can you use new elements and attributes as they become available? For the most part, yes. By the time many popular elements and attributes become part of a standard, they already work with many or most browsers. However, some elements and attributes (including some that were introduced with HTML 4) did not have wide or stable browser support when that specification was released and, to this day, do not have nearly the breadth of support that some other elements and attributes enjoy. We'll point these out throughout this book and show you how they differ from previous versions of HTML.

Monitor Netscape and Microsoft Sites

When HTML was the prevailing web markup standard, each time Netscape or Microsoft released a new browser version, it would also add new markup *extensions*, which are browser-specific, nonstandard elements and attributes. Some of these extensions were useful, some less so. However, as a whole, any nonstandard elements introduced into HTML caused problems both for web developers and for users. Fortunately, far fewer extensions seem to be introduced now that XHTML has appeared on the scene, but you should still be aware of what's added with each new browser release, if only to know what progress the browsers have made in supporting the elements and styles that are already defined.

If you're considering using extensions in your XHTML documents, keep in mind that they're not standard and that the W3C validator will not recognize or validate nonstandard markup. Also, extensions that are specific to a particular browser (for example, Netscape) will probably not work in other browsers (such as IE or Opera). For this reason, we strongly recommend that you refrain from using extensions and use only standard HTML or XHTML elements and attributes. That way, you'll not only be able to validate your documents to make sure they're syntactically correct, but you also can be reasonably sure that all your users can access the information you provide.

You can find Netscape's elements and attributes at `http://developer`
`.netscape.com/docs/manuals/htmlguid/index.htm`.

You will find Microsoft's elements and attributes at `http://msdn`
`.microsoft.com/library/` under Web Development ➢ HTML and Dynamic HTML ➢ SDK Documentation ➢ Reference ➢ HTML Elements. (These pages move frequently, so you may need to browse a little to get there.)

Monitor Other Sites

Although definitive information comes from the W3C, you also should check other reliable resources for information about HTML and XHTML. Here's a list of sites to check regularly.

Organization	URL
Web Design Group	`www.htmlhelp.com`
Web Developer's Virtual Library	`www.wdvl.com`
HTML Writer's Guild	`www.hwg.org`
WebMonkey	`www.webmonkey.com`
CNET's Builder.com	`www.builder.com`
Oasis	`www.oasis-open.org`
Zvon	`www.zvon.org`

Google Web Directory	`http://directory.google`
	`.com/Top/Computers/Data_`
	`Formats/Markup_Languages/`
	`HTML/References/`

WebReference.com	`www.webreference.com`

WHAT'S NEXT?

This chapter gave you a brief overview of HTML and XHTML—what they are, what they're used for, how to enter their tags and attributes correctly, and what supplemental resources might be helpful to you. Although you haven't done any HTML or XHTML coding yet, you now should possess a good foundation of basic concepts and terminology.

In the next chapter, you'll learn more about XHTML document syntax and structure and will create your first HTML or XHTML document.

Chapter 3

CREATING YOUR FIRST HTML OR XHTML DOCUMENT

If you're ready to create your first HTML or XHTML document, you're in the right chapter! We'll help you start a new HTML or XHTML document and save it, using the appropriate file formats, show you how to add document structure elements (which help browsers identify your document), and show you how to apply some common formatting elements.

If you're new to HTML or XHTML (or rusty at hand-coding), you might want to review the element and attribute information in Chapter 2, "Getting Acquainted with HTML and XHTML." Before starting this chapter, you should be familiar with elements and attributes, as well as how to apply them to your content.

Throughout this chapter, we provide lots of code samples and figures to help guide you and to show you what your results should look like. You can substitute your own text if you prefer, or you can duplicate the examples in the chapter. The step-by-step instructions will work regardless of the specific content you use.

Adapted from *Mastering HTML and XHTML*,
by Deborah S. Ray and Eric J. Ray
ISBN 0-7821-4141-2 $49.99

After you work through this chapter, you'll have developed your first document, complete with text, headings, horizontal rules, and even some character-level formatting.

CREATING, SAVING, AND VIEWING DOCUMENTS

Exactly how you start a new document depends on which operating system and editor you're using. In general, you'll find that starting a new document is similar to starting other documents you've created. You'll make your new document an official HTML or XHTML document by saving it as such, which is discussed next.

Before you begin hand-coding HTML or XHTML, be aware that you should save and view your work frequently so that you can see your progress. By doing so, you can make sure that things appear as you expect them to and catch mistakes within a few new lines of code. For example, we typically add a few new lines of code, save the document, then view it. Then we add a few more lines of code, save the document, then view it. Exactly how often you save and view your documents depends on your preference. Chances are that you'll save it frequently at the beginning.

You create an HTML or XHTML document in much the same way that you create any plain-text document. Here's the general process:

1. Open your text editor.

2. Start a new document. If you're using Windows, Macintosh, or Linux/Unix GUI applications, choose File ➢ New. If you're using Unix, type **vi** or **pico** to start a text-based editor.

3. Enter the code and text you want to include. (You'll have plenty of practice in this chapter.)

TIP

We recommend that you practice using HTML or XHTML by completing the examples throughout this and other chapters.

4. Save your document. If you're using Windows, Macintosh, or Linux/Unix GUI applications, choose File ➢ Save or File ➢ Save As. Otherwise, use the commands required by your editing program.

GUIDELINES FOR SAVING FILES

As you work your way through this chapter, keep these saving and viewing guidelines in mind:

▶ Name the file with an `htm` or `html` extension (even if you're creating an XHTML document, and even if you're working on a Mac). Choose one or the other (`htm` or `html`) and be consistent— consistency will save you a lot of time in troubleshooting when your files aren't working as you'd expect.

▶ If you aren't using a text-only editor such as Notepad or TeachText, verify that the file type is set to Text or ASCII. If you use word processing programs to create HTML or XHTML documents (and remember our caveat about this from Chapter 2), save your documents as Text Only, ASCII, DOS Text, or Text with Line Breaks. The specific options will vary according to the word processor you use.

▶ Use only letters, numbers, hyphens (–), underscores (_), and periods (.) in your filename. Most browsers also accept spaces in filenames; however, spaces often make creating links difficult, as you will see in Chapter 4, "Stepping Out: Linking Your Way Around the Web," so we recommend avoiding them.

▶ Save the document and any other documents and files associated with a particular project all in one folder. You'll find that this makes using links, images, and other advanced technologies easier.

▶ Double-check after you've saved your files to be sure that they really have an `htm` or `html` extension. Depending on Windows Explorer settings (Hide Extensions for Known File Types), it might look like `filename.htm` but really be `filename.htm.txt` because of some unneeded help from Windows.

WARNING

If you're using Notepad for creating your HTML and XHTML documents, be sure to select All Files from the option Save as Type. Otherwise, Notepad will save your file as a text file, even if you give the file an `.html` extension, and when you view the file in a browser, it will be displayed as a text file, not as HTML or XHTML.

Viewing the HTML or XHTML documents that you develop is as simple as opening them from your local hard drive in your browser. If you're working with an open document in your editor, remember to save your latest changes and then follow these steps in your browser:

1. In Internet Explorer, choose File ➤ Open and type the local filename or browse your hard drive until you find the file you want to open. In Netscape Navigator, choose File ➤ Open File and then navigate to the file on your hard drive. Your particular menu command might be File ➤ Open Page or Open File, but it's all the same thing.

2. Select the file and click OK to open it in your browser.

TIP

You don't have to be connected to the Internet to view your file in a browser. You can view HTML and XHTML files in a browser even when you're offline as long as the HTML or XHTML file is on your hard drive.

ALTERNATIVE WAYS TO VIEW FILES

Most browsers provide some clever features that can make developing HTML and XHTML files easier.

You can easily see your editing changes in a file by reloading it. For example, after you view a document and save some editing changes, you can reload the document and see the latest changes. You'll probably find that clicking a Reload button is much easier than going back through the File ➤ Open and browse sequence. Generally, you reload documents by clicking a Refresh or Reload button or by choosing a similar option from the View menu. If you make an editing change but it does not seem to show up in your browser, make sure you've saved it in your text editor, then try holding down the Shift key and clicking Refresh or Reload to force it to reload your latest changes.

In addition, you can open a file by selecting it from a list of bookmarks or favorites. *Bookmarking* a file means adding a pointer to the file so that you can open the file quickly, just as a bookmark

CONTINUED ➡

makes it easier to open a book to a specific page. Creating book-marks or favorites is as easy as clicking a menu option (or just typing a keyboard shortcut) while viewing a page. Whenever you want to go back to that page, simply click the bookmark rather than choosing File ➢ Open and selecting the file. Most browsers have bookmark options; just look for a button or a menu command.

APPLYING DOCUMENT STRUCTURE ELEMENTS

After you create a new document, your first task is to include *document structure elements*, which provide browsers with information about document characteristics. For example, document structure elements identify the version of HTML or XHTML used, provide introductory information about the document, and include the title, among other similar things. Most document structure elements, although part of the HTML or XHTML document, do not appear in the browser window. Instead, document structure elements work behind the scenes and tell the browser which elements to include and how to display them. Although these elements do not directly produce the snazzy results you see in web pages or help files, they are essential.

TIP

Most browsers, including Netscape Navigator and Microsoft Internet Explorer, correctly display documents that do not include document structure elements. However, there's no guarantee that future versions will continue to do so or that your results will be consistent. Document structure elements are even more important in the latest versions (6.0 and later) of Netscape Navigator and Microsoft Internet Explorer. These newer browsers make decisions about how to display certain elements on your page based on the document structure elements included in your file. We strongly suggest that you use the document structure elements, because they're required by the HTML and XHTML specifications and because they can affect the way your page is displayed.

All HTML documents should include five document structure elements, nested and ordered as in the following sample markup:

```
<!DOCTYPE HTML PUBLIC
"-//W3C//DTD HTML 4.01 Transitional//EN"
        "http://www.w3.org/TR/html4/loose.dtd">
<html>
  <head>
    <title>Title That Summarizes
the Document's Content</title>
  </head>
  <body>
    HTML Document Body
  </body>
</html>
```

All XHTML documents should include five document structure elements, nested and ordered as in the following sample markup:

```
<!DOCTYPE HTML PUBLIC
"-//W3C//DTD XHTML 1.0 Transitional//EN"
    "http://www.w3.org/TR/xhtml1/DTD/xhtml1-transitional.dtd">
<html xmlns="http://www.w3.org/1999/xhtml">
  <head>
    <title>Title That Summarizes
the Document's Content</title>
  </head>
  <body>
    XHTML Document Body
  </body>
</html>
```

TIP

You can save time when creating future HTML or XHTML documents by saving document structure elements in a template document. That way, you can easily reuse them in subsequent documents, rather than retyping them time after time. If you use an HTML or XHTML authoring program, such as Macromedia's HomeSite, this markup (or something similar to it) is usually the base of a new document.

The *DOCTYPE* Declaration

The DOCTYPE declaration tells browsers and validation services which version of HTML or XHTML the document complies with. The important part of the DOCTYPE declaration is the Document Type Definition (DTD) attribute, which specifies the DTD your document follows. In brief, your HTML and XHTML documents need to comply with some basic rules— rules about what the documents can include and not include and some guidelines about how you need to structure the documents. These rules are outlined in DTDs.

NOTE

A DTD serves two purposes: to specify which elements and attributes you can use to develop markup language documents and to specify the document structure and rules you must adhere to while developing markup language documents.

Both HTML and XHTML DOCTYPE declarations come in three varieties: Strict, Transitional (Loose), and Frameset. Exactly what these declarations include depends on whether you're developing HTML or XHTML documents.

If You're Developing HTML Documents

Strict   This version prohibits everything except "pure" HTML, and you're not likely to use it unless you're writing HTML documents that use no formatting elements and that rely only on style sheets to make them look good. To indicate that your document complies with the Strict specification, use this:

```
<!DOCTYPE HTML PUBLIC "-//W3C//DTD HTML 4.01//EN"
    "http://www.w3.org/TR/html4/strict.dtd">
```

Transitional   This version is the most flexible for accommodating deprecated elements and attributes (those that are still useful but that may be phased out in favor of newer or different ones). In most cases, you'll want to use the Transitional DOCTYPE element. To indicate that your document complies with the Transitional specification, use this:

```
<!DOCTYPE HTML PUBLIC
"-//W3C//DTD HTML 4.01 Transitional//EN"
    "http://www.w3.org/TR/html4/loose.dtd">
```

Frameset   This version is similar to the Transitional specification, but it also supports the elements and attributes needed to use frames:

```
<!DOCTYPE HTML PUBLIC "-//W3C//DTD HTML 4.01 Frameset//EN"
    "http://www.w3.org/TR/html4/frameset.dtd">
```

TIP

For both HTML and XHTML documents, we recommend using the Transitional DOCTYPE element for most of your HTML document needs, unless you are planning to use frames, as discussed in Chapter 8, "Dividing a Window with Frames." The Strict DTD generally is too restrictive to be useful except in fairly unusual situations.

If You're Developing XHTML Documents

XHTML document DOCTYPE declarations are similar to those of HTML declarations, except that they specify different DTDs.

Strict   This version prohibits everything except "pure" XHTML, and you're not likely to use it unless you're writing XHTML documents that use no formatting elements and that rely exclusively on style sheets to make them look good. To indicate that your document complies with the Strict specification, use the following:

```
<!DOCTYPE html PUBLIC "-//W3C//DTD XHTML 1.0 Strict//EN"
    "http://www.w3.org/TR/xhtml1/DTD/xhtml1-strict.dtd">
```

Transitional   This version is the most flexible for accommodating deprecated elements and attributes (those that are still useful but that may be phased out in favor of newer or different ones). In most cases, you'll want to use the Transitional DOCTYPE element. To indicate that your document complies with the Transitional specification, use this:

```
<!DOCTYPE html PUBLIC
"-//W3C//DTD XHTML 1.0 Transitional//EN"
    "http://www.w3.org/TR/xhtml1/DTD/xhtml1-transitional .dtd">
```

TIP

We recommend using the Transitional DOCTYPE element for most of your XHTML document needs, unless you are planning to use frames, as discussed in Chapter 8.

Frameset   This version is similar to the Transitional specification, but it also supports the elements and attributes needed to use frames:

```
<!DOCTYPE html PUBLIC "-//W3C//DTD XHTML 1.0 Frameset//EN"
    "http://www.w3.org/TR/xhtml1/DTD/xhtml1-frameset.dtd">
```

The *html* Element

The html element identifies the document as an HTML or XHTML document. But wait. Didn't the DOCTYPE element just specify this? Yes, but the html element, enclosing the entire document, is still a required component in both the HTML and XHTML specifications.

If you're developing an HTML document, you add just the html element below the DOCTYPE declaration, like this:

```
<!DOCTYPE HTML PUBLIC
"-//W3C//DTD HTML 4.01 Transitional//EN"
        "http://www.w3.org/TR/html4/loose.dtd">
<html>
</html>
```

If you're developing an XHTML document, you should also add the xmlns namespace to the html element. A *namespace* uniquely identifies a set of elements that belong to a given document type, and it ensures that there are no element name conflicts. Remember that XHTML is a subset of XML (Extensible Markup Language), so the specification calls for using the xmlns namespace attribute in the html element, like this:

```
<!DOCTYPE html PUBLIC
"-//W3C//DTD XHTML 1.0 Transitional//EN"
  "http://www.w3.org/TR/xhtml1/DTD/xhtml1-transitional.dtd">
<html xmlns="http://www.w3.org/1999/xhtml">
</html>
```

The *head* Element

Required in every HTML and XHTML document, the head element contains information about the document, including its title, scripts used, style definitions, and document descriptions. Additionally, the head element can contain other elements that have information for search engines and indexing programs.

Few browsers actually require this element, but most browsers expect to find any available additional information about the document within the head element. To add the head element to either an HTML or XHTML document, enter it between the html opening and closing elements, as in this incomplete XHTML document (the next several sections will show how additional elements fit into place to complete an HTML or XHTML document):

```
<!DOCTYPE html PUBLIC
"-//W3C//DTD XHTML 1.0 Transitional//EN"
```

```
     "http://www.w3.org/TR/xhtml1/DTD/xhtml1-transitional.dtd">
<html xmlns="http://www.w3.org/1999/xhtml">
   <head>

   </head>
</html>
```

TIP

Don't confuse this document head element, which is a structure element, with *heading* elements such as h1, which create heading text in a document body. We discuss heading elements in the "Creating Headings" section, later in this chapter.

The head element must contain other child elements (that is, other elements that nest within the head element), including the title and meta elements, along with a few less commonly used elements. Let's take a look.

The *title* Element

The title element, which both HTML and XHTML specifications require, contains the document title. The title does not appear within the browser window, although it's usually visible in the browser's title bar (often the blue bar at the top of your screen). To use the title element, enter it between the opening and closing head elements, as shown in this sample XHTML document:

```
<!DOCTYPE html PUBLIC
"-//W3C//DTD XHTML 1.0 Transitional//EN"
   "http://www.w3.org/TR/xhtml1/DTD/xhtml1-transitional.dtd">
<html xmlns="http://www.w3.org/1999/xhtml">
   <head>
      <title>
         Title That Summarizes the Document's Content
      </title>
   </head>
</html>
```

Because the title bar has limited space, take care to ensure the title briefly summarizes your document's content and keeps key words at the beginning of the title. Titles should represent the document, even if the document is taken out of context. Some good titles include the following:

▶ Sample XHTML Code

- Learning to Ride a Bicycle
- Television Viewing for Fun and Profit

Less useful titles, particularly taken out of context, include the following:

- Examples
- Chapter 2
- Continued

TIP

Watch out for the default titles produced by WYSIWYG editors. Always be sure to put in your own title. Take care when choosing the content for the title. Some search engines use the words in your title as keywords in classifying your site, so take advantage of this and consider what keywords would be useful for site promotion. Also, don't forget that the title can serve as a navigational aid— users may use the title to identify their current location in your site.

The *meta* Element

The meta element is used to embed document meta information. *Meta information* contains information about the contents of the document, such as keywords, author information, and a description of the document. The primary advantage to including meta elements in your HTML and XHTML document is that these elements make it possible for search engine robots and spiders to identify, catalog, and find the information in your document.

For both HTML and XHTML documents, you can include author information, keywords, and a description of the document contents using the empty meta element in combination with name= and content= attributes. Here's an example of some meta information in an XHTML document:

```
<!DOCTYPE html PUBLIC
"-//W3C//DTD XHTML 1.0 Transitional//EN"
   "http://www.w3.org/TR/xhtml1/DTD/xhtml1-transitional.dtd">
<html xmlns="http://www.w3.org/1999/xhtml">
   <head>
      <meta name="author" content="Your name" />
      <meta name="keywords" content="A keyword,a keyword,a
         keyword" />
```

```
    <meta name="description"
        content="This is the Home Page
        of the Website of Your Name. " />
    <title>
        Title That Summarizes the Document's Content
    </title>
  </head>
</html>
```

TIP

When using the meta element in XHTML, remember to close it with a space and a slash before the final angle bracket (/>) because it's an empty element. In HTML, you may omit the / symbol.

Other Children of the *head* Element

In addition to the title and meta elements, the head element may contain the following child elements:

script   Instructs the browser that the enclosed content is part of a scripting language such as JavaScript (also called JScript or ECMAScript) or VBScript.

style   Contains internal Cascading Style Sheets (CSS) information. See Chapter 16, "Using Style Sheets," for more information about style sheets.

link   Defines a link. This element functions somewhat like the anchor (a) element (discussed in detail in Chapter 4). The link element is most commonly used to link external CSS style sheets to a document.

base   Defines a document's base Uniform Resource Locator (URL) using the href attribute. It must occur as a child of the head element, and it establishes a base URL for all relative references. This element is often used in conjunction with anchors to enable navigation within a single document or within documents in a single directory or folder.

TIP

A URL is a type of Uniform Resource Identifier (URI). The value of the `href` attribute can be any type of URI, such as a Uniform Resource Name (URN).

The *body* Element

The body element encloses all the elements, attributes, and information that you want a user's browser to display. Almost everything else we talk about in this book takes place between the opening and closing body elements (unless you're creating a framed document—see Chapter 8 for more information). To use the body element, enter it below the closing head element and above the closing html element, like this:

```
<!DOCTYPE html PUBLIC
"-//W3C//DTD XHTML 1.0 Transitional//EN"
  "http://www.w3.org/TR/xhtml1/DTD/xhtml1-transitional.dtd">
<html xmlns="http://www.w3.org/1999/xhtml">
    <head>
        <title>
            Title That Summarizes the Document's Content
        </title>
    </head>
    <body>
        All the elements, attributes, and information in the
        document body go here.
    </body>
</html>
```

TIP

Throughout this book, we'll provide examples for you that won't include these structural elements. This doesn't mean you shouldn't include them; it just means that we're focusing on the immediate topic.

If you've been following along, save your document, view it in a browser, and compare it with Figure 3.1 to confirm that you're on the right track. The title appears in the title bar, and some text appears in the document window.

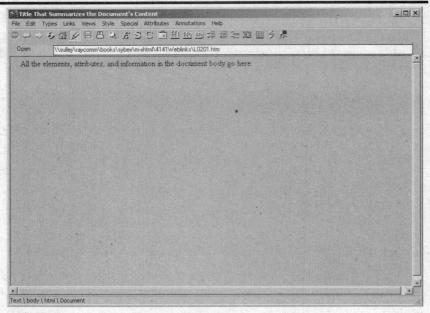

FIGURE 3.1:   Your first XHTML (or HTML) document, including all structure elements

APPLYING BASIC ELEMENTS

After you include the structure elements, you're ready to start placing basic content in the document body. The following sections show you how to include paragraphs, headings, lists, and rules (horizontal lines). These elements constitute the basic HTML and XHTML document components and, unlike the structure elements, appear in the browser window. Learning to apply these basic elements and attributes will prepare you to apply practically any element or attribute.

As you create your content, keep in mind that its exact appearance will vary from browser to browser. As we said in Chapter 2, two browsers will both display a heading bigger and bolder than body text, but the specific font, size, and emphasis will vary. In addition, the user may have specific browser settings on his machine that will affect the display of the document.

Finally, in several places, we've included information on how to change the appearance of some elements—for example, how to right-align a heading or how to change a paragraph's text color. As you work through this chapter, note that many of these formatting level elements have been *deprecated* in HTML 4.01 (and thus, also in the XHTML specification)—meaning that technically they're still available and most browsers will still interpret and display them, but that the HTML and XHTML specifications are now using new elements (or, in most cases, style sheets) to create the same effects. On a more practical level, this means that, while you can use these formatting elements and attributes, you should consider specifying formatting-related information using style sheets, which are covered in Chapter 16. The following sidebar, "Deprecated Elements," specifies which elements have been deprecated and lists reasons not to use deprecated elements in general.

TIP

Throughout the rest of this chapter, we primarily use XHTML sample code. However, keep in mind that these examples will work in either HTML or XHTML. You'll find detailed information about the (slight) differences between HTML and XHTML code in Chapter 2.

DEPRECATED ELEMENTS

One of the original goals of markup languages in general was to separate document structure from presentation—although HTML 3.2 and browser support veered a long way from this goal. In an effort to get back on track, the presentational elements in HTML (and thus XHTML) have been "deprecated." *Deprecated elements* are those that may be phased out of the next version of HTML (even though there may not *be* a next version). They're more likely to disappear from future versions and revisions of XHTML.

Although the HTML 4.01 and XHTML 1.0 Transitional DTDs permit the use of many of these deprecated elements, it's really better to think toward the future and avoid their use altogether in favor of other elements or other options, such as CSS (explained in Chapter 16). Why?

Consider the long-term publication of your documents. Right now, browsers support these elements, but it's hard to say which browsers will support them in the future. Also, consider the difficulties of using these elements now and then changing to CSS in the future. Although developing a style sheet and applying it to your documents isn't that big a deal, *removing* all the character-level formatting *is* a big deal. Character-level formatting overrides

CONTINUED ➤

formatting specified in the style sheet, so you would likely need to remove the character-level formatting for style sheet formatting to be visible. Removing character-level formatting from more than just a few documents is very tedious and time consuming, to say the least.

These HTML elements have been deprecated in HTML 4.01 and XHTML 1:

font   Local change to font. Deprecated in favor of CSS.

center   Shorthand for `div align="center"`. Deprecated in favor of CSS.

s or strike   Strikethrough text. Deprecated in favor of CSS.

u   Underlined text. Deprecated in favor of CSS.

applet   Java applet. Deprecated in favor of the `object` element.

basefont   Base font size. Deprecated in favor of CSS.

dir   Directory list. Deprecated in favor of unordered lists (the `ul` element).

isindex   Single-line prompt. Deprecated in favor of the use of `input` to create text input controls.

menu   Menu list. Deprecated in favor of unordered lists (the `ul` element).

Additionally, virtually all attributes that specify appearance or formatting are deprecated.

When we show you how to apply these elements throughout this chapter, we note that they are deprecated and give alternatives where possible.

Creating Paragraphs

One of the most common elements you'll use is the paragraph element, p, which is appropriate for regular body text. In HTML, you could use just the opening p element to mark your paragraphs. However, in XHTML, the paragraph element must be paired—use the opening element <p> where you want to start a paragraph and the closing element </p> to end the paragraph. It's easier to identify where the element begins and ends if you use both opening and closing elements.

To use the paragraph element, enter the opening and closing elements around the text you want to format as a paragraph, like this:

```
<p>
A whole paragraph goes right here.
</p>
```

TIP

You don't have to type an element's content on a separate line; `<p>Paragraph goes here.</p>` is also valid. We do this just to make the sample code easier to read.

Figure 3.2 shows a few sample paragraphs.

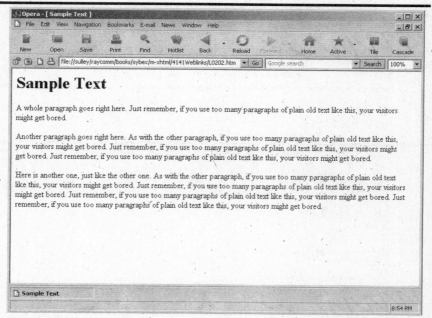

FIGURE 3.2:   Paragraph text is the most common text in HTML and XHTML documents.

You can also use the `align` attribute with the paragraph element, which has values of `left`, `center`, `right`, and `justify`. To apply this attribute, include it in the opening paragraph element, like this:

```
<p align="center">
Paragraph of information goes here.
</p>
```

NOTE

Note that the `align` attribute is deprecated, so we suggest using style sheets to achieve the same effect.

You can also apply other paragraph-level (or block-level) elements instead of the p element to achieve some slightly different effects, as explained in Table 3.1.

TABLE 3.1: Other Paragraph-Formatting Elements

ELEMENT	EFFECT
address	Used for address and contact information. Often appears in italics and is sometimes used as a footer.
blockquote	Used for formatting a quotation. Usually appears indented from both sides and with less space between lines than a regular paragraph.
pre	Effective for formatting program code or similar information (short for *preformatted*). Usually appears in a fixed-width font (such as Courier) with even space between words and letters.

Figure 3.3 shows how the `address` and `pre` elements appear in Internet Explorer.

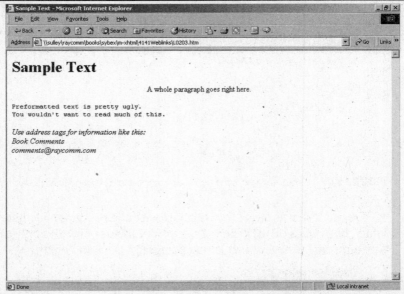

FIGURE 3.3: Special paragraph-level elements make information stand out.

Creating Headings

Headings break up large areas of text, announce topics to follow, and arrange information according to a logical hierarchy. In HTML and XHTML, you can use up to six levels of headings; h1 is the largest of the headings, and h6 is the smallest. The paired elements look like this:

```
<h1>...</h1>
<h2>...</h2>
<h3>...</h3>
<h4>...</h4>
<h5>...</h5>
<h6>...</h6>
```

TIP

For most documents, limit yourself to two or three heading levels. After three heading levels, users begin to lose track of your hierarchy. If you find that you're using several heading levels, consider reorganizing your document or dividing it into multiple documents—too many heading levels often indicates a larger organizational problem.

Here's an example of how to use the heading elements:

```
<!DOCTYPE html PUBLIC
"-//W3C//DTD XHTML 1.0 Transitional//EN"
  "http://www.w3.org/TR/xhtml1/DTD/xhtml1-transitional.dtd">
<html xmlns="http://www.w3.org/1999/xhtml">
  <head>
      <title>Sample Headings</title>
  </head>
  <body>
      <h1>First Level Heading</h1>
      <h2>Second Level Heading</h2>
      <h3>Third Level Heading</h3>
  </body>
</html>
```

Figure 3.4 shows how Netscape 6 displays a few heading levels.

In general, you should use heading elements only for document headings—that is, don't use heading elements for figure captions or to emphasize information within text. Why? First, you don't always know how browsers will display the heading. It might not create the visual effect you intended. Second, some indexing and editing programs use headings to generate tables of contents and other information about your document. These programs won't exclude a heading from the table of contents or other information just because you used it as a figure caption, for example.

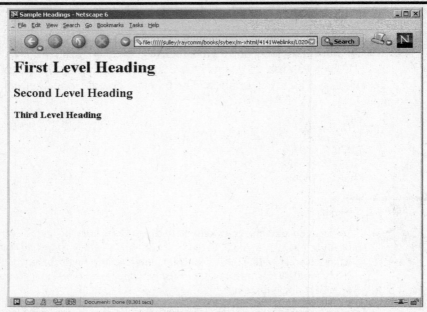

FIGURE 3.4: Heading levels provide users with a hierarchy of information.

WARNING

Just because Navigator and Internet Explorer display headings in bold and change the font size, not every browser does so. A text-to-speech browser might represent a heading by using extra pauses or emphasis. Text-only browsers such as Lynx use different levels of indentation to show headings. Other graphical browsers, such as Opera and Mosaic, allow users to customize the font face, color, and size used for each heading. In short, don't use an <h1> tag just because you want some text to be large and bold—instead, use the text-level elements <strong> and <big> for the same effect.

By default, all browsers align headings to the left. However, most browsers support the align attribute, which also lets you right align, center, and justify headings. To use the align attribute, include it in the heading elements, like this:

```
<h1 align="left">Left-aligned Heading</h1>
<h1 align="center">Centered Heading</h1>
<h1 align="right">Right-aligned Heading</h1>
```

Figure 3.5 shows headings aligned left, center, and right.

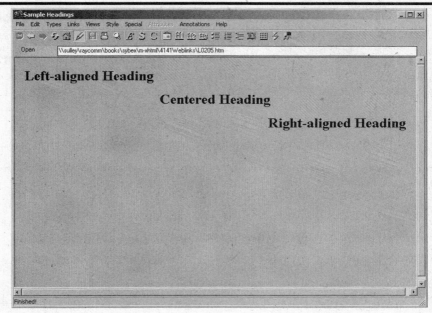

FIGURE 3.5:   Headings aligned left, center, and right

TIP

The HTML and XHTML specifications strongly discourage the use of the `align` attribute. Therefore, although this attribute is still supported at this time, if your users will be using current browsers, you should consider using CSS for your formatting needs. You can control the appearance and alignment of headings with great precision and flexibility through the use of style sheets. You'll find how-to information about CSS in Chapter 16 and a comprehensive list of CSS options in Appendix B, "Cascading Style Sheets Reference."

Creating Lists

Lists are a great way to provide information in a structured, easy-to-read format. They help your users spot information easily, and they draw attention to important information. A list is also a good format for a procedure. Figure 3.6 shows the same content formatted as both a paragraph and a list.

Lists come in two varieties: numbered (called *ordered* lists) and bulleted (called *unordered* lists). To create either kind of list, you first specify that you want information to appear as a list, and then you identify each line item in the list. Table 3.2 shows the list and line item elements.

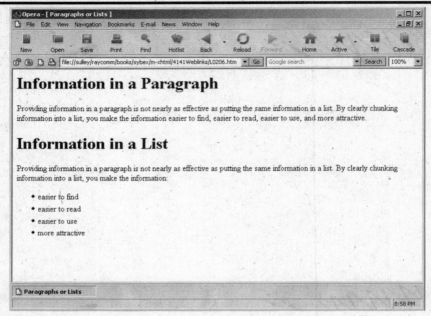

FIGURE 3.6:   Lists often are easier to read than paragraphs.

TABLE 3.2:   List and Line Item Elements

ELEMENT	EFFECT
ol	Specifies that the information appear as an ordered (numbered) list. Ordered lists are appropriate for listing steps or information that needs to be presented or completed in a specific order.
ul	Specifies that the information appear as an unordered (bulleted) list. Unordered lists are appropriate for drawing attention to bits of information that do not need to be presented or completed in a specific order.
li	Specifies a line item in either an ordered or an unordered list.

The following steps show you how to create a bulleted list; use the same steps to create a numbered list but use the ol element instead of the ul element.

1. Start with text you want to format as a list, such as the following:

    ```
    Lions
    Tigers
    Bears
    Oh, My!
    ```

2. Insert the ul elements around the list text:

```
<ul>
Lions
Tigers
Bears
Oh, My!
</ul>
```

3. Put the li opening elements and closing elements around each list item.

```
<ul>
<li>Lions</li>
<li>Tigers</li>
<li>Bears</li>
<li>Oh, My!</li>
</ul>
```

The resulting list, viewed in a browser, looks similar to that shown in Figure 3.7.

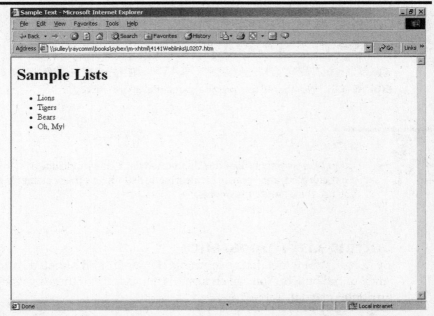

FIGURE 3.7: Bulleted lists make information easy to spot on the page and can draw attention to important points.

To change your list from unordered (bulleted) to ordered (numbered), change the ul element to ol. The resulting numbered list is shown in Figure 3.8.

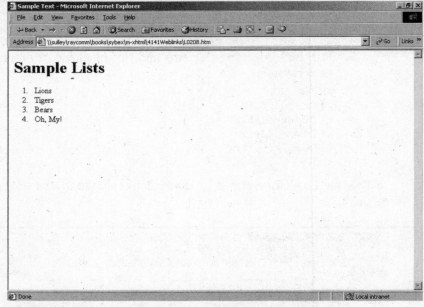

Sample Lists

1. Lions
2. Tigers
3. Bears
4. Oh, My!

FIGURE 3.8:   Numbered lists provide sequential information.

TIP

Other, less commonly used and deprecated list elements include dir, to create a directory list, and menu, to create a menu list. You use these elements just as you use the ul and ol elements.

Setting List Appearance

By default, numbered lists use Arabic numerals, and bulleted lists use small round bullets. You can change the appearance of these by using the attributes listed in Table 3.3.

TABLE 3.3:   List Attributes

Element	Effect
For numbered lists:	
type="A"	Specifies the number (or letter) with which the list should start: A, a, I, i, or 1 (default).
type="a"	
type="I"	
type="i"	
type="1"	
For bulleted lists:	
type="disc"	Specifies the bullet shape.
type="square"	
type="circle"	

To use any of these attributes, include them in the opening ol or ul element or in the opening li element, like this:

```
<ol type="A">
<li>Outlines use sequential lists with letters.</li>
<li>So do some (unpopular) numbering schemes for
    documentation.</li>
</ol>
```

Or like this:

```
<ul type="square">
<li>Use bullets for non-sequential items.</li>
<li>Use numbers for sequential items.</li>
</ul>
```

Or this:

```
<ul>
<li type="circle">
Use bullets for non-sequential items.</li>
<li type="square"> Use different bullets for visual
    interest.</li>
</ul>
```

Figure 3.9 shows how these attributes appear in a browser.

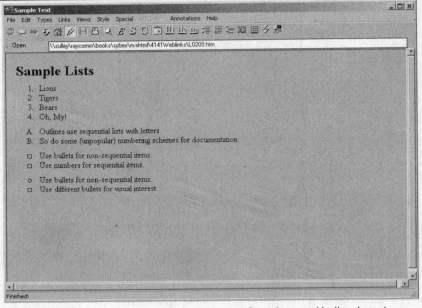

FIGURE 3.9:   You can change the appearance of numbers and bullets by using list attributes.

TIP

You can add the `compact` attribute in the opening `ol` or `ul` element to tell browsers to display the list as compactly as possible. Generally, this setting will make little difference, because most browsers render lists this way by default. This attribute is deprecated.

TIP

The `type` attribute for unordered lists currently is supported by many (but by no means all) browsers; it is also deprecated in favor of using style sheets to accomplish the same thing.

More Options for Ordered Lists

Ordered lists have additional attributes that you can use to specify the first number in the list, as well as to create hierarchical information.

First, you can start a numbered list with a value other than 1 (or A, a, I, or i). Simply include the `start` attribute in the initial `ol` element, as in `<ol start="51">`, to start the list at 51. You even can change specific numbers within a list by using the `value` attribute in the `li` element, as in `<li value="7">`.

TIP

Both the `start` and `value` attributes are deprecated.

To use these attributes, include them in the `ol` element, like this:

```
<ol start="51">
    <li>This is the fifty-first item.</li>
    <li>This is the fifty-second.</li>
    <li type="i" value="7">
        This item was renumbered to be the
        seventh, using lowercase roman numerals,
        just because we can.</li>
</ol>
```

Figure 3.10 shows how this code appears in a browser.

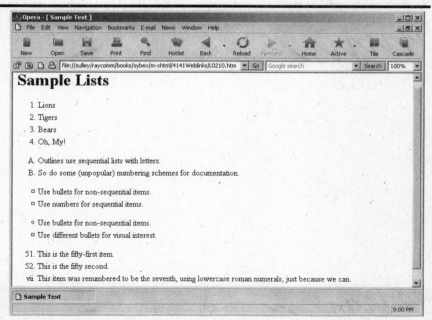

FIGURE 3.10:   Attributes let you customize ordered lists in several ways.

Second, you can use nested ordered lists and different `type` attributes to create outlines. The numbering continues past each lower-level section without the need to renumber manually with a `value` attribute. Here's an example of what the code looks like:

```
<ol type="I">
    <li>Top Level Item</li>
    <li>Another Top Level Item</li>
    <ol type="A">
        <li>A Second Level Item</li>
        <li>Another Second Level Item</li>
        <ol type="1">
            <li>A Third Level Item</li>
            <li>Another Third Level Item</li>
        </ol>
        <li>Another Second Level Item</li>
    </ol>
    <li>A Top Level Item</li>
</ol>
```

As you can see, to nest a list within another one, you just include the opening element, line items, and closing element within part of the main list's code. The result is shown in Figure 3.11.

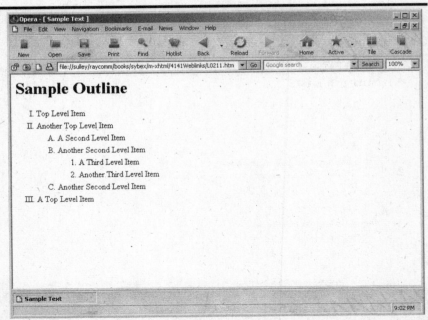

FIGURE 3.11:   Ordered lists are even flexible enough to format outlines.

Using Definition Lists

Finally, one special list variant, *definition lists*, can be useful for providing two levels of information. You can think of definition lists as dictionary entries—they have two levels of information: the entry and a definition. You can use these lists to provide glossary-type information, or you can use them to provide two-level lists. Table 3.4 lists the elements and their effects.

TABLE 3.4:   Definition List and Item Elements

ELEMENT	EFFECT
dl	Specifies that the information appear as a definition list.
dt	Child of dl; identifies definition terms.
dd	Child of dl; identifies definitions.

WARNING

Many web authors have discovered that a <dd> tag when used by itself (out of the context of a definition list) is rendered by Navigator and Internet Explorer as a tab. We recommend you not adopt this practice, because the indenting behavior is not a part of the HTML/XHTML specification, and the indentation will not work on all browsers. For indenting text, the safest method is to use multiple nonbreaking spaces ( )—although even that method is not guaranteed to work. Alternatively, it's better to create indents with style sheets (Chapter 16) or, if you really have no alternative, to use tables for indenting (Chapter 11, "Presenting Information in Tables").

To create a definition list as shown in Figure 3.12, follow these steps:

1. Enter the dl opening and closing elements to start the definition list.

   ```
   <dl>
   </dl>
   ```

2. Add the dt opening and closing elements around the definition terms.

   ```
   <dl>
   <dt>XHTML</dt>
   <dt>Maestro</dt>
   </dl>
   ```

3. Add the dd element to identify individual definitions.

```
<dl>
<dt>XHTML</dt>
<dd>Extensible Hypertext Markup Language is used to create
    web pages.</dd>
<dt>Maestro</dt>
<dd>An expert in some field. See "Readers of <i>Mastering
    HTML and XHTML</i>" for examples.</dd>
</dl>
```

TIP

A great way to apply definition lists is in "What's New" lists—a special page that tells people what's new and exciting on your site or at your organization. Try putting the dates in the dt element (maybe with boldface and italics) and the information in the dd element.

FIGURE 3.12: Definition lists are a formatting option that is useful when presenting dictionary-like information.

Applying Bold, Italic, and Other Types of Emphasis

In addition to creating paragraphs, headings, and lists, you can apply formatting to individual letters and words: For example, you can make a word appear italic, bold, underlined, or subscript, as in H_2O. You use these character-level formatting elements only within paragraph-level elements—that is, you can't put a <p> element within a character-level element such as <b>. You have to close the character-level formatting before you close the paragraph-level formatting.

Correct:

```
<p><b>This is the end of a paragraph that
also uses boldface.</b></p>
<p>This is the beginning of the following paragraph.</p>
```

Incorrect:

```
<p>This text <b>is boldface.</p>
<p>As is this.</b></p>
```

Although many character-formatting elements are available, you'll probably use b (for **boldface**) and i (for *italic*) most often. Table 3.5 lists the most common character-formatting elements.

TABLE 3.5: Common Character-Formatting Elements

ELEMENT	EFFECT
b	Applies boldface.
blink	A proprietary Netscape element that makes text blink; usually considered highly unprofessional. Not supported in some current browsers.
cite	Indicates citations or references.
code	Displays program code; similar to the pre element.
em	Applies emphasis; usually displayed as italics.
i	Applies italics.
s or strike	Apply strikethrough to text; deprecated.
strong	Applies stronger emphasis; usually displayed as bold text.
sub	Formats text as subscript.
sup	Formats text as superscript.

TABLE 3.5 continued: Common Character-Formatting Elements

ELEMENT	EFFECT
tt	Applies a fixed-width font.
u	Applies underline; deprecated.
var	Displays variables or arguments.

To use these elements, enter them around the individual letters or words you want to emphasize, like this:

```
Making some text <b>bold</b> or <i>italic</i> is a useful
technique, more so than <strike>strikethrough</strike> or
<blink>blinking</blink>.
```

Figure 3.13 shows some sample character formatting.

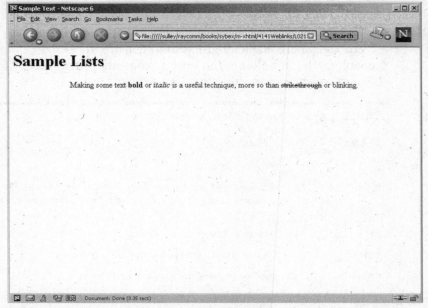

FIGURE 3.13: Character formatting helps you emphasize words or letters.

TIP

Spend a few minutes trying out these character-formatting elements to see how they work and how they look in your favorite browser.

CONSIDER CSS INSTEAD OF FORMATTING ELEMENTS

The HTML and XHTML specifications strongly encourage using CSS for your formatting needs. Although the specification still supports many deprecated individual formatting elements, the use of CSS is the recommended way to include formatting in your XHTML and HTML documents. Using CSS, you can apply the following:

▶ Character-level formatting such as strikethrough and underline

▶ Paragraph-level formatting such as indents and margins

▶ Other formatting such as background colors and images

See Chapter 16 and Appendix B for CSS information.

Including Horizontal Rules

Horizontal rules are lines that break up long sections of text, indicate a shift in information, or help improve the overall document design. To use a horizontal rule, which is an empty element, include the hr element where you want the rule to appear, like this:

```
<p>Long passages of text should often be broken into
sections with headings and, optionally,
horizontal rules.</p>
<hr />
<h3>A Heading Also Breaks Up Text</h3>
<p>A new long passage can continue here.</p>
```

By default, horizontal rules appear shaded, span the width of the browser window, and are a few pixels high. You can change a rule's shading, width, height, and alignment by including the appropriate attributes. Note that all horizontal rule attributes have been deprecated in favor of CSS. Table 3.6 shows horizontal rule attributes.

TIP

Pixels are the little dots on your screen that produce images; *pixel* is an abbreviation for *picture element*. If your display is set to 800 × 600, you have 800 pixels horizontally and 600 pixels vertically.

TABLE 3.6: Attributes of the Horizontal Rule (hr) Element
(All Deprecated)

ATTRIBUTE	SPECIFIES
align="..."	Alignment to left, center, or right
noshade="noshade"	That the rule has no shading
size="n"	Rule height measured in pixels
width="n"	Rule width (length) measured in pixels
width="n%"	Rule width (length) measured as a percentage of the document width

To use any of these attributes, include them in the hr element, like this:

```
<hr width="80%" size="8" />
<hr width="50%" />
<hr width="400" align="right" />
<hr noshade="noshade" align="center" width="200" />
```

Figure 3.14 shows some sample horizontal rules with height, width, alignment, and shading attributes added.

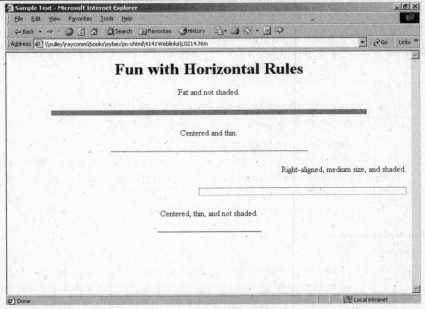

FIGURE 3.14: Horizontal rules can help separate information, improve page design, and simply add visual interest to the page.

Specifying Line Breaks

Sometimes you need to break a line in a specific place, but you don't want to start a new paragraph (with the extra spacing). For example, you might not want lines of poetry text to go all the way across the document; instead, you might want to break them into several shorter lines. You can break paragraph lines easily by inserting the empty element br where you want the lines to break, like this:

```
<p>
There was an XHTML writer<br />
Who tried to make paragraphs wider<br />
He found with a shock<br />
All the elements did mock<br />
The attempt to move that text outside-r.<br />
Mercifully Anonymous
</p>
```

INCLUDING FANCIER FORMATTING

Now that you have a firm grip on using common document elements, you can dive into some of the fancier formatting effects. In the following sections, we'll show you how to add colors and specify fonts and sizes.

Note that most of the elements in the following sections have been deprecated in favor of style sheets. While you can use these formatting elements and attributes, you should strongly consider specifying formatting-related information using style sheets, which we cover in Chapter 16 and Appendix B. Also see the sidebar "Deprecated Elements," earlier in this chapter, for a list of deprecated elements and a brief discussion of why we shouldn't use them.

Adding Colors

One of the easiest ways to jazz up your documents is to add colors to the background or text. You can liven up an otherwise dull web page with a splash of color or an entire color scheme. For example, add a background color and change the text colors to coordinate with the background. Highlight a word or two with color and make the words leap off the page. If you're developing a corporate site, adhere to the company's color scheme to ensure a consistent look.

WARNING

You can also make your pages completely unusable with a poorly selected color scheme or make it very difficult for users with vision problems to access your pages. See Chapter 6, "Planning for a Usable, Maintainable Website," for more information about accessibility issues.

TIP

As you'll see in Chapter 6, developing a color scheme is a great way to help unite your pages into a cohesive website.

The drawback to setting colors is that you really don't have control over what your users see. A user might set his browser to display colors he likes, or he might be using a text-only browser, which generally displays only black, white, and gray.

You specify colors using hexadecimal numbers, which combine proportions of red, green, and blue—called *RGB numbers*. RGB numbers use six digits, two for each proportion of red, green, and blue. As you're choosing colors, remember that not all RGB numbers are displayed well in browsers; some colors *dither*, meaning that they appear spotty or splotchy. We recommend that you select RGB values that are appropriate for web page use, as listed in Table 3.7, which illustrates that R, G, and B can each take on the values 00, 33, 66, 99, CC, or FF—giving you 256 possible combinations. Although you'll most likely never go wrong with these "safe" colors, it's most important to use these colors in page backgrounds or in places with large patches of color, where dithering may occur if you don't use these number combinations.

TABLE 3.7:   Recommended RGB Values

R	G	B
00	00	00
33	33	33
66	66	66
99	99	99
CC	CC	CC
FF	FF	FF

To create an RGB number from the values in this table, simply start with a pound sign (#) to indicate the hexadecimal system and then select one option from each column. For example, choose FF from the R (red) column, 00 from the G (green) column, and 00 from the B (blue) column to create the RGB number #FF0000, which has the largest possible red component but no blue and no green; it therefore appears as a pure bright red.

NOTE

Note that the color values are not case sensitive in either HTML or XHTML.

Setting Background Colors

Using a *background color*, which is simply a color that fills the entire browser window, is a great way to add flair to your web pages. By default, browsers display a white or gray background color, which may be adequate if you're developing pages for an intranet site where flashy elements aren't essential. However, if you're developing a public or personal site, you'll probably want to make your site more interesting and visually appealing. For example, if you're developing a public corporate website, you might want to use your company's standard colors—those that appear on letterheads, logos, or marketing materials. You might want to use your favorite color if you're developing a personal site. In either case, using a background color can improve the overall page appearance and help develop a theme among pages.

TIP

Check out Chapter 6 for tips and information about developing coherent websites.

As you'll see in the following section, pay careful attention to how text contrasts with the background color. If you specify a dark background color, use a light text color. Conversely, if you specify a light background color, use a dark text color. Contrast is key for ensuring that users can read information on your pages.

To specify a background color for your documents, include the bgcolor attribute in the opening body element, like this:

```
<body bgcolor="#FFFFFF">...</body>
```

Setting Text Colors

Similar to background colors, text colors can enhance your web pages. In particular, you can specify the color of the following:

▶ Body text, which appears throughout the document body

▶ Unvisited links, which are links not yet followed

▶ Active links, which are links as they're being selected (clicked)

▶ Visited links, which are links previously followed

Changing body text is sometimes essential—such as if you've added a background color or an image. If you've added a dark background color, the default black body text color won't adequately contrast with the background, making the text difficult or impossible to read. In that case, you'd want to change the text color to one that's lighter so that it contrasts with the background sufficiently.

Changing link colors helps keep your color scheme intact—for unvisited as well as visited links. Set the visited and unvisited links to different colors to help users know which links they've followed and which ones they haven't. That said, remember that users expect that links they've not yet visited are blue and underlined, while others are a different shade. Be sure that any changes you make help—rather than thwart—your users.

To change body text and link colors, simply add the attributes listed in Table 3.8 to the opening body element.

TABLE 3.8:   Text and Link Color Attributes (All Deprecated)

ATTRIBUTE	SETS COLOR FOR
text="..."	All text within the document, with a color name or a #RRGGBB value
alink="..."	Active links, which are the links at the time the user clicks them, with a color name or a #RRGGBB value
link="..."	Unvisited links, with a color name or a #RRGGBB value
vlink="..."	Links the user has recently followed (how recently depends on the browser settings), with a color name or a #RRGGBB value

TIP

We recommend setting all web page colors at one time—that way, you can see how background, text, and link colors appear as a unit.

To change text and link colors, follow these steps:

1. Within the body element, add the text attribute to set the color for text within the document. This example makes the text black:

   ```
   <body text="#000000">
   ```

TIP

When setting text colors, using a "safe" color is less important for text than for backgrounds. Dithering is less apparent in small areas, such as text.

2. Add the link attribute to set the link color. This example uses blue (#0000FF) for the links:

   ```
   <body text="#000000" link="#0000FF">
   ```

3. Add the vlink attribute to set the color for visited links. If you set the vlink attribute to the same as the link, the link will not change colors even after the user follows it. This could be confusing, but it also serves to make it look as if there is always new material available. This example sets the visited link to a different shade of blue:

   ```
   <body text="#000000" link="#0000FF" vlink="#000099">
   ```

4. Finally, set the alink, or active link, color. This is the color of a link while the user is clicking it and will not necessarily be visible in Internet Explorer 4, depending on the viewer's settings. This example sets alink to red:

   ```
   <body text="#000000" link="#0000FF" vlink="#000099"
      alink="#FF0000">
   ```

TIP

Specify fonts and increase font sizes to improve readability with dark backgrounds and light-colored text.

Specifying Fonts and Font Sizes

You can use the font element to specify font characteristics for your document, including color, size, and typeface. However, it's worth noting that the font element and its attributes have been deprecated in favor of CSS. We suggest you check out the font properties in CSS and use them instead of the font element. Table 3.9 describes the elements and attributes you'll use to set font characteristics.

TABLE 3.9: Font Characteristics (All Deprecated)

ITEM	TYPE	DESCRIPTION
font	Element	Sets font characteristics for text.
color="..."	Attribute of font element	Specifies font color in #RRGGBB numbers or with color names. This color applies only to the text surrounded by the font elements.
face="..."	Attribute of font element	Specifies possible typefaces as a list, in order of preference, separated by commas—for example, "Verdana, Arial, Helvetica".
size="n"	Attribute of font element	Specifies font size on a scale of 1 through 7; the default or normal size is 3. You can also specify a relative size by using + or − (for example, +2).
basefont	Element	Sets the default characteristics for text that is not formatted using the font element or CSS.

As you're determining which font face to use, keep in mind that the font must be available on your users' computers for them to view the fonts you specify. For example, if you specify the Technical font and your users do not have it, their computers will substitute a font—possibly one you'd consider unacceptable. As a way of partially overcoming this problem, you can list multiple faces in order of preference; the machine displays the first available. For example, a list of "Comic Sans MS, Technical, Tekton, Times, Arial" will display Comic Sans MS if available, then try Technical, then Tekton, and so forth.

Which fonts should you choose? Table 3.10 lists fonts that are commonly available on Windows, Mac, and Unix platforms.

TABLE 3.10:   Commonly Available Fonts

WINDOWS	MACINTOSH	LINUX/UNIX
Arial	Helvetica	Helvetica
Courier New	Courier	Courier
Times New Roman	Times	Times

TIP

For more information on web typography, check out Chapter 12, "Web Typography."

To specify font characteristics, follow these steps. You can set some or all of the characteristics used in this example.

1. Identify the text to format with the font element.

   ```
   <font>Look at this!</font>
   ```

2. Select a specific font using the face attribute. Refer to Table 3.10 for a list of commonly available fonts.

   ```
   <font face="Verdana, 'Times New Roman', Times">
      Look at this!</font>
   ```

3. Change the font size using the size attribute. You set the size of text on a scale from 1 to 7; the default size is 3. Set the size either absolutely, with a number from 1 to 7, or relatively, with + or – the numbers of levels you want to change. Almost all browsers support size to set font size. The only significant downside to setting the font size is that your user might already have increased or decreased the default font size, so your size change might have more of an effect than you expect.

   ```
   <font face="Technical, 'Times New Roman',
      Times" size="+2">
      Look at this!</font>
   ```

4. Add a color attribute to set the color, using a color name or a #RRGGBB value.

   ```
   <font face="Technical, 'Times New Roman',
      Times" size="+2"
      color="#FF0000">Look at this!</font>
   ```

Figure 3.15 shows the result.

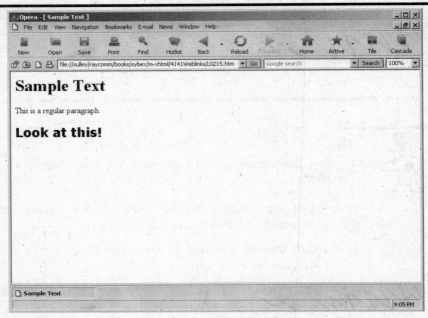

FIGURE 3.15:   Setting font characteristics can spiff up your pages and help you achieve the visual effect you want.

What's Next?

Congratulations! You've just learned to apply HTML and XHTML code, and you even learned some of the most common elements and attributes. In the next chapter, you'll learn how to link your web pages to other pages on your site and on other sites. You'll also learn how to create links to specific parts of pages on your site, and how to use graphics as links.

Chapter 4

STEPPING OUT: LINKING YOUR WAY AROUND THE WEB

Being able to link your web page to other pages is the most innovative and compelling aspect of the web, and it is certainly a huge part of the web's success. Links are convenient—and also exciting—because they provide related information to anyone viewing your page.

In this chapter, we'll review link basics and then learn much more about links, including how to use advanced anchor attributes and how to name sections of your document so that you can create tables of contents with links to particular parts of your document.

We'll see the two major categories of links: *external links*, links to files not on your own site (created by someone else), and *internal links*, links to files that are part of your site (created by you). Even though you'll use the same anchor element for both types of links, it's worth looking at them separately because they involve different concepts. We'll start by looking at external

Updated from *HTML 4.0: No Experience Required*
by E. Stephen Mack and Janan Platt Saylor
ISBN 0-7821-2143-8 $29.99

links and then learn how to integrate anchors with other HTML/XHTML tags; then we'll talk about internal links.

Finally, we'll discuss how to maintain links and check automatically for faulty links.

CREATING AN EXTERNAL LINK

The anchor element uses the <a> and </a> tags. The anchor element is used to create both external links and internal links (both of which are otherwise known as *hyperlinks*).

NOTE

These anchor links are not to be confused with the link element (which uses the <link> tag); the link element establishes different types of relationships between your document and other affiliated documents, and anchors create physical links in the body of your document. The link element is covered in detail in Chapter 16, "Using Style Sheets."

The anchor element takes several attributes. First we'll look at the attributes href, title, target, name, and id separately, and then we'll see some other attributes, including rel, rev and generic HTML 4.01 attributes. We'll also discuss some tips for your anchor text while we discuss the href attribute.

Because external links use the URL addressing scheme, we'll talk about anchors in the context of external links first.

Using the *href* Attribute and Anchor Text

Most of the time, you must use the anchor element's href attribute to specify the hyperlink reference (that is, a reference to a link's address). The href attribute must point to a URL, and the URL should appear in quotes, like this:

```
<a href="http://www.construct.net/">Construct</a>
```

NOTE

A Uniform Resource Locator (URL) is a unique address for a web page or any other file on the Internet.

In this example, `href` is pointing to a web page at the URL `http://www.construct.net/`.

TIP

When adding a link to your page, it's sometimes difficult to make sure that the URL is typed correctly. (One typo and it might not work at all.) Instead, you can visit the page you want to link to, copy the address from the location bar, and then paste it into your text editor between the quotes of your `href` attribute.

You don't have to link to web pages—you can link to any type of file on the web, including images, sounds, and movies. For example, here's some text that includes a link to a movie that's in Microsoft's AVI format:

```
<p>You can see a five-megabyte movie of two guys playing
souped-up <a href="http://www.unrealities.com/robj/videos/
roshambo.avi">Roshambo</a>.
```

(You'll learn more about images in Chapter 10, "Adding Graphics"; you'll see more about multimedia, including movies and sounds, in Chapter 15, "Including Multimedia.")

TIP

When linking to a format that's not commonly used on the web, it's polite to put some details about that format in your anchor text. For example, if you have a Zip file containing some PowerPoint documents, your anchor might look like this: `<a href="files.zip">A Zipped Archive of PowerPoint files, 104K</a>`.

You also can use links that don't use the HTTP protocol, such as links to files served by File Transfer Protocol (FTP):

```
<p>If you have trouble downloading this
<a href="ftp://ftp.emf.net/users/estephen/file.txt">
file</a>, then go ahead and
<a href="mailto:estephen@emf.net">send me a message</a>.
```

Whenever you link to a resource, the text enclosed within the anchor element is highlighted as a link and serves as the *anchor text* that somehow introduces the resource to which you are linking. For example, in the link `<a href="http://www.suite101.com/">Visit Suite 101</a>`, `Visit Suite 101` is the anchor text. By default, anchor text is blue and underlined in Netscape Navigator and Microsoft Internet Explorer.

NOTE

You can set the link color in your browser to whatever color you want. You also can select whether links are underlined. Therefore, a good web author won't include a statement such as, "Click on the blue and underlined word Next above to see the next page!"—the word "Next" may not be underlined or blue at all.

It's best not to use device-specific terms in your anchor text. For example, web authors commonly use statements such as this:

```
<p>Click <a href="http://www.sybex.com/">here</a>
to read about the latest in quality computer books!
```

However, not everyone viewing your page has a mouse, so what if they can't click anything? Also, the anchor text is just the word here, which isn't much of a description—some browsers remember pages you visit by their anchor text. Anyone viewing a list of recently visited pages may see your document listed as just the word here, which won't help them remember what the here document is about.

Instead, use the anchor element to surround the most relevant description of the resource to which you're linking:

```
<p>Read about <a href="http://www.sybex.com/">
the latest in quality computer books</a>!
```

Now the person viewing your page can select the link (whether by mouse or another method) and also knows exactly what page he's visiting; the page's description will appear in any lists of visited documents, and this approach is more concise than the "click here" approach.

To continue our discussion of anchor text, some links use straightforward anchor text.

```
<p>Kyrie works for <a href="http://www.sgi.com/">SGI</a>.
```

In this case, SGI (Silicon Graphics, Inc.) is the name of the company, and clicking the company name will lead to SGI's main website. It might be misleading for the word SGI to lead anywhere other than a main SGI home page.

Sometimes, web authors create anchor text that is subtle so that people are surprised when they follow the link. For example:

```
<p>Partha told me he thought we should sue
<a href="http://www.tickettricks.com/">
those jerks</a>.
```

It's not clear from the context of the page who "those jerks" is meant to refer to—until you point to the words those jerks and see TicketTricks' URL on the status bar. At that point, you understand the object of Partha's ire.

This "misleading" use of anchor text is all part of the fun of the web and is quite common.

WARNING

Some corporations do not take kindly to the appropriation of their logos or people "misrepresenting" their name. One web author, John Klopp, actually received a nasty phone call from a Pacific Bell lawyer for putting a link similar to this one on his page: `<a href="http://www.playboy.com/">Pacific Bell</a>`. Some companies have threatened to sue web authors who use their company names in a disparaging way. Your chances of being sued successfully depend on whether you are misusing a trademarked logo and whether you are running a commercial page that makes money—as well as the truth of your claims about the company.

Creating Advisory Titles for Your Links with the *title* Attribute

One anchor attribute that provides more information about a link is the title attribute. The title attribute allows an "advisory title" that explains the resource in more detail. Using the previous example, you can make it clearer who Partha dislikes by adding the following HTML code, which differs only by including a title attribute in the anchor element:

```
<p>Partha told me he thought we should sue <a href="http://
www.tickettricks.com/" title="TicketTricks">those jerks</a>.
```

Browsers may choose different methods of showing the advisory title attribute, such as displaying the title in a *tooltip* or *balloon help* (a little box that appears when the mouse pointer is pointing to the link), or the title might appear on the status bar. Currently, the title attribute in a link is supported by Internet Explorer 4 and above and Netscape Navigator 4 and above. Both browsers display it as a tooltip (as shown in Figure 4.1 for Internet Explorer).

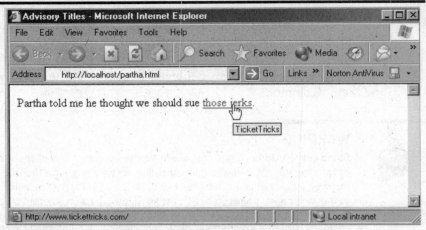

FIGURE 4.1:   Internet Explorer displays a tooltip for this link, thanks to the use of the `title` attribute in the anchor element.

CHANGING THE STATUS BAR TEXT FOR YOUR LINKS

When you point to a link, Navigator and Internet Explorer display the URL of the link's target in the status bar. A commonly used attribute (similar in intent to the `title` attribute) changes the browser's status bar to display a specific phrase when pointing to the link.

Consider this code:

```
<title>Text in the Status Bar</title>
<body>
We buy all of our books from
<a href="http://www .sybex.com/"
onmouseover="window.status='Click Here For Computer
    Books!';
  return true">Sybex</a>.
```

When the mouse pointer crosses over the anchor text (Sybex), the status bar doesn't display the link's URL as it normally would. Instead, the phrase Click Here For Computer Books! is displayed, as shown here.

· CONTINUED ➡

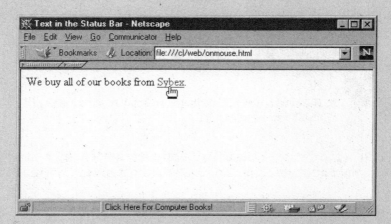

Part I

The attribute value for onmouseover in this HTML code (beginning with window.status) is not HTML at all—instead, this line contains two JavaScript commands. JavaScript is a scripting language created by Netscape that can change how web pages behave. This particular JavaScript code is fairly simple (just one line and two commands) and causes a visible change to the way web pages behave, so it's easy to understand why it is popular.

The onmouseover attribute is one example of HTML 4.01's event attributes; the event attributes can be used with many different elements, not just anchors. While we're discussing this status bar example, we should point out that it has a major drawback: Many people like to see the URL of the link on a page, and they get annoyed when the URL is replaced with a different message in the status bar. In general, users should be able to use their browsers normally when they view web pages. Every time you change the normal behavior of the browser, you risk confusing or annoying people. (For an irreverent look at many of the ways poor design choices can undermine the effectiveness of a website, see *Son of Web Pages That Suck*, by Vincent Flanders (Sybex, 2002).) Also, some visitors to your page might not be able to see the JavaScript message, so you shouldn't rely on the status bar to convey important information.

The `title` attribute can provide a description for links to images or other file types that don't have a full title. For example:

```
<p>You can see <a href="http://www.construct.net/images/
goolnut.jpg" title="Construct's Hand Logo">a logo</a>
that I admire.</p>
```

NOTE

The advisory `title` attribute can apply to almost every HTML element, not just the anchor element.

The anchor element's `title` attribute is not nearly as important as the `href` attribute or the `name` and `id` attributes, which we will discuss next.

Labeling Sections of Your Document with the *name* Attribute

Another important attribute of the anchor element is the `name` attribute, which labels a section of an HTML document with a specific reference name. The `name` attribute enables links to point to a specific section within a document (instead of links always leading to the top of a document).

For example, suppose you want to link to the street directions on a particular page at your site. The page is a long one, and the directions are near the bottom. If you link to the page itself, no one will see the directions unless they read all the way to the bottom of the page. Fortunately, you can link straight to the directions. It's a two-step process: First, you must edit the target document and give a name to the section where the directions begin, using the `name` attribute of the anchor element. Second, you must specify that name in your link.

The appropriate section of the page (where the street directions are located) can be named using this anchor element:

```
<a name="directions">
Here are the directions to our office:</a>
```

NOTE

The anchor element here isn't supposed to affect this text's appearance, but some older browsers change the enclosed text by making it bold.

Once you've added this code, you can link to the directions by taking a normal link tag and adding a number sign (#) and the name assigned (in this case, `directions`) to the URL. If the normal URL for the page is `http://www.foo.com/`, you specify the link for the direction's name like this:

```
The <a href="http://www.foo.com/#directions"> directions to
our office</a> are available
```

HTML 4.01 uses the term *fragment identifier* for the part of the URL starting with #; for example, in the code above, the fragment identifier is `#directions`.

TIP

You can link only to named sections; you can't arbitrarily link to the middle of a document unless the `<a name="`*name*`">` (or `id="`*name*`"`) and `</a>` tags have been added to that document.

Let's take a real-life example. Suppose you want to link to a particular poem in Shakespeare's play *The Tempest* (available from MIT at `http://the-tech.mit.edu/Shakespeare/works.html`). Let's say the section you want occurs in Act I, Scene 2. MIT has broken up each scene of *The Tempest* into a separate file, so the desired URL turns out to be `http://the-tech.mit.edu/Shakespeare/tempest/tempest.1.2.html`. However, the scene contains 593 lines, and your poem is near the bottom.

Fortunately, MIT has added a `name` attribute anchor to each line of every Shakespeare play. The `name` attribute anchor is simply the line number, anchored around a word in that line. For example, the line you're interested in is line number 461 of this scene. (You can discover this by searching the Shakespeare site for the word or phrase in which you're interested.) Here's the `name` attribute anchor that's used by MIT:

```
<a name="461">fathom</a>
```

You can now link straight to your poem by adding #461 to the end of the URL for the scene, which creates a fragment URL. You can use the fragment URL in your link like this:

```
<p>One of my favorite poems is sung by a character named
Ariel in William Shakespeare's <cite>The Tempest</cite>, at
<a href="http://the-tech.mit.edu/Shakespeare/tempest/
    tempest.1.2.html#461">line 461 of Act I, Scene 2</a>.
This verse was used in a song by Laurie Anderson.</p>
```

WARNING

The fragment URL used here is very long; it must be typed in one continuous line, with no line breaks or spaces at all. Remember, any white space in any URL will prevent it from working.

Now, when someone clicks on the link text (line 461 of Act I, Scene 2), he'll see the poem at the top of the screen, with the rest of the play continuing beneath. Figure 4.2 shows the result—note the extra information in Internet Explorer's location bar URL, and you can judge by the vertical scroll bar how far down in the document this line occurs.

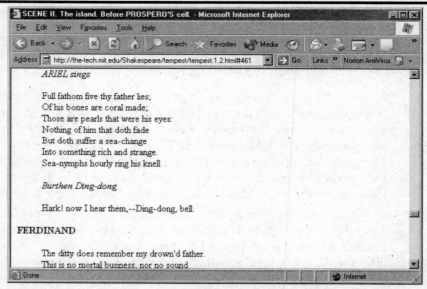

FIGURE 4.2:   Internet Explorer uses a fragment URL to fetch this verse from Shakespeare's *The Tempest*.

NOTE

Since you don't have control over whether named anchor elements exist in an external file, sometimes you won't be able to link to a specific section of an external document.

There's more to learn about named sections and using named links. We'll return to the topic of anchor names later in this chapter.

Changing Browser Windows with the *target* Attribute

Another attribute you can use in an anchor element's `<a>` tag is `target`. The `target` attribute normally is used with frames (as we'll see in Chapter 8, "Dividing a Window with Frames"). However, you can use the `target` attribute even if you don't use frames.

When you specify a `target` for your links, you indicate the name of a window where you'd like the linked page to appear. For example, a link can be specified like this:

```
<a href="http://www.walrus.com/~gibralto/" target="window2">
Acorn Mush</a>
```

When this link is followed, a new window (internally named `"window2"`) is created, containing the Acorn Mush page.

The browsers that obey target attributes (including Internet Explorer and Navigator) create new windows that look as if an extra copy of the browser is running. The old window is located behind the new window, and the old page that contained the link is still visible if the browser does not take up the full screen. If a browser does take up the full screen, the only way to see the old window is for the user to switch windows and go back to the old page.

The new window, with the new page, functions like a normal copy of the browser in every respect. Eventually, the viewer will close the new window, revealing the old window again—which in effect guarantees that the viewer will return to the original site at some point.

Web designers like the idea of letting people follow a link from their site while still keeping their site visible somewhere.

The main drawback of the `target` attribute is that some users can get confused by the unexpected behavior of their browsers when they follow a targeted link. Since each browser window maintains its own history of documents viewed, viewers can get confused when they can't seem to return to a recently visited page—until they notice their old window with their old history.

Also, if a viewer switches back to the old window while leaving the new window open but hidden, then any other links that he selects with the same `target` window (for example, a second link that also specifies `target="window2"`) will appear to be do nothing at all. The viewer will be confused about why links have stopped working in his browser. In reality, the links are working—but the link is only causing a change in a *hidden* window, so it *seems* as if nothing is happening.

Using Other Anchor Attributes

There are several other attributes used in an anchor element's <a> tag.

Although rarely used, the rel and rev attributes theoretically can mark relationships between the current document and the resource in the link. Here's an example:

```
<p>For another view on this issue, see the
   <a rel="alternate" href="http://www.example.com/
   theotherside.html">latest news report</a>.</p>
```

This link specifies that the "latest news report" has an "alternate" relationship to the current document. The important thing to realize about this attribute is that it must be used with an href attribute if you want to create a link.

The rev attribute specifies a reverse relationship. Using the latest news report example shown earlier, a reverse link could be created as in the following:

```
<p>For another view on this issue, see the
   <a rev="alternate" href="http://www.example.com/
   thesameside.html">old news report</a>.
```

In this example, href refers to a document that links to the page containing this link.

NOTE

The value of the rel and rev attributes must be one of the valid link types listed in the HTML 4.01 specification. For more information on link types, see the link types section of the HTML 4.01 specification at www.w3.org/TR/html4/types.html#type-links.

Every popular browser currently ignores these kinds of relationship attributes, so there's not much point in using them yet.

HTML 4.01 allows several new attributes to be used with anchors. First we'll discuss the new accesskey attribute, and after that we'll look at how you can use HTML 4.01's generic attributes with the anchor element to produce some useful effects.

Specifying Keyboard Shortcuts for Links

One drawback with a graphical browser is that it usually is very mouse dependent. For example, you have to click on links to follow them if you use Navigator 3 or earlier. (Internet Explorer 3 and later and Navigator 4 and later all let you use the Tab key to select a link and then Enter to follow it.)

If a page has many links, this keyboard method is a bit cumbersome and can be difficult to use, especially for people with disabilities. HTML 4.01 addresses this problem with the `accesskey` attribute, which lets you specify a shortcut key to be used to follow a link (for example, you can specify that a link should be followed whenever a user presses the A key).

Using the `accesskey` attribute with an anchor is simple: specify a single character as an attribute value. When the surfer presses the equivalent keyboard shortcut command, the browser should automatically select and follow the link.

For example:

```
<a href="http://www.yahoo.com/" accesskey="Y">Yahoo!</a>
```

specifies that the Y key should take your readers to Yahoo!'s URL. However, Windows users must press Alt+Y, and Macintosh users must press Command+Y to follow the Yahoo! link. In Internet Explorer, users must press Alt+Y and then press Enter. In Netscape, users first must put the focus on the page by clicking somewhere on the page and then press Alt+Y. Other systems may use different shortcuts or perhaps allow the shortcut key to be used by itself (without a modifier key).

According to the HTML 4.01 specification, browsers should indicate the Y key as the shortcut in some fashion. You shouldn't have to write, "Press the Y key to visit Yahoo!" anywhere on your page (and that description wouldn't be accurate for all systems or browsers, anyway). However, you may need to include the name of the access key in the anchor text so that it can be highlighted. For example, if you want to use Z as the `accesskey` value for your Yahoo! link, use anchor text such as `"Z: Yahoo!"` or `"Yahoo! (Z)"` to provide a visual indication that Z is the shortcut key.

NOTE

Internet Explorer 4 and above and Netscape 6 and above support the use of the `accesskey` attribute. For more information on the use of the `accesskey` attribute, see `www.cs.tut.fi/~jkorpela/forms/accesskey.html`.

Using Language Attributes

The generic `lang` and `dir` attributes can be particularly useful with anchors, since you can indicate what language is being used in the linked document, as well as the direction (left-to-right or right-to-left) that is used in that document.

In addition, the anchor element allows a special `charset` attribute to declare what character encoding (that is, what set of foreign language characters) is used in the linked-to resource.

For example:

```
<a href="http://www.jmas.co.jp/FAQs/"
lang="jp" charset="euc-jp">Index to various FAQs</a>
```

is a link to a page on a server located in Japan. The language of the page is declared to be Japanese by the `lang` attribute. The `charset` attribute indicates that browsers should use a particular character encoding to display the Japanese characters that are used on the page. In this case, the character encoding is called `"euc-jp"`, but other charsets are possible as well. Unfortunately, charsets are not yet in wide enough use for there to be a definitive list of them anywhere. More details about charsets can be found online (`http://www.ietf.org/rfc/rfc2045.txt`).

Using Reference, Style, and Script Attributes

By defining a style sheet and applying one of those attributes to an anchor element, you can control a wide range of possibilities for the appearance of links and anchor text. In addition, HTML 4.01 specifically allows the use of `id` attribute values as a target for named anchors. Instead of using an anchor with a `name` attribute to label a particular part of your document, you can use an element's `id` attribute. For example, you could name a section of bold text with the identity `"Greg"` as shown here:

```
<b id="greg">Greg Burrell</b> is an expert on this subject.
```

Later in your document (or in a different document), you can link to the `"Greg"` section using a fragment URL that ends with `#greg`.

The `id` attribute is similar to the `name` attribute, although not exactly the same. Both the `id` attribute and the `name` attribute must be unique—a specific `id` or `name` attribute value can be used only once within the same HTML/XHTML document. Both `id` and `name` are designed to be used as fragment identifiers and can be used with the `a`, `applet`, `form`, `frame`, `iframe`, `img`, and `map` elements in HTML 4.01.

In XHTML 1.0, the `name` attribute is deprecated in favor of the use of the `id` attribute. For backward compatibility as well as forward compatibility, the name attribute and the id attribute can be used together. In this case, as shown here, they must have exactly the same value.

```
<a name="461" id="461">fathom</a>
```

Valid content for the name attribute and the id attribute is not exactly the same, but letters and numbers are valid values for either one. For more information on valid content for name and id, see Section C.8 in the XHTML 1.0 specification at www.w3.org/TR/xhtml1/#guidelines.

Using Event Attributes with Anchors

Earlier in this chapter, we discussed the use of the onmouseover attribute and a piece of JavaScript code to change the content of the browser's status bar. A wide range of event attributes can affect the contents or appearance of an attribute. One possible use is a message or confirmation dialog box to give the surfer some information about the link he's about to follow.

In the next section, we'll discuss how to use the anchor element with other elements (for example, to create a list of links).

USING ANCHOR ELEMENTS WITH OTHER HTML ELEMENTS

Before we proceed to some new uses of anchor elements, let's see how well the anchor element interacts with other tags. Specifically, we'll look at how the anchor element should be nested.

An anchor element cannot be nested within other anchor elements. Therefore, this use of an anchor element is illegal:

```
<a href="http://www.yahoo.com/">There are a whole range
of categories in Yahoo's listings, including general
categories like Computers and Entertainment, and specific
categories for <a href="http://www.yahoo.com/Entertainment/
Actors_and_Actresses/Bacon__Kevin/">Kevin Bacon</a>
and Coca-Cola.</a>
```

Instead, separate your anchors into separate elements. Anchor text should be relatively short—a few words should be sufficient. Try this as a replacement for the previous listing:

```
There is a whole range of categories in
<a href="http://www.yahoo.com/">Yahoo's listings</a>,
including general categories like Computers and
```

```
Entertainment, and specific categories for
<a href="http://www.yahoo.com/Entertainment/
Actors_and_Actresses/Bacon__Kevin/">Kevin Bacon</a>
and Coca-Cola.</a>
```

It's legal to put an anchor element inside a heading:

```
<h1><a href="http://www.jazzflavor.com/">It's About Jazz,
    Daddyo!</a></h1>
```

The anchor here would take on the quality of the heading, as shown in Figure 4.3.

FIGURE 4.3:   An anchor nested within a heading appears the same as a heading, but also with the qualities of a link.

Since headings are block-level elements and anchors are text-level elements, the heading must contain the anchor for a link and not vice versa.

Similarly, you can use text-level elements either inside or outside the anchor element to affect the quality of links. This allows you to color-code or otherwise flag certain links. Some websites use this technique to make a distinction between internal and external links.

For example, you can make a link appear in italics by enclosing it in the italic element:

```
<i><a href="http://www.example.com/home/jef/">Jef's
    Home</a></i>
```

The order here doesn't matter, so this similar construction would also render the anchor text in italics:

```
<a href="http://www.example.com/home/jef/"><i>Jef's
    Home</i></a>
```

As you can see from Figure 4.4, both links appear the same way.

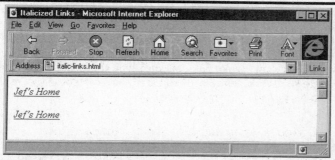

FIGURE 4.4:   Two italicized links, each nested in a different order but with an
identical result displayed by Internet Explorer

NOTE

Actually, it's slightly preferable to put the anchor element *inside* the italic element so that any software that is using the anchor text to index or store links
doesn't get confused by the italic element and store the link as `"I Jef's Home
I"` or `"<i>Jef's Home</i>"`.

You also can color-code links, but the `font` element that contains the
`color` attribute must occur nested within the anchor element. If you put
the `font` element outside the anchor element, the default color of the
link takes precedence over the `font` element. To see this in action, we'll
see the following two links:

```
<font color="green">
 <a href="http://www.example.com/~drkeith/hoot/">
 Hootenanny</a>
</font>
<p>
<a href="http://www.example.com/~drkeith/hoot/">
    <font color="green">Hootenanny</font>
</a>
```

The first link will appear in blue, the default color for a link, because
the inner anchor element has a default color that takes precedence
over the outer `font` element. The second link will appear in green, as
specified, since the inner `font` element takes precedence over the default
link color.

NOTE

If you color your links, be sure to choose colors that are consistent and easy to read. Some HTML style guides recommend against coloring individual links because it may be confusing to users who are used to seeing links in blue or the color they've specified for links. Others designers recommend you use style sheets if you want to color links, because style sheets keep the presentation separate from the content. Since HTML is all about content and not really about formatting, this approach makes sense.

One issue to consider is that if you color a link, surfers won't be able to see if they've visited the link. Your color specification will override the browser's standard behavior of having two different link colors: one for visited links and another for unvisited links.

WARNING

Although Navigator 4 (and above) and Internet Explorer 4 (and above) can color links, earlier versions of those browsers have problems. Internet Explorer 3 cannot display links in different colors at all. Navigator 3 displays colored links only if the anchor is within a table cell (see Chapter 11, "Presenting Information in Tables," for the use of table cells).

For our final example of using anchors with other HTML tags, we'll use lists of links. Since lists are a good way to organize information, they're a natural way of presenting a group of links.

For example, consider the following section of HTML code:

```
<p>There are several good HTML references on the web.
Here are some recommended online references:
<ul>
<li><a href="http://webreference.com/html/">HTML with
Style</a></li>
<li><a
    href="http://www.eskimo.com/~bloo/indexdot/html/
    index.html">Index Dot HTML's Advanced HTML Reference
</a></li>
<li><a href="http://www.w3.org/MarkUp/">W3C HTML Reference
</a></li>
</ul>
```

This code would create a nice bulleted list of HTML references, as shown in Figure 4.5.

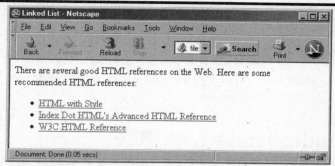

FIGURE 4.5: Each of these links is a list item in an unordered list, displayed by Navigator.

Feel free to experiment with other text-level elements and anchors; most of them work just as you might expect. For example, you can make a link bigger by surrounding it with the `<big>` and `</big>` tags:

```
<big><a href="http://www.levity.com/corduroy">Bohemian Ink
  </a></big>
```

CREATING AN INTERNAL LINK

Now that we've discussed external links, it's time to talk about internal links. *Internal links* refer to pages within your own website.

Internal links behave identically to external links with one exception: You can use *relative URLs* for internal links, which saves typing. We'll discuss how relative URLs work in a moment. First we'll define the concept of absolute URLs.

Understanding Absolute URLs

Absolute URLs are simply fully specified URLs.

If your web page's URL is `http://www.example.com/rupert-links` `.html`, you can refer to other individual pages on your website with the appropriate absolute URL, as we've seen. Each page can be reached simply by changing the individual filenames at the end. The sample file we used in the previous section had several such absolute URLs. Take this example:

```
<a href="http://www.example.com/history.html">Rupert's
  History Page</a>
```

In the `history.html` file, there might be a link back to the Rupert's Recommend Links page with an element like this one:

```
<a href="http://www.example.com/rupert-links.html">
    Rubert's Recommend Links</a>
```

These two URLs are called absolute URLs because the address is fully specified. The URL is 100 percent, absolutely complete.

Understanding Relative URLs

Both of the previous absolute URLs contain the same stuff at the beginning: `http://www.example.com/`. It's a pain to have to retype the full address every time. It's also more likely that you'll make a mistake if you have to type an absolute URL over and over; in addition, if your web page ever moves for some reason (for example, from www.example.com to www.t-shirts .com), you'll have to go through and correct every link.

Relative URLs prevent these problems. A relative URL simply drops the common part from the URL and lets the browsers automatically figure out the part that's missing.

For example, in `http://www.example.com/rupert-links.html`, instead of specifying this:

```
<a href="http://www.example.com/history.html">
    Rupert's History Page</a>
```

just specify the part that's different from the current page's URL:

```
<a href="history.html">Rupert's History Page</a>
```

Whenever anyone chooses the link to `history.html`, the browser will automatically change the relative URL into the fully specified absolute URL, `http://www.example.com/history.html`, and the correct page will be retrieved.

Relative URLs such as this assume that the files are in the same directory; in a moment, we'll discuss what to do if the files are in different directories on the same system. In general, if you create a link such as `<a href="joe.html">All About Joe Thomas</a>`, choosing the link just causes the browser to look for a file named `joe.html` in the current directory.

As you might imagine, you can use relative URLs for all sorts of files, including images. For example, you can specify an inline image with an `<img>` tag that uses a relative URL, like this one:

```
<img src="pluto.gif">
```

If there's an image file in the current directory that is called `pluto.gif`, it will be displayed properly by the `<img>` tag.

Using Relative URLs with Different Directories

We'll assume you know how directories and subdirectories (also known as *folders*) work on your operating system. (If you don't, check with the documentation that came with your computer or your operating system's online help.)

Suppose you have a subdirectory called `faculty`, and you want to link to a file in `faculty` called `smith.html`. If you were to use an absolute URL, it would be `http://www.example.com/faculty/smith.html` (assuming we're still using the `example.com` example from the previous two sections).

If you want to link to the `smith.html` file from `rupert-links.html` (which is at the top level of the server), instead of having to use that absolute URL, you can use a relative URL such as this one:

```
<a href="faculty/smith.html">Rupert's pal, Prof. Smith</a>
```

NOTE

The slash used to separate folders is always a forward slash (/), never a backslash (\).

How do you make a link that goes back to `rupert-links.html` in the `smith.html` file? You can't simply say `<a href="rupert-links.html">Rupert's Links</a>`, because those two files aren't in the same directory.

You could use the absolute URL, `<a href="http://www.example.com/rupert-links.html">Rupert's Links</a>`, but we've already learned that absolute URLs aren't as desirable as relative URLs, so it would be a shame to have to rely on this method.

Fortunately, there's an abbreviation that means "the directory above the current directory" (also known as the parent directory). This abbreviation is two periods (`..`).

If you're a DOS or UNIX user, you are probably familiar with this "dot-dot" notation; older versions of Windows also use the `..` abbreviation in directory lists.

NOTE

Periods are sometimes called *dots*.

Using this abbreviation, you can specify a relative URL in `smith.html` that leads to `rupert-links.html`:

```
<a href="../rupert-links.html">Rupert's Links</a>
```

You even can use multiple `..` references. If you have a file deeply buried in a series of subdirectories, it can link to a file much higher up on the directory tree with a link such as this one: `<a href="../../../icecream .html">Vanilla Ice Cream</a>`. This relative URL means "go to the folder three levels above the current folder, and get the file there named `icecream.html`."

Relative URLs are commonly used, and we recommend you use them whenever possible.

Troubleshooting Relative URLs

If your relative URLs aren't working for some reason, you should try using the `<base>` tag. A `<base>` tag tells the browser the correct absolute URL of your document, which might fix the relative URLs used on that page. (If you already have a `<base>` tag, try removing it.) If worse comes to worst, and the relative URLs still don't work (and you've checked to make sure the files are in same directory and are properly readable), you always can use the absolute URL. If *that* doesn't work, then something is wrong with your server or your files, or else you're not using your URL correctly at all. In that case, it might be time to call in your Internet service provider's technical support.

Using Default Pages

You might be puzzled by one thing we haven't explained before: Why does a URL that doesn't specify an `html` filename still retrieve an HTML file?

For example, when you type in a URL such as `http://www.yahoo.com/`, it's clear you're retrieving an HTML file of some kind. (If you don't believe us, just view the page's source, and you'll definitely see HTML code there.) You didn't specify the name of this HTML file in your URL, as you would in a URL such as `http://www.yahoo.com/help.html`.

The answer to this puzzle is that each server is programmed to send a certain page if no other page is specified in the URL. The name of this default page is usually `index.html`.

NOTE

The term *default* just means the usual or expected choice. If Scott always orders cappuccino whenever he's in a coffee shop, you can assume that if he doesn't specify his order, he still wants cappuccino. You could say that Scott orders cappuccino "by default." This terminology is used with computers and the web all the time.

Try it: Go visit http://www.yahoo.com/index.html, and you'll notice that the page displayed is *exactly* the same as what's displayed with http://www.yahoo.com/. These two URLs both refer to the same file. When you leave off the index.html part, Yahoo!'s server still sends the index.html page—your browser just doesn't tell you in the address box exactly what happened.

Some HTTP servers use a different filename for the default page—for example, Default.html, default.htm, or index.htm instead of index.html. Other servers let you specify the default file independently for each directory so that you can specify that your bacon directory sends the kevin.html file by default. That would mean, for example, that the URLs http://www.samplepage.com/bacon/ and http://www.samplepage.com/bacon/kevin.html both would display the same page.

HOW TO MAKE A RELATIVE LINK TO AN *INDEX.HTML* FILE WITHOUT USING THE WORD *INDEX.HTML*

The last point we have to make here about the index.html default filename is that it can be a little tricky to link to it. You can always refer to it as index.html (with an element such as <a href= "index.html">Rupert's Main Page</a>), but then you might be pointing to the same file with two different names, which could be confusing. After all, the other name for the same file is http:// www.example.com/, and your visitors (and search engines) might not know that you're talking about the same file.

If your index.html file is in a subdirectory called faculty, it's simple to refer to it: Just use a relative link such as href="faculty/".

If you're linking back to your index.html file from a subdirectory, you can use the .. shortcut that we saw earlier, with a relative link like href="../".

CONTINUED ➡

Part I

If your index.html file is in your main directory, you have a choice. You can link to it with its absolute URL, such as href="http://www.example.com/" (which is equivalent to http://www.example.com/index.html but shorter). Or you can use the special abbreviation for the current directory, a single period (.), which would make your relative URL look like this: href="./".

In all of these examples, it's not strictly necessary to include the final slash, but the correct name does include the slash—and using the correct name is a safer practice than leaving off the slash, since some servers and browsers can get confused if the final slash is missing.

JUMPING TO A NAMED ANCHOR WITH INTERNAL LINKS

It's time to return to a topic we first brought up earlier in this chapter: named anchors. In this section, we'll expand on the concept of naming a section of your document by seeing how you can jump from one part of the document to another. This makes it easy, for example, to link from the top of the document to the bottom. In turn, this enables you to put a table of contents at the top of a particular document.

First, however, we'll review the use of named anchor elements in light of what you've just learned about relative URLs.

Using Named Anchor Elements with Internal Links and Relative URLs

As we mentioned, you can link to a specific part of a document by adding its name to the URL after a # character. (We call the section starting with # a *fragment identifier*.) For example, linking to:

```
http://www.emf.net/~estephen/facts/lefthand.html#scientific
```

opens a file called lefthand.html and then jumps down to the scientific section.

These types of links will work only if the file has a section with a named anchor element. For example, you'll need to use a tag such as

`<a name= "scientific">` and then put an `</a>` tag at the end of the section's anchor text.

When you see a fragment identifier like the one above, you can assume that there is a section of the `lefthand.html` file named `scientific`. It turns out that there is such a file with a named anchor as described. The specific HTML code to name the section looks like this:

```
<h4><a name="scientific">Scientific Articles and
    Sites</a></h4>
```

Since you don't have control over whether a named anchor element exists in an external file, sometimes you won't be able to link to a specific section of an external document. However, when you're linking to your own internal files, you'll always be able to add the necessary name or `id` attribute to an anchor element in the appropriate section of your document.

If you want to jump to a certain section within one of your documents, just use a relative URL with the label in your anchor. For example:

```
<p>Please <a href="mary.html#contact">contact Mary</a>
    for more information.</p>
```

To make this link work, make sure that the `mary.html` file exists in the same directory as the file containing the previous code, and make sure that `mary.html` contains the following HTML code somewhere:

```
<a name="contact">My Contact Information</a>
```

NOTE

The specification for HTML says that the names should not be case sensitive. However, anchor names are case sensitive in older browsers, so you should not use `<a name="CONTACT">` if you later use `<a href="#contact">`. Instead, make sure that your name always uses the same case in the name anchor and the fragment identifier.

WARNING

Don't name your sections with illegal characters. Names should be unique in each document, and they must consist of letters and numbers, without spaces or punctuation other than the period (.) and hyphen (–). Also, be careful not to leave off one of the quotation marks in your anchor. Finally, don't try to use an empty name anchor, like this: `<a name="foo"></a>`. Some browsers get confused by empty anchors, so you should always wrap the anchor around some text.

Linking to Different Parts of the Same Document

In addition to linking to other internal files, you also can use anchor elements to name and link to parts of the same document. For example, suppose you're creating a very long document. If there's important information that has to be at the bottom of the document, put a link at the top of the document that lets your viewers quickly jump to the bottom (without having to scroll all the way down).

```
<p><a href="#bottom">Jump to the bottom of this document
    </a> to see some important information.</p>
```

At the bottom of your document, name a section with the following tag:

```
<p><a name="bottom">Here's the important information:</a></p>
<p>(Important information goes here.)</p>
```

We mentioned earlier that you can't nest anchors inside other anchors. Sometimes you'll need to create an href link and a name at the same time, for the same text. This would be impossible without nesting, except for the fact that an anchor element can include both attributes, like this:

```
<a href="next.html" name="next-section">The next section
    describes Monarch butterflies.</A>
```

WARNING

If your document is *really* long, your viewers will have to wait until the document is loaded before they can jump to the bottom. That's because browsers can't jump to a label if they haven't yet loaded the part of the document that contains the named label.

Creating a Table of Contents Using Named Anchors

Now that you've seen how to link to named anchors within the same file, you can create a table of contents.

If you create a long document, you can divide it into sections with headers. It's a good idea to add an anchor element with the name attribute within each header element and use a single-word name for each section that's a relevant keyword, like this:

```
<h2><a name="history">History of the Sonnet</a></h2>
```

This enables other documents to link straight to the history section, by adding #history to the URL.

TIP

Even if you don't plan to link straight to a particular section yourself, perhaps other web authors will want to, so they will appreciate it if you take the time to put in the name anchors.

The best reason to name each section is that it enables you to create a table of contents for your page. This table of contents can occur anywhere in the document or in a different document.

Each item in the table of contents simply contains a link that leads to the particular section, like this:

```
<a href="#history">History of the Sonnet</a>
```

If the table of contents is in a different file, it has to include the filename in the URL, like this:

```
<a href="sonnets.html#history">History of the Sonnet</a>
```

Here's a simplified version of a table of contents, with links at the top of the page that include fragment identifiers to named anchors further down on the page.

Listing 4.1: anchors.html

```
<!DOCTYPE html PUBLIC
"-//W3C//DTD XHTML 1.0 Transitional//EN"
 "http://www.w3.org/TR/xhtml1/DTD/xhtml1-transitional.dtd">
<html xmlns="http://www.w3.org/1999/xhtml">
<head>
<title>Named Anchors</title>
<meta http-equiv="Content-Type"
content="text/html; charset=iso-8859-1" />
</head>
<body>
<h3>We can create a group of named anchors, so that the
links on the top of the page go to specific sections of
that page or another page. This technique is often used on
FAQ pages.<br />
For example:</h3>
<h3><a href="#apple">apple</a></h3>
<h3><a href="#banana">banana</a></h3>
```

```
<h3><a href="#orange">orange</a></h3>
<h3>This allows visitors to go to a specific section of the
page easily. Generally, you also want to add links back to
the top of the page after each separate section so that the
viewer can return easily to the group of links and make
another selection.</h3>
<p><a name="apple" id="apple">
An apple</a> is a red fruit.</p>
<p><a href="#">Return to Top</a></p>
<p><a name="banana" id="banana">
A banana</a> is a yellow fruit.</p>
<p><a href="#">Return to Top</a></p>
<p><a name="orange" id="orange">
An orange</a> is an orange fruit.</p>
<p><a href="#">Return to Top</a></p>
</body>
</html>
```

Figure 4.6 shows the previous HTML code displayed by Internet Explorer.
Each of the links leads to the appropriate section in the same document.

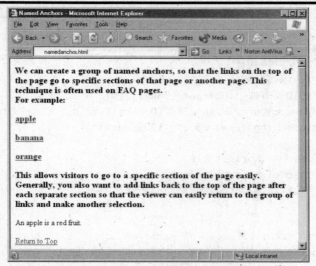

FIGURE 4.6:   Our table of contents page

We've now seen just about every possible use of the anchor element. We'll
round out this chapter with a look at some methods of making sure your
links can be verified and maintained.

VERIFYING AND MAINTAINING LINKS

One of the problems a web author faces is that external links are beyond his control. If someone moves or removes his web page, your link to it will be broken—it will lead nowhere.

When someone tries to follow one of your links that leads to a missing page, he'll get an error message—usually the infamous "404 - Document Not Found" error message.

NOTE

The numbers attached to web error messages are assigned by the protocol specification for HTTP. The article at this address explains the errors in plain English: http://home.cfl.rr.com/eaa/ServerCodes.htm.

For example, trying to view a nonexistent page from the sonic.net Internet service provider results in the error message shown in Figure 4.7.

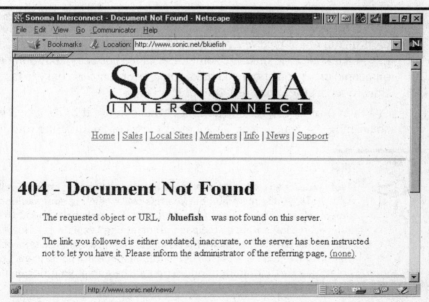

FIGURE 4.7:   We tried to display a page called bluefish from sonic.net, but it no longer exists. Instead, we're greeted with this error message, a 404 - Document Not Found error.

You can prevent having bad links in two ways. The first is not to link to any external sites at all. This is an extreme measure, and the drawback is that you can't link to a lot of useful material (and if you don't link to other people, it's less likely other people will want to link to you unless your content is very compelling). The second way is to choose your external links with care, tending toward documents that have been around a long time or are maintained by responsible people or stable companies.

TIP

When you link to someone's web page, it's polite (but not necessary) to write a brief e-mail saying that you've linked to them. Send along your e-mail address and the URL of your page. That way, they are able to link back to you (if they want to), and they can let you know if they move or delete the page.

There really is no alternative but to check your links often and replace any bad links. You can replace a missing link with a different resource, or you can try to search for the old resource to see if it's moved without leaving a forwarding address.

To verify the links on your pages, you should go through all of your external links and follow them to make sure the pages on the other side are still valid. You should do this at a regular interval, perhaps once a month. You might receive e-mail from people who have noticed that a link of yours is stale (bad links are sometimes called *cobwebs*), but don't count on people to tell you about bad links—most people are too busy to take the time to report every bad link they see.

When (not if) you find a bad link, either remove it or replace it with something else that works. This is the process of maintaining your links.

TIP

Avoid putting an excessive number of links on your page; not only is it more difficult for you to maintain, but you risk overwhelming your audience, and they won't know which links are useful. Lots of people have already tried the "link every single word on the page to something" experiment. However, it's worthwhile to create a link whenever you are using a technical term or abbreviation or mentioning a person or institution that has a home page. Consider creating a Further Information section at the end of your document with relevant links.

Verifying and maintaining links is a time-consuming process. Fortunately, computers are quite adept at helping you out with this task. Several good link verification tools can help you weed out the bad links.

Using External Link Verification Tools

There are two types of tools that can verify your external links. One type is a web page service in which you indicate pages that need to have their links verified; the service will go through all of the links on your pages and create a report to let you know which links are bad.

WARNING

This process is not foolproof. Sometimes a good link might be reported as bad because the link is not working temporarily. Sometimes a bad link will seem to be good because the page on the other side is present but empty. Link verification tools can check only whether the external page exists—they don't tell you if a page is no longer worth a link.

Here are a couple of link verification tools available from the web:

▶ NetMechanic (http://www.netmechanic.com/) can run an exhaustive check on the links in your site in the background, and when it's finished it can mail you a pointer to its report.

▶ Doctor HTML (http://www2.imagiware.com/RxHTML/) includes link verification as one of its tests of a page. (If you want the Doctor to check more than one page at a time, you'll have to pay for the service.)

The second type of link verification tool is a program you run on your server or local computer that goes through the links. Some of these programs are freeware or shareware, and others are commercial software.

Here are some link verification tools you can download or purchase:

▶ MOMSpider, a robot that searches for bad links from your site and runs on UNIX-based systems (as long as they have the Perl language available). Freeware from the University of California, Irvine (http://www.ics.uci.edu/pub/websoft/MOMspider/).

▶ Linklint, a fast HTML link checker available for DOS, UNIX, and Windows machines, but only if they have the Perl language interpreter available. By Jim Bowlin (http://www.linklint.org/).

▶ WebQA, a Windows-based commercial link checker from Watchfire (http://www.watchfire.com/products/webqa.asp). An evaluation version is available to download.

Part I

No matter what tool you use, you'll still want to check your links yourself from time to time.

NOTE

In addition, page- and site-creation tools such as Macromedia Dreamweaver, Adobe GoLive, and Microsoft FrontPage include built-in link verification commands.

WHAT'S NEXT?

In this chapter, we discussed just about everything there is to know about anchors and links, from external links to internal links, some general advice and examples on how to use the anchor element and its attributes, as well as how to create a table of contents. In the next chapter, Deborah Ray and Eric Ray show you how to publish your web page and present it to the World Wide Web.

Chapter 5

PUBLISHING YOUR (X)HTML DOCUMENTS

So far in this book, you've learned what HTML and XHTML documents are, what they look like, and why you'd use them, among many other topics. If you've been doing the examples, you've also created a few documents of your own. To this point, you've been developing and viewing the HTML and XHTML documents on your local computer. However, for other people to use and enjoy them, you must *publish* your documents.

In this chapter, we'll show you options for publishing your documents, and we'll walk you through the publishing process.

Adapted from *Mastering HTML and XHTML*,
by Deborah S. Ray and Eric J. Ray

ISBN 0-7821-4141-2 $49.99

PLACES TO PUBLISH

When you publish your HTML and XHTML documents, all you're doing is putting a copy of the documents on a *server* so that the documents are available on the Internet. You might think of a server as a waiter at a restaurant. You tell the server specifically what you want—"I'll have the BigFuzz Cheeseburger, a Load-o-Fries, and a Choc-o-Yumm, please"—and the waiter gets the order and brings it to you. Likewise, when you visit a website, you ask the server to display a certain page—such as the page on the web server (www), at the raycomm.com domain, and specifically the page called index.html (www.raycomm.com/index.html). You type that in the browser's location box and press Enter, the browser contacts the server, and the server brings you the page you requested. To publish your HTML and XHTML documents, you need to make them available on a server so that the server can make them available to the people (uh, computers) that request them.

In general, you can publish your documents in three different ways:

▶ Your Internet service provider (ISP)

▶ Your corporate IS department

▶ Your own server

Publishing Through Your ISP

One of the most common places to publish documents is on web space provided by an Internet service provider (ISP). ISPs usually provide a slew of Internet-related services—including web space—and help with your web development needs. You can find out more about ISPs in your area by researching the following resources:

The Web   For a comprehensive list of ISPs, along with contact information and services, visit your favorite search engine and search for "ISP" and your geographic area; for example, search for "ISP TX" if you live in Texas. Also, check out www.cnet.com/internet/0-3761.html.

Your Local Paper or Yellow Pages   Often, you'll find ads for local ISPs in the Technology or Business section of your daily newspaper or in the Internet section of your local yellow pages.

Other People   Ask friends, neighbors, business associates, or folks at your local computer store about the services they use and their experiences. The quality, reliability, and service of both ISPs and web-hosting services vary, so get all the advice and input you can before you commit.

TIP

Look for a guaranteed uptime figure, and always ask what you get if they fail to meet the guarantee. Then, after you find an ISP that appears to suit your needs, start by signing a short contract—no longer than six months—until you know that the service is satisfactory.

ISPs often provide a range of services, and you'll need to do some research to find out about them, as well as about startup and monthly costs. In general, though, most ISPs offer either individual or business accounts.

FINDING A WEB-HOSTING SERVICE

Another option—one that's not quite an ISP, but similar—is a web-hosting service. A web-hosting service does not provide dial-up Internet access but simply provides a home from which you can serve your sites.

Generally, you use web-hosting services in conjunction with an ISP, thus combining the best web-hosting deal with reliable dial-up access. Although it's possible that a single company could meet all your needs, shopping for these services separately can be useful. For a fairly comprehensive list of web-hosting services, check out this long but excellent URL:

```
http://dir.yahoo.com/Business_and_Economy/Business_
    to_Business/
Communications_and_Networking/Internet_and_World_
    Wide_Web/
Network_Service_Providers/Hosting/Web_Site_Hosting/
    Directories/
```

Alternatively, follow these steps in Yahoo! to find the web-hosting information: Go to Home ➢ Business And Economy ➢ Business To Business ➢ Communications And Networking ➢ Internet And

CONTINUED ➡

World Wide Web ➤ Network Service Providers ➤ Hosting ➤ Web Site Hosting. (The web changes frequently, so these steps may not be identical by the time you read this book.)

Note that many free services (including GeoCities, owned by Yahoo!) get you on the web, but at the price of putting their ads in your pages (and in the pop-up pages that spring up when your page is accessed). For only a little money each month, you can avoid all that and keep your viewers happier.

About ISP Individual Accounts

Generally, ISPs provide individual subscribers—as opposed to business subscribers—with access to the Internet, to e-mail, and to a relatively small amount of space on a web server. Many ISPs also provide other services, such as sending you the results of a form via e-mail. Exactly which services you'll need depends on what you want to do with your web pages. For example, if you plan to create and publish a few documents, you may need only a little bit of web space. On the other hand, if you plan to create a larger website loaded with multimedia and downloadable files or an e-commerce site, you'll need more space. If you want to include forms or use server-specific capabilities, you may need some server access or specific programs. Therefore, when choosing an ISP account, determine how big a site you'll be developing and what functionality it will include, and then find an ISP that can meet your needs.

In addition to finding out what general services an ISP provides, you may also want to ask these questions, depending on your needs:

What kind of server is it, and what platform does the server run on?   If you know the server and the platform, you can find the documentation on the web, which should tell you which scripts you can add easily. For example, if an Apache server is running on a Sun workstation or a Linux system (likely ISP scenarios), you can reasonably request that your server administrator install specific Perl scripts. However, if you're on an intranet with a Windows 2000–based IIS server and you hear of a cool enhancement to the WebStar server on a Macintosh, you can save yourself some embarrassment and just not ask for it.

Can I restrict access to my pages? When testing pages on the server, you don't want the whole world to see them—setting password-restricted access to the whole site helps with this. Additionally, if you have some pages that you want to make available to only a few people (or to everyone except a few people), you need to be able to set passwords and do that with little hassle and without wasting time.

WARNING

Be careful about publishing pages on the Internet. Even if you don't provide links to a page or publish a page's URL, people may still come across it. Additionally, search engines can also index such pages, making them available.

Can I install and run my own scripts? If you can, you'll have a lot more flexibility and capabilities than you would otherwise. If you're limited to what your ISP has already installed for your use, you're likely to have access to certain limited special capabilities, such as chat rooms, but not the flexibility to go with what you really want.

Do you maintain access logs? How can I find out how many hits my site gets? If you're selling services, promoting your company, or doing anything else that involves a significant number of people seeing your message, make sure that accesses are logged, and learn how to get to those logs.

TIP

Ask your server administrator what kinds of tools are available to view and sort web server access logs—the "raw" (unprocessed) logs are an ugly mess, but lots of neat programs exist to parse the logs into something useful. Although your server administrator might have some of those programs installed, the access instructions may not be publicized.

TIP

Free or inexpensive services on the web can provide logging and access counting for your pages. Look at www.hotscripts.com/Remotely_Hosted/ and browse to Counters (but check out the other cool stuff, too).

Who do I call if the server fails to respond at 2 p.m.? How about 2 a.m.? Does the ISP make backups, or do you need to back up your own site? Under what circumstances will the ISP restore backup files—only if the server crashes or also if you make a mistake and delete your files?

TIP

You might also ask these questions if you're thinking about an ISP business account or publishing on a corporate server.

About ISP Business Accounts

If you're running a business and using the Internet (or if you're moving in that direction), consider getting a business account with an ISP. Business accounts, although somewhat more expensive than individual accounts, usually include more web space, better access to server-side programs, and more comprehensive services, with guaranteed uptime, backups, and more attention to individual needs.

Many ISPs require a business account to have its own *domain name*, which replaces the ISP's name in the URL. For example, instead of our business's URL being:

    www.example.com/~raycomm/index.html

(which includes the ISP name and a folder designated for us), it simply reads:

    www.raycomm.com

Having your own domain name also offers a few practical advantages:

▶ It can enhance your professional appearance and help make your business appear larger than it really is.

▶ It helps establish your identity. Each domain name is unique and can include the business name itself or other names. For example, our business name is RayComm, Inc., and our domain name is www.raycomm.com.

▶ You can keep a consistent address even if you move or change ISPs. Users (who may be your customers or potential customers) will always be able to find you because your address remains constant.

▶ You can easily expand your website as your needs grow. If you start by having your service provider host your domain (called a *virtual domain*), you can easily expand your capacity or add services without changing your address or revising your advertising materials.

VIRTUAL DOMAINS

As an information provider, you're not limited to using the ISP's server name as the hostname portion of your URL. Instead, you can use a virtual domain, which gives you a hostname of your own, but your files still reside on a host computer. Virtual domains are a very popular way for small companies and organizations to look bigger than they really are.

For example, if you put your files on a server called `example.com`, your web address might look something like this:

```
http://www.example.com/~accountname/filename.html
```

In this example, the address includes the protocol indicator, a special folder on the server (indicated by the tilde [~]), an account name, and a filename.

A virtual domain changes the address to eliminate the special folder and account name and replaces these with a new host (domain) name. For example, a web address using a virtual domain might look like this:

```
http://www.accountname.com/filename.html
```

This example includes the protocol indicator, the domain name (`www.accountname.com`), and the filename (`filename.html`).

The easiest way to get a virtual domain is to ask your ISP to set it up for you. You may pay in the neighborhood of $50 to $100 for setup, plus anywhere from $10 to $70 for registering your domain name for two years with one of the official Internet domain name registrars.

If you do a little homework with your ISP, however, you can set up a virtual domain yourself and save a few dollars. You can find a list of accredited registrars at `www.icann.org/registrars/accredited-list.html`.

TIP

If you're thinking about getting your own domain name, start your research and claim the name of your choice as soon as you can. If you don't claim the domain name you want, someone else likely will.

If you have a company name under which you operate, get a domain name immediately, even if you won't use it in the near future. Most of the most popular names are already taken. If you have a small business and aren't incorporated or are just thinking of incorporating, consider getting the domain name first and then incorporating under that name. It seems a little backward, but a domain name must be unique, and competition for good names is stiff. After you obtain your domain name, take care of registering to do business under that name.

Let's look at an example. Suppose your business's name is Laura's Toys and More. You look up www.laurastoysandmore.com, and the domain name is already taken. You can try several variations, such as www.laurastoysnmore.com or www.laurastoystore.com, until you find one that is not taken.

At the time this book is being written, "registrar" companies such as Network Solutions or InterAccess handle most registrations for .com, .org, and .net names. However, you also can access a list of accredited domain registrars at the Internet Corporation for Assigned Names and Numbers (ICANN) site at www.icann.org/registrars/accredited-list.html.

TIP

Check with friends or acquaintances about registrars and recommendations. You can save quite a bit of money if you use an off-brand registrar (particularly if you are registering several names). In our experience, the customer service and support with the smaller registrars (one that we have used is www.gandi.net) is actually better than with the big names.

To register a domain name, follow this process:

1. Go to www.internic.net/whois.html. (InterNIC is the official body that supervises Internet naming; this is their "lookup" page.)

2. Enter your prospective domain name in the query field and press Enter. If you're lucky, you'll see a No Match message, which means that your domain name is available. If you're less fortunate, you'll see the InterNIC records for whoever owns the name you entered. If you want, you can contact them and see if they want to sell it or give it to you, but you're likely to have more success if you simply look for another name.

3. Either register the name or ask your ISP to do it for you. Most ISPs will register domain names for free if they'll be hosting them, or they charge a reasonable fee ($100 or less) for the service, plus hosting charges. If your ISP attempts to charge significantly more than $100, you might consider either doing it yourself or finding another ISP.

If you want to do it yourself, all the information and instructions you'll need are available at the sites owned by the various registrars, although you'll need to get a little information and cooperation from your ISP to complete the process.

Publishing Through a Corporate Server

Another place you might publish your documents is on a corporate server—at your place of employment, most likely. If you work for a large company or an educational institution or if you work with an organization that handles system administration tasks, you'll probably have little to do when it comes to accessing a web server. All the necessary pieces—access, administration, and security—are probably in place, and you'll simply step in and start using the server. This situation can be either the ideal or the worst possible case, depending on the group that actually runs the web server.

The level of access and control you have on a corporate server varies from company to company. In the ideal situation, someone else takes care of running the server but lets you do anything you want, within reason. You get help setting up and running server-side programs and can essentially do anything you need to provide information. At the other extreme, you must adhere to a rigid process to submit information to the intranet. You'll submit documents and then have little control over where they're placed or how they're linked.

In all likelihood, your company will be somewhere in the middle, with an established procedure for accessing the corporate intranet but a substantial amount of freedom to do what you need to do. If not, or if the process of providing content is tightly controlled, you may want to see about running your own server. In any event, you'll need to find out how to contact the server administrators, get emergency contact numbers, find out about the corporate intranet policies, and go from there.

Publishing Through Your Own Server

Finally, you might choose to publish your documents on your own server. If you have the technical savvy and existing infrastructure, running your own server affords you the most flexibility and best range of resources. One good reason to run your own server is that it's a more authentic environment for developing and testing pages. For example, if you have server-relative URLs in links, they'll work properly if you're loading the files from a server, but not if you're loading the same file locally.

Particularly in a corporate or educational environment, where a network infrastructure exists, installing and running a server is straightforward. To run a public server, whether at home or at work, you'll need a dedicated network connection—anything from a full-time DSL line or cable modem (assuming you're allowed to run a web server) to a T1 or similar commercial-grade connection will work. If you're just setting up a local server for your own testing purposes, you can even run the server on a stand-alone machine.

If you plan to host your own server, we suggest that you have a dedicated web server with as few applications as possible on it. That will free up the computer for simply hosting the web pages.

ASSESSING AND ADDRESSING SECURITY RISKS

As a small business owner or someone just interested in publishing documents on your own server, you may not think that you're at risk for being hacked—for computer hackers to break into your computer and read your documents, manipulate your computer, or even plant malicious software on your computer (which might lurk on your computer and relay information to the hacker or be used to attack other computer systems). With scripts and programs available on the Internet to let anyone—regardless of skill or expertise—become a hacker, you may be at risk. How do you assess your own security risks? Ask yourself these questions:

▶ Are you publishing information about your product or services that would be of interest to competitors or potential competitors?

▶ Are you storing source material or raw data about your products or services on your Internet-connected computer?

CONTINUED ➡

▶ Do you run instant messaging applications, file-sharing applications, or other software that you've downloaded from the Internet?

▶ Do you have a continuous Internet connection, or do you stay online for extended periods of time?

▶ Do you have personal or private information anywhere on a computer connected to the Internet?

If you answered yes to one or more of these questions, you may be exposed to hackers, and your server could be used to stage attacks on others. You should take security measures. Consider these options:

▶ Change your passwords often—at least once per month.

▶ Use a firewall if you're running your own server. Check out the Firewall FAQ at www.interhack.net/pubs/fwfaq/ to find out more about firewalls.

▶ Use antivirus software regularly, and scan all incoming files you receive via e-mail before opening them, even if you know and trust the person who sent the file. Check out Google's Web Directory at directory.google.com/Top/ Computers/Security/Anti_Virus/ for more information and resources.

▶ Delay upgrades to software from all vendors as long as possible so that security holes are found and patched before you are vulnerable.

▶ Install patches and security upgrades as quickly as possible.

▶ Monitor antivirus sites, CIAC (Computer Incident Advisory Capability), and CERT (which, at one time, stood for Computer Emergency Response Team) for announcements of problems or security issues that affect your operating system or software.

▶ Monitor other sites for exploits that affect your operating system or software. Good starting points are www.securityfocus .com and www.counterpane.com/alerts.html.

CONTINUED ➡

> ▶ Find, download, and use network security products, including port scanners, intrusion-detection software, and published exploits against your system. Start at www.insecure.org and go from there.
>
> ▶ Educate yourself about network security and how computers and the Internet work, starting with www.insecure.org/reading.html.

If you're considering running your own server, here are some issues to consider:

Security   Web servers present a security risk, although not a huge one. Letting other people access files on your computer, through any means, is inherently a little iffy. On an intranet, assuming you don't have highly confidential material on the server machine, you should be fine.

Uptime and Access   If you're going to set up and publicize a server, you must ensure that it stays up and available all the time. If you don't have a continuous Internet connection, you shouldn't host your own public web server.

Time   Running a web server takes some time. If all you're doing is serving pages, it doesn't take much, but expect a certain investment. If you'll be generating pages from a database or installing and running other add-in programs, it'll take more time, both to keep the server going and to monitor security issues.

Capacity   If your web server provides only plain documents and a few graphics to others on an intranet, or if it's just for testing purposes, almost any computer will do. If you expect heavy traffic or lots of access, however, be sure that the computer you use can handle the load or can be upgraded easily. If you choose a Windows operating system to host your pages, you'll need about 256MB of RAM and 8GB of hard disk space. For a Linux server, you could probably get away with 128MB of RAM and 4GB of hard disk space.

Backups   If you're running your own server, you're responsible for back-ups. If the hard disk on your server suddenly stops working, will you be in a position to restore everything and get it all back up and running?

LEARNING MORE ABOUT RUNNING YOUR OWN SERVER

Installing, configuring, and running a server is beyond the scope of this book; however, if you'd like more information, you can visit the following websites:

www.microsoft.com

At this site, you can learn about the latest Microsoft web server options. At the time of writing, Windows 2000 Server, Windows 2000 Professional, and Windows XP Professional ship with Internet Information Services (IIS) 5. Additionally, the Microsoft products also come with FrontPage, which is handy if you use that for web development.

www.apache.org

At this site, you'll find Apache, the most popular Unix-based server software, although it's also available for other platforms, including Windows.

Finally, get the definitive server information at http:// serverwatch.internet.com/webservers.html.

THE PUBLISHING PROCESS

Before you get started, you'll need the following information:

The address of the HTTP server   For example, www.raycomm.com. Depending on your situation, you may need to know the folder name from which your files will be accessed.

The address of the FTP server, if required   For example, ftp:// ftp.raycomm.com. Depending on how you get your files onto the server, you might have to use the File Transfer Protocol (FTP). Of course, it's also possible, particularly in a corporate or educational environment, that you would simply copy the files to a specific folder on a network drive, and that would be that.

Password and access restrictions   You need a user ID and password to upload files to the server.

Table 5.1 summarizes this information and provides space for you to include your specific information.

TABLE 5.1:   Information You'll Need Before Using FTP

INFORMATION	EXAMPLE	YOUR INFORMATION
FTP server address	`ftp.raycomm.com`	
User ID	`jsmith`	
Password	`JB14mN`	Don't write it down or allow the FTP software to save it for you!
Folder on server to use	`public_html`	

TIP

Passwords should always be something hard to guess, with a combination of lowercase and uppercase letters and numbers. You shouldn't write down your entire password near your computer or save it on your computer. Another option is to break your password into two parts: something you know and something you write down.

Armed with this information, you're ready to upload your files to the server, which essentially just means to put a copy of your documents on the server. The process for uploading your documents to a server will be different for most servers and installations. It can be as easy as copying a file to a folder (on a corporate intranet) or as idiosyncratic as completing multiple-page online forms and copying files to a folder (on intranets in Dilbert-esque companies—yes, we have examples). It also can be a straight-forward process involving an FTP application (the common process on intranets and with ISPs).

The easiest way to upload files to a server is by using the publishing tools included in many high-end HTML editing applications. These tools work well if all the files belong in one folder and if you're comfortable letting the programs "adjust" links as the files are uploaded.

However, you'll likely use either an FTP program or your browser to upload your documents, as described next.

Uploading with FTP

FTP is the Internet standard tool for transferring files. Regardless of which FTP program you choose, you'll probably be dealing with the commands outlined in Table 5.2. As you'll see in the following two sections, you can use these commands when uploading with a text-based FTP program or a graphical FTP program.

TABLE 5.2: FTP Commands for Transferring Files

COMMAND	DESCRIPTION
ftp	Starts an FTP application.
open "..."	Opens an FTP connection to the server name specified.
close	Closes an FTP connection without exiting the FTP application.
quit	Closes an FTP connection and the application.
put	Uploads files to the server computer.
get	Downloads files from the server computer.
ascii	Sets the file type to ASCII, to upload XHTML or other text documents.
binary	Sets the file type to binary, to upload image or class files and other binary documents.
cd	Changes directory on the server. Follow cd with a folder name to change to that folder; follow cd with .. to move up out of the current folder.
pwd	Tells you what folder you're in (stands for *print working directory*).

Uploading Files with a Text-Based FTP Program

Before you get started, you'll need the information specified in Table 5.1, and you'll need your documents and related files at hand. Follow these steps:

1. At a text prompt (a DOS prompt or a Linux/Unix shell), switch to the folder that contains the files you want to upload. For example, if you are at a c: prompt and your files are in the TestWeb subfolder, type **cd testweb**.

2. Type **ftp** to start the FTP application.

3. At the FTP> prompt, type **open** and the address of the FTP server—for example, open ftp.raycomm.com.

4. When prompted, enter your user ID and then your password. Remember that these are case sensitive.

5. Change to the folder where you want to store the files. If you're uploading files to an ISP, your folder name will probably be `public_html`, www, or something similar, such as cd `public_html`.

6. To upload HTML and XHTML documents, set the file type to ASCII. Type **ascii**.

7. Now, upload the documents with the `put` command. For example, type **put filename.htm**.

   If you have multiple files to upload, you can use the `mput` command and a wildcard. For example, to upload all files in the folder that have filenames ending with `.htm`, type **mput *.htm**.

8. To upload binary files (such as graphics), first set the file type to binary. Type **binary**.

9. Now, upload the documents with the `put` command. For example, type **put filename.htm**.

   If you have multiple files to upload, use the `mput` command and a wildcard. For example, to upload all files in the folder that have names ending with `.gif`, type **mput *.gif**.

10. When you've finished, type **quit** to leave the FTP application.

Now, open your web browser and try to access the files you just uploaded. If you find broken image icons, odds are that you didn't specify binary before you uploaded the files (a common problem). Try again, being careful to specify binary.

TIP

If you used a WYSIWYG editor and your links do not work correctly, check out the raw HTML or XHTML code to verify that the links were not changed.

Uploading Files with Graphical FTP Programs

An arguably easier procedure is available if you have a graphical FTP application (such as FTP Explorer for Windows, available from www.ftpx.com) or Fetch for Macintosh (available from http://fetchsoftworks.com).

The specific procedure depends on the software, but generally it resembles the following. Before you start, have at hand the same information you gathered for the text-based FTP application.

Use the following procedure to upload files with FTP Explorer, a Windows application:

1. Start the application, probably by double-clicking its icon.

2. Enter a name for the site and the hostname or IP address in the Connect dialog box that appears.

3. In the appropriate fields, fill in your login name, password, and any other information that your system administrator gave you.

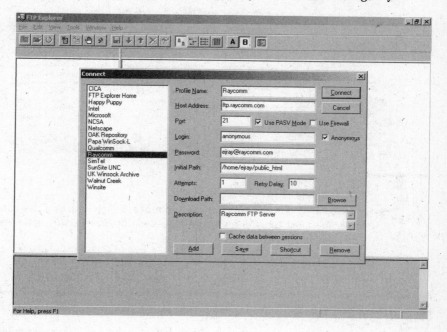

TIP

Both your user ID and password are case sensitive—if you substitute uppercase for lowercase or vice versa, access will be denied.

4. Click Connect. You'll see a connecting message as your FTP client connects to the FTP server; then you'll see your folders and files on the server.

5. Drag files from your Windows Explorer window to the FTP Explorer window to upload; drag the other way to download.

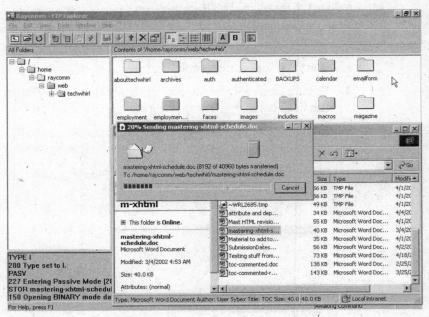

TIP

If you can't open and read the file in Notepad, SimpleText, or Vi, it's not a text file. You must transfer all word processed documents, spreadsheets, and multimedia files as binary.

That's all there is to it. Now, test your uploaded files.

UPLOADING WITH HTTP

Some automatic publishing tools offer the option of uploading via HTTP instead of FTP. However, relatively few ISPs support HTTP uploads because of security considerations.

The primary difference is that with HTTP, you need to provide only the web address at which your files should end up, rather than the FTP server address.

For you, the web developer, there's no real benefit to either approach as long as the files transfer correctly.

Uploading with Other Tools

In addition to using an FTP program to upload your documents, you can upload them through your browser or through specialized tools that come with various HTML editing software. Dreamweaver has an excellent site management tool, illustrated in Figure 5.1. The remote site appears on the left, and the local folders are on the right. This utility works much like an FTP utility and is very convenient. You can develop your pages and upload them to your server, all from the same interface.

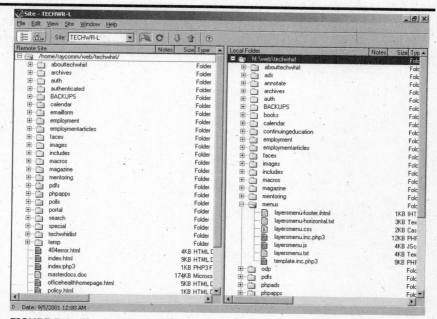

FIGURE 5.1: The Dreamweaver site management tool

You often can upload files by entering **ftp://yourid@yourftpserver.com/** in the location box of your favorite browser. You'll be prompted for your password. The only drawback to this approach is that you must be familiar with the structure of the files on the server. After you browse to the correct folder, choose File ➣ Upload File to select the file to upload (you can upload only one file at a time).

TIP

If you upload through your browser, take a second to bookmark that long URL location of your files so you won't have to browse to it again.

WHAT'S NEXT?

There you have it! You can publish your documents using an ISP, on a corporate network, or on your own server just by transferring a copy of the documents from your computer to a server. By doing so, you make your documents accessible to other people, either at your company or on the Internet. In the next chapter, you'll learn techniques for making your site useable and accessible, as well as some tips for site maintenance.

Chapter 6

PLANNING FOR A USABLE, MAINTAINABLE WEBSITE

Throughout this book, we've been looking at the document-level development process—that is, the steps for adding elements and attributes to pages so that you can include various features, capabilities, and functionality. In most cases, you won't just be creating and publishing a single document or even a handful of documents. Instead, you'll likely be creating documents that will be part of a bigger whole—for a website most likely, or possibly for a kiosk, help system, or personal digital assistant (PDA).

This chapter provides you with the tools, knowledge, and resources you'll need to develop sets of HTML or XHTML documents that are cohesive, maintainable, and accessible. The principles and steps offered in this chapter will work equally well if you're developing documents for nonprofit organizations, corporate intranets, or departmental sites, as well as for other document uses.

We recommend that you start at the beginning and read through the sections in order. Along the way, you'll find advice that will help you make decisions that will improve your site.

Adapted from *Mastering™ HTML and XHTML*, by Deborah S. Ray and Eric J. Ray
ISBN 0-7821-4141-2 $49.99

Planning for Site Development and Maintenance

You might be wondering why we're starting off with planning for site development and maintenance when we haven't even talked about content. Before you start typing those elements and attributes that comprise HTML and XHTML documents, you should think about the long-term goals for your website and realize that the site you create is probably going to start changing as soon as you publish it. Therefore, a little planning is in order.

Planning for a Smooth Development (and Redesign) Process

You can take steps to help ensure that the site development—and "redesign" process—goes as smoothly as possible. Why are we talking about redesigning the site, even before you develop the first site? Just as you have to update site content over time to meet users' changing needs, you also must take into account the fact that the initial site design will not meet user needs forever. Applying the following techniques will help ensure that designing the site goes as smoothly as it can and also help make sure your site is as "redesign-able" as possible:

Use XHTML and Style Sheets   As we mentioned in Chapter 2, "Getting Acquainted with HTML and XHTML," web browsers handle HTML and XHTML equally well, and XHTML is not much more difficult to implement than HTML. XHTML is more flexible and more forward-looking than HTML, and using it can make moving toward XML much easier than if you are using HTML. Further, style sheets replace several elements and attributes in HTML that have been deprecated. If you use deprecated elements and attributes now, changing to style sheets later will require not only that you apply style sheets to the new site's documents but also go through and remove all the deprecated elements and attributes. Even for a small site, removing deprecated elements is tedious and time consuming—especially if you're doing so manually, but also if you develop a script or program to automate some of the process.

Part I

NOTE

In Chapter 16, "Using Style Sheets," you'll learn to create and use style sheets for your HTML and XHTML documents.

Use Standard HTML or XHTML   As tempting as it may be to include an element that's supported only by a specific browser or to use deprecated elements and attributes to achieve a particular effect, don't. By sticking to standard HTML or XHTML, you ensure that the features, functionality, and effects you include are available to the vast majority of your users. Perhaps more important in the context of planning for site updates, using standard HTML or XHTML helps ensure that your code is valid and that you won't have to weed out (or otherwise address) nonstandard code or features manually when you redesign your site.

Consider Your File Structure   If you haven't worked with large websites, you may find it easy to create a single site folder and save all of the site's files in that folder. For smaller sites (that will remain small), that process may work fine. However, if your site is more than just a few pages, or you expect it to grow, consider adding some structure to the files by grouping and saving them in different file folders. That is, rather than creating a single site folder, create a separate folder for each category of information you include on the site.

Doing so offers a few benefits. For example, a user will be able to tell from the URL in his browser's location line where he is in the site:

```
www.wammi.org/troubleshooting/brakes/index.html
```

indicates that the page is the home page of the brakes section of the troubleshooting area on the site. Along those same lines, creating separate folders can enable you to use "breadcrumbing," which is another navigation aid (discussed in the section "Determining How to Organize the Information," later in this chapter). From a maintenance standpoint, having separate folders for separate areas of the site can help you more quickly locate files as you're maintaining them.

TIP

Develop your file structure as you're planning site contents, organization, and navigation, which we discuss next.

Plan for Site Styles and Guidelines   Before you start developing content and pages, take time to develop a site style guide—a reference document that includes rules and suggestions for writing style and presentation. By choosing or developing a style guide before creating the website, you can use the style guidelines to achieve consistency in the HTML and XHTML documents you create. Also, developing documents with consistent styles is much easier than editing and changing documents for consistency.

Often, the site style guide may be the same or similar to the corporate style guide for other documents your company creates, or it may be based heavily on a commercial style guide, such as *Chicago Manual of Style*, *Microsoft Manual of Style*, *Read Me First! A Style Guide for the Computer Industry*, or any number of style guides available. Remember, a style guide doesn't necessarily include the "right" styles or guidelines; it includes the styles that your company wants to apply consistently across a collection of documents. By choosing or developing a style guide before creating the website, you can achieve consistency in the HTML and XHTML documents you create.

TIP

For more information about style guides, see www.raycomm.com/techwhirl/magazine/writing/styleguide.html, then search for "style guide" at your favorite online bookstore for ideas about the range of style guides available.

TIP

At the end of this chapter, we discuss developing a master document, which is a template of sorts that includes some basic design elements that you'll use throughout your site. Although your site design—and therefore your master document—will depend a lot on issues discussed in this chapter, you might start thinking about the overall site theme as you're going through the rest of this chapter.

Planning for Development

Creating a development plan can ease the overall process significantly. If you're reading this chapter, you likely already have some idea of the development needs and expectations for your site. However, taking time to assess the resources you have available and the resources you need to develop the site can help smooth the process, minimize surprises, and ensure that you have the resources necessary to complete the project:

▶ What resources do you have available? What tools (for example, editors, browsers, validators, and conversion tools) do you have at your disposal? How about people resources—who can you call on? How about content resources (for example, existing documents that you can use as source material)? What kind of web server space do you have?

▶ What resources do you have yet to acquire? For example, will you be developing content from scratch? Do you need to gather existing documents and information? Will you be adding team members who haven't been hired yet?

▶ Which team members will be working on the website? This list should include managers, worker-bees, technical folks, content folks, reviewers, testers, editors, and support people, as well as anyone else who might have a say in decisions, content, design, maintenance, administration, or production. Also, what is each team member responsible for? Be specific!

▶ What is the realistic schedule to complete phases of the project? Planning? Master document development? Content development? Document development? Testing? Revision? Additional testing? Publishing?

These questions are by no means exhaustive—issues can vary significantly according to the company and site you're developing. However, these questions are a good starting point before you begin developing your site.

TIP

Create the site development plan collaboratively with input from others on the site development team, and then have the team review the plan before implementing it.

Planning for Maintenance

Maintaining documents is the process of updating and revising existing pages, adding new pages, and deleting outdated pages. Regularly maintaining documents is essential if you want users to keep returning to your site; regular maintenance also helps make long-term maintenance less cumbersome.

Determining Maintenance Needs

Website documents contain two types of information: static and dynamic. *Static* information remains constant. The company logo, most menus, and even product descriptions are examples of static information. Static information is usually what's included in your style sheet.

Dynamic information, on the other hand, must be changed or updated regularly. Prices, schedules, specific or timely information, and product lists are examples of dynamic information. Figure 6.1 shows a web page that includes both types.

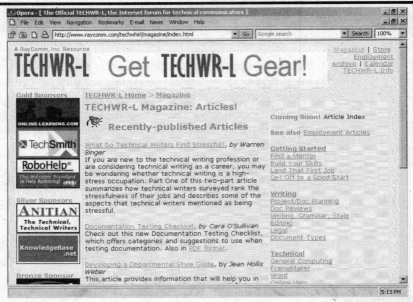

FIGURE 6.1:   Static information remains constant (here, the logo and menus); dynamic information changes frequently (such as articles and ads).

With the exception of a few static elements such as the logo, navigation links, contact information, and a few other page elements that likely won't change much, consider that other dynamic elements can—and should—be updated as needed to keep up with users' changing needs. In general, the more people involved in maintaining the site, the more time, effort, and coordination these process will take:

▶ Will more than one person be involved in developing the content?

▶ Will more than one person play an active role in maintaining the site?

▶ Will your site include more than about 20 documents?

▶ Will you frequently add or modify a significant numbers of pages—more than 20 to 25 percent of the total number of documents?

Developing a Maintenance Plan

If you know that you'll be adding only tidbits of information every few weeks, you probably don't need a formal maintenance plan. However, if you're likely to receive pages and pages of information to add, or if you're likely to make significant changes, you should determine how you can make those additions and changes most effectively.

At a minimum, the maintenance plan should address the following areas:

▶ The site's purpose and goals

▶ The process for determining content

▶ Who provides content

▶ Who edits and prepares content

▶ When content providers should submit information, and how

▶ How content accuracy is tested, reviewed, or assessed

▶ When content is added to the site, and how

▶ What tools are required to maintain content

In addition, the maintenance plan should include a schedule for ensuring that the site in general is working as it should. For example, the following tasks often are included as regular site maintenance:

▶ Checking for links that don't work or that point to outdated information (also known as link rot)

As you add and remove information from your site, you'll find that some pages suddenly have no links to them, or that existing links don't go anywhere. Browse all your links manually, and take advantage of link-checking programs on the web. (Look on sites such as www.tucows.com and www.zdnet.com and search for "link checkers".)

▶ Ensuring that older pages still look good in new versions of browsers

Often, changes in browser software affect how some elements—such as images, tables, and forms—are displayed.

▶ Checking older pages for references to outdated information

For example, you might want to update present tense references to past presidential elections, sports records, or even products, prices, and schedules.

TIP

Develop the maintenance plan collaboratively with input from others on the site development team, and then have the team review the plan before implementing it, as with the site development plan.

DETERMINING WHAT INFORMATION TO PROVIDE

In using HTML or XHTML, you're most likely developing documents that provide information to those who need it. In this capacity, HTML and XHTML authoring is *user centered*—in other words, it focuses on determining what users want and then providing that information.

However, websites have evolved into a marketing tool for millions of companies, organizations, and individuals worldwide. Rather than strictly providing information, the purpose of many websites is to tell users what a company wants them to know, to persuade them to purchase a product or service, and to keep them coming back for more. As a result, HTML and XHTML development is simultaneously user centered and *author centered*. You need to consider not only what your users want to know, but also what information your organization wants to provide.

Therefore, before you start producing documents, you should do some content planning. In particular, you must determine what information your users want and what your organization wants to provide. Your goal is to reconcile these "wants" into a single list that accommodates both your users and your organization.

What Do Your Users Want?

When you visit a website, you usually have a reason for going there. Although you often stumble onto a site that interests you while browsing, you normally have something specific in mind when you start.

Therefore, as you begin the planning phase, you'll want to think about what users expect to see at your site. The process of figuring out what your users want to know often is called *audience analysis* or *user analysis*. As the name implies, you analyze aspects of known and potential users to find out what information they want, need, or expect to find on your site.

How do you determine what your users want or need? The best way to find out is from the users themselves:

- ► Ask existing customers (or co-workers, if you're developing an intranet), because they can provide firsthand information about what they want and need. Often, asking about their wants and needs will result in minimal feedback; asking about what *problems* they have encountered related to the product, service, or other information resources often will result in more useful information.

- ► Check with your company's customer service center; it can provide information about what customers are calling and asking about.

- ► Read any communication, such as customer service e-mail messages, phone logs from customer calls, or notes or logs obtained from customer visits.

By starting with your customers, you can get an idea of what information they want and need. What if you don't have direct access to customers or definitive information about their needs? That's a bit trickier, although you may have more information available to you than you realize. For example, other departments in your company may have information about users, or they may have results of needs analyses or documents that were developed based on audience analysis. For example, the product development team likely has design specifications that are based on user needs. The documentation department may have user documents that can provide valuable information about what people aim to *do* with a product. The marketing team may have information about existing customers that can help you determine what information potential users may want or need. Whatever the size or industry of your company, you probably have reliable customer information available to you.

If you don't have information available, you can make some informed guesses about user needs. For example, suppose you have general information about your company and its general products and services, and you have specific product information, contact information, troubleshooting advice, safety information, prices, schedules, and order forms available. With those categories of information in mind, ask yourself:

- ▶ What skills, knowledge, or experience do users have in using the product or service?

- ▶ What additional information will users need in order to use the product or service?

- ▶ What information would be especially helpful or convenient for users to access through your website?

TIP

Often, your competitors' websites can be a good resource for determining what information to include on your website. Of course, you can't use a competitor's framework or information, but you can look at the types of information they're providing to the same pool of users and potential users.

Finally, use yourself or your co-workers as guinea pigs for determining what information to provide on the website. What questions did you have when using (or learning to use) the product or service? What obstacles did you encounter? What tidbits of information would have been useful to you? What information was tedious to look up (but would have been handy to have on the website)?

At WAMMI, our fictitious auto manufacturer, a survey revealed that users were interested in knowing what models were available, their cost, and their reliability and safety records. They also wanted to be able to request brochures and locate local dealerships. Their list of wants looked like this:

Available models

Cost

Safety record

Reliability record

Contact information

Request brochure

List of dealerships

What Do You Want to Provide?

Ideally, your website will provide all the information your users want; however, what they want isn't necessarily what you can or want to provide. For example, you might not want to publicize a product's repair history—at the very least, you might want to downplay it. If you're developing pages for a corporate intranet—for instance, the R&D department—you don't want to publish *all* the information the department has available. You probably want to include just information about upcoming projects, recent successes and failures, and planned product improvements.

As mentioned in the context of assessing users' needs, you can start determining what information your company wants to provide by looking at materials your company already has on hand. For example, marketing material often includes information about the company, products, and services, information that is suitable for use on a website. Even if you're developing pages for an intranet, marketing materials often provide a jumping-off place.

If you don't have access to marketing materials (or the marketing guru), ask yourself a few questions:

- ▶ What do people want to know about my organization? What is my organization's mission statement? What are its goals?

- ▶ Why are we on the web? What do we want out of it? Who are our users?

- ▶ What are our company's products or services? How do they help people? How do people use them?

- ▶ How do customers order our products?

- ▶ Is repair history or safety information so positive that we want to publicize it?

- ▶ Can we include product specifications?

- ▶ What product information can we send to people if they request it? Will customers download it, or will we e-mail or mail the information to them?

- ▶ Can we provide answers to frequently asked questions? What are the frequently asked questions and their answers?

► Do we want to include information about employees? Do their skills and experience play a big part in how well our products are made or sold?

► Can we provide information that is more timely, useful, or effective than what is provided by other marketing materials such as brochures or pamphlets?

After you answer these and any other questions that are helpful in your situation, you should be able to develop a list of what you want to provide. WAMMI decided to provide general information about the company, tell potential customers about the various models, show a few snazzy pictures, and brag about the cars' reliability records. WAMMI was unsure about discussing prices because they were higher than those of its competitors. Likewise, WAMMI was unsure whether to publicize safety records, which were only average. The final list looks like this:

Definite

Company information

Car models

Photos

Contact information

Maybe

Prices

Safety records

Reconciling the Want Lists

You may find that users want information that you simply can't provide. For example, they might want to know product release dates or be privy to product previews, which is probably information your company doesn't want to disclose. Other times, you might want to provide your audience with information that they don't necessarily care about. For example, you might want to tell people that your company received a big award or just reached one million dollars in sales this year—certainly interesting information that's good for marketing, but not on your users' priority lists.

As you can see, what WAMMI wanted and what its users wanted didn't necessarily coincide:

Users Want	Company Wants
company information	company information
car selection	car selection
reliability records	
contact information	contact information
	photos
car cost	prices
safety records	safety records
request brochure	
list of dealerships	

Although these two lists have items in common, each list also contains unique items. At the very least, we want to include all the items common to both lists. At WAMMI, the reconciled list includes the following:

Company information

Car selection

Safety records

Contact information

What about the items that are unique to each list? We suggest that you consult some of your colleagues, particularly those in marketing or public relations, and see what they think.

TIP

Getting a consensus before you start to build your website is always a good rule to follow. The last thing you want after your site goes public is a vice president announcing that you can't publish information that's already flaunted on your website. The information in this chapter will help you avoid encountering such problems.

WAMMI decided to classify the items common to both lists as primary website information and to classify items unique to one list as secondary information.

Determining How to Organize the Information

After you decide what information to include in your site, you need to determine how you will arrange individual documents. Taking the time to organize the information carefully often makes the difference between having frequent users to your site and having none at all. How often do you return to a site that's not well organized? If you can't find what you need easily and quickly, you have no reason to go there, and the same will be true of visitors to your site.

You can use one or all of these types of organization, depending on your needs:

▶ Hierarchical

▶ Linear

▶ Webbed

Hierarchical Organization

When you organize information in a hierarchical structure, you present a group of equally important topics, followed by another group of equally important topics, and so on. If you've ever created or used an organizational chart, you're familiar with this technique. The hierarchy starts with top officials and then shows the managers who work for them, the employees who work for those managers, and so on. A document outline is another example of hierarchical organization. Multiple main points are followed by subpoints, which are followed by more subpoints. In both an organizational chart and a document outline, hierarchical organization enables you to provide multiple levels of structured information.

You can do the same with a website. You can provide several main points, and under each point you can include subpoints. For example, the WAMMI website uses hierarchical organization to structure the main pages according to the major topics, as shown in Figure 6.2.

If you choose a hierarchical organization scheme, keep these guidelines in mind:

▶ Keep it simple. Visitors to your site will click through three or four levels of information, but after that, they're likely to give up.

► Provide an overview of the organization. You can do this by showing the categories and subcategories of information on the home
page or by providing a site map.

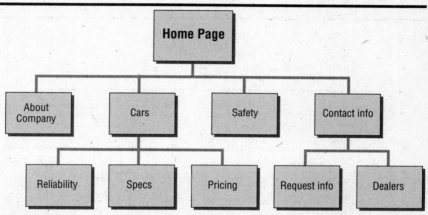

FIGURE 6.2:   Hierarchical organization accommodates several main topics and
subtopics.

TIP

Regardless of the type of site organization you choose, site maps and site
indexes are excellent tools to help users determine the extent of information
on your site, the topics your site covers, and the depth of information included.
Check out HTML Indexer at www.html-indexer.com for a starting point on an
index; site maps tend to be best handled as a special HTML or XHTML page that
you create along with the rest of your site.

Linear Organization

When you organize information in a linear structure, you impose a particular order on it. Instructions and procedures are examples of this type
of organization. If you've ever used a Microsoft Windows–type wizard,
you've seen linear organization in action. You start the wizard and then
proceed in order from one screen to the next until you click Finish. You
can back up a step or two if necessary, but if you don't complete all the
steps, you terminate the procedure.

On a website that uses linear organization, a user can move forward
and backward within a sequence of pages but cannot jump to other pages.

Because this can frustrate users who want to get to other pages, you should use linear organization only when it's necessary. For example, at our WAMMI site, we used linear organization to walk a user through requesting a brochure, as shown in Figure 6.3.

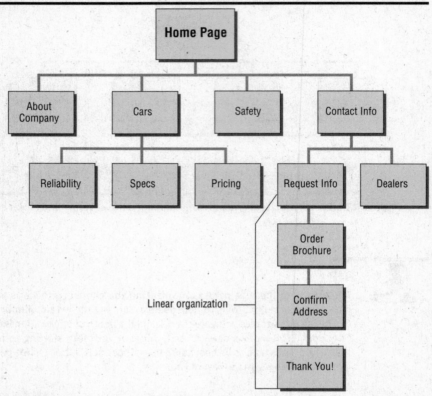

FIGURE 6.3:   Linear organization works well when you want users to perform actions in a specific order.

Here are some guidelines to keep in mind when you employ linear organization:

▶ When your site users are working through linear pages, they can't roam to other pages. Therefore, be sure the linear process is essential to the task at hand.

▶ Keep the linear sequence as short as possible so that users focus on the process and complete it successfully.

▶ Provide prerequisites at the beginning of the process so that users know what information or other resources they should have on hand before starting. For example, if the process requires a product identification number or other information they may not have handy, suggest that they get this information before starting the procedure.

▶ Provide cues to users to let them know the extent of the linear process, as well as where they are in the process while completing it. For example, you might state that the upcoming process has eight steps, or let them know "you are on step 3 of 8 in this process" (or whatever) so they know how far they've come and how far they have yet to go.

▶ Provide cues, as necessary, to let users know they've completed steps successfully. Many times this will be obvious at the end of the process, but if interim steps have to be completed correctly in order for subsequent steps to work, provide a screen capture or description during interim steps so that users know they've completed a step correctly and completely before moving on.

▶ Include a "success page," which acknowledges that a user has successfully completed the steps. This page might include just a short statement, a summary of what the user just did, a summary of what he should do next, or information he should keep on hand.

Webbed Organization

Webbed organization provides users with multiple, unorganized paths to resources on a site. A user can link from one web page to many other pages at the same website or at another website. You often hear stories about web surfers becoming disoriented or lost—they don't know where they are or where they've been. Webbed organization often is the culprit.

An example of effective webbed organization, however, is an online index that's extensively cross-referenced. The WAMMI site provides an index of the available models and cross-references each model to its specific features and to other models. Figure 6.4 shows how this works.

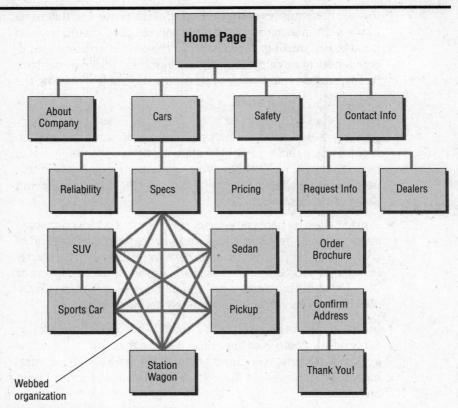

FIGURE 6.4:   Webbed organization is a good technique to use when you want to cross-reference information.

Here are some guidelines to keep in mind when you're using webbed organization:

▶ Provide navigation information consistently across the site so that readers can orient themselves even though content changes from page to page. For example, include a running footer or company logo on each page (keep it small).

▶ Provide a link to your home page on all pages. If you do so, users can return to a familiar page easily.

▶ Provide "breadcrumbs" on the site, which are navigation links that indicate where a user is in the site, as in Home ➢ Trouble-shooting ➢ Brakes.

STORYBOARDS: AN ESSENTIAL ORGANIZATIONAL TOOL

Storyboarding is the process of breaking information into discrete chunks and then grouping related chunks together. It's a technique that web authors borrowed from the film industry, and it's a great way to help determine the best organizational approach for your site.

Here's one way to do it (and the way the WAMMI site was storyboarded):

1. Write each topic or group of information on a separate note card.

2. Pin the note cards to a wall or spread them out on a table or the floor.

3. Group and rank related information.

4. Continue moving cards around until all the information is organized and ranked to your satisfaction.

5. When you've decided what should link to what, connect those note cards with string.

The resulting groups of information should follow one of the three organizational approaches we just discussed or some combination.

PLANNING SITE NAVIGATION

Part of what makes a website usable is how easily users can access it, browse through it, and find the information they want. Most users access your site through a home page, which typically is a single document that provides links to the other pages in the site. However, not all your users will drop in by way of the home page. They can go directly to a page they've bookmarked, or they can access your site through a search engine and go straight to a specific page. In either case, you have little control over how users move through your site.

To ensure that your users can link to the information they're looking for and to encourage them to browse your site, you need to make your site easily navigable—that is, make accessing, browsing, and finding information intuitive and inviting. You can do this by using *navigation menus*, which are sets of links that appear from page to page.

Navigation menus come in two varieties:

▶ Textual, which is a set of text links

▶ Graphical, which is a set of images (or icons) used as links

Textual Navigation

Textual navigation is simply text that links users to other information in the website. As shown in Figure 6.5, a textual navigation menu doesn't offer glitz, but it effectively conveys what information resides at the other end of the link.

FIGURE 6.5:   Textual navigation often is the most informative.

Textual navigation, though somewhat unglamorous, offers several advantages over graphical navigation. Textual navigation is more descriptive than graphical navigation because, done right, the text tells users clearly about the information in the site. Textual navigation links can be as long as necessary to describe the information at the end of the link; the description is not limited by the size of a button. The smaller the button (and thus faster to download), the less text you can fit on it.

Textual navigation also is more reliable than graphical navigation because the link itself is part of the document, not a referenced element such as a navigation button.

Finally, text links download much faster than graphical navigation. The links download as part of the page, without the delays associated with images.

If you're considering using textual navigation, follow these guidelines:

▶ If your textual navigation menu appears as a vertical list, place the most important or most accessed links at the top.

▶ Make the text informative. Rather than calling links "More Information," "Contact Information," and "Related Information," add specific summaries. For example, call them "Product Specs," "Contact Us!," and "Other Sportswear Vendors." Whatever you do, don't use instructions such as "Click Here," which is uninformative and wastes valuable space. Additionally, words such as *Information* rarely do anything but take up space. After all, what would be at the other end of the link besides information?

▶ Provide the same menu—or at least a very similar one—on each page. As your users link from page to page, they become familiar with the setup and location of the menu and (unconsciously) begin to expect that it contains certain information in a certain place.

▶ Customize the menu on each page so that the current page is listed, but not as a link. This approach helps users actually see where they are within the site, and it keeps menu locations consistent.

Graphical Navigation

Graphical navigation is a set of images that link to other information in the site. Most commonly, graphical navigation appears in the form of images with text on them, as shown in Figure 6.6. Graphical navigation also can be images that are pictures (called *icons*) representing what the buttons link to.

Graphical navigation has the distinct advantage of being more interesting visually than textual navigation. For example, because buttons and icons can include colors or patterns and can be almost any shape you can imagine, they are outstanding theme-bearing elements.

As colorful and interesting as graphical navigation might be, it has a few drawbacks. Primarily, it takes longer—sometimes much longer—to download than textual navigation. The download time depends on the file size and your user's connection speed, among other variables that aren't in your control.

FIGURE 6.6:   These navigation buttons include both text and images.

TIP

Chapter 10, "Adding Graphics," provides information about resizing images and making images quick to download, and also includes details about using images as graphical links.

Graphical navigation also tends to be less informative than textual navigation. For example, if you're using buttons with text on them, you might be limited by the size of the button. The text can be difficult to read, depending on the size of the button and the resolution of the user's computer.

If you want to use graphical navigation, consider these guidelines:

▶ Be sure that button text is easily readable. Sometimes, when images used to create buttons are made smaller to fit within a navigation menu, the text becomes too small to read or the letters get compacted. Your best bet is to try several button sizes to get a feel for which size is most effective.

▶ Be sure that the navigation menu integrates well with the other page elements. Images—including graphical navigation—are visually weighty page elements and often make other elements less apparent.

▶ Be sure you include `alt` text for the graphics and provide a text-based alternative menu to accommodate users who cannot or will not use graphical menus.

▶ Plan the navigation menu before you create it. Graphical navigation takes longer to develop than textual navigation, and it's much more difficult to change once it's in place. Even if all the pages aren't in place (or fully planned yet), at least create a placeholder for the navigation menu so that you don't have to revise the menu as you develop new content.

▶ Provide the same menu—or as close as possible—on every page. As with textual menus, users link from page to page and expect to see the same menu options in the same location on each page. Also, developing only one menu that you can use from page to page saves your time; you create it once and reuse it on each page.

TIP

Rather than creating several navigation buttons, you can create one image that includes several links. This single image with multiple links is called an *image map*. See Chapter 10 for more information.

Placing Navigation Menus

After you determine which kind of navigation menu to use, decide where to place the menu on your web pages. Regardless of whether you use textual or graphical navigation, be sure to place menus where users are most likely to use them.

Because navigation menus, particularly graphical ones, often take up a lot of valuable page space, be sure to choose menu locations that don't interfere with other page elements. Here are some considerations when choosing a location for navigation menus:

Top of the Page   Locating a navigation menu at the top of your pages is particularly useful because it's easy to find and access. Users casually surfing your pages can link in and out easily, and those who link to a page in error can get out of the page easily. The big advantage to using the top of the page (from the user's perspective) is that he isn't forced to wade through information to access the menu.

Middle of the Page   This location is effective in long pages because users can read through some of the information but are not forced to return to the top or scroll to the bottom just to leave the page. Usually, with mid-page navigation menus, you'll want to use targeted links, as described in Chapter 4, "Stepping Out: Linking Your Way Around the Web."

Bottom of the Page   This location works well in a couple of situations. For example, you can put the navigation menu at the bottom when you want users to read the material that precedes it. Keep in mind that users don't want to be forced to read information they're not interested in, but they don't mind browsing through a short page to get to a navigation menu at the bottom. Bottom navigation also works well on pages that already include many elements at the top, such as logos or descriptions; adding a navigation menu would crowd other important information.

Right and Left Sides of the Page   These locations are becoming increasingly common with the use of tables and frames. Although you can put the navigation on the right or left side, it's more commonly found on the left side of the page, with the content located in the larger area on the right. For example, you can use a framed layout to place the menu on the left side of the page and the information on the right. A menu at the left creates a two-column page appearance, which can make the page visually interesting and shorten the width of the right column to help readability. In addition, if the navigation menu appears in a separate frame, it can remain on screen at all times, regardless of which pages users link to or how far they scroll down a page. This is very useful for long documents. See Chapter 8, "Dividing a Window with Frames," and Chapter 11, "Presenting Information in Tables," for more information on frames and tables, respectively.

Multiple Locations   For most websites, you'll likely use a combination of locations, which is fine, as long as you use at least one combination consistently. For example, you could place a main menu at the top of all pages, place a menu of what's on the actual page on the left, and include a smaller text version of the main menu at the bottom of the page. Don't use this combination if you're space conscious.

Global Navigation   For large websites, you might choose to have a high-level menu with links to the major sections of the site and submenus within each of the major sections. The global menu would be available on all pages, but the section-specific submenus would be available only within the sections. The menus on www.amazon.com are a good example of this technique.

PLANNING FOR ACCESSIBILITY

As a website developer, you may assume that your potential users will interact with online information in the same way you do. However, a significant number of users—those with visual impairments—do not interact in the same way. Instead, many visually impaired people rely on adaptive technologies, such as screen readers, enlargers, or a combination of these, to access and use the information you provide. Although adaptive technologies help make documents accessible and usable to that audience, they are not a panacea; they cannot deal with many of the visual communication techniques available to help make information more accessible and usable, such as tabular or column formats, frames, graphics, or colors. Because adaptive technologies cannot adequately accommodate these visual-communication techniques, you should take steps during the planning stages to help ensure that the information your site provides is accessible to everyone.

NOTE

The United States federal government now has Section 508 accessibility guidelines in place for companies selling anything to the government. See www.section508.gov for details.

Understanding the Need to Address Accessibility Issues

According to the American Foundation for the Blind, an estimated 12 million people in the United States alone (5 percent of the population) have some degree of visual impairment. Other studies estimate that visual impairments affect up to 20 percent of the population. "Visual impairment," however, doesn't necessarily mean total blindness; it also refers to people with *low vision*, which includes any visual impairment that requires a person to use large type or a magnifying device, that requires a person to read at extremely close range, or that prevents a person from reading for long stretches of time.

What does this mean in terms of what visually impaired people might see when they try to access and use information? Consider the following examples of low vision and their effects. Figure 6.7 shows a screen as it's intended to be viewed, and Figures 6.8 through 6.12 illustrate how low vision might alter how the screen is perceived.

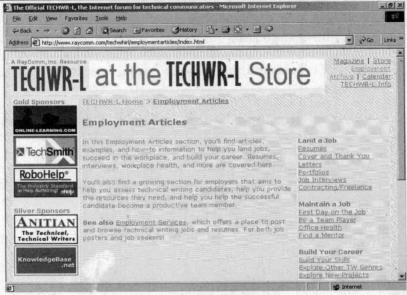

FIGURE 6.7:   People with normal vision would see this screen.

Tunnel Vision   A person with tunnel vision can see only a portion of the normal field of vision. For example, instead of the normal 150 to 180 degree field of vision, people with tunnel vision might be able to see only the width of a piece of paper or a small circle and have to rely on memory to assemble the pieces into a coherent whole.

FIGURE 6.8:   People with tunnel vision might see as if looking through a paper towel tube.

Colorblindness   A person who is colorblind cannot distinguish between certain colors. Most common are problems distinguishing red from green, although some people cannot distinguish yellow from blue or cannot differentiate colors at all.

Age-Related Macular Degeneration   People with this visual impairment cannot see fine detail—they see only faded colors and shapes. This impairment occurs as part of the aging process and therefore is extremely common.

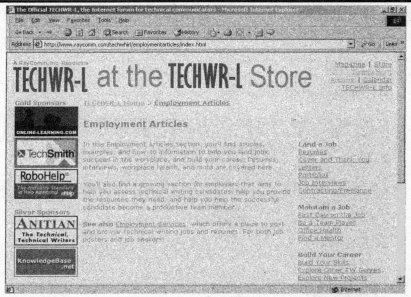

FIGURE 6.9:   People with age-related vision impairments might not be able to see fine details.

Diabetic Retinopathy   This is a visual impairment that affects a person's ability to focus; the severity can vary on a day-to-day basis. Additionally, blood vessels in the eye may leak, causing blood clots and scars that distort vision, turn it red, or possibly cause total blindness.

Cataracts   Cataracts cloud vision and affect the amount of light that enters the eye. This results in very hazy vision, as if you are looking through translucent glass.

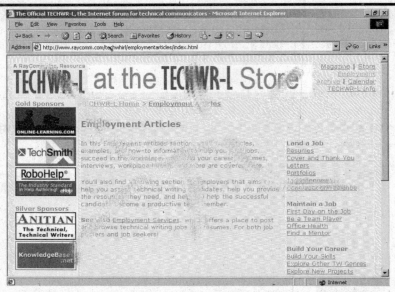

FIGURE 6.10:   People with diabetic retinopathy might see distorted images, resulting from scarring within the eye.

FIGURE 6.11:   People with cataracts experience cloudy vision that makes it very difficult to see anything.

Vision Field Loss   This visual impairment affects how messages are translated by the brain. For example, a person might see only part of an image.

FIGURE 6.12:   People with vision field loss perceive images incorrectly, often seeing only part of the image.

TIP
With this range of visual impairments in mind, you should take the time and effort to accommodate potential users who may have one or more of these impairments and ensure that they can access the information your site provides.

For much more information on accessibility, see the W3C's Web Accessibility Initiative (WAI) pages at www.w3.org/WAI.

Understanding Adaptive Technologies

Despite technological advances in screen readers and enlargers, they actually have become *less* effective for visually impaired people because they do not provide complete access to increasingly complex graphical interfaces or complex document designs and layouts. In this sense, trends in web design have been a step backward for accessibility and usability for that community. Although these trends often improve communication for sighted people, they hinder adaptive technologies' capability to make information accessible and usable. As you'll see in the next two sections, screen readers and enlargers do not offer visually impaired people complete access to the information they need.

Screen-Reading Technology

Screen-reading technology enables people with little or no vision to navigate a graphical interface using keyboard tabs and arrows or using a "talking mouse cursor" to move through menus, buttons, icons, and other interface elements. Screen readers work by reading text associated with on-screen content—that is, text within a document, text descriptions of graphics, and text built into software programs (such as a name associated with a toolbar icon). For their users, screen readers identify interface elements, identify content, and then output the information through a synthesized voice or translate the information into Braille. For example, to oversimplify somewhat, if the user navigates to a Save button, he might hear "button, save," which tells him specifically what he's pointing to (a button) and what the button is labeled (save).

Screen readers are not an ideal technology, however; many cannot interpret special formatting or graphics, so they cannot translate many visual cues that a sighted person might use to access information. For example, we commonly use multicolumn or tabular formats in documents to help group related information or to make information easier to access and read, as in this table:

Publication	Contact Information
TECHWR-L	Visit www.Raycomm.com/techwhirl
A RayComm, Inc.	to learn how to subscribe to the
Resource for the Technical	discussion list and to browse
Writing Community	the variety of free resources.

This table breaks the information into clear and manageable pieces and communicates information one cell at a time. Rather than reading the content of each cell, however, screen readers read from left to right.

In this case, screen readers *technically* can provide access to the information because it's rendered as text; however, the rendition is essentially unintelligible, making the content completely unusable. Perhaps a user could glean the URL from the mass of text, but the URL would have little value or context without the other pieces of information put in order.

Additionally, screen readers cannot make information provided through graphics available without the help of accompanying descriptive text. For example, if you use a chart to summarize data, screen readers would rely on the text—a caption or description within a paragraph—to convey the chart's contents. Without the descriptive text, the chart contents would be completely inaccessible to visually impaired people.

Likewise, screen readers also require descriptive text to interpret colors. For example, in an ordered list, we might use red text to show completed tasks and green text for the tasks yet to be done. Screen readers cannot convey the colors' implications without supplemental text to explain the context at each use. For example, we could add "You've just finished Lesson 1" at the end of a section of red text and add "You're about to begin Lesson 2" before the following section of green text. Only then could screen readers help visually impaired people discern the end of one lesson and the beginning of the next.

Essentially, screen readers can provide access to information, but only if the information is presented through simple text formats and descriptions.

Screen Enlarger Technology

Screen enlarger technology, used by those with various degrees of low vision, helps people more easily access and use on-screen content. Screen enlargers magnify a small portion of the screen, enlarging the content by a factor the user chooses according to the software's capabilities. For example, a user can enlarge an entire screen, specified screen portions (such as a single line), or just the area around the mouse (see Figure 6.13).

Screen enlargers enable visually impaired people to read screen content themselves, rather than having the content read to them or translated into Braille. Like screen readers, though, screen enlargers pose several problems for visually impaired people. For example, as shown in Figure 6.13, enlarged content can be extremely difficult to use. If enlarged enough, text might be read only one letter at a time, which requires the user to assemble the pieces mentally and remember where on-screen elements are located, adding to the already cumbersome process. Also, many fonts become jagged—almost impossible to read—when magnified to that extent.

Screen enlargers don't make intricate page layouts easy to navigate. For example, multicolumn formats, headers, footers, and other page features are difficult to read because they make the document flow difficult to follow.

FIGURE 6.13:   Some screen enlargers magnify the area around the mouse.

Finally, screen enlargers can't always make graphics usable. Large graphics in particular often become unusable because much of the image isn't visible when magnified, making it necessary to scroll around the graphic to access it fully. Also, depending on the graphic's quality, even smaller graphics might be unusable because of jagged lines or other problems with magnification. Screen readers make content *more* accessible, but the content can often remain difficult to use, accessible only in part, or inaccessible without extraordinary effort on the part of users.

Planning for Accessibility

As you're planning your website, plan to implement the following techniques and strategies in your documents. As you'll see, these techniques aren't beyond the normal realm of what we've described in other parts of this book; you'll just need to ensure that these techniques are applied— and applied consistently—across your site.

Keep Page Layouts and Designs Simple   Adaptive technologies can make information fully accessible and usable only with simpler layouts and designs. If you must use multicolumn formats, visually complex spreads, or intricate headers or footers, provide an alternate, text-only format that screen readers and enlargers can accommodate. See Chapters 8 and 11 for more information about the downsides of using frames and tables.

Include a Text-Based Navigation Option   The information you provide is not usable unless people can access all pages, which may not be possible through graphical navigation. See the section "Planning Site Navigation," earlier in this chapter, for more about text-based navigation.

Include Text Alternatives   Adaptive technologies can make graphics and significant colors accessible only through the descriptive text provided with them, such as captions, descriptions in paragraphs, alternate text, or supplemental explanations. See Chapter 10 to learn about using alternate text with images, and see Chapter 4 for information on using alternate text with links.

Develop Informative Text Alternatives   Text descriptions should focus on a graphic's content, not its appearance. For example, if you're describing your e-mail program's interface, stress the conceptual issues (the program presents a list of mail folders, showing one as "open," and lists the contents of the open folder on the screen), rather than the visual appearance (at the left of the window you have a list of mail folders, and the right side shows a list of mail messages).

Use Readable Fonts   Use good quality fonts that scale well, such as TrueType fonts for online presentation, rather than built-in, lower-resolution system fonts. See Chapter 3, "Creating Your First HTML or XHTML Document," for information about using the deprecated font element, and see Chapter 16 about specifying fonts using style sheets.

Use High-Contrast Colors   Choose colors that contrast well (not black on dark blue, for example). Ideally, use system default colors, which make it easier for the reader to adapt the display to specific needs. See Chapter 1, "Introduction to Web Design," for information about choosing colors.

Use Enhancements Sparingly   Adaptive technologies may not interpret bold, italic, underline, or special fonts at all. In some cases, the reader will have to keep track of how the fonts are interpreted. See Chapter 3 for information about applying enhancements.

Clearly Label and Separate Links   Use the descriptive terms "Glossary," "Table of Contents," or "Related Article," rather than "Click here for the Glossary, here for the Table of Contents, and here for a Related Article" or "Choose Glossary, Table of Contents, Related Article." See Chapter 4 for information about creating links.

CREATING A MASTER DOCUMENT

A *master document* contains the necessary structure elements, presentation elements rendered via Cascading Styling Sheets (CSS), and the general document format you want to use. You might think of a master document as being a template—a foundation—for all pages on the site. Creating a master document has several benefits.

TIP

In developing a master document, take into consideration all the aspects discussed in this chapter, including development and maintenance needs, content, navigation, and accessibility issues.

▶ You establish the look-and-feel of the site before you start adding content. By doing so, you can have the look-and-feel reviewed separately from the content. Reviewers can therefore focus on one aspect at a time, and you can incorporate changes on each issue separately, which is often easier than trying to incorporate changes to both issues at the same time.

▶ You can save time and effort by having to type only once any elements that will be included on every page.

▶ You can provide the master document to other people who will be contributing to the site.

TIP

After you create a master document, have it reviewed by others on the site development team *and* tested by potential users of your site to be sure that it appears the way you want, that it is usable and readable, and that it is error free. Finding and solving problems early on will save you lots of time in the overall process.

TIP
You can use style sheets to create a template for your documents. See Chapter 16 for more on style sheets.

A master document should include elements that you want to appear on every page, such as these:

- ► Background
- ► Navigational links
- ► Repeating images
- ► The corporate logo
- ► Icons
- ► Footer information

You might think of elements you include in the master document as being *theme-bearing elements*, which are web page components that help unite multiple pages into a cohesive unit and convey the "brand" of the site. Your users might not notice that you've included theme-bearing elements, but they certainly will notice if you haven't or if you've used them inconsistently from page to page. In this sense, theme-bearing elements set up users' expectations. If your users browse several pages that contain a logo, they'll begin to expect to see the same logo in the same place on each page. They may not consciously notice that it's there, but they'll certainly notice if it's missing or in a different location—just as you never pay attention to that broken-down car at the house on the corner until it's gone.

Used correctly, theme-bearing elements make your site appear complete and professional, and they also help users know that they are in *your* site as they link from page to page. A user can view only one page at a time, so be sure that each page obviously belongs to the rest of the site and not to a page outside your site. The following sections describe the theme-bearing elements you can use in your master document to unify pages in your site.

Adding Backgrounds

Using consistent backgrounds—colors or images—is one of the easiest and most effective ways to unify web pages, just as using the same color and style paper for multipage written correspondence identifies the material as a cohesive package. Using a different background for each web page can lead to some unwanted results. A user might think he's somehow linked outside your site, or he might pay more attention to the differences in design than to your content.

TIP

Have you ever received business correspondence in which the first page is on heavy, cream-colored, linen-textured letterhead, and the second page is on cheap 20-pound copier paper? Using different backgrounds for web pages produces a similar effect—users will notice.

Whether you use a solid color or an image depends on the effect you want to achieve. Background colors are less obtrusive and can effectively mark pages as belonging to a specific site. Imagine Figure 6.14 without the background color—just a plain white or gray background. You could use a solid color to contrast the page elements adequately and unify the other page elements without attracting attention to itself. The textured background in Figure 6.14, on the other hand, doesn't unify the page elements but instead becomes a visually interesting part of the page. Although the image background isn't overwhelming, it does make reading a little more difficult.

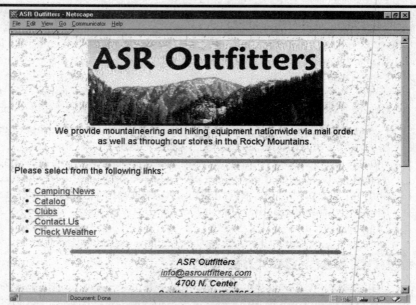

FIGURE 6.14:   Images create backgrounds that are more visually complex, but they can complement—not overwhelm—page elements.

Some websites combine colors and images by using a mostly solid color but adding a small repeating graphic, such as the ASR logo shown in Figure 6.15.

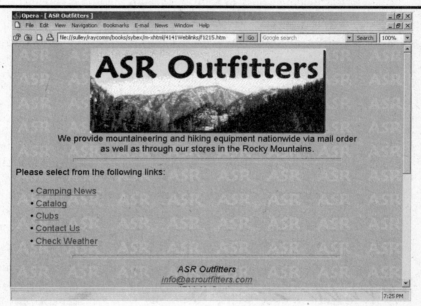

FIGURE 6.15:   You can combine colors and images (or text) to create a subtle background.

By using a small logo—which, in Figure 6.15, appears more like a watermark than an image—you ensure that the image is less apparent and fades into the background. This is a great way to include a logo without significantly increasing download time or taking up valuable page space.

Regardless of whether you choose a color or an image background, follow these guidelines:

▶ Be sure that the background adequately contrasts with the text. Remember that online reading is inherently difficult because of monitor size and quality, resolution, lighting, and screen glare. If you use dark text, use a light background; if you use light text, use a dark background. If you have any doubt about whether the background contrasts adequately, it doesn't.

▶ Be sure that the background complements—not competes with—other elements such as images. For example, if you include images, be sure that the background doesn't overwhelm them. Often, placing a busy or colorful background under equally busy or colorful images makes online reading more difficult.

▶ Be sure that the background matches the style and tone of the website content. A solid black background makes an impression, but it doesn't necessarily soothe and calm the user. It's not a good choice, for example, for the ASR Outfitters pages because it's quite obtrusive.

▶ Be sure that the foreground text is large and bold enough to be easily read against the background. Use the CSS font properties (or the deprecated font element) to increase the size and, optionally, set a font to help your users easily read text. A slightly increased font size can overcome the visual distractions of a textured or patterned background. (You'll find more information about changing fonts and font sizes in Chapter 3 and more about CSS in Chapter 16.)

▶ Be sure to choose a nondithering color (one that appears solid and nonsplotchy in web browsers). Because backgrounds span the entire browser window, the colors you choose make a big difference in how the background integrates with the page elements. If, for example, you use a dithering color as a background, the resulting splotches may be more apparent than the page's content. Your best bet is to choose one of the 216 safe colors. To find out more, read the excellent article at http://hotwired.lycos.com/webmonkey/00/37/index2a.html.

▶ Be sure you view your web pages in multiple browsers and with various color settings—particularly if you use an image background or don't choose from the 216 safe colors. A good background test includes changing your computer settings to 256 colors and then viewing all your pages again. Reducing the computer system's color depth may degrade the quality of the background.

TIP

You'll find information about how to include background colors in Chapter 3 and how to add background images in Chapter 10.

Choosing Colors

In most websites these days, colors abound—you see them in text, links, images, buttons, icons, and, of course, backgrounds. The key is to use color to enhance your web pages and identify a theme from page to page.

When developing a color scheme, consider which elements you want to color—text (regular text as well as links, active links, visited links), logos, buttons, bullets, background, and so on. For smaller color areas—text or links—you can choose any color you can imagine. For larger color areas, such as panes or backgrounds, stick to one of the 216 safe colors. The goal is to choose the colors you'll use for each element and use them consistently.

Most web development software, from Netscape Composer to Microsoft FrontPage to Macromedia Dreamweaver, comes with prepared color schemes. If you're not good with colors, consider using the prematched colors. Because color is the primary visual element in your pages, problematic color choice will be woefully apparent to all users.

The colors you choose should match the site's content. For example, if you're developing a marketing site for a high-tech company, you'll probably choose small areas of bright, fast-paced colors (reds, bright greens, or yellows) that correspond to the site's purpose of catching and holding users' attention. If you're developing an intranet site, you're likely to choose mellow colors such as beige and blue or dark green or make the colors match the company colors, because the site's purpose is to inform users, not dazzle them.

If you choose particularly vivid colors, use them in small areas. As the old commercial goes, a little dab will do ya! A small area of red, for example, can attract attention and hold users to the page. A broad expanse of red—such as a background—will likely scare them off or at least discourage them from hanging around.

Including Logos

If you're developing a corporate website, consider using a logo on each page. In doing so, you not only help establish a theme, but you also explicitly provide readers with the name of your company or organization throughout the site. You can even make the logo a link to your home page, so regardless of which page users are on, they can jump to the home page via your logo. Logos often include multiple theme-bearing elements: the logo itself, its colors, and the fonts or emphasis of the letters. Take a look at Figure 6.16, which shows a sample logo used on the ASR Outfitters page.

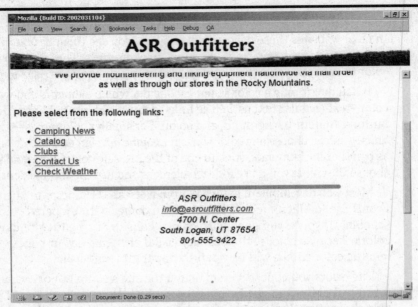

FIGURE 6.16:   ASR Outfitters' home page uses a nonscrolling logo as a theme-bearing element.

The logo helps set up other page elements. For example, the font appears in other places on the page, the colors are consistent throughout the page, and the image used as the foundation for the logo conveys the appropriate impression.

You may have no control over the logo you use—sometimes you're required to use your company's logo, for example. If you can develop a logo or enhance an existing logo, do so. Logos used online, particularly in websites, must carry more information about the company or organization and its style than a logo designed primarily for hard copy. A traditional logo is established by determining paper choice, paper texture, and other elements. Often, an online logo stands nearly alone without the help of other images or background images.

Where you place the logo depends on its emphasis. Many sites use a fairly large logo on the home page and a smaller version on subsequent pages. The logo thus appears on all pages, yet more space on subsequent pages is reserved for content.

An effective presentation is to combine small, classy logos with a clever arrangement of frames. For example, as shown in Figure 6.16, a logo can reside in a small frame that does not scroll at the top of a page, remaining visible while users are at the site. Because it does not have to be reloaded, other pages load more quickly.

Incorporating Other Graphical Elements

Other theme-bearing elements include buttons, graphical links, icons, and bullets. These elements, even more than colors and logos, add interest to your pages because they combine color and shape. What's more, these can be (and should be) small; you can include them throughout a page, adding a splash of color with each use.

You also can enhance a page with animated GIF images, which add visual attraction without increasing load time too much. See Chapter 15, "Including Multimedia," for more information about animated GIF images.

WHAT'S NEXT

This chapter provided an overview of the HTML and XHTML document lifecycle. In particular, it covered planning and organizing issues as well as issues about creating, publishing, publicizing, and maintaining HTML and XHTML documents. If you understand these topics, you'll be able to develop documents and use them for a variety of applications, including web pages and sites, intranet sites, help files, and kiosks.

In the next chapter, you will learn more about the elements that can be used in the body section of an HTML or XHTML document.

Part II
PLANNING AND DESIGNING YOUR WEB PAGE

Chapter 7

FORMATTING THE BODY SECTION OF YOUR PAGES

I n this chapter, you'll learn about the elements used in the body section of an HTML document. We'll show you simple examples of how individual elements' tags mark up bits of text. We'll also show you examples from some of our favorite personal web pages so that you can examine other source code by "real people" and try out their HTML on your own test pages.

NOTE

This chapter presents an opportunity to review the structure and function of the body section of an HTML document. Some of this material is also presented in Chapter 3, "Creating Your First HTML or XHTML Document," but this chapter includes additional material.

There are two types of body section elements: block-level elements, which are used to define sections of text (such as a paragraph), and text-level elements, which affect smaller bits of text (for example, making a word bold).

Updated from *HTML 4.0: No Experience Required*, by E. Stephen Mack and Janan Platt Saylor
ISBN 0-7821-2143-8 $29.99

Part II

In this chapter, we'll also see that some of the text-level elements can be divided into two categories: font-style elements, which change the physical appearance of text (such as bold and italic), and phrase elements, which define certain logical roles for text (such as a citation).

At the end of the chapter, we'll learn about two HTML elements that are used to mark changes to a document.

We'll start by learning about all of the different block-level elements before moving on to the text-level elements.

USING BLOCK-LEVEL ELEMENTS TO STRUCTURE YOUR DOCUMENTS

Block-level elements contain blocks of text and can organize text into paragraphs. Some common block-level elements are headings (`<h1>` and `</h1>`, `<h2>` and `</h2>`), paragraphs (`<p>` and `</p>`), horizontal rules (`<hr>`), and centered text (`<center>` and `</center>`). We'll look at these and the rest of the block-level elements in this section.

WARNING

HTML element and attribute names must be in lowercase in an XHTML document.

A block-level element, according to the W3C standard for HTML 4.01, should have a line break or paragraph break before and after the element. (The actual method used by a browser to display the paragraph break varies from browser to browser.) According to HTML's rules of nesting, block-level elements can be container tags for other block-level and text-level elements. Some block-level elements are "empty," however, meaning that the element doesn't contain anything and that the end tag is not allowed. For example, `<hr>` creates a horizontal rule by itself, and the horizontal rule element can't contain text—you can't use an `</hr>` tag because the end tag for the horizontal rule element doesn't exist in HTML.

NOTE

In XHTML, empty elements must have a closing tag, such as `<hr></hr>`, or it must include a space and a forward slash, such as `<hr />`. Technically, the extra space is not required for XHTML compliance, but it is recommended to ensure compatibility in older browsers. For more information on HTML compatibility with XHTML, see the guidelines at www.w3.org/TR/xhtml1/#guidelines.

We'll divide the block-level elements into two categories: block-level elements used to create functional and logical divisions and block-level elements used to create lists. We'll start with the functional and logical block-level elements.

Functional and Logical Divisions

The main purpose of HTML is not so much to be a page layout and presentation language as it is to be a markup language that classifies each part of your document by its role. When you use HTML, you're indicating, for example, which part of your document is a heading and which part is a paragraph. That way, it's easy for software programs to do tasks such as to create an outline of your document (by listing the headings), translate your paragraphs into foreign languages, or insert paragraph breaks between your paragraphs.

Logical HTML markup identifies the text within the start and end tags. For example, the `<address>` and `</address>` tags identify the words within these two tags as authorship and other contact information. The `<div>` and `</div>` tags mark up logical divisions in your text.

The basic functional units of your document are its paragraphs and headings. In this section we'll look first at headings and then at paragraphs, address information, forms, tables, horizontal rules, hierarchical divisions, centering, block quotations, and preformatted text.

For each tag, we'll discuss its use and some examples. We'll also present the attributes that can be used in each element's start tag to change the element's behavior. When an element has more than one possible attribute, the attributes can appear in any order.

WHEN DO YOU NEED TO PUT QUOTES IN AN ATTRIBUTE?

You may notice that we've put quotes around attributes (for example, `<font color="red">`. On the web, however, some authors just say `<font color=red>`.

Quotes are needed around an attribute value whenever it includes any character other than letters, digits, periods, or hyphens. This includes punctuation common to URLs (such as the colon and slash). In addition, you need quotes whenever there is any type of white space in the attribute value, such as a space.

CONTINUED ➡

Part II

You can use either double quotes (color="red") or single quotes (color='red'), but some browsers can get confused by single quotes.

There's no difference between saying <font color="Red">, <font color=red>, and <font color="red">.

WARNING

All XHTML attribute values must be quoted, such as <body bgcolor="red">.

Using HTML 4.01's Generic Attributes

Before we discuss the individual elements that can be used in the body section, we'll briefly mention the generic attributes that can be used with almost every element. There are four sets of generic attributes:

Language Attributes   The lang attribute can be used to specify which natural language is being used within an element. The dir attribute can specify the direction (left to right or right to left) that should be used with a language.

Style and Identification Attributes   Three attributes are used in conjunction with style sheets to specify how an element should appear. The class and id attributes mark an element as belonging to a particular class of styles or with a particular identification for an individual style. The style attribute can apply style information directly.

WARNING

The style attribute has been deprecated since XHTML 1.1 in favor of the id attribute for inline styles. For more information on deprecated elements and attributes, see Chapter 3.

Event Attributes   There is a wide class of attributes that can be used with individual elements to make documents more dynamic.

Advisory Titles   Many attributes can take an advisory title attribute that adds more information about an element.

In general, you can be reasonably sure that all four groups of attributes apply to all of the elements we discuss in this chapter. To make sure that a particular attribute applies to a particular element, see Appendix A, "HTML and XHTML Elements and Attributes."

With this little preamble about attributes out of the way, we can proceed to learn about the block-level elements, starting with the six different heading elements.

Adding Heading Elements

The heading elements (<h1>, <h2>, <h3>, <h4>, <h5>, and <h6>) define different levels of headings for your page, much like the headlines and sub-headings in a book, a newspaper article, or an essay written with an outline. There are six levels of headings, from most important to least important; for example, <h1> would be used for the largest and most important heading, and <h6> would be used for the smallest and least important heading.

NOTE

For additional information on using heading elements, see the section "Creating Headings" in Chapter 3.

Creating Paragraphs with the Paragraph Element's *<p>* Tag

The paragraph element's <p> tag marks the beginning of a paragraph. The end of a paragraph can be marked with </p>.

NOTE

In XHTML, all non-empty elements must include both an opening and a closing tag, such as <p> and </p>.

In general, the <p> tag is used to separate text into different paragraphs, such as this:

```
<p>This is a paragraph.</p>
<p>So is this.</p>
```

The paragraph element has the same alignment attributes as headings:

```
align="left"
align="center"
align="right"
align="justify"
```

WARNING

All attributes that specify appearance or formatting, including the `align` attribute, are deprecated in favor of Cascading Style Sheets (CSS). For more information on CSS, see Chapter 16, "Using Style Sheets."

The default horizontal alignment is left alignment—unless your paragraph is enclosed within a `<div>` or `<center>` element (described later) that changes the default. Browsers take care of word-wrapping your paragraphs to fit the available space.

Anything before the `<p>` start tag and after the `</p>` end tag is separated by two line breaks (a paragraph break).

THE PERILS OF `<p>`

The presence of the `<p>` or `</p>` tag can sometimes cause a paragraph break to appear where it normally wouldn't appear, in violation of the HTML specification of how paragraphs should behave.

This is because browsers often behave a little inconsistently from the specifications of HTML. Consider this example of rules and paragraphs in which `<p>` and `</p>` create a paragraph break:

```
<html><head><title>Paragraphs and Rules</title> </head>
<body>
<hr>
<p>A wonderful paragraph describing my friends Rick and
Janet's new baby T.R.</p>
<hr>
<p>Another paragraph detailing my childhood in England,
only not closing the paragraph. (In HTML, the paragraph
end tag is optional, after all.)
<hr>
A third and final paragraph with no p. This paragraph
mentions dinosaurs solely to make this example more
popular with children.
<hr>
</body></html>
```

When this HTML code is displayed by Internet Explorer or older versions of Navigator or Lynx, there will be a paragraph break whenever

CONTINUED ➡

a <p> or </p> tag is used, despite the fact that <hr> is a block-level element that should cause a paragraph break itself. (The same behavior occurs with other block-level elements, such as <form> and <table>, substituted for <hr>.)

Figure 7.1 shows the difference in paragraph breaks according to whether a <p> or </p> is present. As you can see from Figure 7.1, there is no paragraph break between the <hr> and the paragraph unless a <p> or </p> tag is used. However, Netscape 7 displays this code correctly, with a paragraph break between the <hr> and the paragraph.

By the way, a strict approach to HTML requires that every bit of text appear inside some kind of block-level container. The third paragraph in the previous example is contained only in the body of the document; technically, therefore, it is considered body text and not a paragraph. (This distinction is important when you use a style sheet that defines how paragraphs appear. If you do use such a style sheet, only text that is nested in a paragraph element will appear in the "paragraph style.")

Part II

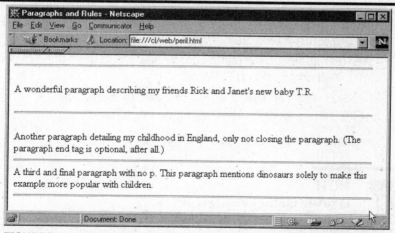

FIGURE 7.1:   The <p> and </p> tags create space around the <hr> tag in this Navigator display.

As a general rule, don't use multiple paragraph tags to create vertical white space in a document; most browsers will collapse multiple paragraph breaks into a single paragraph break. For example, this code:

```
<p>Waiting for Godot seems to take forever. </p>
<p></p>
<p></p>
<p></p>
<p>In fact we're still waiting.</p>
```

is treated by most browsers as if it were the following:

```
<p>Waiting for Godot seems to take forever. </p>
<p>In fact we're still waiting.</p>
```

In other words, the empty paragraphs are simply ignored. HTML 4.01's specification describes empty paragraphs as "bad form." You can create vertical white space by using style sheets.

You also can force an extra paragraph break by putting an invisible space in the paragraph. To use an invisible space, we'll use the nonbreaking space entity:

```
<p>Waiting for Godot seems to take forever.</p>
<p> </p>
<p>In fact we're still waiting.</p>
```

This code will cause an empty paragraph to appear between the first and last paragraphs. However, future browsers might not allow even this construction to cause a blank paragraph, and this use of a nonbreaking space is a controversial area.

Another approach to creating empty space is to use a line-break tag (<br>), as shown in this HTML code:

```
<p>Waiting for Godot seems to take forever.</p>
<br>
<br>
<p>In fact we're still waiting.</p>
```

NOTE
In XHTML, the line break tag is <br />.

Even this approach may not work in every browser. It's best to accept that HTML doesn't have an easy way of creating white space. The best way to create vertical white space is with style sheets (see Chapter 16).

Marking the Author's Address with an *address* Element

The address element uses the <address> start tag and the </address> end tag to mark up addresses and other contact information. The text in your address element is recognized by search engines and indexers as your address information.

Navigator and Internet Explorer put any text inside the address element in italics. Here's an example of an address element that includes a link to an e-mail address for a web author named Malcolm Humes:

```
<address>
<a href="mailto:mal@emf.net">Malcolm Humes: mal@emf.net</a>
</address>
```

Here's another example of an address element showing some information that's useful to put at the end of your home page:

```
<address>
Ankiewicz Galleries<br>
P.O. Box 450 Kendall Square<br>
Cambridge, MA 02142<br>
</address>
```

As you can see, address elements can contain a single line or multiple lines of text (often using line breaks created with a <br> tag).

Getting Information with *form* Elements

You can use the form element's <form> and </form> tags to mark an area where people viewing your web page can fill in fields and send data to you. There are all sorts of options for forms, including drop-down lists, text areas, and radio buttons (just like a dialog box). You'll read all about forms in Chapter 17, "Developing Forms."

Presenting Data in Tables

The table element is used to create a table of data. The <table> start tag and </table> end tag mark the start and end of the table's position in your document. Tables have many different uses, and there are a number of special elements used to create table cells and rows. You'll find a more detailed discussion of tables in Chapter 11, "Presenting Information in Tables."

Drawing a Line with the *horizontal rule* Element

The horizontal rule element is simply the <hr> tag. Each <hr> tag in your document creates a shaded horizontal rule between text. (A *rule* is just a fancy word for a line.) This rule appears in the same color as the document background. For example, this HTML code:

```
Hello
<hr>
World!
```

would appear in Internet Explorer or Navigator as shown in Figure 7.2.

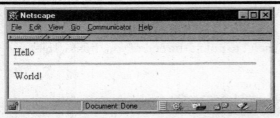

FIGURE 7.2:   Navigator displays a simple horizontal rule dividing two words.

Horizontal rules have many attributes. Here's a list of the possible attributes and attribute values:

```
align="left"
align="right"
align="center"
noshade
size="[number]"
width="[number]"
width="[percent]"
```

You can use one align attribute, a size attribute, a width attribute, or a noshade attribute—or a combination of the four.

. The align attribute positions the rule on the page either flush left, flush right, or centered. Since a rule normally fills the entire width of the screen, aligning a rule is useful only if you have changed the width of the rule with the width attribute.

The noshade attribute renders the horizontal rule as an unshaded dark gray line (or whatever color the system colors define), without the hollow and slightly three-dimensional appearance that Navigator and Internet Explorer give to a rule.

NOTE

In XHTML, attribute values cannot be minimized. This means that both the name and the value must be included for an attribute, even when they are the same. For example, while <hr noshade> is valid HTML, the same code must be written as <hr noshade="noshade" /> in XHTML.

The size attribute is a measurement of how thick the rule is. The number must be in pixels. (*Pixels* are "picture elements," the smallest unit of your computer screen's resolution. Each pixel is simply a dot on the screen.) If you don't specify the size attribute, Navigator and Internet Explorer display the rule at size 2. Here's a fragment of HTML code that uses several sizes of horizontal rules:

```
Hello <hr> World
<hr noshade>
<hr size="1">
<hr size="2">
<hr size="3">
<hr size="4">
<hr size="5">
<hr size="10">
<hr noshade size="10">
<hr size="15">
<hr size="15" noshade>
```

Internet Explorer would display this code fragment as shown in Figure 7.3.

TIP

Internet Explorer also supports a proprietary color attribute for the hr element, for example, <hr color="green">.

The width attribute can be specified with either a numeric value or a percentage value. A numeric value is measured in number of pixels, just like the size attribute. Alternately, you can specify a percentage of the browser window's width, such as <hr width="50%">. Setting a percentage is a good idea in order to make your rule consistent no matter what screen resolution is being used by the surfer viewing your page.

Here's a final example of an <hr> tag that uses several different attributes:

```
<hr size="4" noshade width="40%" align="right">
```

Part II

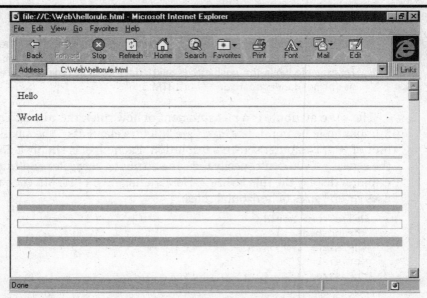

FIGURE 7.3:   Various sizes of horizontal rules in Internet Explorer

WARNING

The HTML 4.01 specification does not recommend using the `size`, `align`, `width`, or `noshade` attribute; you should use a style sheet instead.

Dividing Sections with the *division* Element

The `division` element divides your document into sections. The division element consists of the `<div>` and `</div>` tags, which mark the logical divisions in your text. The division element can be used to create a hierarchy of divisions within your document. In HTML 3.2, the main use of the division element was to indicate the default alignment of a section. In HTML 4.01, you can use divisions with style sheets to change the appearance of different sections of a document; you'll see how to do this in Chapter 16.

The `<div>` tag's attributes are the same as those for paragraphs and headings:

```
align="left"
align="right"
align="center"
align="justify"
```

The division element can have other block-level elements, such as tables and paragraphs, nested within it. This enables you to center a big chunk of your document: You just put a <div align="center"> tag at the beginning of the chunk and a </div> tag at the end. Everything wrapped within this division element will be centered.

However, just as with paragraphs and headings, HTML 4.01 does not recommend using the alignment attribute—it recommends that you use style sheets instead. Unlike most block-level elements, the division element creates a line break instead of a paragraph break when displayed by Navigator and Internet Explorer.

If you use a block-level element with another align attribute inside the division element, the innermost element's alignment will override the division element's align attribute. Listing 7.1 shows an example called happydiv.html.

Listing 7.1: happydiv.html

```
<!DOCTYPE HTML PUBLIC
"-//W3C//DTD HTML 4.01 Transitional//EN">
<html>
<head>
<title>HappyFunCo Divisions</title>
</head>
<body>
<p>HappyFunCo Presents...</p>
<div align="right"><p>The Newly Revised</p>
<h1>HappyFunCo Home Page</h1>
<p>Welcome!</p>
<p align="center">We sell used junk at low prices!</p>
</div>
<p>Give us a call at 1-800-555-1223.</p>
</body>
</html>
```

This HTML code contains six block-level elements (five paragraphs and one heading). The <div align="right"> tag causes all of the following elements to be right-aligned by default, until the division element is closed with the </div> end tag. Because the next three elements (The Newly Revised, HappyFunCo Home Page, and Welcome!) are within the division element, they normally would be aligned to the right side of the document. However, the We sell used junk line is centered because the align attribute of the <p> tag overrides the align attribute of the <div> tag.

Figure 7.4 shows Navigator's rendering of this code. Headings and paragraphs, like most block-level elements, cause a paragraph break. Bear in mind that not every browser will show paragraph breaks in the same way.

FIGURE 7.4:   Using the division element to change default alignment

Centering Items with the *center* Element

The center element (`<center>` and `</center>`) will center large blocks of text. A line break (not a paragraph break) is rendered before the start tag and after the end tag. The following example would center the words "Hello, World!" on a line:

```
<center>Hello, World!</center>
```

The `<center>` tag is a synonym for `<div align="center">`. There's absolutely no difference between them, except that `<center>` has had a longer history (it was introduced by Netscape as an extension to HTML 2.0). Because `<center>` has been around longer, it has slightly more support among various browsers.

Like the division element, the center element can be used to center a whole chunk of a document, as well as tables and other block-level elements.

NOTE

The center element is deprecated in favor of `<div align="center">` or the use of style sheets for setting alignment.

Quoting Sections with the *blockquote* Element

The blockquote element (<blockquote> and </blockquote>) marks up quotes that take more than a few lines (*blocks of quotation*). You use this tag when you are quoting one or more paragraphs from another source. Navigator and Internet Explorer indent the entire block of quoted text.

Here's some sample HTML markup for a blockquote:

```
<p>From The Bridges of New York City,
Queensboro Ballads by Levi Asher
    (http://www.levity.com/brooklyn/index.html):
<blockquote>
It isn't just that everybody hates the city; the more time
I spend with these people the more I understand that they
hate everything. Or at least they seem to, because it is
the culture of Wall Street to never show joy. Maybe some
of my co-workers lead wonderful lives at home; similarly,
I bet some of the Puritans of colonial New England had
great sex behind closed doors. In public, though, we are
busy, busy, busy.
</blockquote>
</p>
```

Figure 7.5 shows how Internet Explorer renders the blockquote element.

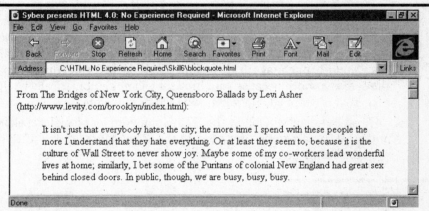

FIGURE 7.5:   In this Internet Explorer screen shot, you can see how Levi's blockquoted text is indented from the introductory text.

It's tempting to use the blockquote element to indent general text, but this may misguide search engines and page indexers. Even though

Navigator and Internet Explorer indent blockquoted text, other browsers don't; some browsers may put quote marks around blockquoted text or render it in italics. (If you want to indent text, you can use a style sheet or use <pre>. Browsers may render the text contained in <pre> tags in a monospaced font such as Courier, which may not be the look you want. We'll see how to use the <pre> tag in the next section.)

NOTE

In HTML 4.01, the <blockquote> tag can take an optional cite attribute to indicate where the quote came from. For example, we could have used <blockquote cite="http://www.levity.com/brooklyn/index.html"> instead of <blockquote> in our previous example. Current browsers don't do anything with the cite attribute, but future browsers will probably display the information in some fashion or allow you to look up the quote from the cite attribute's URL.

Later in this chapter you'll see another element used for quotations: the HTML 4.01 quote element (which uses the <q> and </q> tags).

Preserving White Space with the *preformatted* Element

The preformatted element (<pre> and </pre>) enables you to include preformatted text. Text contained within the preformatted text element defaults to a fixed pitch font (typically Courier). Your browser will preserve the white space (line breaks and horizontal spacing) of your text within the <pre> and </pre> tags. This means that your text can continue past the screen's width because your browser will not automatically wrap the text. Text is wrapped only when you include a line break.

Most browsers will follow the HTML standard for block-level elements and create a paragraph break before the <pre> start tag and after the </pre> closing tag.

WARNING

It's best to use the spacebar rather than the Tab key to create spaces within your text. When you or someone else goes back to edit your pages, the text editor you use may have the tab spacing set to a different value, and your text may become misaligned.

As an example of preformatted text, we'll show a haiku by poet and teacher Tom Williams, with and without the <pre> tag.

```
<p> morning wind
my hair moves
  with the clouds and trees
<pre> morning wind
my hair moves
  with the clouds and trees</pre>
morning wind
my      hair moves  with the      clouds
and trees</p>
```

Figure 7.6 shows how this HTML code will be displayed by a browser.

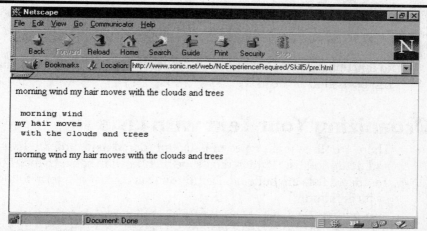

FIGURE 7.6:   A haiku by Tom Williams, displayed with and without the use of a <pre> tag

The <pre> tag takes one attribute:

```
width="number"
```

This number indicates how wide the text is (in columns). In theory, a browser would adjust the font size of the preformatted text to fit the <pre> text into the entire browser window. However, this attribute isn't supported by most browsers at this time and is now deprecated in favor of style sheets.

Using Other Block-Level Elements

HTML 4.01 uses three other block-level elements in particular types of documents:

▶ The `noframes` element (`<noframes>` and `</noframes>`) is used to indicate what should be displayed if a browser can't display frames. See Chapter 8, "Dividing a Window with Frames," for more information about frames and alternate content.

▶ The `noscript` element (`<noscript>` and `</noscript>`) enables you to specify alternate content for browsers that don't display scripts, if you're using a script.

▶ The `fieldset` element (`<fieldset>` and `</fieldset>`) is a special element used to group different parts of a form.

Now that we've seen the last of the block-level elements that are related to functional and logical divisions, it's time to see the HTML tags that can be used to create lists.

Organizing Your Text with Lists

There are three main types of lists: unordered lists, ordered lists, and definition lists. Ordered lists are numbered in some fashion, and unordered lists are bulleted. Definition lists consist of a term followed by its definition.

Both ordered and unordered lists require start and end tags as well as the use of a special element to indicate where each list item begins (the `<li>` and `</li>` tags).

▶ Unordered lists can be preceded by one of several bullet styles: a closed circle, an open circle, or a square. The tags for an unordered list are `<ul>` and `</ul>`.

▶ Ordered lists can be preceded by Arabic numerals, uppercase or lowercase Roman numerals, or uppercase or lowercase alphanumeric characters. The tags for an ordered list are `<ol>` and `</ol>`.

▶ Definition lists require a start tag (`<dl>`) and end tag (`</dl>`) and two special elements: one for definition terms (the `<dt>` tag) and one for definitions (the `<dd>` tag).

NOTE

For more information on using lists, see the section "Creating Lists" in Chapter 3.

Using Text-Level Elements

Text-level elements mark up bits of text in order to change the text's appearance or function. You use text-level elements to make words or sentences bold, for example, or to turn something into a link.

NOTE

The HTML 4.01 specification uses the term *inline elements* to refer to text-level elements. (Older versions of HTML called these elements *text-level elements*, as we do.) To reinforce the contrast between block-level elements and text-level elements, we'll continue to use the older term.

The main contrast between text-level and block-level elements that you should remember is that text-level elements don't start new paragraphs—instead, text-level elements are usually used *within* a paragraph.

Text-level elements can be used only as containers for other text-level elements. (We've referred to this structuring of tags within tags as *nesting*.) As with any HTML element, disordered nesting, missing end tags, extra start tags, or missing portions of tag attributes (such as an ending quote or an equals sign) may cause a browser to ignore huge portions of your page.

Let's look at some general rules of text-level elements:

- ▶ They can define character appearance and function.

- ▶ They must be nested in the proper order.

- ▶ They generally don't cause paragraph breaks.

- ▶ They can contain other text-level elements but not block-level elements.

After examining some general purpose text-level elements (including anchors, line breaks, images, and maps), we'll discuss fonts in some detail. Then we'll look at two general categories of text-level elements: font-style elements and phrase elements.

Creating Links with the Anchor Element's `<a>` Tag

The anchor element (`<a href="url">` and `</a>`) is used to create links. Links (otherwise known as *hyperlinks*) point to different files on the web.

WARNING

Anchors cannot be nested within other anchors.

The text or image enclosed within the `<a>` and `</a>` tags is a link; this link is clickable in a graphical browser. With most browsers, text within the anchor tags is displayed in a different color (the link color) and underlined (unless the person viewing your page has customized his browser not to display links with underlines).

Here's an anchor element that leads to Mark Napier's home page:

```
<a href="http://www.interport.net/~napier/">
   Mark Napier's Home Page</a>
```

NOTE

The name attribute also is used to create labels in a document, and it's possible to link to different named parts of a document (rather than always linking to the top of each document).

To create a link, the anchor element's `<a>` tag requires an `href` attribute. For more information on linking, you can refer back to Chapter 4, "Stepping Out: Linking Your Way Around the Web."

Creating New Lines with the Line-Break Element

The line-break element (an empty element consisting of the `<br>` tag) forces a line break. For example:

```
Hello<br>
World!
```

would force `World!` to appear on the line after `Hello`. Line breaks are useful for addresses and other short items.

A very simple tag, <br> has these attributes:

```
clear="left"
clear="right"
clear="all"
clear="none"
```

The clear="none" attribute has no effect whatsoever (it's the same as a regular <br> tag). The other three attributes all force the line break to be tall enough that the margin is clear on either the left side, the right side, or both sides (depending on which attribute you choose). These attributes are meaningful only when there are images (or other objects) on the page—so we'll discuss these attributes again in Chapter 10, "Adding Graphics," which is about images.

Using more than one <br> tag to create vertical white space may not give the same effect in all browsers; some browsers collapse multiple <br> tags into a single line break. See our earlier discussion about the <p> tag for more about vertical blank space.

Adding Graphics with the Image Element

The image element is an empty element consisting of the <img> tag. The image element adds images to the body of a document. These images are referred to as *inline images* because the images often are inserted within a line of text. The various attributes for the <img> tag tell the browser how to lay out the page so that text can flow properly around the image.

Images are a complex subject; we'll take a much longer look at the <img> tag in Chapter 10.

Making Imagemaps with the Map Element

The map element (<map> and </map>) is used for imagemaps. An *imagemap* is an image that contains *hotspots;* these hotspots can take a surfer to different URLs. An imagemap is simply an image that can be used to take a surfer to different places, depending on where he clicks in the image. Imagemaps are useful, for example, with geographical maps or with an image showing the different areas of your site. You'll find a discussion of imagemaps in Chapter 10.

The Quote Element

HTML 4.0 added the quote element for citing inline quotes. The quote element uses <q> as a start tag and </q> as an end tag. The quote element is very similar to the blockquote element; the main difference is that since the quote element is not block level, it doesn't start a new paragraph. Instead, it's used within a paragraph to mark a quotation. For example:

```
<p>Churchill said, <q>We have chosen shame and will get war, </q>
    but he wasn't talking about 1066.</p>
```

Most versions of Internet Explorer wrongly display the content of the quote element as plain text, but Netscape Navigator and Opera automatically (and correctly) add quote marks.

The specification for HTML does say that browsers should control the presence of quote marks (and that they should be appropriate for the language being used, because different languages use different quote marks than English).

TIP

Until Internet Explorer supports the quote element by adding quote marks to text enclosed in <q> and </q> tags, there's no real advantage to using the quote element for quotes in your web pages.

Like the blockquote element, the quote element can take an optional cite attribute to point to a URL from which the quote was taken.

The Subscript Element

The subscript element (_{and}) renders the enclosed text in subscript (a bit lower than regular text). This element is useful for mathematical or scientific formulas.

For example, this line of HTML code contains the chemical formula for water:

```
We all need H<sub>2</sub>O.
```

The Superscript Element

The superscript element (^{and}) renders the enclosed text in superscript (a bit higher than regular text). This element also is useful for formulas.

For example, here's Einstein's most famous equation:

```
E=MC<sup>2</sup>
```

Another good use of the `<sup>` tag is for the trademark symbol:

```
Eat A Bulky Burger<sup>TM</sup> today!
```

WARNING

Another way to get the trademark symbol is to use the `&trade;` entity, which is one of the "extended" entities in HTML 4.01.

We'll see an illustration of the superscript and subscript elements later in this chapter.

Using Other Text-Level Elements

In addition to the text-level elements we've seen in this section, there are a few other text-level elements that need to be mentioned:

► The `object` element (`<object>` and `</object>`) is used to insert images, movies, and multimedia in your document.

► The bidirectional override element (`<bdo>` and `</bdo>`) controls the direction in which text is displayed for foreign languages (left to right or right to left text).

► The `script` element (`<script>` and `</script>`) can be used as a text-level element in HTML 4.01.

► The `span` element (`<span>` and `</span>`) is similar to the division element (`<div>` and `</div>`) in some ways; the difference is that the span element is a text-level element and the division element is a block-level element. Both elements are commonly used with style sheets, so we'll return to the topic of the span element in Chapter 16.

► There are five elements used to create buttons and other form components that are considered to be text-level elements: the `input` element, the `select` element, the `textarea` element, the `label` element, and the `button` element.

► Finally, the `iframe` element is a text-level element used to insert another HTML document within an inline frame.

In the next sections, we'll build on the introduction to text formatting that you received in Chapter 3 as we discuss the font and font-style elements.

Changing Font Size, Face, and Color with the *font* Element

The font element (`<font>` and `</font>`) is used to format the size, typeface, and color of the enclosed text.

WARNING

The font element should not be used as an alternative to the header element. If your text is actually a header, you should put it inside a header element. Indexers and search engines don't recognize `<font>` as a way to generate a hierarchical outline of your page.

Here's a haiku by Tom Williams dressed up with the use of a `<font>` tag:

```
<font color="blue" size="+1" face="verdana,arial,helvetica">
    flock of geese,<br>
the same shape<br>
as his slingshot<br></font>
```

The `<font>` tag can be used with three different attributes: `size`, `face`, and `color`.

The `size` attribute can be specified in absolute or relative values ranging from 1 (smallest) to 7 (largest). Using a relative font size (putting a plus or minus sign before the number) will change the font size relative to the default font size. For example, `<font size="+4">` makes the font size four steps bigger than the current size. The seven different font sizes are shown here compared to the default font size.

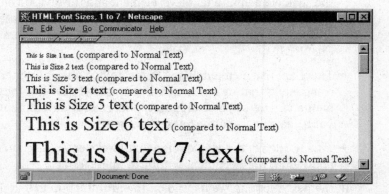

The `color` attribute is specified with an RGB value, or you can specify a color name. Color is discussed in Chapter 10.

The face attribute specifies a typeface that you'd like to use for the text enclosed by the font element; you can use a single typeface (such as Arial or Courier), or you can give a list of typefaces separated by commas. You'll learn more about typefaces in the next section of this chapter and in Chapter 12, "Web Typography."

WARNING

Like many of the earlier attributes and elements discussed in this chapter, the HTML 4.01 specification deprecates the use of the font element. Instead, the use of style sheets is recommended. (For a detailed explanation of what deprecation actually means, see "Deprecated Elements" in Chapter 3.)

Using Fonts Securely

HTML wasn't designed for page layout or word processing, so initially there wasn't any way to specify a typeface for your HTML documents. After all, because HTML was a cross-platform language, there was no way to know what font faces were available—and the concept of a typeface is meaningless for a document being spoken through a text-to-speech reader.

However, many web designers pushed for a way to specify the typeface in HTML. By default, most browsers used Times Roman for normal body text and Courier for preformatted text. Many web designers consider those two typefaces ugly or boring, and Navigator eventually introduced an extension to HTML in the form of the face attribute to the <font> tag. Internet Explorer followed Navigator's lead.

Although HTML 3.2 did not officially recognize the use of the face attribute to the <font> tag, HTML 4.01 allows you to use the face attribute—but at the same time, recommends that you use style sheets instead.

The current browsers don't agree universally on font properties, so the same font type might have different names on different systems, or the same font name might look different on different systems. Another deterrent to using fonts securely is that, although operating systems come with default fonts, users can install additional fonts onto their computers and remove or change the default ones. You have no control over which fonts each user may have on his system. What looks beautiful on your system may look horribly ugly on someone else's system.

Microsoft's web typography site (http://www.microsoft.com/typography) freely distributes several popular fonts for both Macintosh and Windows users, just in case you don't have them on your system.

One trouble with specifying font names is that similar fonts are known by different names. What is called Helvetica on one system may be known as Arial or Univers on another.

WARNING

Even worse, two different fonts can share the same name, and fonts can look completely different from platform to platform. Courier, for example, looks fine on Macintosh computers and Unix workstations, but at most point sizes it is a profoundly ugly font on Windows systems.

With the font element face attribute and with style sheets, font types can include generic family choices. Fonts in the same general category (with similar properties) are offered as a choice so that your browser can pick the best face from its current font possibilities. Some examples of the generic font families are these, with an example of each:

- ▶ Cursive (Zapf-Chancery and Mistral)
- ▶ Fantasy (Western)
- ▶ Monospace (Courier)
- ▶ Sans serif (Helvetica)
- ▶ Serif (Times New Roman)

NOTE

Serif fonts, such as the one used for the main text of this book, have flags (serifs), or decorations, on the letters. *Sans serif* fonts, such as the one used in this Note, are unadorned (without serifs).

In Chapter 16, you'll see how to use style sheets to specify fonts in your HTML documents.

Now that we've learned about fonts, we're ready to move on to the last two categories of text-level elements: font-style elements and phrase elements.

USING FONT-STYLE ELEMENTS

Font-style elements change the appearance of text (for example, making text bold, underlined, or stricken through). These font-style elements are also known as *physical markup*.

NOTE

Don't confuse "font-style elements" with the `font` element; they are separate things. The `font` element is a text-level element that uses the `<font>` and `</font>` tags to change a font size, font face, or font color. Font-style elements are a category of elements, such as the bold and italic elements, that change the way text itself is displayed.

Among HTML purists, there is something of a stigma against font-style elements because font-style elements are device dependent (that is, they assume that the display device is a computer screen capable of showing bold, italic, and so forth). Phrase elements (covered in the following section), such as em and `strong`, are preferred over font-style elements. Despite this stigma, font-style elements still are commonly used.

WARNING

You can't guarantee that your font-style elements will work on every system, so make sure your document is comprehensible even with plain text. In other words, don't depend on font-style elements to convey vital information.

Font-style elements are a subcategory of text-level elements, and they all require both start and end tags. They all can be nested according to the normal rules of nesting text-level elements.

We'll look briefly at each of the seven font-style elements and the tags they use: bold (`<b>`), italic (`<i>`), underline (`<u>`), strikeout (`<strike>` or `<s>`), big (`<big>`), small (`<small>`), and teletype (`<tt>`).

The *bold* Element

The bold element (`<b>` and `</b>`) causes text to appear in a bold typeface.

The bold element does not indicate strong emphasis when read by some text-only or text-to-speech browsers. Instead, use the `strong` element (a phrase element we'll see shortly) to mark important information.

TIP

The `<b>` tag is easier to type than the `<strong>` tag, so you may want to use the `<b>` tag when you create your web pages and then use your HTML tool's search and replace feature to change `<b>` tags into `<strong>` tags and `</b>` tags into `</strong>` tags.

Part II

The *italic* Element

The `italic` element (`<i>` and `</i>`) marks up text in italics (text slanted diagonally upward to the right)—for example, `<i>Hello, World!</i>`.

The italic element carries no other meaning than that text is to be rendered in italics. It's appropriate to use the italic element to indicate text in a foreign language—for example, `<i>carpe diem</i>`. (But using `<i lang="LA">carpe diem</i>` is even better because it indicates that the language used is Latin, thanks to the `lang` attribute.)

There are several phrase elements that we'll see in the section "Using Phrase Elements," later in this chapter, that are appropriately used instead of the italic element. For example, use the emphasis element (`<em>` and `</em>`) for emphasis or the citation element (`<cite>` and `</cite>`) for a citation to indicate why text is displayed in italics.

The *underline* Element

The `underline` element (`<u>` and `</u>`) underlines text:

```
<u>Hello, World!</u>
```

WARNING

Readers may confuse underlined text with hyperlinked text that isn't working properly. You should avoid using the underline element.

The *strike* Element

The `strike` element (`<strike>` and `</strike>` or `<s>` and `</s>`) indicates that the enclosed text should have a line drawn through the middle of the text.

```
<strike>Yikes! I'm some helpless text and I'm struck.</strike>
```

WARNING

Not all browsers and HTML page creation tools know how to deal with the strike element. In HTML 4.01, the use of the strike element is highly discouraged, and the new `ins` and `del` elements are recommended instead. We'll see the `ins` and `del` elements at the end of this chapter. If you do use the strike element, be aware that the `<strike>` tag is more widely understood than the `<s>` tag.

Figure 7.7 shows some strikeout text in Internet Explorer.

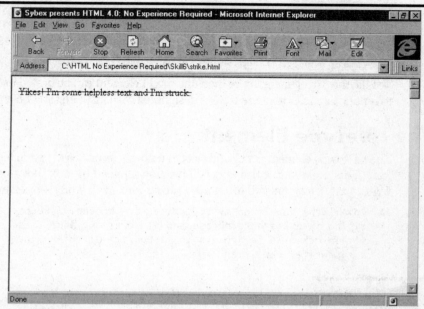

FIGURE 7.7:   You can see in this Internet Explorer example that the text, though stricken, is still quite readable.

The *big* Element

The big element (<big> and </big>) renders the enclosed text in a larger font (unless the document's font size already is as large as possible). The <big> tag has the same effect as <font size="+1">.

```
<big>The Big and Tall Company</big>
```

More than one big element can be nested to render text larger than is achieved with just one big element, but it might be clearer to say this:

```
<font size="+2">The Very Big and Tall Company</font>
```

rather than this:

```
<big><big>The Very Big and Tall Company</big></big>
```

The *small* Element

The small element (`<small>` and `</small>`) renders the enclosed text in a smaller font; if your text is already at size 1 (the smallest size possible), the tag is ignored. The `<small>` tag has the same effect as `<font size="-1">`.

```
<small>The Small and Short Company</small>
```

Like the big element, more than one small element can be nested in order to render a smaller text size than is designated with just one small element.

The *teletype* Element

The teletype element (`<tt>` and `</tt>`) renders the enclosed text in teletype font. This means that the text will be monospaced to look like a typewriter font (browsers will often use Courier font by default). For example:

```
<p>All the vowels on my typewriter are broken. I keep
typing in a standard phrase and it comes out like this:
<tt>Th qck brwn fx jmps vr th lz dg</tt>. I think I need
a typewriter repairman.</p>
```

NOTE

Don't confuse `<tt>` and `<pre>`. The teletype element (`<tt>`) is a text-level element that doesn't affect the rules of white space, whereas the preformatted text element (`<pre>`) is a block-level element that can be used to create indents and carriage returns or draw ASCII art.

Now we've seen all of the font-style elements. Before we move on to phrase elements and finish this chapter, let's see how all of these font-style elements are displayed. Figure 7.8 shows all the font-style elements used in this section, along with the superscript and subscript elements from the previous section, as displayed by Navigator.

NOTE

The underline (`<u>`) and strikeout (`<strike>` or `<s>`) elements are deprecated in favor of style sheets.

NOTE

You'll find more information on font and font-style elements in Chapter 12, which is devoted to the topic of web typography.

FIGURE 7.8:   Navigator's display of all of the font-style elements and the superscript and subscript elements

USING PHRASE ELEMENTS

Phrase elements are used to mark up small sections of text. They're especially useful for readers who use a nongraphical browser, for search engines and indexers that refer to your HTML code to categorize sections of your document for their site outlines, and for other computer programs that need to interact with your web pages to extract data for other useful purposes. For example, text rendered with the <cite> tag may render visually the same as italicized text, but the underlying HTML code indicates that the text is a citation.

Start and end tags are necessary for all phrase elements. We'll see the nine different phrase elements briefly: acronyms (<acronym>), citations (<cite>), computer code (<code>), definitions (<dfn>), emphasis (<em>), suggested keyboard sequences (<kbd>), sample output (<samp>), strongly emphasized text (<strong>), and computer variables (<var>).

After we've defined all nine phrase elements, we'll see how a browser displays them.

The *acronym* Element

The acronym element's <acronym> and </acronym> tags indicate the presence of an abbreviation (FBI, WWW, and so on). Text marked within the acronym element may not necessarily appear any differently, but spell-checkers and speech synthesizers may find it useful to know that the marked text is an acronym, and an advanced program could use the acronym element to help construct a glossary for your document.

You can use the advisory title attribute to define the acronym. For example:

```
I spy for the <acronym title="Federal Bureau of
    Investigation">FBI</acronym>.
```

WARNING
The acronym element is supported in newer versions of Netscape Navigator, but it is not yet supported in Internet Explorer.

The *citation* Element

The citation element's <cite> and </cite> tags are used to indicate that the enclosed text is a citation (titles of excerpts, quotes, or references) from another source.

WARNING
Don't use the <cite> tag except to indicate the title of a cited work.

Text within <cite> and </cite> is usually rendered in italics (although you can't always depend on every browser doing so).

For example:

```
<p>I have read and reread <cite>Moby Dick</cite>, but I
still can't make heads nor tails of it.</p>
```

The *code* Element

The code element's <code> and </code> tags are used for examples of program code. Text nested in the code element usually is rendered in a monospaced typeface, just like text inside <tt> and </tt> tags.

For example:

```
<p>To use the automatic date feature in Excel, just enter
   <code>=Date()</code> into a cell.</p>
```

The *definition* Element

The definition element's <dfn> and </dfn> tags are intended to be used to mark the first time you define a term. For example:

```
<p>It's not strange that <dfn>SGML</dfn> (Standard
   Generalized Markup Language) is so eerily similar
   to HTML.</p>
```

By marking your definitions this way, special software programs can create an index or a glossary for your document. Most browsers will display the definition text in italics.

The *emphasis* Element

The emphasis element is a popular way to emphasize text. Any text between <em> and </em> tags will be emphasized. Most browsers render the emphasized text in italics, but a text-to-speech browser knows to give spoken emphasis to text within an emphasis element.

TIP

Many style guides recommend using the emphasis element instead of the italic element.

For example:

```
<p>I simply <em>must</em> get your recipe for chili,
   Karen Dodson!</p>
```

The *keyboard* Element

The keyboard element's <kbd> and </kbd> tags indicate text that the viewer should type. Some browsers render this text as monospaced (some also may view the text as bold). Unlike with the <pre> tag, though, multiple spaces within the keyboard element are collapsed.

For example:

```
<p>To start the program, hit the <kbd>S</kbd> key and press
   the <kbd>Carriage Return</kbd>, then hold onto your hat!</p>
```

The *sample* Element

The sample element uses the `<samp>` and `</samp>` tags to indicate sample output text from a computer program. An example might be a directory listing or sample form output from a script program used to process your website's access log.

As with the keyboard element, the sample element's text often is rendered in a monospaced font, and multiple spaces are collapsed. The keyboard element is used for text that a user must enter, whereas the sample element is used for text that a computer generates in response to a user's action.

For example:

```
<p>Instead of giving me the expected results, the computer
kept printing <samp>All work and no play makes Jack a dull
boy</samp> over and over again.
I'm not sure what it means.</p>
```

The *strong* Element

The strong element's `<strong>` and `</strong>` tags are used to indicate strong emphasis. Text within a strong element usually is rendered as bold or given a strident pronunciation by a text-to-speech reader.

TIP

Many style guides recommend using the strong element instead of the bold element.

For example:

```
<p>I swear, if they don't give me that raise
<strong>tomorrow</strong>, I quit.</p>
```

The *variable* Element

The variable element (`<var>` and `</var>`) marks up the variables used in computer programs or the parts of a computer command chosen by the user. The text is usually rendered as italic.

For example:

```
<p>The formula for the <var>distance traveled</var>
(in miles) is <var>speed</var> (in miles per hour)
multiplied by <var>time</var> (in hours).</p>
```

Now let's see how Internet Explorer displays all the phrase elements we've seen. Figure 7.9 shows them in action.

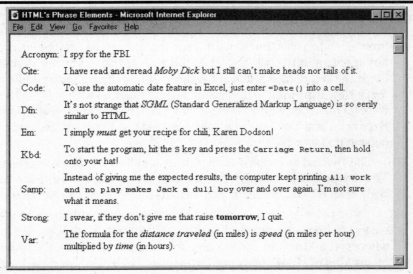

Acronym: I spy for the FBI.

Cite: I have read and reread *Moby Dick* but I still can't make heads nor tails of it.

Code: To use the automatic date feature in Excel, just enter =Date() into a cell.

Dfn: It's not strange that *SGML* (Standard Generalized Markup Language) is so eerily similar to HTML.

Em: I simply *must* get your recipe for chili, Karen Dodson!

Kbd: To start the program, hit the s key and press the Carriage Return, then hold onto your hat!

Samp: Instead of giving me the expected results, the computer kept printing All work and no play makes Jack a dull boy over and over again. I'm not sure what it means.

Strong: I swear, if they don't give me that raise **tomorrow**, I quit.

Var: The formula for the *distance traveled* (in miles) is *speed* (in miles per hour) multiplied by *time* (in hours).

FIGURE 7.9:   All the phrase elements

You can always nest multiple phrase elements. For example, you might use the following phrase elements if you were writing a web page about the anchor element:

```
<p>When using an anchor element, make sure to use the
    <code>href="<var>URL</var>"</code> attribute.</p>
```

Whew! That's it for phrase elements, which means we've finished the text-level elements. In the last section of this chapter, we'll introduce two new elements that are neither text-level nor block-level elements and that are used for marking changes to a document: the ins and del elements.

MARKING CHANGES WITH THE *INS* AND *DEL* ELEMENTS

Users of a word processor such as Word or WordPerfect may be familiar with an automatic feature that compares two different documents and marks the changes between them. Newly added phrases appear in a highlighted color, and deleted phrases are shown in a strikeout font.

HTML 4.01 has two elements intended for the same purpose: the `ins` element (with required `<ins>` and `</ins>` tags) to mark inserted text, and the `del` element (with `<del>` and `</del>` tags, naturally) to mark deleted text.

The actual methods used to display these elements will vary from browser to browser, but usually a section marked as deleted either will not appear at all or will appear as if it were within a `strike` element (with the standard stricken appearance—a line through the middle of the text). Newly inserted material could be highlighted with a different font color, in italics, or with a different font face. The newer browsers (Internet Explorer 6 and Netscape 7) display inserted text as underlined and display deleted text as strikethrough.

The `ins` and `del` elements are neither text-level nor block-level elements. They are unique in this respect—they are the only two elements used in the body of an HTML document that aren't text-level or block-level elements.

These two elements are closest in behavior to the phrase text-level elements; however, phrase elements can't contain block-level elements, whereas the `<ins>` and `<del>` tags, for example, can mark the beginning of any kind of HTML body section element before they're closed with `</ins>` and `</del>`. This makes it convenient to mark three paragraphs as being inserted.

Another difference is that while phrase elements can't take any special attributes, both the `<ins>` and `<del>` tags can be used with the following attributes:

```
<ins cite="URL"> or <del cite="URL">
<ins datetime="DATE & TIME"> or <del datetime="DATE & TIME">
```

The `cite` attribute can be used to point to a URL that contains information about why a change was made.

The `datetime` attribute can be used to indicate when the change was made. However, the date and time format must be specified in a very exact way. The format is YYYY-MM-DDThh:mm:ssTZD, where:

- ▶ YYYY = four-digit year

- ▶ MM = two-digit month (01=January, and so on)

- ▶ DD = two-digit day of month (01 through 31)

- ▶ T = the letter "T"

- ▶ hh = two digits of hour (00 through 23; A.M./P.M. *not* allowed)

► mm = two digits of minute (00 through 59)

► ss = two digits of second (00 through 59)

► TZD = time zone designator (either the letter Z to indicate UTC/GMT, an offset such as +04:00 to indicate four hours ahead of UTC, or -02:30 to indicate two-and-a-half hours behind UTC).

Here's a quick (and quite hypothetical) example that uses the ins element to mark a new section:

```
<h2>Latest News</h2>
<ins datetime="2000-04-22T11:38:00-07:00"
   cite="http://www.tori.com/updatelog.html">
<p>We've just received some new information.</p>
<p>Apparently there will be
<strong>two shows</strong> on Sunday. </p>
</ins>
<p>The show will start at 7:00 p.m.</p>
```

This code marks the middle two paragraphs as new. They were changed on April 22, 2000, at 11:38 A.M. (at 7 hours behind UTC/GMT); information about the change (perhaps who made the change or where the new information came from) can be found at the URL listed in the cite attribute. The ins and del elements are the last of the elements that are used in the body section.

WHAT'S NEXT?

You've already learned a lot about formatting your web pages—in fact, you've now been exposed to nearly all the basic elements you'll need to put together the body section. In Chapter 12, you'll learn more about the type-related elements that have already been introduced and also see suggestions on how to use type to get your ideas across on the web. But first we'll move on to the love-em or hate-em topic of frames.

Part II

Chapter 8

DIVIDING A WINDOW WITH FRAMES

In previous chapters, you've learned how to create HTML and XHTML documents that take up the entire browser window. What if you want to create a document that can divide the browser window into different parts and can show more than one document at once? HTML 4.01 lets you use *frames* to do just that.

In this chapter, we will teach you how to create a *frameset document*, which is a document that defines one or more frames by using the `frameset` and `frame` elements. You'll learn how to specify different sizes and properties for the `frameset` element and how to target your links from one frame to another.

We'll consider the advantages and disadvantages of frames and create alternate content for browsers that can't display frames. We'll also create an inline frame, which is a region of an HTML document that contains another document.

Updated from *HTML 4.0: No Experience Required*, by E. Stephen Mack and Janan Platt Saylor
ISBN 0-7821-2143-8 $29.99

UNDERSTANDING THE USE OF FRAMES

Frames allow multiple HTML or XHTML documents to be presented as independent windows (or subwindows) within one main browser window. This enables you to present two or more documents at once.

For example, a pair of simple vertical frames is shown in Figure 8.1 as displayed by Netscape Navigator. A frameset document has declared that one HTML file should be shown on the left and a different HTML file should be shown on the right.

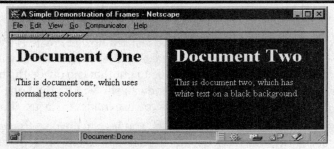

FIGURE 8.1: There are two frames here—one on the left and one on the right.

·NOTE

In Figure 8.1, you're looking at three different files at once. The frameset document contains the main title element (you can see the title on the title bar) and creates the frames (the two different framed documents shown here). The contents of each frame, Document One and Document Two, are separate files.

Frames also can be horizontal, as shown here using Microsoft Internet Explorer:

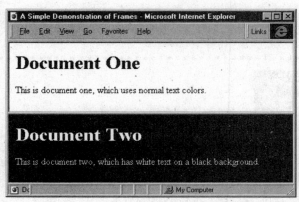

Each frame is resizable and scrolls separately by default (we'll show you how to change this behavior later in this chapter). You specify the initial size of each frame when you create the frameset document.

While these examples have shown only sample documents so far, you can probably see how frames can be useful. One frame can be used to keep some information static (such as a navigation bar or a site logo), and the other frame can contain the actual content of different sections of a website. We'll teach you to how to set up your links so that clicking on an item in one frame can change information in another frame.

WARNING

You should use frames only if you have a good reason. If you don't feel confident about your web design skills, adding frames can easily confuse your audience.

HTML 4.0 was the first version of HTML officially to include frames. They are supported on Internet Explorer and Netscape browsers and are now used on many websites. Nonetheless, there are some things any web author planning to use them should know about.

Knowing the Limitations of Frames

Although nearly all browsers support frames, not all do. In particular, text-to-speech browsers (designed to be used with adaptive devices, as discussed in Chapter 6, "Planning for a Usable, Maintainable Website") cannot read them, and some browsers for handheld devices do not support frames.

(Browsers that can display frames are called *frames-enabled*, and those that can't are called *non–frames-enabled* browsers.) Later in this chapter, we'll explain a few ways you can include alternate content for non–frames-enabled browsers by using the noframes element.

Even among frames-enabled browsers such as Internet Explorer and Navigator, the browsers don't always display framed pages the same way. There are even significant differences between the Macintosh and Windows versions of the same browser.

For example, one platform's browser may center each frame so that the text and images are easily viewable. Another browser may display a frame such that the bottom of a line of text or an image is cut off. These limitations mean that framed pages must be tested thoroughly to ensure that your viewers won't become frustrated.

Since you don't usually know the size of the window being used to view your site (or if a screen is being used at all), it's hard to decide on the right size for each frame. You run the risk of having a frame too small to display its content, forcing surfers to constantly scroll to read an entire line or see all of the options.

The user interface also can cause problems when a browser displays a frame page. After all, browsers were designed originally to display only one document at a time. The capability to show more than one document with frames was an afterthought. Because of this, browsers cannot assign a bookmark to an individual frame, only to an entire frameset document.

Similarly, it's impossible to link to a particular set of framed pages after you've followed a link. You can link only to a document in an individual frame or to the initial frameset. Also, most browsers cannot print the entire frameset page, and some browsers can print only the first frame in a frameset. The Back and Forward buttons behave differently when used while viewing a frameset, which can make frame navigation confusing. It's also harder to view the source of framed pages.

NOTE

Netscape 4, Internet Explorer 4, and Opera 4 and later browsers can deal with frames relatively well, providing bookmarks and appropriate Back and Forward button operations.

The initial frames created by the frameset document will change as soon as someone follows a link (or if a page is updated dynamically, such as through meta refresh). The URL in the browser's location bar doesn't change, still pointing to the initial frameset and its default frames. The frameset document's source code no longer shows the true content of each frame. This is another source of confusion.

WARNING

Some search engines are confused by frames and may not be able to index a framed site properly.

Before you give up on frames, however, try out their innovative inter-face. Some sites are improved with a frame-based design. If you're designing pages for an intranet (where you know what browser is being used by other employees in your organization), or if you make sure to offer both framed and non-framed alternatives, frames might be right for your website. Frames offer some useful advantages for navigation, as we'll discuss next.

Understanding the Advantages of Frames

Frames enable web designers to present multiple documents in one window. In one frame, for example, you can present a static list of the sections of your site. This frame becomes a table of contents that's always available. Another frame might contain a logo and a help button that won't scroll off the screen. Other frames can contain your site's content. Each frame can be scrolled through separately (enabling you to present and compare two documents side by side, for example), or you can replace the content of each frame with a different page every time the surfer follows a link.

These navigation features are useful when a website contains many levels of pages and when viewers might get lost searching through the content to find specific information. Next, we'll show you how to use frames by creating a frameset document.

Part II

CREATING FRAMESET DOCUMENTS

Frameset documents have a different structure than normal HTML documents. A regular HTML or XHTML document has a head element and a body element, but a frameset document has a head element and a `frameset` element.

NOTE

When you create a frameset document in HTML, you should use a special DOCTYPE declaration on the first line: `<!DOCTYPE HTML PUBLIC "-//W3C/DTD HTML 4.0 Frameset//EN">`. For XHTML frameset documents, you must include the required special DOCTYPE declaration: `<!DOCTYPE html PUBLIC "-//W3C//DTD XHTML 1.0 Frameset//EN" "http://www.w3.org/TR/xhtml1/DTD/xhtml1-frameset.dtd">`.

As an example, consider the HTML code used in a frameset document to create the two simple frames shown previously in Figure 8.1:

```
<!DOCTYPE HTML PUBLIC "-//W3C//DTD HTML 4.0 Frameset//EN">
<html lang="en">
  <head>
    <title>A Simple Demonstration of Frames</title>
  </head>
```

```
<frameset cols="50%,50%">
  <frame src="document1.html">
  <frame src="document2.html">
  <noframes>
    <body>
      <p>Your browser does not display frames. Please read
      <a href="document1.html">Document One</a>
      and
      <a href="document2.html">Document Two</a>.</p>
    </body>
  </noframes>
</frameset>
</html>
```

Here is the HTML code for document1.html, as referenced in the preceding code:

```
<html>
<body>
<h1>Document One</h1>
<p>This is document one, which uses normal text colors.</p>
</body>
</html>
```

Here is the HTML code for document2.html:

```
<html>
<body bgcolor="black" text="white">
<h1>Document Two</h1>
<p>This is document two, which has white text on a black
   background.</p>
</body>
</html>
```

NOTE

We'll discuss the new frameset element in the next section and the frame element in a section that follows.

As you can see, the code doesn't contain a normal body element. Instead, the body element is contained in an optional noframes element, which is used for displaying alternate content for non–frames-enabled browsers. Therefore, the noframes element's body section here is displayed only if the browser isn't displaying frames.

We'll learn more about how alternate content works near the end of this chapter, after we learn about the frameset and frame elements and their attributes.

XHTML AND FRAMES

XHTML is a reformulation of HTML in the strict syntax of XML. Using frames in XHTML depends on which version of XHTML you are using. We'll review briefly the development history of XHTML as it relates to using frames. More information about XHTML is covered in Chapter 19, "XHTML: HTML Goes XML."

▶ HTML 4.0 was introduced in 1997. This was the first version of HTML to include frames as well as a special frameset document type.

▶ HTML 4.01 was released in 1999. This is the last version of HTML and continues to include support for frames.

▶ XHTML 1.0 was introduced in early 2000 and revised on 8/1/2002. This version of XHTML includes support for frames that is similar to HTML 4.01, including a special frameset document type.

▶ XHTML Basic was released at the end of 2000. It is designed for devices such as mobile phones, PDAs, and pagers. XHTML Basic does not support the use of frames.

▶ XHTML 1.1 was introduced at the end of 2001. It is based on modules. The modules are subsets of XHTML that include different functions, such as frames. Some modules are required, but most of them are optional, including the frames module. These modules are combined using a special hybrid document type. To use frames in XHTML 1.1, you must include the frames module in your document type.

▶ XHTML 2.0 was released as a W3C Working Draft on August 5, 2002, and can be viewed at www.w3.org/TR/xhtml2/. This version of XHTML includes updated modules, but it does not include support for frames.

▶ XFrames was released as a W3C Working Draft on August 6, 2002, and can be seen at www.w3.org/TR/2002/WD-xframes-20020806/. XFrames is an XML application and technically not part of XHTML. However, XFrames is a module designed to replace HTML (and XHTML) frames and to address many of the problems (as discussed previously) with using frames.

To summarize, XHTML documents can use frames in XHTML 1.0, as a module in XHTML 1.1, and (soon!) as an XFrames module.

Part II

Using the *frameset* Element

The frameset element consists of the <frameset> and </frameset> tags, which contain one or more frame elements. The frameset element uses a couple of attributes (rows and cols) that define the layout of the frames.

The frame element uses the src attribute to point to the document that you want to display in each frame; we'll discuss it in more detail later in this chapter.

We'll see in a coming example that you can nest one or more framesets to divide a page in a complex way. We'll also learn that the frameset element can contain a noframes element if you want to present alternate text for non–frames-enabled browsers.

WARNING

Text and random HTML elements that appear before the frameset document's frameset element may be ignored or may prevent the frameset element from working properly.

This HTML code shows a simple two-column frames page with a navigation bar frame and a main content frame:

```
<!DOCTYPE HTML PUBLIC "-//W3C//DTD HTML 4.0 Frameset//EN">
<html lang="en">
  <head>
    <title>Frames - Two Columns</title>
  </head>
  <frameset cols="1*,3*">
    <frame src="navbar.html">
    <frame src="main.html">
  </frameset>
</html>
```

Here is the HTML code for the navigational frame, navbar.html:

```
<html>
<body bgcolor="black" text="white">
<p>Primary Colors</p>
<ul>
<li><font color="red">Red</font></li>
<li><font color="yellow">Yellow</font></li>
<li><font color="blue">Blue</font></li>
<li><font color="white">Main frame</font></li>
</ul>
</body>
</html>
```

Here is the HTML code for the starting main frame, `main.html`:

```html
<html>
<body bgcolor="black" text="white">
<p>Red, Yellow, Blue</p>
<p>
Click on the words in the left navigation frame to
  load a new page into this right main frame.</p>
</body>
</html>
```

Figure 8.2 shows the result of this code.

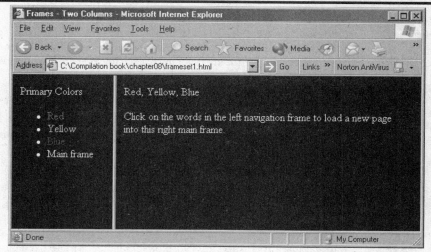

FIGURE 8.2:   A two-column frames page with a navigation bar frame (left) and a main content frame (right)

WARNING

This document would be completely blank for a non–frames-enabled browser. Always include a `noframes` element to display alternate content. We'll teach you how to use the `noframes` element near the end of this chapter.

You might notice from this example that instead of using percentages to size the frames, we used the asterisk width notation.

Next we'll take a look at the `cols` and `rows` attributes. Most `frameset` elements use one or the other of these attributes. If no columns or rows are defined, you can have only a single frame that takes up the entire page.

NOTE

The frameset element also can take the optional onload and onunload attributes, which are used to trigger scripts.

Creating Vertical Frames with the *cols* Attribute

The cols attribute is used within the frameset element's <frameset> tag to specify the size of two or more vertical frames. Each column's width is a value separated by a comma.

NOTE

The default value for the cols attribute is 100 percent, so if you don't specify a number of columns by giving each column a width, you will have only one column. If the cols attribute is not used, each row is set to the entire width of the window.

Each column's width may be an absolute width (a percentage of the window or a number of pixels) or a relative width (a value followed by an asterisk, *) that assigns a part of the window in proportion to the amount requested.

Absolute values have highest priority and are assigned first, and then the remaining space is divided among the columns with relative values next.

WARNING

You can't specify the exact size of the browser window on a user's computer using HTML/XHTML, so you must give the browser some ability to control the relative size of the frames. You must either give the cols attribute percentage values or use absolute pixel numbers combined with at least one relative width (*).

Let's take a look at some uses of the cols attribute:

```
<frameset cols="25%,75%">
```

This element specifies two columns. The first column (on the left) takes 25 percent of the browser's window space. The second column (on the right) takes 75 percent of the browser's window space.

WARNING

The results are unpredictable if you specify percentages that don't add up to 100 percent, but the browser should adjust your percentages proportionally until they do add up to 100 percent.

This element also specifies two columns:

```
<frameset cols="1*,3*">
```

The first column takes the relative value of one part of the browser window. The second column takes the relative value of three parts of the browser window. Since there is a total of four parts requested, the first column will get one quarter (25 percent) of the window's width, and the second column will get three quarters (75 percent).

This element creates four columns:

```
<frameset cols="100, 25%, 2*, 3*">
```

If you have a window that's 500 pixels wide, this element will assign 100 pixels of space to the first column (which could be useful if you'd like to have the first frame contain an image that's exactly 100 pixels wide). The second column will get 25 percent of the total space, or 125 pixels. That leaves 275 pixels for the last two columns. Two-fifths of this remaining space will go to the third column (110 pixels). The last column will receive three-fifths of the remaining space (165 pixels).

NOTE

Browsers will recalculate the space for each frame every time you resize the browser window.

Creating Horizontal Frames with the *rows* Attribute

The rows attribute works similarly to the cols attribute, except for horizontal frames instead of vertical frames.

If you don't specify a rows attribute, each column will take up the entire height of the window.

Horizontal frames are created from top to bottom. As with the cols attribute, you specify the height of frames using either absolute values (percentages or pixels) or relative values.

For example, this frameset:

```
<frameset rows="34%,33%,33%">
```

would create three horizontal frames, each taking up about one-third of the height of the window.

Part II

Creating Grids of Frames by Specifying Rows and Columns

You can use a frameset that specifies both the rows and cols attributes to create a grid of frames.

For example:

```
<frameset cols="250,*" rows="50%,25%,25%">
```

would create two columns and three rows, for a total of six frames. The frames appear from left to right and then from top to bottom. The first column is 250 pixels wide, and the second column gets the remaining space (* is equivalent to 1*). The first row is half the window's height, and the second and third rows are each a quarter of the window's height. The result is shown here:

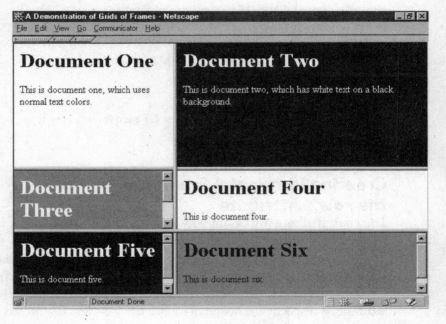

Nesting Framesets to Create Subdivided Frames

By nesting a frameset within another frameset, you can create complex frames. Each nested frameset replaces a single frame with two or more frames.

The following example uses a frameset to create a page with two rows. The lower row is a nested frameset, which splits the row into two equal frame columns, for a total of three frames:

```
<frameset rows="25%,75%">
  <frame src="topnavbar.html">
  <frameset cols="50%,50%">
    <frame src="left.html">
    <frame src="right.html">
  </frameset>
</frameset>
```

NOTE

By studying the previous examples in this chapter, you should have an understanding of how to create the basic HTML or XHTML files that go into each frame, so we will leave the code up to you for the three HTML files referenced in this code sample.

Figure 8.3 shows a sample document created with the nested frames.

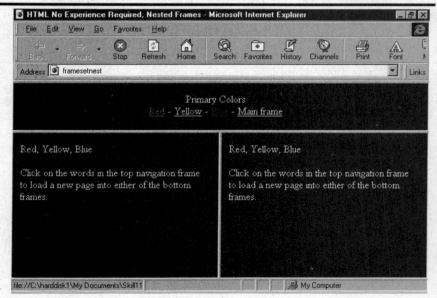

FIGURE 8.3:   Internet Explorer displays a frames page with two rows. The second row is split into two equal frames. This creates a total of three frames.

It's possible to use a series of nested framesets to continuously divide frames into more frames. This takes a lot of trial and error, however. It's

Part II

possible to make documents with even more frames, such as the nine frames we see on this page:

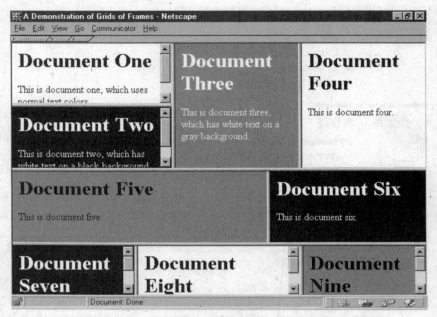

One way to make complex frames is to have more than one frameset document. If one of your frames contains a frameset document, that frame will be subdivided into smaller frame windows. The first frameset document is called the *parent frameset*, and the other embedded frameset documents are called *child framesets*.

Using the *bordercolor* Attribute

One other attribute often is used with the frameset element: The bordercolor attribute can set the color of a frame's border (instead of the default gray). For example, <frameset bordercolor="#FF0000"> sets the frame's border to red.

This attribute is not mentioned in the HTML 4.01 or XHTML specification. Instead, it's an extension to HTML that happens to be recognized by Internet Explorer and Navigator.

All of the frameset document's frame border colors are set universally with this attribute value. (Border colors also can be set individually with the frame element's bordercolor attribute, another extension to HTML, as we'll see a little later.)

WARNING

Be careful with this attribute, because it produces invalid HTML and XHTML that can't be checked easily for errors by a validation program.

Now that we've shown you how the frameset element works, we'll discuss the frame element and its attributes.

Putting Documents Inside Frames with the Frame Element

The frame element's <frame> tag defines the content of a single frame. The most important attribute for the frame element is the src attribute, which specifies the URL of the document inside the frame.

The frame content must be located in a separate file. For example, <frame src="document1.html"> specifies that the document to be displayed inside the frame is document1.html. You can use relative or absolute URLs. You don't have to link to HTML or XHTML files; you can put any kind of file in a frame, including images and multimedia files.

You can use several other attributes with the frame element in order to change the frame's appearance and the way it works. We'll learn about them now.

Adding Frame Borders with the *frameborder* Attribute

The frameborder attribute determines if there is a separator border between the frame and its neighboring frames. The default behavior is for each frame to have a gray border. By specifying <frame src= "document.html" frameborder="0">, you can remove the border.

You can specify frameborder="1" to mean that a border should be visible, but this is the default value.

You must specify frameborder="0" for both neighboring frames in order to remove a frame border. If one of the two frame elements doesn't include this attribute, the border will appear.

The HTML code for one frame with borders on and one frame with no borders is as follows:

```
<frameset rows="25%,75%">
    <frame frameborder="0" src="topnavbar.html">
    <frameset cols="50%,50%">
```

Part II

```
        <frame frameborder="0" src="left.html">
        <frame frameborder="1" src="right.html">
    </frameset>
</frameset>
</html>
```

NOTE

frameborder="yes" is equivalent to frameborder="1", and frameborder=
"no" is equivalent to frameborder="0". These values for the frameborder
attribute enable or disable frame borders but don't specify the size of those
borders. You can use a border attribute in addition to a frameborder
attribute to specify the border size. The frameborder attribute is a nonstandard extension to HTML, and browsers vary in their interpretation of it.
If you decide to use it, be sure to test your page in different browsers.

Coloring Individual Frame Borders with the *bordercolor* Attribute

You can use an HTML extension to specify the color of a frame's border.
The latest versions of Internet Explorer and Navigator recognize the
bordercolor attribute, which you can use to color individual frame borders.
For example, <frame src="document.html" bordercolor="yellow">
would create a frame with a yellow border.

NOTE

As mentioned earlier, all the frame border colors can be set at once with the
bordercolor attribute in the frameset element.

Specifying Frame Margins with the *marginheight* and *marginwidth* Attributes

Two attributes can be used to set the margins of a frame. Because regular
documents can't have margins without style sheets, this is one advantage
to using frames.

The marginheight attribute determines the number of pixels (which
must be greater than one pixel) between the frame's content and the
frame's top and bottom edges.

Similarly, the marginwidth attribute determines the number of pixels
between the frame's content and the frame's left and right edges.

For example:

```
<frame src="document2.html" marginheight="100"
 marginwidth="200">
```

creates a frame filled by the document2.html file, which would be displayed with top and bottom margins of 100 pixels and left and right margins of 200 pixels.

Preventing Frame Sizing with the *noresize* Attribute

Normally, each frame is resizable. By pointing your mouse at a frame border, you can drag the frame border to make the frame larger or smaller.

Sometimes you will want to prevent surfers from being able to resize your frames. The noresize attribute accomplishes this. For example, <frame src="document.html" noresize> means that this frame window is not resizable.

WARNING

Don't use the noresize attribute without a good reason; surfers will have different screen resolutions and font sizes, and often they will need to be able to resize a frame to see all of its contents.

NOTE

XHTML requires that all attributes have a specified value, even if that value is the same as the name of the attribute, such as noresize="noresize".

Removing Scroll Bars with the *scrolling* Attribute

Each frame will be displayed with a vertical or horizontal scroll bar (or both) if the contents of the frame won't fit in the frame's current dimensions. By default, scroll bars appear only when necessary. You can choose to have scroll bars always appear, or you can make them never appear. These examples show the three possibilities:

```
<frame src="document.html" scrolling="yes">
<frame src="document.html" scrolling="no">
<frame src="document.html" scrolling="auto">
```

The scrolling="auto" value is the default behavior.

By including a scrolling="yes" attribute, the frame's window will always include a scroll bar. Similarly, scrolling="no" prevents a scroll bar from appearing, even when it's necessary to scroll to see a frame's contents.

WARNING

You might have predicted that we'd warn against using scrolling="no" unless you have some compelling reason. You don't know what size window a surfer will have or what size fonts he uses, so there's really no way you can tell whether scrolling will be required to display a frame's entire contents.

Naming Frames for Targeting with the *name* Attribute

The name attribute sets a name for the frame. This name then can be used in links located in other frames to target the named frame.

For example, suppose we create a frameset document with two frames. We can name the second frame so that the links in the first frame will target it.

```
<!DOCTYPE HTML PUBLIC "-//W3C//DTD HTML 4.0 Frameset//EN">
<html lang="en">
<head>
    <title>Named Frames</title>
</head>
<frameset cols="1*,3*">
    <frame src="navbar.html">
    <frame src="main.html" name="main">
</frameset>
```

The first frame, on the left, is static. It contains a document called navbar.html. Because this frame has not been named, links in other frames can't target it. The second frame, on the right, is given the name main.

NOTE

Frame names must start with an alphanumeric character. It's safest always to use lowercase frame names, because some browsers are confused by uppercase names. Also, frame names are case sensitive in Internet Explorer.

In the next section, we'll see why naming a frame with the name attribute is useful.

USING TARGETED LINKS

We first discussed how to target links in Chapter 4, "Stepping Out: Linking Your Way Around the Web," where we used the `target` attribute to cause links to create a new window. In this section, you'll learn how to have links target a particular frame.

You'll also learn about the use of the `base` element to set a default target, see a concrete example of how frames can be useful for large files, and then see how to use four special predefined target names.

Targeting Frames

Once you've named a frame, you can create links that target the named frame by using the `target` attribute.

In this section, we'll use the HTML example from the previous section about the `name` attribute (which created two frames: a navigation bar on the left and a document named `main` on the right).

You can create links in the left frame's document (navbar.html) that target the right frame. For example, any links in the navbar.html document can use the anchor element's `target` attribute (as described in Chapter 4) to cause the contents of the frame on the right to change whenever a link is followed.

A sample link in navbar.html might look like this:

```
Read <a href="page2.html" target="main">page two</a> for
   more information.
```

When anyone clicks on page two, the frame on the right will no longer display main.html but will show page2.html, instead. The navbar.html file will still be displayed in the left frame.

NOTE

If most of the links in your document use the same target, you can set the default target by using a base element, as we'll explain in the next section.

Consider the frameset document shown back in Figure 8.2. When you click the word Red in the left frame, the page that appears on the right changes. Figure 8.4 shows how the left frame remains static, but the right frame is replaced.

Part II

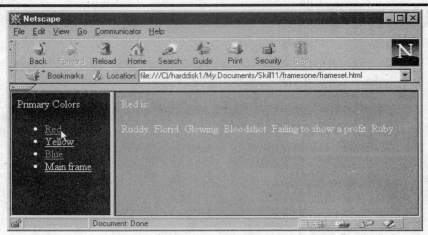

FIGURE 8.4:   When the Red link in the left frame is clicked, the initial document in the right frame, named `main.html`, is replaced with the linked document named `red.html`.

The HTML code for `navbar.html`, contained in the first frame, includes the HTML code with targeted links to the frame named `main`:

```
<!DOCTYPE HTML PUBLIC "-//W3C//DTD HTML 4.0 Frameset//EN">
<html lang="en">
<head>
    <title>Frames Navigation Bar</title>
</head>
<body bgcolor="#000000" text="#ffffff">
<p>Primary Colors</p>
<ul>
<li><a href="red.html" target="main">Red</a></li>
<li><a href="yellow.html" target="main">Yellow</a></li>
<li><a href="blue.html" target="main">Blue</a></li>
</ul>
</body>
</html>
```

Clicking any of the four targeted links in `navbar.html` replaces the current document in the right frame, named `main`, with the linked page.

It's essential to use targeted links if you want to keep a navigation element in one frame while having another frame's content change. If you don't specify a `target` attribute in the link, the link opens in the current frame and replaces its contents.

NOTE
Area elements and anchors in imagemap elements and form elements also can use the `target` attribute to target different frames.

If you use a targeted link such as `<a href="page2.html" target="foo">` and there is no frame named `foo`, the browser will create a new, full-size window.

Using the *base* Element to Set a Default Target

Sometimes a page will contain many links that you want targeted to a different frame. It's inconvenient to use the `target="framename"` attribute in each link. Fortunately, you can use the `base` element to set the default target frame.

For example, putting a `<base target="main">` tag in the head of a document would make every link in that document change the content of the frame named `main`.

To make this use clear, we'll create a longer example. We'll create one frame with a long page full of alphabetized entries and another frame with 26 links (one for each letter) that jump from the first frame to the appropriate spot in the alphabet.

To do this, we'll need three HTML files: the frameset document (which we'll call `alphadict.html`), the first frame's long list of alphabetized entries (`dictionary.html`), and the second frame's alphabet navigation page (`alphabet.html`).

The contents of `alphadict.html` might look like this:

```
<!DOCTYPE HTML PUBLIC "-//W3C//DTD HTML 4.0 Frameset//EN">
<html lang="en">
<head>
    <title>The Modern Hacker's Dictionary</title>
</head>
<frameset rows="80%,20%">
    <frame src="dictionary.html" name="dictionary">
    <frame src="alphabet.html">
</frameset>
</html>
```

This will create the two frames (one on top of the other), with the dictionary in the top frame (taking up 80 percent of the screen) and the alphabet links in the bottom frame (in the remaining 20 percent of the window's height). The top frame is given the name `dictionary` so that it can be targeted. (We could have used any name.)

The `dictionary.html` file will need 26 named anchors in the appropriate spots, such as:

```
<h2><a name="q">The Q Section</a></h2>
<h2><a name="r">The R Section</a></h2>
```

TIP

See Chapter 4 for a thorough discussion of named anchors and partial URLs.

The `alphabet.html` document needs 26 targeted links that used partial URLs and a `target` attribute, such as this:

```
<a href="dictionary.html#q" target="dictionary">Q</a>
<a href="dictionary.html#r" target="dictionary">R</a>
```

Instead of using the `target` attribute 26 times, you can simply create a head section in `alphabet.html` that includes a targeted `<base>` tag, and then you can leave out the `target` attribute from the 26 links. The resulting `alphabet.html` file is shown here:

```
<!DOCTYPE HTML PUBLIC "-//W3C//DTD HTML 4.0//EN">
<html lang="en">
<head>
    <title>Index To The Modern Hacker's Dictionary</title>
    <base target="dictionary">
</head>
<body>
<center><big>
<a href="dictionary.html#a">a</a>
<a href="dictionary.html#b">b</a>
[the other twenty-four letters follow...]
</big></center>
</body>
</html>
```

Here's how this setup might appear:

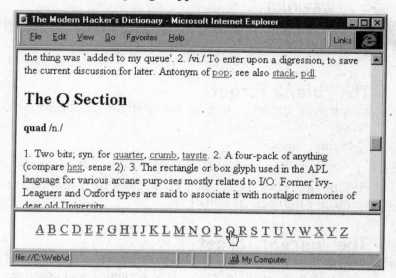

You can make this example more complex if you like by adding additional frames. Most agree that being able to jump instantly from letter to letter while keeping the alphabet links constantly visible makes this a handy use of frames.

In this example, both `alphabet.html` and `dictionary.html` are given `title` elements, like any HTML document. However, Navigator and Internet Explorer don't display the two frame's titles anywhere—only the frameset document's title is displayed in the title bar. However, the `title` element still is required for the frame documents, and the title will be displayed if the frame document ever becomes unframed.

Using Special Target Names

You've seen how you can specify a `target` attribute to change the contents of a particular frame if that frame was named with the `frame` element's name attribute.

Four predefined names also can be targeted by an anchor. These four targets have special meanings. They all start with an underscore (_), which normally is an illegal character for a target name.

WARNING

All four of these special target names are case sensitive. (Most target names are not case sensitive.)

The _blank Target

By specifying `target="_blank"`, you can cause the document to be loaded into a new window.

In this example:

```
<a href="document.html" target="_blank">My Document</a>
```

clicking on My Document would cause a new browser window to appear, containing the `document.html` file.

The _parent Target

The _parent target name refers to the parent frameset. Most of the time, you won't have multiple framesets in separate files (so you won't have parent framesets or child framesets), but in the rare cases where you do have nested framesets, you may need to refer to the parent frameset without using the frame's name.

If the current frame is part of a child frameset (that is, it is part of a nested frameset in a separate file), you can use the `_parent` target to dismantle the child frameset and target the frame from the initial frameset (before it was subdivided).

In this example:

```
<a href="document.html" target="_parent">My Document</a>
```

clicking on My Document would cause the `document.html` file to appear in the parent frameset, if the parent had been defined in another file.

NOTE

If there is no parent, the document loads into the current frame.

The _self Target

The _self target loads the document into the current frame (the same frame as the HTML code that contains the anchor). Since this is the default behavior, the only reason that _self is useful is if you've used a base element to set a default target and want to make an exception.

For example, suppose you've previously declared <base target="mary"> to have links target a frame named mary by default. You can use this:

```
<a href="document.html" target="_self">My Document</a>
```

When someone clicks on My Document, the file document.html will replace the contents of the current frame instead of the mary frame.

The _top Target

The most useful of the four special target names is _top, which removes frames altogether.

In this example:

```
<a href="document.html" target="_top">My Document</a>
```

clicking on My Document would cancel all the frames and replace the entire frameset with the document.html file.

NOTE

You can use the browser's Back button to return to the frameset.

You can use the base element with any of the four special target names. For example, using <base target="_top"> in a document's head section would cause any link on that page to cancel frames (thus "unframing" the page).

We'll discuss more about unframing documents a little later in this chapter.

PROVIDING ALTERNATE CONTENT WITH THE *NOFRAMES* ELEMENT

The specification for HTML 4.01 strongly recommends that each frameset document include an alternate method of accessing the framed information.

Everyone using a non–frames-enabled browser will see a completely blank page if they view a frameset document that doesn't include alternate content. Therefore, it's imperative to use the noframes element to explain what's going on and enable people to access the content of your website. The `noframes` element consists of the `<noframes>` and `</noframes>` tags, which contain the alternate content. The alternate content is displayed *only* by a browser that is not displaying frames.

NOTE

When a search engine searches and indexes (or *spiders*) a website for inclusion in its search listings, the content of the `<noframes>` tags is added to the listings. If you have placed a string such as `Your browser doesn't support frames` there, then your search engine listing will more than likely have "Your browser doesn't support frames" as the description of your website. To avoid this situation, put meaningful text in this location, including links to some of the other primary pages on your site.

Here's an example of how to include the `noframes` element in a frameset document:

```
<!DOCTYPE HTML PUBLIC "-//W3C//DTD HTML 4.0 Frameset//EN">
<html lang="en">
<head>
    <title>NOFRAMES Alternative Text Example</title>
</head>
<frameset cols="50%,50%">
    <frame src="document1.html">
    <frame src="document2.html">
    <noframes>
      <body>
      <p>Please visit the <a href="noframes.html">
         Anderson Manufacturing website</a>
         to see our new online catalog.</p>
      </body>
    </noframes>
</frameset>
</html>
```

In Figure 8.5, we see how the Opera browser shows this page when frames are disabled (File ➤ Preferences ➤ Page Style).

TIP

Some sites create two versions of their pages: one for frame-enabled browsers and one for non–frame-enabled browsers. However, this is a lot of work, and it's difficult to maintain two sets of pages accurately.

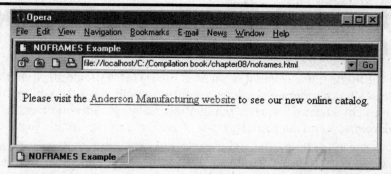

FIGURE 8.5: Opera 6 displays the alternate content when frames are disabled.

HTML 4.01 enables you to include a `noframes` element in regular documents. The content of the `noframes` element will be shown only if the document is not being displayed as part of a frameset. Unfortunately, this use of the `noframes` element is not yet supported by any browser— so the contents of the `noframes` element will be displayed regardless.

Part II

NOTE

In our example of the `noframes` element, we included the body element's `<body>` and `</body>` tags inside the `noframes` element, but those tags are not required here. Some browsers like to see them, however.

Many web authors include only a brief "Get Navigator or Internet Explorer" statement in the `noframes` element (sometimes they'll link to Netscape's or Microsoft's home page). Most surfers are aware that they need a frames-enabled browser to see frames, and many even know where they can get such a browser—they may have disabled frames by choice or are using a computer system on which they can't possibly install a frames-enabled browser. No text-to-speech browsers can handle frames properly. For these users, it's not polite to tell them to update their browser. Instead, you should link to the individual documents or an alternate document.

NOTE

Frames have been supported in Netscape since version 2.0 and in Internet Explorer since version 3.0.

USING THE INLINE FRAME ELEMENT TO CREATE INLINE FRAMES

The inline frame element is a part of the HTML 4.01 specification that can show a separate document within part of a page. The inline frame element is related to frames, but they're actually two different things. Internet Explorer 3 and later and Navigator 6 and later recognize this element.

The inline frame element uses the <iframe> and </iframe> tags, along with the same attributes used in the frame element and optional width, height, and align attributes.

Inline frames can be included within a block of text. The inline frame element should contain alternate text that is displayed only if the inline frame element can't be displayed.

The following HTML code inserts three inline frames centered within the document after the words "Primary Colors."

Listing 8.1: iframe1.html

```
<!DOCTYPE HTML PUBLIC "-//W3C//DTD HTML 4.0//EN">
<html lang="en">
<head>
    <title>First Inline Frames Example</title>
</head>
<body bgcolor="#000000" text="#ffffff">

<p>Primary Colors</p>

<center>

<iframe src="red.html" marginheight="0" frameborder="10"
width="300" height="25">
<p>The <a href="red.html">red</a> file is available.</p>
</iframe>
<br>
<iframe src="yellow.html" marginheight="0" frameborder="10"
width="300" height="25">
<p>The <a href="yellow.html">yellow</a> file is available.
</p>
</iframe>
```

```
<br>
<iframe src="blue.html" marginheight="0" frameborder="10"
width="300" height="25">
<p>The <a href="blue.html">blue</a> file is available.</p>
</iframe>

</center>
</body>
</html>
```

Each inline frame defaults to automatic scrolling, just like regular frames. Figure 8.6 shows how these three inline frames would be displayed by Internet Explorer.

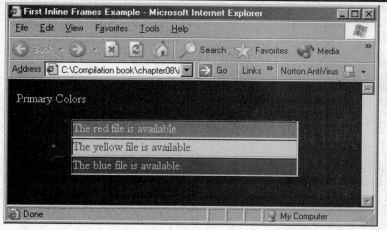

FIGURE 8.6:   Internet Explorer displays three centered inline frames.

NOTE

Just as with other frames, you'll have to create each of the files displayed by the inline frame element ahead of time. Figure 8.6 shows the contents of four different files (the main content file and the three inline frame files).

On the other hand, a pre–Navigator 6 browser, which wouldn't recognize the iframe element, will display whatever is between the <iframe> and

`</iframe>` tags, as shown here:

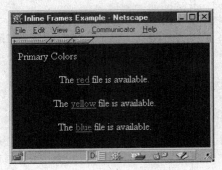

The `object` element can be used to include an HTML file within another HTML file. The only difference between using an `object` element and an inline frame element is that you can use the `name` attribute with an inline frame to create links that target the inline frame.

NOTE

If you are using the Strict XHTML DTD, you must use the `object` element rather than `iframe`. The `iframe` element is available only in the Transitional DTD. See Chapter 3, "Creating Your First HTML or XHTML Document," and Chapter 19 for more information about DTDs and XHTML.

Listing 8.2: `iframe2.html`

```
<!DOCTYPE HTML PUBLIC "-//W3C//DTD HTML 4.0//EN">
<html lang="en">
<head>
    <title>Second Inline Frames Example</title>
</head>
<body>

<p>
Primary Colors -- pick one:
<a href="yellow.html" target="centerframe"><font
    color="yellow">yellow</font></a>,
<a href="red.html" target="centerframe"><font
    color="red">red</font></a>, or
<a href="blue.html" target="centerframe"><font
    color="blue">blue</font></a>.
</p>
```

```
<center>
<iframe width="300" height="75" name="centerframe">
<p>Choose a color from the list above.</p>
</iframe>
</center>

</body>
</html>
```

This example creates an empty inline frame in the center of the document, named centerframe. (We could have given it any legal name.) By clicking on any of the three links, the inline frame will display the appropriate document. The inline frame is initially empty, as shown here.

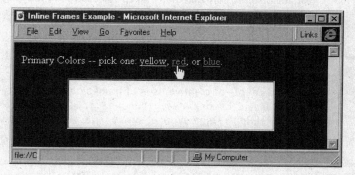

UNFRAMING PAGES

It's easy to create a set of framed documents, but not so easy to remove them. Because the default action for a link is to replace only the current frame, a link to an external site might leave one or more of your frames still on-screen. That external site might have frames of its own, which will be added to your frames. Pretty soon, the screen is cluttered with all sorts of frames containing menus and logos.

WARNING

Another problem is that if one of the framed pages links to the frameset document without using a special target name, the frameset will be repeated on-screen—displaying duplicate navigation bars, for example.

To prevent this from happening, it's important to unframe pages for external links or internal links to frameset documents.

The easiest way to unframe pages is to use either the `_blank` or the `_top` special target, discussed earlier in this chapter. If you're careful always to include a `target` attribute with one of those targets for all of your external links (or internal links to pages that you want to display full-screen), then you'll never create a problem of too many frames on-screen. For example:

```
<a href="document.html" target="_top"> See this document
    unframed.</a>
```

TIP

Sometimes you'll find that people are linking to one of your pages as part of a frame. To make sure that their frames don't surround your page for long, put a `<base target="_top">` in the head section of your document. The next link that's followed on your page will be shown full-screen.

NOTE

To see a couple of creative uses of frames on the web, try Scot Hacker's Spong Classic (`http://www.birdhouse.org/images/scot/spong/`) and Robert Kendall's Frame Work at `www.uiowa.edu/%7Eiareview/tirweb/hypermedia/robert_kendall/`.

HOW TO UNFRAME A PAGE IN A BROWSER

Sometimes when you're surfing, you'll want to unframe the pages that you see on-screen. In order to view each separate document in a frames page, Navigator can open new browser windows for each document within a frames page. That way, you can view each document unframed, which lets you print or view source normally. To unframe a page in Navigator 4 or later, perform the following steps:

1. To select the frame you want to unframe, click inside it.

2. Click the right mouse button (or hold the mouse button down with the Command key if you're using a Macintosh) to open the shortcut menu.

3. From the shortcut menu, choose the Open Frame in New Window command.

CONTINUED ➡

Navigator will open a new window for that framed document.

In Opera 3.60 or later, choose Frame ➢ Maximize from the right mouse button shortcut menu.

Internet Explorer doesn't have an easy way for you to unframe an individual page, although you can use a similar technique to open each link in a new window. Internet Explorer 4 and above makes it easy to print each separate frame document. In Internet Explorer 4 or above, click inside the frame you want to print and then choose the Print command. You'll have three options: As Laid Out on Screen, Only the Selected Frame, or All Frames Individually.

WHAT'S NEXT?

In the next chapter, Molly Holzschlag offers an overview of layout technology, taking a close look at how layouts are constructed. She'll also explore how HTML and XHTML syntax combine with space, shape, and object placement, resulting in the blueprint of your website's layout design.

Chapter 9

LAYOUT TECHNOLOGY

In this chapter, you'll explore layout control. You'll delve into standard and tables-based technologies and look at how HTML and XHTML syntax combines with space, shape, and object placement to result in the blueprint of your website. Then you will be introduced to document templates as a quick and effective means of creating pages that have the same design features as documents made from scratch.

NOTE

The basics of frames were covered in Chapter 8, "Dividing a Window with Frames," and therefore will not be covered here.

Certainly, one chapter devoted to the complex and emerging technologies of web design layout is not going to be enough. Therefore, you'll see plenty of references to resources that will help you master the areas of layout that interest you most.

Adapted from *web by design: The Complete Guide* by Molly E. Holzschlag
ISBN 0-7821-2201-9 $49.99

STANDARD HTML AND XHTML FORMATTING

Standard HTML and XHTML formatting involves breaking up the page with balanced amounts of text, graphics and other media, and space. Your sketches can prepare the foundation for this, but you'll need to get up close and personal with HTML and XHTML code to really manipulate blocks of text or media.

The first step in managing text with standard techniques is to determine *how much* text you have for the entire site. This will help you break up text into focused pages. For individual pages within the site, a reasonable layout runs from one to three screens per page (see Figure 9.1). Remember, though, that no one wants to scroll through text alone; therefore, that figure will probably be higher.

FIGURE 9.1:   Once we add white space and artwork, this text will take up about three screens

The following code shows about three screens' worth of text before any text formatting has been added. Pay attention to how this amount of text changes visually in the figure examples throughout the process.

NOTE

The code examples in this chapter are done in XHTML. For more information on XHTML, see Chapters 2, 3, 5, and 19.

```
<!DOCTYPE html PUBLIC
    "-//W3C//DTD XHTML 1.0 Transitional//EN"
    "http://www.w3.org/TR/xhtml1/DTD/xhtml1-transitional.dtd">

<html xmlns="http://www.w3.org/1999/xhtml">

<head>
<title>Text Example</title>
</head>

<body bgcolor="#FFFFFF" text="#000000" link="#999999"
vlink="#CCCCCC" alink="#FFFFCC">
<p>
Duis autem vel eum iriure dolor in hendrerit in vulputate
    velit esse molestie consequat, vel illum dolore eu
    feugiat nulla facilisis at vero eros et accumsan et
    iusto odio dignissim qui blandit praesent luptatum
    zzril delenit augue duis dolore te feugait nulla
    facilisi. Nam liber tempor cum soluta nobis eleifend
    option congue nihil imperdiet doming id quod mazim
    placerat facer possim assum.

Accumsan et iusto odio dignissim qui blandit praesent
    luptatum zzril delenit augue duis dolore te feugait
    nulla facilisi. Eros Et Accumsan dignissim qui blandit
    praesent luptatum zzril delenit augue duis dolore te
    feugait nulla facilisi. Nam liber tempor cum soluta
    nobis eleifend option congue nihil imperdiet doming id
    quod mazim placerat facer possim assum. Iusto odio
    dignissim qui blandit praesent luptatum zzril delenit
    augue duis dolore te feugait nulla facilisi.

Nam liber tempor cum soluta nobis eleifend option congue
    nihil imperdiet doming id quod mazim placerat facer
    possim assum. Accumsan et iusto odio dignissim qui
    blandit. Vendrerit In Vulputate Duis autem vel eum
    iriure dolor in hendrerit in vulputate velit esse
    molestie consequat, vel illum dolore eu feugiat nulla
    facilisis at vero eros et accumsan et iusto odio.
    Occumsan Aliquam dignissim qui blandit praesent
```

```
            luptatum zzril delenit augue duis dolore te feugait
            nulla facilisi. Nam liber tempor cum soluta nobis
            eleifend option congue nihil imperdiet doming id quod
            mazim placerat facer possim assum.

        Eros Et Accumsan dignissim qui blandit praesent luptatum
            zzril delenit augue duis dolore te feugait nulla
            facilisi. Nam liber tempor cum soluta nobis eleifend
            option congue nihil imperdiet doming id quod mazim
            placerat facer possim assum. Iusto odio dignissim qui
            blandit.

        Accumsan dignissim qui blandit praesent luptatum zzril
            delenit augue duis dolore te feugait nulla facilisi.
            Nam liber tempor cum soluta nobis eleifend option
            congue nihil imperdiet doming id quod mazim placerat
            facer possim assum. Iusto odio dignissim qui blandit
            praesent luptatum zzril delenit augue duis dolore te
            feugait nulla facilisi.

        Nam liber tempor cum soluta nobis eleifend option congue
            nihil imperdiet doming id quod mazim placerat facer
            possim assum. Accumsan et iusto odio dignissim qui
            blandit. Duis autem vel eum iriure dolor in hendrerit
            in vulputate velit esse molestie consequat, vel illum
            dolore eu feugiat nulla facilisis at vero eros et
            accumsan et iusto odio.
        </p>
        </body>
        </html>
```

Now see what happens when margins are added via the <blockquote> tag (see Figure 9.2). The blockquote element is necessary to create that all-important white space. The updated code follows.

```
<!DOCTYPE html PUBLIC
    "-//W3C//DTD XHTML 1.0 Transitional//EN"
    "http://www.w3.org/TR/xhtml1/DTD/xhtml1-transitional.dtd">
<html xmlns="http://www.w3.org/1999/xhtml">

<head>
<title>Text Example</title>
</head>

<body bgcolor="#FFFFFF" text="#000000" link="#999999"
vlink="#CCCCCC" alink="#FFFFCC">
```

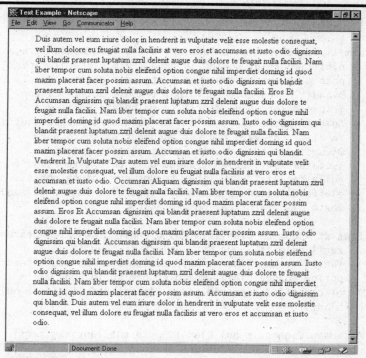

FIGURE 9.2: The blockquote element creates that all-important white space.

```
<blockquote>
<p>
```
Duis autem vel eum iriure dolor in hendrerit in vulputate
velit esse molestie consequat, vel illum dolore eu
feugiat nulla facilisis at vero eros et accumsan et
iusto odio dignissim qui blandit praesent luptatum
zzril delenit augue duis dolore te feugait nulla
facilisi. Nam liber tempor cum soluta nobis eleifend
option congue nihil imperdiet doming id quod mazim
placerat facer possim assum.

Accumsan et iusto odio dignissim qui blandit praesent
luptatum zzril delenit augue duis dolore te feugait
nulla facilisi. Eros Et Accumsan dignissim qui blandit
praesent luptatum zzril delenit augue duis dolore te
feugait nulla facilisi. Nam liber tempor cum soluta
nobis eleifend option congue nihil imperdiet doming id
quod mazim placerat facer possim assum. Iusto odio

```
              dignissim qui blandit praesent luptatum zzril delenit
              augue duis dolore te feugait nulla facilisi.

          Nam liber tempor cum soluta nobis eleifend option congue
              nihil imperdiet doming id quod mazim placerat facer
              possim assum. Accumsan et iusto odio dignissim qui
              blandit. Vendrerit In Vulputate Duis autem vel eum
              iriure dolor in hendrerit in vulputate velit esse
              molestie consequat, vel illum dolore eu feugiat nulla
              facilisis at vero eros et accumsan et iusto odio.
              Occumsan Aliquam dignissim qui blandit praesent
              luptatum zzril delenit augue duis dolore te feugait
              nulla facilisi. Nam liber tempor cum soluta nobis
              eleifend option congue nihil imperdiet doming id quod
              mazim placerat facer possim assum.

          Eros Et Accumsan dignissim qui blandit praesent luptatum
              zzril delenit augue duis dolore te feugait nulla
              facilisi. Nam liber tempor cum soluta nobis eleifend
              option congue nihil imperdiet doming id quod mazim
              placerat facer possim assum. Iusto odio dignissim qui
              blandit.

          Accumsan dignissim qui blandit praesent luptatum zzril
              delenit augue duis dolore te feugait nulla facilisi.
              Nam liber tempor cum soluta nobis eleifend option
              congue nihil imperdiet doming id quod mazim placerat
              facer possim assum. Iusto odio dignissim qui blandit
              praesent luptatum zzril delenit augue duis dolore te
              feugait nulla facilisi.

          Nam liber tempor cum soluta nobis eleifend option congue
              nihil imperdiet doming id quod mazim placerat facer
              possim assum. Accumsan et iusto odio dignissim qui
              blandit. Duis autem vel eum iriure dolor in hendrerit
              in vulputate velit esse molestie consequat, vel illum
              dolore eu feugiat nulla facilisis at vero eros et
              accumsan et iusto odio.
          </p>
          </blockquote>
          </body>
          </html>
```

Attention span on the web is short. It's in your best interest to serve
your audience by ensuring that paragraphs are equally short. Therefore,
after breaking up text into pages, break your page into logical sections of

short paragraphs (see Figure 9.3). The following code shows the paragraph tags added.

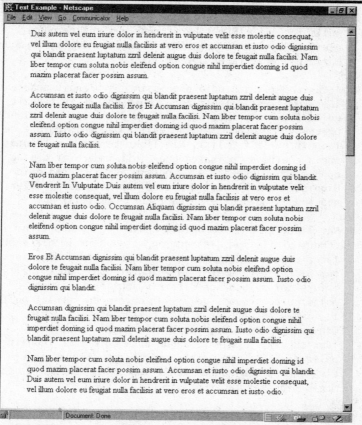

FIGURE 9.3: Paragraphs should be short and to the point.

```
<!DOCTYPE HTML PUBLIC
    "-//W3C//DTD XHTML 1.0 Transitional//EN"
    "http://www.w3.org/TR/xhtml1/DTD/xhtml1-transitional.dtd">
<html xmlns="http://www.w3.org/1999/xhtml">

<head>
<title>Text Example</title>
</head>
<body bgcolor="#FFFFFF" text="#000000" link="#999999"
vlink="#CCCCCC" alink="#FFFFCC">
<blockquote>
```

```
<p>Duis autem vel eum iriure dolor in hendrerit in
   vulputate velit esse molestie consequat, vel illum
   dolore eu feugiat nulla facilisis at vero eros et
   accumsan et iusto odio dignissim qui blandit praesent
   luptatum zzril delenit augue duis dolore te feugait
   nulla facilisi. Nam liber tempor cum soluta nobis
   eleifend option congue nihil imperdiet doming id quod
   mazim placerat facer possim assum.
</p>
<p>Accumsan et iusto odio dignissim qui blandit praesent
   luptatum zzril delenit augue duis dolore te feugait
   nulla facilisi. Eros Et Accumsan dignissim qui blandit
   praesent luptatum zzril delenit augue duis dolore te
   feugait nulla facilisi. Nam liber tempor cum soluta
   nobis eleifend option congue nihil imperdiet doming id
   quod mazim placerat facer possim assum. Iusto odio
   dignissim qui blandit praesent luptatum zzril delenit
   augue duis dolore te feugait nulla facilisi.
</p>
<p>Nam liber tempor cum soluta nobis eleifend option
   congue nihil imperdiet doming id quod mazim placerat
   facer possim assum. Accumsan et iusto odio dignissim
   qui blandit. Vendrerit In Vulputate Duis autem vel eum
   iriure dolor in hendrerit in vulputate velit esse
   molestie consequat, vel illum dolore eu feugiat nulla
   facilisis at vero eros et accumsan et iusto odio.
   Occumsan Aliquam dignissim qui blandit praesent
   luptatum zzril delenit augue duis dolore te feugait
   nulla facilisi. Nam liber tempor cum soluta nobis
   eleifend option congue nihil imperdiet doming id quod
   mazim placerat facer possim assum.
</p>
<p>Eros Et Accumsan dignissim qui blandit praesent
   luptatum zzril delenit augue duis dolore te feugait
   nulla facilisi. Nam liber tempor cum soluta nobis
   eleifend option congue nihil imperdiet doming id quod
   mazim placerat facer possim assum. Iusto odio
   dignissim qui blandit.
</p>
<p>Accumsan dignissim qui blandit praesent luptatum zzril
   delenit augue duis dolore te feugait nulla facilisi.
   Nam liber tempor cum soluta nobis eleifend option
   congue nihil imperdiet doming id quod mazim placerat
   facer possim assum. Iusto odio dignissim qui blandit
   praesent luptatum zzril delenit augue duis dolore te
   feugait nulla facilisi.
```

```
</p>
<p>Nam liber tempor cum soluta nobis eleifend option
    congue nihil imperdiet doming id quod mazim placerat
    facer possim assum. Accumsan et iusto odio dignissim
    qui blandit. Duis autem vel eum iriure dolor in
    hendrerit in vulputate velit esse molestie consequat,
    vel illum dolore eu feugiat nulla facilisis at vero
    eros et accumsan et iusto odio.
</p>
</blockquote>
</body>
</html>
```

Some people choose to use the nonbreaking space character ( ) to create indentation in paragraphs. The results are quite readable, as you can see in Figure 9.4.

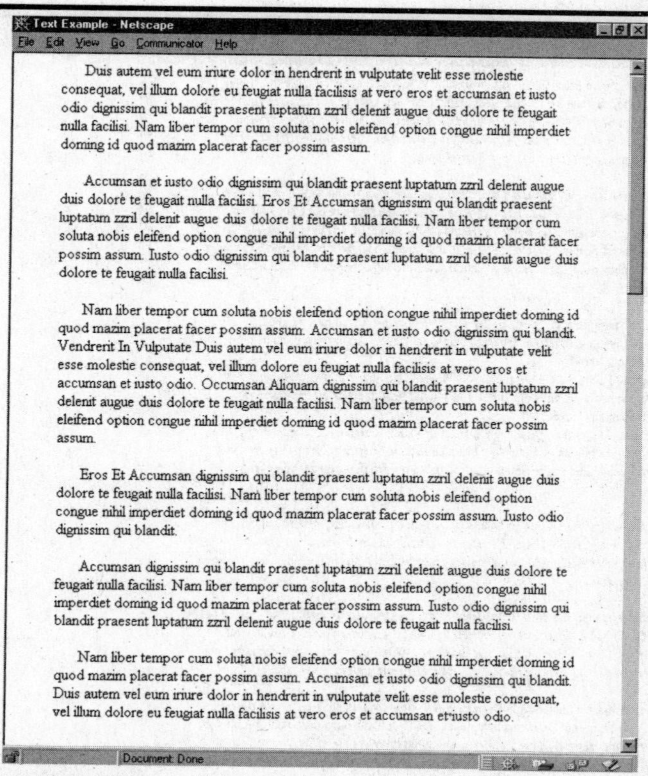

FIGURE 9.4: You can use nonbreaking space characters to achieve paragraph indentation.

The following three nonbreaking space characters before the paragraph show you how to achieve the technique:

```
<p>      Duis autem vel eum iriure dolor
    in hendrerit in vulputate velit esse molestie
    consequat, vel illum dolore eu feugiat nulla facilisis
    at vero eros et accumsan et iusto odio dignissim qui
    blandit praesent luptatum zzril delenit augue duis
    dolore te feugait nulla facilisi. Nam liber tempor cum
    soluta nobis eleifend option congue nihil imperdiet
    doming id quod mazim placerat facer possim assum.
</p>
```

Remember also that lists are a good way to break up space and help shape a page's layout. You can add them wherever your design calls for them or where they seem logical. Figure 9.5 shows the use of lists with the same text.

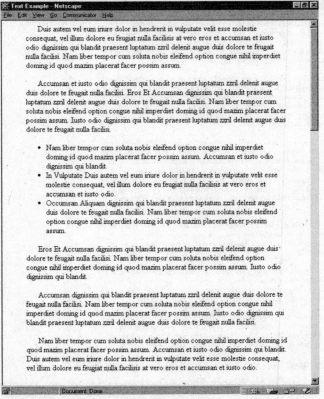

FIGURE 9.5:   The page with a list added

Here is the code:

```
<!DOCTYPE HTML PUBLIC
    "-//W3C//DTD XHTML 1.0 Transitional//EN"
    "http://www.w3.org/TR/xhtml1/DTD/xhtml1-transitional.dtd">
<html xmlns="http://www.w3.org/1999/xhtml">

<head>
<title>Text Example</title>
</head>

<body bgcolor="#FFFFFF" text="#000000" link="#999999"
vlink="#CCCCCC" alink="#FFFFCC">

<blockquote>

<p>      Duis autem vel eum iriure dolor
    in hendrerit in vulputate velit esse molestie
    consequat, vel illum dolore eu feugiat nulla facilisis
    at vero eros et accumsan et iusto odio dignissim qui
    blandit praesent luptatum zzril delenit augue duis
    dolore te feugait nulla facilisi. Nam liber tempor cum
    soluta nobis eleifend option congue nihil imperdiet
    doming id quod mazim placerat facer possim assum.
</p>

<p>      Accumsan et iusto odio dignissim
    qui blandit praesent luptatum zzril delenit augue duis
    dolore te feugait nulla facilisi. Eros Et Accumsan
    dignissim qui blandit praesent luptatum zzril delenit
    augue duis dolore te feugait nulla facilisi. Nam liber
    tempor cum soluta nobis eleifend option congue nihil
    imperdiet doming id quod mazim placerat facer possim
    assum. Iusto odio dignissim qui blandit praesent
    luptatum zzril delenit augue duis dolore te feugait
    nulla facilisi.
</p>

<ul>
<li>Nam liber tempor cum soluta nobis eleifend option
    congue nihil imperdiet doming id quod mazim placerat
    facer possim assum. Accumsan et iusto odio dignissim
    qui blandit.</li>
<li>In Vulputate Duis autem vel eum iriure dolor in
    hendrerit in vulputate velit esse molestie consequat,
    vel illum dolore eu feugiat nulla facilisis at vero
    eros et accumsan et iusto odio.</li>
```

```
<li>Occumsan Aliquam dignissim qui blandit praesent
    luptatum zzril delenit augue duis dolore te feugait
    nulla facilisi. Nam liber tempor cum soluta nobis
    eleifend option congue nihil imperdiet doming id quod
    mazim placerat facer possim assum.</li>
</ul>

<p>      Eros Et Accumsan dignissim qui
    blandit praesent luptatum zzril delenit augue duis
    dolore te feugait nulla facilisi. Nam liber tempor cum
    soluta nobis eleifend option congue nihil imperdiet
    doming id quod mazim placerat facer possim assum.
    Iusto odio dignissim qui blandit.
</p>

<p>      Accumsan dignissim qui blandit
    praesent luptatum zzril delenit augue duis dolore te
    feugait nulla facilisi. Nam liber tempor cum soluta
    nobis eleifend option congue nihil imperdiet doming id
    quod mazim placerat facer possim assum. Iusto odio
    dignissim qui blandit praesent luptatum zzril delenit
    augue duis dolore te feugait nulla facilisi.
</p>

<p>      Nam liber tempor cum soluta nobis
    eleifend option congue nihil imperdiet doming id quod
    mazim placerat facer possim assum. Accumsan et iusto
    odio dignissim qui blandit. Duis autem vel eum iriure
    dolor in hendrerit in vulputate velit esse molestie
    consequat, vel illum dolore eu feugiat nulla facilisis
    at vero eros et accumsan et iusto odio.
</p>
</blockquote>
</body>
</html>
```

Finally, you will want to use graphics or other media for functional purposes; graphics can function as linked graphics, navigation buttons, and imagemaps. You can include graphics, such as a photograph, as design enhancements (see Figure 9.6) or as a main splash graphic. The code for the text example, with an added graphic, follows. Notice how the page is beginning to take on an attractive shape and that, with the addition of space and other layout techniques, the original jumbled text is formatted into three full screens of information.

Duis autem vel eum iriure dolor in hendrerit in vulputate velit esse molestie consequat, vel illum dolore eu feugiat nulla facilisis at vero eros et accumsan et iusto odio dignissim qui blandit praesent luptatum zzril delenit augue duis dolore te feugait nulla facilisi. Nam liber tempor cum soluta nobis eleifend option congue nihil imperdiet doming id quod mazim placerat facer possim assum.

Accumsan et iusto odio dignissim qui blandit praesent luptatum zzril delenit augue duis dolore te eugait nulla facilisi. Eros Et Accumsan dignissim qui blandit praesent luptatum zzril delenit augue duis dolore te feugait nulla facilisi. Nam liber tempor cum soluta nobis eleifend option congue nihil imperdiet doming id quod mazim placerat facer possim assum. Iusto odio dignissim qui blandit praesent luptatum zzril delenit augue duis dolore te feugait nulla facilisi.

- Nam liber tempor cum soluta nobis eleifend option congue nihil imperdiet doming id quod mazim placerat facer possim assum. Accumsan et iusto odio dignissim qui blandit.
- In Vulputate Duis autem vel eum iriure dolor in hendrerit in vulputate velit esse molestie consequat, vel illum dolore eu feugiat nulla facilisis at vero eros et accumsan et iusto odio.
- Occumsan Aliquam dignissim qui blandit praesent luptatum zzril delenit augue duis dolore te feugait nulla facilisi. Nam liber tempor cum soluta nobis eleifend option congue nihil imperdiet doming id quod mazim placerat facer possim assum.

Eros Et Accumsan dignissim qui blandit praesent luptatum zzril delenit augue duis dolore te feugait nulla facilisi. Nam liber tempor cum soluta nobis eleifend option congue nihil imperdiet doming id quod mazim placerat facer possim assum. Iusto odio dignissim qui blandit.

Accumsan dignissim qui blandit praesent luptatum zzril delenit augue duis dolore te feugait nulla facilisi. Nam liber tempor cum soluta nobis eleifend option congue nihil imperdiet doming id quod mazim placerat facer possim assum. Iusto odio dignissim qui blandit praesent luptatum zzril delenit augue duis dolore te feugait nulla facilisi.

Nam liber tempor cum soluta nobis eleifend option congue nihil imperdiet doming id quod mazim placerat facer possim assum. Accumsan et iusto odio dignissim qui blandit. Duis autem vel eum iriure dolor in hendrerit in vulputate velit esse molestie consequat, vel illum dolore eu feugiat nulla facilisis at vero eros et accumsan et iusto odio.

FIGURE 9.6:   A graphic added to the page

```
<!DOCTYPE HTML PUBLIC
    "-//W3C//DTD XHTML 1.0 Transitional//EN"
    "http://www.w3.org/TR/xhtml1/DTD/xhtml1-transitional.dtd">
<html xmlns="http://www.w3.org/1999/xhtml">

<head>
<title>Text Example</title>
</head>
<body bgcolor="#FFFFFF" text="#000000" link="#999999"
vlink="#CCCCCC" alink="#FFFFCC">

<blockquote>
```

```
<p>      Duis autem vel eum iriure dolor
   in hendrerit in vulputate velit esse molestie
   consequat, vel illum dolore eu feugiat nulla facilisis
   at vero eros et accumsan et iusto odio dignissim qui
   blandit praesent luptatum zzril delenit augue duis
   dolore te feugait nulla facilisi. Nam liber tempor cum
   soluta nobis eleifend option congue nihil imperdiet
   doming id quod mazim placerat facer possim assum.
</p>

<img src="sydney.jpg" width="146" height="98" hspace="5"
   vspace="5" border="0" align="right" alt="sydney opera
   house at night" />

<p>      Accumsan et iusto odio dignissim
   qui blandit praesent luptatum zzril delenit augue duis
   dolore te eugait nulla facilisi. Eros Et Accumsan
   dignissim qui blandit praesent luptatum zzril delenit
   augue duis dolore te feugait nulla facilisi. Nam liber
   tempor cum soluta nobis eleifend option congue nihil
   imperdiet doming id quod mazim placerat facer possim
   assum. Iusto odio dignissim qui blandit praesent
   luptatum zzril delenit augue duis dolore te feugait
   nulla facilisi.
</p>

<ul>
<li>Nam liber tempor cum soluta nobis eleifend option
   congue nihil imperdiet doming id quod mazim placerat
   facer possim assum. Accumsan et iusto odio dignissim
   qui blandit.</li>

<li>In Vulputate Duis autem vel eum iriure dolor in
   hendrerit in vulputate velit esse molestie consequat,
   vel illum dolore eu feugiat nulla facilisis at vero
   eros et accumsan et iusto odio.</li>

<li>Occumsan Aliquam dignissim qui blandit praesent
   luptatum zzril delenit augue duis dolore te feugait
   nulla facilisi. Nam liber tempor cum soluta nobis
   eleifend option congue nihil imperdiet doming id quod
   mazim placerat facer possim assum.</li>
</ul>
```

```
<p>      Eros Et Accumsan dignissim qui
   blandit praesent luptatum zzril delenit augue duis
   dolore te feugait nulla facilisi. Nam liber tempor cum
   soluta nobis eleifend option congue nihil imperdiet
   doming id quod mazim placerat facer possim assum.
   Iusto odio dignissim qui blandit.
</p>

<p>      Accumsan dignissim qui blandit
   praesent luptatum zzril delenit augue duis dolore te
   feugait nulla facilisi. Nam liber tempor cum soluta
   nobis eleifend option congue nihil imperdiet doming id
   quod mazim placerat facer possim assum. Iusto odio
   dignissim qui blandit praesent luptatum zzril delenit
   augue duis dolore te feugait nulla facilisi.
</p>

<p>      Nam liber tempor cum soluta nobis
   eleifend option congue nihil imperdiet doming id quod
   mazim placerat facer possim assum. Accumsan et iusto
   odio dignissim qui blandit. Duis autem vel eum iriure
   dolor in hendrerit in vulputate velit esse molestie
   consequat, vel illum dolore eu feugiat nulla facilisis
   at vero eros et accumsan et iusto odio.
</p>
</blockquote>
</body>
</html>
```

When graphics and media are being used as functional media, such as a link, place them using the <img> or <object> tag and any alignment attribute you want.

Graphics and media used to enhance the page should be arranged in the fashion you've determined with your layout sketches. Typically, standard HTML and XHTML layouts will apply to most simple pages, such as those with limited text and graphics, or splash pages where a map or hyperlinked graphic is the main attraction.

Splash-Screen Example

Let's look at a plain splash page with a graphic as its main feature. Figure 9.7 and the standard XHTML code used to create the page follow.

FIGURE 9.7:   The splash page as it appears in a browser

```
<!DOCTYPE HTML PUBLIC
    "-//W3C//DTD XHTML 1.0 Transitional//EN"
    "http://www.w3.org/TR/xhtml1/DTD/xhtml1-transitional.dtd">
<html xmlns="http://www.w3.org/1999/xhtml">

<head>
<title>Splash Screen</title>
</head>
<body text="#000000" bgcolor="#FFFFFF" >
<div align="center">
<a href="storyboard.htm">
    <img border="0" src="splash.gif" height="323"
    width="432" alt="Site Splash Screen" /></a>
</div>
</body>
</html>
```

No surprises here! It's a very straightforward page with the layout design relying heavily on the graphic.

WARNING

Splash pages, although widely used, have some disadvantages that make them controversial in the field of web design. First, they take some time to download, which means your site visitor may lose interest and click away to somewhere else. Second, they make it harder for search engines to index your site. Placing anything other than meaningful text, in "clean" HTML, can result in a lower ranking from search engines. See *Son of Web Pages That Suck: Learning Good Design by Looking at Bad Design*, by Vincent Flanders (Sybex, 2002), for an entertaining look at these issues and ways to minimize them. Also, see www.searchenginewatch.com/searchday/01/sd0918-design.html for tips on optimizing your site for search engines.

TABLES

Now take a look at how tables are constructed. Table tags are very simple, but with the variety of attributes available to you, the application is somewhat complicated.

Only three elements are absolutely necessary when designing with tables:

▶ table

This element determines the beginning of a table within an HTML or XHTML document. As with the majority of HTML and XHTML elements, the end of a table is denoted by a closing tag, in this case </table>.

▶ tr

Table rows are identified with this element, which determines a row—the left to right, horizontal space within a table. Table rows are closed with the </tr> tag.

▶ td

Individual table cells are defined by this element, which also is referred to as the *table data* element. The table cell tags are particularly critical for a number of reasons, which you'll see as you look at various applications of the element. Remember that the information contained within the td element determines the columnar structure of a table. The td element closes with the </td> tag.

TIP

For additional information on using tables, see Chapter 11, "Presenting Information in Tables."

Now that you've got the basics, I'll review the attributes you might want to use with these core elements. There are many, and they make HTML and XHTML more complicated; however, they also contribute to making HTML and XHTML serious layout technologies. The attributes are as follows:

▶ align="*x*"

Use this attribute to align tables on a page. Options allow x to equal left or right. Because the latest browsers default alignment is to the left and it's commonplace to center tables using other tags, the only effective use of this attribute is when you specifically want an entire table placed to the far right of the browser field, as in Figure 9.8.

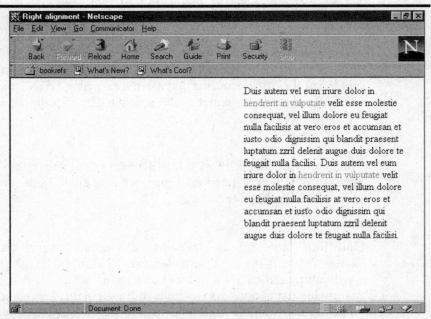

FIGURE 9.8:   A right-aligned table

Part II

TIP

Want to center your table on the page? There are several legal ways to do so. The simplest way is to place the table between the `<div align="center">` tag and its closing `</div>` tag. Division tags are stable in cross-platform environments.

▶ `border="x"`

The x is replaced with a value from 0 up, which defines the width of the visual border around the table.

▶ `cellspacing="x"`

The `cellspacing` attribute defines the amount of space between individual table cells—in other words, between visual columns. The x requires a value from 0 up.

▶ `cellpadding="x"`

This attribute defines the space around the edges of each cell within the table—literally, its "padding."

▶ `width="x%"` or `width="x"`

To define the width of a table, you can use a number that relates to the percentage of browser space you want to span or a specific numeral that will be translated into pixels of width.

When given the option of defining a table by percentage or pixel width, it's generally better to use pixels because you can count each pixel in a space. For example, if you have a table that is 595 pixels wide, you must be sure that all the elements within that table *do not exceed* 600 pixels. Percentages are less accurate, but they can be handy when you want to use a visual portion of a space that is not dependent on literal pixel count. An example of this is creating a table that is 75 percent of the browser area—the section will remain proportionately the same no matter what the screen resolution is when you're viewing the page.

TIP

Be sure to read the latest release notes applicable to your version of the browser for specific and timely information regarding that browser's technology. Ultimately, you must test your work in different browsers to see the results firsthand.

With the `table`, `tr`, and `td` elements, you have the foundation for all table-based layout design. It seems simple and, in many ways, it is. However, knowing when to use a row or a column sometimes can be very challenging.

NOTE

Web browsers are essential to the way HTML and XHTML are deciphered. Tables are well supported in most recent browsers. As you may already know, computer platform, monitor size and type, and screen resolution all may influence the way an HTML or XHTML page looks. It's always wise to test your work with a variety of browsers and, when possible, to try and view your work on different platforms.

Rows and Columns

I learned about the application of tables through the wise guidance of Wil Gerken, CEO of DesertNet and Weekly Wire. Like many other people with limited natural spatial abilities, I was having a very difficult time interpreting how to relate table syntax to layout.

When I was working on the original design of the Film Vault, Wil made me take the layout and try to work *from* the design *to* the XHTML. I had to take the image and figure out how cells and rows would configure most simply to create the layout.

After making several erroneous attempts with the sketches, I became so frustrated that I gave up for a while. It took some time for the exercise to sink in (see Figure 9.9), but once it did, the understanding was total and remained with me—enough for me to venture out on my own, designing interesting table-based layouts.

FIGURE 9.9:   The Film Vault's table configuration with columns and spanning

If you don't have good spatial ability, you can develop it with practice. Approach tables first from the columnar layout. What can you control vertically? Through the vertical, you can control the table column layout by first spatially placing items and then confirming their placement with cell attributes allowed in the td, or table data, element.

Keep in mind that graphics can be stacked and placed in tables, too, so don't get stumped by graphics that run vertically, such as the two graphics in Figure 9.10 that are in the same table cell. Remember also that graphics are used in tables as backgrounds, such as the black left panel and the white main section of the Design Studio site (see Figure 9.11), and as unseen holders that fix space on both the horizontal and vertical lines in a design (see Figure 9.12).

FIGURE 9.10:   This vertical graphic is actually two sections placed together by the table.

FIGURE 9.11:   A page from the Design Studio—the black and white sections are created by a graphic with a table laid on top.

FIGURE 9.12:   Arrows indicate where spacer GIFs have been used to fix positioning.

Attributes that are helpful within table-cell tags are these:

▶ `align="x"`

When you use this attribute within a table cell, the data inside the cell will align with the literal value you assign to the attribute. In other words, a `left` value will left justify the text or graphic you place within the cell, a `center` value will center the information, and a `right` value will right justify the information.

▶ `colspan="x"`

This attribute refers to the number of columns the cell will span.

▶ `rowspan="x"`

As with `colspan`, `rowspan` refers to the span of the cell—that is, how many rows the cell will stretch.

▶ `valign="x"`

The vertical alignment of a table cell will place the information at the top, middle, or bottom of the cell.

The two notable attributes for use in rows include `align`, which controls the row's horizontal spatial alignment, and `valign`, which determines the vertical placement of all the data within a row. It's rare to see table-row attributes used. Most designers prefer the surrounding HTML and XHTML `table` attributes and `td` table-data attributes to determine the attributes applied to table layouts. The table-row attributes are described as follows:

▶ `align="x"`

Here, the possible values for *x* are `left`, `right`, and `center`.

▶ `valign="x"`

Vertical alignment can be `top`, `middle`, `bottom`, or `baseline`.

You will need to think very carefully about `rowspan` and `colspan`. With these attributes, you can have one cell spanning multiple columns or rows, as shown in Figure 9.13 and in the following code, or many cells using a variety of span attributes to create a wide selection of visual field options.

Part II

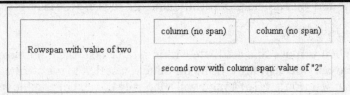

FIGURE 9.13:   An example of colspan and rowspan

```
<!DOCTYPE html PUBLIC
    "-//W3C//DTD XHTML 1.0 Transitional//EN"
    "http://www.w3.org/TR/xhtml1/DTD/xhtml1-transitional.dtd">
  <html xmlns="http://www.w3.org/1999/xhtml">

<head>
<title>colspan and rowspan</title>
</head>
<body bgcolor="#FFFFFF" text="#000000">

<table border="1" cellspacing="20" cellpadding="10">
  <tr>
    <td rowspan="2">
    Rowspan with value of two
    </td>
    <td>
    column (no span)
    </td>
    <td>
    column (no span)
    </td>
  </tr>

  <tr>
    <td colspan="2">
    second row with column span: value of "2"
    </td>
  </tr>

</table>
</body>
</html>
```

TIP

Use the border attribute of the table element to visualize your table layout. Set border="1" to visualize the borders, and then set border="0" to turn off border display.

TEST YOUR LAYOUT SKILLS

Visit any website that uses tables and attempt to reconstruct it by drawing out what you think the table cell and row structure is. Build a table using that configuration and see if it works. Only then should you peek at the source code for that page.

A Table-Based Design

Here you'll look at the site for Bernstein Communications, which uses a straightforward table-based design. Figure 9.14 shows that page, and the code follows. Take a close look at the table's structure and identify how the various attributes control the layout.

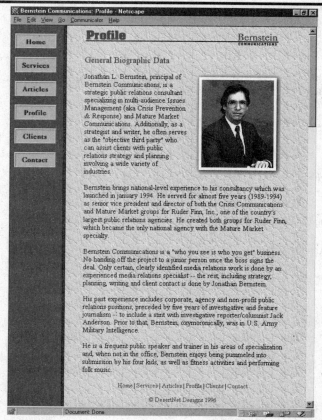

FIGURE 9.14: A page from the table-based Bernstein Communications site

```
<!DOCTYPE html PUBLIC
    "-//W3C//DTD XHTML 1.0 Transitional//EN"
    "http://www.w3.org/TR/xhtml1/DTD/xhtml1-transitional.dtd">
<html xmlns="http://www.w3.org/1999/xhtml">

<!-- site by desertnet designs: sales@desert.net -->
<!-- design director: molly holzschlag -->
<!-- graphic design: amy burnham -->
<!-- online editor: molly holzschlag -->
<!-- content provided by bernstein communications -->

<!-- begin header -->

<head>
<title>Bernstein Communications: Profile</title>
</head>
<!-- end header -->
<body bgcolor="#FFFFFF" text="#000000" link="#0000FF"
    vlink="#0000CC" alink="#FFFFFF"
    background="brn_bkgd.gif">

<table border="0" cellspacing="0" cellpadding="0"
    width="600">
<tr>
<!-- begin menu column -->

<td valign="top" align="left" width="97">

<img src="brn_nav.gif" alt="Navigation (text at bottom)"
    width="87" height="298" border="0" usemap="#brn_nav" />

<!-- begin spacer -->

<td width="55">
<img src="spacer.gif" width="55" height="1"
    alt="spacer image" />
<br />
</td>

<!-- end spacer -->

<td valign="top">
<p>

<img src="brn_h3.gif" alt="Profile Header" width="406"
    height="35" border="0" />
```

```
</p>
<p>
<font size="+1" color="#990000">General Biographic
    Data</font>
</p>
<p>
<img src="brn_ph1.gif" alt="Jonathan Bernstein"
    width="179" height="219" hspace="15" border="0"
    align="right" />
</p>
<p>Jonathan L. Bernstein, principal of Bernstein
    Communications, is a strategic public relations
    consultant specializing in multi-audience Issues
    Management (aka Crisis Prevention and Response) and
    Mature Market Communications. Additionally, as a
    strategist and writer, he often serves as the
    "objective third party" who can assist clients with
    public relations strategy and planning involving a
    wide variety of industries.
</p>

<p>Bernstein brings national-level experience to his
    consultancy which was launched in January 1994. He
    served for almost five years (1989-1994) as senior
    vice president and director of both the Crisis
    Communications and Mature Market groups for Ruder
    Finn, Inc., one of the country's largest public
    relations agencies. He created both groups for Ruder
    Finn, which became the only national agency with the
    Mature Market specialty.
</p>

<p>Bernstein Communications is a "who you see is who you
    get" business. No handing off the project to a junior
    person once the boss signs the deal. Only certain,
    clearly identified media relations work is done by an
    experienced media relations specialist -- the rest,
    including strategy, planning, writing and client
    contact is done by Jonathan Bernstein.
</p>

<p>His past experience includes corporate, agency and
    non-profit public relations positions, preceded by
    five years of investigative and feature journalism --
    to include a stint with investigative
    reporter/columnist Jack Anderson. Prior to that,
```

```
        Bernstein, oxymoronically, was in U.S. Army Military
        Intelligence.
    </p>

    <p>He is a frequent public speaker and trainer in his
        areas of specialization and, when not in the office,
        Bernstein enjoys being pummeled into submission by his
        four kids, as well as fitness activities and
        performing folk music.
    </p>

    <p align="center">
    <font size="2">
    <a href="index.html">Home</a> |
    <a href="services.html">Services </a> |
    <a href="articles.html">Articles</a> |
    <a href="profile.html">Profile </a> |
    <a href="clients.html">Clients</a> |
    <a href="contact.html">Contact</a>
    </font>
    </p>
    <p align="center">
    <font size="2">
    <a href="http://desert.net/designs/">&#169; DesertNet
        Designs 1996</a>
    </font>
    </p>

    </td>

    <!-- begin spacer -->

    <td width="30" rowspan="2">
    <img src="spacer.gif" width="30" height="1"
        alt="spacer image" />
    <br />
    </td>

    <!-- end spacer -->

    </tr>
    </table>

    <map name="brn_nav">
    <area shape="rect" coords="0,10,86,41"
        href="index.html" />
```

```
<area shape="rect" coords="0,60,86,92"
    href="services.html" />
<area shape="rect" coords="0,113,86,143"
    href="articles .html" />
<area shape="rect" coords="0,162,85,194"
    href="profile.html" />
<area shape="rect" coords="0,213,85,246"
    href="clients.html" />
<area shape="rect" coords="1,267,85,296"
    href="contact.html" />
<area shape="default" nohref="nohref" />
</map>

</body>
</html>
```

If you paid close attention to the code, you should have noticed the use of graphics as background and placeholders within this layout.

NOTE

You also may have noticed the use of an imagemap in this code (<map name="brn_nav">). Imagemaps are an effective way to use one graphic to include multiple links. For more details on imagemaps, see Chapter 10, "Adding Graphics."

TEMPLATES

Using a template to format information in the same or a similar appearance is an old technique. Microsoft started using templates with Word way back when Word was just a baby. Although HTML and XHTML don't include any features that enable you to create templates, many software programs, such as Macromedia Dreamweaver and Microsoft FrontPage, create a template for you and adjust all your links according to the permanent location of the documents created from the template.

Dreamweaver templates, for example, include everything required for your document from the headings, titles, table structures, layer structures, and base images and body elements that will stay the same for all pages. Dreamweaver allows you to insert specific areas of your document that can be modified—for instance, the document title, as well as any other areas you specifically want to include. What you modify can be something as simple as a single cell of a table or as complex as a series of locations within the text of a document that enable you to personalize information using a server-side language such as ColdFusion.

You can create your own templates for formatting your documents by creating a basic HTML or XHTML document and saving it with a name such as `template.html`. Then, in your normal HTML editor, you can open your `template.html` document, save your document with a new name, make your updates, and save those changes to the new document.

WARNING

If you save your template document with a new name when you first open it, you do not have to worry about inadvertently using the Save command or the keyboard shortcut and saving over your default template.

WHAT'S NEXT?

With the concepts of layout method and technology in mind, you're ready to think about adding graphics to your pages. In the next chapter, E. Stephen Mack and Janan Platt Saylor teach you how to work with image files and formats while building your site.

Chapter 10

ADDING GRAPHICS

Graphics, images, pictures, photographs—whatever you call them, a visual element makes your page more compelling and is the easiest way to give your page a unique look. In this chapter, we'll show you all the ways you can add images to your pages using the `<img>` tag and its many attributes. You'll also learn how to use images as links.

Throughout this chapter, you'll find suggestions on how you can make your images useful and functional even when viewed by a browser that doesn't display images. Toward the end of the chapter, we'll take a look at the different image formats and discuss how you can create images (including interlaced images, transparent images, and animated images).

Adapted from *HTML 4.0: No Experience Required*, by E. Stephen Mack and Janan Platt Saylor
ISBN 0-7821-2143-8 $29.99

ADDING GRAPHICS WITH THE IMAGE ELEMENT

The purpose of the image element (which consists of the <img> tag) is to include graphic images in the body of your web page.

NOTE

HTML 4.01 recommends using the object element (the <object> and </object> tags) instead of the image element. However, <img> is still common, and HTML 4.01 and XHTML 1.0 and 1.1 fully support it. In the XHTML 2.0 Working Draft (August 2002), img is deprecated in favor of the use of object for images. The object element isn't currently as widely supported as <img>.

Images sometimes are referred to as *inline images* because the images are inserted within a line of body text. Because the image element is a text-level element, it should be nested inside a paragraph or other block-level container, and it doesn't start a new paragraph automatically.

NOTE

The sample code in this chapter is formatted in XHTML. For more information on XHTML, see Chapter 2, "Getting Acquainted with HTML and XHTML," Chapter 3, "Creating Your First HTML or XHTML Document," and Chapter 19, "XHTML: HTML Goes XML."

To make an image appear as a separate paragraph, enclose it within the paragraph element, like this:

```
<p>
<img src="http://www.emf.net/~estephen/images/
    turtleshirt.jpg" />
</p>
```

NOTE

In XHTML, empty elements include a space and a forward slash, for example, <hr />, <br />, and <img />.

If you have an image in the same directory as your HTML/XHTML file, you can abbreviate the URL and use a tag like this:

```
<img src="turtleshirt.jpg" />
```

This inserts an image called `turtleshirt.jpg` on a page, but it will work only if the `turtleshirt.jpg` file exists in the same directory as the HTML/XHTML file.

TIP

Many web authors like to keep their images together in one (or more) subdirectories, such as `images`, separate from their HTML/XHTML files. This practice helps keep images organized. If you decide to do this, you can use a tag such as `<img src="images/turtleshirt.jpg" />` to refer to your image files.

For the first part of this chapter, don't worry too much about the format of image files or how you create them. For now, just remember that most graphical browsers can display images only if they are in a particular format. The two most popular image formats are GIF and JPEG (with the `.gif` and `.jpg` file extensions, respectively). We'll learn more about these two image formats later in this chapter, as well as a newer image format called PNG.

NOTE

The sample image tags you've just seen would not work as written. As you'll see in a moment, they lack some required attributes.

USING IMAGE ELEMENT ATTRIBUTES

In this section, we'll expand on the possibilities of the `<img>` tag and see how its attributes work. The `<img>` tag's attributes are intended primarily to tell a browser how the page should be laid out with the image so that text can flow properly around the image.

WARNING

Since HTML and XHTML are about structure and not presentation, the HTML 4.01 and XHTML specifications recommend you use style sheets to control an image's appearance on a page, instead of using `<img>` appearance attributes. (See Chapter 16, "Using Style Sheets," for information on style sheets.)

Describing Images with Alternate Text

You always should use two attributes with any `<img>` tag: the `src` and `alt` attributes, both of which are required. The `alt` attribute is used to describe the image in some way. For any browser that isn't displaying images, the alternate text contained inside the `alt` attribute is displayed instead. Here's an example of an image element using alternate text:

```
<img src="images/mickeymouse.jpg" alt="Mickey Mouse" />
```

If you use this tag, browsers can display the words "Mickey Mouse" instead of displaying an image of Walt Disney's famous rodent.

Here are five reasons why a browser would use the alternate text instead of the image itself:

► The browser is text only and can't display images. If there is no alt attribute in the <img> tag, a text-only browser such as Lynx will display the word [INLINE] on the screen instead of the image itself. However, if alternate text is present, Lynx displays the alternate text in place of the image.

► The browser is programmed to read the alternate text aloud instead of displaying an image. That way, the alt attribute can explain your image to blind surfers or surfers who are using a speaking machine.

► The person using the browser has chosen not to display images. Because images often are large files that are slow to display, many people surf with their browser set *not* to autoload images or view pictures. Instead, browsers show an empty frame as a placeholder for the image, and the alternate text is displayed inside the frame (see Figure 10.1).

► Navigator and Internet Explorer display an image's alternate text while the image is being loaded.

WARNING

Some people use alternate text such as "Please switch on images" or "Please wait for this image to load." These descriptions don't actually describe the image, and they make assumptions about what browser is being used.

► Finally, Internet Explorer 4 and above as well as Navigator 4 and above display the alternate text as a tooltip whenever you point your mouse cursor at the image for a few seconds. (If the <img> tag has an advisory title attribute, that's shown instead.)

NOTE

For more details on the use of the title attribute, see Chapter 4, "Stepping Out: Linking Your Way Around the Web."

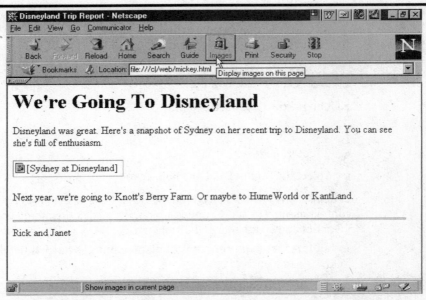

FIGURE 10.1: Navigator puts the alternate text for this image in a frame, with an icon to show there's an image not being displayed.

TURNING OFF IMAGES

Images load slowly. To surf quickly (and avoid advertising banners in the process), set your browser so that it doesn't display images automatically.

To set Navigator 4 not to load images automatically, follow these steps:

1. Select Edit ➢ Preferences.

2. Choose the Advanced category.

3. Deselect Automatically Load Images. (For Navigator 3, you can use the Options ➢ Auto Load Images command.)

To set Navigator 6 to not load images automatically, follow these steps:

1. Select Edit ➢ Preferences.

2. Choose the Advanced category.

3. Select the Do Not Load Any Images radio button.

CONTINUED ➡

Part II

To set Navigator 7 to not load images automatically, follow these steps:

1. Select Edit ➤ Preferences.

2. Choose the Advanced category.

3. Select the Privacy and Security category.

4. Choose Images.

5. Select the Do Not Load Any Images radio button

To display an individual image, choose View Image from the image's context menu. (To see a context menu, right-click the image on a PC or hold down the mouse button on a Mac.)

To tell Internet Explorer 4 not to display images automatically, follow these steps:

1. Choose View ➤ Options.

2. Deselect Show Pictures from the Advanced tab.

To tell Internet Explorer 5 not to display images automatically, follow these steps:

1. Choose Tools ➤ Internet Options.

2. Deselect Show Pictures from the Advanced tab.

To tell Internet Explorer 6 not to display images automatically, follow these steps:

1. Choose Tools ➤ Internet Options.

2. Select the Advanced tab.

3. Deselect Show Pictures from the Multimedia section.

To display an image in Internet Explorer 4, 5, or 6, right-click it and choose Show Picture. Internet Explorer 6 also includes the Image toolbar, which appears automatically when you roll over an image. The Image toolbar displays icons for automatically saving, printing, and e-mailing images. The Image toolbar also can be turned off in the Multimedia section of the Advanced tab.

CONTINUED ➡

To set Opera 5 and above to not load images automatically, follow these steps:

1. Select File ➢ Preferences.

2. Choose the Multimedia category.

3. Select the Show No Images radio button.

You also can toggle the display of all images and applied background colors by using the G key to toggle the page images or Ctrl+G to toggle the display of background colors.

As you can see, using alternate text is important. Fortunately, it's an easy task: Just put a meaningful description as the attribute value for `alt` for every image (except for purely decorative images).

TIP

Some HTML and XHTML style guides recommend using empty alternate text for purely decorative images (that is, putting nothing within the quotes for the alternate text: `alt=""`). We agree, unless the image is being used as an anchor for a link, as we describe in the section "Using Images as Links," later in this chapter. Using nonexistent alternate text means that, for example, your page's decorative borders won't distract users of text-only or text-to-speech browsers.

Here are some guidelines to follow when describing an image with alternate text:

▶ Put brackets around the description (for example, `alt="[Me at age 12.]"`) to distinguish the description from regular text.

▶ Leave off the words "image" or "picture." It's better to describe the image itself rather than its media. "[President Lincoln at the White House]" is a more compact and useful description than "[Image of President Lincoln at the White House]".

▶ Don't be vague. For example, don't use `alt="[Company Logo]"` for your company logo. Instead, use `alt="[RadCo Spinning R Logo]"`.

▶ Remember that text-only and speech browsers place the alternate text wherever the image occurs in a sentence, so be sure your alternate text is clear in context. "Another excellent website from [Picture of a Tree] [Company Logo]" will raise some eyebrows.

▶ Use the alternate text to duplicate the image's purpose. If you use an image of a yellow star next to several items in a list, don't use `alt="Pretty yellow star"`; instead, use `alt="*"`. For the alternate text for an image of a decorative horizontal line, try `alt="------------"`.

▶ Alternate text can subtly present two different versions of a page. If you've used `alt="[New!]"` for a "new" icon, you can then explain at the top of your page that "New information is denoted by `<img src="new.jpg" alt="[New!]">`." Users with graphics will see your new icon in the explanation; users without graphics also will see an explanation that correctly matches their view of your page.

▶ Some art sites place copyright information along with the image's description; other sites put secret messages in an image's alternate text.

▶ You can use entities (such as `&copy;`) in alternate text.

▶ For full compatibility, keep your alternate text on one unbroken line of your document; some browsers have problems with a carriage return in the middle of the alternate text.

TIP

For detailed information on the use of the `alt` attribute and accessibility issues, see "Guidelines on `alt` texts in `img` elements" by Jukka Korpela at `www.cs.tut.fi/~jkorpela/www.html`.

You can't use tags inside `alt` text, so `alt="[I'm <em>beating</em> Hemingway at wrestling]"` is not valid. However, the `<img>` tag, including the alternate text, is subject to whatever elements it's nested within. To make your alternate text bold, enclose the `<img>` tag within `<b>` and `</b>` tags; for example:

```
<b><img src="new.jpg" alt="[New!]" /></b>
```

Now that we've seen the use of alternate text, the next attribute we'll discuss determines how images are aligned on a page.

Placing Images with Alignment Attributes

When you align images with an alignment attribute (`align`), there are two entirely separate results:

- ▶ Inline images occur in the middle of a line of text. If the image is large, the line becomes very tall, and a lot of white space will appear.

- ▶ Floating images cause text to wrap around the image. Images can be either left aligned or right aligned. The paragraph will flow around the image for several lines if the image is large.

The two different behaviors are caused by choosing the attribute value for `align`. We'll discuss the values for inline images first, then floating images.

WARNING

Using `align` to place images is not recommended by either the HTML 4.01 or XHTML standards, because alignment is a presentational feature, not a structural feature. Instead, both standards recommend using style sheets (see Chapter 16).

Aligning Inline Images

To align an image in a line, choose one of the following attributes for the image element:

```
align="top"
align="middle"
align="bottom"
```

The default behavior is `align="bottom"`, which means that the bottom of an image will align with the bottom of the line of text. By choosing `align="top"`, you request that the browser display the top of your image so that it aligns with the top of the line of text. (This will push down the next line of text.) Similarly, by choosing `align="middle"`, the browser will align the middle of the image with the middle of the line of text. Figure 10.2 shows an image aligned to the middle of its line of text.

The XHTML code that produces the image in Figure 10.2 is fairly simple.

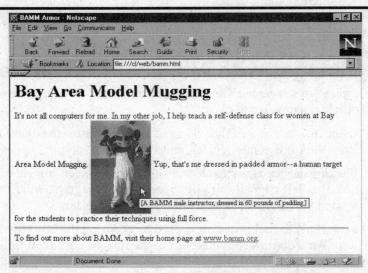

FIGURE 10.2:   The middle of an image (shown here in Navigator) is aligned to the middle of the second line of text. The first and last lines are pushed apart by the image. (Notice the alternate text appearing as a tooltip.)

Listing 10.1: `bamm.html`

```
<!DOCTYPE html PUBLIC
"-//W3C//DTD XHTML 1.0 Transitional//EN"
"http://www.w3.org/TR/xhtml1/DTD/xhtml1-transitional.dtd">
<html xmlns="http://www.w3.org/1999/xhtml">
 <head>
  <title>BAMM Armor</title>
 </head>
 <body>
  <h1>Bay Area Model Mugging</h1>
  <p>
  It's not all computers for me. In my other job, I help
  teach a self-defense class for women at Bay Area Model
  Mugging.
   <img src="http://www.emf.net/~estephen/sbamm.jpg"
   align="middle"
   alt="[A BAMM male instructor, dressed in 60 pounds of
   padding.]" />
  Yup, that's me dressed in padded armor----a human
  target for the students to practice their techniques
  using full force.
```

```
    </p>
    <hr />
    <p>
        To find out more about BAMM, visit their home page at
        <a href="http://www.bamm.org/">www.bamm.org</a>.</p>
    </body>
    </html>
```

If we had used `align="top"` instead of `align="middle"`, the first and second lines would be next to each other, and there'd be a large space between the second and third lines. If we had used `align="bottom"` (or no `align` attribute at all), there would have been a big space between the first and second lines. (Try these examples on your own; simply make the change to the `align` attribute in your editor, save the XHTML file, switch to your browser, and reload the file using the Reload button.)

Creating Floating Images

To make an image "float" to the left or right side and cause paragraphs to wrap around the image, choose one of the following attribute values for the `align` attribute:

```
    align="left"
    align="right"
```

Choosing `left` or `right` as the value for `align` causes the image to be placed directly against the left or right margin. Text after the `<img>` tag will flow around the image. Shown here is the result of taking the code we used in the previous section and using `align="right"` as the alignment attribute:

Bay Area Model Mugging

It's not all computers for me. In my other job, I help teach a self-defense class for women at Bay Area Model Mugging. Yup, that's me dressed in padded armor--a human target for the students to practice their techniques using full force.

To find out more about BAMM, visit their home page at www.bamm.org.

This result might not be quite what we want, so let's move the `<img>` tag up to the beginning of the first paragraph. Here's the result:

Bay Area Model Mugging

It's not all computers for me. In my other job, I help teach a self-defense class for women at Bay Area Model Mugging. Yup, that's me dressed in padded armor--a human target for the students to practice their techniques using full force.

To find out more about BAMM, visit their home page at www.bamm.org.

One drawback to this result is that the horizontal rule (from the `<hr />` tag) and the last paragraph are next to the picture. We might want to push these items down so that they're below the image. In Chapter 7, "Formatting the Body Section of Your Pages," we mentioned that the line-break element has attributes that can be used to clear the margin. The line-break element is simply the `<br />` tag. By itself, the `<br />` tag won't do what we want (it will just create a single blank line that wouldn't be big enough to push the horizontal rule below the image). If we use the `clear` attribute and the appropriate margin value, the horizontal rule and the last paragraph will be forced down below the image. Since the image is on the right margin, we want to use a `<br clear="right" />` tag (placed immediately before the `<hr />` tag or before the `</p>` tag). Shown here is the effect of the line-break element with a `clear` attribute:

Bay Area Model Mugging

It's not all computers for me. In my other job, I help teach a self-defense class for women at Bay Area Model Mugging. Yup, that's me dressed in padded armor--a human target for the students to practice their techniques using full force.

To find out more about BAMM, visit their home page at www.bamm.org.

If your page has images on both the left and right sides, use `<br clear="all">` to force the next line of text to appear below the lowest image.

Sizing an Image with *width* and *height* Attributes

Two attributes are used with the `<img>` tag to specify an image's width and height. The `width` and `height` attributes indicate the exact size of your image in pixels. For example:

```
<img src="sbamm.jpg" width="109" height="175"
alt="[A BAMM male instructor, dressed in 60 pounds of
    padding.]" />
```

TIP

To find out the size of an image in pixels, you'll have to use an image utility. See the section "Using Image Tools to Create and Edit Images," later in this chapter. If you are viewing the image in a browser, you can right-click on the image and select Properties (select Image Properties in Opera) to view the image dimensions as well as other image-specific information. In Netscape Navigator, you can also choose View Image from the context menu. The image's width and height display in the title bar of the window displaying the image.

One overwhelming advantage to adding the height and width to an `<img>` tag is that when you specify the image size for all of your images, browsers take a lot less time to render your page. That's because the browser can determine the layout of the page without having to retrieve each image separately to find out what size it is.

However, there are two drawbacks to specifying the height and width:

▶ The height and width are presentational attributes, so ideally they belong in a style sheet instead of in your `<img>` tag.

▶ If you have a very small image and specify its height and width, Navigator and Internet Explorer won't be able to fit the alternate text inside the small image box for those users not displaying images.

Figure 10.3 shows the difference in Internet Explorer between setting and not setting the `height` and `width` attributes when images aren't displayed.

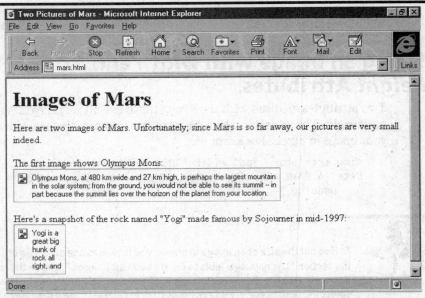

FIGURE 10.3:   Internet Explorer displays a page with two image areas showing alternate text instead of the images; the first alternate text is fully displayed, but the second is cut off.

In Figure 10.3, the user has set Internet Explorer not to display images. The first image does not have its height and width specified in the HTML code, so the entire alternate text is shown. For the second image, the height and width were specified (in the <img> tag). If images were to be displayed, both would be only 80 pixels wide and fit the frame shown for the second image. However, since Internet Explorer allocates the specified size for the second image even when the image itself is not displayed, the alternate text cannot fit inside this small area, so it is cut off by Internet Explorer. (Navigator does the same thing but displays none of the second image's alternate text at all.) Newer versions of both browsers would allow the alternate text to be seen via tooltips, but only if the mouse is pointed to the image area.

The speed advantages of setting the width and height attributes may outweigh the two drawbacks, especially if you are not using small images with a lot of alternate text.

There's one other use of the height and width attributes: to scale an image.

Scaling Images with *width* and *height* Attributes

You can specify an image to have a particular height or width, even if the original dimensions of the image don't match. Navigator and Internet Explorer then will scale your image, stretching it accordingly.

For example, if your original image's dimensions are 50 by 50, you can specify an <img> tag with a width of 200 and a height of 25. Graphical browsers (which know how to scale images) will stretch the image's width to quadruple the normal size, while at the same time squeezing the image's height so that it's half as tall as normal.

You can create interesting and artistic effects with this technique, but not every browser knows how to scale images. Most browsers do a poor job (leaving jagged edges or strange distortions), so if you want to resize an image permanently, it's better to use an image tool for that purpose.

By specifying a width of 350 pixels and a height of 100 pixels, we've distorted our sample image significantly, as shown here:

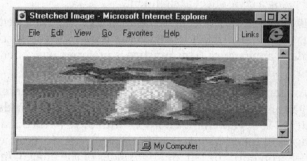

NOTE

To scale an image vertically, you can specify just the height and leave the width at automatic. You can scale an image horizontally by specifying the width and leaving the height with its default value.

Both the HTML and XHTML specifications recommend against using the height and width attributes to scale images.

Setting an Image's Border Width

By default, no border appears around an image unless that image is a link (as we'll see in the section "Using Images as Links," a bit later in this chapter). However, you can specify a border for an image. If you use the border="1" attribute in an <img> tag, a thin border will appear around the image. You can specify larger values for the border attribute, as well. XHTML recommends that you use style sheets for controlling image borders.

There's no need to specify border="0" for a normal image, because borders do not appear by default.

WARNING

Internet Explorer 3 does not display image borders and ignores the value of border unless the image is a link. All newer versions of Internet Explorer, as well as Netscape Navigator and Opera, will display image borders.

An image border always will be colored black in Internet Explorer 4, and in Navigator it's the same color as the text. In Internet Explorer 5 and above and Netscape Navigator 6 and above, image borders can be modified using a style sheet assignment.

If you use a style sheet (see Chapter 16), you can specify whatever color you want for image borders, and you'll have far better control over the border's appearance. This practice is preferred over border attributes by the HTML 4.01 and XHTML specifications.

An image's border width does not count toward determining an image's height or width. If you specify an image to be 100 pixels wide (with width="100") and have a border width of 10 (with border="10"), the image will take 120 pixels of horizontal space (because the border appears on both the left and right sides of the image). In addition, the image will take a few pixels more than 120 because browsers will put a small amount of space between an image and text. The amount of space allocated is determined by the hspace and vspace attributes.

Adding White Space with *hspace* and *vspace*

Internet Explorer and Navigator do not place images right next to text. Instead, they put a small margin of a few pixels between text and an image. You can control the amount of horizontal space with the hspace attribute and the amount of vertical space with the vspace attribute:

▶ The value of the hspace attribute sets the number of pixels of horizontal white space around the image (both left and right).

▶ The value of the vspace attribute sets the number of pixels of vertical white space around the image (both top and bottom).

For example, suppose we edit our bamm.html document to add 50 pixels of horizontal space around the image by putting an hspace="50" attribute in the <img> tag. Figure 10.4 shows the result.

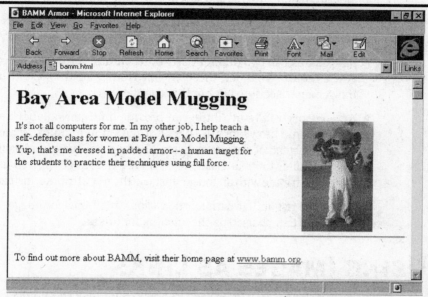

FIGURE 10.4: Internet Explorer displays 50 pixels to both the left and right of the image, thanks to the hspace attribute.

Using Other Attributes with Images

In addition to the image attributes, HTML 4.01 and XHTML 1.0 and 1.1 allow some generic attributes that apply to almost every element, including the image element:

▶ The lang and dir attributes can be used to indicate what language an image's alternate text is written in and which direction the alternate text should be displayed (left to right or right to left).

▶ The style, id, and class attributes can be used with an <img> tag to allow precise formatting and control over an image's appearance on a page.

▶ A new attribute, longdesc, points to a URL of the image's description. It is not yet supported.

▶ Several event attributes (such as onclick and onmouseover) can have a dramatic effect on images. In particular, you can use an onmouseover attribute to change an image when someone points his mouse cursor to it. This special effect is quite common on the web.

▶ The <img> tag takes a special attribute, name, when you are using an image as a button on a form.

▶ Imagemaps use two different attributes in the <img> tag: ismap and usemap. We'll see these two attributes in the "Creating Imagemaps" section, later in this chapter.

▶ An advisory title attribute can provide information about an image. Some browsers put this information in a tooltip, which appears instead of the alternate text. Because an image's advisory title is similar to its alternate text, there's not much need to use a title attribute with an image. Just use the alt attribute, instead.

Now that we're familiar with all the various attributes for images, we'll see how images can be used as the anchors for links.

USING IMAGES AS LINKS

Images, as well as text, can be used as anchors for hypertext links.

Suppose we want to make the bamm.jpg image of the self-defense instructor take us to more information about BAMM when we click on it. Instead of using a text-anchored link, we can make the image itself a link:

```
<a href="http://www.bamm.org/"><img src="sbamm.jpg" alt=
    "[BAMM]" /></a>
```

NOTE

Using alternate text for an image is even more important if the image is being used as a link. Lynx displays the image link as just the word [LINK] if there's no alternate text for the image.

You also can have both text and image in a link anchor:

```
<a href="http://www.bamm.org/">Find out about BAMM! <img
    src="bammlogo.gif" alt="[Bamm's Logo]" /></a>
```

By default, Navigator and Internet Explorer place a blue border around image links to show that clicking the image will take you to a URL (shown in the status bar), just as with a text link. (Users of non-graphical browsers also can follow image links, provided the alternate text is present.)

The blue border placed by Navigator and Internet Explorer normally is two pixels wide. You can make the border width bigger, smaller, or nonexistent by specifying a value for the border attribute that we described earlier. Specifying an <img> tag with border="0" means not to use any border at all.

Figure 10.5 shows what happens when you set the border to a large value for an image used as a link. We used this code:

```
<a href="http://www.bamm.org/"><img src="sbamm.jpg" align=
    "right" border="10" width="109" height="175"
alt="[A BAMM male instructor, dressed in 60 pounds of
    padding.]" /></a>
```

FIGURE 10.5:   A wide border around this image in the link color is a strong visual clue that it's a link.

TIP

If you see an extraneous blue underlined space next to your document's image links in Internet Explorer and Navigator, make sure that the </a> tag that closes the anchor is right next to the <img> tag and not separated by a space or carriage return.

Part II

CREATING IMAGEMAPS

We've just learned how clicking an image can lead to a link. Imagine if you have an image of a map of the United States, with five different branch offices of your company highlighted in different states. It would be nice if, depending on where the user clicks, he could see information about a specific branch—the California branch if he clicks California, or the Idaho branch if he clicks Idaho.

That kind of image setup is called an *imagemap*. Imagemaps don't have to be geographic maps. You can create a custom image and divide it into whatever regions you like.

In general, an imagemap is an image that contains *hotspots*, or *active regions*. Your readers access your predefined hotspots by passing the mouse pointer over an area and then clicking the mouse. Just by passing the mouse over the hot area, the browser usually will display the URL of the hotspot in the status bar.

Imagemaps are useful for directing viewers to options in a menu bar image. You can create an image that names the major features of your website and then use an imagemap to direct visitors to the appropriate place; these kinds of imagemaps are called *navigation imagemaps*.

Imagemaps were once fairly common on the web, but they have become less common recently due to their drawbacks. You can duplicate the effects of an imagemap by placing several linked images next to each other. Just make sure to set the hspace, vspace, and border attributes of each image to zero, and if your images are on the same line, they'll be right next to each other, just like an imagemap.

Understanding Imagemap Types

There are two distinct kinds of imagemaps. The older type is called a *server-side imagemap* because a web server is responsible for determining where each region leads when you click on the image. The newer and more efficient kind of imagemap is called a *client-side imagemap* because a client (that is, a viewer's web browser) determines where each region is supposed to lead when you click the image.

For both types of imagemaps, you must first create an image to use as a map. Next, divide it into regions that lead to different URLs. For a server-side imagemap, you'll need to create a special map file and make sure that the server is set up to deal with imagemaps. For a client-side imagemap, you'll use special area and map elements.

Finally, in the image tag itself, you'll include a special attribute to indicate that the image is actually an imagemap. For a server-side imagemap, use the ismap attribute. For a client-side imagemap, use the usemap attribute with the name of a map element.

WORKING WITH IMAGE FILES

Now that we've discussed the HTML/XHTML code for using images, it's time to discuss the different image formats used on the web and how to create and edit images in those formats.

Entire books are written about creating images, and we're certainly not going to be able to tell you even a fraction of everything there is to know on the topic. However, we'll give you enough information to get you going by recommending some tools and approaches and pointing out some pitfalls to avoid.

Understanding Image Formats

Two different image formats are common on the web: GIF and JPEG. We'll give each a rundown, along with some less frequently seen formats.

GIF Images

GIF images (with a file extension of .gif) are the most common type of images used on the web. *GIF* stands for Graphic Interchange Format and was developed by CompuServe (with the compression scheme patented by UNISYS) in the late 1980s.

NOTE
The word "GIF" is commonly pronounced with a hard *g* sound like the first part of the name "Gifford," but officially it's pronounced with a soft *g* as if it were spelled "Jif."

GIFs are used for all types of images, but GIF is an especially good format for line drawings, icons, computer-generated images, simple cartoons, and any images with big areas of solid colors. GIFs are compact because the GIF format uses the same LZW compression routine found in Zip files (which is why zipping GIFs is not effective).

The biggest limitation of GIFs is that they can contain only up to 256 different colors.

There are two common varieties of GIF: GIF87A and GIF89A. The difference won't normally be important to you, but basic GIF images are GIF87A, and more complicated GIFs are usually in GIF89A format. (A third variety, GIF24, was proposed by CompuServe but has never become popular.)

One particular advantage of GIF images is their flexibility, because GIF89A images can be transparent, animated, or interlaced. These three kinds of GIFs are defined in a later section, "Working with Special Image Formats."

JPEG Images

JPEG stands for the Joint Photographic Experts Group, a committee organized to develop advanced image formats. JPEGs started becoming popular in 1993. JPEGs have a file extension of .jpg (or less commonly, .jpeg) and are the second most common format for images on the web.

NOTE
The word "JPEG" is pronounced as "jay-peg."

JPEG is a remarkably compact format, designed for photographs and other images without big patches of solid colors. JPEGs are *lossy*, which means that they achieve their amazing compression by eliminating data that the human eye does not perceive. When creating JPEGs, it's possible to specify an amount of lossiness. At the highest levels of lossiness, the image becomes visibly crude. At normal levels of lossiness, you probably won't be able to detect the difference between a GIF and a JPEG on-screen. You'll notice the file size difference, however, because a JPEG is usually one fourth the size of a GIF.

The largest difference between JPEGs and GIFs is that JPEG images are always 24-bit—in other words, they allow up to 16 million different colors in an image.

JPEGs are not very effective for icons or logos with lots of solid colors. Both GIFs and JPEGs have their role, and it's usually not too hard to decide which format to use. You'll probably end up using a mix of GIF and JPEG images.

The biggest limitation of JPEGs (aside from the lossiness that can accumulate if you repeatedly compress and decompress a JPEG in the process of editing it) is that they can't be transparent or animated. A special type of JPEG called "progressive JPEG" is similar to an interlaced GIF and is discussed a little later in the section, "Working With Special Image Formats."

WARNING

Don't convert GIFs to JPEGs without being very careful. GIFs are only 256 colors (8-bit) at most, while JPEGs use millions of colors (24-bit). If a photograph already is in GIF format, it has lost most of its color information, and it may get worse if you convert it into a JPEG. To make the best JPEGs, start with a file format that has full 24-bit color information, such as a TIFF file. (TIFF files are a common format used when you scan a photograph into your computer using an image scanner.)

Other Image Formats

The only other image format that's a contender for web popularity is the PNG format. *PNG* stands for Portable Network Graphics, and the format was devised in 1995 by the W3C and CompuServe in response to controversies over GIF licensing. PNG is superior to GIF in just about every way possible: PNGs are smaller, have more colors, and have more capabilities. Two things hamper the PNG format:

▶ PNG images cannot be animated images (although a companion design promises to take care of that).

▶ Most important, the major browsers did not support PNG at all until recently, and support is still not complete. The most serious gap in PNG support by browsers is Internet Explorer's continuing lack of full support for alpha transparency in PNG.

NOTE

For more information about PNG, visit the PNG home page (http://www .libpng.org/pub/png/) or see W3C's PNG information (http://www.w3 .org/Graphics/PNG/Overview.html).

Several other miscellaneous image formats are used infrequently on the web, such as Tagged Image File Format (TIFF), Portable Bitmap (XBM), Windows Bitmap (BMP), Macintosh Bitmap (PICT), Computer Graphics Metafile (CGM), and PostScript (a common printing format). There's also Portable Document Format (PDF), advocated by Adobe for its Acrobat Reader. *Bitmap* is simply a generic term for an image, and many bitmap formats produce huge file sizes because the images aren't compressed.

It's not worth going into much more detail about any of these formats here because they aren't very popular or well supported on the web.

Working with Special Image Formats

GIF images can have three special capabilities: transparency (one color of an image is invisible and reveals the background), interlacing (the image is formatted so that it appears in stages), and animation (two or more image frames appear in sequence). JPEGs can't be transparent or have animation, but they do feature a kind of interlacing called progressive JPEGs.

Creating Interlaced GIFs and Progressive JPEG Images

Images are often large and therefore slow to load, and it's annoying for viewers to have to wait a long time before they can see your image. Normally, images load from top to bottom, a line at a time. However, if you use a special image format of GIF, you can *interlace* your image so that it loads in a mixed order of different segments instead of simply top-to-bottom. First the top line of the image appears, then every fifth line appears, down to the bottom. Then the second line appears, followed by the sixth line, and so on. Thus, the image appears in four passes. After the first pass, the viewer has a good idea of what the image will look like. The second pass adds more detail, the third pass even more detail, and the image is complete after the fourth pass.

To save your image in interlaced format, check with your image tool (we'll discuss image tools in the section "Using Image Tools to Create and Edit Images," later in this chapter). Usually, you can select an option if you want your image interlaced. Interlacing makes your image's file size slightly larger (which actually makes it load slower), so not every image should be interlaced.

Progressive JPEGs are similar in theory to interlaced GIFs. To quote Tom Lane's JPEG frequently asked question file (*FAQ*), which can be found online http://www.faqs.org/faqs/jpeg-faq/), a progressive JPEG "divides the file into a series of scans. The first scan shows the image at the equivalent of a very low quality setting, and therefore it takes very little space. Following scans gradually improve the quality. Each scan adds to the data already provided so that the total storage requirement is about the same as for a baseline JPEG image of the same quality as the final scan. (Basically, progressive JPEG is just a rearrangement of the same data into a more complicated order.)"

However, progressive JPEGs are not as widely supported as interlaced GIFs. Even though most browsers now know how to display progressive JPEGs, a lot of image tools don't know how to create them.

Creating Transparent GIF Images

HTML and XHTML images always are square or rectangular. However, you can create the illusion that your image is shaped differently in several ways. For example, if your page has a white background, you can create an image of a dog on a white background. The white colors will blend and it will appear as if the image is shaped like a dog (and it will fit better with your page).

WARNING

Not all white colors are the same. Be sure that the different whites match. A true white has an RGB value of #ffffff (which is equivalent to the decimal values of 255, 255, and 255 for red, green, and blue). Some image tools use decimal values, and others use hexadecimal values.

An image with a white background does not match a page with a gray background. If you assume that your background page color is white, you might end up with an ugly result if your page's background ends up a different color, such as the old default of gray. If that happens, you'll end up with the white and gray background color clash shown in Figure 10.6.

WARNING

You can't guarantee that your page's background always will be displayed with the color you select. Many surfers will override the default document color with their own preferences, particularly if they have vision problems or are colorblind. Therefore, the background color of your images might not match the background color of your page. It is always best to make the background of images transparent, if possible, using either a PNG or GIF format.

When you have specified a background color or image for your page, often you'll want to ensure that the page background shows through the background parts of an image. The only way to do this is to make an image transparent. A transparent image has a color that has been set to be "invisible" so that whatever is behind the image shows through. Using a transparent image will save you from having to match an image's background with your page's background. Transparency is easier seen than explained, so examine Figure 10.7, which shows a transparent image compared to its nontransparent counterpart.

FIGURE 10.6:   The "New!" image has a white background, and the page has
a default gray background (common for users who haven't
customized the default background color).

FIGURE 10.7:   Two "New!" images on a cloud background; the color white in the
left image is transparent (allowing the cloud background to show
through), and the right image is not transparent.

NOTE

The techniques for making GIFs transparent vary wildly from program to program, but only GIF89A format GIFs can have a transparent color—make sure you're saving in the right format. Check your image tool's Help program and try searching for "Transparent" to find out how transparency works in your program.

Some image tools can make transparent GIFs only if the transparent color is black or white, and other image tools let you make any color transparent. However, only one color can be transparent. JPEGs cannot have a transparent color, and PNGs allow more complex types of transparency than GIFs.

TIP

An excellent website that can help you with your GIFs is OptiView (www .optiview.com).

Creating Animated GIF Images

One type of image really jumps out on the web: animated GIFs. An *animated GIF* is a series of two or more normal GIF images that have been combined into one file and are displayed by the browser frame by frame in the same space. This creates the illusion of animation.

Animated GIFs are popular because they don't require special software or a complicated program to be displayed. Any graphical browser from Navigator 2 or Internet Explorer 2 on will show animated GIFs, although early browsers had glitches. (The newer versions of Navigator and Internet Explorer allow you to switch off animation.)

WARNING

Some surfers become annoyed and distracted by animated images. Use them sparingly. Certain animated GIFs are in widespread use (such as the spinning globe or the animated mailbox), and using one of them on your page is trite.

To create an animated GIF, you'll first need to create each frame of the animation as a separate image. Then, use a special image tool to combine the images and set the amount of delay between each frame.

Animating an image is a special art, and an exhaustive review of the technique is beyond the scope of this book. However, we'll list several

GIF animation tools in the following section on image tools; each of the packages we mention will come with sufficient documentation to get you started.

Using Image Tools to Create and Edit Images

When it comes time to add an image to your page, you have two choices: either create your own images or use and edit existing images. For different reasons, you'll also probably want to edit your images (such as to change a color scheme, modify a design, or convert from one format to another).

No matter what you're doing with an image, you'll need an image tool. There are numerous image tools to choose from, but you're already equipped with a fairly capable one: Your browser at least knows how to display images in several different formats, and it also can save images you see on the web.

We're not going to go into a lot of detail on the different image tools, but we will take a brief look at some broad categories of image tools and name the major players.

Image Applications

Most people have heard of the popular image applications. The application that's probably mentioned most often is Photoshop by Adobe. Photoshop was designed, as its name implies, to edit photographs. It features many advanced tools for creating and editing images (not just photographs), but it may not be as easy to use Photoshop to create logos and images as other tools. For example, there's no simple way to create a circle in Photoshop, and its text tools are not sophisticated, though they improve with each new version. However, Photoshop's capabilities can be extended through the use of plug-ins.

If you use Photoshop and want to work with more powerful text-editing features, you can give Extensis' PhotoTools plug-in a try. Visit its home page (http://www.extensis.com/) to download a trial version.

Unfortunately, Photoshop is extremely expensive. However, its powerful filters can apply professional effects to your images (just be careful not to overuse the "lens flare" filter, for example).

Illustrator is another expensive and powerful application sold by Adobe that's often used to create graphics. Illustrator emphasizes creating images more than Photoshop does. However, Photoshop and Illustrator are two of the more complicated applications in existence, and both will take you some time to learn.

Photoshop and Illustrator are both available for Windows PC, Macintosh, and Unix systems. More information is available from Adobe's website (http://www.adobe.com/).

For Windows users, Paint Shop Pro is a popular program used to edit and create images. Created and distributed by Jasc, Inc., more information can be found on its home page (http://www.jasc.com/).

CorelDRAW and related software packages also are popular image applications. Find out more from Corel's home page (http://www.corel.com/).

In addition, Deneba (http://www.deneba.com/) sells the popular Canvas application for Windows and Macintosh users.

TIP

Microsoft FrontPage and some other HTML editors come with image editors. Most of the recent versions of FrontPage ship with the Microsoft Image Composer, which is a capable image tool. FrontPage itself can be a handy image tool because it can make images transparent with a click of a button.

You may be able to adapt your existing applications' drawing capabilities. Popular word processors such as WordPerfect and Microsoft Word have drawing tools, and Microsoft PowerPoint (normally used to create business presentations) may be able to handle your image needs. The main issue involved in using these tools is their inability to save the images in a useful web format.

On the low end, you can always create images with a drawing program that may have been provided free with your operating system (such as the Paint program that comes with Windows). However, these simple drawing programs don't have a lot of features and often don't save files in GIF or JPEG format (so you'll have to use a utility or conversion tool before you can add your drawings to your web pages).

The image applications usually know how to convert images fairly effectively, but they aren't really optimized for creating images in GIF or JPEG formats For that, you should check out an image utility. Newer versions of Photoshop (5.5 and above), however, include an integrated image utility application (ImageReady).

Part II

Image Utilities and Conversion Tools

A large number of popular utilities are available; most of them are shareware and can be downloaded from the web. All of these utilities can display images quickly and convert images between GIF and JPEG formats as well as other popular image formats (some of the tools are solely designed for converting images from one format to another).

Most of these utilities also can make simple and complex changes to an image, such as changing an image's size, orientation, color, contrast, and rotation. Some can handle more advanced editing, such as rearranging the image and changing the number of colors.

NOTE

The process of reducing the number of colors in an image is called *dithering*, and it's usually wise to get a utility that's good at dithering if you want to convert a 24-bit image into GIF format.

For Windows, popular image utilities include LView Pro, WinGIF, ACDSee, and PolyView. One popular commercial image utility is HiJaak Pro.

For Macintosh, check out DeBabelizer, JPEGView, GIFConverter, GraphicConverter, and GifBuilder.

GIF Animators

The best-known GIF animator is Alchemy Mindwork's GIF Construction Set (available from http://www.mindworkshop.com/). This package is a bit unconventional, but it contains everything you need to animate images, including an animation wizard to guide you through the process. It's a capable image utility as well, and it includes several shortcuts for creating animated images, such as a scrolling marquee image with a message you specify or a special transition between two images.

Other GIF animators include PhotoImpact GIF Animator, Animagic, VideoCraft, Jasc Animation Shop, and webImage.

Creating Images

Creating images is difficult work and requires a lot of time and energy—not to mention talent. There's no shortage of graphic designers and design firms that would be happy to design a coordinated series of images for you.

If you create images for your websites yourself, you should use the best image tool available. Take the time to learn how your tool or application works (finish the online tutorials and look into computer training classes) and find out what it's capable of. Scour the web for inspiration in the form of design ideas and fresh approaches—don't always rely on the drop shadows and neon effects that are so commonplace.

TIP

If you're creating a simple image, it's often best to work on a version that's much larger than what you intend as your final size and then scale down your work to the desired size.

The easiest type of image for most people to create is a photograph. Using either a conventional camera or a newer digital camera, you can take a wide variety of photographs to help illustrate your page. You can scan photographs or have them developed onto CD-ROM and then converted into JPEG format. However, an amateur photograph with ineffective lighting or poor composition will hamper your page as much as a crudely drawn image will.

TIP

When you create images, decide if you're designing for 256 colors or 24-bit color. If you're using 256 colors, try to see if your application has a web-compatible palette of colors that won't dither—that is, colors that will be displayed as solids that resemble the colors you intend. Visit the browser-safe palette page (http://www.lynda.com/hex.html) for a tutorial on the 216 "safe" colors and to pick up a web palette for Photoshop.

If you're good at illustrating on paper (or know someone who is), buy or rent a scanner to convert paper illustrations into computer files. (You also can find scanners at many copy stores and find scanning services in the Yellow Pages. Some scanners are sold with bundled image applications, such as Photoshop.)

However, if (like most of us) you're no artist, then it's time to consider using existing images.

Using Existing Images

You can use existing images on your web pages in several ways. Here are some methods:

Legacy Material   Perhaps your organization has some image material that you can use (such as logos, street maps, slide presentations, or previously commissioned material) once you convert it into the correct format.

Part II

Clip Art Collections   There are several commercial and shareware packages of clip art and stock photographs that are licensed for nonprofit use on your web pages. (Check the license of the package carefully before using a clip art image on your website.)

Public Domain Material   Certain illustrations and images are public domain and can be included on your web page once you find the image (and convert it if necessary). However, be careful, because most images are copyrighted and are not in the public domain.

Freely Licensed Material   Many companies create special images and logos (also known as *badges* or *banners*) for the express purpose of use on a web page when you link to that company. For example, Netscape freely licenses the ubiquitous "Netscape Now" image that many people use to link to Netscape's site.

TIP

Check a site that you want to link to and see if it has a logo page that explains its licensing and linking policies. Using a badge to link to a company is free advertising for them, so think twice before you send your audience away to such a site.

Freeware Collections and Libraries   There are a number of collections of images (such as background images and common icons) to which the artist has relinquished copyright or allows you to use his images on your web pages with no restrictions (or sometimes simply in exchange for author credit and a link back to his site).

NOTE

Here are several freeware image collections of links (aside from the ones you can find at Yahoo!): Clipart.com (http://www.clipart.com/) and Clip Art Review (http://www.webplaces.com/html/clipart.htm).

Material That You May Use After You Buy a License   Many web artists display images in their online galleries and will sell an inexpensive image license. If you see an image that you want to use on a web page, it doesn't hurt to inquire if it is available for licensing.

WARNING

In the early days of the web, fan sites used copyrighted material (such as images of U2 album covers or pictures of *Star Trek* characters) unchecked. These days, corporate crackdowns on illegally used copyrighted material are common. You must assume that any image you see is copyrighted unless there is a specific statement to the contrary. U.S. copyright law grants copyright protection even if there is no explicit copyright statement.

It's all too easy to see an image, background, or icon that you like and save it to your hard drive. (Using Navigator or Internet Explorer, all you have to do is use the Save command on the image's context menu—right-click the image on the PC, or hold down the mouse button over an image with a Mac. In Internet Explorer 6.0, you can use the Image toolbar.) Once the image is saved on your hard drive, you can edit it and include it on your web pages with little difficulty. However, just because you *can* use other people's images on your web pages doesn't mean it's legal to do so. In general, this practice is quite widespread—and also quite immoral. Using another person's copyrighted work without his permission is a crime. (There are exceptions to copyright law for fair use or parody, but we're not lawyers, so you're on your own to determine what's fair use and parody.)

NOTE

It's considered bad manners to include an <img> tag or background attribute that links to another site's image without permission. You're just using someone else's work without giving them credit. (Whether this practice is actually illegal hasn't been settled.)

If you own the material or if your license allows it, use the image tools we described earlier to modify existing images for your own purposes. Add your company name to a stock photograph of the Golden Gate Bridge, or change the contrast of *Mona Lisa* and add your logo to replace her head. Above all else, be creative by trying things you haven't seen on other websites. The more unique your images are, the more your site will stand out. Our best advice is to start experimenting with images and practicing to feel comfortable with them.

Part II

What's Next?

The knowledge you've gained in this chapter will serve you well as you begin to use images to diversify the content of your website. The next chapter will enable you to apply your knowledge of design, color, and images to the process of laying out your page. We'll take a close look at using HTML to create tables. We'll tell you how to organize your data with tables, discuss the different methods for creating them, and show you how to use tables effectively to display your website's content to the world.

Chapter 11

PRESENTING INFORMATION IN TABLES

In this chapter, you'll learn a variety of ways to present your web page data in table format. We'll cover all of the elements and attributes for tables in detail so that you can become a master at using tables.

You'll learn about the advantages—and the limitations—to using tables. We'll show you many useful examples so that you can learn how to create tables that organize your data. We'll also show you different ways you can use tables to enhance the layout of the text on your pages. Tables are extremely popular on the web because they are a flexible and attractive way of presenting information.

NOTE

In Chapter 9, "Layout Technology," tables were introduced as one form of layout technology for web page display. This chapter presents a different view of using tables and provides many additional details about creating HTML and XHTML tables.

Adapted from *HTML 4.0: No Experience Required*, by E. Stephen Mack and Janan Platt Saylor

ISBN 0-7821-2143-8 $29.99

UNDERSTANDING THE USE OF TABLES

HTML tables organize the display of data that should be presented in a table structure, instead of in paragraphs or other block-level structures. With tables, you can present data organized in rows and columns. For example, two types of data that can easily be organized into a table structure are yesterday's high and low temperatures by city (see Table 11.1).

TABLE 11.1:   Yesterday's Weather

CITY	HIGH	LOW	WIND
Alameda	70	53	south
Bakersfield	83	54	south
Barstow	93	65	south
Beaumont	89	52	west
Big Bear	72	40	south

Even though this isn't an HTML table, it's a good illustration of the concept of a table, and we can use it to establish some vocabulary:

▶ The *caption* is an optional description of the table. In Table 11.1, the caption is "Yesterday's Weather."

▶ A table's *rows* are the horizontal lines of data. Table 11.1 has six rows, starting with the "City" row and ending with the "Big Bear" row.

▶ The *columns* are the vertical lines of data. There are four columns in this example, starting with "City" and ending with "Wind."

▶ Each piece of data is at the intersection of a column and a row, and those intersections are called *cells*. Since there are six rows and four columns, Table 11.1 has 24 cells.

▶ Finally, the first four cells ("City," "High," "Low," and "Wind") show labels for the type of information in each column. These special cells are called *headings*.

Figure 11.1 shows how Internet Explorer would display the Yesterday's Weather table if it were created in HTML code. (We'll see the actual

HTML code used to create this table in the "Creating an Example Table" section, later in this chapter.)

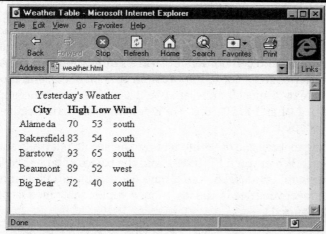

FIGURE 11.1: An HTML table showing yesterday's weather by city

NOTE

Tables sometimes are used for general page layout—for example, to organize paragraphs into columns or to create margins. This has varying results, depending on which browser is used to view your pages. We'll talk about using tables as a layout tool later in this chapter, and we'll see some reasons why this is discouraged. For an alternate view on using tables for layout, see Chapter 9.

When you create a table in HTML/XHTML, you'll use the `table` element, which starts with the `<table>` tag and ends with a `</table>` tag. In order to create a table, you'll need to understand the rules of what elements should appear between the two tags.

Understanding Table Models

The rules of which elements occur in a table (and in what order) create what is called a *table model*. In this chapter, we'll present two important table models. Originally created by Netscape and later adopted by the W3C, the HTML 3.2 table model used a fairly simple set of elements, and it resulted in widespread use of tables. Tables have become fully supported in all recent versions of Navigator, Internet Explorer, Mosaic, and Lynx.

However, text-to-speech browsers and older versions of Lynx have trouble dealing with tables.

HTML 4.01 expanded on the older, simple table model with new elements and attributes while still remaining compatible with the earlier table model. The main difference is that HTML 4.01 allowed rows and columns to be grouped together and introduced several useful new attributes for alignment and cell borders. XHTML's table model is designed to make tables richer, easier to import from spreadsheets, and more accessible to text-to-speech browsers. We'll see other differences in the "Using HTML 4.01 and XHTML `table` Elements and Attributes" section, later in this chapter.

We're going to learn the older model first and see its relatively simple set of elements. When you fully understand the basics of tables, we'll talk about the new table model. You can always use as simple a table model as necessary to meet your needs and use more complex table models only when really required.

Introducing the Simple Table Model and Its Elements

We will discuss four elements of the simple table model:

- ▶ The optional `caption` element consists of the `<caption>` and `</caption>` tags containing the table's description.

- ▶ The table row element (`<tr>` for *table row*, with the `</tr>` end tag) creates a horizontal row of cells and contains the table headings and table data.

- ▶ The table data element uses the `<td>` (*table data*) tag (with the `</td>` end tag) to create each individual cell. (The number of cells in a row determines how many columns will be displayed by the browser, so there is no separate element for table columns in the simple HTML table model.)

- ▶ The table heading (`<th>` for *table heading* and the `</th>` end tag) element creates the heading cells.

We'll discuss each of these new elements in more detail later in this chapter, and we'll learn about their attributes and capabilities. For now, the next section will show these four elements in action by showing some code for our example table.

Creating an Example Table

Study the following XHTML code to see how Figure 11.1 was created. To create this example on your own, type the code into your text editor and save it as weather.html.

Listing 11.1: weather.html

```
<!DOCTYPE html PUBLIC
"-//W3C//DTD XHTML 1.0 Transitional//EN"
  "http://www.w3.org/TR/xhtml1/DTD/xhtml1-transitional.dtd">

<html xmlns="http://www.w3.org/1999/xhtml">
<head>
      <title>Weather Table</title>
</head>
<body>

<table>
    <!-- This is the table's caption. -->
    <caption>
        Yesterday's Weather
    </caption>

    <!-- This is the first row of the table. -->
    <tr>
        <th>City</th>
        <th>High</th>
        <th>Low</th>
        <th>Wind</th>
        <!-- Each of these words is marked as a heading. -->
    </tr>

    <!-- This is the second row of the table. -->
    <tr>
        <td>Alameda</td>
        <td>70</td>
        <td>53</td>
        <td>south</td>
        <!-- Each of these pieces of information
        is a cell, or "table data." -->
    </tr>
```

```
        <tr>
            <td>Bakersfield</td>
            <td>83</td>
            <td>54</td>
            <td>south</td>
        </tr>

        <tr>
            <td>Barstow</td>
            <td>93</td>
            <td>65</td>
            <td>south</td>
        </tr>

        <tr>
            <td>Beaumont</td>
            <td>89</td>
            <td>52</td>
            <td>west</td>
        </tr>

        <!-- This is the sixth and final row of the table.-->
        <tr>
            <td>Big Bear</td>
            <td>72</td>
            <td>40</td>
            <td>south</td>
        </tr>

    </table>
    </body>
    </html>
```

In this example, we've used indentations and comments to make the
code easily comprehensible. We've also used the `</tr>`, `</td>`, and
`</th>` closing tags for clarity. The `</table>` end tag always is required,
but the `</tr>`, `</td>`, and `</th>` closing tags are optional in HTML and
required in XHTML. Note also that the tags are not capitalized in the
above XHTML code listing. XHTML is case sensitive and requires—with
few exceptions—that all elements and attributes be typed using lowercase
letters.

You'll see some HTML/XHTML authors code table rows this way:

```
<table>
<tr><td>Beaumont</td><td>89</td><td>52</td>
<td>west</td></tr>
<tr><td>Big Bear</td><td>72</td><td>40</td>
<td>south</td></tr>
</table>
```

However, you may find this method a little harder to follow and edit.

Our sample table does not have a border or any gridlines. We can use the border attribute of the <table> tag to cause a line to appear around each cell. By adding this attribute to the <table> tag, you can dramatically change the visual appearance of your table, as Figure 11.2 shows. (We'll see more about the border attribute in the "Creating Border Lines with the border Attribute" section, later in this chapter.)

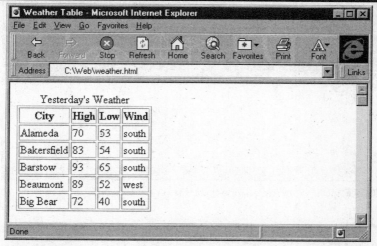

FIGURE 11.2:   The same weather table now has a border. Notice that the caption appears outside the border.

You can use a table to highlight a particular paragraph with a border. Here's the XHTML code for a one-cell table with a border:

```
<!DOCTYPE htmlPUBLIC
"-//W3C//DTD XHTML 1.0 Transitional//EN"
   "http://www.w3.org/TR/xhtml1/DTD/xhtml1-transitional.dtd">
<html xmlns="http://www.w3.org/1999/xhtml">
```

```
<head>
    <title>Boxing "Hello, World"</title>
</head>
<body>
    <table border="2">
        <tr>
            <td>
                Hello, World!
            </td>
        </tr>
    </table>
</body>
</html>
```

Figure 11.3 shows how Navigator renders this one-cell table with borders turned on.

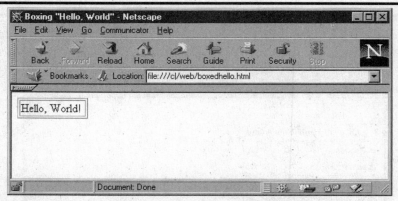

FIGURE 11.3:   A bordered, one-cell table rendered in Navigator

TIP

You may have noticed a small space between the exclamation point and the border. This is a consequence of putting the `</td>` tag on the following line. To avoid that space, use `<td>Hello, World!</td>` on one line.

WARNING

Using a table for a boxed paragraph effect can bring special attention to an important paragraph. However, the paragraph really doesn't belong in a table, because it's not a table of information. If your only goal is to get a border around a paragraph, style sheets are better suited to that task. (Chapter 16, "Using Style Sheets," discusses style sheets.)

The smallest table you can make has only one cell (that is, one row and one column), but there's no limit to how large you can make your tables. Although HTML/XHTML does not impose any theoretical limits on how many rows or cells you can have, in practicality, if you use more than 10 columns you'll probably force the table to be wider than the window (and a horizontal scroll bar will appear in Navigator and Internet Explorer).

The only limit to the number of columns is how wide you want your table to be; there is no limit to the number of rows you can include in a table. There also is no limit to the number of separate tables that can appear on a page.

Advantages of Tables

One of the greatest advantages of tables is that your data is much easier to read when structured properly on the page. A properly designed table gives your readers a clear and quick way to evaluate your content. A table can contain many different types of content other than just text—such as lists, forms, nested tables (tables within tables), images, preformatted text, and paragraphs.

NOTE
You'll learn about tables inside of other tables in the "Nesting Tables" section, later in this chapter.

The use of a table also can break up a plain page with an interesting visual feature (an attractive table is nicer to look at than just a bunch of numbers). We'll see some examples later in this chapter.

Limitations of Tables

One of the biggest limitations to tables is the amount of time it can take to create a complex table structure, as well as the amount of time it can take a browser to decipher the code in order to display a complex table. A medium-size table's HTML/XHTML code can take up several pages if hand-coded properly for readability.

Making your tables easy to read is important so that the data can be updated quickly later. With so many nested tags and attributes, there's more room for error when you're coding a table than with other elements. It's harder to find errors, and if one tag is left off or put in the wrong place, the entire table may not appear.

It's very tempting to try to use tables to solve a lot of your page layout challenges. Be careful that your HTML/XHTML coding follows the HTML/XHTML standards for tables that we present in this chapter, and verify that both Navigator and Internet Explorer display your tables properly.

One example of using tables for layout is multiple columns of text (similar to the columns in a newspaper article). There's no standard HTML/XHTML tag available to create multiple text columns. Web authors discovered that they could duplicate the appearance of text columns in graphical browsers by using tables. Starting when Navigator 2 came out, tables were (and still are) often used (with borders turned off) to create the look of multicolumn text.

However, tables used for multiple text columns will produce extremely varied results. Web page designers might spend a long time trying to get two columns to be exactly the same height, but that is a foolhardy quest. Internet Explorer and Navigator don't always display fonts the same way. With multiple columns created in tables, depending on the font, the automatic line breaks in Internet Explorer may not be rendered the same way in Navigator. Also, as soon as someone resizes the browser window, the line breaks will readjust, and the bottom of the columns will probably not match because of the relative lengths of the words in each column. Figure 11.4 shows how the bottoms of two columns that were even don't match up when we resize the Navigator window to a narrower width.

The moral here is that tables can't always be used reliably for multiple text columns, and you should be careful to check your tables with a few different browsers. This is a lesson in HTML/XHTML's purpose: HTML/XHTML elements are designed to indicate the structure of your document. Just because certain browsers happen to display some elements a certain way doesn't mean you should abuse the meaning of the tags to create a certain visual effect. If your document doesn't contain tables of data, it shouldn't have table elements.

Earlier versions of HTML had no way to change a page's layout without tables, so many web designers ignored this advice. Now that HTML 4.01 (and XHTML) and the newer (4.0 and above) browsers are able to work with style sheets, you always can get the visual layout effects by using style sheets instead of tables. (You'll learn how in Chapter 16.)

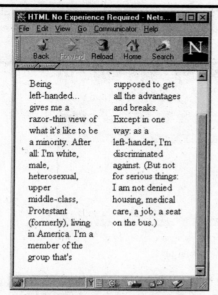

FIGURE 11.4:   Navigator, with a reduced window width, renders our example of a two-column table of text in a less than desirable way.

USING THE SIMPLE TABLE MODEL'S ELEMENTS AND ATTRIBUTES

The elements used in tables all must be nested within the beginning `<table>` and ending `</table>` tags. First we'll show you the `<table>` tag and its attributes, and then we'll show you all the uses of the elements that create rows, cells, headings, and captions.

Defining Tables with the *table* Element

The `<table>` start tag and the `</table>` end tag both are required for every table you create. All of the `<table>` tag's attributes, however, are optional.

Even with the simple table model, the tables themselves can be very simple or very complex, as we've seen. Here's an example of the HTML code for an unbordered table that has one row (within the `<tr>` tags), one cell (within the `<td>` tags that contain the words "Hello, World!"), and no attributes:

```
<table><tr><td>Hello, World!</td></tr></table>
```

If you exclude table attributes, the table's position defaults to left alignment with no border. This table would look like regular text, as we see in Figure 11.5.

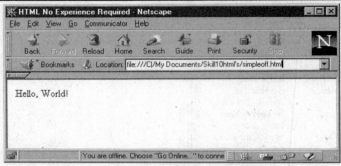

FIGURE 11.5:   "Hello, World!" inside a single-cell table with no attributes; it looks exactly like normal text.

However, you can make this table appear very differently using the table element's attributes.

Using the *table* Element's Attributes

By using table attributes in the <table> tag, you can determine the following formatting options for your table:

- ▶ Width of the entire table
- ▶ Alignment of the entire table
- ▶ Cell borders and table border width
- ▶ Spacing between neighboring cells
- ▶ Padding within a cell (between the cell's content and the cell border)

Let's take a look at each <table> tag attribute and try out some simple examples of tables created by hand. As you're reading along, you might want to experiment with a few more sample tables yourself. It's easiest to start with a basic table, such as the weather.html example we used earlier, and try out the different attributes one at a time.

The <table> tag can include any of following attributes, listed in any order: align, width, border, cellspacing, cellpadding, and bgcolor.

We'll be discussing the bgcolor attribute (used to set a table's background color) a little later, in the "Coloring Parts of the Table with the bgcolor Attribute" section, but we'll talk about the rest of the table element's attributes in the next few sections, starting with the align attribute.

Positioning Tables with the *align* Attribute

There are three possible uses of the align attribute (left is the default):

```
<table align="left">
<table align="center">
<table align="right">
```

The align attribute specifies the horizontal alignment of the table. This means that the table itself is aligned, not the content of individual cells.

The weather table we saw in Figure 11.1 is shown here, but with the align ="right" attribute added:

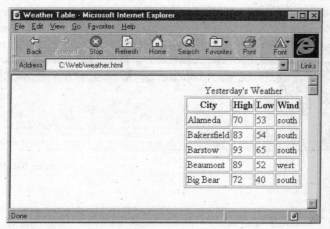

Part II

WARNING

Using align to place tables is not recommended by either the HTML 4.01 or XHTML standard, because alignment is a presentational feature, not a structural feature. Instead, both standards recommend using style sheets (see Chapter 16).

Sizing Tables with the *width* Attribute

There are two ways to specify the width of a table using the width attribute:

```
<table width="percent">
<table width="number">
```

If you don't specify the width, the table will be only as wide as absolutely necessary to display the included content.

You can force a table to take up more room if you don't like the way it appears. To do this, either you set the width of the table to a percentage of the window's horizontal width (for example, `width="50%"`) or you set `width` to a fixed pixel value (with an attribute such as `width="100"` to make a table 100 pixels wide).

WARNING

Don't leave off the percent sign if you want a table to be a certain percentage of your page. There's a *big* difference between 100 *percent* (`width="100%"`) and 100 *pixels* (`width="100"`).

Figure 11.6 shows examples of two tables displayed in Navigator. The first table uses the table attribute `width="150%"`. The second table uses the table attribute `width="500"`. You can see how the first table is 50 percent wider than the horizontal width of the window (use the horizontal scroll bar to see the rest of the table). Specifying a percentage allows your table and its contents to adjust to fit the browser window whenever it is resized.

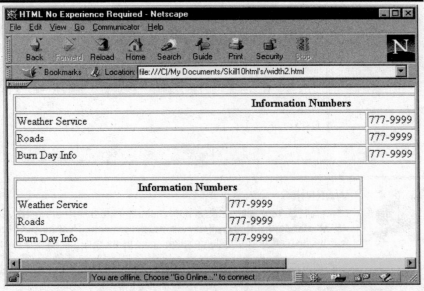

FIGURE 11.6: Navigator shows two examples of tables using the `width` attribute.

Creating Border Lines with the *border* Attribute

The border attribute is used to make a table and its cells appear with lines:

```
<table border="number">
```

The default border size, if you don't specify a value, is 1 pixel wide. Omitting the border tag or using `border="0"` indicates no border. Really thick borders, such as `<table border="5">` or `<table border="10">` can produce interesting results.

WARNING

In HTML, a value is not required for the `border` attribute, and a 1 pixel border can be specified by `<table border>` or `<table border="1">`. In XHTML, all attributes must have values. To be XHTML compliant, if you use a `border` attribute, you must specify a value for it.

The border size applies *only* to the outside table border. If there is a border for your table, the inner cells will have a cell border that is always only 1 pixel thick, regardless of the setting of the `border` attribute. There is no way to set the size of a cell's border yet.

If you specify a border of 50 pixels for the table in the `weather.html` example (with `<table border="50">`), you'll see a result similar to Figure 11.7.

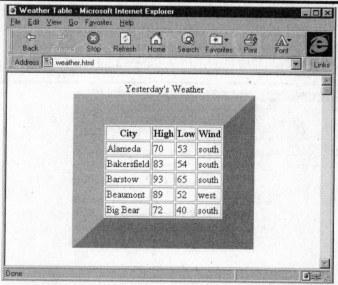

FIGURE 11.7: Your viewers won't be able to overlook this weather table with a 50 pixel border. Internet Explorer (shown here) and Navigator give a three-dimensional appearance to the border, but not every browser does so.

Spacing Cells with the *cellspacing* Attribute

You can create more space between each cell in your table by using the `table` element's `cellspacing` attribute, which looks like this:

```
<table cellspacing="number">
```

The amount of cell spacing, indicated in pixels, is the common border width around each cell. For example, specifying `cellspacing="5"` in the `<table>` tag would space each cell apart by 5 pixels (including 5 pixels between the first cell and the outside border).

This sample HTML fragment creates a table with a border of 5 pixels and cell spacing of 50 pixels:

```
<table border="5" cellspacing="50">
<tr>
    <td>Sunday</td>
    <td>Monday</td>
    <td>Tuesday</td>
</tr>
<tr>
    <td>First</td>
    <td>Second</td>
    <td>Third</td>
</tr>
</table>
```

Figure 11.8 shows how Internet Explorer would display this table.

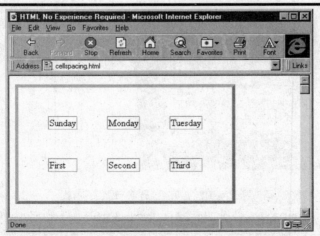

FIGURE 11.8:   Internet Explorer renders a six-celled table with the cell spacing between each cell (and the spacing between each cell and the table's border) equal to 50 pixels.

When the `cellspacing` attribute is not supplied or is unrecognized, Navigator and Internet Explorer use a default value of 2. If you specify a `cellspacing` of 0, table cells will appear right next to each other.

Making Cells Bigger with the *cellpadding* Attribute

Within each cell, the data normally appears right next to the cell's border. You can increase the amount of space between the cell border and the cell data with the `cellpadding` attribute:

```
<table cellpadding="number">
```

The padding between each cell border and the cell contents is indicated in pixels, such as `cellpadding="10"`.

The default value for `cellpadding` used by Navigator and Internet Explorer is `cellpadding="1"`, so you can squeeze each table cell down by specifying `cellpadding="0"` or you can make each cell larger by specifying a larger attribute value for `cellpadding`.

TIP

It's easy to confuse `cellspacing` and `cellpadding`. Remember that `cellspacing` determines the space *between* each cell, and `cellpadding` determines the space *within* each cell.

Figure 11.9 shows various values for `cellpadding` in several different tables.

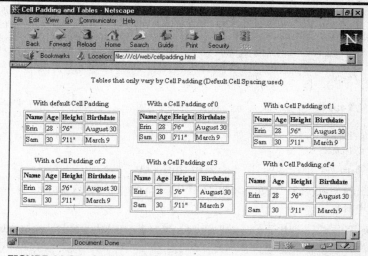

FIGURE 11.9:   Six tables that differ only by how `cellpadding` is specified (shown in Navigator)

Putting All of the *table* Element's Attributes Together

The following HTML code includes all of the `<table>` tag's attributes listed previously and creates a basic table with two side-by-side cells. The left cell includes two lines of the text separated by a line break. The right cell contains one line of text.

```
<!DOCTYPE html PUBLIC
"-//W3C//DTD XHTML 1.0 Transitional//EN"
  "http://www.w3.org/TR/xhtml1/DTD/xhtml1-transitional.dtd">
<html xmlns="http://www.w3.org/1999/xhtml">
<head>
      <title>Two Competing Philosophies</title>
</head>
<body>

<table align="center" width="50%" border="5"
 cellspacing="10"  cellpadding="5">

<tr>

<td>
Make Love<br />
Not War
</td>

<td>
Show Me The Money!
</td>

</tr>

</table>

</body>
</html>
```

Figure 11.10 shows the result of this code.

The two-celled table contains the following effects created by attributes:

▶ The `align` attribute makes the table (but not the table's contents) centered on the page. (You could use `<center>` and `</center>` tags around the table instead or use `<div align="center">` and `</div>` tags around the table.)

▶ The width attribute makes the table width equal to 50 percent of the browser window's horizontal width.

▶ The border attribute calls for cell borders and creates an outer border equal to 5 pixels.

▶ The cellspacing attribute puts 10 pixels of space between the two cells and 10 pixels of space between each cell border and the table's outer border.

▶ The cellpadding attribute puts 5 pixels of space between the cell data (the words) and the cell borders.

FIGURE 11.10: A simple two-column, one-row table using five table element attributes

Now that you've learned about the table element's attributes, it's time to learn more about the elements contained within the <table> and </table> tags. We introduced the four elements earlier in the chapter, but now we'll discuss their uses and their attributes.

Using the Simple Table Model's Elements

The following elements are all nested within the <table> and </table> tags. These elements create captions, table rows, table data, and table headings. Their attributes can determine a variety of formatting options for the table and its individual cells.

Describing Tables with the *caption* Element

The caption element (which requires both a <caption> start tag and a </caption> end tag) is used to create a caption on top of (the default) or below the table. This positioning is specified with the `caption` element's `align` attribute:

```
<caption align="top">
<caption align="bottom">
```

As we've seen, the caption is displayed outside the table's border. A caption will not make a table wider; instead, the contents of the caption element wrap within the available space (which will make the table taller).

NOTE

HTML 4.01 and XHTML allow you to specify `align="left"` and `align="right"` for the caption so as to place it to the left or the right of the table. Browser support for these options varies. Newer versions of Internet Explorer support left and right alignment of table captions and display them appropriately. The newest versions of Netscape (7) and Opera (6) do not yet support right and left alignment of table captions.

Only text and text-level elements are allowed within the `caption` element. The `caption` element must appear before the first row of the table, immediately after the `<table>` tag.

Creating Rows with the Table Row (*tr*) Element

The table row element consists of a `<tr>` start tag and one or more table data elements or table head elements, followed by a `</tr>` end tag. Each use of a table row element begins a new table row.

The `<tr>` tag can include several attributes: `bgcolor`, `align`, and `valign`.

The `bgcolor` attribute determines the background color of the row. See the discussion of this attribute in the section "Coloring Parts of the Table with the `bgcolor` Attribute," later in this chapter.

Since the `align` and `valign` attributes also can be used with the `<td>` and `<th>` tags, we'll talk about them separately after we discuss more about the table heading and table data elements.

A row must contain at least one table data element or table heading element. Furthermore, the *only* two things that legally can be placed inside a table row element are table heading and table data elements. (The data itself must be contained in the cell, not the row.) We'll see how to use these cell elements in the next section.

Creating Cells with Cell Elements: Table Headings with *<th>* and Table Data with *<td>*

You've already learned that the table data element (<td>) creates cells and the table heading element (<th>) creates headings. These two elements are referred to as the *cell elements*.

The two cell elements are identical to each other except that a heading cell is specially marked. (We've seen that Navigator and Internet Explorer display table heading text centered and in bold, but other browsers can use different methods.)

Cell elements can contain many different types of items, including text, images, and other tables. We'll see some examples of what you can put in a cell a little later in this chapter.

Cells also may be empty if you don't want them to contain data. (Simply use a <td> tag followed immediately by a </td> tag.) Navigator and Internet Explorer will not display a cell border around the empty cell. If you want a cell to have a border but still be empty, put a nonbreaking space inside the cell (<td> </td>).

There are several attributes for cells that can be used in the <td> and <th> tags; we'll see them in the next few sections.

Using Attributes with the Simple Table Model's Elements

In this section, we'll discuss the different attributes that can be used with table row elements and cell elements. We'll also show you how to use the bgcolor attribute to set the color of a table, row, or cell.

The attributes for cells include alignment (with align and valign), background color (with bgcolor), the nowrap attribute to prevent word wrapping in a cell, and attributes to make a cell span one or more rows or columns (rowspan and colspan). You also can specify the width and height of cells.

Aligning the Contents of Cells and Rows

The align attribute indicates the default horizontal alignment of cell data. The <tr>, <td>, and <th> tags all can include an align attribute. The possible values are these:

```
align="left"
align="center"
align="right"
```

As you may have noticed from all the figures so far in this chapter, table data is left aligned by default.

NOTE

HTML 4.01 and XHTML allow some new horizontal alignment choices. In addition to the three possibilities for HTML 3.2, you can use align="justify". Also, there are attributes for aligning cell data on a particular character. We'll discuss this type of alignment in the section about the HTML 4.01 and XHTML table model, later in this chapter.

You also can specify the vertical alignment of cell data with the valign attribute in the <tr>, <td>, or <th> tags. The valign attribute has four values:

```
valign="top"
valign="middle"
valign="bottom"
valign="baseline"
```

WARNING

Don't confuse the middle and center attribute values. middle is for vertical alignment, and center is for horizontal alignment.

The default value for the valign attribute is middle. Because all the cells in a row always will have the same height, the vertical alignment only makes a difference if some cells in a row take up fewer lines than the biggest cell. (For example, look at Figure 11.10 and see how the "Show Me The Money!" line is halfway between the two text lines of its neighboring cell.)

NOTE

The valign="baseline" value is only subtly different from valign="top". The difference is in the exact placement of the bottom of the first line of text in a cell. With the baseline value specified, the bottom of the first line of each cell will always line up, even if the font size used in different cells varies. When the top value is used, the bottoms of words in different cells won't necessarily line up.

If a cell and its row both include different align or valign attribute values, the cell's specified alignment takes precedence. You can take advantage of this to make an entire row centered and then make specific cells in that row right aligned.

Coloring Parts of the Table with the *bgcolor* Attribute

You can change the background color of different parts of a table with the bgcolor attribute. You can change the background color of an entire table, a single row, or an individual cell, depending on where you specify the bgcolor attribute. Here are the possibilities:

```
<table bgcolor="color name or color value">
<tr bgcolor="color name or color value">
<td bgcolor="color name or color value">
<th bgcolor="color name or color value">
```

NOTE

HTML 3.2 and earlier did not allow you to specify bgcolor for a table, although it was common practice (because Navigator and Internet Explorer both understood the attribute as an extension to HTML). HTML 4.01 and XHTML allow the bgcolor attribute to be used with some of the different elements of a table.

Although you can't change the color of a caption separately, if you specify the bgcolor in the <table> tag, your background color applies to the entire table, including the caption.

WARNING

It's somewhat dangerous to color a table, because current browsers don't let users override your table color choices, as they can with document colors (unless they use a user-defined style sheet). For example, if you specify a color that is hard to read, people who are colorblind may not be able to read the contents of your table at all.

Disabling Word Wrapping with the *nowrap* Attribute

You can disable the default word wrapping of cell text with the nowrap attribute in a table cell (specified in either a <td> tag or a <th> tag). This means that the cell will be guaranteed to be displayed on one line. Here is how you can use the nowrap attribute:

```
<td nowrap>
<th nowrap>
```

Using the nowrap attribute is equivalent to changing all of the spaces in a cell to the nonbreaking space entity, .

WARNING
You can make your table cell unnecessarily wide if you don't use the nowrap attribute carefully. Because style sheets can control word wrap more effectively, nowrap is deprecated as of the HTML 4 specification.

NOTE
In XHTML, all attributes must have a value. If you use the nowrap attribute in XHTML, you must give it the value nowrap, such as <td nowrap="nowrap">.

Spanning Cells with the *colspan* and *rowspan* Attributes

The colspan attribute can be used in a cell to make the cell's contents merge with another cell. You can use colspan in either a table data cell or a table heading cell:

```
<td colspan="number">
<th colspan="number">
```

To span two columns, for example, specify colspan="2".

The colspan attribute is useful if you have a heading that you want to cover two different columns of data.

Similarly, the rowspan attribute specifies how many rows a cell should take up:

```
<td rowspan="number">
<th rowspan="number">
```

Here's a fragment of HTML code for a two-row, three-column table, where the first cell is made two rows tall using rowspan:

```
<table border="2">
<tr>
    <td rowspan="2">Burger Emperor</td>
    <td>Royale Burger</td>
    <td>690 calories</td>
</tr>
<tr>
    <td>Royale with Cheese</td>
    <td>750 calories</td>
</tr>
</table>
```

The first cell in the second row (Royale with Cheese) is automatically moved over to make room for the spanned cell, as shown here:

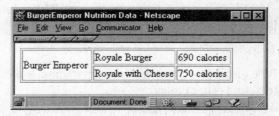

Setting Cell Widths and Heights

You can set the width of an entire table using the `<table>` tag's width attribute. You also can specify the widths of individual cells in the simple table model.

When a browser displays a table constructed with the simple table model, each column will be as wide as the widest cell in that column. (Because it can take some time for a browser to retrieve the entire table and work out how wide each column should be, tables sometimes can be slow to display if you don't specify width values.) Each column will have a different width.

NOTE

In HTML 4.01 and XHTML's table model, you also can specify column widths individually or by groups, using the new column elements that you'll see later in this chapter.

You can specify the minimum width of a column by using the width attribute on a cell. (Best results are achieved by specifying the widths for all the cells in the first row.) The width is specified in pixels, and the width attribute can be used only in a table data element or table heading element. For example:

```
<td width="number">
<th width="number">
```

The height attribute is a new attribute in HTML 4.0. (However, Navigator and Internet Explorer have supported this attribute as an extension for quite a while.) It's important to remember that both the width and the height attributes are recommendations: Browsers often will override your specified dimensions. The advantage to specifying width and height is that your tables will be displayed much faster.

Putting Images and Other Elements Inside Cells

As a general rule, a cell can contain almost anything that you can put inside the body section of your document. This means that you can include the following:

- ▶ Text

- ▶ Block-level elements (including paragraphs, lists, preformatted text, and other tables)

- ▶ Text-level elements (including font and phrase elements, anchors, line breaks, and images)

NOTE

When you use an image within a cell, it's a good idea to specify the height and width of the image and also specify the width of the image's cell (as we discussed in the previous section). This will help your table be displayed as quickly as possible.

Nesting Tables

Including a table inside another table's cell is called *table nesting*. One common use of table nesting is to create two tables that are side by side (normally, each table would be in a separate paragraph).

Listing 11.2 gives an example of the XHTML code for two tables nested inside of another table.

Listing 11.2: `toriamos.html`

```
<!DOCTYPE html PUBLIC
"-//W3C//DTD XHTML 1.0 Transitional//EN"
   "http://www.w3.org/TR/xhtml1/DTD/xhtml1-transitional.dtd">
<html xmlns="http://www.w3.org/1999/xhtml">
<head>
<title>Tori Amos Music Catalog Numbers</title>
</head>
<body>
<table border="0" cellspacing="20" bgcolor="#cccccc">
   <caption>Tori Amos Album and Single Catalog Excerpt
   </caption>
   <tr>
      <td>
         <table border="10" cellpadding="4">
            <caption>Albums</caption>
```

```
              <tr>
                 <td><i>Little Earthquakes</i></td>
                 <td>82358-2</td>
              </tr>
              <tr>
                 <td><i>Under the Pink</i></td>
                 <td>82567-2</td>
              </tr>
              <tr>
                 <td><i>Boys For Pele</i></td>
                 <td>82862-2</td>
              </tr>
           </table>
        </td>
        <td>
           <table border="10" cellpadding="4">
              <caption>Singles</caption>
              <tr>
                 <td>"Crucify"</td>
                 <td>82399-2</td>
              </tr>
              <tr>
                 <td>"God"</td>
                 <td>85687-2</td>
              </tr>
              <tr>
                 <td>"Cornflake Girl"</td>
                 <td>85655-2</td>
              </tr>
              <tr>
                 <td>"Caught A Lite Sneeze"</td>
                 <td>85519-2</td>
              </tr>
           </table>
        </td>
     </tr>
  </table>
  </body>
  </html>
```

In Figure 11.11, Internet Explorer renders this HTML code. The outer table contains no direct content of its own; it just specifies some attributes (including the light gray color) and contains a caption and two cells.

Each cell contains a nested table. The inner tables have a 10 pixel border and a number of cells each (six for the left table, eight for the right table).

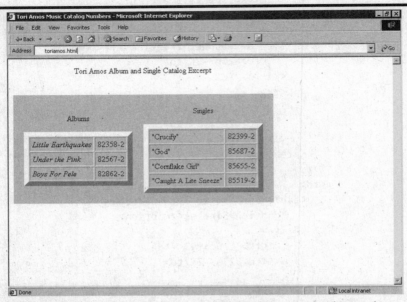

FIGURE 11.11:   Internet Explorer renders two tables nested within another table, allowing the two tables to exist side by side.

NOTE

An earlier figure, Figure 11.9, was created by nesting six tables inside a larger table.

UNOFFICIAL HTML EXTENSIONS TO THE SIMPLE TABLE MODEL

A few other attributes can be used with the simple table model, but they aren't official HTML or XHTML attributes—they're browser extensions to HTML 4. You can use a background image in a table or in a table cell by specifying a background attribute, just like the one used in the body tag. Netscape 4.x, however, will display a specified table background image in each individual table cell rather than behind the entire table.

CONTINUED ➡

You also can specify the height of an entire table; this will help your tables to be displayed more quickly.

Table widths also can be specified using percentage values as well as pixels (for example, <td width="33%">). If you specify a width for a table and then specify the width of a cell, you can request that another table cell be assigned the rest of the available width by using <td width="*">.

These are useful extensions, but they are understood only by certain versions of Internet Explorer and Navigator, so be sure your table does not depend on these attributes.

Once you understand the simple table model and feel that the four basic table model elements make sense, you're ready to move on to the more complex HTML 4.01 and XHTML table model.

Using HTML 4.01 and XHTML Table Elements and Attributes

The HTML 4.01 table model builds on the simple table model and adds a few new elements and attributes to make tables richer and more capable, but also more complex.

TIP

If you're not comfortable with the simple table model from the first half of this chapter, you might want to work with it for a while before reading about the HTML 4.01 and XHTML table model.

The changes from the HTML 3.2 table model improve the simple table model in key areas. First, the simple table model resulted in slow display times for a large table because a browser had to read through the entire table before figuring out how wide each column needed to be. Second, it was difficult to import information from spreadsheets because the table models differed so much. Finally, it was impossible to group data by row or by column. To solve these problems, the HTML 4.0 table model introduces new elements for columns and groups of columns as well as groups of rows.

Part II

Here are some other changes in the table model, introduced by popular demand:

▶ The capability to align on a specific character, such as " . " or " : " (to allow numbers to be decimal aligned).

▶ More flexibility in specifying table borders, especially borders around individual row and column groups.

▶ Better support for breaking tables across multiple pages when printing.

▶ Setting the alignment of cells by column or by groups of rows.

WARNING

Currently, only Internet Explorer 4 and above and Netscape 6 and above support the new table model.

To see how these changes work, we'll discuss the HTML 4.01 and XHTML table model's structure.

Understanding the Structure of the HTML 4.01 and XHTML Table Model

In HTML 4.01 and XHTML, tables have the following structure:

▶ The required table element start tag (<table>) must start a table, followed by an optional caption (with the caption element, same as in the simple table model), followed by:

    ▶ One or more groups of columns (using the new column group and column elements), followed by:

    ▶ One or more groups of rows. You can have an optional table head row group and an optional table foot row group, and you must have one or more table body row groups (using the new <thead>, <tfoot>, and <tbody> tags).

▶ Each row group must consist of one or more rows (using the table row element, same as in the simple table model).

▶ Each row must consist of one or more cells (using the table data and table heading elements, same as in the simple table model).

▶ The required `table` element end tag (`</table>`) must finish a table, same as in the simple table model.

The new elements in the HTML 4.01 and XHTML table model are the column group element (which uses the `<colgroup>` tag), the column element (which uses the `<col>` tag), and the three new elements for row groups: table headers (the `<thead>` tag), table bodies (the `<tbody>` tag), and table footers (the `<tfoot>` tag).

Each table is assumed to have one column group and one table body row group, even if those elements are not specified explicitly with tags. (This is how the new table model is able to stay backward compatible with the simple table model.)

Because the new table model is backward compatible, none of the five new elements are *required* if you want to make an HTML 4.01 or XHTML table.

We'll see other new attributes and attribute values after we see the new elements for tables. There are five elements to consider; we'll start with the two new column group elements and then see the three new row group elements.

Creating Columns and Groups of Columns

HTML 4.01 and XHTML tables always have at least one column group. If you don't specify your column group (using a `<colgroup>` tag), every column in your table is assumed to make up the column group.

You can define one or more groups of columns; each `<colgroup>` tag defines a new group. (There is an end tag, `</colgroup>`.) Each column group must have one or more columns; we'll see how to define columns in the next section.

The `<colgroup>` tags are used immediately after the `caption` element if there is one. If there's no `caption` element, the `<colgroup>` tags should be put immediately after the `<table>` tag.

The advantage to defining column groups is that you can apply attributes to every cell in the column group. For example, if you want to specify that every cell in a group of columns should be centered, you can simply use a `<colgroup align="center">` tag. In the simple table model, you would have had to apply the `align` attribute to every cell you wanted centered, one at a time.

Another advantage to column groups is that you can specify column widths. This allows browsers to begin displaying your table immediately because they don't have to read through the entire table to find out how many columns there are and how wide they should be. For long tables, this can make a tremendous difference in the time it takes to display your document (especially for someone viewing your page on a slow Internet connection).

NOTE
You also can specify column widths without the use of colgroup by adding a width attribute to td or th tags.

Using the Column Group (*colgroup*) Element

There are two ways to use the column group element, and you must use one or the other:

▶ Within the column group, you can use one or more column elements. The column element uses the <col> tag. Each <col> tag creates one column. We'll see how to use the column element in the next section.

▶ You can create a group of columns by using the <colgroup> tag with a span attribute. The number of columns in the column group is equal to the attribute value of span. For example, <colgroup span="4"> creates a group of four columns. The span attribute's value defaults to 1. We'll see some examples of this method in this section.

In addition to the span attribute, the <colgroup> tag can contain an align attribute, a valign attribute, and a width attribute. The values for these attributes can be the same as in the simple table model, or they can have new possibilities discussed later in this chapter, when we introduce the new HTML 4.01 table model's attributes.

Following are some examples of the <colgroup> tag. The first example creates a column group with only one column (because the span attribute is not specified). Every cell in the column will be right aligned:

```
<colgroup align="right">
...
</colgroup>
```

This example creates a group of five columns, each one centered, top-aligned, and 100 pixels wide:

```
<colgroup span="5" valign="top" align="center" width="100">
...
</colgroup>
```

This example creates two groups of columns. The first group has eight columns that are fully justified, and the second group has four columns, each 50 pixels wide:

```
<colgroup span="8" align="justify">
...
</colgroup>
<colgroup span="4" width="50">
...
</colgroup>
```

The width attribute is an important part of column groups. If you don't specify the width, either the browser will divide all of the columns equally across the width of the screen or it will have to read through your entire table to determine the column widths.

We'll see other examples of the use of <colgroup> in our HTML 4.01 and XHTML table examples in the next section and at the end of the chapter.

Using the Column (*col*) Element

The column element uses a <col> tag. The column element is empty, so there's no required </col> end tag. The column element can be placed only inside a column group element. Each <col> tag creates a column.

NOTE

In XHTML, empty elements include a space and a forward slash, such as <hr />, <br />, <img />, and <col />.

Like <colgroup>, you can use attributes in the <col> tag to apply to each cell in a column. For example, you could begin a table like this:

```
<table>
    <caption>the "six columns of fun" table</caption>
    <colgroup span="2" align="center" width="50" />
    <colgroup align="right">
        <col width="150" />
        <col width="100" valign="top" />
```

Part II

```
        <col width="50" />
        <col width="*" align="left" />
    </colgroup>
</table>
```

Assuming you finished this example (with some table rows, cells, and a `</table>` end tag), the code would define a table with six columns. The first two columns are created by the first `<colgroup>` tag (thanks to the `span="2"` attribute). Both of these first two columns have their cell data centered and are 50 pixels wide. The next four columns are created by the four `<col>` tags inside the second column group element. By default, these four columns will be right aligned. The third column will be 150 pixels wide. The fourth column will be 100 pixels wide, and its cells will be top aligned. The fifth column is 50 pixels wide.

The sixth column uses a special width value, which means "give this column the rest of the available width"; we'll see more about the asterisk and its use in the "New Alignment Attributes" section, later in this chapter. The sixth column also specifies left alignment for its cells, which will override the default of right alignment set by the second `<colgroup>` tag.

When you complete the rest of the table, make sure not to include more than six cells in a row, because you've already specified a maximum of six columns for this table. Browsers might not display any extraneous cells or will possibly become confused.

Once you define your column groups and columns, you can next include elements that define one or more row groups.

Grouping Rows with Row Group Elements

In the simple table model, the `table` element simply contains an optional caption and one or more table row elements. In the HTML 4.01 and XHTML table model, all of the table rows (and the `<tr>` tags) are contained in row groups. A *row group* is simply one or more table rows that are grouped together for common formatting or positioning.

There are three types of row groups:

▶ An optional table head row group: `<thead>` tag (for the top of each page)

▶ An optional table foot row group: `<tfoot>` tag (for the bottom of each page)

▶ At least one required table body row group: `<tbody>` tag (for the bulk of the table's data)

The order of these row groups in a table is important.

▶ If there's a table head row group, it must occur before the table foot row group and the table body row group.

▶ If there's a table foot row group, it must occur before the table body row group.

▶ You can have one or more table body row groups. There's no limit to how many table body row groups your table can contain.

There is not much of a difference between these three types of row groups: Table head row groups go on the top of a table (and are repeated on the top of each page if a table is printed out), and table foot row groups go on the bottom of a table (and are repeated at the bottom of each page in a printout). Other than that, the main reason for these three row group sections is to enable you to assign attributes to groups of rows. The table head row group and the table foot row group are completely optional.

If you want just one table body row group (without any table head or table foot row groups), you don't have to specify any row group elements at all—the presence of the table body row group element is assumed if there's not a <tbody> tag in your table. For the required table body element, there's no difference between nesting the table row elements within plain <tbody> and </tbody> tags and not doing so.

NOTE

Remember that if you want a table head row group or table foot row group, you have to use the <thead>, <tfoot>, and <tbody> tags (in that order).

It can be useful to specify a table body row group element in your table, because (just as with columns and column groups) you can apply an attribute to the <tbody> tag that will affect an entire group of rows (and the cells contained in those rows). For example:

```
<table border="1">
 <thead align="center">
  <tr>
   <td>B1</td><td>B2</td><td>B3</td><td>B4</td><td>B5</td>
  </tr>
 </thead>
 <tbody align="right">
  <tr>
   <td>1</td><td>23</td><td>04</td><td>23</td><td>2</td>
  </tr>
```

```
  <tr>
   <td>5</td><td>39</td><td>93</td><td>10</td><td>2</td>
  </tr>
 </tbody>
</table>
```

This example creates a table with two row groups. The first row group (a table head row group) contains just one row with all five cells in that row center aligned. The second row group (a table body row group), contains two rows—and both of those rows will have right-aligned cells. In the simple table model, you would have had to apply the alignment attributes to the <tr> tags. In this example, with only three rows, it would not have been time consuming to do so, but imagine a table where you want 700 right-aligned rows, and you'll understand the motivation for row groups.

NOTE

One main idea behind row groups is to enable the display of a very large table within a scrolling frame region. The head section and foot section would stay constant at the top and bottom of the browser window, while the body section between them would have a separate scroll bar. Alas, browsers have not yet implemented this approach.

WARNING

Only the latest versions of Internet Explorer and Navigator support the header and footer feature of tables when you're printing them out. Navigator 4.01 and earlier and Internet Explorer 4.0 and earlier may not handle printed head and foot row groups properly.

Using the HTML 4.01 and XHTML Table Model's Attributes

Several new attributes can be used in HTML 4.01 and XHTML tables. Some of these attributes can only be used in the <table> tag, and others can be used in a variety of different elements.

NOTE

In addition to these attributes, every element used in tables can take the standard HTML 4.01 attributes, such as the language attributes (lang and dir) and the advisory title attribute, the ID, class, and style attributes that will be discussed with style sheets in Chapter 16, and the event attributes (onmouseover and so on).

The first new attributes we'll see can be used in the <table> tag: the cols attribute to indicate the number of columns and the frame and the rules attributes to specify borders more precisely.

Then we'll discuss some new values for the align attribute and see more about the width attribute.

Specifying the Number of Columns with the *cols* Attribute

Instead of using the column group and column elements we discussed earlier, you can specify a cols attribute in the <table> start tag to indicate how many columns are in your table.

Navigator 4 and above understand this attribute and will display a table with the indicated number of columns, using width="100%" (instead of the default width).

Internet Explorer 4 and earlier, along with earlier versions of Navigator, ignore this attribute. The specifications for HTML 4.01 and XHTML recommend that you use the column group elements to specify columns instead, because you also can use those elements to specify column widths, which speeds up display time.

Using Advanced Borders with the *frame* and *rules* Attributes

The simple table model doesn't give you a lot of flexibility with your table borders: Either you have a border or you don't; you can specify the width of the outside table border, but that's all you can specify. HTML 4.0 introduced the frame and rules attributes for the <table> tag to help improve the amount of control you have over borders.

NOTE

Internet Explorer 3 and later and Navigator 7 recognize the frame and rules attributes. The frame attribute indicates which sides of the table's outside border are rendered.

WARNING

Don't confuse the frame attribute with the HTML frames feature; frames are used to subdivide the browser window with different documents (frames are discussed in Chapter 8, "Dividing a Window with Frames").

The `frame` attribute's values are shown in Table 11.2.

TABLE 11.2: Values for the `frame` Attribute

FRAME VALUE	EFFECTS
`frame="above"`	The top
`frame="below"`	The bottom
`frame="border"`	All four sides—the same as specifying the `border` attribute
`frame="box"`	Same as `frame="border"`
`frame="hsides"`	The top and bottom ("horizontal sides")
`frame="lhs"`	The left side
`frame="rhs"`	The right side
`frame="void"`	No sides rendered (the default value)
`frame="vsides"`	The left and right sides ("vertical sides")

The result of using tables with each of these `frame` values is shown here using Internet Explorer:

The frame attribute applies to the outside of a table. The rules attribute applies to which cell borders will appear between cells within a table.

The rules attribute's values are shown in Table 11.3.

TABLE 11.3: Values for the rules Attribute

rules VALUE	EFFECT
rules="none"	No cell borders; this is the default value and is displayed the same as border = "0" or no border attribute.
rules="groups"	Cell borders will appear only between row groups and column groups.
rules="rows"	Rules will appear only between rows.
rules="cols"	Rules will appear only between columns.
rules="all"	Rules will appear between all rows and columns (same as specifying the border attribute).

The result of using tables with each of these frame values (and the border attribute) is shown here, again using Internet Explorer:

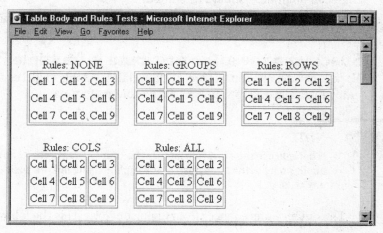

As you can see, the rules attributes apply only to the inside of the table, not the outside border.

Since the border attribute from the simple model is still available and overlaps with the use of frame and rules, it's helpful to know that setting border="0" is the same as rules="none" and frame="void".

Using border="*number*" is the same as using frame="border" and
rules="all". In HTML, using the attribute <table border> by itself is
the same as using <table border="2" frame="border" rules="all">.
However, Internet Explorer 3 and 4 sometimes behave strangely unless
the border attribute is present along with the frame and rules attributes.

New Alignment Attributes

HTML 4.01 and XHTML add align="justify" so that you can use full
justification on paragraphs inside table cells.

They also allow align="char" to specify that cells should be aligned
on a certain character. By default, the character is the decimal sepa-
rator (which is a period if your document is in English). By specifying
align="char", you could cause a row of numbers to be aligned on their
decimal points.

Two other new alignment attributes are char and charoff. Using
char="$" along with align="char" would enable you to align on the
dollar sign. You can specify any character you like.

The charoff attribute specifies an offset (that is, distance) that the
character alignment should be shifted.

Unfortunately, character alignment is not yet supported in browsers.

Specifying the *align* Attribute in Multiple Places

The align attribute can be used in many different table model elements: the
individual cells, the row groups, or the column groups.

NOTE

When you use the align attribute in the <table> tag or the <caption> tag, it
applies only to the table itself or the caption itself, not the position of data in
any cells.

The order of precedence (from highest to lowest) is the following:

1. An element within a cell's data (for example, <p align=
   "center">)

2. The cell (in the <th> or <td> tag)

3. A column or column group (<col> and <colgroup>)

4. A row or row group (<tr>, <thead>, <tfoot>, and <tbody>)

For a `valign` attribute, the order of precedence is this:

1. The cell

2. The row or row group

3. The column or column group

In general, horizontal alignment is determined by columns in preference to rows; it's the reverse for vertical alignment.

New Uses of the *width* Attribute

We saw earlier how the `width` attribute can be used in the column group and column elements to specify the width of a column.

In the simple table model of HTML 3.2, the only way to specify a width for a cell was in pixels. In HTML 4.01 and XHTML's table model, there are two additional ways to specify column widths: using percentages and using relative amounts with an asterisk.

The percentage amount of width is not complicated: simply specify a percentage for each column, such as `<col width="40%">` to give a column 40 percent of the available table width.

We also saw earlier that you could specify `<col width="*">` to mean that a column should be given all of the available space. If two columns both specify the `width="*"` attribute, the amount of space will be divided in half, with equal width for each column.

HTML 4.01 and XHTML enable additional possibilities involving these "relative amounts" of width. The special value `width="0*"` means to use the minimum width possible for the content of the column. You also can use a number with the asterisk to make a column use more of the available space. The bigger the number, the more proportional space the column will receive. (`width="*"` is the same as `width="1*"`.)

Consider this example:

```
<table>
   <colgroup span="2" width="20" />
   <colgroup span="3" width="0*" />
   <colgroup>
      <col width="50">
      <col width="20%">
      <col width="1*">
      <col width="2*">
```

The rest of the table would follow, with table row groups, table rows, data, and the `</table>` tag.

This example creates nine columns in three column groups. When determining the column widths, a browser will give the first two columns 20 pixels each. The next three columns will have a variable amount of width, the minimum possible to display their data. The sixth column has 50 pixels. The seventh column is given 20 percent of the table's total width (assuming that much is still available). The remaining space for the table is divided into thirds. One third is given to the eighth column, and two-thirds is given to the ninth column.

It's common to create a table with a total width of 100 percent and then assign a fixed pixel width to the first column. The remaining columns often are divided using relative amounts, with width="*".

NOTE

It's important to be flexible with table widths. Consider this warning from the HTML 4.0 specification: "A major consideration for the HTML table model is that the author does not control how a user will size a table, what fonts he or she will use, etc. This makes it risky to rely on column widths specified in terms of absolute pixel units. Instead, tables must be able to change sizes dynamically to match the current window size and fonts."

WARNING

Browsers will disobey your column widths whenever they feel it's necessary to override them.

Making Tables Accessible

HTML and XHTML include table elements and attributes that make tables more accessible to users with visual disabilities by making table content more accessible to screen readers. The caption element, discussed earlier in this chapter, can provide a short description of a table's content. In addition, the summary attribute can provide a long description of a table's content, and the headers, scope, and axis attributes enable relational grouping of the data in table cells.

For more information on table accessibility elements and attributes, see:

▶ The HTML 4.01 specification, section 11.4 at www.w3.org/TR/html4/struct/tables.html#h-11.4

▶ "Making Tables Accessible" at www.vsarts.org/bestpractices/culturalaccess/webaccess/tables.html

PUTTING THE NEW TABLE MODEL TO WORK: A FINAL EXAMPLE

We've seen plenty of new features for HTML 4.01 and XHTML's table model. It's time to show a final example that will put it all together.

Here's an example of XHTML code that uses the colgroup and tbody elements to render a television schedule with three different column groups and two different row groups. Through the use of the new rules elements, the cell borders effectively divide the table into different regions.

Listing 11.3: tvscout.html

```
<!DOCTYPE html PUBLIC
"-//W3C//DTD XHTML 1.0 Transitional//EN"
  "http://www.w3.org/TR/xhtml1/DTD/xhtml1-transitional.dtd">
<html xmlns="http://www.w3.org/1999/xhtml">
<head>
  <title>TV Scout's TV Schedule</title>
</head>
<body>

<table border="5" rules="groups" frame="void"
   align="center">
<caption>Television Schedule for Monday</caption>

<!-- first column: headings -->

<colgroup align="center" width="75"></colgroup>
<colgroup> <!--columns 2 and 3: 6am -->
  <col align="center" width="75"/>
  <col width="*" align="left"/></colgroup>
<colgroup> <!--columns 4 and 5: 7am -->
  <col align="center" width="75"/>
  <col width="*" align="left"/>
</colgroup>

<thead valign="bottom" align="center">
  <tr>
    <th rowspan="3">Channel</th>
```

Part II

```
      <th colspan="4">Time</th>
    </tr>
    <tr>
      <th colspan="2">6 am</th>
      <th colspan="2">7 am</th>
    </tr>
    <tr>
      <th>Show</th>
      <th>Description</th>
      <th>Show</th>
      <th>Description</th>
    </tr>
  </thead>

  <tbody align="center">
    <tr>
      <td>3</td>
      <td>CHiPs</td>
      <td>Ponch discovers some stolen Pentium
       processors.</td>
      <td>The Munsters</td>
      <td>Herman creates a family home page. The cops
       confiscate his computer.</td>
    </tr>
    <tr>
      <td>7</td>
      <td>I Love Lucy</td>
      <td>Lucy surfs the Web and accidentally charges
       $50,000 to her VISA.</td>
      <td>The X-Files</td>
      <td>Scully and Mulder investigate some alien-infested
       table cells.</td>
    </tr>
  </tbody>
  </table>
  </body>
  </html>
```

Figure 11.12 shows how this code will be displayed by Internet Explorer 4 (and Navigator 4 in the background). Because Navigator 4 doesn't understand all of the new table model, it displays the table a little differently—but at least all of the data is there.

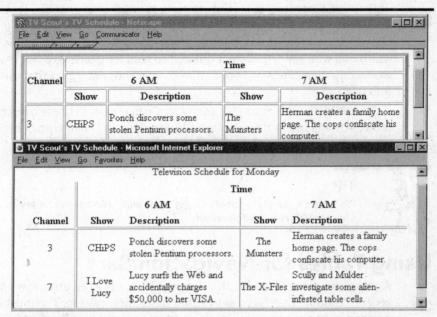

FIGURE 11.12: A table that uses the colgroup and tbody elements displayed by Internet Explorer, with Navigator's window behind Internet Explorer's window

Using a Table as a Layout Tool

HTML and XHTML were not designed to be page layout languages. However, HTML evolved to include a few layout elements. Style sheets were supposed to handle the rest of an author's layout needs, but style sheets were not in wide use until HTML 4.0 arrived. In the meantime, many web authors developed ways of laying out pages using tables.

Even though this is somewhat abusive of HTML's purpose (since, after all, you are not describing table data), it's a common practice, so we'll show you a few techniques for making a table perform as a layout tool.

NOTE

For more information on using a table as a layout tool, see Chapter 9.

Creating Page Margins with Tables

Sometimes it's nice to emphasize a paragraph with white space. The full width of a window can make it difficult to read long passages (we're used to reading magazines or books, which have wider margins than most web pages).

To establish wider margins easily, you can create a simple one-cell table, borders off, and specify a table width or cellpadding. This will separate the text from the left and right margins of the page.

TIP

It's easy to use style sheets to get even more control over margins. Read Chapter 16 for more information.

Using Tables for Navigation Bars

Another nice way to use a table for page layout is to create a row with several columns that serve as a button navigation system. The most basic navigation bar can use a table with text in each cell (see Figure 11.13).

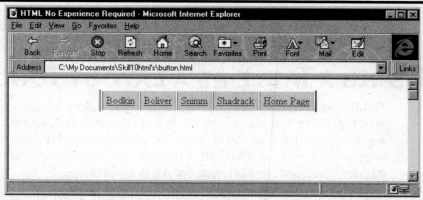

FIGURE 11.13:   Internet Explorer renders a table that serves as a text navigation bar.

Some bars use an image in each cell. Let's take a look at the HTML code for a simple text navigation bar:

```
<table border="3" frame="vsides" align="center"
  cellpadding="5">
```

```
<tr>
  <td bgcolor="aqua"><a href="bodkin.html">Bodkin</a></td>
  <td bgcolor="aqua"><a href="boliver.html">
   Boliver</a></td>
  <td bgcolor="aqua"><a href="snimm.html">Snimm</a></td>
  <td bgcolor="aqua"><a href="shadrack.html">
   Shadrack </a></td>
  <td bgcolor="aqua"><a href="home.html">Home Page</a></td>
</tr>
</table>
```

As we saw earlier, web authors sometimes try to create text columns using tables. Others use other tricks with tables (such as forcing a column to be a certain width by using transparent images). In general, most of those effects can be better achieved with style sheets. Some web authors use tables to split a page into two halves, with navigation links on the left half and page content on the right half, although frames are a more effective way of dividing the browser's screen into regions.

What's Next?

In this chapter, you learned that using tables is an extremely powerful way to arrange data. Tables are both complex and useful, so it's worth taking the time to learn them and use them on your pages. In the next chapter, Molly Holzschlag will give you the details on the type-related elements of web design and provide suggestions on how to use type to get your message across.

Part II

Chapter 12
WEB TYPOGRAPHY

Web typography challenges the best of designers, no matter how skilled they are with type. The reason is simple: Support for type is truly limited. Designers have only three basic alternatives when designing for type on the web: using graphics to handle desired typographic elements, coding type with the HTML <font> tag, and using Cascading Style Sheets (CSS).

Three options doesn't sound limited, but there's a catch: With HTML and style sheets, if a specific typeface doesn't exist on the machine used by your website visitor, that visitor will not see your beautiful type.

A further headache is the often-referred-to browser problem. Microsoft's Internet Explorer 3 and above have good style sheet support. Netscape introduced limited support for style sheets in version 4 but failed to support key features of the CSS2 visual formatting model, such as the float property and absolute positioning. Fortunately, support for style sheets has improved with newer browser versions. Internet Explorer 6 and Netscape Navigator 6 and above support all of CSS level 1 and most of CSS level 2.

• •

Adapted from *Web by Design: The Complete Guide*, by Molly E. Holzschlag
ISBN 0-7821-2201-9 $49.99

NOTE

One advantage if you're using those browsers is that the style sheet interpretation for typographic elements is pretty good, compared to the less stable style sheet positioning, although this has also improved in the newer browsers. It is for this reason alone that I go into such detail with style sheets in this chapter. For more details on using style sheets, see Chapter 16, "Using Style Sheets."

The future holds great hope, however. With Microsoft's embedded fonts and the OpenType initiative, new technologies are on the horizon that will place type within easy reach of designers.

Embedded fonts enable the designer to embed the font information for a specific page into the code of that page. The necessary fonts are then silently downloaded by the visitor's browser, allowing the fonts on that page to be seen. Interestingly, embedded fonts strip out any characters and letters in a font that are not used on the page. This means that the embedded information can transfer with relative speed.

The OpenType initiative is a cooperative effort between Microsoft and Adobe, companies that historically have been at odds. In order to solve some of the typographic problems born of the web environment, they have put aside their differences and are working on fonts that will be instantly accessible to web visitors. Adobe developed 12 original typefaces just for the web. The typefaces include two serifs, a sans serif, a script, and two decorative faces.

ONLINE INFORMATION

Check out these sites for information regarding web typefaces:

Microsoft Typography

For up-to-date news on typographic technology, including Microsoft's new ClearType for improved screen readability, visit `http://www.microsoft.com/typography/default.asp`.

Adobe

This company site has terrific information on general type and web type as well as typographic tools for PC and Macintosh platforms: `http://www.adobe.com/`.

Despite the push-me, pull-you feel of the state of web typography, you can begin working with the technologies that exist. This chapter will help you do just that. You'll examine:

▶ Designing type with graphics

▶ Implementing HTML-based type techniques

▶ Using Cascading Style Sheets to achieve greater typographic control

---

"In a printed piece, or on the web, attractive, well-executed typography adds elegance and improves communication. Poor typographic execution can seriously degrade otherwise inspired design."

—Paul Baker, *PBTWeb*

The most important thing to remember about typography on the web is that advances are made at regular intervals. Keep up with the technology, and you'll stay ahead of the pack when it comes to typographic applications in web design.

APPROACHING WEB TYPOGRAPHY

Whether you're looking to use type in the conservative fashion as a method to deliver your web-based written content or you'd like to be adventurous and use type as artistic design, the more methods you can use to approach web typography, the better equipped you are to achieve your typographic goals.

"Typography is becoming tribal, an initiation rite."

—Joe Clark, writings from Typo Expo 1996

I believe that type should do both—serve its function *and* be used artistically. The web is a perfect opportunity to experiment. Obviously, when your client and audience want you to manage text, you're going to be somewhat reined in by convention. Still, there are times when you will have the opportunity or want to create more cutting-edge designs. Type can help you do this.

Again, web typography currently can be approached with some stability through three vehicles: graphics, HTML, and Cascading Style Sheets.

Graphics and Type

In many ways, putting type on a website as a graphic is currently the most stable method of ensuring that your type design will be seen. Visitors don't have to have the font installed—they are seeing the font as part of a graphic. This gives you lots of control because not only can you select from any type-face you own, you also can color it to your taste and add special effects, too.

Of course, the downside is the time that graphics take to download. Where you use graphics to handle the majority of your type, you'll need to take care to balance the typographic elements with the graphics necessary for your individual pages. Here are a few tips to help you when working with type as a graphic:

- ▶ Select flat colors from the browser-safe palette to ensure the smallest file size even if you're using large type.

- ▶ Save flat-color, simple, graphic-based typeset files as GIFs.

- ▶ If you add special effects such as shadows, gradient fills, and metallic color, or if you use 3D type, try saving your files as GIFs and JPEGs in order to compare the results. You might find that in certain instances, JPEGs will serve you better, and in other cases, you will get smaller files and a terrific look from GIFs.

- ▶ In most cases, you will want to anti-alias your fonts as you set the type on the graphic (see Figure 12.1). However, anti-aliasing can become problematic when you want to set small type. It's espe-cially wise to avoid anti-aliasing on any type that is smaller than 12 points, although you should experiment with both in order to get the best look (see Figure 12.2).

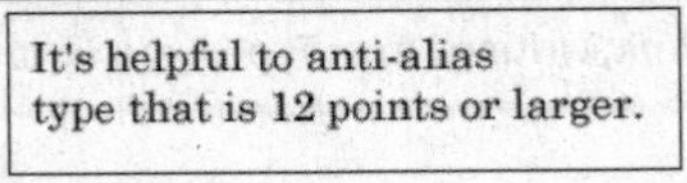

> It's helpful to anti-alias
> type that is 12 points or larger.

FIGURE 12.1:   Type that is 12 point or more typically should be anti-aliased.

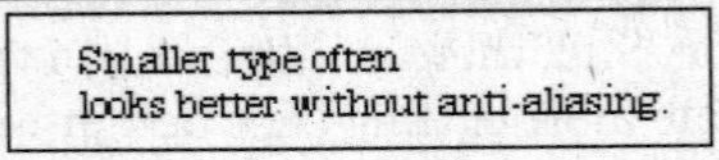

> Smaller type often
> looks better without anti-aliasing.

FIGURE 12.2:   Small type that is not anti-aliased looks fine.

Treat type-based graphics as you would any other graphic when coding. This means to be sure to use the appropriate tag and attributes, including width, height, alt, and any relevant alignment tags:

```
<img src="welcome.gif" width="300" height="100" alt=
    "Welcome to Our House" align="right" />
```

Wherever possible, it's also a good idea to combine graphic-based type with type you create on the page. That way, you lean less on the graphics to get your typographic point across.

WARNING
Remember accessibility issues when you use text as graphics. Be sure to add the graphic text content to the required alt attribute of the img tag.

HTML and Type

Aside from browser and individual users' font library support issues, the main problem with HTML type is that you can use it only along the horizontal. Also, you can't set it in specific points—you must rely on really poor sizing techniques. However, you still can do some interesting things with HTML type.

HTML type is delivered primarily through the <font> tag. The only exception to this is the header tags <h1>...</h1> through <h6>...</h6>, which use a bold Times font to create a variety of headers ranging in size from large (size 1) to small (size 6). You'll want to use them now and then, but with so many other options, you might find them limiting as you work with different typefaces and sizes.

WARNING
The font element and all its attributes are deprecated in favor of the use of style sheets.

The *<font>* Tag

The <font> tag has numerous considerations in terms of widespread compatibility, but it does help designers address type techniques through HTML. The <font> tag allows a number of attributes, including face, size, and color.

The <font> tag follows standard HTML conventions, with an opening and closing tag enclosing the division of information to which you are applying the font attributes:

```
<font>
Love is a smoke raised with the fume of sighs;
```

```
Being purged, a fire sparkling in lovers' eyes;
Being vex'd a sea nourished with lovers' tears:
What is it else? a madness most discreet,
A choking gall and a preserving sweet.
</font>
```

Of course, nothing happens until you add relevant attributes, which I'll show you as we look at the use of typefaces, forms, and color further on in this chapter.

HTML CHARACTER ENTITIES

To make it easier to use unusual numeric, alphabetic, and symbolic characters, the HTML 4.01 specification is compliant with several standardized character sets. These include the ISO Latin-1 character set, mathematical symbols, Greek letters, and assorted other international and markup-significant character sets.

What Is the ISO Latin-1 Character Set?

The International Organization for Standardization (ISO) is the group in charge of managing international standards for everything from computer protocols to character sets. The ISO 8859-1 standard, more commonly known as the ISO Latin-1 character set, is the default character set used by HTML. The term *Latin* refers to the Roman alphabet, which is the basis of the world's Romance languages. The number 1 indicates that this particular character set is the first in the ISO Latin series.

Most of the symbols and special characters used in web pages are found in the ISO Latin-1 character set. Because this is HTML's default character set, you can use its numeric and character entities in your web pages. If you need to use characters that are not in the ISO Latin-1 series—for example, characters found in languages such as Russian and Hebrew—you'll need to use ISO-8859-8 (Hebrew), ISO 8859-5 (Cyrillic), or Unicode. For more information on the ISO-8859 standards, see http://czyborra.com/charsets/iso8859.html.

What's Unicode?

Unicode is the web typographer's Swiss Army knife. Officially known as ISO 10646, Unicode is a way of defining special characters

CONTINUED ➡

for use in HTML, SGML, and the newest metalanguage, XML. The ISO Latin-1 character set is a subset of Unicode, which comprises a huge collection of special characters that covers major languages from throughout the world. That's one big set. How does Unicode do it? It uses unique bit patterns for each character, which computers can recognize and display.

Because Unicode is so extensive (version 3.2.1 includes 49,194 distinct, coded characters), it has been broken up into several subsets called Universal Transformation Formats (UTFs).

HTML 4.01 supports only a selected portion of the Unicode character set. You can find a full list of what is supported at http://www.w3 .org/TR/html4/sgml/entities.html. If you want to know the Unicode number for a certain character or which UTF you should use for a project, check out the Unicode Consortium's website at http://www.unicode.org.

Random Cheats

Getting other typefaces to appear using HTML is a trick many designers use. The most popular of these is the preformatted text tag <pre>, which will force a monospaced (usually Courier) typeface:

```
<pre>
Love is a smoke raised with the fume of sighs;
Being purged, a fire sparkling in lovers' eyes;
Being vex'd a sea nourished with lovers' tears:
What is it else? a madness most discreet,
A choking gall and a preserving sweet.
</pre>
```

Figure 12.3 shows the results.

You also can use the <tt> tag for a monospaced font, but unlike the above example using <pre>, the text will wrap unless a line break <br /> is added at the end of each line:

```
<tt>
Love is a smoke raised with the fume of sighs;
Being purged, a fire sparkling in lovers' eyes;
Being vex'd a sea nourished with lovers' tears:
What is it else? a madness most discreet,
A choking gall and a preserving sweet.
</tt>
```

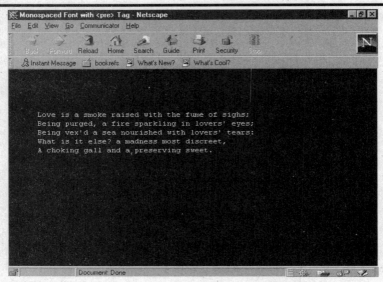

FIGURE 12.3:   Using the `<pre>` tag will force a monospaced font.

Style Sheets and Type

We'll look at style sheets with a focus on how you will work with style sheet code to apply typography in the web environment.

NOTE

To view style sheet information, you'll need a compatible browser. Individuals using Internet Explorer 3 and above or Netscape 4 and above will be able to see style sheets. Of course, if a particular typeface is called for and doesn't exist on your visitor's machine, the type will not be seen in that face.

There are three primary ways to use style sheets. They are the *inline* method, the *embedded* (or individual page method), and the *linked* (or external) method.

Inline Style Sheets

This approach exploits existing HTML tags within a standard HTML document and adds a specific style to the information controlled by that tag. An example would be controlling the indentation of a single paragraph using the `style="x"` attribute within the `<p>` tag. Another method of achieving this is by combining the `<span>` tag and the `style="x"` attribute.

Here is an inline style example:

```
<span style="font: 14pt garamond">
Love is a smoke raised with the fume of sighs;
Being purged, a fire sparkling in lovers' eyes;
Being vex'd a sea nourished with lovers' tears:
What is it else? a madness most discreet,
A choking gall and a preserving sweet.
</span>
```

You could do the same thing with the paragraph tag:

```
<p style="font: 14pt garamond">
Love is a smoke raised with the fume of sighs;
Being purged, a fire sparkling in lovers' eyes;
Being vex'd a sea nourished with lovers' tears:
What is it else? a madness most discreet,
A choking gall and a preserving sweet.
</p>
```

Embedded Style Sheets

This method enables the control of individual pages. It uses the `<style>` tag, along with its companion tag, `</style>`. This information is placed between the `<html>` tag and the `<body>` tag, between the `<head>` and `</head>` tags, with the style attributes inserted within the full `<style>` container:

```
<style type="text/css">
P { font-family: arial, helvetica, sans-serif; }
</style>
```

Linked Style Sheets

All that is required for linked style sheets is to create a style sheet file with the master styles you would like to express, using the same syntax you would with embedded style, as follows:

```
P { font-family: arial, helvetica, sans-serif; }
```

Save the file using the `.css` extension—for example, the file `paragraph` `.css`. Then simply be sure that all the HTML documents that will require those controls are *linked* to that document.

Within the `<head>` tag of any document you want to adopt the style you've just created, insert the following syntax (keep in mind that the reference will have your own location and filename):

```
<link rel="stylesheet" href="paragraph.css" type="text/css" />
```

Style Sheet Syntax

With embedded and linked style sheets, the attribute syntax is somewhat different from standard HTML syntax. First, attributes are placed within curly brackets. Second, where HTML would place an equal sign (=), a colon (:) is used. Third, individual, stacked arguments are separated by a semicolon rather than a comma. Also, several attributes are hyphenated, such as `font-style` and `line-height`. A simple style sheet line looks like this:

```
{ font-style: arial, helvetica; }
```

As with HTML, style sheets tend to be quite logical and easy to understand.

TIP

The `<div>` (division) tag can be used like the `<span>` tag for inline control. The `<div>` tag is especially helpful for longer blocks of text, whereas `<span>` is most effective for adding style to smaller stretches of information, such as sentences, several words, or even individual letters within a word.

In a sense, the inline method of style sheet control defeats the ultimate purpose of Cascading Style Sheets. The main point of the technology is to seek style control of entire pages or even entire sets of pages. The inline method should be used only where touches of style are required.

FAMILIES AND FACES

The capability to use type families and faces can empower web designers because they can use those faces to fully express the emotion within the design being created. Limitations aside, we'll look at how typefaces and families can be used with graphics, HTML, and Cascading Style Sheets.

Typefaces and Graphics

The most important thing to remember is to select the typefaces you want to use for your body and header text *before* sitting down to set your type. Once you've determined what typefaces you'll be using and you know the literal content of the graphic to be designed, the issue boils down to the tool you're going to use to set the type.

Most designers agree that to work with type, the ideal combination is Illustrator and Photoshop. Illustrator allows a lot of control over the type you're setting, including kerning. Once you've set your type in Illustrator, you then can add your effects in Photoshop. The process is a bit time consuming, however, and many web designers have learned to be very creative using Photoshop alone. Newer versions of Photoshop offer much more support for controlling type, and it is becoming more feasible to use Photoshop alone to work with type in graphics. Many designers who use Photoshop alone to set type are perfectly happy doing so.

In Figure 12.4, you can see that the Photoshop 7 Type tool is open and that text is about to be set at 9-point, 14 line-spacing, crisp anti-aliased, Papyrus typeface. Figure 12.5 shows the results.

Adobe Photoshop
File Edit Image Layer Select Filter View Window Help
Papyrus
Regular
9 pt
Crisp
Character
Paragraph
Papyrus
Regular
9 pt
14 pt
Metrics
0
100%
100%
0 pt
Color:
English: USA
Crisp
100%
Doc: 726K/726K

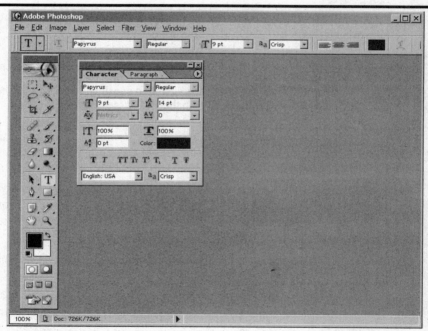

FIGURE 12.4: Using the Character palette of the Type tool in Photoshop 7

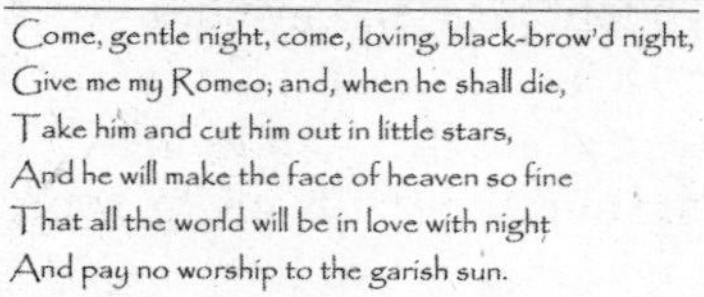

Come, gentle night, come, loving, black-brow'd night,
Give me my Romeo; and, when he shall die,
Take him and cut him out in little stars,
And he will make the face of heaven so fine
That all the world will be in love with night
And pay no worship to the garish sun.

FIGURE 12.5: The type is set.

Typefaces, Families, and the Font Tag

With the HTML <font> tag, you can select any typeface that you like and use it in the face attribute. Again, the limitation is that you will run into a problem with who has what on any given machine.

There is a total of only three type families and specific, related typefaces that you can be almost absolutely sure will show up across platforms and on individual machines.

On the PC, the forms are serif, monospaced, and sans serif. The specific faces are Times New Roman, Courier New, and Arial and Verdana, respectively.

Macintosh offers the same three forms, with Times, Courier, and Helvetica, as well as Arial and Verdana.

TIP

Verdana is a sans-serif typeface designed specifically for easy readability on-screen and is available on both the PC and Mac platforms.

What does this mean to you as a designer? It's simple. The face attribute of the <font> tag has one rather intelligent aspect: You can stack any number of typefaces with a type family and hopefully cover your bases.

After tagging the section of text to which you'd like to apply font styles, you add the face attribute and then define the font names. The browser will look for the first font name called for and, if it doesn't find it, will move on to the next named font:

```
<font face="arial,helvetica">This text will appear as Arial
    or Helvetica, depending upon which font is available</font>
```

If you'd like to add some stability to this syntax, you can add the family name at the end of the stack:

```
<font face="arial,helvetica,sans-serif">This text will
    appear as Arial or Helvetica or the default sans-serif
    font, depending upon which font is available</font>
```

It's important to remember that if a font face isn't available on a given machine, the default face will appear. Default is almost always a serif font such as Times, unless the user has selected another font for his default. If you're mixing fonts, bear in mind that your sans serifs might appear as serifs, and vice versa.

This lack of control can seem maddening! You can always forego using type, but then you run the risk of having ho-hum pages. Go for fonts, but do so thoughtfully and, wherever possible, stack the fonts along with a family name.

Style Sheets

Using a typeface family as a default is an excellent idea all around because it covers the designer's font choices as completely as possible. Even if a specific font face is unavailable on a given computer, it's likely that a similar one in that font's family is available. An aware designer will place the first choice first, second choice second, and so forth, with the family name at the end.

You can approach fonts in style sheets using the `font-family` string. Style sheets will accept this in all three types of style sheets: inline, embedded, and linked.

An inline example (see Figure 12.6) follows:

```
<span style="font-family:garamond,times,serif">
Love is a smoke raised with the fume of sighs;
Being purged, a fire sparkling in lovers' eyes;
Being vex'd a sea nourished with lovers' tears:
What is it else? a madness most discreet,
A choking gall and a preserving sweet.
</span>
```

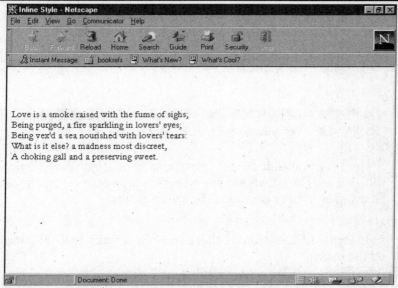

FIGURE 12.6: The result of an inline application of style

Since inline style can be used with any reasonable HTML tag, you could also do this:

```
<blockquote style="font-family:garamond,times,serif">
Love is a smoke raised with the fume of sighs;
Being purged, a fire sparkling in lovers' eyes;
Being vex'd a sea nourished with lovers' tears:
What is it else? a madness most discreet,
A choking gall and a preserving sweet.
</blockquote>
```

The result is that the browser picks up not only the style sheet information, but the HTML blockquote format as well (see Figure 12.7).

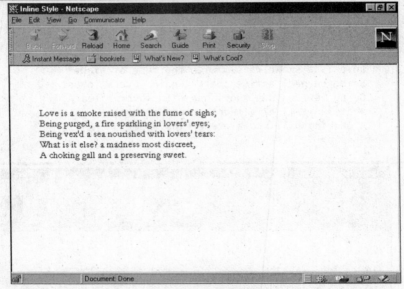

FIGURE 12.7:   Using inline style with the blockquote tag

Here's an embedded example of the same concept (linked style also will look like this). Let's say you want to apply a series of typefaces and a family to an entire paragraph. The syntax is this:

```
P { font-family: garamond, times, serif; }
```

In Figure 12.8, you can see that Garamond appears in all the paragraphs on the page.

You can apply this style to the blockquote as well:

```
blockquote { font-family: arial, helvetica, sans-serif; }
```

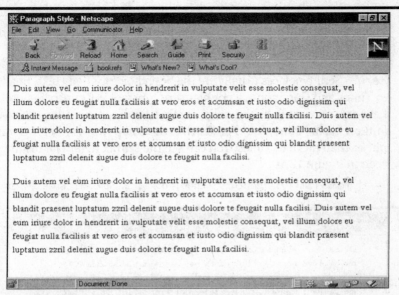

FIGURE 12.8:   Garamond is applied to all the paragraphs.

Figure 12.9 shows the blockquoted section.

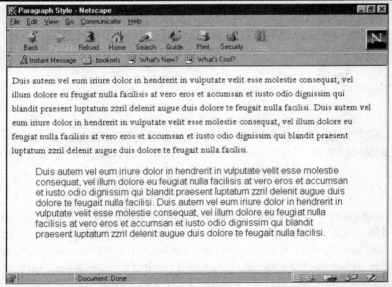

FIGURE 12.9:   In this instance, the embedded style controls the appearance of all the blockquoted material.

Font Family Support

There are specific families supported by style sheets, as discussed in the following sections.

serif   Serif typefaces usually are the best choice for body text. In addition to Times and Garamond, a popular serif typeface is Century Schoolbook. Let's say you want to have that appear first, but if someone doesn't have that font on his machine, you'd prefer that the computer search for Garamond rather than move to Times. You can see the syntax here. The result can be seen in Figure 12.10.

```
{ font-family: "century schoolbook", garamond, times, serif; }
```

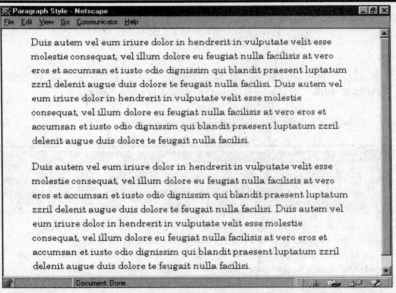

FIGURE 12.10:   My browser shows the Century Schoolbook typeface, because I have that font.

sans serif   This font family includes popular choices such as Arial, Helvetica, and Avant Garde. The same concept applies here, of course—if the user doesn't have Arial on his machine, the browser will then search for Helvetica, then Avant Garde, and finally (if none of the previous choices were found) for the generic sans-serif font.

```
{ font-family: arial, helvetica, "avant garde", sans-serif; }
```

TRY IT ONLINE

Try this one on your own with a style sheet–compatible browser. What is your result? Do you see Arial, Helvetica, Avant Garde, or a default sans-serif font?

cursive   Use this in place of `script`. These are the same as script typefaces—fonts that appear as though they have been handwritten. Figure 12.11 shows the result.

```
{ font-family: embassy, cursive; }
```

Part II

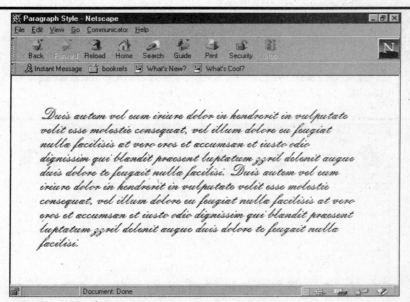

FIGURE 12.11:   This typeface results from embedded style.

fantasy   Fantasy fonts are used for *decorative* type, such as stylish, fun headings and titles. They are not practical for body text. You can see the Whimsy typeface in Figure 12.12.

```
{ font-family: "whimsy icg", fantasy; }
```

monospace   As with serif and sans-serif options, you're familiar with the monospaced font. Figure 12.13 looks like the text was typed on a page.

```
{ font-family: courier, monospace; }
```

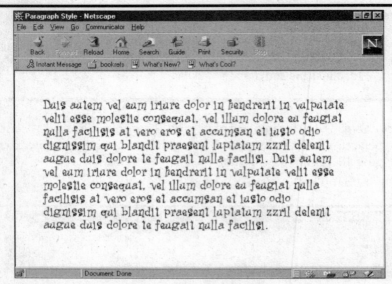

FIGURE 12.12: Here you see the Whimsy typeface.

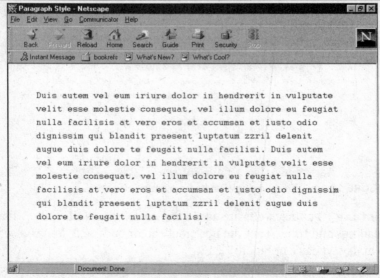

FIGURE 12.13: Using style again, you can ensure a monospaced (in this case, Courier) typeface.

Does *anyone* still use a typewriter?

TYPE FORM

In the world of typographic design, *form* refers to such concerns as weight and posture.

Type Form and Graphics

With graphics, you can address weight by choosing the exact typeface and weight you want for your graphic. Figure 12.14 shows Arial Narrow.

Come, gentle night, come, loving, black-brow'd night,
Give me my Romeo; and, when he shall die,
Take him and cut him out in little stars,
And he will make the face of heaven so fine
That all the world will be in love with night
And pay no worship to the garish sun.

FIGURE 12.14:   Arial Narrow is set on a graphic.

Posture also is dealt with when choosing the typeface. If you select the italic or oblique form of the typeface, you end up with that typeface. Figure 12.15 shows Century Schoolbook italicized. I love the look of this font in italic—it's very evocative of handwriting. Figure 12.16 shows a bold weight Bodoni typeface.

Come, gentle night, come, loving, black-brow'd night,
Give me my Romeo; and, when he shall die,
Take him and cut him out in little stars,
And he will make the face of heaven so fine
That all the world will be in love with night
And pay no worship to the garish sun.

FIGURE 12.15:   Century Schoolbook italicized.

Come, gentle night, come, loving, black-brow'd night,
Give me my Romeo; and, when he shall die,
Take him and cut him out in little stars,
And he will make the face of heaven so fine
That all the world will be in love with night
And pay no worship to the garish sun.

FIGURE 12.16:   Bold Bodoni.

Part II

Type Form and HTML

Standard HTML is more difficult when it comes to weight because you are dependent upon the user's library of fonts. If the user doesn't have the light, narrow, bold, demi-bold, or other weight you specify in the face attribute of the <font> tag, you're going to be out of luck. One thing you can do is stack the weight that you'd prefer with the typeface itself, and in some cases your font will be seen (see Figure 12.17).

```
<font face="arial narrow, arial, helvetica, sans-serif">
Love is a smoke raised with the fume of sighs;
Being purged, a fire sparkling in lovers' eyes;
Being vex'd a sea nourished with lovers' tears:
What is it else? a madness most discreet,
A choking gall and a preserving sweet.
</font>
```

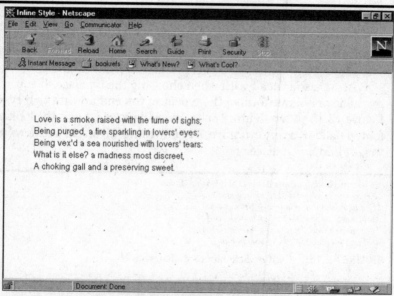

FIGURE 12.17:   Using the <font> tag to achieve Arial Narrow

Italics are easily created with the italic tag, <i>...</i>. Any text between opening and closing italic tags will appear in the italic version of that typeface, provided that the individual has the means of viewing the italic version.

```
<font face="arial narrow, arial, helvetica, sans-serif">
Love is a smoke raised with the fume of sighs;
```

```
Being purged, a fire sparkling in lovers' eyes;
Being vex'd a sea nourished with lovers' tears:
What is it else? a <i>madness</i> most discreet,
A choking gall and a preserving sweet.
</font>
```

Similarly, bold can be created with the bold tag, <b>...</b>.

```
<font face="arial narrow, arial, helvetica, sans-serif">
Love is a smoke raised with the fume of sighs;
Being purged, a fire sparkling in lovers' eyes;
Being vex'd a sea nourished with lovers' tears:
What is it else? a <b>madness</b> most discreet,
A choking gall and a preserving sweet.
</font>
```

Hopefully, Shakespeare will forgive me for forcing emphasis on Romeo's already impassioned speech!

There is no tag for oblique postures, but oblique text can be specified with the CSS font-style property (supported in IE 4 and above, Navigator 6 and above, Opera 3 and above, and IE 5 on the Mac).

NOTE

The use of HTML structural phrase elements such as <strong> and <em> is recommended over the use of presentational font style elements such as <b> and <i>. This is particularly important in aural web browsers.

Type Form and Style Sheets

As with font faces, font weights in style sheets rely on the existence of the corresponding font and weight on an individual's machine. A range of attributes is available in style sheets, including extra-light, demi-light, light, medium, extra-bold, demi-bold, and bold.

Be aware that before assigning font weights, the typeface to which you are applying the weight must have that weight available within the face. It is likely that many people will have the medium, light, or bold version of a typeface; it is much less likely that they will have extra-light or demi-bold—unless they have an extensive font collection on their computer.

A light weight is assigned to the Arial font in Figure 12.18 and a bold weight to the Walbaum font in Figure 12.19.

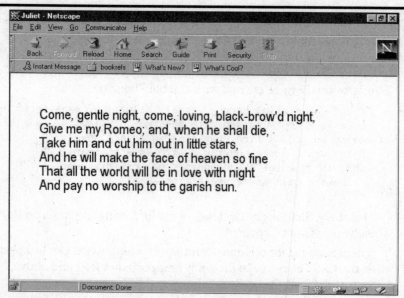

FIGURE 12.18:   Arial Narrow is achieved with style.

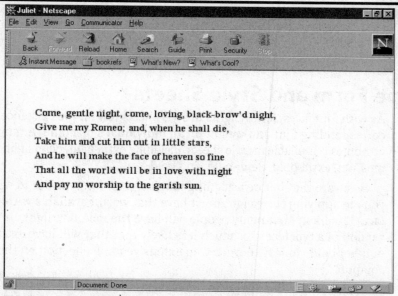

FIGURE 12.19:   Bold gives weight to Walbaum.

To achieve posture, you'll rely on three methods:

- ► The `font-style` attribute

- ► The `text-decoration` attribute

- ► Standard HTML with `bold`, `strong`, `italic`, or `em` tags

Italic can be achieved using the `font-style` attribute. The `font-style` attribute typically dictates the style of text, such as placing it in italic. The syntax to do so is this:

```
{ font-style: italic; }
```

TIP

Dislike underlined links? With Cascading Style Sheets, designers can now use the `{text-decoration: none}` attribute and argue to shut off underlined links globally. In embedded and linked style sheet formats, the syntax would follow the A value: A `{text-decoration: none}`. For inline style, simply place the value within the link you want to control: `<a style="text-decoration: none" href="my.html">this link has no underline!</a>`.

OTHER TYPOGRAPHIC CONSIDERATIONS

Other typographic considerations include size, proportion, leading, and kerning. Size and proportion can be addressed with HTML and Cascading Style Sheets. Leading and kerning are addressed somewhat by Cascading Style Sheets.

Using Graphics

Because you can address almost any kind of typographic issue by using Illustrator and Photoshop to set the type onto a graphic, graphics gives the most flexibility when you're dealing with typographic problems that cannot be dealt with using HTML or style sheets.

Size and proportion depend on your own design and aesthetics. Using points, you can set type as small or as large as you want. Leading (pronounced *ledding*) is addressed within the programs, as is letterspacing and kerning. In Photoshop 7, leading and kerning can be specified in the

Character palette of the Text tool, shown earlier in Figure 12.4. Photoshop 7 also includes options for paragraph formatting via the Paragraph palette of the Text tool (shown in Figure 12.20).

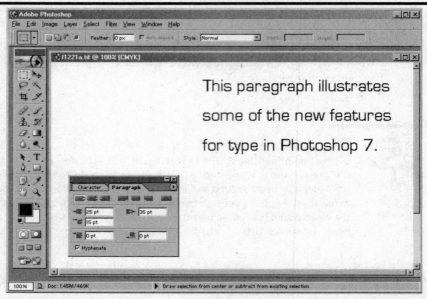

FIGURE 12.20:   Using the Paragraph palette of the Type tool in Photoshop 7

The options available include these:

- ▶ Left last right
- ▶ Justify all
- ▶ Indent left margin
- ▶ Indent right margin
- ▶ Indent first line
- ▶ Add space align text
- ▶ Center text
- ▶ Right align text

▶ Justify last left

▶ Justify last centered

▶ Justify before paragraph

▶ Add space after paragraph

Type Size and HTML

The size attribute of the <font> tag enables you to set type based on a numeric system. Unfortunately, this system does not allow a designer to control type size using points. Furthermore, direction, leading, spacing, and kerning cannot be controlled with standard HTML.

Using the *size* Attribute

Font sizing in HTML is pretty rudimentary, with whole-number values determining the size of the font. Default, standard size is 3; anything higher is going to be larger, and anything lower will be smaller. You can also use negative numbers, such as −1, to get a very small type size. Here's an example of a header using font face and size:

```
<font face="times,garamond,serif" size="5">
```

Anything much bigger than size 5 is ungainly. Small fonts, such as size 1, are good for notes and copyrights. Anything less usually is not viewable to people with average-to-poor eyesight.

Figure 12.21 shows an example with a header, body text, and a copyright notice, each in a different size font. Note the typefaces being used. The header and copyright notice appear in Times, and the body is in Arial. This page looks nice and neat, unlike Figure 12.22, which shows what happens when a coder runs amok. The "wave" effect came into vogue when font sizing first became available.

Some designers will argue that Figure 12.22 looks more interesting. They're right—it does, and I certainly don't want to discourage creativity. This particular effect was fun, but it quickly became cliché. I encourage you to study typography a little more closely and come up with original typographic applications.

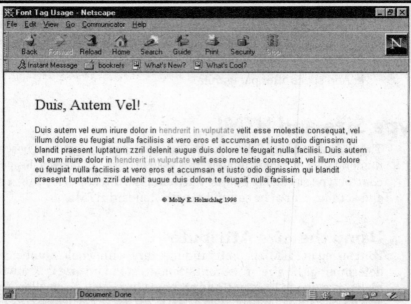

FIGURE 12.21:   Using the <font> tag for page design

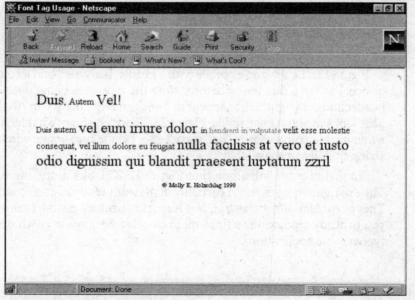

FIGURE 12.22:   The "wave" effect

Style Sheets

Style sheets to the rescue! Size (with choice of measurement units), leading, word spacing, and letterspacing can be applied using style sheets.

Size

Sizing in style sheets gives designers five size options for their fonts.

Points   To set a font in point size, use the abbreviation pt immediately following the numeric size:

```
{font-size: 12pt}
```

Inches   If you'd rather set your fonts in inches, simply place the abbreviation in next to the numeral size, in inches, of the font size you require:

```
{font-size: 1in}
```

Centimeters   Some designers might prefer centimeters, represented by cm and used in the same fashion as points and inches:

```
{font-size: 5cm}
```

Ems   You also can use a relative size measurement. One em is equal to 100% so, for example, if your default for the body text is a font size of 14 point, you can set a paragraph with font size of 1.5em, or 21 point in this case:

```
{font-size: 1.5em}
```

If the user has changed the default font size, any type size defined in ems will be scaled proportionally from the user's choice.

Pixels   Pixels are argued with the px abbreviation:

```
{font-size: 24px}
```

Percentage   You also may choose to set a percentage of the default point size:

```
{font-size: 50%}
```

NOTE

Relative units of measurements, such as ems or percentages, are preferred over absolute units of measurement, such as points and pixels. Using relative units allows text size to scale relative to the default font size or the user's choice of relative font size (View ➤ Text Size in IE or View ➤ Text Zoom in Netscape Navigator).

Leading

Leading is addressed in Cascading Style Sheets with `line-height`. This refers to the amount of spacing between lines of text. This space should be consistent, or the result is uneven, unattractive spacing. The `line-height` attribute enables designers to set the distance between the baselines, or bottoms, of lines of text.

To set the leading of a paragraph, use the `line-height` attribute in points, inches, centimeters, ems, pixels, or percentages in the same fashion you would when describing sizing attributes:

```
P { line-height: 14pt; }
```

Word Spacing and Letterspacing

Kerning is addressed in style sheets through the use of word spacing and letterspacing. Word spacing is used to change the amount of space between words, and letterspacing is used to change the amount of space between the letters in words. Both style properties accept either positive or negative values using absolute or relative measurement units.

To set the word spacing and letterspacing in a paragraph, use the `word-spacing` and `letter-spacing` attributes:

```
P {word-spacing: 0.5em;
   letter-spacing: 0.2em;}
```

COLOR AND TYPE

Color adds interest to type. You can use contrasting colors to gain a variety of effects. You can emphasize certain passages or parts of a word, as in Figure 12.23, or use colored type to separate headers from body text.

COLOR MY WORLD

FIGURE 12.23: Emphasizing type with color

Creating Colored Type with Graphics

Again, graphics are your best bet when you really want to address color effects.

A helpful tip is to select your colors from the safe palette and to be sure always to optimize your graphics appropriately. This will give you the best chance of having smaller file sizes and better matches between HTML and graphic colors.

HTML-Based Type and Color

The `color` attribute enables you to set any hexadecimal value you want when using the `<font>` tag. As always, stick to safe palette values. An example of the `<font>` tag with the `color` attribute added looks like this:

```
<font face="times,garamond,serif" size="5" color="#003300">
```

Use hexadecimal code to select a color; the one you see listed here is forest green. Some people and certain HTML editing programs will use the literal name of standard colors, such as blue, green, red, and the like. However, the hexadecimal codes are much more stable in cross-browser, cross-platform environments.

COLOR ONLINE

You can find hexadecimal color references at these websites:

▶ Nutrockers Web HTML Color Code Chart at `http://www` `.nutrocker.co.uk/colorchart.html` lets you preview colors and obtain the hexadecimal value as you roll over an extensive collection of color swatches.

▶ Download the `nvalue.gif` and `nhue.gif` charts from Lynda Weinman's site at `http://www.lynda.com/files/`.

These charts put color selection and hexadecimal values of the browser-safe color palette right at your fingertips.

Style Sheets and Color

Style sheets allow a great deal of flexibility in adding color. Using hexadecimal codes, RGB triplets, or 16 predefined color names, color can be added to actual attributes, including other HTML tags used in the inline style sheet method:

```
<p style="color: #ff00ff">
All of the text in this paragraph will appear in fuchsia.
</p>
<p style="color: rgb(255,0,255)">
All of the text in this paragraph will appear in fuchsia.
</p>
<p style="color: fuchsia">
All of the text in this paragraph will appear in fuchsia.
</p>
```

The text in each of these paragraphs will display in fuchsia.

With embedded and linked style sheets, you can add the `color` attribute to generalized, rather than specific, sections. In the following example, all level-two heads appear in red. Note that other attributes have been added here, including typeface, size, and style.

```
<style type="text/css">
H2 {font-family: arial, helvetica; sans-serif;
font-size: 14pt;
font-style: italic;
color: #FF0033;}
</style>
```

TIP

The color picker in newer versions (5.5 and above) of Photoshop displays the hexadecimal code for any color you select.

ALL TOGETHER NOW

So far, you've had a look at fragmented pieces of graphics, fonts, and styles. Here are full examples of an HTML page and a CSS page, in text and code.

HTML Example

This example demonstrates the use of the `font` tag and its attributes. I want you first to look at the page, which is shown in Figure 12.24.

Then determine all the different fonts (graphics and HTML included) on the page *just by looking*. Make a list of those fonts.

Now study the following code:

```
<!-- molly e. holzschlag: molly@molly.com -->
<!DOCTYPE html PUBLIC
"-//W3C//DTD XHTML 1.0 Transitional//EN"
   "http://www.w3.org/TR/xhtml1/DTD/xhtml1-transitional.dtd">
<html xmlns="http://www.w3.org/1999/xhtml">
<head>
   <title>molly e. holzschlag: poems and songs</title>
</head>
<body bgcolor="#000000" text="#000000" link="#993300"
   vlink="#993300" background="images/mol-bak.gif">
<table border="0" width="600" cellpadding="5"
 cellspacing="0">
 <tr bgcolor="#cc9966">
```

```
<td valign="top" width="400" bgcolor="#ffffff">
 <img src="images/pm-hed.gif" alt="poetry" width="300"
   height="50" align="right" />
 <br clear="all" />
 <font face="arial,helvetica,sans-serif">
   <h3>Recent Events</h3>
```

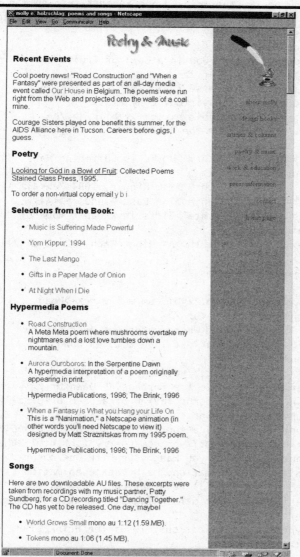

FIGURE 12.24: A Poetry and Music page from molly.com

```
<p>Cool poetry news! "Road Construction" and "When a
Fantasy" were presented as part of an all-day media
event called <a href="http://www.ourhouse.be/">Our
House</a> in Belgium. The poems were run right from
the web and projected onto the walls of a coal
mine.</p>
<p>Courage Sisters played one benefit this summer,
for the AIDS Alliance here in Tucson. Careers before
gigs, I guess.</p>
<h3>Poetry</h3>
<p><u>Looking for God in a Bowl of Fruit</u>:
Collected Poems<br />
Stained Glass Press, 1995.</p>
<p>To order a non-virtual copy email
<a href="mailto:ybi@ybi.com">y b i</a></p>
<h3>Selections from the Book:</h3>
<ul>
<li><a href="p-1.htm">Music is Suffering Made
Powerful</a></li>
<li><a href="p-2.htm">Yom Kippur, 1994</a></li>
<li><a href="p-3.htm">The Last Mango</a></li>
<li><a href="p-4.htm">Gifts in a Paper Made of
Onion</a></li>
<li><a href="p-5.htm">At Night When I Die</a></li>
</ul>
<h3>Hypermedia Poems</h3>
<ul>
<li><a href="http://ybi.com/molly/rc/">Road
Construction</a><br />
A Meta Meta poem where mushrooms overtake my
nightmares and a lost love tumbles down a
mountain.</li>
<li><a href="http://ybi.com/aurora/">Aurora
Ouroboros</a>: In the Serpentine Dawn<br />
A hypermedia interpretation of a poem originally
appearing in print.<br /><br />
Hypermedia Publications, 1996; The Brink, 1996</li>
<li><a href="http://ybi.com/poetry/fant.html">When a
Fantasy is What you Hang your Life On</a><br />
This is a "Nanimation," a Netscape animation (in
other words you'll need Netscape to view it)
designed by Matt Straznitskas from my 1995 poem.
<br /><br />
Hypermedia Publications, 1996; The Brink, 1996</li>
</ul>
<h3>Songs</h3>
```

```
    <p>Here are two downloadable AU files. These excerpts
    were taken from recordings with my music partner,
    Patty Sundberg, for a CD recording titled "Dancing
    Together." The CD has yet to be released. One day,
    maybe!</p>
    <ul>
      <li><a href="images/wrldgrow.au">World Grows
      Small</a> mono au 1:12 (1.59 MB).</li>
      <li><a href="images/tokens.au">Tokens</a> mono au
      1:06 (1.45 MB).</li>
    </ul>
  </font>
</td>
<td valign="top" align="right" width="200">
  <img src="images/poetry.gif" width="108" height="125"
    border="0" alt="pen and ink" />
  <p><a href="molly.htm">about molly</a></p>
  <p><a href="books.htm">design books</a></p>
  <p><a href="write.htm">articles & columns</a></p>
  <p><a href="poems.htm">poetry & music</a></p>
  <p><a href="work.htm">work & education</a></p>
  <p><a href="press.htm">press information</a></p>
  <p><a href="contact.htm">contact</a></p>
  <p><a href="index.html">home page</a></p>
</td>
</tr>
</table>
</body>
</html>
```

If you guessed three for the total number of fonts used on this page, you're correct. First there's the header graphic, which uses the Bergell typeface. Then there's the body text, which will appear as Arial, Helvetica, or whatever sans-serif font you have available if those are not.

Finally, there's the type I've used in the right margin menu. Sharp readers will have noticed that *there is no font tag or attribute* used to create this font. Why?

Think about it for a second.

Can you identify the typeface?

It's a serif.

Specifically, it's Times.

Remember now? Serif is the *default* font. Therefore, I didn't have to code for it.

AN OFFLINE EXERCISE

Have some fun with this code! Change type using the <font> tag as often as you like, trying out different combinations, colors, sizes, and styles.

Style Sheet Example

Here, typeface, form, leading, and color have been assigned to the page using style sheets.

```
<!DOCTYPE html PUBLIC
"-//W3C//DTD XHTML 1.0 Transitional//EN"
   "http://www.w3.org/TR/xhtml1/DTD/xhtml1-transitional.dtd">
<html xmlns="http://www.w3.org/1999/xhtml">
<head>
<title>Style Sheet Example</title>

<style type="text/css">

body { background: #000000; }

h1 { font-family: arial, helvetica, san-serif ;
font-size: 22pt;
color: #FFFF00; }

p { font-family: times, serif;
font-size: 18pt;
color: #FFFFFF;
line-height: 18pt; }

a { text-decoration: none;
font-weight: bold;
color: #CCFFCC; }

</style>

</head>

<body>

<blockquote>

<h1>Juliet Thinks of Romeo</h1>
```

```
<p>
Come, gentle night, come, loving, black-brow'd night,<br />
Give me my <a href="romeo.htm">Romeo</a>; and, when he shall
    die,<br />
Take him and cut him out in little stars,<br />
And he will make the face of heaven so fine<br />
That all the world will be in love with night<br />
And pay no worship to the garish sun.
</p>

</blockquote>

</body>
</html>
```

Figure 12.25 shows the result.

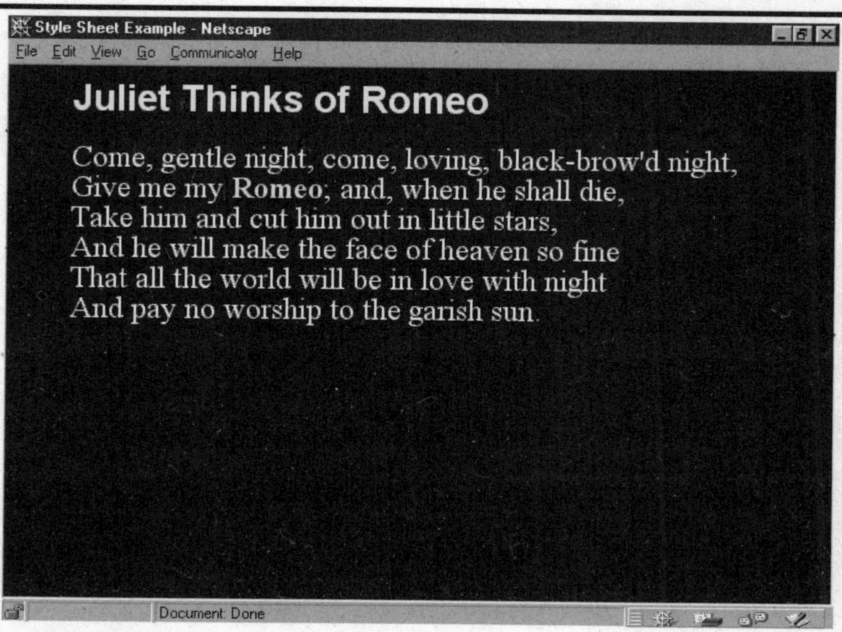

FIGURE 12.25:   Style applied to a page

Obviously, these examples are just the tip of the iceberg in the use of style sheets. Many options and more powerful applications are available, and I highly recommend that you study more about style sheets as you learn more about typography. They will no doubt be a major player in how type on the web is delivered with increasing sophistication.

What's Next?

The typographic tips you've learned in this chapter will take you a long way toward creating an eye-catching web page. Along the way, you were introduced to the use of style sheets, a topic covered in detail in Chapter 16. In the next part of this book, you'll learn how to optimize your pages for the two most popular browsers being used today, and you'll learn other advanced features, including adding multimedia, creating forms, and using dynamic HTML.

Part III

ADVANCED HTML

Chapter 13

OPTIMIZING YOUR WEB PAGES FOR INTERNET EXPLORER

In Chapter 6, "Planning for a Usable, Maintainable Website," you learned about site planning and site maintenance. Another important step in the site planning process is to evaluate your audience and the browsers your audience is most likely to use to view your web pages. This gives you valuable information for making decisions about which features you should include in your pages for the best viewing experience by your target audience.

In this chapter, you'll learn the major features of Internet Explorer 6, the latest version of IE, including its support for technologies, plug-ins, and a variety of scripting, markup, and programming languages. In the next chapter (Chapter 14, "Optimizing Your Web Pages for Netscape Navigator"), you'll learn about Netscape Navigator 6 and 7.

Part III

Written for *HTML Complete*, Third Edition, by Lucinda Dykes

DEFINING THE TARGET AUDIENCE

Browser compatibility continues to be a major problem for web designers and developers, although there has been some improvement with the latest versions of the two most popular browsers, Internet Explorer and Netscape Navigator. Learning the features of the major browsers will help you to design pages that work well when viewed in either browser and save you from having to create a different version of your pages for each browser.

Unless you are designing pages for a very specific audience—an office intranet where everyone is using computers with the same operating system and the same browsers, for example—you need to consider browser compatibility as you design and create pages.

The vast majority of your audience is most likely to be using a computer with the Windows operating system. As of October 2002, according to statistics from TheCounter.com (www.thecounter.com), Windows users comprise about 97 percent of the web audience, Mac users comprise 2 percent, and the remaining 1 percent includes all other platforms combined.

Internet Explorer 5 and 6 currently are the most popular browsers, and the number of Internet Explorer 6 users continues to increase steadily. Overall, as of October 2002, global statistics at TheCounter.com showed that 46 percent of the web audience use Internet Explorer 5, 45 percent use Internet Explorer 6, and the remaining 9 percent use other browsers, including Netscape Navigator, Opera, and Mozilla.

WARNING

Internet Explorer 6 currently is available only for PCs. The latest versions of Internet Explorer for the Mac include version 5.1.6 for Mac OS 8.1 and 9.*x* and version 5.2.2 for Mac OS X.

A recent report from StatMarket (www.statmarket.com) shows that Internet Explorer 6 and Windows XP are the most popular browser–operating system combination on the web. This combination currently is used by about 20 percent of the global web audience.

Keeping these statistics in mind, look at your target audience. Which browsers are they likely to use? Do your pages include JavaScript or CSS (Chapter 16, "Using Style Sheets")? Do your pages include multimedia files (Chapter 15, "Including Multimedia") such as Flash animations, QuickTime movies, or streaming audio? Do your pages include special features that require the latest browsers, such as XML (Chapter 20, "Introduction to XML," and Chapter 21, "Fundamentals of XML") or CSS absolute positioning? Can your pages be viewed by users with disabilities (Chapter 6)? You should review all these issues at the beginning of the site design process and evaluate them again during the testing process.

WEB STANDARDS

As you learned in Chapter 2, "Getting Acquainted with HTML and XHTML," the World Wide Web Consortium (W3C) develops and issues detailed specifications outlining the vocabulary and syntax of HTML and other languages and technologies. Browser support for these specifications, however, has always been incomplete and varies both among the browsers and among different versions of the same browser. Browser differences have included not only proprietary HTML tags that are not part of any specification (for example, Netscape's infamous blink tag or Internet Explorer's marquee tag) but also varying support for features such as Cascading Style Sheets, JavaScript, and other web languages and technologies.

Web designers and developers often have been compelled to create multiple versions of web pages so that their websites could be viewed in more than one browser. As web technologies continued to develop, it became more and more frustrating to design pages that either used only the simplest web technologies in order to function well and be viewable in all browsers or used the new technologies but at the cost of decreased accessibility. The differences between Netscape and Internet Explorer were greatest with the release of the level 4 browsers in 1997, but cross-browser compatibility has improved since that time due to increased attention to compliance with web standards in newer browser versions.

The recommendations issued by the W3C are known as *web standards*. Through the work of many individuals and with the help of organizations such as the Web Standards Project (www.webstandards.org), both the web community and the browser developers have begun to address the problems of browser incompatibility and incomplete support for web standards. Although no browser currently offers complete support of

Part III

web standards, the latest browsers (Internet Explorer 6 and Netscape 6 and 7) support the W3C specifications for HTML 4.01, XHTML 1.0, XML 1.0, ECMAScript 262 (the standard version of JavaScript), Cascading Style Sheets level 1 (CSS1), and most (but not all!) features of Cascading Style Sheets level 2 (CSS2).

The browser manufacturers are not the only ones that need to address the issue of compliance with current web standards. Web designers and developers also must learn to design and create web pages that comply with web standards. This is not only economical; it also ensures that pages created today will continue to be accessible in the browsers of tomorrow.

To learn more about web standards:

- ▶ Visit the Web Standards Project at www.webstandards.org.
- ▶ Check out the specifications themselves on the W3C site at www.w3.org.
- ▶ See the article by Paul Boutin, "Web Standards for Hard Times," at http://hotwired.lycos.com/webmonkey/02/33/index1a.html.

SUPPORT FOR WEB STANDARDS IN INTERNET EXPLORER 6

According to the Web Standards Project (www.webstandards.org/about/), current web standards include four different standards categories.

Structural Languages: HTML 4.01, XHTML 1.0, XHTML 1.1, and XML 1.0

Internet Explorer (IE) 6 supports HTML 4.01 and XHTML 1.0 and offers some support for XHTML 1.1. IE 6 offers the most support for XML 1.0 of any current browser. For example, if an XML document is well formed (in other words, follows the syntax rules of XML), the XML markup will appear in Internet Explorer 6. It is easy to see the overall XML document structure from this display, as shown in Figure 13.1. Netscape Navigator and Opera, on the other hand, show the content contained in the XML markup but do not display document structure. As you can see in Figure 13.2, the XML content is displayed as one line of text in Netscape 7.

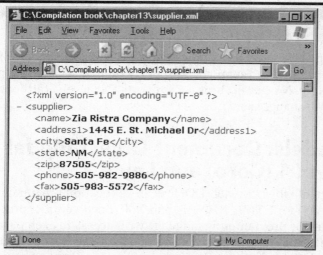

FIGURE 13.1:   supplier.xml displayed in Internet Explorer 6

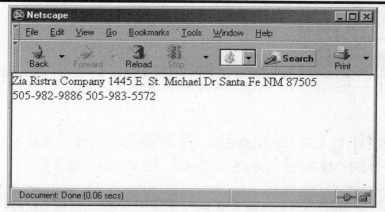

FIGURE 13.2:   supplier.xml displayed in Netscape Navigator 7

Part III

TIP

Both CSS and XSLT (Extensible Style Language Transformations) style sheets can be used to display XML content as HTML and XHTML pages.

Presentation Languages: Cascading Style Sheets (CSS) Levels 1, 2, and 3

Internet Explorer 6 offers complete support for the Cascading Style Sheets level 1 specification and supports most of CSS level 2, including support for positioning. No current browser supports CSS level 3 (although we hope that will change soon!).

Object Models: Document Object Model (DOM) Level 1 (Core) and Level 2

The Document Object Model (DOM) is an application programming interface (API) for HTML, XHTML, and XML documents. It provides any scripting or programming language with access to each part of a document (as long as you use the methods and properties of the Recommendation). Internet Explorer 6 offers complete support for the W3C Document Object Model level 1 (Core) and also supports some features of the Level 2 DOM, including the methods getElementById and getElementsByTagName.

NOTE
To learn more about the DOM and scripting for browsers, see Chapter 18, "Bringing Pages to Life with Dynamic HTML and XHTML."

Scripting Languages: ECMAScript 262 (the Standard Version of JavaScript)

Netscape's JavaScript and Internet Explorer's JScript combined to form the ECMA-262 standard. The third and latest edition of ECMA-262 is supported by Internet Explorer 6, as well as all level 6 browsers and above.

Internet Explorer 6 supports web standards to a greater degree than any previous Internet Explorer release, but support for web standards is not 100 percent in any current browser.

In summary, Internet Explorer 6 supports most web standards and offers strong support for CSS and XML.

USING *DOCTYPE* DECLARATIONS

As you learned in Chapter 3, "Creating Your First HTML or XHTML Document," a DOCTYPE declaration tells the browser which version of HTML or XHTML a document complies with. A DOCTYPE declaration includes a document type definition (DTD) attribute value. This DTD specifies both the elements and attributes that can be used in the document, as well as the rules for the structure of the document. For example, the following DOCTYPE declaration tells the browser that this page complies with the XHTML 1.0 strict DTD:

```
<!DOCTYPE html PUBLIC "-//W3C//DTD XHTML 1.0 Strict//EN"
    "http://www.w3.org/TR/xhtml1/DTD/xhtml1-strict.dtd">
```

This DOCTYPE specifies that the document has a root element of html, uses the elements and attributes of XHTML 1.0, does not include presentational markup (strict), and is in the English language.

TIP

See Chapter 3 for more information about using DOCTYPE declarations in HTML and XHTML documents.

The DTDs are included in the W3C specifications and can be viewed at the W3C site (www.w3.org). Although a DOCTYPE declaration is not required for an HTML or XHTML page to be displayed in a browser, the newer browsers (6 and above) use the DOCTYPE declaration to make decisions about how the page should be displayed.

In Internet Explorer 6, if no DOCTYPE declaration is included, the page will be displayed in what is called "backward-compatibility" or "quirks" mode, which means that the page will be displayed in the same way as it would in earlier versions of Internet Explorer (before version 6). If a DOCTYPE declaration is included, Internet Explorer 6 will do its best to display the page according to the rules of the specified DTD.

NOTE

Browsers that use DOCTYPE to determine how a page is displayed include Internet Explorer 6 and above on Windows, Internet Explorer 5 and above on Macs, and all Mozilla-based browsers, including Netscape 6 and above.

WHAT'S NEW IN INTERNET EXPLORER 6

Internet Explorer 6 was released in August 2001. It includes several new features both for viewers and for web designers and developers. Important new features are discussed in the following sections.

WARNING

Internet Explorer 6 will not work in Windows 95 or earlier versions of the Windows operating system.

The Image Toolbar

The image toolbar is new in Internet Explorer 6. This toolbar appears whenever a viewer moves the mouse across an image on a web page. (The image size must be at least 200 pixels in height and width for the image bar to appear.) It includes four functions that enable the user to save, print, email an image, or open the My Pictures folder easily. These four functions are displayed visually as four icons on a toolbar, as shown in Figure 13.3.

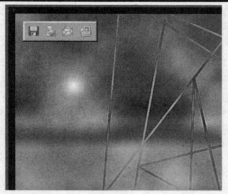

FIGURE 13.3:   The image toolbar in Internet Explorer 6

The image toolbar can be distracting to the visual presentation of a page because it appears whenever the viewer moves the mouse over any image on the page. Although it makes it easier for a viewer to access those four functions, all of the functions can be accessed as usual by right-clicking on the image and using the context menu.

To disable the image toolbar in pages you create, insert the following line of code in the head section of your documents:

```
<meta http-equiv="imagetoolbar" content="no" />
```

To disable the image toolbar for a specific image, add the `galleryimg` attribute to the `img` element, as in the following:

```
<img src="cat.gif" alt="tabby cat" height="250" width="250"
galleryimg="no" />
```

To disable or enable display of the image toolbar in your browser, choose Tools ➢ Internet Options from the Internet Explorer menu bar, and then click on the Advanced tab and check (enable) or uncheck (disable) the Enable Image Toolbar option in the Multimedia section, as shown in Figure 13.4.

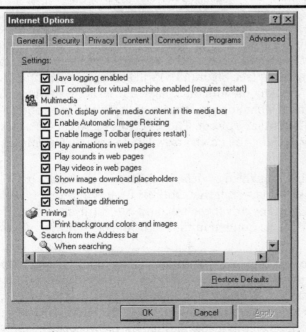

FIGURE 13.4: Disabling the image toolbar in Internet Explorer 6

TIP

For more information on configuring the new features of Internet Explorer 6, see "Customizing New Browser Features" at www.microsoft.com/windows/ie/using/howto/default.asp.

The Media Bar

The media bar enables the viewer to locate and play media files within the browser window itself rather than in a separate media player window. It includes an HTML content area and a media player control that enables the viewer to play music, video, or mixed-media files in the browser window. This can be advantageous if your page includes multimedia content that is viewable in the Windows Media Player and you want the viewer to see the multimedia files in the browser window.

TIP

To learn more about including multimedia in your web pages, see Chapter 15.

The media bar settings can be accessed by clicking the Media icon on the Internet Explorer 6 toolbar or by choosing View ➢ Explorer Bar ➢ Media. The media bar (see Figure 13.5) will also appear the first time a user clicks on a media file link on a page in Internet Explorer 6. The first time the media bar appears, the user is offered the option to play media files in Internet Explorer. Those settings also can be accessed at any time by clicking the down arrow labeled Media Options in the media bar.

The media bar is enabled by default. To disable the media bar in your browser, choose Tools ➢ Internet Options from the Internet Explorer menu bar, click on the Advanced tab, and check (disable) the Don't Display Online Media Content in the Media Bar, as shown previously in Figure 13.4.

You can use scripting to access the mediaBar object and its properties to control the playback, display, and HTML content of the media bar. You also can format links to media files that specify that the files won't play in the browser window, regardless of the user's media preference settings. When the user clicks on this media file link, the file will open in a separate

Windows Media Player window or other appropriate application for the media file type. To ensure that a media file opens in a separate window, include `target="_blank"` in the link, as shown in the following code:

```
<a href="myMusic.wav" target="_blank">My Music</a>
```

FIGURE 13.5:   The media bar in Internet Explorer 6

NOTE

To learn more about scripting for the media bar, see "Using the Media Bar in Internet Explorer" at http://msdn.microsoft.com/library/default.asp?url=/nhp/default.asp?contentid=28000441.

Expanded Privacy Features

Internet Explorer 6 includes enhanced privacy features based on the Platform for Privacy Preferences (P3P) Recommendation of the W3C. The specification became a full W3C Recommendation in April 2002 (after the release of Internet Explorer 6) but was available as a proposed Recommendation at the time Internet Explorer 6 was developed. P3P is a web privacy standard that specifies preferences and guidelines for the use of *cookies* (small text files that websites store on your computer so that they can identify you when you visit the site again).

Internet Explorer 6 allows the user to set preferences for cookies. It includes six levels of preferences, including Accept All Cookies, Reject All Cookies, and four choices in between. The browser monitors all incoming cookie traffic based on the user's chosen privacy level. To access the privacy settings, choose Tools ≻ Internet Options from the Internet Explorer menu bar and then click on the Privacy tab. Figure 13.6 shows details of the Medium High privacy setting. As you can see at the bottom of the figure, the user also can choose to override the chosen setting for individual websites.

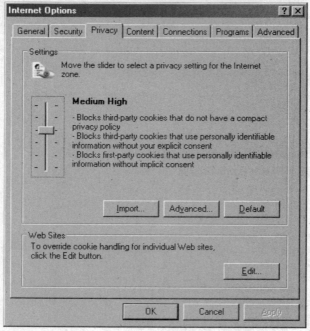

FIGURE 13.6:   Privacy settings in Internet Explorer 6

How does this affect you as the web developer? Websites that distribute cookies and want to be displayed in Internet Explorer 6 need to create a privacy profile and save it as an XML file named p3p.xml that resides in the root directory of the site. When an Internet Explorer 6 user visits the site, the browser reads the p3p.xml file for that site and compares it to the user's chosen privacy preferences. The browser then allows the cookie to be served if the site's privacy profile is compatible with the user's privacy preferences or alerts the user if it is not compatible.

NOTE
For additional information on creating privacy profiles for your websites, see the W3C's "Resources for P3P Implementation" at www.w3.org/P3P/develop.html and the P3P 1.0 specification at www.w3.org/TR/P3P/.

Internet Explorer 6 has deleted some major features from previous versions. Internet Explorer 6 does not support the use of Netscape-style plug-ins and instead supports only the use of ActiveX controls. The main plug-in affected by this decision is the Apple QuickTime plug-in. Apple has provided an ActiveX control for QuickTime that can be downloaded at www.apple.com/quicktime/download/qtcheck/.

Internet Explorer 6 also no longer includes the Java Virtual Machine, so if you want to view some of the million web pages that use Java applets, you will need to install the Java Virtual Machine. If you upgraded to Internet Explorer 6 from a previous version, the Java Virtual Machine will still be available. Otherwise, you can download it at http://java.sun.com/getjava/download.html.

OPTIMIZATIONS FOR INTERNET EXPLORER 6

When we talk about optimization, we are talking about two different things:

- Adding functionality (through elements, attributes, and properties) not present in other browsers.

- Making sure that the code you write is clean and clear and takes the minimum time to load into the browser.

Adding Functionality

This is the most exciting aspect of optimization, so this is where we'll begin. Adding functionality to a web page isn't as complicated as it sounds. You don't need to write pages of HTML or learn complicated scripting languages. Adding functionality generally means only making small adjustments or "tweaks" to the HTML or XHTML and letting the browser do the rest.

Let's begin by looking at how to optimize the layout of the page.

Page Layout

Figure 13.7 shows a web page in Internet Explorer 6 containing a couple of paragraphs of text. Notice the margins around the page. These are set to the default of the browser.

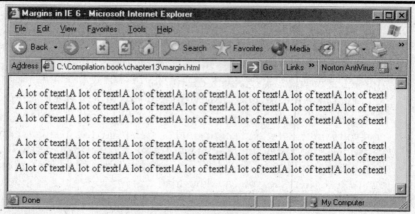

FIGURE 13.7: A web page in IE 6 with default margins

However, you can easily change the margins of the page to any number of pixels you want by using the topmargin and leftmargin attributes of the body element.

```
<body topmargin="0" leftmargin="0">
```

The result is shown in Figure 13.8.

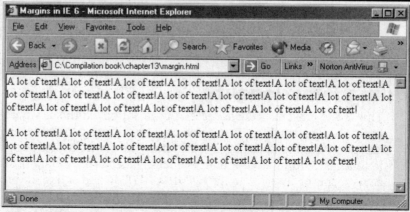

FIGURE 13.8: The same page in IE 6 with top and left margins set to zero

If you wanted to set a large margin at both the top and left side of the page, you would set them as follows:

```
<body topmargin="50" leftmargin="50">
```

The values for topmargin and leftmargin must be positive integers. This means that negative values are invalid, and the browser will revert to the default page margins.

TIP

Neither Netscape Navigator nor Opera supports the use of the topmargin or leftmargin attribute of the body element and will display the page with default margin settings if those attributes are used. Both topmargin and leftmargin are proprietary Internet Explorer attributes that continue to be supported in Internet Explorer 6.

TIP

If your page is created in frames (see Chapter 8, "Dividing a Window with Frames"), you can use marginheight="0" and marginwidth="0". These are valid HTML 4.01 attributes for the frame and iframe elements. If you are using CSS (Chapter 16), you can use body {margin: 0;}.

Making Hyperlinks Hover

Once upon a time, that blue underlined text of a hyperlink was unmistakable. Nowadays, with so much color and excitement on Web pages, hyperlinks can blend too easily into the background. When you want them to stand out, one of the best ways is to use color...but not a single color! It's far better to make them change color as the visitor moves the mouse pointer over them.

The great thing about this is that it is easy to do, and you need to code it only once on the page for all hyperlinks on that page to behave in the same way.

To perform this magic, you'll use a web technology called *Cascading Style Sheets* (CSS). Internet Explorer 6 supports the hover pseudo-class from the CSS level 2 specification, which is the link pseudo-class we'll explore in this section.

NOTE

Cascading Style Sheets are covered in greater depth in Chapter 16.

Part III

Let's start with a web page that has three hyperlinks. The code is shown in Listing 13.1, and the page is shown in Figure 13.9.

Listing 13.1: A Web Page with Three Hyperlinks

```
<!DOCTYPE html PUBLIC
  "-//W3C//DTD XHTML 1.0 Transitional//EN"
   "http://www.w3.org/TR/xhtml1/DTD/xhtml1-transitional.dtd">
<html xmlns="http://www.w3.org/1999/xhtml">
<head>
<title>Links</title>
<meta http-equiv="Content-Type"
 content="text/html; charset=iso-8859-1" />
</head>
<body>
<h1>Links, links, links!</h1>
A link to <a href="mypage.htm">Me</a>!
<br />
A link to <a href="friends.htm">my friends</a>!
<br />
A link to <a href="pets.htm">my pets</a>!
</body>
</html>
```

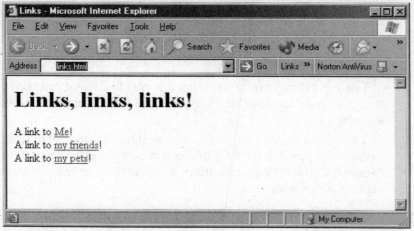

FIGURE 13.9:   A web page with three hyperlinks in Internet Explorer 6

It's quite easy to make these hyperlinks much more visually appealing. Let's look at the steps:

1. First, add a style block to the head element on the web page. This is where the Cascading Style Sheet information will go and consists of the `<style>` opening and closing tags.

```
<title>Links</title>
<style type="text/css">

</style>
</head>
```

2. Next, add XHTML comment tags inside the style block that you just created. These comment tags are put there in case someone visits the page with an older browser that isn't capable of understanding the Cascading Style Sheet information you will add. With comment tags in place, older browsers will simply ignore anything between the `<style>` tags. Without the comment tags, those browsers may throw out error messages or display the page incorrectly.

TIP

It is a good idea to always add the comment tags, even if you *know* that the browser your visitor is using can understand CSS.

```
<title>Links</title>
<style type="text/css">
<!--

-->
</style>
</head>
```

3. Now you can add the Cascading Style Sheet information to the page. The amazing thing is that it consists of just one line!

```
<title>Links</title>
<style type="text/css">
<!--
a:hover { color: red }
-->
</style>
</head>
```

4. Save the web page and view it in Internet Explorer 6. Move the mouse pointer over the hyperlinks, and watch them change color. The hyperlinks should turn red, according to the code above. As the mouse pointer moves off them, they automatically change back to the original color.

5. If you don't like red, you can choose another color.

```
<title>Links</title>
<style type="text/css">
<!--
a:hover { color: teal }
-->
</style>
</head>
```

Once you are more familiar with other CSS properties, you can do a lot more with hyperlinks, such as making them bold or applying an overhead line when the mouse pointer is moved over them.

NOTE
Netscape added support for the CSS level 2 a : hover pseudo-class in Netscape 6.

Adding a Favorites Icon

This feature, first introduced in IE 5, enables you to add an icon to your web pages. The icon will be saved along with the page title when an Internet Explorer user adds your page to his Favorites menu, and the icon also will be displayed in the browser address bar when the page is viewed.

For more information about using this feature, see http://msdn .microsoft.com/library/default.asp?url=/workshop/author/ dhtml/howto/shortcuticon.asp.

Writing Clean Code

In this chapter, you've learned about web standards and about Internet Explorer 6's support for web standards. As a web designer or web developer, how can you be sure that the pages you create support web standards? The easiest way is to validate your pages.

Validating your pages simply means making sure that your pages follow the rules of the language you are using to create them, whether that language is HTML or XHTML.

The W3C offers free validation services for HTML and XHTML and for CSS. Let's test the document from the previous section in the W3C XHTML validator at `http://validator.w3.org/`. The heading on the page says "W3C HTML Validation Service," but it now can validate XHTML documents as well as HTML documents. If your page is available on the web, you can enter the URL and click the button labeled Validate This Page. If your page is not yet available online, you can upload the file from your computer to the validator at `http://validator.w3.org/file-upload.html`.

Let's use the code from Listing 13.1 and see if our page validates as XHTML:

1. Type the code in a text editor such as Notepad or SimpleText and save the file as `pseudoclass.html`. This file includes an XHTML 1.0 Transitional `DOCTYPE` declaration, so it will be validated as an XHTML 1.0 Transitional document.

2. Browse to the `pseudoclass.html` file on your computer.

3. Check the box for Show Source Input. This option shows the source code for your document as part of the validation result. It can be very useful to have the source code at hand when you are evaluating any error messages from the validator. You don't need to specify a Document Type because you have included a `DOCTYPE` declaration in the document.

4. Click the button labeled Validate This Document.

Figure 13.10 shows the validation result. The source code (not seen in the figure) is listed below the results. If we choose, we now can include the W3C graphic that indicates that this page has been tested and validates as XHTML 1.0.

Of course, we knew that our code was valid, so let's test our file after we insert an error. Since we are using XHTML, we used the format <br /> for the line break element. Change one of the <br /> tags to <br>, save the file, and revalidate it. Figure 13.11 shows the result. This time, the validator has pointed out the invalid form of the <br> tag for an XHTML document.

As you can see, using a validator is a free and easy way to test your pages for compliance with web standards, and it is also a great way to learn web standards.

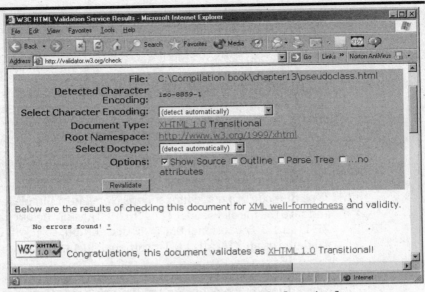

FIGURE 13.10: Using the W3C validator for `pseudoclass.html`

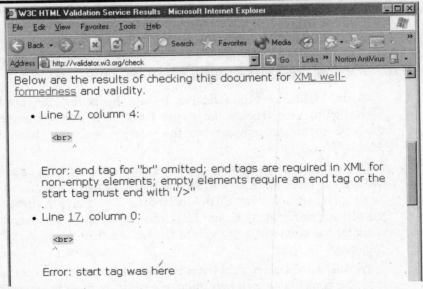

FIGURE 13.11: Validator results point out an error in the document.

The Web Design Group also offers a free validation service for HTML and XHTML documents at www.htmlhelp.com/tools/validator/. The site also includes many support documents for using the validator. The error message text generated by the Web Design Group validator generally is much more helpful than the sometimes cryptic error messages generated by the W3C validator.

IMPLEMENTING BROWSER DETECTION

With improved compliance with web standards in the new browsers, directing users to a specific version of a page should be a rare event! However, Internet Explorer and Netscape Navigator, although certainly more alike than in the past, still differ. Even if your pages are compliant with web standards, those standards may not yet be supported in both Internet Explorer and Netscape Navigator. Making separate versions of site pages is costly, but occasionally it still is necessary. If you have had to create separate versions of web pages for different browsers, consider implementing JavaScript to detect which browser your users are using. Remember, if users are not using the browser for which the documents were developed, they'll get error messages.

Browser detection in the past generally was a simple matter of determining whether users were using Netscape Navigator or Internet Explorer, using two simple JavaScript methods and properties:

▶ navigator.appName to determine the browser name

▶ navigator.appVersion to determine the browser version

This worked well for both Netscape Navigator and Internet Explorer version 4.*x* or lower and enabled site developers to redirect users to an appropriate page with the appropriate JavaScript for the version of the browsers that they were using and the DOM that the version implemented. With the introduction of newer versions of Internet Explorer (6) and Netscape Navigator (6 and 7), other browsers such as Opera, and the multitude of possible operating systems, browser detection became much more complex.

Current browser detection usually makes use of the userAgent string. The HTTP 1.1 specification uses a header called userAgent. This header identifies the client to the server and includes information about the operating system, the browser name, and the browser version. If you use the

Part III

following simple script, you can find out the userAgent string returned by your current browser:

```
<script type="text/javascript" language="javascript">
    var agent = navigator.userAgent;
    document.write ("userAgent string: " + agent);
</script>
```

Here are a few examples of the userAgent string returned by this script:

```
userAgent string: Mozilla/4.75 [en] (Win98; U)
userAgent string: Mozilla/3.0 (compatible; Opera/3.0;
    Windows 95/NT4)
userAgent string: Opera/6.05 (Windows XP; U) [en]
userAgent string: Mozilla/5.0 (Windows; U; Win98; en-US;
    CDonDemand) Gecko/20010131 Netscape6/6.01)
userAgent string: Mozilla/4.0 (compatible; MSIE 6.0;
    Windows NT 5.1)
```

The first string is returned from a computer running Netscape 4.75 on the Windows 98 platform, the second from Opera 3.0 on Windows 95, the third from Opera 6.05 on Windows XP, the fourth from Netscape 6 on Windows 98, and the last from Internet Explorer 6 on Windows XP (note that the value returned for Windows XP is Windows NT5.1). You can see how browser detection has become much more complex!

It's beyond the scope of this chapter to go into the details of pulling out the needed pieces of information from the userAgent string, but for more information on how browser detection works, see the Browser Detection tutorial by Richard Blaylock at http://hotwired.lycos.com/webmonkey/99/02/index2a.html?tw=authoring.

If you choose to use browser detection, how can you do so? How do you sort out Internet Explorer 6 users from those using Netscape Navigator 7? A few years ago, developers placed links on their web pages that said something such as, "If you are viewing with Internet Explorer, CLICK HERE...". This had many drawbacks, one of the biggest being that many of the users themselves didn't know which browser they were using. Of those who did, not many understood the relevance of choosing the correct link.

The best solution is one that removes the responsibility from the visitors and does the sorting out in the background, while they are waiting for the page to load. In order to do this, you need to insert some code into your web pages that will find out which browser the visitor is using and, if it is a different browser from the one you are expecting, redirect the user to the appropriate web page suited to his browser.

The code that you will use, called a *script*, is written in a scripting language called JavaScript. If you're now beginning to worry because you haven't used a script before, don't. The great thing about this script is that you don't need to know how it works. You just need to add it to the web page and watch it work.

WARNING

According to November 2002 statistics at www.thecounter.com, 10 percent of web users have JavaScript turned off in their browsers.

Adding the Script

Let's start off with an empty XHTML page and look at how to add the script to it. Here's the script for the empty page:

```
<!DOCTYPE html PUBLIC
"-//W3C//DTD XHTML 1.0 Transitional//EN"
    "http://www.w3.org/TR/xhtml1/DTD/xhtml1-transitional.dtd">
<html xmlns="http://www.w3.org/1999/xhtml">
<head>
<title>Browser Detection</title>
</head>
<body>
</body>
</html>
```

The JavaScript we are going to add will be inserted inside the <head> tag, after the <title> tag. The script is as follows:

```
<script type="text/javascript" language="JavaScript">
<!--
var browser = "unknown"
var version = 0
var detected = false
var ua = window.navigator.userAgent

if (ua.substring(0,7) == "Mozilla") {
    if (ua.indexOf("MSIE") > 0) {
        browser = "Microsoft"
    }
```

```
   if (ua.indexOf("6.") > 0) {
      version = 6
   }
}

//Find Internet Explorer 6 users and do nothing
if (browser == "Microsoft" && version == 56) {
   detected = true
}

//Find other JavaScript-enabled browser here and move
//them to another, more suitable page!
if (detected == false) {
   location.href = "alternate.html"
}
//-->
</script>
```

Notice the line `location.href = "alternate.html"`. This is the line that decides where visitors not using Internet Explorer 6 go. Remember to change the page name referred to in the script to correspond to the name of the page you want visitors to be redirected to. A common mistake made by beginners is to forget to do this and redirect to the same page every time. This can leave the visitor going around in a loop or going to a dead link.

The complete code containing the JavaScript to redirect those users who are not using Internet Explorer 6 to a page called `alternate.html` is shown in Listing 13.2. The code for the alternate page is shown in Listing 13.3.

Listing 13.2: browser_detect.html

```
<!DOCTYPE html PUBLIC
"-//W3C//DTD XHTML 1.0 Transitional//EN"
   "http://www.w3.org/TR/xhtml1/DTD/xhtml1-transitional.dtd">
<html xmlns="http://www.w3.org/1999/xhtml">
<head>
<title>Browser Detection</title>
<script type="text/javascript" language="JavaScript">
<!--
var browser = "unknown"
var version = 0
var detected = false
var ua = window.navigator.userAgent

if (ua.substring(0,7) == "Mozilla") {
   if (ua.indexOf("MSIE") > 0) {
```

```
      browser = "Microsoft"
   }

   if (ua.indexOf("6.") > 0) {
      version = 6
   }
}

//Find Internet Explorer 6 users and do nothing
if (browser == "Microsoft" && version == 6) {
   detected = true
}

//Find other JavaScript-enabled browser here and move
//them to another, more suitable page!
if (detected == false) {
   location.href = "alternate.html"
}
//-->
</script>
</head>
<body bgcolor="green">
<h2>This browser is Internet Explorer 6.</h2>
</body>
</html>
```

Listing 13.3: alternate.html

```
<!DOCTYPE html PUBLIC
"-//W3C//DTD XHTML 1.0 Transitional//EN"
   "http://www.w3.org/TR/xhtml1/DTD/xhtml1-transitional.dtd">
<html xmlns="http://www.w3.org/1999/xhtml">
<head>
<title>Alternate Document</title>
</head>
<body bgcolor="teal">
<h2>This browser is not Internet Explorer 6.</h2>
</body>
</html>
```

Note that we have used different background colors and have also included different messages in the body section of these pages to tell them apart as we test our code. Figure 13.12 shows the page displayed when `browser_detect.html` is opened in Internet Explorer 6, and Figure 13.13 shows the page displayed when `browser_detect.html` is opened in any browser other than Internet Explorer 6.

FIGURE 13.12: `browser_detect.html` in Internet Explorer 6

FIGURE 13.13: `browser_detect.html` redirects to `alternate.html` when opened in Netscape 7.

NOTE

For a common sense approach to the use of browser detection in your pages, see "Browser Detection and Cross-Browser Support" at http://devedge .netscape.com/viewsource/2002/browser-detection/.

WHAT'S NEXT?

In this chapter, you learned about Internet Explorer 6, web standards, and testing your pages for compliance with web standards. Now it's time to look at that other major web browser and learn about Netscape Navigator 6 and 7.

Chapter 14

OPTIMIZING YOUR WEB PAGES FOR NETSCAPE NAVIGATOR

In this chapter, you'll learn the major features of the latest versions of the Netscape browser—Netscape Navigator 6 and 7—including details on support for technologies, plug-ins, and the variety of scripting, markup, and programming languages.

Part III

Written expressly for *HTML Complete*, Third Edition, by Lucinda Dykes

Netscape Navigator 4

As we discussed in Chapter 13, "Optimizing Your Web Pages for Internet Explorer," the differences between Netscape Navigator and Internet Explorer were the greatest with the release of the level 4 browsers in 1997. Internet Explorer became much more compliant with web standards with the release of Internet Explorer 5 (March 1999), and web standards compliance continued and expanded in Internet Explorer 6 (August 2001). However, Netscape did not release Netscape Navigator 5, so Netscape users could use only Netscape 4.x (or earlier versions) until the release of Netscape 6 in November 2000.

According to statistics at www.upsdell.com/BrowserNews/stat.htm, about two to four percent of the current web audience uses Netscape 4.x.

Problems in Netscape 4.x include issues with table layout, DHTML, and certain features of CSS1 (including lack of support for absolute positioning and float).

As web developers decided to develop pages that complied with web standards, some developers made the decision not to create web pages for the noncompliant Netscape 4.x.

For more details, see these sources:

▶ "Why Don't You Code for Netscape?" at www.alistapart.com/stories/netscape/

▶ "To Hell with Bad Browsers" at www.alistapart.com/stories/tohell/

▶ "Will Browsers Ever Not Suck?" at http://hotwired.lycos.com/webmonkey/99/52/index2a.html

For a contrary view of this argument, see

▶ "Return of the 'Best Viewed With' Parochialism" at http://gutfeldt.ch/matthias/articles/bestwievedwith.html

Netscape Navigator 6

The release of Netscape 6 heralded a major change in the Netscape browser. Netscape 6 is not just an updated version of Netscape 4—it's a new browser that's compliant with most web standards and that no longer supports several features in previous versions of Netscape. Netscape 6 is based on a Mozilla open-source base and the Gecko engine. For more information on Mozilla and Gecko, visit www.mozilla.org.

Proprietary Netscape elements (for example, the blink element) and proprietary document objects (layer and ilayer elements) are no longer supported in Netscape 6 and later versions.

Unlike Internet Explorer 6, which supports both the proprietary Internet Explorer DOM (accessed with document.all) as well as the W3C Level 1 Document Object Model (DOM), Netscape Navigator 6 supports only the W3C DOM and no longer supports Netscape's proprietary DOM (accessed with document.layers). This change in document object support affects dynamic web pages using scripts that access Netscape's proprietary document objects. The DOM is discussed further in the following section of this chapter.

TIP

For more details on the Document Object Model (DOM) and dynamic web pages, see Chapter 18, "Bringing Pages to Life with Dynamic HTML and XHTML."

TIP

For information on updating dynamic web pages for newer browsers, see "Updating DHTML Web Pages for Next Generation Browsers" at http://devedge.netscape.com/viewsource/2001/updating-dhtml-web-pages/.

The major change from Netscape 4.x to Netscape 6 is the broad support for web standards in Netscape 6. The details are outlined in the following section.

SUPPORT FOR WEB STANDARDS IN NETSCAPE NAVIGATOR 6

The previous chapter reviewed web standards support in Internet Explorer 6. Now let's look at the same four categories in Netscape Navigator 6. According to the Web Standards Project (www.webstandards.org/about/), current web standards include four different standards categories:

▶ Structural Languages: HTML 4.01, XHTML 1.0, XHTML 1.1, and XML 1.0

▶ Presentation Languages: Cascading Style Sheets (CSS) levels 1, 2, and 3

▶ Object Models: Document Object Model (DOM) Level 1 (Core) and Level 2

▶ Scripting Languages: ECMAScript 262 (the standard version of JavaScript)

Netscape Navigator 6 supports web standards to a far greater degree than any previous Netscape release.

Netscape Navigator 6 supports HTML 4.01, XHTML 1.0, XHTML 1.1, and XML 1.0. As detailed in the previous chapter, IE 6 offers the most support for XML 1.0 of any current browser, and it displays document structure for any well-formed XML document. Netscape Navigator and Opera, on the other hand, display the content contained in XML markup but do not display document structure.

Netscape Navigator 6 offers complete support for the Cascading Style Sheets level 1 specification and supports most of CSS level 2, including support for positioning. There are some problems with support for fixed positioning and with full support for the `float` property. For more details on bugs in CSS support in Netscape Navigator 6, see `www.richinstyle.com`.

The DOM is an Application Programming Interface (API) for HTML, XHTML, and XML documents. Netscape Navigator 6 offers complete support for the W3C Level 1 Document Object Model (Core and HTML) and also supports some features of the Level 2 DOM, including the `getElementById` and `getElementsByTagName` methods.

Netscape's JavaScript and Internet Explorer's JScript combined to form the ECMA-262 standard. The third and latest edition of ECMA-262 is supported by Netscape Navigator 6, as well as all level 6 browsers and above.

In summary, Netscape Navigator 6 supports most web standards and offers strong support for CSS and Level 1 DOM.

Using *DOCTYPE* Declarations

As you learned in Chapter 3, "Creating Your First HTML or XHTML Document," a DOCTYPE declaration tells the browser which version of HTML or XHTML a document complies with. Netscape Navigator 6 (and all other level 6 browsers) uses DOCTYPE to determine how to display HTML/XHTML documents.

TIP

See Chapter 3 for more information about using DOCTYPE declarations in HTML and XHTML documents.

In Netscape Navigator 6, if no DOCTYPE declaration is included, the page will be displayed in what is called "backwards-compatibility" or "quirks" mode, which means that the page will be displayed in the same way as it would in earlier versions of Netscape Navigator (before version 6). Netscape Navigator 6 also displays pages in quirks mode if a transitional or frameset HTML 4.0 DTD is used or if a transitional or frameset HTML 4.01 DTD is used without an accompanying URL. Netscape's use of DOCTYPE is not straightforward. For details, see the Doctype switch table at `http://gutfeldt.ch/matthias/articles/doctypeswitch/table.html`.

Optimizations for Netscape Navigator 6

When we talk about optimization, we actually are talking about two different things:

- Adding functionality (through elements, attributes, and properties) not present in other browsers

- Making sure that the code you write is clean and clear and takes the minimum time to load into the browser

The previous chapter includes details on writing clean code and using a validator, and this information applies equally well to Netscape Navigator, Internet Explorer, or any other browser. For further details, see the section "Writing Clean Code," in Chapter 13.

Part III

Adding Functionality

Adding functionality generally means making only small adjustments or "tweaks" to the HTML or XHTML and letting the browser do the rest.

Let's begin by looking at how to optimize the layout of the page.

Page Layout

Figure 14.1 shows a web page in Netscape Navigator 6 containing a couple of paragraphs of text. Notice the margins around the page. They are set to the default of the browser.

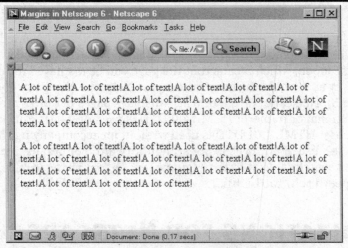

FIGURE 14.1:   A web page in Netscape 6 with default margins

You can change the margins of the page to any number of pixels by using the marginwidth and marginheight attributes with the body element, as shown in the following code:

```
<body marginwidth="10" marginheight="10">
```

However, the display you get depends on the DOCTYPE you use. Using marginwidth and marginheight attributes in the body element is not standards-compliant code; according to the HTML 4.01 specification, these are valid attributes only for the frame and iframe elements.

A common issue for the web designer and developer is how to eliminate the browser default margins and have pages with no margins. The code for this would be this:

```
<body marginwidth="0" marginheight="0">
```

If you use this code on a web page with an XHTML 1.0 Transitional DTD, as shown in the following code snippet, you would expect a level 6 browser such as Netscape Navigator 6 to switch into standards mode for the page display and to display margins with default values rather than the values in nonstandard attributes. However, what actually happens is that Netscape Navigator 6 and 7 display the page with a `marginwidth` of zero, but with a default value for `marginheight`, as shown in Figure 14.2.

```
<!DOCTYPE html PUBLIC
"-//W3C//DTD XHTML 1.0 Transitional//EN"
   "http://www.w3.org/TR/xhtml1/DTD/xhtml1-transitional.dtd">
<html xmlns="http://www.w3.org/1999/xhtml">
<head>
<title>Margins in Netscape 6</title>
<meta http-equiv="Content-Type" content="text/html;
 charset=iso-8859-1" />
</head>
<body marginwidth="0" marginheight="0">
```

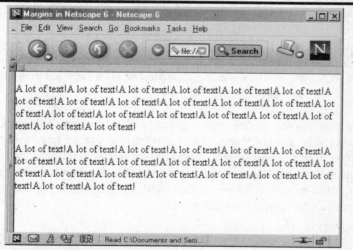

FIGURE 14.2:   The same page in Netscape 6 (standards mode) with `marginwidth` and `marginheight` set to zero

If you use this code on a web page without a DTD, as shown in the following code snippet, you would expect Netscape Navigator 6 (and 7) to switch into quirks mode for the page display and to display no margins. This is what happens, as shown in Figure 14.3.

```
<html>
<head>
<title>Margins in Netscape 6</title>
<meta http-equiv="Content-Type" content="text/html;
 charset=iso-8859-1" />
</head>
<body marginwidth="0" marginheight="0">
```

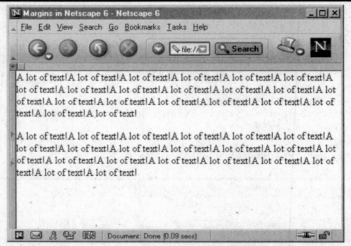

FIGURE 14.3:   The same page in Netscape 6 (quirks mode) with marginwidth
and marginheight set to zero

Although you can get the page to appear with no margins, this works only
in quirks mode. Even if you remove the marginwidth and marginheight
attributes from the body element and use an embedded CSS style to set
margins to zero, as shown in the following code, the results are the same.
In standards mode, only the left and right margins are set to zero; in
quirks mode, all margins are set to zero.

```
<!DOCTYPE html PUBLIC
"-//W3C//DTD XHTML 1.0 Transitional//EN"
    "http://www.w3.org/TR/xhtml1/DTD/xhtml1-transitional.dtd">
<html xmlns="http://www.w3.org/1999/xhtml">
<head>
<title>Margins in Netscape 6</title>
<meta http-equiv="Content-Type" content="text/html;
 charset=iso-8859-1" />
<style type="text/css">
```

```
<!--
body {margin: 0;}
-->
</style>
</head>
<body>
```

Although Netscape Navigator 6 and 7 are standards-compliant browsers, you can see that there are some bugs in the implementation of Netscape's standards compliance.

Styles for Hyperlinks

As detailed in the previous chapter, the hover pseudo-class from the Cascading Style Sheets level 2 specification can be used to make hyperlinks change color as the visitor moves the mouse pointer over them. This feature of CSS level 2 was first supported in Netscape in Navigator 6. It works whether Netscape Navigator 6 displays pages in quirks mode or in standards mode.

The style block to make hyperlinks hover is shown in the following code snippet. This code is the same as that used in the previous chapter. For more details, see the section "Making Hyperlinks Hover," in Chapter 13.

```
<style type="text/css">
<!--
a:hover {color: red;}
-->
</style>
```

NOTE

Cascading Style Sheets are covered in greater depth in Chapter 16, "Using Style Sheets."

You also can use other style properties to change the appearance of hyperlinks, including using the text-decoration property to remove the default underlining of link text. Of course, if you remove the underlining from link text, you need to make it obvious in other ways that the text is a link. Let's look at the steps to remove underlining from link text and add color to each link pseudo-class:

1. First, add a style block to the head element on the web page. This is where the Cascading Style Sheet information will go; it consists of the <style> opening and closing tags.

```
<head>
<title>Link Styles</title>
<style type="text/css">
</style>
</head>
```

2. Next, add HTML/XHTML comment tags inside the style block that you just created. These are there in case someone visits the page with an older browser that isn't capable of understanding the Cascading Style Sheet information you will add. With comment tags in place, older browsers will simply ignore anything between the <style> tags. Without the comment tags, these browsers may throw out error messages or display the page incorrectly.

TIP

It is always a good idea to add the comment tags, even if you *know* that the browser your visitor is using can understand CSS.

```
<head>
<title>Link Styles</title>
<style type="text/css">
<!--

-->
</style>
</head>
```

3. Now you can add the Cascading Style Sheet information to the page.

```
<head>
<title>Link Styles</title>
<style type="text/css">
<!--
a:link {text-decoration: none;}
-->
</style>
</head>
```

4. To apply this style to visited and hover links, not just unvisited links, include selectors for visited and hover links.

```
<head>
<title>Link Styles</title>
<style type="text/css">
```

```
<!--
a:link,a:visited,a:hover {text-decoration: none;}
-->
</style>
</head>
```

5. Add color choices to the link pseudo-classes.

```
<head>
<title>Link Styles</title>
<style type="text/css">
<!--
a:link,a:visited,a:hover {text-decoration: none;}
a:link {color: red;}
a:visited {color: green;}
a:hover {color: teal;}
-->
</style>
</head>
```

6. Save the web page and view it in Netscape Navigator 6. Move the mouse pointer over the hyperlinks, and watch them change color. The hyperlinks should turn teal, according to the code above. As the mouse pointer moves off them, they automatically change back to the original color. The link text should change to green when a link has been visited. The link text should not be underlined, regardless of the state of the link.

The complete code follows in Listing 14.1.

Listing 14.1: Styles for Hyperlinks

```
<!DOCTYPE html PUBLIC
 "-//W3C//DTD XHTML 1.0 Transitional//EN"
  "http://www.w3.org/TR/xhtml1/DTD/xhtml1-transitional.dtd">
<html xmlns="http://www.w3.org/1999/xhtml">
<head>
<title>Link Styles </title>
<meta http-equiv="Content-Type"
 content="text/html; charset=iso-8859-1" />
<style type="text/css">
<!--
a:link,a:visited,a:hover {text-decoration: none;}
a:link {color: red;}
a:visited {color: green;}
a:hover {color: teal;}
-->
```

Part III

```
</style>
</head>
<body>
<h1>Links, links, links!</h1>
A link to <a href="mypage.htm">Me</a>!
<br />
A link to <a href="friends.htm">my friends</a>!
<br />
A link to <a href="pets.htm">my pets</a>!
</body>
</html>
```

Other CSS properties also can be added to hyperlink text, such as formatting the link text in a specific font or making the link text bold. For more details on using Cascading Style Sheets, see Chapter 16.

WHAT'S NEW IN NETSCAPE NAVIGATOR 7?

Netscape Navigator 7 was released in August 2002. It includes several new features both for viewers and for web designers and developers. Important new features include the following.

My Sidebar Tabs for Developers   My Sidebar was introduced in Netscape 6 and continues to be supported in Netscape 7. My Sidebar Tabs are HTML pages that are displayed to the left of a page in Navigator, Mail, and Instant Messenger in Netscape 6 and 7. My Sidebar is accessed via View ➤ Show/Hide ➤ My Sidebar in the main Netscape menu bar. My Sidebar can be customized to include your favorite web pages, and it is useful for pages you access frequently. Netscape DevEdge offers Tabs for quick reference to W3C specifications, including HTML 4.01 (shown in Figure 14.4), CSS 2, CSS 2.1, and DOM 2. The DevEdge Tabs can be downloaded and installed at http://devedge.netscape.com/toolbox/sidebars/. Tabs can be added easily to My Sidebar, and custom Tabs can be created.

TIP

For more information on My Sidebar, see "My Sidebar Developer's Guide" at http://devedge.netscape.com/viewsource/2002/sidebar/.

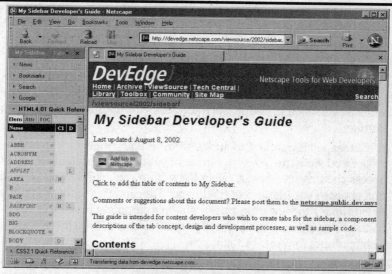

FIGURE 14.4:   The HTML 4.01 specification in My Sidebar in Netscape 7

The terms displayed in the sidebar shown in Figure 14.4 are links to the appropriate section of the HTML 4.01 specification. The linked pages appear in the window on the right.

Web Site Icon Support   Web Site Icons can be added to any web page and promote quick recognition of a site or a product. Company logos often are used as Web Site Icons. Web Site Icons are a specific file type (.ico) and are constructed from several images of different sizes and color depth. A trial version of Icon Forge to create favicons (*favorites icons*) can be downloaded at Favicon (www/favicon.com) or Cursor Arts (www.cursorarts.com/ca_if.html).

Netscape 7 Release Notes (http://wp.netscape.com/eng/mozilla/ns7/relnotes/7.html#new) state that Netscape 7 supports Web Site Icons (favicons), and Web Site Icons show up in the Location bar (next to the URL) and in Tabs (when using Tabbed Browsing) in Netscape 7. However, unlike the Favorites menu in Internet Explorer, icons don't appear in Netscape's Bookmarks menu.

Part III

TIP

For more information on using and creating Web Site Icons, see "All About the Favorites Icon" by Emily Baum at http://hotwired.lycos.com/webmonkey/01/18/index1a.html.

Expanded Privacy Features   Netscape Navigator 7 includes enhanced privacy features based on the Platform for Privacy Preferences (P3P) Recommendation of the W3C (www.w3.org/TR/P3P/). The specification became a full W3C Recommendation in April 2002.

As discussed in Chapter 13, P3P is a web privacy standard that specifies preferences and guidelines for the use of cookies. To create a P3P-compliant website, you need to define a privacy policy for it; Chapter 13 shows how to do that.

Netscape Navigator 7 includes a P3P Privacy Viewer that lets the user locate and view the privacy policies of your P3P-compliant websites. To access the Privacy Viewer, select View from the main Netscape menu bar and choose Page Info, select the Privacy Tab, and then choose Policy and/or Summary to view either the website's complete Privacy Policy page or a summary of the site's privacy policies. Figure 14.5 shows the Privacy Tab contents for www.llbean.com.

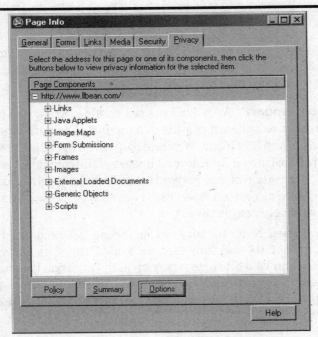

FIGURE 14.5:   The Privacy tab in Netscape Navigator 7

Netscape Navigator 7's privacy features can be accessed from the main menu bar. Choose Edit ➢ Preferences ➢ Privacy & Security ➢ Cookies.

The Cookies preferences display is shown in Figure 14.6. From the Cookies preferences, you can access privacy preferences by clicking the View button, which displays Privacy Settings, as shown in Figure 14.7. Cookie acceptance is based on the selected privacy level (Low, Medium, High, or Custom). Figure 14.7 shows the Custom settings for cookie acceptance.

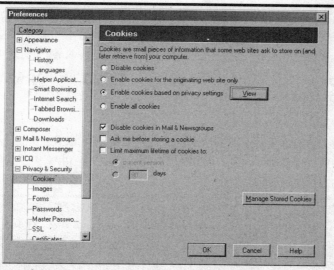

FIGURE 14.6:   Cookie preferences in Netscape Navigator 7

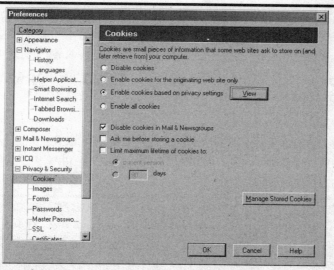

FIGURE 14.7:   Privacy preference settings in Netscape Navigator 7

Tabbed Browsing   Tabbed Browsing enables the user to have several web pages open at once and to move between them easily via a set of organized tabs at the top of the page. If the page you are viewing includes a Web Site Icon (discussed earlier in this section), the icon will be displayed on the tab as well as the page title.

There are four different ways to access Tabbed Browsing:

- ▶ Click the Open a New Tab button at the top left of the tabs
- ▶ From the main menu bar, choose File ≻ New ≻ Navigator Tab
- ▶ Right-click on a hyperlink and choose Open Link in New Tab from the context menu
- ▶ Use the keyboard shortcut Ctrl+T

Figure 14.8 shows a tabbed interface with tabs for four separate web pages. The Netscape Gecko Compatibility page is displayed in the foreground.

FIGURE 14.8:   Tabbed Browsing in Netscape Navigator 7

Netscape Navigator 7 includes several additional new features for users. For more information, see:

- ▶ Netscape 7 and 7.01 Release Notes at http://wp.netscape .com/eng/mozilla/ns7/relnotes/7.html

▶ Netscape 7 FAQs at `http://channels.netscape.com/ns/browsers/7/learnmore/faq.jsp`

INSTALLING MULTIPLE VERSIONS OF NETSCAPE

You can install several versions of Netscape on the same computer as long as you install them in separate folders. Otherwise, the last version you install will overwrite the files of a version installed earlier. For example, on a PC, you can create a folder named `Netscape 6` in the `Program Files` directory, and install Netscape 6 into that folder. (Make sure you choose that folder during the installation process.) Then create a folder named `Netscape 7` in the `Program Files` directory, and install Netscape 7 into that folder. It's possible to install earlier versions of Netscape too, as long as you create separate folders.

For more information, see `http://channels.netscape.com/ns/browsers/7/learnmore/faq.jsp#gen5`.

WHAT'S NEXT?

In this chapter, you learned about Netscape Navigator 6, web-standard compliance in Netscape Navigator 6, and the features of the latest version of Netscape, Netscape Navigator 7. In the next chapter, you will learn about the effective use of multimedia elements in your web pages, including detailed information about adding multimedia files to your pages.

Part III

Chapter 15

INCLUDING MULTIMEDIA

In recent years, web surfers have seen text-only pages transformed into pages that bounce, shimmy, sing, and gyrate. Developers of public sites, in particular, are using flair and excitement in an effort to attract users and to keep them coming back again and again. Flashy elements don't always attract, however. Some users find them such a distraction that they don't continue to browse the site, nor do they return to it. The key is to use glitz wisely and to weigh its benefits and liabilities carefully—and to use it only if it adds to the overall value of the page.

In this chapter, we'll show you how to include special effects—animated Graphics Interchange Format (GIF) files, sounds, videos, Flash animations, Java applets, and ActiveX controls—collectively known as *multimedia*. (In this book, we define multimedia as anything you can include in a web page other than basic HTML or XHTML code and static images.) We'll look at the pros and cons of various elements and discuss how to include them effectively, if you choose to include them.

Part III

Adapted from *Mastering HTML and XHTML*, by Deborah S. Ray and Eric J. Ray
ISBN 0-7821-4141-2 $49.99

DECIDING TO INCLUDE MULTIMEDIA

Animated images, sounds, and video can make your pages come alive. Done correctly, multimedia can also give web pages that "up with technology" look-and-feel. However, before you run off to gather multimedia elements, take heed: Multimedia poses several challenges, both for users and for the developer.

TIP

The principles for including these effects apply to other elements you might discover. For example, if the engineers at your company want to publish their AutoCAD files on your corporate intranet, you can include them in web pages, following the principles outlined in the "Adding Multimedia" section, later in this chapter.

The Challenges for Users

Multimedia can bring your pages to a virtual halt as users sit and wait (and wait!) for the files to download. Although some multimedia files such as animated GIFs can be as small as 2KB, other files, such as video, easily can grow to 5MB or more. Even though many of your users may have fast Internet connections that make multimedia usable and useful, many will likely have much slower connections.

TIP

Of all the various multimedia formats available, Macromedia's Flash (www.macromedia.com/software/flashplayer) is the most widely available on all browsers and operating systems. Therefore, it is the least likely to inconvenience your users.

In addition, some multimedia files require *plug-ins* (programs used to view file types not directly supported in the browser itself). In the past, users had to download and install a separate plug-in for each multimedia file type (for example, one plug-in for one video format, another for a different kind of video, and so on). However, in newer browsers, support for many multimedia elements is part of the basic browser installation package, including support for *streaming* audio and video (which can be listened to or viewed as the download is occurring) and QuickTime video playback, as well as 3D animation and the *Virtual Reality Markup Language* (VRML). (VRML is one way to provide 3D simulations on the Web.)

WARNING

Internet Explorer 6 does not support the use of Netscape-style plug-ins and instead supports only the use of ActiveX controls. The main plug-in affected by this decision is the Apple QuickTime plug-in. Apple has provided an ActiveX control for QuickTime that can be downloaded at www.apple.com/quicktime/download/qtcheck/. For more information about Internet Explorer 6, see Chapter 13, "Optimizing Your Web Pages for Internet Explorer."

TIP

Netscape Navigator also includes another feature for multimedia users. If you go to the Help menu and choose About Plug-ins, you'll find out which plug-ins are currently installed, the version number, and what types of multimedia files they support.

MULTIMEDIA DEVELOPERS

Some multimedia software companies offer integrated packages of free software (you can also purchase expanded versions), which support almost all multimedia file formats available on the Web. If you download and install one or more of those programs, you will be able to view multimedia on the Web with few hassles, but remember that your users will have to do the same to get the same capabilities. Those software programs include the following:

▶ RealOne Player, the latest version of the RealPlayer software, which supports streaming audio and video, including RealAudio and RealVideo, as well as several other media types available as plug-ins. RealOne Player combines features of RealPlayer and RealJukebox so that you can organize your media files or burn CDs. It also includes a built-in web browser for downloading media files. Although the preset defaults in the RealOne Player enable you to use it for every media file type, you can uncheck those selections during the installation process. Download RealOne Player at www.real.com.

▶ QuickTime, which supports more than 200 types of digital media, including MP3, MIDI, AVI, AVR, MPEG-4, AAC audio, streaming media, and digital video. The latest version is QuickTime 6. Download QuickTime at www.apple.com/quicktime.

CONTINUED ➡

Part III

> ▶ Windows Media Player, which includes seven features in a single application: CD player, audio and video player, media jukebox, media guide, Internet radio, portable device music file transfer, and an audio CD burner. The newest version is the Windows Media Player 8 for Windows XP. Windows Media Player 9 is currently available in beta release (XP is recommended, but can be used with Windows 98 Second Edition, Windows 2000, Windows Me). Windows Media Player 7.1 is the latest version for Windows 98, Windows Me, and Windows 2000, and versions are also available for several other platforms, including the Mac OS X platform. Download Windows Media Player at www.microsoft.com/windows/windowsmedia/EN/default.asp.

The Challenges for Developers

In addition to these resounding indictments of carefree multimedia use in web pages, it gets worse. For you, the developer, obtaining relevant and useful multimedia objects often is difficult. Your first option is to create the effects yourself, which requires both raw materials (such as photographs, sounds, and video clips) and often special software that you must purchase and learn to use. In addition, even if you're familiar with the software, developing effective multimedia objects can be time consuming.

You can also browse the Web for multimedia elements, which is a less expensive and less time-consuming option, but you may not find exactly what you want. Although tons of multimedia elements are available on the Web, they're likely to be inappropriate or not freely available for you to use.

Your goal is to consider carefully the advantages and disadvantages of each multimedia element *before* you include it. Start by asking these questions:

▶ Does the multimedia element add content that I cannot otherwise provide?

▶ Does the multimedia element clearly enhance or complement content?

▶ Do the users have browsers that support these elements?

▶ Do the users have fast Internet connections?

▶ Are the users likely to have the appropriate plug-ins or the time, inclination, and technical wherewithal to get and install them?

▶ Do I have the time, skills, and resources to develop or find multimedia elements?

If you answer yes to some or all these questions and you opt to include multimedia, the rest of this chapter is for you.

TIP

Throughout this chapter, we point out that you can find multimedia elements on the Web. However, remember that much of what you find is not available for public use. Before you take a file and use it as your own, be sure that it's clearly labeled "for public use" and that the licensing agreement is compatible with your intended use. For example, many multimedia effects are available for non-commercial use on private web pages but not for a business application. If something is not clearly labeled, you should assume that it's not for you to take and use, or just send the webmaster an e-mail and ask for permission. Nothing ventured, nothing gained.

CONSIDERING MULTIMEDIA USABILITY

Before you commit to pages that are fully multimedia enhanced — or even to a single animated GIF on your home page — consider carefully what including multimedia will do to your site's usability. User Interface Engineering (http://world.std.com/~uieweb/surprise.htm) presents some alarming findings about the usability of web pages that incorporate multimedia elements.

In their pilot study, these authors found that "animation did seem to cause delays in the users' performance" and support that finding with observational research in which website visitors sat and waited through several cycles of an animation in order for the page to finish displaying — which of course it never did, because the animation continued to cycle.

For the full report based on data from their research, see their book *Web Site Usability: A Designer's Guide* (http://world.std.com/~uieweb/bookdesc.htm).

CONTINUED ➡

Part III

> Although some sites were more problematic than others, and other studies show that animations are more effective than static images in advertisements, your site might not benefit from any of these effects.

DEVELOPING AND USING ANIMATED GIFs

Perhaps the easiest multimedia element to include is an animated GIF, which is a file that more or less includes a bunch of images stacked together to give the illusion of movement. Animated GIFs are similar to those little cartoon booklets or "flip books" you had as a kid. When you whirred quickly through the pages, the cartoon seemed to move. Of course, the illusion of movement was nothing more than each drawing being slightly different. Animated GIFs work the same way.

The uses for animated GIFs vary considerably, from flashing commercial messages to elaborate mini-movies to small bullets or arrows that appear to grow or move. Animated GIFs commonly are used to attract users' attention to a specific element.

Developing Animated GIFs

If you're interested in developing your own animated GIFs, we recommend software such as Animation Shop from JASC (maker of Paint Shop Pro, www.jasc.com) or GifBuilder for the Macintosh (www.mac.org/graphics/gifbuilder). These packages provide the tools to combine individual images into an animated GIF; however, you also can develop animated GIFs by developing a set of individual images with any software that can create GIF images, including Photoshop, Paint Shop Pro, ImageReady (included with Photoshop), Gimp, Illustrator, and Fireworks. If you want to see what's available on the Web, go to www.yahoo.com or www.google.com and search on "gif animation" (be sure to use the quotes). You will find lots of information, software, and software reviews.

Developing an animated GIF often takes more time and effort than you expect. The process can become tedious, especially if you're working with longer animations or animations in which the illusion of smooth motion is needed (rather than simply presenting discrete panes of information, as in ad banners).

The first step is to generate the individual images that eventually will be each panel within the animated GIF. For a basic animated bullet that appears to move from left to right, you might create a set of images similar to those shown in Figure 15.1.

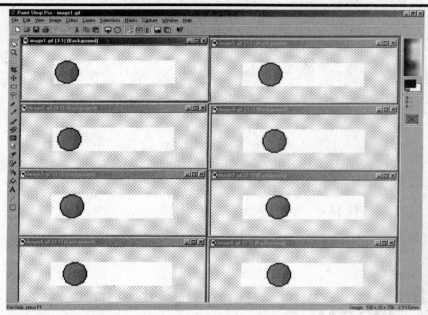

FIGURE 15.1:   Creating a bullet that slides right in Paint Shop Pro

The easiest way to get smooth animation is to create a single image, select the object that changes or moves, move it into each successive position, and then save the image with each new object position. In this example, after creating the small ball, we selected the ball, moved it two pixels to the right, saved the image, moved it again, and so forth. The more pixels between images, the jerkier the motion; the fewer pixels between images, the smoother the motion.

After you create the images, use a GIF animation program such as JASC Animation Shop (see Figure 15.2) or any of the graphics programs mentioned earlier to sequence the images and to set animation properties, such as how often to loop through the animation and how to redraw the images as the animation proceeds.

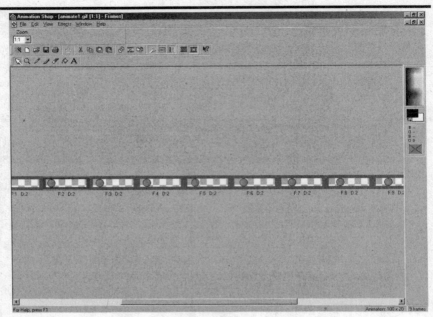

FIGURE 15.2:   Animating the bullet in JASC Animation Shop

After you insert each of the frames and preview the image to your satisfaction, simply save it as a GIF file.

Incorporating Animated GIFs into HTML and XHTML Documents

Table 15.1 lists and describes the elements and attributes you use to include animated GIFs in your XHTML documents. You can treat animated GIFs like any other image. (See Chapter 10, "Adding Graphics," for more information on images.)

TABLE 15.1:   Main Elements and Attributes of Animated GIFs

Item	Type	Description
img	Empty element	Inserts an image in a document.
src="url"	Attribute of img	Specifies the location of the image file; required.
alt="..."	Attribute of img	Provides alternate text for users who don't view the image; required.

To include an animated GIF in your web page, follow these steps:

1. Find or create an appropriate animated GIF image.

2. Place the image in your HTML or XHTML document, with the regular image elements. Your code could look similar to the following:

```
<img src="animate2.gif" width="99" height="16" border="0"
     alt="animated gif" />
<a href="camping.html">Camping News</a> provides the latest
comments from the trails.<br />
```

3. Enjoy the experience!

TESTING MULTIMEDIA

If you're testing your pages either locally or over a direct Internet connection—for example, through your network at the office, connected to the Internet with a dedicated line—take the time to test them with the slowest dial-up connection your users will be using. Check out what happens with 56Kbps (and possibly slower) modems. What's tolerable with a direct connection can seem interminable over a dial-up connection.

In ideal circumstances, a user with a 56Kbps modem can download a maximum of 7KB per second. In real life, that number decreases dramatically, depending on network traffic and a variety of intangibles. If your page contains 2KB of text, a 4KB bullet image, a 20KB photograph, and a 9KB logo, you're already talking about at least a 5-second download. Add a 60KB animation or sound file, and you've just bumped that to 15 seconds—best-case scenario. At this point, the user has likely moved on to another site.

However, this is becoming less of an issue as more users obtain faster Internet connections, such as cable modems and Digital Subscriber Line (DSL) service. As always, have an idea of what your users will have, and cater to the lowest common denominator. At the very least, be aware of what portion of your potential users may not wait for your multimedia elements to download.

Part III

ADDING SOUNDS

Adding audio can produce some fun effects, but if you surf the Web looking for sound, you'll find little of practical use. Generally speaking, web page sounds come in three varieties:

▶ Sounds that play when users access the page

▶ Sounds that play when users click something

▶ Sounds that are part of a multimedia file, such as a Flash animation or a video file

Sounds that play when users access a page are called *background sounds* and can be a short tune or one that plays the entire time a user is at the page. These mooing, beeping, crescendo-ing background sounds usually do nothing more than entertain (or irritate). Figure 15.3 includes a control box that users can click to play a sound.

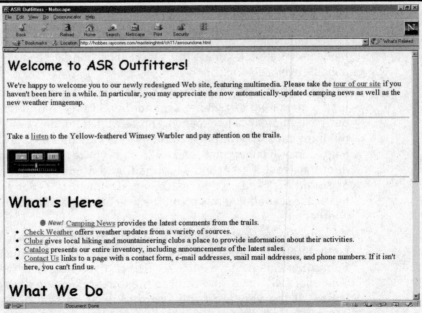

FIGURE 15.3:   The control box lets users choose whether to play the sound.

TIP

Our take on the "it-plays-the-whole-time-you're-visiting" background sounds is that if we want music to play while we're surfing the Web, we'll put a CD in the computer.

Although sounds accessed in this way are primarily for entertainment, they could be of practical use—for example:

► If your car sounds like this *rumble*, you need a new muffler.

► If your car sounds like this *choke*, you might have bad gasoline.

► If your car sounds like this *kaCHUNK* when you shift gears, your transmission is going out.

You get the idea. Instead of adding the whole control box, however, you could just link directly to an audio file, which might well keep readers happier as well.

Some Disadvantages of Sounds

Many of the disadvantages associated with using multimedia elements in general also are associated with using sounds:

► Sound files are usually large and load slowly.

► A user in a corporate environment might not welcome a loud greeting from his computer.

When choosing to add sound to your page, apply the guidelines we mentioned earlier about using multimedia elements in general. If an audio element does not enhance your message or provide content that is not possible in any other way, you're probably better off not using it.

Sound File Formats

If you decide to include a sound in your web page, all you have to do is find a sound file in one of six formats (other formats are available, but are less common):

MIDI (Musical Instrument Digital Interface)   MIDI files (with the `.midi` or `.mid` extension) contain synthesized music. MIDI files are

Part III

supported by most browsers and don't require a plug-in. The sound quality is very good, and the files are relatively small, making MIDI a very good choice for web audio. Special hardware and software are required to synthesize MIDI files.

AIFF (Audio Interchange File Format)   AIFF files (with the .aif or .aiff extension) contain good quality sampled sound. AIFF files are supported by most browsers and don't require a plug-in. You can record your own AIFF files, but large file size limits their use on the Web.

AU (Basic AUdio)   AU files (with the .au extension) also provide acceptable—but not great—quality sampled sound. These files are accessible on the widest range of browsers and computer systems and don't require a plug-in.

WAV (as in WAVe)   WAV files (with the .wav extension) contain high quality sampled sound. WAV files are supported by most browsers and don't require a plug-in. You can record your own WAV files, but as with AIFF files, the large file size limits their use on the Web.

RAM or RA (RealMedia)   RealAudio files (with the .ra, .ram, or .rpm extension) contain high-quality streaming sound in a compressed format. RealAudio files are smaller than MP3 files. RealAudio files require the use of RealPlayer software, either a browser plug-in or a helper application.

MP3 (MPEG Audio Layer 3)   MP3 files (with the .mp3 extension) provide outstanding (nearly CD-quality) sound. (The name MP3 is derived from Moving Picture Experts Group, or MPEG, Audio Layer 3.) MP3 is a compressed format that greatly reduces the size of the files. MP3 files still can be very large, however. The files can be *streamed*—the file plays as it downloads, rather than having to wait for the whole file to download before it starts to play. The disadvantage of the MP3 format is that it requires a browser plug-in or helper application.

If you have a sound card and a microphone, you can record your own sounds. Of course, you can find thousands, if not millions, of sounds and samples on the Web.

TIP

There are many sources for sound files on the Web. Do a search at www.yahoo.com or www.google.com for "audio files," or use Comparisonics' search engine for sound effects on the Web at www.findsounds.com. Many of the sound files on the Web are not public domain, which means you can borrow them to experiment with and learn from, but not to publish as your own.

To include sound files in the easiest and most user-friendly way, link to them. You add a link to a sound file in the same way that you add a link to an image. The code looks like this:

```
<p>Take a <a href="weirdbrd.aif">listen</a>
to the Yellow-feathered Wimsey Warbler and pay attention
on the trails.</p>
```

If you use this option, users can choose whether to hear the sound, which is accessible from most browsers.

If you want to give users additional control over the sound, including volume level, pause, and play, you need to use the `object` element to add the sound file and to create a viewable sound control box on the page. See "Adding Multimedia," later in this chapter, for details on using the `object` element, including a table of supported attributes.

ADDING VIDEO

You'll find that video—in the right situation—is perhaps the most practical multimedia element. In one quick video clip, you can *show* users a concept or a process, rather than describing it in lengthy paragraphs or steps.

Video files can be huge, however, so you must be sure that a large video file is important enough to your presentation to ask a user to wait for it to download. Video technology is continuing to develop, and movie clips of reasonable size are increasingly available. Many news and entertainment sites, such as www.cnn.com/videoselect and www.comedycentral.com, offer short movie clips that download quickly.

Newer versions of Internet Explorer support video streaming, MPEG video, and QuickTime movie playback (for PCs; Mac users must download an ActiveX control) in the basic installation. Netscape Navigator support of video playback and video streaming is more limited, and Netscape requires a plug-in for QuickTime movies. Netscape 7 includes Winamp, RealPlayer 8, and a Flash player as part of the full installation. Opera includes some video support directly but requires a plug-in for QuickTime.

Video File Formats

You can create your own video files or find them on the Web. Look for files in the formats discussed in the following sections.

AVI (Audio Video Interleave)   This format (with the `.avi` extension) originally was supported only on Windows platforms but is now also supported on the Mac platform. AVI files often are used for short video clips that aren't streamed. You can embed the AVI file in your page or create a link to it. In either case, the file must download entirely before playback can begin, so don't forget to keep it short!

MPEG (Moving Picture Experts Group)   MPEG files (with the `.mpg` extension) are the most widely supported video file format on the Web. The MPEG file format is highly compressed so that the video file size can be made as small as possible. MPEG files, like AVI files, often are used for short video clips that aren't streamed. Because it's highly compressed and usable, MPEG is the best universal choice.

QuickTime   QuickTime (with the `.qt` extension), originally a Macintosh standard, is now available for Windows as well. It provides good quality, but users must have the plug-in to view files in Netscape Navigator or Opera. (QuickTime movie playback for PCs is a basic feature of later versions of Internet Explorer.)

TIP

QuickTime, RealMedia, and Windows Media files are the most common web video file formats for streaming video. Each of these file formats requires a helper application unless the specific multimedia player is already installed on the user's computer.

We recommend linking to video files, rather than placing them in a web page directly. When video files are linked, users can choose whether to view them. The code to do this would look similar to this:

```
<p>Take a <a href="weirdbrd.mpg">look at video</a> of the
Yellow-feathered Wimsey Warbler.</p>
```

If you want to add a video file directly to your page rather than linking to it, you need to use the `object` element to add a video file and to create a viewable movie control box on the page. See "Adding Multimedia," later in this chapter.

ADDING JAVA APPLETS

Applets, developed with the Java programming language, are mini-programs that enable you to animate objects, scroll text, or add interactive components to your web pages. Figure 15.4 shows a TicTacToe applet, and Figure 15.5 shows an applet that scrolls a welcome message across the top of a web page.

TicTacToe Applet

FIGURE 15.4:   Even a simple applet adds interest and interactivity to a web page.

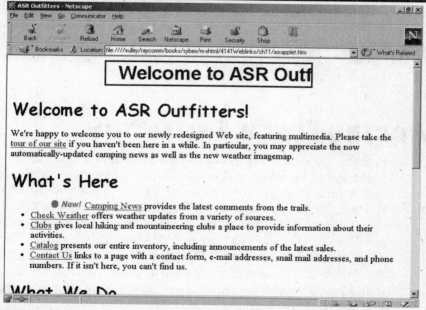

FIGURE 15.5:   The "Welcome" message scrolling across the top of the page is animated by an applet.

Part III

Java applets have the `.class` filename extension. In the simplest cases, you need only the name of the applet to use it—for example, `TicTacToe`
`.class`. With more complex applets, you also must provide *parameters*. You'll have to get the exact information to include in the parameter from the documentation that comes with applets.

The software that enables you to program in Java, available at `www.sun.com`, includes tools for developing applets. Unless you're a programmer or have some time on your hands, you'll be better off using prepackaged applets or tools that develop applets on-the-fly. (Search for "applet" at software archives such as `www.shareware.com`, `www.hotscripts.com`, or `www.developer.com/java/` to find these tools.)

WARNING

Support for Java technologies, such as Java applets, has changed in newer versions of the Windows operating system. For more information on using Java with Windows, visit `www.microsoft.com/java`.

Applet files, like video files, are big and take up to a couple of minutes to download. On the positive side, though, users with most versions of Netscape Navigator or Internet Explorer can use applets without additional software, and the plug-ins for other browsers are easy to come by from `java.sun.com`.

ADDING FLASH ANIMATIONS

Flash animations are created in Macromedia Flash, which is a vector-based animation program. Because they're vector graphics, Flash files can be small enough to be reasonable for use on many websites. Also, it's possible to develop Flash animations that provide additional capabilities and functionality for a website—not just Flash for its own sake. Figure 15.6 shows a page from Michael Jantze's "The Norm" comic strip's website (with HTML and JavaScript-based effects), and Figure 15.7 shows the same content presented (more effectively) with Flash. For more information on Flash, visit Macromedia's site at `www.macromedia.com`.

FIGURE 15.6:   Providing additional information through JavaScript and pop-up windows is awkward, at best.

FIGURE 15.7:   A Flash animation (complete with text that fades in over the picture) provides the same information in a flashier format, which can enhance the user's experience.

Part III

ADDING MULTIMEDIA

The future of developing multimedia elements for the Web is clear: Instead of using several elements and attributes, you'll simply include the `object` element and choose from attributes that support this element. Previously, you needed the `applet`, `embed`, and `object` elements, among others, to provide multimedia to your users. In this respect, the HTML 4.01 and XHTML 1.0 Recommendations accommodate any kind of multimedia element, and most common browsers also support this single element. Wow! You don't need to specify that you're including sound, a video, an applet, or whatever; you simply specify that you're including an object. You use only the `object` element and its attributes, listed in Table 15.2. You no longer need to code separately for both Netscape Navigator and Internet Explorer to use multimedia files on your pages.

TIP

For more information on using the `object` element in Netscape Navigator, see "Plug-in Basics" at `http://devedge.netscape.com/library/manuals/2002/plugin/1.0/intro.html#1001793`.

NOTE

The `object` element has an expanded role in XHTML 2.0—the `img` and `applet` elements are deprecated in favor of the use of `object`. For more information on XHTML 2.0, see `www.xml.com/pub/a/2002/08/07/deviant.html`.

TABLE 15.2:   Object Elements and Attributes

ITEM	TYPE	DESCRIPTION
object	Element	Embeds a software object into a document.
align="..."	Attribute of object	Indicates how the object lines up relative to the edges of the browser window and other elements within the window. Possible values are left, right, bottom, middle, and top.
archive= "url url url..."	Attribute of object	Specifies a space-separated list of addresses for archives containing resources relevant to the object, which may include the resources specified by the classid and data attributes. Preloading archives generally results in reduced load times for objects.

TABLE 15.2 continued: Object Elements and Attributes

ITEM	TYPE	DESCRIPTION
border="n"	Attribute of object	Indicates the width (in pixels) of a border around the object. border="0" indicates no border.
class="..."	Attribute of object	Assigns a class name or set of class names to an object.
codebase="url"	Attribute of object	Specifies the absolute or relative location of the base directory in which the browser will look for data and other implementation files.
codetype="..."	Attribute of object	Specifies the MIME type for the object's code.
class="..."	Attribute of object	Indicates which style class applies to the element.
classid="..."	Attribute of object	Specifies the location of an object resource, such as a Java applet. Use classid= "java:appletname.class" for Java applets.
data="url"	Attribute of object	Specifies the absolute or relative location of the object's data.
height="n"	Attribute of object	Specifies the vertical dimension (in pixels) of the object.
hspace="n"	Attribute of object	Specifies the size of the margins (in pixels) to the left and right of the object.
id="..."	Attribute of object	Indicates an identifier to associate with the object.
name="..."	Attribute of object	Specifies the name of the object.
standby="..."	Attribute of object	Specifies a message that the browser displays while the object is loading.
style="..."	Attribute of object	Specifies style information.
title="..."	Attribute of object	Specifies a label assigned to the element.
type="..."	Attribute of object	Indicates the MIME type of the object.
vspace="n"	Attribute of object	Specifies the size of the margin (in pixels) at the top and bottom of the object.
width="n"	Attribute of object	Indicates the horizontal dimension (in pixels) of the object.

Part III

TIP

Table 15.2 includes the most common attributes of the `object` element, but there are many additional attributes for special circumstances. For more information about the additional attributes, see the HTML 4.01 specification and the XHTML 1.0 Recommendation at `www.w3.org`. Another excellent source of information is the XHTML 1.0 Reference at `www.zvon.org/xxl/xhtmlReference/Output/index.html`.

When objects require more information—for example, a Java applet usually needs specific settings to run—you pass data to the object with the `param` element. Table 15.3 lists and describes the `param` element and attributes.

TABLE 15.3: Parameter Elements and Attributes

Item	Type	Description
param	Empty element	Specifies parameters passed to an object. Use the param element within the object or applet element.
id="..."	Attribute of param	Assigns the object an ID so other items in the document can identify it.
name="..."	Attribute of param	Indicates the name of the parameter passed to the object; required.
type="..."	Attribute of param	Specifies the MIME type of the data found at the specified URL.
value="..."	Attribute of param	Specifies the value associated with the parameter passed to the object.
valuetype="..."	Attribute of param	Indicates the kind of value passed to the object. Possible values are data, ref, and object.

You can use the `object` element to include almost any kind of object. Let's start with the Java TicTacToe applet shown earlier in Figure 15.4.

To add an applet using the `object` element, follow these steps:

1. Start with a basic document, like this:

```
<!DOCTYPE html
  PUBLIC "-//W3C//DTD XHTML 1.0 Transitional//EN"
  "http://www.w3.org/TR/xhtml1/DTD/xhtml1-transitional.dtd">
<html xmlns="http://www.w3.org/1999/xhtml">
<head>
   <title>TicTacToe</title>
```

```
</head>
<body>
   <h1>TicTacToe Applet </h1>
</body>
</html>
```

2. Add the `object` elements:

```
<h1>TicTacToe Applet </h1>
<object>
</object>
```

3. Add alternate text between the `object` elements:

```
<h1>TicTacToe Applet </h1>
<object>
   If your browser supported Java and objects, you could be
   playing TicTacToe right now.
</object>
```

4. Add the `classid` attribute to indicate the name of the Java class file (program file). You use `classid` to incorporate programs, such as applets or ActiveX controls.

```
<h1>TicTacToe Applet </h1>
<object classid="java:TicTacToe.class">
   If your browser supported Java and objects, you could be
   playing TicTacToe right now.
</object>
```

5. Add the `width` and `height` attributes. A square that is 120×120 pixels should be sufficient.

```
<h1>TicTacToe Applet </h1>
<object classid="java:TicTacToe.class" width="120"
   height="120">
   If your browser supported Java and objects, you could
   be playing TicTacToe right now.
</object>
```

6. If you had the `TicTacToe.class` file, and you saved and tested your document, you'd see something similar to the following:

TicTacToe Object

Users with browsers that don't support the `object` element or don't support Java will see something similar to the following:

TicTacToe Object

Unknown Media Ty

If your browser supported Java and objects, you could be playing TicTacToe right now.

TIP

See Chapter 18, "Bringing Pages to Life with Dynamic HTML and XHTML," for tips on handling missing capabilities more cleanly.

The process for adding video and sound is similar. The only difference is that you use the `data` attribute instead of the `classid` attribute. Also, you add a `type` attribute to show the MIME type of the object. (You don't need the `type` when you're adding an applet, because `java:` precedes the name of the applet, making it clear what kind of object it is.)

MAKING IT SOUND EASY

If you're embedding sounds in your pages, consider using a regular link to the sound file rather than using the `object` element to embed it. The only real advantage to using the `object` element is a neat little widget in the web page that users can use to play the sound as if they were using a VCR. However, those neat little widgets aren't the same size in Internet Explorer and Netscape Navigator, so you end up with either a truncated object or one with loads of extra space around it.

We recommend using an icon or a text link to the sound file—it's much easier. Besides, if the sound takes so long to play that the user has time to click Stop or Pause, the sound file is probably too big.

To add a sound using the `object` tags, follow these steps:

1. Start with a document.

2. Add the `object` tags:

```
<object>
</object>
```

3. Add the data attribute along with the filename:

```
<object data="weirdbrd.aif">
</object>
```

4. Add the type attribute to specify the type of multimedia:

```
<object data="weirdbrd.aif" type="audio/aiff">
</object>
```

5. Add the height and width attributes to specify the object's size:

```
<object data="weirdbrd.aif" type="audio/aiff" height="50"
    width="100">
</object>
```

There you go! If you had the weirdbrd.aif file, your document would now look like Figure 15.3, shown earlier in this chapter.

INCLUDING ACTIVEX CONTROLS

ActiveX controls are similar to Java applets—they're little programs that provide enhanced functionality to a web page. For example, ActiveX controls can provide pop-up menus, the capability to view a Word document through a web page, and almost all the pieces needed for Microsoft's HTML Help. These controls—developed by Microsoft and implemented with Internet Explorer 3—are powerful but Windows-centric. Although you can get a plug-in to view ActiveX controls in Netscape Navigator, you'll find that the results are far more reliable when you view ActiveX controls with Internet Explorer.

If you want to try out some controls—both free and licensed varieties—check out CNet's ActiveX site at http://download.cnet .com/downloads/0-10081.html or Gamelan at www.gamelan.com. If you're so inclined, you can create ActiveX controls using popular Windows development packages, such as Visual Basic or Visual C++. You include ActiveX controls in a page just as you include multimedia elements: You use the object element—as discussed earlier in this chapter.

Remember, Internet Explorer 6 does not support the use of Netscape-style plug-ins and instead supports only the use of ActiveX controls.

What's Next?

This chapter showed you some of the more entertaining elements you can include in your HTML or XHTML documents. Although multimedia files don't always have practical uses, they do make your pages more interesting and give them the "up with technology" look-and-feel. You also learned, however, that multimedia effects have a big disadvantage: The files can be enormous, which slows download time considerably.

In the next chapter, you'll learn about using Cascading Style Sheets to greatly increase your ability to format your documents just the way you want!

Chapter 16

USING STYLE SHEETS

Using Cascading Style Sheets (CSS) is one of the best ways to format HTML and XHTML documents easily and consistently. Style sheets are a major step toward separating presentation from content, enabling the document to specify structure and content and giving you almost total control over page presentation. The latest CSS recommendation adds even more control, including aural style sheets for screen-reading software, more options for formatting printed documents from the web, and options for relative and absolute positioning.

Are style sheets here to stay? Yes. In fact, the HTML 4.01 and XHTML 1.0 specifications deprecate formatting elements and attributes (such as the font element and the align attribute) in favor of style sheets, as we've noted in many places throughout this book.

In this chapter, you'll see how style sheets enhance the effectiveness of HTML and XHTML and how you can benefit from using them. We'll discuss the advantages and limitations of style

Adapted from *Mastering HTML and XHTML*,
by Deborah S. Ray and Eric J. Ray
ISBN 0-7821-4141-2 $49.99

sheets to help you decide whether they're right for your needs. And, of course, you'll find out how to implement them in this chapter; see Appendix B, "Cascading Style Sheets Reference," for a complete reference of style sheet options.

How Do Style Sheets Work?

As we mentioned in Chapter 2, "Getting Acquainted with HTML and XHTML," HTML and XHTML are markup languages that you use to identify structural elements in a document. For example, you can specify that one element is a first-level heading, one is a bullet point, one is a block quotation, and so on by manually inserting formatting elements and attributes. Inserting these elements every place they occur quickly can become a tedious process. With style sheets, however, you specify formatting once, and it's applied throughout the document. If you've used styles in a word processor, you're familiar with this concept.

Style sheets—formally known as the World Wide Web Consortium (W3C) *Cascading Style Sheets* Recommendations—promise to give you layout and format control similar to what you may be accustomed to in programs such as PageMaker or Quark. You can control how page elements look, where they appear, their color and size, the fonts they use, and so on—and do so without awkward workarounds. Now, you can determine page appearance to a far greater extent than was possible before.

WARNING

Before you decide to use style sheets, keep in mind that the newest browsers support all the features of CSS level 1 and many features of CSS level 2, with slight differences between level 2 features supported in Internet Explorer and Netscape Navigator. Current versions of Microsoft Internet Explorer (5 and later), Netscape Navigator (6 and later), and Opera (5 and later) browsers offer very good style sheet support (CSS level 1). However, many style sheet features do not work consistently or at all in earlier browser versions. Version 6 browsers generally offer support for many, but not all, features of CSS2.

WARNING

Regardless of style sheet support, remember that your users can override your settings at any time and use their own style sheets. HTML or XHTML, in any form, cannot ensure that your visitors see exactly what you want them to see. For that, you will have to use Adobe Acrobat Portable Document Format (PDF) files (www.adobe.com), which maintain the document formatting you set.

BROWSERS, USERS, AND STYLE SHEETS

Style sheets were introduced in Internet Explorer 3, Netscape Navigator 4, and Opera 3. In the very unlikely event that you have visitors using those browsers or even older ones, they may experience unexpected formatting glitches or, in the case of older browsers, see plain documents that include little more than the logical formatting elements, such as headings, paragraphs, tables, and lists. Very few people use browsers without good style sheet support (at least CSS level 1), however.

The latest browsers (IE 6, Netscape 7, and Opera 6) all come close to supporting web standards, including CSS1 and many elements of CSS2. Support for web standards allows web developers more potential for a consistent appearance of web pages in different browsers and on different platforms.

Also, your users still have final control over the document appearance, regardless of the formatting you supply in the style sheet. They can disable style sheets or override them with their personal preferences for colors and fonts. This rarely happens, but it is possible. CSS2 offers additional support for users, including the capability for users to override the designer's style sheets. This is a very important part of making the web more accessible to users with disabilities, and we can expect more emphasis on users' needs as CSS and the web develop. See Chapter 6, "Planning for a Usable, Maintainable Website," for more information about making your documents accessible to people with visual impairments.

Part III

Some Advantages of Using Style Sheets

In addition to giving you more control over how your documents appear to users, style sheets let you manage documents more easily than if they were filled with formatting elements. When you place formatting markup in the style sheet, your HTML or XHTML document is less cluttered.

Style sheets also reduce the time you spend developing and maintaining documents. Rather than manually formatting paragraphs of text, you simply change the style definition in one place—the style sheet—and the style sheet applies the definition to all occurrences in the document. No muss, no fuss.

Finally, style sheets give you flexibility from document to document within a website. Even if you set up a style sheet that applies to all pages in the site, you can set up individual style sheets to apply to individual documents. The individual style sheet overrides the global one. In addition, you can tweak individual style sheets further to accommodate special text formatting, such as a document in which certain paragraphs should appear in a different color.

Cascading Style Sheets Level 1

Cascading Style Sheets level 1 (CSS1) introduced extensive style properties for many features of page layout and text presentation. The CSS1 Recommendation was adopted by the W3C in December 1996 and revised in January 1999. The CSS1 style properties include the following:

- ▸ Font properties, including expanded options for setting font size and other font features

- ▸ Text properties, including text alignment and decoration

- ▸ Box properties, such as margins, padding, borders, and floating elements

- ▸ Color and background properties, including background repeat options and background color for elements

- ▸ Classification properties, including styles for displaying lists

All these properties are covered in detail in various sections of this chapter.

TIP

The W3C CSS1 recommendation is available online at www.w3.org/TR/REC-CSS1.

Cascading Style Sheets Level 2

The *CSS2* Recommendation was adopted in May 1998. This Recommendation builds on the features included in CSS1 and adds new style properties, including the following:

- ▸ Media types and properties, including aural style sheets and printed media

- ▸ Positioning properties, such as absolute, relative, and fixed positioning

- ▶ Downloadable fonts

- ▶ Table style properties

- ▶ Additional box properties, including new box types

- ▶ Visual formatting model, including properties for overflow, clipping, and visibility

- ▶ Generated content, used to import content from another web location

- ▶ Text shadows

- ▶ System colors

- ▶ Cursor styles

The features of CSS2 that have widespread support as of this writing (and only in newer browsers) are the positioning properties, some of the changes in CSS selectors, and printed media properties. (For more on selectors, see the section "Developing a Style Sheet," later in this chapter.) Internet Explorer 6 supports the visual formatting model when in standards-compliant mode (see Chapter 13, "Optimizing Your Web Pages for Internet Explorer," for more information on Internet Explorer and web standards). Aural style sheets (even though they're not yet supported), printed media properties, and CSS positioning are discussed in detail later in this chapter.

TIP

The W3C CSS2 recommendation is available online at www.w3.org/TR/REC-CSS2.

Cascading Style Sheets Level 3 and Beyond

Although CSS2 has limited support in current browsers, CSS3 is being developed. Unlike previous versions, CSS3 is being developed as individual modules (much as XHTML is evolving into a modularized approach, as we discuss in Chapter 19, "XHTML: HTML Goes XML"). This will make it easier for browsers to support CSS3 on a module-by-module basis, easier for updates in individual modules, and easier for users, web designers, and web developers to figure out easily which modules are supported in a particular browser. Although there will be more modules to manage with this approach, each module will provide a specific kind of functionality, and (presumably) browsers will use some intelligence in their handling of the various modules.

CSS3 is still in Working Draft form, but some of the modules currently being developed are these:

- ▶ User-interface enhancements for dynamic and interactive features
- ▶ Scalable Vector Graphics (SVG)
- ▶ Behavioral extensions (adding the capability to attach dynamic script actions to elements)
- ▶ Expanded accessibility features
- ▶ International layout properties
- ▶ Multicolumn layout

Future additions to CSS will most likely include further accessibility properties, enhanced multimedia support, and expanded dynamic and interactive capabilities.

TIP

For information on all the style sheet types, including the advanced Extensible Stylesheet Language (XSL), check out the W3C's style site at www.w3.org/Style.

Implementing Style Sheets

As you're perusing the rest of this chapter, remember that your documents and the associated style sheets work as a team. HTML or XHTML documents carry the content, and style sheets carry the formatting information. As you'll see, developing style sheets is a two-part process:

1. You associate (or connect) a style sheet with the document.

2. You develop a style sheet's contents, complete with all the formatting information.

TIP

After you become familiar with creating style sheets, you may create the style sheet first and then associate it with an XHTML document. However, for instruction purposes, it makes more sense for us to tell you how to associate the (as yet nonexistent) style sheet first so that you can test the style sheet as you develop it later in the chapter.

Associating Style Sheets with Documents

You can associate style sheets with your HTML or XHTML documents in four ways:

- ▶ You can embed the style sheet in the document by defining it between the opening and closing head elements.

- ▶ You can store the style sheet in a separate document and either link to it or import it.

- ▶ You can apply style definitions to specified parts of the document.

- ▶ You can use inline style definitions.

Embedding the Style Sheet in the Document

Embedding the style sheet is the easiest of the four methods of associating it with your HTML or XHTML documents. To embed a style sheet, you use the style element, along with style information, between the opening and closing head elements.

Embedding style sheets makes developing styles easy because you have to work with only one document, instead of working with a style sheet document and an HTML or XHTML document. You simply open the document and adjust the style sheet code. If you're working with multiple documents or documents that you update frequently, however, you have to adjust the style sheet in every document if you use the internal style sheet. We recommend using the external style sheet method instead unless a specific document has formatting that applies only to it.

TIP

After you develop an embedded style sheet, consider moving the style definitions to a different file and using an external style sheet. This will make it easier to apply the same styles to multiple documents.

To embed a style sheet in a document, you'll apply the items shown in Table 16.1 between the opening and closing head elements.

TABLE 16.1: Style Sheet Code Components

ITEM	TYPE	DESCRIPTION
style	Element	Specifies the style sheet area within a document. Within this section, you can define or import formatting.
<!--...-->	Comment markup	Hides style sheet contents from non–style-capable browsers.
type="text/css"	Attribute of style	Specifies the type of style sheet; required.

To embed a minimal style sheet in an existing document, follow these steps:

1. Start with a functional document header.

```
<!DOCTYPE html PUBLIC "-//W3C//DTD XHTML 1.0 Strict//EN"
    "http://www.w3.org/TR/xhtml1/DTD/xhtml1-strict.dtd">
<html xmlns="http://www.w3.org/1999/xhtml">
<head>
    <title>Embedded Style</title>
</head>
</html>
```

TIP

Choose an appropriate DTD for your document, just as you usually would. Theoretically, you could use the Strict DTD in a document that contains style sheets, because the Transitional DTD allows formatting elements, and the purpose of style sheets is to avoid using them. Realistically, however, the Transitional DTD will meet most needs well.

2. Add opening and closing style elements as well as the type attribute:

```
<head>
    <title>Embedded Style</title>
    <style type="text/css">
    </style>
</head>
```

3. Add the comment markup (<!--...-->), within the style element to hide the contents from non–style-capable browsers.

```
<head>
    <title>Embedded Style</title>
    <style type="text/css">
        <!--
        -->
    </style>
</head>
```

Browsers that do not support style sheets ignore the `style` element but display the text that appears between them. Adding comment markup within the `style` elements ensures that the styles will not appear as content in older or less-capable browsers.

4. Add style definitions within the comment markup. In this (minimal) example, we specify that the paragraph text is red.

```
<head>
    <title>ASR Outfitters</title>
    <style type="text/css">
        <!--
        p {color: red}
        -->
    </style>
</head>
```

5. Add a body element, a p element, and content for the p element, and you're ready to test your embedded style.

```
<!DOCTYPE html PUBLIC "-//W3C/DTD XHTML 1.0 Strict//EN"
    "http://www.w3.org/TR/xhtml1/DTD/xhtml1-strict.dtd">
<html xmlns="http://www.w3.org/1999/xhtml">
<head>
    <title>Embedded Style</title>
    <style type="text/css">
        <!--
        p {color: red}
        -->
    </style>
</head>
<body>
    <p>This paragraph uses an embedded style.</p>
</body>
</html>
```

That's it! To test your embedded style sheet, save this markup and open the document in your favorite browser.

Storing Style Sheets Separately

A separate style sheet (an *external style sheet*) is simply a plain-text file, saved with a `.css` file extension, that includes style definitions. You should develop an external style sheet anytime you're working with several documents that share similar formatting. In this case, you develop a single style sheet and apply it to all the documents, as shown in Figure 16.1. You then can make formatting changes in all the documents simultaneously simply by changing the external style sheet.

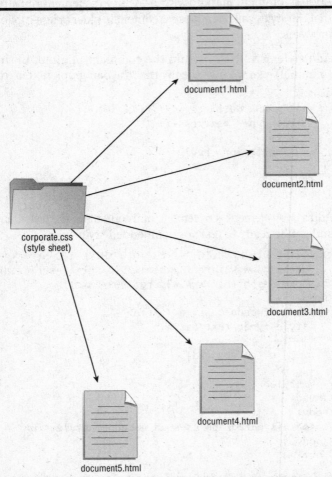

FIGURE 16.1:   When you develop a separate style sheet, you can easily apply styles to many XHTML documents.

TIP

Even if you're working with only a few documents, consider developing an external style sheet. You never know how many documents your site will eventually include.

After you develop the external style sheet document, you associate it with the document(s) using one of two methods: importing or linking.

Importing a Style Sheet

This method is handy when you're developing multiple style sheets, each with a particular function. For example, as illustrated in Figure 16.2, you can develop a page that applies corporate styles, one that applies styles for your department, and another that specifies particular document formatting. Rather than wading through a 10-page style sheet, you work with multiple smaller ones.

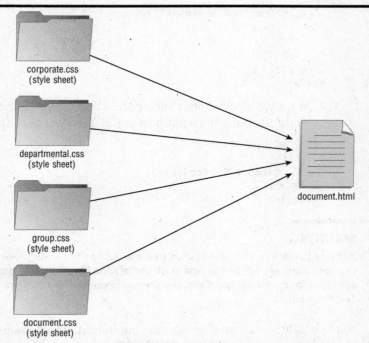

corporate.css
(style sheet)

departmental.css
(style sheet)

group.css
(style sheet)

document.css
(style sheet)

document.html

Part III

FIGURE 16.2:   Importing enables you to maintain a detailed style sheet easily.

TIP

Importing style sheets works well only in some browsers. To find out which browsers currently support importing (as well as other CSS properties), check the most current version of the style sheet Reference Guide Master Grid at `www.webreview.com/style/css1/charts/mastergrid.shtml`.

You import a style sheet by inserting an @import statement within the style element inside the comment delimiters. The syntax for these imports is @import url(...), with the URL of the imported style sheet inside the parentheses.

To import a style sheet, follow these steps:

1.   Start with a complete style block, such as the following code:

```
<!DOCTYPE html PUBLIC "-//W3C/DTD XHTML 1.0 Strict//EN"
    "http://www.w3.org/TR/xhtml1/DTD/xhtml1-strict.dtd">
<html xmlns="http://www.w3.org/1999/xhtml">
<head>
    <title>Imported Style</title>
    <style type="text/css">
        <!--
        -->
    </style>
</head>
```

2.   Within a style block or style sheet, add a line similar to the following (substitute the name of your CSS file for red.css):

```
<style type="text/css">
    <!--
        @import url(red.css);
    -->
</style>
```

WARNING

If you're using @import in addition to other embedded style properties, @import must always be the first style declaration listed, followed by any additional @import declarations, and then followed by the additional style declarations.

A complete style block that does nothing but import two style sheets (red.css and blue.css) would look like the following:

```
<style type="text/css">
    <!--
```

```
        @import url(red.css);
        @import url(blue.css);
    -->
</style>
```

WARNING

Currently, the main advantage of @import over the link method is the fact that it is *not* supported in Netscape 4.x browsers. This means you can write an external style sheet that includes features supported in later browsers and link to it using the @import method. Netscape 4.x will ignore the link.

Linking a Style Sheet

This method has a distinct advantage over the other methods: It gives users a choice of style sheets to use for a specific page. For example, you can link one style sheet to a page for users who will read on-screen and link a different style sheet to the same page for users who will print, as shown in Figure 16.3. Theoretically, you even could develop a style sheet (since browsers implement this functionality) optimized for aural presentation.

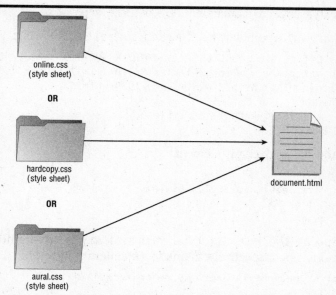

FIGURE 16.3: Linking lets you apply style sheets for specific uses.

Although you can import a style sheet, linking the style sheet is a better long-term choice because future browser versions should offer users more flexibility in handling style sheets, including the option to select from multiple style sheets. Importing offers no choices—it just loads the style sheet. Table 16.2 explains the elements and attributes you use to link style sheets to documents.

TABLE 16.2: Elements and Attributes for Linking Style Sheets

ITEM	TYPE	DESCRIPTION
link	Empty element	References a style sheet.
href="url"	Attribute of link	Identifies the style sheet source as a standard URL.
rel="stylesheet"	Attribute of link	Specifies that the referenced file is a style sheet.
title="..."	Attribute of link	Names the style sheet. Unnamed style sheets are always applied; named style sheets are applied by default or provided as options, depending on the rel attribute used.
type="text/css"	Attribute of link	Specifies the type of the style sheet.

To link a style sheet to a document, follow these steps:

1. Start with a complete head section, such as the following:

```
<!DOCTYPE html PUBLIC "-//W3C/DTD XHTML 1.0 Strict//EN"
    "http://www.w3.org/TR/xhtml1/DTD/xhtml1-strict.dtd">
<html xmlns="http://www.w3.org/1999/xhtml">
<head>
    <title>Linked Style</title>
</head>
```

2. Add the link empty element:

```
<head>
    <title>Linked Style</title>
    <link />
</head>
```

3. Specify the rel and type values of stylesheet and text/css, respectively, to link to a standard style sheet:

```
<link rel="stylesheet" type="text/css" />
```

4. Specify the address of the style sheet with the href attribute. Specify either a relative URL, as in the sample code, or an absolute URL.

```
<link rel="stylesheet" href="blue.css" type="text/css" />
```

There you go! To link your document to more than one style sheet, simply include multiple link elements, complete with each of the style sheets to which they link. For example, you might link a document to a generic style sheet that contains basic style definitions and then also link it to a more specific style sheet that contains definitions suitable to a particular style of document—instructions, marketing, and so on. If you link to multiple style sheets, all take effect. However, if you define the same element in multiple sheets, the later links override the previous links.

The HTML and XHTML specifications indicate that you also can link your documents to optional style sheets using the rel="alternate stylesheet" attribute so that users can choose which styles to use. Theoretically, you can provide optional style sheets that, for instance, let users choose a low-bandwidth style for viewing over a modem connection or a high-bandwidth style with lots of cool images for viewing over a high-speed connection. You can present choices for high-resolution and high color depth monitors and provide alternatives for standard monitors at lower color depths. However, at the time of writing, no browsers support optional style sheets.

Applying Style Sheets to Parts of Documents

So far, you've seen how to apply style sheets to entire documents. You can also apply styles included in a style sheet to specific parts of documents, as shown in Figure 16.4. This is called applying *style classes*, which you define in your style sheet. For example, suppose you specify in a style sheet that the first line of all paragraphs should be indented. You may find that paragraphs after a bulleted list should not be indented because they continue the information from the paragraph before the list.

Part III

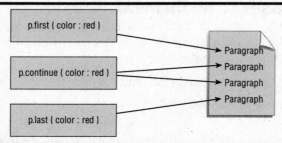

FIGURE 16.4:　Applying style classes, you can specify how parts of XHTML documents appear.

To address this issue, you can format the paragraph manually for that occurrence. However, a better solution is to set up a new paragraph element class within your style definition, called `continue`, for example. You can use this new paragraph class whenever the first line of a paragraph should not be indented. Table 16.3 describes the elements and attributes you use to apply classes.

TABLE 16.3: Elements and Attributes for Applying Classes

ITEM	TYPE	DESCRIPTION
div	Element	Holds style attributes and applies them to the code between the opening and closing elements. Surround paragraphs or other block-level elements with these.
span	Element	Holds style attributes and applies them to the code between the opening and closing elements. Surround letters, words, and other inline elements with these elements.
class="..."	Attribute of various elements	References a style class to apply to a specified part of a document.
id="..."	Attribute of various elements	Specifies a unique name associated with a specific style definition. You can use this only once within a style sheet.

You can apply a class to an existing HTML or XHTML element, or you can use the `div` and `span` elements to specify that the class applies to other elements—such as specific letters or words—not individually specified by an HTML or XHTML element.

Applying Classes to an Element

You apply a class to an existing element—such as p, h1, ul, and so on—to specify formatting for a group of items. To apply classes within an HTML or XHTML document, follow these steps:

1. Start with an existing paragraph within a document.

   ```
   <p>Many people buy ASR products despite the higher
       cost.</p>
   ```

2. Add the `class` attribute to the opening p element, like this:

   ```
   <p class="">Many people buy ASR products despite the
       higher cost.</p>
   ```

3. Add the name of the paragraph class. (You'll see how to define and name classes when you develop the style sheet later in this chapter.)

```
<p class="continue">Many people buy ASR products despite
    the higher cost.</p>
```

That's it!

If you have a specific unique formatting need—a one-time per document need—you can define a style ID and then apply the id attribute in place of the class attribute in the preceding example. You would end up with something like this:

```
<p id="538fv1">Many people buy ASR products despite the
    higher cost.</p>
```

Applying Classes to Other Document Parts

You also can apply classes to specific parts of a document that do not have existing elements. For example, suppose you want to make the first few lines in the document body a different color. Because no specific element exists to designate the first few lines, you must specify the paragraph or text to which the style applies.

To apply classes to specific parts of a document, use the div and span elements, described previously in Table 16.3. Those elements provide a place to apply class formatting when there's no existing formatting.

You use the div element to apply classes to block-level sections of a document—areas where you need the class to apply to more content than just one element. Here are the steps to apply the div class margin, which is defined elsewhere to set the left margin to 40 percent, for example:

1. Start with a section of an existing document:

```
<p>Many people buy ASR products despite the higher
    cost.</p>
<blockquote>"We sell only the highest quality outdoor
    equipment."</blockquote>
```

2. Add the div elements around the section:

```
<div>
<p>Many people buy ASR products despite the higher
    cost.</p>
<blockquote>"We sell only the highest quality outdoor
    equipment. "</blockquote>
</div>
```

3. Add the appropriate class attribute:

```
<div class="margin">
<p>Many people buy ASR products despite the higher
    cost.</p>
<blockquote>"We sell only the highest quality outdoor
    equipment. "</blockquote>
</div>
```

The margin class now will apply to both the p and blockquote elements.

Use the span element to apply classes to characters or words—any stretch of content that's *less* than a full, regular element. For example, to apply the firstuse class (that you define elsewhere) to a word, follow these steps:

1. Start with an existing element—for example, a p element:

```
<p>Many people buy ASR products despite the higher
    cost.</p>
```

2. Add the span opening and closing elements:

```
<p>Many people buy <span>ASR products</span> despite the
    higher cost.</p>
```

3. Add the appropriate class attribute:

```
<p>Many people buy <span class="firstuse">ASR
    products</span> despite the higher cost.</p>
```

TIP

You might use classes in conjunction with tables (covered in Chapter 11, "Presenting Information in Tables"). Table elements accept class attributes to apply formatting—either to the table sections you specify, to individual cells, rows, and columns, or to the table, cells, rows, or columns as a whole. (See the section "Applying Classes to an Element," earlier in this chapter.)

Applying Inline Style Definitions

Applying inline style definitions throughout a document is similar to adding formatting attributes. For example, just as you can apply an align attribute to a paragraph, you can apply a style definition within the p element. Of course, with style sheets you have far more formatting possibilities than with traditional HTML or XHTML formatting commands.

The technique is simple: add the style="..." attribute to any element. Provide the style definition within quotes (and if there are quoted items within the style attribute, put them in single quotes). For that element, these values will override any other style definitions that are defined, imported, or linked into the document.

Although you wouldn't use this method to apply styles throughout a document—it's extremely time consuming and defeats the purpose of having style sheets—you could use it in special cases for a specific instance in an existing style sheet. For example, your style sheet might specify that paragraphs appear in blue text. You then could apply an inline style to specify that one particular paragraph appears in red text.

To add a style definition to an existing element, follow these steps:

1. Start with an existing element—for example, the p element:

   ```
   <p>Many people buy ASR products despite the higher
       cost.</p>
   ```

2. Add the `style` attribute:

   ```
   <p style="">Many people buy ASR products despite the
       higher cost.</p>
   ```

3. Add the style definition(s), separated by semicolons. Substitute single quotes for double quotes within the attribute; otherwise, you'll close the attribute prematurely:

   ```
   <p style="color: red; font-family: 'Times New Roman',
       serif"> Many people buy ASR products despite the higher
       cost.</p>
   ```

TIP

Notice that Times New Roman is in quotes, and serif is not. This is because Times New Roman contains white space and therefore must be in quotation marks. However, serif does not contain white space; therefore, it does not need to be quoted.

WARNING

Using style sheets in this manner negates many of the advantages of style sheets. If you need to apply styles to a specific element in a specific case, use classes or ID attributes, as discussed in the previous section.

What Is Cascading?

As you have seen in the preceding sections, there are several ways to specify styles for a document: external style sheets, embedded styles, and inline styles. Conflicts may exist between these styles; for example, the

Part III

external style sheet specifies that all text in the document is red, and the embedded style specifies blue text for paragraphs. The browser resolves these conflicting style definitions by applying the precedence rules for style sheets; these rules are called *the cascade*.

The two general cascading rules are these:

1. The most specific style rule will be applied—a style that applies only to paragraphs is more specific than a style that applies to all the document text.

2. If two style rules are equally specific, the style rule that occurs *later* is considered more specific and will be the one applied. If you have two different style definitions for paragraph color, such as this:

```
p {color:green}
p {color:blue}
```

the second definition will take precedence; therefore, the paragraph text will be displayed in blue.

Style definitions declared in an external style sheet come before style definitions embedded in a document, and those come before inline style declarations. Therefore, the precedence order, from lowest to highest, is this:

3. External style sheet

2. Embedded styles, including `@import` (if any, override external style sheet)

1. Inline styles (if any, override others)

DEVELOPING A STYLE SHEET

In the previous sections, you learned how to associate a style sheet with a document. Your goal now is to develop the style sheet—to specify the style definitions you want to include. A *style definition* (also called a *style rule*) specifies formatting characteristics.

You can choose from any combination of the eight categories of style properties. We'll cover each of these in its own section later in this chapter.

► Font Properties

Specify character-level (inline) formatting, such as the typeface.

- ▶ Text Properties

  Specify display characteristics for text, such as alignment or letter spacing.

- ▶ Box Properties

  Specify characteristics for sections of text, at the paragraph (or block) level.

- ▶ Color and Background Properties

  Specify color, background color, and images at both the inline and block levels.

- ▶ Classification Properties

  Specify display characteristics of lists and elements (such as p or h1) as inline or block level.

- ▶ Aural Style Sheet Properties

  Control the presentation of documents by sound (CSS2 only).

- ▶ Printed Style Sheet Properties

  Add features specifically to control printed output of documents (CSS2 only).

- ▶ Positioning Properties

  Add features to precisely control the placement of elements on the display (CSS2 only).

You can easily get carried away with formatting options, but start simple. Look through the style sheet information in Appendix B to get an idea of the vast number of options. As you might guess, using even some of these options can quickly get complex.

Before we dive into developing a style sheet, let's take a look at some style sheet code:

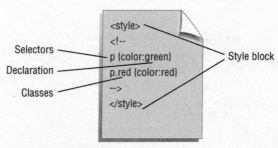

Part III

Here's what each part does:

▶ The Style Block

This includes style elements and comment markup, plus style definitions (or rules).

▶ Selectors

These are HTML or XHTML elements. In this example, the p—as in a paragraph element—is a selector.

▶ Declarations

These are the properties of the elements, such as color, background, alignment, and font. In this example, `color:green` and `color:red` are the declarations. A declaration consists of a property and a value, separated by a colon. In the second example, `color` is the property and `red` is the value. The property/value combination is enclosed within curly brackets, or braces—{ }.

▶ Classes

These specify an additional style definition associated with specific occurrences of an element. For example, paragraphs tagged with `<p class="red">` use this style class.

Each style definition can define the formatting associated with a specific HTML or XHTML element, with a specific `class`, or with a specific ID. The formatting associated with elements appears in the document without any special action on your part (aside from referencing or including the style sheet in your document). Style definitions for classes or IDs also require that you add the `class` or `id` attribute to the appropriate document section before the formatting can appear in the document.

To add these elements in an internal style sheet, follow these steps:

1. Be sure the style block is in place:

```
<style type="text/css">
  <!--
  -->
</style>
```

2. Add a selector and braces:

```
<style type="text/css">
  <!--
    p { }
```

```
    -->
  </style>
```

3. Add the declaration between the braces:

```
<style type="text/css">
  <!--
      p { color: aqua }
  -->
</style>
```

STYLE SHEET TIPS

As you're building a style sheet, the process will be easier and the results more readable if you follow these guidelines:

▶ To include multiple selectors, place them on separate lines, like this:

```
<style type="text/css">
  <!--
      p {color: red}
      h1 {color: blue}
      blockquote {color: green}
  -->
</style>
```

▶ To provide multiple declarations for a single selector, group the declarations within the braces, separated by semicolons. In addition, you might find the style definitions easier to read if you space them out somewhat and put only one declaration on a single line. For example, to define p as red text with a yellow background, use the following markup:

```
<style type="text/css">
  <!--
      p { color: red;
          background: yellow; }
  -->
</style>
```

▶ Start at the highest level—the most general level—within your document, which is probably the body. Format the body as you want most of the document to appear, and then use more specific style rules to override the body settings.

CONTINUED ➡

Part III

▶ White space within style definitions and rules is ignored; each of the following lines of code produces the same result:

```
p{color:red}
p {color:red}
p {color: red}
p { color:red}
p { color:red }
```

In addition, become familiar with ways to specify measurements and values, which are discussed in the following two sections.

Specifying Measurements

When specifying locations of elements, you also might want to specify their size. For example, when specifying that the first line of a paragraph is indented, you can also specify the size of the indention. In general, provide measurements in the units shown in Table 16.4. You also can express most measurements as a percentage of the browser window.

Your measurement might look like one of these:

```
p { text-indent: 2px }
p { text-indent: 1em }
```

TABLE 16.4: Units of Measurement in Style Sheets

UNIT	WHAT IT IS	DESCRIPTION
cm	Centimeter	The measurement in centimeters.
em	Em space	In typography, an em is the width of a capital M in the typeface being used. In CSS, 1 em is equal to the font size—for example, if the font size is 12pt, the size of 1 em is equal to 12 points.
ex	x-height	The height of a lowercase letter x in the typeface being used.
in	Inch	The measurement in inches.
mm	Millimeter	The measurement in millimeters.
pc	Pica	A typographic measurement that equals 1/6 inch.
pt	Point	A typographic measurement that equals 1/72 inch.
px	Pixel	An individual screen dot.

Relative units such as em usually are preferred to absolute units such as pt when specifying font size because relative units are scalable by the user. For example, users with visual disabilities may set their browser preferences to larger text. If the font size is specified in ems, all the text will be scaled proportionately; the same text layout relationships exist, just at a larger size.

Specifying Colors in Style Rules

When using style sheets, you can specify colors in the standard HTML or XHTML ways (as hexadecimal #rrggbb values or as color names), as well as in two other ways, which use a slightly different approach to specify proportions of red, green, and blue. The following shows how to specify red in each method.

Method	Example
Hex Code	p{color: #ff0000}
Color Name	p{color: red}
Decimal	p{color: rgb(255,0,0)}
Percentage	p{color: rgb(100%,0%,0%)}

TIP

Although each of these is equally easy to use, we recommend using the #rrggbb option; it's likely to be more familiar because it matches HTML or XHTML color statements, as described in Chapter 3, "Creating Your First HTML or XHTML Document," and Chapter 7, "Formatting the Body Section of Your Pages."

In the following sections, we'll show you how to develop an embedded style sheet. After you complete an embedded style sheet, you can move it to a separate document and import it or link it.

To follow along with the example, have a document with the complete structure elements ready, or use Listing 16.1.

Listing 16.1: A Document with the Complete Structure Elements

```
<!DOCTYPE html PUBLIC
"-//W3C/DTD XHTML 1.0 Transitional//EN"
  "http://www.w3.org/TR/xhtml1/DTD/xhtml1-transitional.dtd">
```

```
<html xmlns="http://www.w3.org/1999/xhtml">
<head>
  <title>ASR Outfitters</title>
</head>
<body>
  <h1>Welcome to ASR Outfitters!</h1>
  <p>We're happy to welcome you to our newly redesigned web
site, featuring <b>styles</b> (because they look cool) as
well as redesigned graphics. Please take the
<a href="tour.html"> tour of our site</a>
if you haven't been here in a while. In particular,
you may appreciate the now automatically updated
camping news, as well as the new weather imagemap.
Additionally, we've been getting some nice kudos
from frequent and occasional visitors.</p>
  <blockquote>Your site always provides timely and useful
  information. Keep up the good work.<br />
  Jim Smith
  </blockquote>
  <hr />
  <h2>What's Here</h2>
  <ul>
    <li><a href="camping.html">Camping News</a> provides the
    latest comments from the trails.</li>
    <li><a href="weather.html">Check Weather</a> offers
    weather updates from a variety of sources.</li>
    <li><a href="clubs.html">Clubs</a> gives local hiking
    and mountaineering clubs a place to provide information
    about their activities. </li>
    <li><a href="catalog.html">Catalog</a> presents our
    entire inventory, including announcements of the latest
    sales. </li>
    <li><a href="contact.html">Contact Us</a> links to a
    page with a contact form, e-mail addresses, snail mail
    addresses, and phone numbers. If it isn't here, you
    can't find us.</li>
  </ul>
  <h2>What We Do</h2>
  <p>In addition to providing the latest camping and outdoor
  activities news, we also provide mountaineering and hiking
  equipment nationwide via mail order as well as through our
```

```
stores in the Rocky Mountains. Please take a few minutes to
look through our
<a href="catalog.html">online offerings</a>.
</p>
<h2>Other Issues</h2>
<ul>
    <li>As you may know, our URL was misprinted in the
    latest <i>Hiking News</i>. Please tell your hiking friends
    that the correct URL is
    <tt>http://www.asroutfitters.com/</tt>.
    </li>
    <li>To collect a $1000 reward, turn in the name of the
    person who set the fire in the Bear Lake area
    last weekend.
        <ol>
            <li>Call 888-555-1212.</li>
            <li>Leave the name on the recording.</li>
            <li>Provide contact information so we can send
            you the reward.</li>
        </ol>
    </li>
</ul>
<h2>What Would You Like To See?</h2>
<p>If you have suggestions or comments about the site or
other information we could provide, we'd love to know
about it. Drop us an e-mail at
<a href="mailto:asroutfitters@example.com">
asroutfitters@example.com</a>. Of course, you could also
contact us more traditionally at the following address:
</p>
<address>ASR Outfitters<br />
  4700 N. Center<br />
  South Logan, UT 87654<br />
  801-555-3422
</address>
</body>
</html>
```

Without any styles or formatting other than the standard browser
defaults, the document from Listing 16.1 looks something like
Figure 16.5.

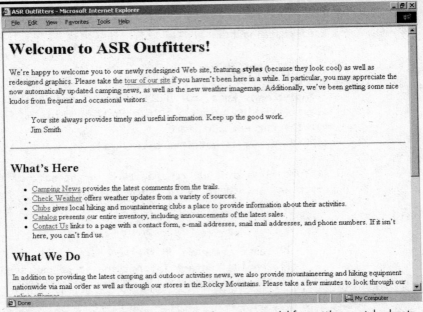

FIGURE 16.5:   An XHTML document without any special formatting or style sheets

To add a style block to the document, follow these steps:

1. Add a pair of opening and closing `style` elements within the document head, as shown in the following code.

```
<!DOCTYPE html PUBLIC
    "-//W3C/DTD XHTML 1.0 Transitional//EN"
 "http://www.w3.org/TR/xhtml1/DTD/xhtml1-
    transitional.dtd">
<html xmlns="http://www.w3.org/1999/xhtml">
<head>
    <title>ASR Outfitters</title>
    <style type="text/css">
    </style>
</head>
```

2. Add the comment markup (`<!-- -->`) within the `style` elements, as shown here:

```
<style type="text/css">
    <!--
    -->
</style>
```

After the `style` element and comment markup are in place, define the style sheet. You specify style properties, such as fonts, text, boxes, colors, backgrounds, and classifications, as discussed in the next section. Think of defining styles as specifying rules for what each element should look like. For example, specify that you want all text blue, all bullets indented, all headings centered, and so on.

SETTING STYLE SHEET PROPERTIES

The following sections cover how to set properties for fonts, text, boxes, colors, backgrounds, and classifications. The sections do not build on one another; instead, they show you how to set each of the properties separately, based on the sample ASR Outfitters page. Through these examples, you'll see *some* of the style sheet effects you can achieve. For a more complete list of style sheet options, see Appendix B.

Setting Font Properties

If the fonts you specify are not available on a user's computer, the browser will display text in a font that is available. To ensure that one of your preferred fonts is used, choose multiple font families and common fonts and, in addition, always include a generic font family choice. Table 16.5 shows some of the basic font properties and values.

TABLE 16.5: Font Properties

PROPERTY	POSSIBLE VALUES
font	Any or all of the following font properties can be set within this combination font property.
font-family	Font names, such as Times New Roman or Arial, or generic font families, such as serif, sans-serif, monospace, fantasy, and cursive.
font-size	xx-small, x-small, small, medium, large, x-large, xx-large, or size measurement in length or percentage.
font-style	normal, italic, oblique.
font-variant	normal, small-caps.
font-weight	normal, bold, bolder, lighter, 100, 200, 300, 400, 500, 600, 700, 800, 900.

Part III

The following example sets a basic font for the whole document—everything between the opening and closing body elements. It sets the basic font for a document to Comic Sans MS, with Technical and Times New Roman as other choices and with a generic serif font as the last choice.

1. Within the style block, add a body selector and braces to hold its properties:

```
<style type="text/css">
   <!--
      body {}
   -->
</style>
```

2. Add the property. To set only the typeface, use font-family:

```
<style type="text/css">
   <!--
      body { font-family }
   -->
</style>
```

3. Add a colon to separate the property from the value:

```
<style type="text/css">
   <!--
      body { font-family: }
   -->
</style>
```

4. Add the value "Comic Sans MS" (the first choice typeface). (If the font family name contains a space, put the name in quotes. Otherwise, quotes are optional.)

```
<style type="text/css">
   <!--
      body { font-family: "Comic Sans MS" }
   -->
</style>
```

5. Add additional values, as you choose, separated by commas. Conclude your list of fonts with either a serif or sans-serif font that's likely to match a font on the user's computer.

```
<style type="text/css">
   <!--
      body { font-family: "Comic Sans MS", Technical,
         "Times New Roman", serif }
   -->
</style>
```

Figure 16.6 shows the resulting page, complete with the new font for the document body.

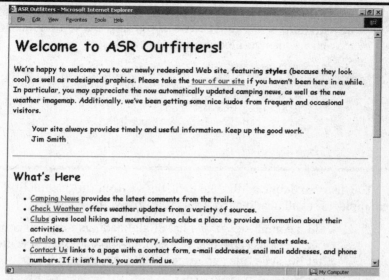

FIGURE 16.6: We've converted our whole page to a new font, without having to insert font elements in the document!

TIP

Newer browsers support three additional choices for generic font families. In addition to serif and sans-serif, the three additional generic font families are cursive, fantasy, and monospace.

SETTING LINK CHARACTERISTICS

You use three special style classes (also known as *anchor pseudo-classes*) along with font style rules to control the colors of links in your document:

▶ a:link

▶ a:active

▶ a:visited

CONTINUED ➡

Use these within your style sheet definition to specify the rules that apply to links, active links, and visited links. For example, to set unvisited links to blue, active links to red, and visited links to magenta, your style block would look like this:

```
<style type="text/css">
  <!--
    a:link { color: blue }
    a:active { color: red }
    a:visited { color: magenta }
  -->
</style>
```

You also can define additional text styles within the document. For example, to set all headings to Arial italic, follow these steps:

1. Add a comma-separated list of all headings to the existing style block as selectors. The comma-separated list specifies that the style rule applies to each selector individually.

    ```
    <style type="text/css">
      <!--
        body { font-family: "Comic Sans MS", Technical,
                            "Times New Roman", serif }
        h1, h2, h3, h4, h5, h6
      -->
    </style>
    ```

2. Add braces:

    ```
    h1, h2, h3, h4, h5, h6 { }
    ```

3. Add the `font-family` property, with `Arial` as the first choice, `Helvetica` as the second choice, and `sans-serif` as the third choice:

    ```
    h1, h2, h3, h4, h5, h6 { font-family: Arial,
                                          Helvetica,
                                          sans-serif }
    ```

4. After the `font-family` values, add a semicolon and a new line so that you can easily enter (and read) the font style rule:

    ```
    h1, h2, h3, h4, h5, h6 { font-family: Arial,
                                          Helvetica,
                                          sans-serif;
                           }
    ```

5. Add the font-style property, a colon, and the italic value:

```
h1, h2, h3, h4, h5, h6 { font-family: Arial,
                                      Helvetica,
                                      sans-serif;
                         font-style: italic }
```

6. Continue adding font properties, separated by semicolons, if you want to define other aspects, such as font size or weight. The following lines of code show the headings set to a larger size and weight than usual. You'll see the results in Figure 16.7:

```
<style type="text/css">
<!--
      body { font-family: "Comic Sans MS", Technical,
                          "Times New Roman", serif }
      h1, h2, h3, h4, h5, h6 { font-family: Arial,
                                            Helvetica,
                                            sans-serif;
                               font-style: italic;
                               font-size: x-large;
                               font-weight: bolder; }

      -->
</style>
```

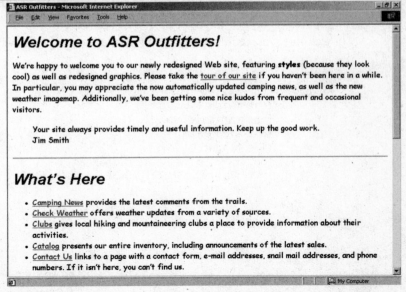

FIGURE 16.7: The result of setting the font family, style, size, and weight for headings

Part III

COMBINING FONT PROPERTIES

If you use the special, combination font property to set several different font properties at once, the properties must be specified in a certain order or they won't display correctly in a browser.

▶ The first are font-style, font-weight, and font-variant. They can be in any order, but they must come before other font properties. Any of these three properties can be omitted, and default values will be used.

▶ Next is font-size, which is required if you use the combination font property.

▶ You can follow font-size by a slash (/) and a line-height value, which specifies how far apart the lines in a paragraph should be:

```
p { font-size: 12pt/14.4pt }
```

Line height also can be set as a separate font property—for example:

```
p { font-size: 12pt; line-height: 14.4pt }
```

(See "Setting Text Properties," the next section in this chapter.)

▶ Last is font-family, which also is required if you use the combination font property.

For example, you could specify each font property separately:

```
<style type="text/css">
   <!--
   body {font-style: italic;
         font-weight: bold;
         font-variant: normal;
         font-size: 1em;
         line-height: 1.2em;
         font-family: "Zapf Renaissance",
                      "Snell Roundhand", cursive}
   -->
</style>
```

The properties could be combined:

```
<style type="text/css"
   <!--
```

CONTINUED ➡

```
body {font: italic bold 1em/1.2em "Zapf Renaissance",
            "Snell Roundhand", cursive}
    -->
</style>
```

Setting Text Properties

Text properties specify the characteristics of *text blocks* (sections of text, not individual characters). Table 16.6 shows some of the most common text properties.

TABLE 16.6: Text Properties

PROPERTY	POSSIBLE VALUES
letter-spacing	Measurement
line-height	Number, measurement, or percentage
text-align	left, right, center, justify
text-decoration	none, underline, overline, line-through, blink
text-indent	Measurement or percentage
text-transform	none, capitalize, uppercase, lowercase
vertical-align	baseline, super, sub, top, text-top, middle, bottom, text-bottom, or a percentage
word-spacing	Measurement

You apply these properties to selectors in the same way you apply font-level properties. To indent paragraphs and set up a special, unindented paragraph class, follow these steps:

1. Within the style block, add a p selector and braces:

   ```
   <style type="text/css">
       <!--
           p { }
       -->
   </style>
   ```

Part III

2. Add the `text-indent` property, with a value of 5% to indent all regular paragraphs by 5 percent of the total window width:

```
<style type="text/css">
   <!--
      p { text-indent: 5% }
   -->
</style>
```

3. Add the `p.noindent` selector (and braces) on a new line within the style block. Using a standard selection, in conjunction with a descriptive term that you make up, you create a new style class within the style sheet:

```
<style type="text/css">
   <!--
      p { text-indent: 5% }
      p.noindent { }
   -->
</style>
```

4. Add the `text-indent` property, with a value of 0% to specify no indent:

```
<style type="text/css">
   <!--
      p { text-indent: 5% }
      p.noindent { text-indent: 0% }
   -->
</style>
```

5. To specify which text should be formatted without an indent, add a new p element with a `class="noindent"` attribute, as shown here:

```
<p>We're happy to welcome you to our newly redesigned web
   site, featuring <b>styles</b> (because they look cool)
   as well as redesigned graphics. Please take the
   <a href="tour.html">tour of our site</a> if you haven't
   been here in a while. In particular, you may appreciate
   the now automatically updated camping news as well as
   the new weather imagemap.</p>
<p class="noindent">Additionally, we've been getting some
   nice kudos from frequent and occasional visitors.</p>
```

Figure 16.8 shows the results. All text tagged with p in the document is indented by 5 percent of the window width, and special formatting, set up with the `class` attribute, does not indent.

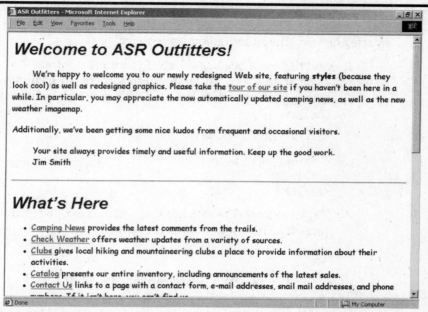

FIGURE 16.8: Setting text properties lets you customize your documents—the second paragraph is not indented, and the first one is, because of a style class.

SPECIFYING GENERIC STYLE CLASSES

You also can specify a class without a selector, as in the following style block:

```
<style type="text/css">
<!--
    .red { color: #ff0000 }
-->
</style>
```

You can use a *generic class*, such as red in this example, with any elements in your document. However, if you specify an element with a class (p.red, for example), you can use that class only with p elements.

You also can use text properties to apply special formatting to headings. To format all headings with a line below them, centered, and with extra spacing between the letters, follow these steps:

1. Add the list of heading selectors you want to format to your basic style sheet. To apply these formats to headings 1 through 3, for example, list h1, h2, h3, with braces following the list:

```
<style type="text/css">
  <!--
    h1, h2, h3 { }
  -->
</style>
```

2. To place a line below each heading, add the text-decoration property with underline as the value:

```
<style type="text/css">
  <!--
    h1, h2, h3 { text-decoration: underline }
  -->
</style>
```

3. Add a semicolon to separate the rules, and add the text-align property with a value of center to center the headings:

```
<style type="text/css">
  <!--
    h1, h2, h3 { text-decoration: underline;
                 text-align: center }
  -->
</style>
```

4. Finally, add another separation semicolon and the letter-spacing property with a value of 5px (5 pixels):

```
<style type="text/css">
  <!--
    h1, h2, h3 { text-decoration: underline;
                 text-align: center;
                 letter-spacing: 5px }
  -->
</style>
```

The sample page looks like Figure 16.9.

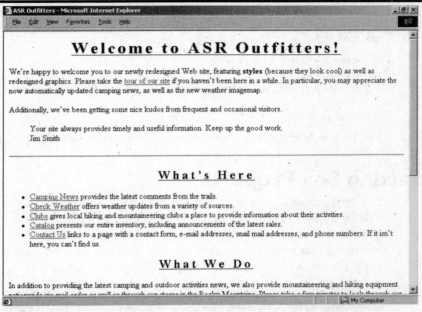

FIGURE 16.9: You can apply text properties to several elements at once—for example, centering all headings.

SPECIFYING STYLE IDS

You can specify an ID for a one-time use—for example, if you're developing a Dynamic HTML or XHTML document and want to format specific elements in specific contexts. Use a # at the beginning of the `id` selector, as in the following style block:

```
<style type="text/css">
  <!--
      #firstusered { color: red }
  -->
</style>
```

You can use an ID, such as `firstusered` in this example, with any single `id` attribute in your document. If you specify an element with the `id` attribute (`<p id="firstusered">`, for example), you can use that ID only once in the document.

Sometimes you may want to set links without underlines. You can use the anchor pseudo-classes and set the text-decoration property to a value of none, as in the following example:

```
<style type="text/css">
    <!--
        a:link, a:visited, a:active {text-decoration: none}
    -->
</style>
```

Just be sure to make it obvious from your page design that these are links!

Setting Box Properties

You use box properties to create box designs—a feature that's not available in standard HTML or XHTML. You can box text to call attention to it, such as cautions or contact information. You can adjust the margins to control how close text is to the border, and you also can remove the border to create floating text. Table 16.7 lists some commonly used box properties.

TABLE 16.7:   Box Properties

PROPERTY	POSSIBLE VALUES
border	Any or all of the following border- attributes
border-color	#rrggbb
border-style	none, dotted, dashed, solid, double, groove, ridge, inset, outset
border-width	Measurement, thick, medium, thin
clear	right, left, none, both
float	right, left, none
height	Measurement or auto
margin	Measurement or percentage of parent
margin-bottom	Measurement or percentage of parent
margin-left	Measurement or percentage of parent
margin-right	Measurement or percentage of parent
margin-top	Measurement or percentage of parent
width	Measurement, percentage, or auto

TIP

Older versions of Internet Explorer (before version 6) did not support box properties correctly—in particular, the relationship between the surrounding text and the box, the size of the box around text, and the interpretation of the width value were quite inconsistent. In standards-compliant mode (see Chapter 13), Internet Explorer 6 fully and correctly supports the CSS box model.

To create a box, apply these box-level characteristics to existing text in a document, including paragraphs, block quotes, and headings. The following steps show you how to create a box using an existing block quote. This box will float close to the right margin with a 2-pixel border and will occupy only 50 percent of the window width.

1. Within the style block, add a blockquote selector and braces:

```
<style type="text/css">
  <!--
    blockquote { }
  -->
</style>
```

2. Add a width property, with a value of 50%:

```
<style type="text/css">
  <!--
    blockquote { width: 50% }
  -->
</style>
```

3. Add a semicolon as a separator and the float property with a value of right:

```
<style type="text/css">
  <!--
    blockquote { width: 50%;
                 float: right }
  -->
</style>
```

4. Add another semicolon as a separator and the border property. In this example, we provide the individual border properties together, rather than as individual entities.

```
<style type="text/css">
  <!--
```

```
blockquote { width: 50%;
             float: right;
             border: 2px solid black }
     -->
</style>
```

Figure 16.10 shows the result.

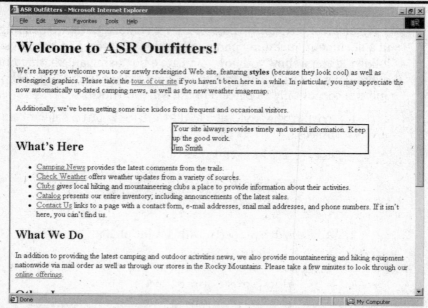

FIGURE 16.10:   Using boxes is an excellent way to call attention to information.

WARNING

The float property is fully supported in only the relatively recent browsers (Netscape 6, IE 5.5, Opera 5, and later versions). Although float is partially supported in previous browser editions, results tend to be inconsistent and unpredictable in older browsers.

Setting Color and Background Properties

To establish color and background properties for the sample document or for any block-level elements, use the properties and values shown in Table 16.8.

TABLE 16.8: Color and Background Properties

PROPERTY	POSSIBLE VALUES
background	Any or all of the following background- properties
background-color	#rrggbb, transparent
background-image	url(http://example.com) or none
background-repeat	repeat, repeat-x, repeat-y, no-repeat
color	#rrggbb

To include a background color, add the properties to the body element, as shown in the following steps, which add #ffffcc (light yellow) to the background:

1. Within the style block, add a body selector:

```
<style type="text/css">
  <!--
    body
  -->
</style>
```

2. Add braces, the background-color property, and the #ffffcc value, which specifies the light yellow color:

```
<style>
  <!--
    body { background-color: #ffffcc }
  -->
</style>
```

When viewed in a browser, the background will appear lightly colored, just as it would if the bgcolor attribute were applied to the body element. Each element within the document inherits the background color from the body. However, you also can specify a separate background color for any inline or block-level element, even if you set a background color for the body element. The more specific style rules override the more general style rules.

You also can add a background image to the body element or other block elements. Remember that a block element is any element with a line break before and after—for example, body, p, and h1.

As shown in the following steps, you can tile the background image either vertically or horizontally:

1. To add a background image to the document body, add the `background-image` property, separated from the previous property with a semicolon:

    ```
    <style type="text/css">
       <!--
          body { background-color: #ffffcc;
                 background-image: }
       -->
    </style>
    ```

2. Add the value for the background image as `url(pattern.gif)`. Use any absolute or relative URL in the parentheses:

    ```
    <style type="text/css">
       <!--
          body { background-color: #ffffcc;
                 background-image: url(pattern.gif) }
       -->
    </style>
    ```

3. Add `background-repeat: repeat-x` to specify that the background image repeat horizontally (in the direction of the x-axis). To repeat only vertically, use `repeat-y`; use `no-repeat` if you don't want a repeat.

    ```
    <style type="text/css">
       <!--
          body { background-color: #ffffcc;
                 background-image: url(pattern.gif);
                 background-repeat: repeat-x; }
       -->
    </style>
    ```

Setting Classification Properties

You use classification properties to change specific elements from inline (such as i or b) to block elements with line breaks before and after (such as p and h1), as well as to control the display of lists. Table 16.9 lists some classification properties and their values.

TABLE 16.9: Classification Properties

PROPERTY	POSSIBLE VALUES
display	inline, block, list-item
list-style-image	url(http://example.com/image.gif)
list-style-type	disc, circle, square, decimal, lower-roman, upper-roman, lower-alpha, upper-alpha, none

To specify that an unordered list use square bullets, follow these steps:

1. Within the style block, add a ul selector followed immediately by an li selector on the same line. By combining these, the style rule will apply only to an li element within a ul element. If you set a rule for only the li element, it would affect all numbered and bulleted lists in your document, not just those within ul elements.

```
<style type="text/css">
  <!--
    ul li
  -->
</style>
```

2. Add braces:

```
<style type="text/css">
  <!--
    ul li {}
  -->
</style>
```

3. Add a list-style-type property with the value of square:

```
<style type="text/css">
  <!--
    ul li { list-style-type: square }
  -->
</style>
```

You also can set a specific image for use as a bullet by using `list-style-image: url(figure.gif)`, as shown here:

```
<style type="text/css">
    <!--
        ul li { list-style-image: url(figure.gif) }
    -->
</style>
```

TIP

If you specify a `list-style-image` property, it's a good idea to also include a `list-style-type` property in case the image is not displayed (that is, if the browser is unable to download or display the image). The image will be used if available, but if not, `list-style-type` will be used instead.

By changing the display property, you can change a list from a vertical list, as is customary, to an inline list in which each item appears within a line of text. To do so, use the following style rule:

```
<style type="text/css">
    <!--
        ul li { display: inline }
    -->
</style>
```

WARNING

Display properties are supported only in recent browsers: Netscape 6, IE 5.5, and Opera 4 and later.

See Listing 16.2 for an example of a document with a link to an external style sheet and the code needed to apply those style definitions. Listing 16.3 details the external style sheet code.

Listing 16.2: An XHTML Document Linked to an External Style Sheet

```
<!DOCTYPE html PUBLIC
"-//W3C/DTD XHTML 1.0 Transitional//EN"
    "http://www.w3.org/TR/xhtml1/DTD/xhtml1-transitional.dtd">
<html xmlns="http://www.w3.org/1999/xhtml">
<head>
    <title>ASR Outfitters</title>
    <link rel="stylesheet" type="text/css" href="0903.css">
```

```
</head>
<body>
  <h1>Welcome to ASR Outfitters!</h1>
  <p>We're happy to welcome you to our newly redesigned web
  site, featuring <span class="emph">styles</span> (because
  they look cool) as well as redesigned graphics. Please
  take the <a href="tour.html">tour of our site</a> if you
  haven't been here in a while. In particular, you may
  appreciate the now automatically updated camping news, as
  well as the new weather imagemap. Additionally, we've
  been getting some nice kudos from frequent
  and occasional visitors.</p>
    <blockquote>Your site always provides timely and useful
    information. Keep up the good work.<br />
    Jim Smith</blockquote>
  <hr />
  <h2>What's Here</h2>
  <div class="text"><ul>
    <li><a href="camping.html">Camping News</a> provides the
      latest comments from the trails.</li>
    <li><a href="weather.html">Check Weather</a> offers
      weather updates from a variety of sources.</li>
    <li><a href="clubs.html">Clubs</a> gives local hiking
    and mountaineering clubs a place to provide information
      about their activities.</li>
    <li><a href="catalog.html">Catalog</a> presents our
    entire inventory, including announcements of the latest
    sales. </li>
    <li><a href="contact.html">Contact Us</a> links to a
    page with a contact form, e-mail addresses, snail mail
      addresses, and phone numbers. If it isn't here, you
      can't find us.</li>
    </ul></div>
  <h2>What We Do</h2>
  <p>In addition to providing the latest camping and outdoor
  activities news, we also provide mountaineering and hiking
  equipment nationwide via mail order as well as through our
  stores in the Rocky Mountains. Please take a few minutes
  to look through our
  <a href="catalog.html">online offerings</a>.
  </p>
  <h2>Other Issues</h2>
```

Part III

```
<div class="text"><ul>
  <li>As you may know, our URL was misprinted in the
  latest <span class="ital">Hiking News</span>.
  Please tell your hiking friends that the correct URL is
  <span class="inlineurl">
  http://www.asroutfitters.com/</span>.
  </li>
  <li>To collect a $1000 reward, turn in the name of the
    person who set the fire in the Bear Lake area last
    weekend.
    <ol>
      <li>Call 888-555-1212.</li>
      <li>Leave the name on the recording.</li>
      <li>Provide contact information so we can send
      you the reward.</li>
    </ol>
  </li>
</ul></div>
<h2>What Would You Like To See?</h2>
<p class="diff">If you have suggestions or comments about
the
site or other information we could provide, we'd love
to know about it. Drop us an e-mail at
<a href="mailto:asroutfitters@raycommexample.com">
asroutfitters@raycommexample.com</a>. Of course, you could
also contact us more traditionally at
the following address:</p>
<div class="text"><address>ASR Outfitters<br />
  4700 N. Center<br />
  South Logan, UT 87654<br />
  801-555-3422
</address></div>
</body>
</html>
```

Listing 16.3: An External Style Sheet

```
body
{background-color: #ffffcc;
 margin: 5%;
 font-style: normal;
 font-family: "Comic Sans MS", Verdana, Arial, Helvetica,
              sans-serif;
```

```
  font-size: 12pt;
  line-height: 16.5pt}

h1, h2
{font-family: "Comic Sans MS", Verdana, Arial, Helvetica,
              sans-serif}

p
{font-style: normal;
 font-family: "Comic Sans MS", Verdana, Arial, Helvetica,
              sans-serif;
 font-size: 12pt;
 line-height: 16.5pt}

blockquote
{color: red;
 font-family: "Comic Sans MS", Verdana, Arial, Helvetica,
              sans-serif;
 font-size: 11pt;
 line-height: 15pt;
 margin-left: 15%;
 width: 300px}

li
{list-style-type: disc;
 font: bold 12pt/16.5pt "Comic Sans MS", Verdana, Arial,
       Helvetica, sans-serif}

li li
{list-style-type: circle}

address
{font-style: normal;
 font-weight: bold;
 font-size: 13pt;
 line-height: 17.5pt}

.emph
{font-weight: bolder}

.ital
{font-style: italic}
```

```
.inlineurl
{font-family: Courier, monospace;
 font-size: 10pt}

.diff
{color: red}

.text
{font-style: normal;
 font-family: "Comic Sans MS", Verdana, Arial, Helvetica,
              sans-serif;
 font-size: 12pt;
 line-height: 16.5pt}
```

Setting Aural Style Sheet Properties

One of the more recent additions to style sheet capabilities is aural properties, which enable you to set properties for documents that will be read aloud by a device. Visually impaired users use these properties; you could use them as supplements to visual presentations or in situations in which reading is not possible—for example, in the car. Aural style sheet properties let you specify that documents be read aloud, specify sound characteristics, and specify other auditory options.

WARNING

At this time, most browsers do not yet support aural style sheets. One exception is Emacspeak (`www.cs.cornell.edu/Info/People/raman/emacspeak/emacspeak.html`), which you can use for testing these style sheets.

Table 16.10 lists some aural style sheet properties and their values. See the expanded Appendix B on the Sybex website (`www.sybex.com`).

TABLE 16.10: Aural Style Sheet Properties

PROPERTY	POSSIBLE VALUES
pause	Time, percentage
pitch-range	Value
speech-rate	Value, x-slow, slow, medium, fast, x-fast, faster, slower
volume	Value, percentage, silent, x-soft, soft, medium, loud, x-loud

To specify that the document be read aloud with loud volume and fast speech (for efficiency), follow these steps:

1. In a new style block, provide a body selector to apply your settings to the entire document, followed by braces:

```
<style type="text/css">
   <!--
      body { }
   -->
</style>
```

2. Add a volume property with the value of loud:

```
<style type="text/css">
   <!--
      body { volume: loud; }
   -->
</style>
```

3. Add a speech-rate property with the value of fast:

```
<style type="text/css">
   <!--
      body { volume: loud; speech-rate: fast;}
   -->
</style>
```

Aural style sheets are part of the CSS2 specification and currently are not supported by browsers. Check the W3C's Accessibility Features of CSS (www.w3.org/TR/CSS-access) for the latest on these features. You also can check Webreview.com's Style Sheet Reference Guide at www.webreview.com/style/index.shtml. Note that although the most recent major browsers do not support these features, there are some specialized browsers that render these style rules appropriately.

Setting Printed-Media Properties

Printed-media properties can help you accommodate users who print your documents rather than read them online. These CSS2 properties let you set values for the page box, which you might think of as the area of your printout. For example, in hardcopy, your page box might be the 8.5" × 11" piece of paper; the page box includes the content, margins, and edges. Table 16.11 lists some of the more common printed-media properties and their values. Appendix B provides additional information.

TABLE 16.11:   Printed-Media Style Sheet Properties

PROPERTY	POSSIBLE VALUES
margin	Length, percentage, auto
marks	crop, cross, none
orphans	Value
page-break-after	auto, always, avoid, left, right
page-break-before	auto, always, avoid, left, right
page-break-before	auto, always, avoid, left, right
page-break-inside	auto, always, avoid, left, right
size	Value, auto, portrait, landscape
widows	Value

To specify a page break before all h1 elements in a printed version of your document, follow these steps:

1. In a style block, provide an h1 selector and braces to apply your settings to all first-level headings in the entire document:

```
<style type="text/css">
   <!--
      h1 { }
   -->
</style>
```

2. Add a page-break-before property with the value of always:

```
<style>
   <!--
      h1 { page-break-before: always; }
   -->
</style>
```

See the websites listed in the previous section for more on CSS2 features.

Setting Positioning Properties

With positioning, you can add properties to style rules to control element positioning. For example, you can identify specific locations for elements, as well as specify locations that are relative to other elements. Positioning properties are part of the CSS2 specification, and only the newer browser versions support them. Table 16.12 lists some positioning properties and their values.

TABLE 16.12:   Positioning Properties

Property	Possible Values
float	left, right, none
overflow	visible, scroll, hidden, auto
position	static, absolute, relative, fixed
top, bottom, left, and right	Length, percentage, auto

Let's look at an example of how positioning properties work. To specify that the `.warning` classes in the document float to the left with text wrapping around to the right and that the `p.logo` class sits at the bottom of the window, follow these steps:

1. In a new style block, provide a `.warning` selector and braces to hold its properties:

```
<style type="text/css">
  <!--
      .warning { }
  -->
</style>
```

2. Add a `float` property with the value of `left`:

```
<style type="text/css">
  <!--
      .warning { float: left }
  -->
</style>
```

3. Add a `p.logo` selector and braces:

```
<style type="text/css">
  <!--
      .warning { float: left }
      p.logo { }
  -->
</style>
```

4. Add a `position` property and a `fixed` value:

```
<style type="text/css">
  <!--
      .warning { float: left }
      p.logo { position: fixed }
  -->
</style>
```

Part III

5. Add bottom and right properties and a length of 0 (use any units) for each value:

```
<style type="text/css">
   <!--
      .warning { float: left }
      p.logo { position: fixed; bottom: 0px; right: 0px }
   -->
</style>
```

Positioning properties are a part of the CSS2 specification that is supported by newer browsers. However, relative positioning is supported more fully than absolute positioning at the present.

THE FUTURE OF STYLE SHEETS

It seems likely that *external* style sheets will be the preferred way to use styles with HTML and XHTML documents in the future. Embedded and inline styles options are available in XHTML 1.0; however, XHTML 1.1 requires the use of the style sheet module in order to use the style element. Using CSS with XML is possible only with external style sheets. External style sheets offer ways to use all the features of both embedded and inline styles through specifying classes and IDs as well as XHTML element selectors.

In addition, if you're going to venture more into XML, you should check out the Extensible Stylesheet Language (XSL) and XSL Transformations (XSLT). You can find out more at www.w3.org/Style/XSL.

WHAT'S NEXT?

In this chapter, you learned how style sheets and HTML or XHTML documents relate and how to develop style sheets for your own needs. As you can see, style sheets certainly are more comprehensive than any formatting option previously available.

Next, you'll learn about adding HTML and XHTML forms to your pages to obtain user input from your pages.

Chapter 17
DEVELOPING FORMS

When you submit credit card information to purchase something online, search the web with Google or Yahoo!, participate in a web-based chat room, or even select a line from a web-page drop-down menu, you're using a form. Within the scope of plain HTML or XHTML—as opposed to extensions such as JavaScript, Java applets, and other embedded programs—a form is the only method of two-way communication between web browsers and web servers.

Perhaps because of the name, web developers tend to assume that forms are just for collecting pages of data. In fact, you can use forms to get any kind of information from users without giving them the feeling of "filling out a form." A form is often as simple as a blank entry field and a Submit button.

In this chapter, we'll look at how to develop forms using standard elements and attributes, which virtually all browsers support. We'll develop a form piece by piece, including all the essential tasks in using forms effectively.

Part III

Adapted from *Mastering HTML and XHTML*, by Deborah S. Ray and Eric J. Ray
ISBN 0-7821-4141-2 $49.99

DETERMINING FORM CONTENT

The first step in developing a form is determining which information to include and how to present it—that is, how to break it into manageable pieces. You then need to ensure that users can provide the information you want from them easily, which means that your form needs to be both functional and visually appealing.

Information Issues

When deciding which information to include and how to break it down, consider your purposes for creating the form. You might begin by answering these questions:

- ▶ What information do I want? Customer contact information? Only e-mail addresses so that I can contact users later? Opinions about the site?

- ▶ Why will users access the form? To order something online? To request information? To submit comments or questions about products or services?

- ▶ What information can users readily provide? Contact information? Descriptions of their product use? Previous purchases?

- ▶ How much time are users willing to spend filling out the form? Would they be willing to describe something in a paragraph or two, or would they want to select from a list?

After determining what information you want and what information your users are willing to provide, break the information into the smallest chunks possible. For example, if you want users to provide contact information, divide contact information into name, street address, and city/state/postal code. You could even go a step further and, for example, collect the city, state, and postal code as separate items so that you can sort data according to customers in a particular area. If you don't collect those items separately, you won't be able to sort on them individually.

TIP

Although it's possible to go back and change a form after you implement it, careful planning will save a lot of trouble and work later. For example, if you complete and implement a form and then discover that you forgot to request key information, the initial responses to the form will be less useful or skew the resulting data. Fixing the form takes nearly as much time as doing it carefully at first.

Our site, TECHWR-L ("tech-whirl"), hypothetically might include a form to collect targeted addresses for future product and sale announcements. Although you could just as easily (but not as cheaply) use regular mailings by purchasing mailing lists, a website form avoids the cost of traditional mailings, collects information from specifically interested users (respecting their privacy, of course, and also addressing any governmental regulations regarding data collection and use), and keeps the Internet-based company focused on the web.

Because filling out a web page form takes some time, TECHWR-L created a form, shown in Figure 17.1, that includes only the essentials.

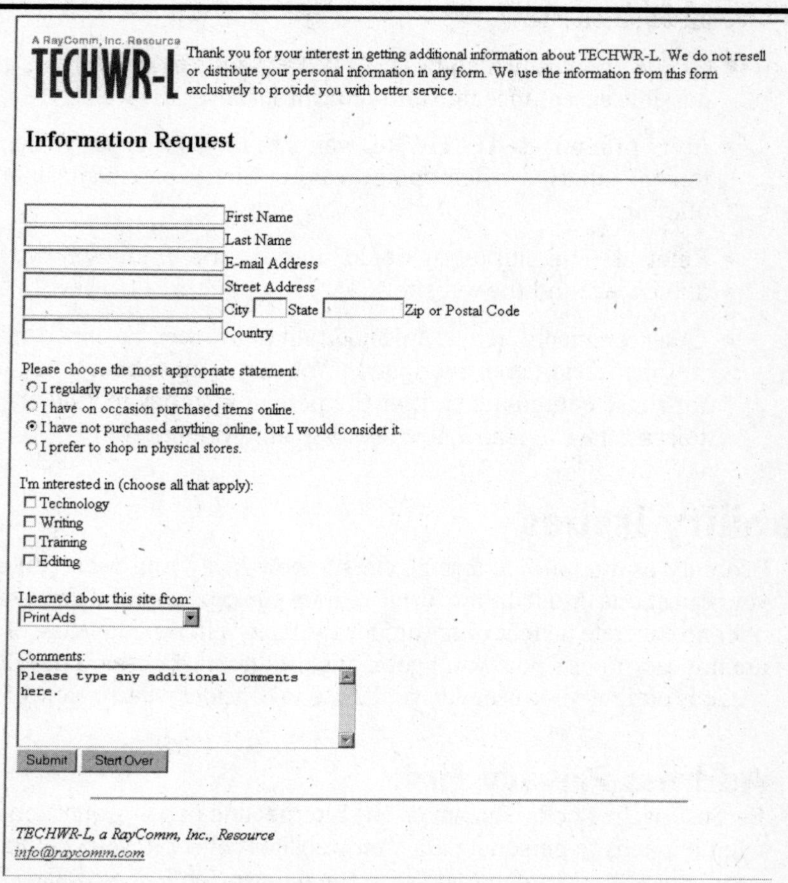

FIGURE 17.1:   TECHWR-L's form collects only basic demographic and marketing information.

In this case, a little demographic information is needed:

▶ First name—This is necessary to help personalize responses.

▶ Last name—This also is necessary to help personalize responses.

▶ E-mail address—Collecting this information is the main purpose of the form.

▶ Street address, city, state, postal code—These are all necessary for future snail-mailings and demographic analysis. Collecting the address, even with no immediate intent to use it, is probably a wise move because it would be difficult to ask customers for more information later.

▶ Online purchasing habits—TECHWR-L wants to learn about the possible acceptance rate for taking orders over the web.

▶ Areas of interest—TECHWR-L wants to find out about the customer's interests to determine areas in which to expand its online offerings.

▶ Referral—The marketing department wants to know how the audience found the website.

▶ Other comments—It's always important to give users an opportunity to provide additional information. You may want to limit the space for these comments so that the person who has to read them doesn't have to read a novel's worth of information.

Usability Issues

Usability, as it applies to forms, refers to how easily your users can answer your questions. Most online forms require some user action and usually offer no concrete benefit or reward for the users' efforts. Therefore, if forms are not easy to use, you won't get many (or any) responses. The following sections outline some usability guidelines to consider when creating forms.

Address Privacy First

Because of the floods of spam on the Internet and ongoing questions about what happens to personal data after websites collect it, you should state explicitly what you plan to do with the data you collect as well as link to privacy policies or similar information available on your site. By including a statement or privacy policy, you indicate to your users that you acknowledge and care about their concerns, and you inform them of your intentions:

▶ Take time to plan your intentions for using the information after it's collected, and ensure that your company can live by the policy it outlines. Changing a privacy policy after it has been implemented would be difficult to do, if not impossible, depending on what the original policy states.

▶ Make sure that the people receiving or using collected information know the details of the privacy policy.

▶ Ensure that people across your company also know the uses for the information collected. For example, if your policy says that your company will use the information for product shipping purposes only, make sure that product developers and the marketing team know that the user information is not for their purposes.

▶ Consult an attorney to ensure the policy is adequate both for your company's needs as well as your users' needs.

Group Similar Categories

When you group similar categories, as previously shown in Figure 17.1, the form appears less daunting, and users are more likely to fill it out and submit it. TECHWR-L can group the information it's soliciting from users into three main categories:

▶ Contact information

▶ Purchasing habits and areas of interest

▶ Referrals and other information

Make the Form Easy

If you've ever completed a long form, you know how tedious it can be. Think of a tax form for an example of how *not* to do it. Although the specifics depend greatly on the information you'll be collecting, the following principles remain constant:

▶ Whenever possible, provide a list from which users can choose one or more items. Lists are easy to use, and they result in easy-to-process information.

▶ If you can't provide a list, ask users to fill in only a small amount of text. Again, this takes minimal time, and it provides you with data that is fairly easy to process.

▶ Ask users to fill in large areas of text only if it's absolutely necessary. Large blocks of text take a lot of time for the user to enter and for you to process. Additionally, many users are likely to ignore a request that requires them to enter a great deal of information.

TIP

For more information about how to create lists and areas to fill in, see the section "Creating Forms," later in this chapter.

Provide Incentives

Provide users with incentives to fill out the form and submit it. Offer them something even if its value is marginal. Studies show that a penny or a stamp included in mailed surveys often improves the response rate significantly. Consider offering a chance in a drawing for a free product, an e-mailed list of tips and tricks, or a discount on services.

TECHWR-L could have offered anything from a free tote bag to an e-mailed collection of tips to a discount on the next purchase but chose to settle for a small giveaway book.

WARNING

Most drawings and giveaways are legally binding in some way, and you need to be sure of their legal standing.

Design Issues

Perhaps because of the need to address all the technical issues, web authors often neglect design issues. However, a well-designed form encourages users to give you the information you want.

TIP

For information on how to incorporate sound web design on your site, check out the **Web Page Design for Designers** site at www.wpdfd.com.

What constitutes good form design? Good form design is visually appealing, graphically helpful, and consistent with the remainder of the site. A form at an intranet site that has a white background and minimal graphics and that is managed by conservative supervisors would likely have a simple, vertical design and be none the worse for it. However, a visually interesting or highly graphical website calls for a form in keeping with the overall theme.

Although the visual interest of the form should not overwhelm the rest of the page, you'll want to make judicious use of color, alignment, small images, and font characteristics. Here are some guidelines:

▶ Use headings to announce each new group of information. This helps users move through the form easily.

▶ Be sure to separate groups visually. This makes a form easier to use because sections become shorter and easier to wade through. You can use horizontal rules or the `fieldset` element to do this.

▶ Use text emphasis to draw the audience to important information. Use emphasis sparingly; emphasize only a few words so that they stand out on the page.

▶ Specify how users should move through the form. Don't make your users scroll horizontally to access information. Consider making a narrow, longer form rather than a wider, shorter form to accommodate users who have lower monitor resolution. If your survey is in multiple columns, make different categories visually obvious.

▶ Use arrows to help users move through the page in a specified order.

▶ Be sure that it's clear which check boxes and fields go with the associated descriptive information. For example, if you have a long row of check boxes and labels, users may have a hard time figuring out whether the check box goes with the text on the right or the text on the left. Use line breaks and spacing to differentiate clearly.

▶ Specify which fields are optional and which are required:

> ▶ Lump all required fields together under a "Required" heading and all optional ones under an "Optional" heading, or put "Required" beside each required field.
>
> ▶ Put asterisks (*) by optional fields, with a note indicating that asterisks indicate optional fields.
>
> ▶ Put the word "optional" in parentheses next to each optional field.

Regardless of how you indicate what's required and what's optional, understand that some processing programs reject incorrectly filled out or incomplete forms, which can cause frustration for you and your users.

▶ Use a background image. Forms with some texture tend to seem friendlier. However, be sure that the image doesn't outweigh the content and that the text adequately contrasts with the image so the text is not difficult to read.

▶ Make all the text-entry fields the same width and put them on the left if you have a vertical column of name and address information. This enables all the text to align vertically and looks much better. If the text labels go on the left, the fields will not (cannot) align vertically and, therefore, will look more random and less professional.

TIP

Check out Appendix A, "HTML and XHTML Elements and Attributes," for a comprehensive list of form elements and attributes.

TIP

You also can use tables to align form fields; for example, right-align all the labels in table cells in one column, and then place all the text-entry fields in table cells in an adjacent column. See Chapter 11, "Presenting Information in Tables," for more details on using tables.

CREATING FORMS

Forms have two basic parts:

▶ The part you can see, which a user fills out

▶ The part you can't see, which specifies how the server should process the information

In this section, we'll show you how to create the part that you can see. We'll show you how to create the other part later in this chapter, in the section "Processing Forms."

HAND-CODE FORMS OR USE A WYSIWYG EDITOR?

You can create forms using any HTML or XHTML development tools—singly or in combination. For example, if you plan to develop a lot of forms, you might consider using a WYSIWYG ("What You See Is What You Get") editor such as Macromedia Dreamweaver, Adobe GoLive, or Microsoft FrontPage to create the basic form. Those editors don't always produce consistently good results, but they help ensure that you don't leave out any elements or necessary attributes. You then can modify the formatting manually as necessary. However, if you'll only be doing one or two forms, creating them manually or with the help of a code-based editor is more than adequate and is probably easier than learning how to use a WYSIWYG editor effectively.

Understanding Widgets

Forms consist of several types of widgets, also called *controls*, which are fields you can use to collect data, including these:

▶ *Submit and Reset buttons* send the form information to the server for processing and return the form to its original settings.

▶ *Text fields* are areas for brief text input. Use these for multiple-word responses such as names, search terms, or addresses.

▶ *Select lists* are sets from which users can choose one or more items. Use them to present a long but finite list of choices— for example, choosing a state or province from a list or choosing one of 17 options.

▶ *Check boxes* enable the user to select none, one, or several items from a list. Use them to elicit multiple answers. For example, TECHWR-L used check boxes to get information about the activities of its customers.

▶ *Radio buttons* give users an opportunity to choose only one item— for example, gender, a preference, or anything else that can be only one way or one value from a group.

▶ *Text areas* are areas for lengthy text input, as in open-ended comments or free-form responses.

Figure 17.2 shows a sample form that includes these widgets.

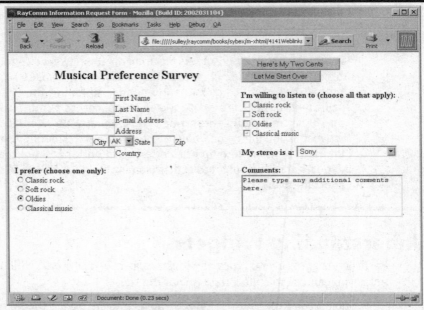

FIGURE 17.2: Forms give users different ways of entering information.

WHICH WIDGETS ARE BEST?

When deciding which widget to use, consider the information you want to collect. For example, start by deciding if you can collect information using check boxes and radio buttons. These are generally the easiest to use because they specify the options and require only the click of a mouse. Then, look for places you can use select lists, which also are easy to use. Finally, include text areas only if users need to respond in their own words.

In general, radio buttons, check boxes, and select lists all are better for accepting input than text areas. If users are selecting choices from a list, you don't need to be concerned with misspellings, inconsistent answers, or free-form answers that don't fit the categories. If you can provide choices and let users choose from them, do so.

Creating a Form and Adding Submit and Reset Buttons

The first step in creating a form is to insert the form element and add Submit and Reset buttons. Submit and Reset buttons are essential components because they enable users to submit information and, if necessary, clear selections. Although you must add other form fields before the form will do anything worthwhile, the Submit button is the key that makes the form go somewhere.

TIP

Forms require two form element attributes (action and method) to specify what happens to the form results and which program on the server will process them. We'll look at these attributes in the section "Processing Forms," later in this chapter.

Table 17.1 lists and describes the basic form button elements. (See Table 17.2 for more attributes to use with the input element.)

TABLE 17.1:   Basic Elements for Form Buttons

ELEMENT	PROVIDES
`<input type="submit" value="..." />`	A Submit button for a form. The value attribute produces text on the button.
`<input type="image" name="..." src="urlv />`	A graphical Submit button. The src attribute indicates the image source file.
`<input type="reset" value="..." />`	A Reset button for a form. The value attribute produces text on the button.

In the following example, we'll create a form for the TECHWR-L site as we show you how to start a form and then add Submit and Reset buttons. The code in Listing 17.1 produces the page shown in Figure 17.3.

NOTE

The examples in this chapter use XHTML, rather than HTML.

Part III

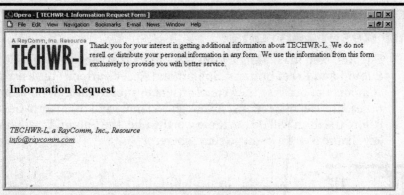

FIGURE 17.3:   The TECHWR-L form page, sans form

Listing 17.1: The TECHWR-L Information Page, Without Form

```
<!DOCTYPE html PUBLIC
"-//W3C//DTD XHTML 1.0 Transitional//EN"
"http://www.w3.org/TR/xhtml1/DTD/xhtml1-transitional.dtd">
<html xmlns="http://www.w3.org/1999/xhtml">
  <head>
    <title>TECHWR-L Information Request Form</title>
  </head>
  <body>
    <table>
      <tr>
        <td valign="top"><img src="techwhirllogo.gif" alt=
          "TECHWR-L Logo" border="0" />
        </td>
        <td>
          <p>
          Thank you for your interest in getting additional
          information about TECHWR-L. We do not resell or
          distribute your personal information in any form.
          We use the information from this form exclusively
          to provide you with better service.
          </p>
        </td>
      </tr>
    </table>
    <h2>Information Request</h2>
    <hr width="80%" />
```

```
    <hr width="80%" />
    <address>
      <br />
      TECHWR-L, a RayComm, Inc., Resource<br />
      <a href="mailto:info@raycomm.com">
      info@raycomm.com</a><br />
    </address>
  </body>
</html>
```

To add a form to the page, follow these steps:

1. Add the form element where you want the form. We're going to put ours between the horizontal rules.

   ```
   <hr />
   <form>
   </form>
   <hr />
   ```

TIP

You can avoid problems with your forms by properly nesting your form within other elements in the document. Be careful to place the form outside paragraphs, lists, and other structural elements. For example, you do not want to open a table within the form and close it after the end of the form. Also, be sure to test your forms carefully.

2. Create a Submit button by adding the input empty element, the type="submit" attribute, and the value attribute. Although the Submit button traditionally goes at the bottom of the form (immediately above the closing form tag), it can go anywhere in the form. You can set the text on the face of the Submit button to any text you want—simply substitute your text for the text in the value attribute (just be sure it's still obvious that this button submits something).

   ```
   <form>
   <input type="submit" value="Submit" />
   </form>
   ```

3. Create a Reset button by adding the input empty element, the type="reset" attribute, and the value attribute. Again, although the Reset button traditionally goes at the bottom of the form with the Submit button, immediately above the closing form tag, it can go anywhere in the form. The Reset

button can have any text on its face, based on the value attribute. The following example has Start Over on the face.

```
<form>
<input type="submit" value="Submit" />
<input type="reset" value="Start Over" />
</form>
```

Figure 17.4 shows what the buttons look like in a completed form.

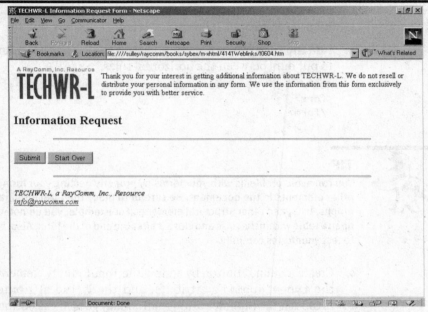

FIGURE 17.4: The Submit and Reset (Start Over) buttons are added to the form.

WARNING

To be valid HTML or XHTML, the form element must include an action attribute. The action attribute is a URL which specifies the location of the script that processes the submitted form data. More information on the action attribute is included in the "Processing Forms" section later in this chapter.

TIP

You cannot control button size directly; the length of the text displayed on the button determines the size of the button.

If the appearance of your form is extremely important to you, consider using a graphical Submit button. However, be sure that your users are using browsers that can handle them.

WARNING

If you use something other than a Submit button (one that says Submit on it), be sure it's obvious what it's supposed to be. Most users are familiar with "Submit" and may not readily understand other text you choose.

If you want to use an image for your Submit button, substitute the following code for the Submit button (substituting your own image for `submitbutton.gif`):

```
<input type="image" name="submitbutton"
src="submitbutton.gif" />
```

The `type="image"` attribute specifies that an image is used to submit the form when clicked. The `name="submitbutton"` attribute specifies that the x,y-coordinates where the mouse is located will be returned to the server when the image is clicked. Finally, the `src` attribute works just as it does with regular images.

Figure 17.5 shows the complete TECHWR-L form with a graphical Submit button.

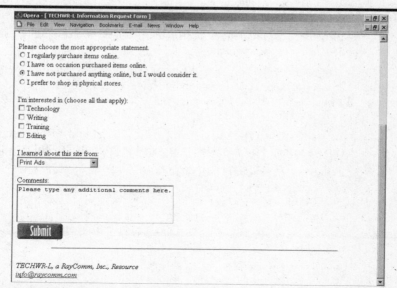

FIGURE 17.5: Graphical Submit buttons can make your form more interesting.

Part III

WARNING

XHTML makes no direct provision for a Reset button with an image; therefore, if you want to use an image for your Submit button, you might choose to dispense with a Reset button. If you don't, you'll have to deal with the potentially poor combination of an image and a standard Reset button.

OPPORTUNITIES

Assuming that your users are using browsers that comply with HTML 4.01 and later versions (and they probably are, for the most part), you can use the button element to create a button that you can include instead of or in conjunction with Submit and Reset buttons. Buttons created with the button element have no specific action associated with them, as the Submit and Reset buttons do. However, if you're so inclined, you can link the button to JavaScript. Doing so gives you all sorts of functional and flashy possibilities.

To provide a Submit button using the button element, use code similar to the following:

```
<button type="submit" value="submit" name="submit">
    Click to Submit Form
</button>
```

To provide a graphical Reset button using the button element, use code similar to the following:

```
<button type="reset" value="reset" name="reset">
    <img src="gifs/resetbuttonnew.gif" alt="Reset
    button" />
</button>
```

If you want to use a button element to call a script that, for example, verifies a form's contents, you might use something like this:

```
<button type="button" value="verify" name="verify"
    onclick="verify(this.form)">
    Click to Verify Form
</button>
```

Including General Input Fields

You also can develop other types of input fields using various attributes in the input element, an empty element that sets an area in a form for user input. Table 17.2 shows the most frequently used attributes of the input element. (See Appendix A for a complete listing of attributes you can use with the input empty element.)

TABLE 17.2:   Most Common Input Field Attributes

ATTRIBUTE	USE
accept="..."	Specifies the acceptable MIME types, in a comma-separated list, for file uploads. Wildcards are acceptable, as in accept="image/*".
maxlength="n"	Sets the maximum number of characters that can be submitted. Use this attribute with text fields.
name="..."	Specifies the name of the field for the program that processes form results.
selected="selected"	Indicates the default selection to be presented when the form is initially loaded or reset.
size="n"	Sets the visible size for a field. The number *n* equals characters with text input fields and pixels in other fields.
type="..."	Sets the type of input field. Possible values are text, password, checkbox, radio, file, hidden, image, submit, button, and reset.
value="..."	Provides content associated with name="...". Use this attribute with radio buttons and check boxes because they do not accept other input. You also can use this attribute with text fields to provide initial input.

Part III

Text Fields

A text field is a blank area within a form and is the place for user-supplied information. As you can see, text fields commonly are used for a name, an e-mail address, and so on:

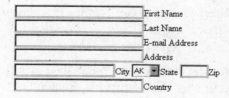

To add a text field to an existing form, follow these steps:

1. Add an `input` element where you want the field:

    ```
    <form>
    <input />
    </form>
    ```

2. Specify the type of input field. In this case, use `type="text"`.

    ```
    <form>
    <input type="text" />
    </form>
    ```

3. Add the `name` attribute to label the content. For example, one of the first fields in the TECHWR-L form is for the first name of a user; therefore, the field name is `firstname`.

    ```
    <input type="text" name="firstname" />
    ```

TIP

The values for `name` should be unique within the form. Multiple forms on the same site (or even on the same page) can share values, but if different fields share the same `name` value, the results will be unpredictable.

4. Specify the size of the field in the form by including the `size` attribute. Although this is optional, you can ensure your user has ample space and can make similar text fields the same size. For example, 30 is a generous size for a name, but still not overwhelmingly large, even on a low-resolution monitor.

    ```
    <input type="text" name="firstname" size="30" />
    ```

5. Add the `maxlength` attribute if you want to limit the number of characters your users can provide (for example, if the field passes into an existing database with length restrictions). Keep in mind that `maxlength` settings should not be less than the `size` attribute; otherwise, your users will be confused when they can't continue typing to the end of the field.

    ```
    <input type="text" name="firstname" size="30"
      maxlength="30" />
    ```

6. Add text outside the `input` field to indicate the information your user should provide. Remember that the name of the field is not visible in the browser; up to this point, you've

created a blank area within the form, but you have not labeled that area in any way. You also may want to add a br element because the input element doesn't insert line breaks.

```
<input type="text" name="firstname" size="30"
   maxlength="30" />First Name<br />
```

Figure 17.6 shows the resulting text field in the context of the form. Use the same process to add other text fields with the name to the right of the element.

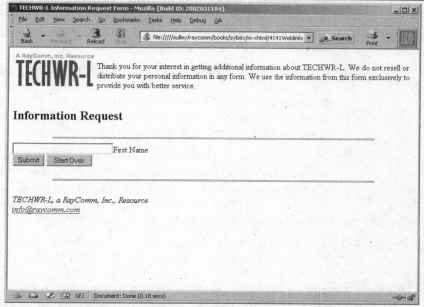

FIGURE 17.6: Users can enter information in text fields.

GUIDELINES FOR INCLUDING MULTIPLE TEXT FIELDS

As a rule, forms are much more attractive if the fields are aligned. If they're nearly but not exactly aligned, the form looks sloppy, just as a misaligned paper form looks sloppy.

CONTINUED ➡

Part III

Here are some guidelines to follow when you include multiple text fields in your form:

▶ Place the fields at the left margin of your page, followed by the descriptive text. If you place the descriptive text (such as First Name or Last Name) to the left of the fields, the fields will not line up vertically. Alternatively, consider putting your form fields and descriptive text in a table so that you can ensure that the rows and columns are evenly aligned. Set the text fields to the same size when appropriate. Of course, you wouldn't set the field for entering an official state abbreviation to 30 characters, but there's no reason that First Name, Last Name, and Company Name couldn't all be the same length.

▶ As you add descriptive labels, remember also to add line breaks (
 or <p>...</p>) in appropriate places. None of the form elements forces a line break, so your form elements all will run together on a single line if you do not include additional elements. In some cases, this is fine, but it also can look a little odd.

▶ Optionally, you can add a value attribute to the text input element to "seed" the field with a value or to provide an example of the content you want. For example, you could add value="First Name Here" to the input field used for the first name to let your users know what information to type.

If you're taking a survey, seeding a field is of questionable value. If your users can't figure out what to put in a field, you probably have a design problem. If you include some text, your users are more likely not to complete the field (and submit your sample) or to accidentally leave part of your sample text in the field, thereby corrupting your data.

The best—possibly only—time to seed a field is if you do not have space on the form for descriptive labels.

Radio Buttons

A *radio button* is a type of input field that enables users to choose one option from a list. Radio buttons are so named because you can choose only one of them, just as you can select only one button (one station) at a time on your car radio. When viewed in a browser, radio buttons usually are small circles, as shown here:

I prefer (choose one only):
○ Classic rock
○ Soft rock
◉ Oldies
○ Classical music

In the TECHWR-L questionnaire, we wanted to find out if users were inclined to make purchases online; the choices range from refusing to purchase to purchasing online regularly. Each choice is mutually exclusive—choosing one excludes the remainder. Radio buttons were our obvious choice.

To add radio buttons to a form, follow these steps:

1. At the point where the buttons should appear, add any introductory text to lead into the buttons. Also add descriptive text and formatting commands as appropriate. The text of the TECHWR-L example looks like this:

    ```
    <p>
    Please choose the most appropriate statement.<br />
       I regularly purchase items online.<br />
       I have on occasion purchased items online.<br />
       I have not purchased anything online, but I would
       consider it.<br />
       I prefer to shop in physical stores.<br />
    </p>
    ```

2. Add the input element where the first radio button will go:

    ```
    <input />I regularly purchase items online.<br />
    ```

3. Add the type="radio" attribute:

    ```
    <input type="radio" />I regularly purchase items
       online.<br />
    ```

4. Add the name attribute. The name applies to the collection of buttons, not just to this item (all the radio buttons of a given set repeat the same name attribute value), so be sure the value is generic enough to apply to all items in the set.

    ```
    <input type="radio" name="buying" />I regularly purchase
       items online.<br />
    ```

5. Add the value attribute. In text input areas, the value is what the user types; however, you must supply the value for radio

buttons (and check boxes). Choose highly descriptive, preferably one-word values (such as "regular" rather than "yes" or "of course").

```
<input type="radio" name="buying" value="regular" />
    I regularly purchase items online.<br />
```

6. If desired, add the attribute checked to one of the items to indicate the default selection. Remember that only one radio button can be selected, so only one button can carry the checked attribute.

```
<input type="radio" name="buying" value="regular"
    checked="checked" />I regularly purchase items
    online.<br />
```

TIP

In general, make the most likely choice the default option, both to make a user's job easier and to minimize the impact of his not checking and verifying the entry for that question. Although adding the checked attribute is optional, it ensures that the list records a response.

7. Add the remaining radio buttons.

Use the same name attribute for all radio buttons in a set. Browsers use the name attribute on radio buttons to specify which buttons are related and, therefore, which ones are set and unset as a group. Different sets of radio buttons within a page use different name attributes.

The completed set of radio buttons for the TECHWR-L form looks like the following:

```
<p>
Please choose the most appropriate statement.<br />
    <input type="radio" name="buying" value="regular" />
        I regularly purchase items online.<br />
    <input type="radio" name="buying" value="sometimes" />
        I have on occasion purchased items online.<br />
    <input type="radio" name="buying" value="might"
        checked="checked" />I have not purchased anything
        online, but I would consider it.<br />
    <input type="radio" name="buying" value="willnot" />
        I prefer to shop in physical stores.<br />
</p>
```

When viewed in a browser, the radio buttons look like those in Figure 17.7.

FIGURE 17.7: A user can select a radio button to choose an item from a list.

USING *FIELDSET* TO GROUP ELEMENTS

XHTML lets you group related items easily using the fieldset element. For example, in the TECHWR-L form, several fields collect personal information, and you could group them within a fieldset element, like this:

```
<fieldset>
...various input fields for personal information go
    here...
</fieldset>
```

Additionally, by adding legend elements (aligned to the top, bottom, left, or right), you can label content clearly:

```
<fieldset>
<legend align="top">Personal Information</legend>
...various input fields for personal information
    go here...
</fieldset>
```

CONTINUED ➡

Part III

A `fieldset` element with a `legend` element can look quite sophisticated, as shown here:

> **TECHWR-L Information Request Form - Microsoft Internet Explorer**
>
> File Edit View Favorites Tools Help
>
> ⇐ Back ▾ ⇒ ▾ ⊗ ⊠ ⌂ | ⊗Search ⊕Favorites ⊕History | ⊠▾ ⊜ ⊠ ▾ ⊟ ⊚
>
> Address ⊠ \\sulley\raycomm\books\sybex\m-xhtml\4141Weblinks\g0603.htm ▾ ⟨∂Go⟩ | Links »
>
> ## Information Request
>
> ┌─ Personal Information ─────────────────────────────────────
> │ [   ] First Name
> │ [   ] Last Name
> │ [   ] E-mail Address
> │ [   ] Street Address
> │ [   ] City [   ] State [   ] Zip or Postal Code
> │ [   ] Country
> └──
>
> Please choose the most appropriate statement.
> ○ I regularly purchase items online.
> ○ I have on occasion purchased items online.
> ◉ I have not purchased anything online, but I would consider it.
> ○ I prefer to shop in physical stores.
>
> I'm interested in (choose all that apply):
> ☐ Technology
> ☐ Writing
> ☐ Training
>
> ⊠ Done   ⊞ Local intranet

Check Boxes

Users can also use *check boxes* to select an item from a list. Each check box works independently from the others; users can select or deselect any combination of check boxes. Using check boxes is appropriate for open questions or questions that have more than one "correct" answer.

In most browsers, check boxes appear as little squares that contain a check mark when selected:

> **I'm willing to listen to (choose all that apply):**
> ☐ Classic rock
> ☐ Soft rock
> ☐ Oldies
> ☐ Classical music

The TECHWR-L form is designed to find out about activities that interest customers. Any combination of answers, from none to all, might be possible, so this is a good place to use check boxes.

To add check boxes to your form, follow these steps:

1. Enter the lead-in text and textual cues for each item, as in the following code sample:

```
<p>I'm interested in (choose all that apply):<br />
   Technology<br />
   Writing<br />
   Training<br />
   Editing<br />
</p>
```

2. Add an input element before the first choice in the list:

```
<input />Technology<br />
```

3. Add the type="checkbox" attribute to set the input field as a check box:

```
<input type="checkbox" />Technology<br />
```

4. Add the name attribute to label the item. For check boxes, unlike radio buttons, each item has a separate label. Although the check boxes appear as a set, logically the items are completely separate.

```
<input type="checkbox" name="tech" />Technology<br />
```

5. Add the value attribute for the item. In the TECHWR-L form, the value can be yes or no—indicating that technology is or is not an area of interest. However, when the form is returned through e-mail, it's useful to have a more descriptive value. If the value here is tech, the term *tech* returns for a check mark, and nothing returns for no check mark. The e-mail recipient can decipher this easier than a yes or a no.

```
<input type="checkbox" name="tech" value="tech" />
   Technology<br />
```

6. Add a checked attribute to specify default selections. With check boxes, you can include a checked attribute for multiple items, but be careful not to overdo it. Each checked attribute that you include is an additional possible false positive response to a question.

```
<input type="checkbox" name="tech" value="tech"
   checked="checked" />Technology<br />
```

7. Repeat this process for each of the remaining check boxes, remembering to use different name attributes for each one (unlike radio buttons).

In the TECHWR-L form, the final code looks like this:

```
<p>I'm interested in (choose all that apply):<br />
<input type="checkbox" name="tech" value="tech" />
Technology<br />
<input type="checkbox" name="writing" value="writing" />
Writing<br />
<input type="checkbox" name="training" value="training" />
Training<br />
<input type="checkbox" name="editing" value="editing" />
Editing
</p>
```

When viewed in a browser, the check boxes look like those in Figure 17.8.

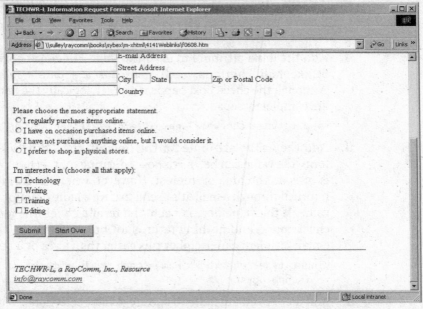

FIGURE 17.8:   Users can use check boxes to choose multiple items from a list.

Password Fields

Password fields are similar to text fields, except the content of the field is not visible on the screen. (They're not encrypted or otherwise secured, but are hidden from casual eyes.) Password fields are appropriate whenever the content of the field is confidential—as in passwords, Social Security numbers, or the mother's maiden name. For example, if a site is accessed from a public place and requires confidential information, a user will appreciate your using a password field. Of course, because your users cannot see the text they type, the error rate and problems with the data rise dramatically.

To establish a password field, follow these steps:

1. Add the `input` field:

   ```
   <input />
   ```

2. Set the `type="password"` attribute:

   ```
   <input type="password" />
   ```

3. Add the `name` attribute:

   ```
   <input type="password" name="newpass" />
   ```

4. Specify the visible size and, if appropriate, the maximum size for the input text by using the `maxlength` attribute:

   ```
   <input type="password" name="newpass" size="10"
      maxlength="10" />
   ```

Viewed in the browser, each typed character appears as an asterisk (*), like this:

Password

Hidden Fields

Hidden fields—obviously—are not visible to your users. However, they are recognized by the program receiving the input from the form and can provide useful additional information. For example, TECHWR-L uses the program cgiemail to process its form, which includes a hidden field that essentially says, "When this form is submitted, show the user the Thanks page." Therefore, when the user submits the form, cgiemail recognizes this hidden field and renders the Thanks page shown in Figure 17.9.

TIP

The cgiemail program, which is software for a Linux/Unix web server to return form results with e-mail, is discussed at length in the final section of this chapter, "One Solution: Processing Results with cgiemail."

Part III

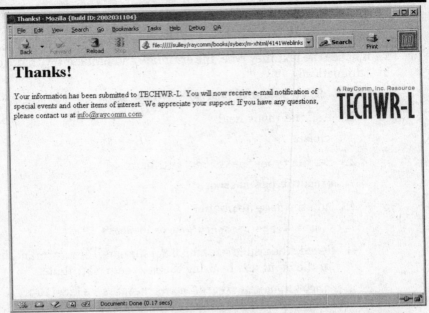

FIGURE 17.9:   A hidden field can tell the server to send a reference page (like this one) to the user or pass other information to the server.

If you need hidden fields, the program that requires them usually includes specific documentation for the exact values. The cgiemail program that TECHWR-L uses requires a hidden field such as the following:

```
<input type="hidden" name="success"
   value="http://www.example.com/techwhirl/
   techwhirl-mail-thanks.html" />
```

The type="hidden" attribute keeps it from being shown, and the name and value attributes provide the information that cgiemail expects.

Hidden fields can go anywhere in your form, but it's usually best to place them at the top, immediately after the opening form tag, so that they aren't misplaced or accidentally deleted when you edit the form.

File Fields

HTML and XHTML also support a special input field, a *file field*, to allow users to upload files. For example, if you want a user to submit a picture, a scanned document, a spreadsheet, or a word-processed document, he can use this field to upload the files without the hassle of using FTP or e-mailing the file.

This feature must be implemented both in the web browser and in the web server because of the additional processing involved in uploading and manipulating uploaded files. After verifying that the server on which you'll process your form supports file uploads, you can implement this feature by following these steps:

1. Add the appropriate lead-in text to your XHTML document:

   ```
   Upload this picture:
   ```

2. Add an `input` field:

   ```
   Upload this picture:
   <input />
   ```

3. Add the `type="file"` attribute:

   ```
   Upload this picture:
   <input type="file" />
   ```

4. Add an appropriate name attribute to label the field:

   ```
   Upload this picture:
   <input type="file" name="filenew" />
   ```

5. Optionally, specify the field's visible and maximum lengths with the `size` and `maxlength` attributes:

   ```
   Upload this picture:
   <input type="file" name="filenew" size="30"
      maxlength="256" />
   ```

6. Optionally, specify which file types can be uploaded by using the `accept` attribute. For example, add `accept="image/*"` to accept any image file:

   ```
   Upload this picture:
   <input type="file" name="filenew" size="30"
      maxlength="256" accept="image/*" />
   ```

The values for the `accept` attribute are MIME types. If you accept only a specific type, such as `image/gif`, you can specify that. If you'll take any image file but no other files, you can use `image/*`, as TECHWR-L did. Finally, if you will accept only a few types, you can provide a list of possible types, separated by commas:

```
<input type="file" name="filenew" size="30"
   maxlength="256" accept="image/gif, image/jpeg" />
```

Part III

TIP
To download a complete list of MIME types, visit `ftp://ftp.isi.edu/in-notes/iana/assignments/media-types/`.

When rendered in most browsers, this code results in a text area plus a button that enables users to browse to a file, as shown in Figure 17.10.

FIGURE 17.10:   You can use file fields to upload files.

Including Text Areas

Text areas are places within a form for extensive text input. One of the primary uses for text areas is to solicit comments or free-form feedback from users, as shown here:

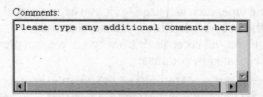

The textarea element sets an area in a form for lengthy user input. Initial content for the text area goes between its opening and closing elements. Table 17.3 lists and describes the chief attributes used for text areas within forms.

TABLE 17.3: Major Attributes of the textarea Element

ATTRIBUTE	USE
cols="*n*"	Sets the number of columns (in characters) for the visible field.
name="..."	Establishes a label for an input field. The name attribute is used for form processing.
rows="*n*"	Sets the number of rows (lines of type) for the visible field.

TIP

Don't confuse text fields with text areas. Text fields are appropriate for shorter input; text areas are appropriate for longer input.

To include a text area in a form, follow these steps:

1. Enter any lead-in text to set up the text area wherever you want it to appear:

   ```
   <p>Comments:</p>
   ```

2. Add the opening and closing textarea elements:

   ```
   <p>Comments:</p>
   <textarea></textarea>
   ```

3. Add a name attribute to label the field:

   ```
   <textarea name="comments"></textarea>
   ```

4. Add rows and cols attributes to set the dimensions of the text area. The rows attribute sets the height of the text area in rows, and cols sets the width of the text area in characters.

   ```
   <textarea name="comments" rows="5" cols="40"></textarea>
   ```

5. Enter some sample information to let your users know what to type by adding the text between the opening and closing textarea tags.

   ```
   <textarea name="comments" cols="40" rows="5">
   Please type any additional comments here.</textarea>
   ```

Part III

This `textarea` markup produces a text area field in the XHTML document similar to the one shown in Figure 17.11.

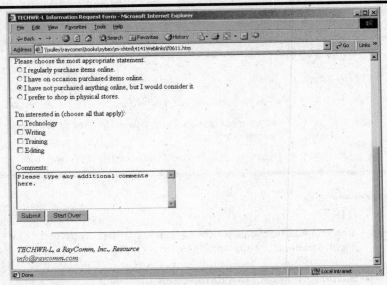

FIGURE 17.11:   A user can type comments in a text area.

Including Select Fields

A select field is one of the most flexible fields used in developing forms because you can let users select single and multiple responses. For example, suppose you need users to tell you the state or province in which they live. You could list the regions as a series of radio buttons, but that would take up tons of page space. You could also provide a text field, but users could make a typing mistake or spelling error.

Your best bet is to use a select field, which lets you list, for example, all 50 U.S. states in a minimal amount of space. Users simply select a state from the list without introducing spelling errors or typos.

Select fields, such as the one shown here, can provide either a long (visible) list of items or a highly compact listing, similar to the Fonts drop-down list in a word-processing program.

 State

The `select` element defines an area in a form for a select field. Table 17.4 lists and describes the elements and attributes used to create select fields.

TABLE 17.4:   Important Select Field Elements and Attributes

Item	Type	Use
select	Element	Sets an area in a form for a select field that can look like a drop-down list or a larger select field.
multiple="multiple"	Attribute of select	Sets the select field to accept more than one selection. Use this attribute along with the size attribute to set to a number as large as the maximum number of likely selections.
name="..."	Attribute of select	Establishes a label for an input field. The name attribute is used for form processing.
size="n"	Attribute of select	Sets the visible size for the select field. The default (1) creates a drop-down list. You can change the default (to 2 or higher) if you want more options to be visible.
option	Element	Marks the items included in the select field. You'll have an option element for each item you include.
selected="selected"	Attribute of option	Lets you specify a default selection, which will appear when the form is loaded or reset.
value="..."	Attribute of option	Provides the content associated with the name attribute.

Use a select field anytime you need to list many items or ensure that users don't make spelling or typing errors. To include a select field in a form, follow these steps:

1. Enter the lead-in text for the select field:

```
I learned about this site from:<br />
```

2. Add the opening and closing select elements:

```
I learned about this site from:<br />
<select>
</select>
```

3. Enter a name attribute to label the select field:

```
<select name="referral">
</select>
```

Part III

4. Add the choices your users should see. Because the select field and `option` element insert line breaks and other formatting, do not include any line break elements.

```
I learned about this site from:<br />
<select name="referral">
  Print Ads
  In-Store Visit
  Friend's Recommendation
  Sources on the Internet
  Other
</select>
```

5. Add the opening and closing `option` tags for each possible selection:

```
<select name="referral">
  <option>Print Ads</option>
  <option>In-Store Visit</option>
  <option>Friend's Recommendation</option>
  <option>Sources on the Internet</option>
  <option>Other</option>
</select>
```

6. Provide a `value` attribute for each `option` element. These values are what you will see when the form is submitted, so make them as logical and descriptive as possible:

```
I learned about this site from:<br />
<select name="referral">
  <option value="print">Print Ads</option>
  <option value="visit">In-Store Visit</option>
  <option value="rec">Friend's Recommendation</option>
  <option value="internet">Sources on the Internet</option>
  <option value="other">Other</option>
</select>
```

7. Optionally, let users select multiple items from the list by including the `multiple` attribute in the opening `select` element:

```
<select name="referral" multiple="multiple">
```

TIP

If you include `multiple`, your user can select one or all options; you cannot restrict the choices to only two of four items, for example.

8. Optionally, add the `selected` attribute to the `option` element to specify a default selection. You can offer more than one default setting if you use the `multiple` attribute.

```
<option value="print" selected="selected">
```

With this, the basic select field is complete. Browsers display this select field as a drop-down list, as in Figure 17.12.

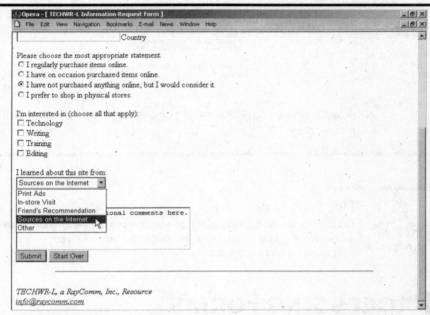

FIGURE 17.12: Select fields let you provide many choices in a compact format.

DESIGNING LONG SELECT FIELDS

When developing particularly long select fields—those that include many items—be sure to make the area as easy to use as possible. Here are some guidelines:

▶ Be sure that the select field appears within one screen; don't make users scroll to see the entire select field.

CONTINUED ➡

Part III

▶ Add a `size` attribute to the opening `select` element to expand the drop-down list to a list box, like this:

```
<select name="referral" multiple="multiple"
    size="5">
```

The list box can have a vertical scroll bar, if necessary, to provide access to all items, as shown here:

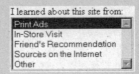

Select boxes are fixed horizontally, meaning that they cannot scroll horizontally.

TIP

You can use JavaScript to validate form input. For example, you can ensure that users fill out contact information or credit card numbers you need to process their information or requests.

PROCESSING FORMS

In general, after a user clicks the Submit button on a form, the information is sent to the web server and to the program indicated by the `action` attribute in the form. What that program then does with the data is up to you. In this section, we'll look at some, but not nearly all, of your options. The server can do these things:

▶ Send the information to you via e-mail

▶ Enter the information into a database

▶ Post the information to a newsgroup or a web page

▶ Use the input to search a database

When you're working out what to do with the data you collect, or if you're just checking out what others have done to get some inspiration, your first stop always should be your web server administrator. In particular, ask which programs are installed to process form input. Depending on what's available, you might be able to take advantage of those capabilities.

Regardless of how you want the information processed, you include specific attributes in the opening `form` element, as explained in Table 17.5.

TABLE 17.5: Processing Attributes for the `form` Element

ATTRIBUTE	USE
`action="..."`	Indicates the program on the HTTP server that will process the output from the form.
`method="..."`	Tells the browser how to send the data to the server, with either the post method or the get method.

The `action` and `method` attributes depend on the server-side program that processes the form.

In general, the documentation that came with your form processing script or with your web server will tell you what to use for `post` and `get`. For example, TECHWR-L's Internet service provider (ISP), `www.example.com`, publishes information on its website about how to set up a form to mail the results (using a CGI script called cgiemail, discussed later in this chapter). In this case, the proper opening `form` element is as follows:

```
<form method="post" action="http://www.example.com/cgi-bin/
    cgiemail/~user/user-mail.txt">
```

WARNING

Remember that we have to break long lines, like this one, to fit the page width of this book. You should type this code all on one line because including hard returns in attribute values can lead to unpredictable browser behavior.

Of course, the attributes you use depend on the program processing the information. By changing the attributes, you also can specify a different program. Because this single line of code within a form determines how the information is processed, you can change what happens to the data without significantly changing the form itself.

Why would you want to change what happens to the data? You'd do so primarily because you discover that there are better ways to manipulate the data. For example, if you want feedback about your company's new product, you want the quickest way to collect the data, which is probably to have it e-mailed to you. Later, you can investigate ways to have the data written directly to an automated database—which isn't as speedy to set up as e-mail but could save you some work.

Some web servers have built-in scripts or commands to process form results. Others, particularly Linux/Unix servers, require additional programs.

In the following sections, we discuss your form-processing options—sending with e-mail, writing to a database, posting to a web page, and other possibilities. Because your ISP's particular setup can vary significantly, we've provided general information that you can apply to your specific situation—probably with the help of your server administrator. The final section in this chapter gives you a specific example of setting up an e-mail return—an option you're likely to use.

TIP

To learn your form processing options, check with your server administrator or visit your ISP's website.

ABOUT USING FORM DATA

Getting a good response rate is the single biggest challenge to survey takers. Using a form to collect information puts you in a similar role, with the added complication that your users must find your website to complete it. After you get the data, you need to use it wisely. Here are some guidelines:

▶ Tell your users how you're going to use the information. For example, if you ask for a user's e-mail address, let him know if you plan on sending him e-mail about your product. Better yet, ask whether he wants information sent. See the "Usability Issues" section earlier in this chapter for more information about including privacy policy information.

CONTINUED ▶

▶ Consider the source carefully, and don't read more into the data than you should. It's quite tempting to assume that the available information is representative of what you might collect from an entire population (customers, users, and so on).

▶ Take the time to analyze your data carefully, determining what it does and doesn't tell you.

For example, after TECHWR-L implements its form and receives a few hundred responses, it will have a general idea of how many customers are willing to make purchases online, how many are located in specific areas, how many have certain interests, and even how many use online services. Much of this information was not previously available to TECHWR-L, and it is tempting to assume that the data is representative of all TECHWR-L customers.

The results of TECHWR-L's online survey reflect only the preferences and opinions of that small set of customers who use the Internet, visited the site, and took the time to fill out the survey. Even if 95 percent of the people who complete the survey express interest in technology, that might not reflect the interests of the overall TECHWR-L customer base.

Processing Forms via E-mail

Having the server return form results to you via e-mail isn't always ideal (although it can be, depending on your situation); however, it's often useful, nearly always expedient, and cheap. Using e-mail to accept form responses simply sends the information the user submits to you (or someone you designate) in an e-mail message. At that point, you have the information and can enter it (manually) in a database, send a response (manually), or do anything else you want with the data.

If you're collecting open comments from a relatively small number of people, receiving the results via e-mail is a reasonable, long-term solution. That is, it's a reasonable solution if you—or whoever gets the e-mail—can address the volume of form responses easily. E-mail is also a good solution if you do not know what level of response to expect. If the volume turns out to be manageable, continue. If the volume is high, consider other solutions, such as databases.

Database Processing

Writing the information that respondents submit to a database is a good solution to a potentially enormous data management problem. If you're collecting information about current or potential customers or clients, for example, you probably want to call up these lists quickly and send letters or e-mail or provide demographic information about your customers to potential website advertisers. To do that, you'll want to use a database.

Although the specifics of putting form data into a database depend on the server and the software, we can make some generalizations. If you work in a fairly large company that has its own web server onsite, you'll encounter fewer problems with tasks such as putting form results directly into a database or sending automatic responses via e-mail. If you represent a small company and rely on an ISP for web hosting, you may have more of a challenge.

If your web server uses the same platform on which you work—for instance, if you use Windows 2000 and your web server is a Windows 2000 web server—feeding the form results directly into a database is manageable. However, if your web server is on a Linux/Unix platform, for example, and you work on a Windows machine, you may face some additional challenges getting the information from a form into a readily usable database.

Posting to a Web Page

Depending on the information you're collecting, you might want to post the responses to a web page or to a discussion group. For example, if TECHWR-L sets up a form to collect information, the natural output might be a web page.

Other Options

If you find that the options available on your system do not meet your needs, look for form processing scripts at Matt's Script Archive at www.scriptarchive.com/, HotScripts at www.hotscripts.com, or Extropia's scripts at www.extropia.com/applications.html.

These scripts offer a starting point for either you or your server administrator to handle form processing effectively. In particular, the form processing script from Selena's archive (www.extropia.com) offers everything from database logging to giving users the opportunity to verify the accuracy of the data they enter.

Keep in mind, if you choose to install and set up these scripts yourself, that the installation and debugging of a server-side script is considerably more complex and time consuming than installing a new Windows program. It isn't impossible for the novice to do it successfully, but set aside some time.

If you choose to download and use scripts from the web, be sure that you get them from a reliable source and that you or your server administrator scans the scripts for possible security holes. Form-processing programs must take some special steps to ensure that malicious users don't use forms to crash the server, send spam, or worse. Unless you take precautions, forms can pass commands directly to the server, which will then execute them with potentially disastrous results.

One Solution: Processing Results with cgiemail

Because you'll likely choose—at least initially—to have form results e-mailed to you, we'll walk you through a form-to-e-mail program. The cgiemail program is produced and distributed for free by MIT, but it's available only for Linux/Unix servers. Check out http://web.mit.edu/wwwdev/cgiemail/index.html for the latest news about cgiemail (yes, it looks old, but it works very well and currently is used widely across the web). This program is a good example because many ISPs offer access to it and because it's also commonly found on corporate Internet and intranet servers.

TIP

You can find a comparable program for Windows 95/98/NT/2000, MailPost for Windows 32-bit web, at www.mcenter.com/mailpost.

Part III

Here is the general process for using cgiemail:

1. Start with a complete form—the one developed earlier in this chapter or a different one. Without a functional form, you cannot have the results sent to you via e-mail.

2. Add the action and method attributes with values you get from your server administrator. (See the "Processing Forms" section, earlier in this chapter, for more information about the action and method attributes.)

3. Develop a template for the e-mail message to you. This template includes the names of each of your fields and basic e-mail addressing information.

4. Develop a response page that the user sees after completing the form.

Now, let's look at how TECHWR-L can use cgiemail to implement its form.

1. The Form

You don't need to do anything special to use forms with cgiemail. You have the option of requiring some fields to be completed, but that's not essential. For example, because the purpose of the TECHWR-L form is to collect e-mail addresses, TECHWR-L should make the e-mail address required.

The solution? Rename the name field from emailaddr to required-emailaddr. The cgiemail program then will check the form and reject it if that field is not complete. The actual code for that line of the form looks like this:

```
<br /><input type="text" name="required-emailaddr"
    size="30" />
  E-mail Address
```

Optionally, add required- to each field name that must be completed.

2. The *action* and *method* Attributes

The server administrator provided TECHWR-L with the action and method attributes shown in the following code:

```
<form method="post" action="http://www.example.com/cgi-bin/
    cgiemail/techwhirl/techwhirl-mail.txt">
```

The file referenced in the action line is the template for an e-mail message. In this case, the http://www.example.com/cgi-bin/cgiemail part of the action line points to the program itself, and the following part (/techwhirl/techwhirl-mail.txt) is the server-relative path to the file. (With a server-relative path, you can add the name of the server to the front of the path and open the document in a web browser.)

3. The Template

The plain-text template includes the bare essentials for an e-mail message, fields in square brackets for the form field values, and any line breaks or spacing needed to make it easier to read.

In general, you can be flexible when setting up the template, but you must set up the e-mail headers exactly as shown here. Don't use leading spaces, but do capitalize and use colons as shown. The parts after the colons are fields for the From e-mail address, your e-mail address (in both the To: line and in the Errors-To: line), and any subject field you choose:

```
From: [emailaddr]
To: Webmaster <webmaster@raycomm.com>
Subject: Web Form Submission
Errors-To: Webmaster <webmaster@raycomm.com>
```

Format the rest of the template as you choose—within the constraints of plain-text files. If you want to include information from the form, put in a field name (the content of a name attribute). The resulting e-mail will contain the value of that field (either what a user enters or the value attribute you specify, in the case of check boxes and radio buttons).

Be liberal with line breaks, and enter descriptive values as you set up the template. E-mail generated by forms may make sense when you're up to your ears in developing the form, but later it's likely to be so cryptic that you can't understand it.

Following is the complete content of the techwhirl-mail.txt file:

```
From: [emailaddr]
To: Webmaster <webmaster@raycomm.com>
Subject: Web Form Submission
Errors-To: Webmaster <webmaster@raycomm.com>
Results from Information Request Web Form:
[firstname] [lastname]
[emailaddr]
[address]
[city], [state] [zip]
[country]
Online Purchasing:
[buying]
Interested In:
[tech]
[writing]
[training]
[editing]
Referral:
[referral]
Comments:
[comments]
```

The cgiemail program completes this template with the values from the form, resulting in an e-mail message similar to the following:

```
Return-path: <www@krunk1.example.com>
Delivery-date: Sat, 25 May 2002 10:03:55 -0600
Date: Sat, 25 May 2002 10:03:51 -0600 (MDT)
X-Template: /home/users/e/public_html/techwhirl/
  techwhirl-mail.txt
From: mjones@example.com
To: Webmaster <webmaster@raycomm.com>
Subject: Web Form Submission
Errors-To: Webmaster <webmaster@raycomm.com>
Results from Information Request Web Form:
Molly Jones
mjones@example.com
402 E 4th
South Logan, UT 84341
USA
Online Purchasing:
might
Interested In:
tech
writing
Referral:
rec
Comments:
I'd also like information about online help.
Thanks!
```

4. Success Page

The only step remaining is to set up a success page—a document that is returned to the user to indicate that the form has been received. Although a success page is optional, we recommend that you use one. In the form code, a success field is actually a hidden input field that looks like this:

```
<input type="hidden" name="success"
   value="http://www.example.com/techwhirl/
   techwhirl-mail-thanks.html" />
```

A success page can contain any content you choose. If you want, you can point the success page back to your home page or to any other page on your site. On the other hand, many developers use the success page as a place to thank the user for taking the time to fill out the form, to offer an opportunity to ask questions or make comments, or to confirm what the user submitted.

WARNING

A less-robust way of returning forms is to use a `mailto` URL in the `action` line, as in `action="mailto:webmaster@raycomm.com"`. However, that solution does not consistently and reliably deliver form results. A much better solution, unless you can closely control the browsers your users use, is a server-based e-mail program, which can process, validate, and help control the data you collect.

WHAT'S NEXT?

In this chapter, you learned how to determine what information to include in forms and to develop them using a variety of widgets. Additionally, you learned about the different ways to process forms and get the data back. In the next chapter, you will learn about additional ways to include interactivity in your pages with Dynamic HTML (DHTML).

Chapter 18

BRINGING PAGES TO LIFE WITH DYNAMIC HTML AND XHTML

When you develop a web page using dynamic HTML or XHTML, your users can view new content without reloading the page, change screen colors with a mouse click, and view animations without installing a plug-in. Dynamic HTML or XHTML uses style sheets and scripting (such as JavaScript)—in tandem with standard HTML or XHTML—to produce dynamic effects. Only browsers that support style sheets and scripting can support dynamic HTML or XHTML.

In addition, you implement dynamic HTML or XHTML one way if you're developing for Microsoft Internet Explorer (IE) or current versions of Netscape Navigator and Opera (all of which support the Document Object Model (DOM) and another way if you're developing for Netscape version 4. For example, IE users may encounter errors or see nothing at all if they open a page designed for Netscape Navigator. Therefore, taking advantage of the latest and greatest can be problematic if the new feature is

Adapted from *Mastering HTML and XHTML*, by Deborah S. Ray and Eric J. Ray

ISBN 0-7821-4141-2 $49.99

Part III

not designed for your users' browsers. The introduction of fairly standards-compliant versions of browsers such as Netscape Navigator 6 and IE 6 makes it easier to write dynamic cross-platform and cross-browser code, but you will still have to accommodate older browsers for a while.

If you're developing for newer browsers and you want to include dynamic effects on your pages, you'll want to know about and use dynamic HTML and XHTML. In this chapter, we introduce you to the technologies, look at some of the advantages and disadvantages associated with using them, and show you how to use them in your documents—for both Netscape Navigator and IE. We'll then use dynamic HTML and XHTML to develop a practical application: collapsing pages.

WHAT ARE DYNAMIC HTML AND XHTML?

Dynamic HTML and XHTML expand on standard HTML or XHTML by giving you the formatting control of style sheets combined with the interactive capabilities of scripting languages such as JavaScript. When you develop pages with dynamic HTML or XHTML, users can spend far less time accessing information because it's available directly within the browser, rather than needing to be retrieved from the server.

TIP
You may see dynamic HTML or XHTML referred to as "DHTML" or "DXHTML." But because there's no defined DHTML or DXHTML language, we stick with calling it dynamic HTML or dynamic XHTML.

WARNING
Dynamic HTML and XHTML are not languages; they're simply combinations of technologies.

For example, suppose you have a table of contents page. If you develop it with standard HTML or XHTML, users click an item; the browser then requests the document from the server and displays it when it arrives. If you develop the table of contents page with dynamic HTML or XHTML, however, the trip to the server is eliminated. Figures 18.1 and 18.2 show this process.

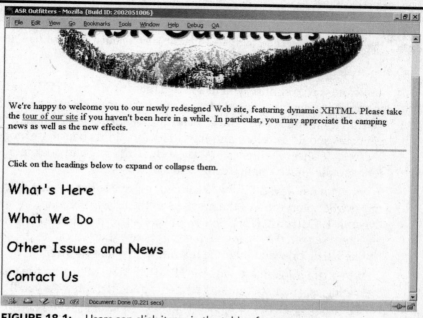

FIGURE 18.1:   Users can click items in the table of contents.

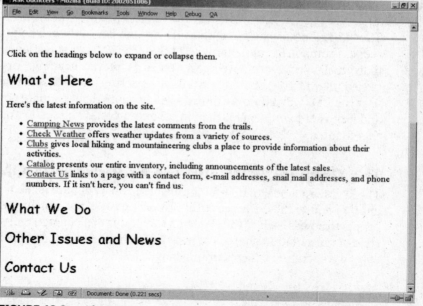

FIGURE 18.2:   After selecting an item, the user can view the expanded content.

Part III

TIP

We show you how to create collapsible information in the section "Creating a Collapsible Document," later in this chapter.

Before you go sprinting off to add dynamic HTML or XHTML capabilities to your documents, you need to be familiar with style sheets and JavaScript. Within dynamic HTML and XHTML, style sheets tell browsers what elements should look like, and JavaScript functions change the properties set by style sheets, which is how page elements know to do something— for example, move, change colors, and so on.

You can use JavaScript's onmouseover event handler to change an image when a user moves the mouse over the image. For many browsers, dynamic HTML or XHTML and event handlers can do this with just about any page element. For example, you can change the color of text, increase the text size, or even make the text jump to a new location.

When you implement dynamic HTML or XHTML using the standard technologies, you use standard elements and attributes. As you'll see in the following section, this approach offers wider support along with better functionality, and it promises more in terms of long-range stability.

The Document Object Model (DOM)

The W3C's *Document Object Model* (DOM) is a key (although behind-the-scenes) component of dynamic HTML or XHTML. It specifies how individual objects within web pages (such as images, headings, or other tagged information) should be available to scripts. In browsers that support the DOM, dynamic documents will be more flexible, more powerful, and far easier to implement than in other browsers. This is illustrated in this chapter.

The Original DOM and the Proprietary DOMs

The DOM is a model of how all the elements on a page are related to one another and to the document itself. Knowing these relationships enables scripts to access each of the elements (or groups of elements) and apply style or presentation changes to just that element (or group of elements) using JavaScript or other scripting languages.

NOTE

The DOM Level 1 specification became a W3C recommendation in October 1998. You can view the full text of the recommendation at www.w3.org/TR/1998/ REC-DOM-Level-1-19981001.

The easiest way to understand the DOM is by looking at a document as a tree structure. The highest level of the tree is the document itself, and all other elements on the page, including the body element, are classified as children of the document.

For example, let's look at a simple piece of code:

```
<html>
<body>
<h1>The document tree</h1>
<p>This is an example of a child element.</p>
<p>This is also a child element.</p>
```

This code can be illustrated as a tree:

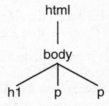

In this simple form of a document tree, html is the parent element. It has one child, body, and the first child element of html (body) also has three children (h1, p, and p).

The original DOM (Level 0) was developed by Netscape for use in Netscape Navigator 2 with the newly developed scripting language JavaScript. It allowed access only to forms and links. In Netscape 3, access to images was added. IE 3 also added implementation of the Level 0 DOM; however, the implementation did not work quite like Netscape's implementation.

Netscape Navigator 4 and IE 4 continued to support the Level 0 DOM, but each added its own proprietary DOMs to supplement the Level 0 DOM. The Netscape proprietary DOM is accessed using document.layers in the JavaScript code, and the IE proprietary DOM is accessed using `document.all` in the JavaScript code, so code that takes advantage of the fourth-generation browser DOM features cannot work on both Netscape and IE.

TIP

Browser-detection scripts can determine which browser a visitor is using to access a site so that the browser is provided with the correct version. More details on browser detection, as well as a browser-detection script, are included in Chapter 13, "Optimizing Your Pages for Internet Explorer."

Up through fourth-generation browsers, you've had two main choices for implementing dynamic documents:

► Using a browser-detection script and creating at least three versions of each page that includes dynamic features—a Netscape Navigator version, an IE version, and a version for browsers that don't support style sheets and JavaScript.

► Writing a complex script that includes the options for all three but implements them all from a single document.

Even with different versions of dynamic pages, the features supported by Netscape's DOM and IE's DOM are not the same, so similar effects are not always possible in both browsers. We explore some features of each proprietary DOM in more depth in the following section, and then we return to the Level 1 DOM and the newest generation of web browsers (version 6 for IE, Opera, and Netscape). According to statistics from www.thecounter.com, about 3 percent of the web audience currently uses Netscape 4.*x* or IE 4.*x*, so it may be important to you to know how to use both of the proprietary DOMs—but, as always, it depends on what your users need.

Level 1 DOM and the Sixth-Generation Browsers

The W3C Level 1 DOM was designed to provide access to every part of an XML document. Because HTML and XHTML documents also can be *parsed* (broken down into component parts) like an XML document, this DOM also is accessible to JavaScript and other scripting and programming languages.

The Level 1 DOM treats each object of the document as a *node*, and the corresponding tree diagram is based on nodes.

If we look at the code sample from the previous section again, we can make a new tree diagram based on nodes:

```
<body>
<h1>Heading text</h1>
<p>This is a child element.</p>
<p>This is also a child element.</p>
```

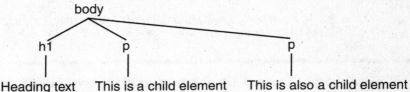

In this diagram, the parts break down as follows:

- ▶ body is an element node.
- ▶ h1 is an element node (and first child of body).
- ▶ Heading text is a text node, which is a child of h1.
- ▶ p is an element node (and a child of body).
- ▶ This is a child element is a text node.
- ▶ The second p also is an element node (and child of body).
- ▶ This is also a child element is a text node and a child of the second p.

You'll use three main node types for scripting: element nodes, text nodes, and attribute nodes. For example, if you add an align attribute to the second paragraph, align is an attribute node, and right is a child of this attribute node.

```
<p align="right">This is also a child element.</p>
```

This node structure enables you to access any node individually by giving it an id and by using two very useful access methods: getElementsBy-TagName and getElementById. Through these methods and id, you can apply a style or a script to a particular node.

The Level 1 DOM is supported by Netscape 6 and above, IE 5 and above, and Opera 4 and above (although Opera 4 and 5 did not support all of the methods and properties of the Level 1 DOM).

Part III

ADDITIONAL LEVEL 1 DOM INFORMATION

Peter-Paul Koch's website offers several resources for more information on the Level 1 DOM:

▶ For more information on using the Level 1 DOM, see "Level 1 DOM—Introduction" at www.xs4all.nl/~ppk/js/dom1.html.

▶ For details on browser support and DOM, check out "Browsers" at www.xs4all.nl/~ppk/js/browsers.html.

▶ For a detailed chart of support for DOM properties and methods, see www.xs4all.nl/~ppk/js/version5.html.

Although IE 5.*x* and 6 implement most of the Level 1 DOM, they also support IE's proprietary DOM. On the other hand, Netscape 6 and above support the Level 1 DOM but do *not* offer support for Netscape's proprietary DOM. This means that scripts written for Netscape 4.*x* will not work in Netscape 6 and above. Although you still need to use a browser-detection script for Level 4 browsers (if your audience includes users of those browsers) and separate scripts for Netscape 4.*x* and Netscape 6 and above, the move toward standards compliance in the latest browsers offers the hope that eventually you'll have to create only one version of a web page for all browsers and all platforms.

IE 6 takes a different approach to backward compatibility by making it dependent on the DOCTYPE declaration used on your page. If you use a DOCTYPE declaration with an HTML 3.2 DTD, your pages will appear in IE 6 as they did in IE 4.*x* and 5.*x*. However, if you use a DOCTYPE declaration with the Strict form of the HTML 4.0 DTD or XHTML DTD, it will use the Level 1 DOM when executing your scripts.

TIP

For more details on using DOCTYPE declarations, see Chapter 3, "Creating Your First HTML or XHTML Document."

TIP

For more information on DOCTYPE and browser mode—standards-compliant or backward-compatibility ("quirks")—see the Doctype switch table at http://gutfeldt.ch/matthias/articles/doctypeswitch/table.html.

For more details on creating dynamic pages in Netscape Navigator 6 and IE 6, check out the following resources:

▶ "Scripting for the 6.0 Browsers," by Scott Andrew LePera, at www.scottandrew.com/index.php/articles/dom_1.

▶ "Mozilla Document Object Model Information," by Dave Eisenberg, at www.alistapart.com/stories/dom/article.html.

▶ "IE 6 Switches to Standards," by Jeffrey Veen, at http://hotwired.lycos.com/webmonkey/01/14/index0a.html?tw=authoring.

TIP

For an extensive script library to help support cross-browser scripting, see www.cross-browser.com.

Understanding the Standard Implementation

Dynamic HTML or XHTML in standards-compliant browsers exposes all page elements to scripting; that is, each page element can be manipulated—recolored, scrolled, jiggled, and so on. If you can specify what the element is, you can format it with style sheets and then change the style sheets using JavaScript. For example, you can identify a heading, specify in the style sheet that the heading is red, and then specify in the JavaScript that the red heading changes to green when a user passes the mouse pointer over the heading.

Part III

TIP

IE 6 offers implementation of most of the W3C DOM properties and includes backward compatibility for its proprietary DOM (document.all). Therefore, scripts written for IE 4.x also will work in later versions. IE 5.x and 6 offer access to the DOM objects through scripting and also through Component Object Model (COM) interfaces.

TIP

If you haven't already done so, you might take a quick look at Chapter 16 before starting these examples. In particular, look closely at the id attribute description in Chapter 16.

Let's take a look at the general process for adding dynamic capabilities to your documents using a standards-compliant implementation (good for current versions of IE, Opera, Mozilla, and Netscape):

1. Start with a functional document. The following code includes the XHTML structural elements and style sheet elements:

```
<!DOCTYPE html PUBLIC
"-//W3C/DTD XHTML 1.0 Transitional//EN"
  "http://www.w3.org/TR/xhtml1/DTD/xhtml1-
     transitional.dtd">
<html xmlns="http://www.w3.org/1999/xhtml">
<head>
  <title>Fix Colors</title>
  <style type="text/css">
<!--
   h1 {color :red }
//-->
</style>
<script type="text/javascript" language="javascript">
<!--
// -->
</script>
</head>
<body>
<h1>Changing Color</h1>
<p>
If you'd like to change the color of the heading above
from black to red for better contrast and easier reading,
just move your mouse over this paragraph.</p>
</body>
</html>
```

2. Add the `id` attribute for each instance that will be affected by a dynamic XHTML function. In this example, we'll change a text color and apply the `changeme` `id` to a heading. Remember that `id` attributes must be unique in each instance.

```
<h1 id="changeme">Changing Color</h1>
```

3. Add the JavaScript event handlers. In this example, each event handler calls a function—`swapit()` or `revert()`—to switch the color when a user clicks the text. Because standards-compliant dynamic document technology exposes *all* elements to scripting and style sheets, you can add the event handlers

directly to the p elements. Because these functions are generic (so you could use the same function to change different elements at different times), you have to include in the function call the id of the element to change.

```
<h1 id="changeme">Changing Color</h1>
<p   onmouseover="swapit('changeme')"
     onmouseout="revert('changeme')">
If you'd like to change the color of the heading above
from black to red for better contrast and easier reading,
just move your mouse over this paragraph.</p>
</body>
</html>
```

4. Add the JavaScript functions, which change the colors on command from the event handlers to the head section of the document (before the closing head element, for example). Each function sets the myElement variable to the element that should be changed (as specified in the event handlers added in the previous step). Next, each function specifies the color property of the element and sets it to a specific color.

```
<!--
function swapit(element) {
var myElement = document.getElementById(element);
myElement.style.color="red"
}
function revert(element) {
var myElement = document.getElementById(element);
myElement.style.color="black"
}
// -->
</script>
```

See the complete code in Listing 18.1.

Listing 18.1: Dynamic Color Changes Using Standards-Compliant Dynamic XHTML

```
<!DOCTYPE html PUBLIC
  "-//W3C/DTD XHTML 1.0 Transitional//EN"
  "http://www.w3.org/TR/xhtml1/DTD/xhtml1-transitional.dtd">
<html xmlns="http://www.w3.org/1999/xhtml">
<head>
```

```
<title>Fix Colors</title>
<style type="text/css">
 <!--
   h1 {color :red }
  // -->
</style>
<script type="text/javascript" language="javascript">
<!--
function swapit(element) {
var myElement = document.getElementById(element);
myElement.style.color="red"
}
function revert(element) {
var myElement = document.getElementById(element);
myElement.style.color="black"
}
// -->
</script>
</head>
<body>
<h1 id="changeme">Changing Color</h1>
<p  onmouseover="swapit('changeme')"
onmouseout="revert('changeme')">
If you'd like to change the color of the heading above
from black to red for better contrast and easier reading,
just move your mouse over this paragraph.</p>
</body>
</html>
```

When writing a function, you need to specify exactly which character-istics of which page element (technically, which *object*) the function applies to, and you do this most easily by setting a variable for the specific object name (think of it as an address) and then modifying the properties. For example, in step 4, the variable myElement is set to an element identified with a unique id by using document.getElement-ById(element), and then the properties of myElement are modified. As a result, the element with the id changeme changes color when a user moves the mouse over the paragraph. Table 18.1 shows you other sample addresses.

TABLE 18.1:   Dynamic XHTML Sample Object and Property Identifiers

THIS SAMPLE ADDRESS	DOES THIS
`document.body.style.color`	Specifies the `color` property of the style of the body of the document.
`document.myElement.top`	Specifies the `top` position property of the style for the `myElement` variable.
`document.form(0).style.background`	Specifies the background of the first form in the document.

TIP

Elements in arrays are numbered starting with 0, as in `form(0)` in Table 18.1. If your document has three form elements, the `form` array would include `form(0)`, `form(1)`, and `form(2)`. The numbering is based on when the form element is specified in the document code; the first form is `form(0)`, and so on. The length of the array is 3 because there are three form elements.

CREATING A COLLAPSIBLE DOCUMENT

A useful dynamic HTML or XHTML capability is providing collapsible information, such as the table of contents you saw earlier. The following section shows you how to develop such a feature for standards-compliant browsers such as IE 5.5 and later, Netscape 6 and later, and Opera 6 and later.

TIP

If your audience uses older browsers (which is possible, but fairly unlikely), you need to provide additional scripts to accommodate those browsers and use a browser-detection script to switch. See Chapter 13, "Optimizing Your Web Pages for Internet Explorer," for more information on browser detection and a sample script. Check out `http://javascript.internet.com/` for additional script samples.

Part III

Collapsing a Document

To create a collapsible document similar to the document shown in Figure 18.1 earlier in this chapter, follow these steps:

1. Start with a basic document.

```
<!DOCTYPE html PUBLIC
 "-//W3C/DTD XHTML 1.0 Transitional//EN"
  "http://www.w3.org/TR/xhtml1/DTD/xhtml1-transitional
      .dtd">
<html xmlns="http://www.w3.org/1999/xhtml">
<head>
<title>ASR Outfitters</title>
<style type="text/css">
<!--
body {font-size : 110% }
h1, h2, h3 {font-family : "Comic Sans MS"}
h1 {font-size : 180% ; font-weight : bold}
// -->
</style>
</head>
<body>
<center>
<img src="asrlogo.gif" alt="ASR logo" />
</center>
<p>We're happy to welcome you to our newly redesigned web
    site, featuring dynamic XHTML. Please take the
    <a href="tour.html">tour of our site</a> if you haven't
    been here in a while. In particular, you may appreciate
    the camping news as well as the new effects. </p>
<hr />
<p>Click on the headings below to expand or collapse them.
  </p>
<h2>What's Here</h2>
<p>Here's the latest information on the site.</p>
<ul>
<li><a href="camping.html">Camping News</a> provides the
latest comments from the trails.</li>
<li><a href="weather.html">Check Weather</a> offers weather
    updates from a variety of sources. </li>
<li><a href="clubs.html">Clubs</a> gives local hiking and
    mountaineering clubs a place to provide information about
    their activities.</li>
<li><a href="catalog.html">Catalog</a> presents our entire
inventory, including announcements of the latest sales.
  </li>
```

```
<li><a href="contact.html">Contact Us</a> links to a page
with a contact form, e-mail addresses, snail mail addresses,
 and phone numbers. If it isn't here, you can't find us.
</li>
</ul>
<h2>What We Do</h2>
<p>In addition to providing the latest camping and outdoor
    activities news, we do also provide mountaineering and
    hiking equipment nationwide via mail order as well as
    through our stores in the Rocky Mountains. Please take a
    few minutes to look through our <a href="catalog.html">
    online offerings</a>.</p>
<h2>Other Issues and News</h2>
<ul>
<li>As you may know, our URL was misprinted in the latest
    <i>Hiking News</i>. Please tell your hiking friends that
    the correct URL is
    <a href="http://www.asroutfitters.com/">
    http://www.asroutfitters.com/</a>.</li>
<li>To collect a $1000 reward, turn in the name of the
person who set the fire in the Bear Lake area last weekend.
<ol>
<li>Call 888-555-1212. </li>
<li>Leave the name on the recording. </li>
<li>Provide contact information so we can send you the
    reward.</li>
</ol>
</li>
</ul>
<h2>Contact Us</h2>
<p>If you have suggestions or comments about the site or
other information we could provide, we'd love to know
about it. Drop us an e-mail at
<a href="mailto:asroutfitters@raycomm.com">
    asroutfitters@raycomm.com</a>.
    Of course, you could also contact us more traditionally
    at the following address: </p>
<address>ASR Outfitters<br />
4700 N. Center <br />
South Logan, UT 87654<br />
801-555-3422</address>
</body>
</html>
```

2. Add `div` elements around each of the elements that should individually expand or collapse. Add a unique `id` attribute to each. You'll use the `id` attribute to specify the name for later reference from scripts.

```
<h2>What's Here</h2>
<div id="whathere">
<p>Here's the latest information on the site.</p>
<ul>
<li><a href="camping.html">Camping News</a> provides the
latest comments from the trails.</li>
<li><a href="weather.html">Check Weather</a> offers weather
    updates from a variety of sources. </li>
<li><a href="clubs.html">Clubs</a> gives local hiking and
    mountaineering clubs a place to provide information about
    their activities.</li>
<li><a href="catalog.html">Catalog</a> presents our entire
    inventory, including announcements of the latest sales.
</li>
<li><a href="contact.html">Contact Us</a> links to a page
with a contact form, e-mail addresses, snail mail addresses,
 and phone numbers. If it isn't here, you can't find us.
</li>
</ul>
</div>
<h2>What We Do</h2>
<div id="whatwedo">
<p>In addition to providing the latest camping and outdoor
    activities news, we do also provide mountaineering and
    hiking equipment nationwide via mail order as well as
    through our stores in the Rocky Mountains. Please take a
    few minutes to look through our <a href="catalog.html">
    online offerings</a>.</p>
</div>
<h2>Other Issues and News</h2>
<div id="otherstuff" >
<ul>
<li>As you may know, our URL was misprinted in the latest
    <i>Hiking News</i>. Please tell your hiking friends that
    the correct URL is
    <a href="http://www.asroutfitters.com/">
    http://www.asroutfitters.com/</a>.</li>
<li>To collect a $1000 reward, turn in the name of the
person who set the fire in the Bear Lake area last weekend.
<ol>
<li>Call 888-555-1212. </li>
```

```
<li>Leave the name on the recording. </li>
<li>Provide contact information so we can send you the
    reward.</li>
</ol>
</li>
</ul>
</div>
<h2>Contact Us</h2>
<div id="contactus">
<p>If you have suggestions or comments about the site or
other information we could provide, we'd love to know
about it. Drop us an e-mail at
<a href="mailto:asroutfitters@raycomm.com">
    asroutfitters@raycomm.com</a>.
    Of course, you could also contact us more traditionally
    at the following address: </p>
<address>ASR Outfitters<br />
4700 N. Center <br />
South Logan, UT 87654<br />
801-555-3422</address>
</div></body>
</html>
```

3. Add an event handler that invokes a script to make the display change. Note that each of the event handlers includes the unique id of the following div section, so the click that each event handler processes will control the display of the following section.

```
<h2 onclick="showOne('whathere')">What's Here</h2>
<div id="whathere">
<p>Here's the latest information on the site.</p>
<ul>
<li><a href="camping.html">Camping News</a> provides the
latest comments from the trails.</li>
<li><a href="weather.html">Check Weather</a> offers weather
    updates from a variety of sources. </li>
<li><a href="clubs.html">Clubs</a> gives local hiking and
    mountaineering clubs a place to provide information about
    their activities.</li>
<li><a href="catalog.html">Catalog</a> presents our entire
    inventory, including announcements of the latest sales.
</li>
<li><a href="contact.html">Contact Us</a> links to a page
with a contact form, e-mail addresses, snail mail addresses,
 and phone numbers. If it isn't here, you can't find us.
```

Part III

```
</li>
</ul>
</div>
<h2 onclick="showOne('whatwedo')">What We Do</h2>
<div id="whatwedo">
<p>In addition to providing the latest camping and outdoor
   activities news, we do also provide mountaineering and
   hiking equipment nationwide via mail order as well as
   through our stores in the Rocky Mountains. Please take a
   few minutes to look through our <a href="catalog.html">
   online offerings</a>.</p>
</div>
<h2 onclick="showOne('otherstuff')">Other Issues and News
</h2>
<div id="otherstuff" >
<ul>
<li>As you may know, our URL was misprinted in the latest
   <i>Hiking News</i>. Please tell your hiking friends that
   the correct URL is
   <a href="http://www.asroutfitters.com/">
   http://www.asroutfitters.com/</a>.</li>
<li>To collect a $1000 reward, turn in the name of the
person who set the fire in the Bear Lake area last weekend.
<ol>
<li>Call 888-555-1212. </li>
<li>Leave the name on the recording. </li>
<li>Provide contact information so we can send you the
   reward.</li>
</ol>
</li>
</ul>
</div>
<h2 onclick="showOne('contactus')">Contact Us</h2>
<div id="contactus" >
<p>If you have suggestions or comments about the site or
other information we could provide, we'd love to know
about it. Drop us an e-mail at
<a href="mailto:asroutfitters@raycomm.com">
   asroutfitters@raycomm.com</a>.
   Of course, you could also contact us more traditionally
   at the following address: </p>
<address>ASR Outfitters<br />
4700 N. Center <br />
South Logan, UT 87654<br />
801-555-3422</address>
```

```
</div>
</body>
</html>
```

4. Add the script at the top that controls all this. The first function hides all of the div sections within the document by looping through each and setting the display property to hidden. The second function (showOne()) first closes all the div elements and then displays the element belonging to the id passed to it. This function enables users to toggle the headings to collapse and expand with each click.

```
<script type="text/javascript" language="javascript1.3">
<!--
function closeall() {
var divs = document.getElementsByTagName('div')
var elements = divs.length
for(var i = 0;i < elements;i++)
    {
    var divStyle = divs.item(i)
        divStyle.style.display = 'none';
            }
return;
}
function showOne(element) {
closeall()
var element = document.getElementById(element)
element.style.display = 'block'
return;
}
// -->
</script>
```

5. Finally, add an onload event handler to the body element to close all of the div elements as the page loads. This serves two purposes: First, it collapses all of the div elements. Second, it ensures that browsers (such as Opera) that incorrectly claim to support display properties still will display everything to their users. (If we used a style sheet to hide those elements and then scripts to display them, the Opera users could not see them. By using the same script to hide and display, we ensure that, at the worst, the page will simply not be dynamic.)

```
<body onload="closeall()">
```

The complete code for a standards-compliant collapsible document is shown in Listing 18.2. This document works well in Netscape 6 and above and IE 6, but it is not dynamic in Opera 6 because Opera does not properly support the CSS display property.

Listing 18.2: Collapsible Document Using Dynamic XHTML

```
<!DOCTYPE html PUBLIC
"-//W3C/DTD XHTML 1.0 Transitional//EN"
   "http://www.w3.org/TR/xhtml1/DTD/xhtml1-transitional.dtd">
<html xmlns="http://www.w3.org/1999/xhtml">
<head>
<title>ASR Outfitters</title>
<style type="text/css">
<!--
body {font-size : 110% }
h1, h2, h3 {font-family : "Comic Sans MS"}
h1 {font-size : 180% ; font-weight : bold}
// -->
</style>
<script type="text/javascript" language="javascript1.3">
<!--
function closeall() {
var divs = document.getElementsByTagName('div')
var elements = divs.length
for(var i = 0;i < elements;i++)
    {
    var divStyle = divs.item(i)
        divStyle.style.display = 'none';
            }
return;
}
function showOne(element) {
closeall()
var element = document.getElementById(element)
element.style.display = 'block'
return;
}
// -->
</script>
</head>
<body onload="closeall()">
```

```
<center>
<img src="asrlogo.gif" alt="ASR logo" />
</center>
<p>We're happy to welcome you to our newly redesigned web
    site, featuring dynamic XHTML. Please take the
    <a href="tour.html">tour of our site</a> if you haven't
    been here in a while. In particular, you may appreciate
    the camping news as well as the new effects. </p>
<hr />
<!--<a onclick="closeall()" href="javascript:closeall();">
Close All</a> -->

<p>Click on the headings below to expand or collapse them.
</p>
<h2 onclick="showOne('whathere')">What's Here</h2>
<div id="whathere">
<p>Here's the latest information on the site.</p>
<ul>
<li><a href="camping.html">Camping News</a> provides the
latest comments from the trails.</li>
<li><a href="weather.html">Check Weather</a> offers weather
    updates from a variety of sources. </li>
<li><a href="clubs.html">Clubs</a> gives local hiking and
    mountaineering clubs a place to provide information about
    their activities.</li>
<li><a href="catalog.html">Catalog</a> presents our entire
    inventory, including announcements of the latest sales.
</li>
<li><a href="contact.html">Contact Us</a> links to a page
with a contact form, e-mail addresses, snail mail addresses,
 and phone numbers. If it isn't here, you can't find us.
</li>
</ul>
</div>
<h2 onclick="showOne('whatwedo')">What We Do</h2>
<div id="whatwedo">
<p>In addition to providing the latest camping and outdoor
    activities news, we do also provide mountaineering and
    hiking equipment nationwide via mail order as well as
    through our stores in the Rocky Mountains. Please take a
    few minutes to look through our <a href="catalog.html">
    online offerings</a>.</p>
</div>
```

```
<h2 onclick="showOne('otherstuff')">Other Issues and News
</h2>
<div id="otherstuff" >
<ul>
<li>As you may know, our URL was misprinted in the latest
    <i>Hiking News</i>. Please tell your hiking friends that
    the correct URL is
    <a href="http://www.asroutfitters.com/">
    http://www.asroutfitters.com/</a>.</li>
<li>To collect a $1000 reward, turn in the name of the
person who set the fire in the Bear Lake area last weekend.
<ol>
<li>Call 888-555-1212. </li>
<li>Leave the name on the recording. </li>
<li>Provide contact information so we can send you the
    reward.</li>
</ol>
</li>
</ul>
</div>
<h2 onclick="showOne('contactus')">Contact Us</h2>
<div id="contactus" >
<p>If you have suggestions or comments about the site or
other information we could provide, we'd love to know
about it. Drop us an e-mail at
<a href="mailto:asroutfitters@raycomm.com">
    asroutfitters@raycomm.com</a>.
    Of course, you could also contact us more traditionally
    at the following address: </p>
<address>ASR Outfitters<br />
4700 N. Center <br />
South Logan, UT 87654<br />
801-555-3422</address>
</div>
</body>
</html>
```

The resulting collapsible document should look similar to Figures 18.1 and 18.2, earlier in this chapter.

What's Next?

As you learned in this chapter, dynamic HTML and XHTML offer lots of potential for making your pages leap off the screen. Although this chapter covered only the basics, you can combine any style sheet characteristic with a JavaScript function to make your pages flash, change, and move.

If you feel confident using style sheets and JavaScript, we recommend that you experiment with combining these two aspects.

In the next chapter, you'll learn how to extend XHTML through the use of XHTML modules.

Part IV

XML

Chapter 19
XHTML: HTML GOES XML

HTML as you may have once known it may someday be nothing more than an artifact of what will be considered the horse and buggy days of the web. In its place will be XHTML, which will be used as the main language driving a wide variety of browsers built into everything from the kind of navigation tools we are used to seeing today to cell phones, PDAs, and maybe even refrigerators.

XHTML stands for Extensible Hypertext Markup Language, and the W3C places enough importance on it that XHTML is considered the definitive current specification regarding HTML. That old standby HTML, and in particular version 4.0, while obviously still a valid language because of the sheer volume of web pages adhering to its definitions, is being replaced. This process will take a long time—maybe a decade, maybe more. There are hundreds of millions of web pages out there. Many of them may never disappear. Considering the extensibility offered by XHTML

Adapted from *Mastering XML*, by Chuck White, Liam Quin, and Linda Burman
ISBN 0-7821-2847-5 $49.99

and an ease of use that compares with HTML (although the document type definitions [DTDs] themselves are highly complex), you risk ignoring it at your own peril, especially if you are a professional web developer.

XHTML is different from HTML. For one thing, it's an XML-based language. Tags all must close, attributes must be in quotes and in attribute/value pairs, and every other rule of XML must be followed. Another key difference is that it is extensible. XHTML consists of not only a core language set, but also a large group of modules that can be used and extended by developers for their own purposes. In fact, you can develop your own modules as long as you follow a specific set of guidelines. These guidelines can be found at the W3C site at www.w3.org/TR/2000/CR-xhtml-modularization-20001020/abstraction.html#s_abstraction.

THE THREE "FLAVORS" OF XHTML 1.0

Your transition to XHTML 1.0 can be reasonably painless because there are three kinds of DTDs to choose from when validating XHTML 1.0 documents. They are comparable to the three similarly named HTML 4.0 DTDs, except they are XML compliant.

NOTE

XHTML 1.0 is the first version of XHTML in the W3C specifications. For a historical look at XHTML development, see the sidebar "XHTML and the W3C," later in this chapter.

XHTML 1.0 Transitional

Like HTML 4.0 Transitional, with this DTD you can use deprecated elements such as font, applet, and center. (Deprecated elements are those elements that, although legal within the framework of a given DTD, are expected to be removed from future DTDs.) Generally, in HTML, these relate to styling elements. The DOCTYPE declaration should look like this:

```
<!DOCTYPE html PUBLIC
"-//W3C//DTD XHTML 1.0 Transitional//EN"
"http://www.w3.org/TR/xhtml1/DTD/xhtml1-transitional.dtd">
```

XHTML 1.0 Strict

This is for those of you who are up to the challenge of writing a completely XML-conformant document that also avoids deprecated elements. The DOCTYPE declaration should look like this:

```
<!DOCTYPE html PUBLIC "-//W3C//DTD XHTML 1.0 Strict//EN"
"http://www.w3.org/TR/xhtml1/DTD/xhtml1-strict.dtd">
```

XHTML 1.0 Frameset

This is for developing frames-based XHTML documents. The DOCTYPE declaration should look like this:

```
<!DOCTYPE html PUBLIC "-//W3C//DTD XHTML 1.0 Frameset//EN"
"http://www.w3.org/TR/xhtml1/DTD/xhtml1-frameset.dtd">
```

NOTE

You also can find the W3C XHTML Basic Recommendation in bonus Appendix A, "XHTML Basic Specification," on the Sybex website (www.sybex.com).

MANAGING XHTML DOCUMENT CONFORMANCE

To be considered conformant XHTML, a document must follow these rules:

- ▶ There must be a DOCTYPE declaration in the document prior to the document instance and, by extension, the root element.

- ▶ The document must be validated against one of the three DTDs shown in the previous section.

- ▶ The root element must be html.

- ▶ The root element also must contain the xmlns attribute with the following namespace as its value: http://www.w3.org/1999/xhtml.

Listing 19.1 shows a very simple XHTML document.

Listing 19.1: A Simple XHTML Document

```
<?xml version="1.0" encoding="UTF-8"?>
<!DOCTYPE html PUBLIC "-//W3C//DTD XHTML 1.0 Strict//EN"
```

```
    "http://www.w3.org/TR/xhtml1/DTD/xhtml1-strict.dtd">
    <html xmlns="http://www.w3.org/1999/xhtml"
     xml:lang="en" lang="en">
    <head>
       <title>Foo Fighters</title>
    </head>
    <body>
       <p>Not all references to foo are necessarily about
          computer programming.</p>
    </body>
    </html>
```

You can see a few things going on in Listing 19.1 that demonstrate a clear difference between XHTML and HTML. First, the file is clearly an XML file, because it starts with a document prolog. Second, the DOCTYPE declaration makes it possible to validate against the strict DTD. Note also that the xmlns attribute is used to declare the XHTML namespace. You may run into other namespaces for XML-compliant HTML but, officially, they won't be XHTML-conformant documents unless they possess that namespace.

XHTML MODULARIZATION

One of the most significant traits of XHTML is modularization. XHTML is designed to function within the range of different modules that use subsets of the entire language. This is because cell phones designed for browsing web pages, for example, would have a difficult time loading a traditional web page in memory. By requiring cell phone browsers to understand a much smaller set of tags, there is less of a strain on its processor resources.

The W3C therefore has decided to create a fairly extensive set of prebuilt modules for XHTML that can be used either on their own or as building blocks for your own DTDs.

XHTML Module Implementations

A *module* is a set of element types, a set of attribute-list declarations, and a set of content-model declarations. Attribute-list and content-model declarations in a module may modify an element type outside the element types or typesets that were defined in the module.

XHTML 1.1 was the first version of XHTML to implement modules by transforming XHTML 1.0 Strict into a module framework. The use of modules has been expanded in XHTML 2.0.

XHTML AND THE W3C

The mission of the W3C HTML Working Group is "to develop the next generation of HTML as a suite of XML tag sets with a clean migration path from HTML 4" (www.w3.org/MarkUp/#xhtml11). A brief review of the W3C documents and Recommendations for XHTML details the path from HTML to XML and, in particular, the development of XHTML modularization.

▶ XHTML 1.0

The XHTML 1.0 Recommendation (www.w3.org/TR/xhtml1) was released in January 2000 and revised in August 2002. XHTML 1.0 is a reformulation of HTML 4 as an XML 1.0 application.

▶ XHTML Basic

The XHTML Basic Recommendation (www.w3.org/TR/xhtml-basic) was released in December 2000. XHTML Basic is designed for users of information appliances, including these:

    Mobile phones

    Televisions

    PDAs

    Vending machines

    Pagers

    Automotive navigation systems

    Mobile game machines

    Digital book readers

    Smart watches

XHTML Basic includes text structure elements and attributes, links, forms, tables, and meta elements, but it does not include the full set of HTML 4.01 or XHTML 1.0 features.

▶ Modularization of XHTML

The Modularization of XHTML Recommendation (www.w3.org/TR/xhtml-modularization) was released in April 2001. This document defines abstract modules and the DTDs to implement them. An abstract module is a set of elements, attributes, and content models.

CONTINUED ▶

▶ XHTML 1.1—Module-Based XHTML

The XHTML 1.1 Recommendation (www.w3.org/TR/xhtml11) was released in May 2001. The current XHTML 1.1 modules are shown in Table 19.1, later in this chapter. Additional modules may be added in the future.

▶ XHTML 2.0

XHTML 2.0 was released as a working draft (www.w3.org/TR/xhtml2) in August 2002. XHTML 2.0 includes modules from the Modularization of XHTML Recommendation and modules from the following:

RUBY: Ruby Annotation (www.w3.org/TR/ruby) provides a pronunciation guide for Japanese and Chinese base text.

XML Events: This is an XML events syntax (www.w3.org/TR/xml-events) based on Level 2 DOM.

XForms: This is the successor to HTML forms. XForms separate the content (data collection) and presentation of forms.

An XHTML document type consists of any series of one or more abstract modules; these can be combined as you see fit within the constraints of the definitions contained within the various modules. A module is a specific DTD that can contain other modules within it as part of its definition set. As a simple non-XHTML example, imagine defining an XML DTD with just one element, foo. You might call that the foo module. Then, imagine defining another module that adds to that and creating a separate DTD for your new module. That module might be called fooFun. It may be defined with one additional element, named fooFun, which is an extension of the foo module, which in turn contained only that one element initially. The new set would thus contain a total of two elements: foo and fooFun.

There are many different module implementations within the current XHTML 1.1 framework. Table 19.1 lists and describes these modules.

TABLE 19.1: XHTML 1.1 Modules

MODULE	DESCRIPTION OF ELEMENTS	ASSOCIATION WITH OTHER MODULES	FILENAME
Structure	title, head, body, html	html acts as the root element for all XHTML family document types.	xhtml-struct-1.mod
Hypertext	a	Adds the a element to the Inline content set of the Text module.	xhtml-hypertext-1.mod
List	dl, dt, dd, ol, ul, li	Adds list-oriented elements to the Flow content set of the Text module.	xhtml-list-1.mod
Text	Heading content set: h1, h2, h3, h4, h5, h6 Block content set: address, blockquote, div, p, pre Inline content set: abbr, acronym, br, cite, code, dfn, em, kbd, q, samp, span, strong, var Flow content set includes Heading, Block, and Inline content sets	Contains Presentation, Edit, and Bi-directional Text modules.	xhtml-text-1.mod
Presentation	b, big, i, small, sub, sup, tt	Adds hr to the Block content set of the Text module, and b, big, i, small, sub, sup, and tt to the Inline content set of the Text module.	xhtml-pres-1.mod
Edit	ins, del	Adds del and ins to the Inline content set of the Text module.	xhtml-edit-1.mod
Bi-directional Text	bdo	Adds bdo to the Inline content set of the Text module.	xhtml-bdo-1.mod

TABLE 19.1 continued: XHTML 1.1 Modules

MODULE	DESCRIPTION OF ELEMENTS	ASSOCIATION WITH OTHER MODULES	FILENAME
Forms	form, label, input, select, optgroup, option, textarea, fieldset, legend, button	Contains Basic Forms module; adds the Form content set to the Block content set of the Text module and the Formctrl content set to the Inline content set of the Text module.	xhtml-form-1.mod
Basic Forms	form, label, input, select, option, textarea	Subset of Forms module; contains a limited set of forms-related elements.	xhtml-basic-form-1.mod
Tables	table, caption, thead, tfoot, tbody, colgroup, col, tr, th, td	Contains Basic Tables module; adds table to the Block content set as defined in the Text module.	xhtml-table-1.mod
Basic Tables	table, caption, tr, th, td	Subset of Tables module; contains a limited set of tables-related elements.	xhtml-basic-table-1.mod
Base	base	Adds base to the content model of the head element in the Structure module.	xhtml-base-1.mod
Client-side Image Map	area, map	Adds map to the Inline content set of the Text module; Image module (or another module that supports img) must also be included.	xhtml-csismap-1.mod
Image	img	Adds img to the Inline content set of the Text module.	xhtml-image-1.mod
Intrinsic Events	attributes for XHTML-based events	Adds specific attributes to elements when modules containing those elements are included, for example, adds onblur and onfocus to button element when Forms module is included.	xhtml-events-1.mod
Link	link	Adds link to the content model of the head element in the Structure module.	xhtml-link-1.mod

TABLE 19.1 continued: XHTML 1.1 Modules

MODULE	DESCRIPTION OF ELEMENTS	ASSOCIATION WITH OTHER MODULES	FILENAME
Metainformation	meta	Adds meta to the content model of the head element in the Structure module.	xhtml-meta-1.mod
Object	Object, param	Adds object to the Inline content set of the Text module.	xhtml-object-1.mod
Scripting	script, noscript	Adds script and noscript to the Block and Inline content sets of the Text module, adds script to the content model of the head element in the Structure module.	xhtml-script-1.mod
Server-side Image Map	ismap attribute for img, input	Image module (or another module that supports img) must also be included.	xhtml-ssismap-1.mod
Style Attribute	style attribute	N/A	xhtml-inlstyle-1 .mod
Stylesheet	style	Adds style to the content model of the head element in the Structure module.	xhtml-style-1.mod
Ruby Annotation	ruby,rbc,rtc,rb,rt,rp	Supports elements and attributes for Ruby Annotation markup.	xhtml-ruby-1.mod

NOTE

The Style Attribute module is deprecated in favor of the use of the Stylesheet and Link modules.

NOTE

The Frames, iframe, Legacy, Name Identification, Target, and Applet modules were defined in "Modularization of XHTML," but are not included in XHTML 1.1.

As an example of using one of the modules in Table 19.1, take a look at the Text module. This module consists of four core content types: headings, block elements, inline elements, and flow content. It also contains

Part IV

other modules: the Presentation, Edit, and Bi-directional Text modules. If you look at the Bi-directional Text module, in turn, you will see that it contains the inline content of the Text module, as well as one additional element: the bdo element.

As another example, consider the Edit module. This module consists simply of an extension of the Text module's inline entity. Two elements are added to the Text module to complete the Editing module: the del element and the ins element. Each module typically contains parameter entities, such as the inline entity of the Text module. We have not described each of these entities in Table 19.1 because of space constraints, but you can find that information in the associated DTDs.

Each of the modules listed in Table 19.1 consists of its own DTD, corresponding to the filename in the last column of the table. Each of these is a public resource that is identified like so:

```
PUBLIC "-//W3C//ELEMENTS XHTML fooModule 1.0//EN"
```

In the case of the Hypertext module, for instance, the public identifier would look like this:

```
PUBLIC "-//W3C//ELEMENTS XHTML Hypertext 1.0//EN"
```

Similarly, each module has a system identifier, which takes this general format:

```
http://www.w3.org/TR/xhtml-modularization/DTD/foo.mod
```

To find the Hypertext module, you would point to this resource:

```
http://www.w3.org/TR/xhtml-modularization/DTD/
xhtml-hypertext-1.mod
```

NOTE

XHTML 2.0 adds the nl element (for navigation lists), expands the use of the href attribute to every element, and deprecates img and applet elements in favor of an expanded use of the object element. For more information on the features of XHTML 2.0, see "XHTML 2.0: The Latest Trick," by Kendall Grant Clark, at www.xml.com/pub/a/2002/08/07/deviant.html.

DIFFERENCES BETWEEN HTML AND XHTML

XHTML is a language that is strictly adherent to XML. Therefore, not only are there specific differences between HTML and XHTML, but those differences are enough that if your background is as an HTML developer, you'll have to make some substantial adjustments to the way you think.

A few years ago, many serious HTML developers would not close p elements because they didn't have to, and also because some felt it was a waste of bandwidth to close them. Each character was considered a drain on resources that, if not necessarily make a web page slower to load, would at least have a cumulative effect on the performance of the Internet as a whole.

Worthy as such thinking may be, it won't work in an XML-based world. XML is not bandwidth friendly, and XHTML is no exception. XML and XHTML require all elements to have closing tags, attribute values to have quotes around them, and so on. Understanding XHTML is almost as simple as understanding that any HTML element needs to be converted to an XML-friendly format.

Let's take a look at some of the differences between HTML and XHTML:

▶ Nested elements must be closed.

▶ End tags are not optional.

▶ XHTML elements are case sensitive, and the case is always lowercase, meaning <p> is a valid element, but <P> is not.

▶ Empty elements must be terminated with an end tag.

▶ All attribute values must be wrapped in quotes.

▶ Attributes cannot be minimized, which simply means an attribute cannot stand alone without some value attached to it, because XML requires attribute value *pairs*.

▶ White space in attribute values is normalized according to Section 3.3.3, "Attribute-Value Normalization," of the XML specification.

▶ Script and style elements are contained within CDATA sections.

▶ Element exclusions (as in SGML) are not allowed. Nevertheless, the XHTML recommendation does specify a normative list of elements for which no nesting is allowed. These are shown in Table 19.2.

NOTE

In W3C documentation, rules that are non-normative are informative and are not mandatory but only a recommended best practice. Rules that *must* be followed are called *normative*.

Part IV

TABLE 19.2:   Elements That Cannot Be Nested in XHTML

ELEMENT	MAY NOT CONTAIN
a	Other a elements
button	button, fieldset, form, iframe, input, label, select, textarea
form	Other form elements
label	Other label elements
pre	big, img, object, small, sub, sup

Compatibility with Older HTML Browsers

In addition to the normative rules outlined in the previous section, the XHTML recommendation consists of several recommendations that are not strict requirements. These are called non-normative, or informative, rules. They are designed primarily to aid in the construction of HTML code that pre-XHMTL browsers will interpret correctly.

Add a Space Before Terminating an Empty Element

Browsers interpreting an XHTML empty element such as <br/> usually will not do it properly, so you should add a single space before the / markup, like this: <br />.

Follow the Content Model when Managing Empty Elements

Empty elements that don't have empty content according to the XHTML DTDs should never have an XML empty element construct like this: <p />. The p element is an example of an element that does have content according to the XHTML DTDs, so you should develop both a beginning tag and an ending tag: <p> </p>.

Don't Use Line Breaks and White Space in Attribute Values

Don't trust that, just because the XHTML Recommendation normalizes white space in attribute values, a user agent will do it. Avoid white space and line breaks in attribute values altogether.

Use Both *lang* and *xml:lang* Attributes

The xml:lang attribute takes precedence officially, but because the support of these two attributes is not reliable, you should include both when specifying the language of an element.

Use Both *id* and *name* Attributes when Identifying URI Fragments

In XHTML, to maintain backward-compatibility, you should use both the id attribute and the name attribute when creating identifiers:

```
<a id="foo" name="foo">...</a>
```

However, the name attribute is deprecated in XHTML 1.0 in favor of the id attribute.

Specify Character Encoding Both in the XML Declaration and in a *meta* Tag

If you specify character encoding, you should do it in two places: in the XML declaration and through the meta http-equiv statement:

```
<?xml version="1.0" encoding="EUC-JP"?>
<meta http-equiv="Content-type" content='text/html;
    charset="EUC-JP"' />
```

Using Ampersands in Attribute Values

Ampersands in XML declare the beginning of an entity reference. When using attribute values with an ampersand, you need to use a character reference for the ampersand (&). For example, if you are using an a element with an href attribute that refers to a script that takes parameters, the ampersand must be denoted with the ampersand character reference:

```
<a href="www.example.com/cgibin/formscript.pl?
class=user&amp;name=guest">
```

instead of:

```
<a href=www.example.com/cgi-bin/formscript.pl?
class=user&name=guest">
```

PORTING HTML INTO XHTML

The HTML Tidy utility is a tool developed within the auspices of the W3C by Dave Raggett, the editor of the HTML 4.0 Recommendation. He originally wrote the Tidy program to help web developers write cleaner

HTML documents and clean up documents produced by WYSIWYG editors that dumped all kinds of garbage into the source code. HTML Tidy also can be used to help you convert HTML documents to XML.

NOTE

HTML Tidy can be downloaded from `http://tidy.sourceforge.net`.

Some HTML and XML editors, such as Macromedia HomeSite, also incorporate Tidy as a component.

Sometimes, of course, you just have to tidy up the code yourself. This means paying close attention to the DTDs, as well as the guidelines outlined earlier in this chapter. Remember that if you follow the basic rules of XML, keep all of your element names in lowercase, close all tag sets, and place all attribute values in quotes, you will go a long way toward developing a valid XHTML document.

WHAT'S NEXT?

In this chapter you learned about the transformation of HTML into XML via the XHTML language. In the next chapter, you'll learn more about XML itself.

Chapter 20

INTRODUCTION TO XML

The storage and exchange of information has been a problem in the world of computers since they were invented. In essence, files fit into one of two categories: Either they are basic text or they are binary.

Text files are the most compatible. They use standard 8-bit characters using the ASCII system to store information. ASCII is universally accepted—from the workhorse mainframes of the late 1970s to the first "toy" personal computers of the early 1980s to the modern PC, Mac, and Unix workstations, they all read and write ASCII data. ASCII is not without problems—for example, different machines use different characters for line termination—but these are not impossible to overcome.

However, there are problems with ASCII as a storage format for anything beyond letters, numbers, and basic punctuation. One of the fundamental problems with ASCII text is that essentially we are limited to 128 different characters, consisting of the main letters (upper- and lowercase), numbers, and basic characters, such as the comma, dollar sign, and mathematical symbols.

Adapted from *XML Processing with Perl, Python, and PHP*, by Martin C. Brown
ISBN 0-7821-4021-1 $49.99

Part IV

With standard ASCII, there is no way to represent anything beyond those standard characters, so accented characters and other currency symbols are missing. We don't even have access to the accent symbols, so we can't mark them up in the text so that a program such as Word will understand what we mean.

This representation issue is the main complaint about plain text as a file. By definition, plain text is an unformatted and unstructured solution for storing information. There are solutions for imposing structure, such as Comma Separated Values (CSV) and Tab Delimited Fields (TDF), but both of these are completely unsuitable for anything other than tabular data.

Suppose you want to store a marked-up document that uses bold and italic, different fonts, and special characters and incorporates images, movies, and sound? The obvious option is to produce your own proprietary binary format. You get to use 8-bit, full-width characters and, instead of relying on a text representation of what you are doing, you can format and structure your document however you like. It doesn't matter that the document isn't readable by anything other than your application. If someone wants to read your document, he can just buy a copy of your application, right?

Proprietary Data Formats

Although these proprietary formats are fine as long as you are using your application, what happens when you want to exchange that document with someone else? If you are transferring it over e-mail, you probably need to encode it into an ASCII-based format—normally handled automatically by your e-mail software—then decode it back to its binary format.

When your recipient gets the document, he still needs a copy of the application that created it, or at least one that is able to import or read that binary format. This presents something of a problem. There are lots of different word processors out there; if you're sending a copy of a letter that you wrote in Word, and your recipient uses AppleWorks, what do you do?

You could try saving to a compatible format. Both applications support Rich Text Format (RTF), which is actually a structured text format that retains most of the formatting for a document, though it's not infallible. Congratulations, you've just solved your first data exchange problem!

Now do the same with your latest database application. The first problem is that there's no direct equivalent of the RTF format for exchanging information. Sure, we can export the data in Data Interchange Format

(DIF), Sylk Symbolic Link (SYLK) format data file, or the previously mentioned CSV and TDF formats. We'll need to do that for each table in our database, and we'll need to set up the database at the other end to hold the information we need to import.

If we take a specific example, such as a contacts database, we can be more specific. Exchanging entire tables between systems isn't a problem, but pulling out a single record can be. If the database is modeled with three different tables containing contact names, addresses, and contact numbers, then that single contact will mean taking only a few rows from each table. You'll have to import each table individually, and woe to you if your record IDs don't match!

Although transferring information between two database systems that you've created is relatively simple, try repeating the exercise with two databases that are not identical, such as the contacts database in the e-mail software on your Desktop and the equivalent database in your handheld. The field names don't match, and in all likelihood the number and type of fields don't match either.

Modifying the raw text data generated when you did the export would solve the problem, but you'd probably lose some data in the process. In addition, you would be adding a manual element to something that should really be automatic. Computers are supposed to make your life easier, right?

XML — Making Data Portable

By now you should have started to spot a trend. Exchanging data between applications, even those that you've created and written yourself, is not easy. In fact, it's often the single most frustrating process in using your application and one of the most asked-about topics in user forums and to helpdesk managers.

Data exchange happens all the time. Everything from your latest credit card purchase to clicking on a URL in an e-mail message triggers some form of data exchange. Get more adventurous and you find that exchanging documents with your friends, importing graphics into your newsletter or catalog, doing a mail merge, or even sharing data between your Desktop and your handheld all rely on the exchange of information.

The critical area in each case is how to model the data in a format that is as portable as possible and still retain the data structure. RTF, CSV, TDF, and a myriad of other formats all have tried to fit that particular niche.

The problem is that each is targeted at solving a particular problem, which means that each essentially uses its own proprietary format. We're back to square one.

In 1974, Charles F. Goldfarb invented Standardized General Markup Language (SGML). This system represented the contents of complex documents using standard text. Tags were used to help describe the content and format of the text so that it was possible to convert a raw SGML document and extract data from it, either to produce a final document or to extract elements. Everything from a full book to a quick reference card could be pulled from a raw SGML file, all without ever modifying or copying the contents. In order to accomplish all these things, however, SGML developed into a massive and complicated specification. Until the development of HTML and other markup languages developed from SGML, SGML was used mainly by large electronic libraries such as those developed by IBM and the Department of Defense.

In 1991, Tim Berners-Lee used the basic mechanisms provided by SGML to create a way to mark up text for formatting it on-screen; he called it Hypertext Markup Language (HTML). Although the Internet was nothing new by the time HTML came on the scene, HTML did revolutionize the way we use the Internet and browse and exchange information.

In about 1997, it became apparent that many of the principles that applied to SGML and HTML could be applied equally for modeling data. If SGML declares document elements so that we can pick out individual paragraphs, chapters, and other specific fragments and HTML defines text formatting, then Extensible Markup Language (XML) can be used to store data in a structured format.

XML enables us to mark up a text document so that we can identify different pieces of information. For example, we could mark up a contact record like this:

```
<contact>
    <name>Martin Brown</name>
    <address>The House</address>
    <town>Sometown</town>
    <postcode>AB12 3CD</postcode>
    <contact_numbers>
        <phone>01234 567890</phone>
        <mobile>09876 543210</mobile>
        <email>mc@mcslp.com</email>
    </contact_numbers>
</contact>
```

We can now pick out from this XML document the name of the contact, the address, and a list of phone numbers.

The entire document is in text, so we don't have to worry about dealing with or programming a reader for a proprietary format. The fields are easily marked up; we needn't doubt which of these fields is my phone number, and for all we know the entire record could have come from seven different tables in a database. We also haven't lost any information in the translation.

Going back to our original problem—that of exchanging data between applications—you can see that we've just solved all the problems we had with either the binary formats or the CSV, RTF, and other text- and data-specific formats we've been using up to now.

Using our contact XML document, if we'd exported that from our e-mail application on the Desktop and then transferred it over to our handheld, we'd have copied the information easily, efficiently, and without any manual intervention. If the handheld was unable to cope with mobile phone numbers, it could have ignored the field. If it used a single field to hold the address, city, and postcode information, it could have bonded all that together when the record was imported.

This is what XML is all about: modeling data in a structured way so that we can exchange information between applications easily. XML is a solution for making data portable.

XML GOALS

Extensible Markup Language (XML) is a side-set of SGML. Although it follows most of the basic premises of the SGML system, some of the complexity has been removed in order to make it easier to use as a way of displaying and formatting information for the web. The original design goals of the World Wide Web Consortium (W3C) when developing XML were these:

1. XML shall be straightforwardly usable over the Internet.

2. XML shall support a wide variety of applications.

3. XML shall be compatible with SGML.

4. It shall be easy to write programs to parse XML documents.

5. The number of optional features of the XML standard should be kept to an absolute minimum (preferably zero).

6. XML documents should be human-readable and reasonably clear.

7. The XML design should be prepared quickly.

8. The design of XML should be formal and concise.

9. XML documents should be easy to create.

10. Terseness in XML markup is of minimum importance.

For the most part, W3C succeeded. XML is easy to use, create, parse, and understand, even when reading it in its raw format. The XML 1.0 specification has been set in stone, with the formal ratification taking place on February 10, 1998.

XML FEATURES

We can list the primary features that XML provides in six simple statements:

- ▶ XML enables you to store and organize information that can be tailored to your needs, rather than being controlled by the application that created the information.

- ▶ XML uses the Unicode character set, which means we are not limited to ASCII or indeed any character set for any language. XML documents can be written in English, Chinese, Gujarati, Greek, or Sanskrit.

- ▶ XML is an open standard, which means that nobody owns the standard, it's not reliant on a single company, and it's not part of or reliant on the features of a single application.

- ▶ XML documents can be as open or strict as we like. We can check the quality of the document by examining syntax, the data content, or the document structure.

- ▶ XML is clear and easy to read. People can read and write XML documents, and documents can be written and modified using a standard text editor.

- ▶ XML is a system for modeling data. We can convert the data into a formatted document using style sheets, without the need to convert the data into another format.

XML: PAST, PRESENT, AND FUTURE

Despite its apparent age, XML is still a relatively new technology. At the time I write this, January 2003, XML is 3.5 years old, and yet many of the features, applications, and promises made in XML's infancy have yet to be realized.

This is not in any way a criticism. HTML is just 12 years old, and even now we are only beginning to realize its potential. Most people use HTML every day, and a significant proportion of them write it, but still there are issues surrounding how best to use the language. Compatibility issues (different browsers displaying the same HTML in different ways), tags, and where HTML fits into the whole scheme of document formatting are topics still to be decided. As you learned in the previous chapter, XHTML is a reformulation of HTML with the strict syntax of XML. XHTML is now three years old, and the XHTML language continues to evolve and expand as XML continues its development.

XML is actually a family of technologies. The XML standard itself defines how to specify elements and their attributes within your XML documents. Behind the scenes sits the document type definition (DTD) or the schema document (XML Schema or any of several alternative schema languages such as Relax NG and Schematron). Both DTDs and schemas are optional elements that define the structure, layout, and validity of the fields and data that you can incorporate into your XML document. DTDs and schemas make it possible to validate XML documents against their specific definitions of a valid document.

There are extensions to the XML standard that enable you to define and specify other elements in the document, such as XLink for adding hyperlinks, XPath and XPointer for pointing and referring to areas of an XML document, XFrames for HTML frames functionality without the accessibility problems of HTML frames, XForms for separating content and presentation in forms, and XQuery for querying a broad variety of XML sources, including documents and databases. "Coming attractions" (still in Working Group form) are XML Encryption, XML Signature, and XML Key Management.

For converting the XML document into HTML for display on a web page, we have Cascading Style Sheets (CSS), Extensible Stylesheet Language (XSL), and XSL Transformations (XSLT). XML languages for specific graphic and display functions include Synchronized Multimedia Integration Language (SMIL), Scaleable Vector Graphics (SVG) and Graph Markup Language (GraphML).

Finally, there are technologies for reading XML documents, such as Simple API for XML (SAX) and Document Object Model (DOM). There are the technologies that use XML, such as Resource Description Format (RDF), which is used to model metadata, RDF Site Summary (RSS), which is used to stream news information in a structured format, and the rapidly developing area of Web Services for application-to-application communication via remote technologies such as XML-RPC and SOAP, which use XML to exchange requests and responses with a remote server to enable you to execute functions remotely.

At the present time, XML is still in the "let's see what we can do" stage. Standards are being discussed and agreed upon, and many companies and developers are converting their systems to use XML. Most of the topics already mentioned in this chapter are still in development, and although it's true that most things evolve over time, many of these haven't yet made it to the growing-legs and breathing-air stage.

In the future, XML will be a major part of your computing experience. Whether you are aware of this or not will depend on how it is advertised.

Other companies are creating groups that will agree on standards for communicating between systems. Already there are groups for our contact database and Desktop/handheld data problem. There also are companies developing solutions for Electronic Data Interchange (EDI), a system that requires the definition of hundreds or even thousands of fields just to hold the information for an order.

You'll wake up in the morning, read the news through a set of RSS feeds, send an XML-formatted e-mail to your friends, exchange an XML document with your bank to find your latest balance, and raise orders and receive invoices from your suppliers and clients by sending them an XML document, rather than printing them out and faxing or posting them.

WHAT'S NEXT?

In this chapter, you got an overview of using XML for information exchange and learned the history and basic functions of the XML family of technologies. In the next chapter, you'll learn more about XML syntax, including elements, attributes, and the rules for "well-formed" XML documents.

Chapter 21

FUNDAMENTALS OF XML

In the previous chapter, you learned about the history of XML and the XML family of technologies. This chapter features background information on what XML is and what the different components are that make up an XML document.

XML is incredibly simple, and if you know HTML you are already more than halfway there. XML itself is an extensible markup language; it uses the same tag style as an HTML document. Unlike HTML, which has a specific set of tags, with XML you can create your own.

The difference between HTML and XML is in the information that is contained in the eventual document. An HTML document contains text with links (hence *hyperlink*) and other embedded elements such as graphics and movies. The eventual aim is to produce a document that looks good on-screen and has links and jump points to similar documents in order to build an information source—whether that be a website, online help in an application, or an interactive info guide.

Adapted from *XML Processing with Perl, Python, and PHP*, by Martin C. Brown

ISBN 0-7821-4021-1 $49.99

Part IV

XML, on other hand, is designed to represent information in a structured and ultimately transparent and portable way. As we saw in the previous chapter, one of the problems with modern computing is that we have no portable way of transferring data, and that's what XML aims to solve. The way it does this is to use the tags and existing structure and features of HTML (actually, SGML, the precursor of HTML, XHTML, and XML) in a more flexible way.

In this chapter, we're going to look at what makes up an XML document, what the different components are, how we can use this information to format data, and how the different elements are identified and processed within a typical XML parser.

XML STRUCTURE

As you can see from the following example, all XML documents are made up of a number of different components. The text below is a typical XML document, in this case describing a video and some links that enable us to buy the product through Amazon UK's referral service:

```
<video>
<video_base>
<title>Alien Resurrection</title>
<subtitle>Witness the Resurrection</subtitle>
<stars>Sigourney Weaver, Winona Ryder</stars>
</video_base>
<buylinks>
<!-- The product code references go here -->
<azuk id="B00004S8GR">Buy Alien Resurrection on DVD</azuk>
<azuk id="B00004S8K7">Buy the Alien Box Set on DVD</azuk>
</buylinks>
</video>
```

The important fragments of the document are the elements (also known as *tags*), which are the portions of text between the < and > characters, the attributes within some of the tags, and the character data (the information not between the <> characters. One other piece of information that might be important is the comment text, enclosed by <!-- and -->.

The whole document structure also should be noted. The information in the document is divided between the XML elements and the character data. We start with a single element, <video>, which contains all the other elements.

It should be obvious from this small example that XML documents are organized so that the elements define the data we are storing, and the character data is the actual information. For example, our video contains a piece of information about its title, subtitle, and stars, and the actual data component of the title is Alien Resurrection. Information may also be included as attributes. For example, the azuk elements contain id attribute information.

You also should note that, although the tags within the XML document define different fields, there is no limit to the number of tags or their structure. In our example, the video_base section includes the basic information on the video in question—the title, subtitle, and stars—and we also have a buylinks section that contains two azuk tags.

Elements and Attributes

An XML element defines an area of information within the document. In our example, our first XML element is <video>, and it defines the start of the information on a video title. The end of the video title information is indicated by the </video> tag. Those familiar with HTML will recognize this structure from many tag pairs, such as those used for table specifications, <td> and </td>.

Like HTML, XML also supports individual (that is, non-paired) tags for empty elements. Empty elements contain no content. Unlike HTML, which uses empty tags such as <hr>, empty elements in XML include a slash mark, such as <mytag/>.

Some naming rules apply to the text you use for element names. The following sidebar explains.

XML ELEMENT NAMING RULES

The XML specification includes the following guidelines for tag and attribute names:

▶ Names are case sensitive: <account> and <Account> are treated as different tags.

▶ A name must start with a character or an underscore, but after that it can continue with any combination of letters, digits, underscores, or periods.

CONTINUED ➡

Part IV

> ▶ Names beginning with xml (in any combination of uppercase and lowercase) are reserved for use by the XML specification and any of its associated systems.

An *attribute* is an additional piece of information defined within a specific tag. For example, in our azuk elements, we included an ID number to be used when referring to the product on the Amazon UK website. Attributes can be used to give an element a unique label or to add properties to an element.

In HTML, you use attributes to include information such as the URL of a link when defining a hyperlink or the location of a graphics file when inserting an image.

Any element can have as many attributes as necessary, as long as each attribute has its own unique name (see the "XML Element Naming Rules" sidebar for more information on what's supported). You also should note the following:

- ▶ Individual attributes should be separated by spaces. For example, the following fragment is invalid:

    ```
    <chapter section="1"subsection="2">
    ```

    It should be written:

    ```
    <chapter section="1" subsection="2">
    ```

- ▶ Attribute data should be enclosed in either single or double quotes. The following is an example of how *not* to quote information:

    ```
    <chapter title=The Long and Winding Road
     section=1 subsection=2>
    ```

    The problem here is that we (and therefore an XML parser) have no way of knowing where the data for the title attribute ends.

Elements are handled in a *parser* (software that divides code into smaller sections that can then be analyzed) by accessing them either by name or by the name of an attribute being supplied to a handler function. Attributes are usually handled in the same way; with most scripting languages, an attribute is supplied as a hash, an associative array, or a dictionary (depending on what your language calls it).

ARRAYS

An array, a hash, and a dictionary are all objects that can store a sequence of values. The location of a value in the array is indexed.

In the following JavaScript code, a new array named MyGroup is created, and then populated with the four names that comprise the group. Note that the first position in the array is [0].

```
MyGroup = new Array(4)
MyGroup[0] = Bob
MyGroup[1] = Carol
MyGroup[2] = Ted
MyGroup[3] = Alice
```

Comments

You can introduce comments into an XML document just as you can with HTML. However, unlike HTML, where comments are used to annotate the code for human readers and to pass instructions to a server or to an application, XML comments are used strictly for annotations. HTML comments frequently are used for everything from processing instructions (the Server Side Includes (SSI) system on the web, for example) to adding application-specific data within tools such as ColdFusion and other HTML authoring systems.

In XML, processing instructions are handled completely differently (see the section "XML Processing Instructions," later in this chapter, for more information) and we no longer need to use an existing tag in the HTML specification to hold information. XML lets us define our own tags for that.

XML comments are formatted in the same way as HTML comments, starting with <!-- and ending with -->:

```
<!-- This is a comment -->
```

You can include as much text as you like within a comment, even XML tags:

```
<!-- Please ignore this section
<options>Rear seatbelts, heated windscreen</options>
-->
```

Most XML parsers completely ignore comments. Others allow you to read and access comments through the same mechanism as you normally would use to access XML tags and character data.

Character Data

Character data essentially is all the information within an XML document that doesn't appear within the constraints of an XML tag or its attributes. For example, in our sample XML document, the following fragment contains two pieces of information—the XML tag `<title>` and the character data `Alien Resurrection`:

```
<title>Alien Resurrection</title>
```

In the majority of XML documents, it's actually the character data that contains the real information. The tags often just define the type of field to which the character data refers.

Note that, as with XML in general, character data contents are treated verbatim—newlines, spaces, and other white space are significant. This can cause problems if you are used to building HTML documents, in which white space is largely ignored. For example, this XML fragment:

```
<title>
Alien Resurrection
</title>
```

is different from this one:

```
<title>Alien Resurrection</title>
```

Different parsers handle the issue of white space in different ways. For example, some would treat the first item as three separate blocks of character data: the first newline, the actual text, and then the final newline at the end of the text. Others return any data between two tags as a single character data block, and it's up to you to handle the information accordingly.

XML also allows you to insert large chunks of character data that are not subject to the normal conversion and translation handled by entity references (which we'll see later). In those situations, you can insert a special CDATA block. A CDATA block starts with the prefix `<![CDATA[` and terminates with the `]]>` character sequence. For example, the following fragment normally would fail because of the use of < and & characters:

```
<example>$a << 8; output($a && $b);</example>
```

We could resolve the problem with entity references:

```
<example>$a &lt;&lt; 8; output($a &amp;&amp; $b);</example>
```

However, not only is this difficult to read, it's also difficult to write. We can get around this by using a CDATA block:

```
<example><[CDATA[ $a << 8; output($a && $b); ]]></example>
```

CDATA blocks are better used in large pieces of text where the normal entity references would be difficult to use and include. For very short pieces of code, including the examples above, the use of entity references is much better.

Within most XML parsers, character data is considered to be another vital element in the processing sequence, in the same way that start and end tags are. Some also support the identity of the start and end of character data sections.

WELL FORMED XML DOCUMENTS

There are lots of ways to validate and verify that the structure of an XML document is correct, including the use of document type definitions (DTDs) and schema documents. However, at the basic level, all XML documents should be formatted correctly according to the rules of XML syntax. Documents that conform to this are said to be *well formed*.

NOTE
In order to validate an XML document against a DTD or schema, the XML document must be well formed.

It is not a requirement that a document be well formed, but most XML processors will raise an error if the document is not. To get the full details of the rules that define being well formed, see the W3C's XML specification at http://www.w3.org/TR/REC-xml#sec-well-formed.

In a nutshell, the rules are these:

▶ There should be one root element (called the *parent*), from which all other elements (known as *children*) are derived. Documents with more than one root element are not well formed.

▶ Nested elements should be opened and closed in the correct sequence. For example, the following is not well formed because the </foo> tag closes before the </bar> tag has been completed:

```
<foo><bar></foo></bar>
```

▶ A child tag should be closed before its parent. For example, the following is wrong because <bar> is not closed:

```
<foo><bar></foo>
```

Part IV

▶ Attribute values should be enclosed in double quotes. This fragment is not well formed because `hello` should be in quotes:

```
<foo value=hello></foo>
```

ENTITY REFERENCES

Entity references are merely ways of introducing a standard piece of text by name, rather than explicitly within the text itself. There are two reasons for using entities. The first is to get around the problem of introducing characters into character data that would otherwise be identified as special XML characters. The second is to provide an easy means for introducing repeating elements of text into your XML documents without the risk of introducing errors.

This first problem is covered in the next section, "Character Entities." The second problem is covered in the "Mixed-Content Entities" section that follows.

There is a third entity type, the *unparsed entity*, which is used to insert binary data into an XML document. It's unparsed because including the information in the XML document would probably confuse the typical XML parser. We don't cover or use unparsed entities in this book. See *XML Complete*, published by Sybex, for a complete discussion of entities, their types, and their definition.

Character Entities

The XML specification supports five standard character entities, listed in Table 21.1.

TABLE 21.1: Standard XML Character Entities

NAME	VALUE
amp	&
apos	'
gt	>
lt	<
quot	"

To insert these entities into your XML documents, use the form *&entity;*, where *entity* is one of the names in Table 21.1, such as in the following:

```
<condition>Where x &lt; 10</condition>
```

In addition to these standard character entities, you also can introduce a character by its numerical value. For example, to introduce the ampersand character (&) by its numerical value, you'd use &. The # sign indicates that what follows is a number and should be used as a numerical value within the Unicode table.

NOTE

Unicode is a standard for representing characters as integers; it provides a unique number for any character. For more information on Unicode, see the Unicode home page at www.unicode.org.

Finally, we also can refer to certain characters within the Unicode database by name if they've been declared within an external DTD. A DTD already exists that enables characters to be inserted by name from the Latin, Greek, Cyrillic, and Nordic scripts used in the majority of Western Europe and the Americas.

Mixed-Content Entities

Mixed-content entities can be either internal or external. *Internal* entities are used when you want to insert the same block or section of text into an XML document. For example:

```
<?xml version="1.0"?>
<!DOCTYPE doc SYSTEM "http://www.mcwords.com/generic.dtd"
[
    <!ENTITY title "Alien Resurrection">
]>
<title>&title;</title>
<review>&title; is a great film, but it plays more like
a sequence of individual scenes than a connected whole.
One of the problems that you notice throughout &title;
is that the story doesn't really flow. </review>
```

Here we've used the `title` entity so that we can keep referring to the film without having to type it each time. This prevents you from entering it incorrectly; we know that each time we use `&title;`, it'll appear correctly in the text.

Entities are defined as part of a DTD—the DTD in this case is defined inline within the XML document itself. The entity definition consists of the name we want to use for the entity—title—and the text that we want to be inserted each time the entity is referenced. The text can be anything, including more XML.

External entities can be used to insert the content of an external file into the current XML document. You can use this to insert repeating or large chunks of data into a number of documents. For example, when writing the contents of a Help document, you might want to include the same static XML fragment at the head of each XML document. That fragment would contain the generic help information, such as the product, product version, and other static information.

You specify the location of an external file by using the SYSTEM keyword within the entity declaration:

```
<?xml version="1.0"?>
<!DOCTYPE doc SYSTEM "http://www.mcwords.com/generic.dtd"
[
    <!ENTITY docheader SYSTEM "header.xml">
]>
<chapter>
&docheader;
<chapter_title>Help on Help</chapter_title>
</chapter>
```

Note that the filename following the SYSTEM keyword could just as easily be a URL to an external XML document.

Providing the parser has been configured properly, most entities should be automatically inserted into the document while it is being parsed. You normally have some flexibility over the parsing and inclusion process, including being given triggers when a parsed entity is found within a document.

XML PROCESSING INSTRUCTIONS

XML itself is designed to hold data. You shouldn't use XML to hold either presentational information (such as fonts or layout) or instructions about how to handle or process the information contained within the XML document.

However, there are times when you want to be able to give an instruction to the processor to treat a piece of information in a specific way within an

XML document. For example, you may want to force a particular paragraph or piece of text to be formatted in a particular way (perhaps because of style or trademark guidelines), or you may want to introduce a fixed element such as a linebreak into an otherwise free-form character data section.

Processing instructions are very simple: They follow this form:

```
<?name data ?>
```

where *name* is the name used to describe the processing instruction in question; it's used in the same way as tags are to identify the instruction. *data* is any information in the form of strings or attribute/value pairs. For example, all the following are examples of processing instructions:

```
<?font MCSLPStandard?>
<?breakline?>
<?parseasrecipe id=567 title="parsnips on parade"?>
```

Although processing instructions appear to give some information, that's not the intention. Whether you actually use processing instructions or follow them is entirely up to you when parsing the document. The result of the instruction also is up to you, although presumably you'll be defining what a processing instruction does as part of the definition of the XML structure itself.

THE XML DECLARATION

The XML declaration is a special type of processing instruction. It sits at the top of an XML document and tells the parser what the document is (XML), what version of XML is in force, what encoding system you are using to introduce text into the document, and whether the document stands alone or requires additional documents.

- ▶ version defines the version number of the XML specification to which the document applies. At the time of this writing, there is only one specification, 1.0, but it's likely that other versions will be added in the future.

- ▶ encoding specifies the character encoding used in the document. Unless you are using characters other than the standard Latin set (as used by most Western and European languages), this item is optional. Valid values depend on the Unicode standard.

- ▶ standalone defines whether the document is fully contained or requires other documents to be loaded to be processed properly.

Typically, you would set this to no if there were no external entities, DTDs, or schemas to the XML document and to yes if there
were. You can use this value to improve performance: If the value
is set to no, processing can begin instantly. If it is set to yes, you
know you first must parse the document to determine what other
files are needed before you can parse the document fully.

All of these properties are configured in the XML declaration just like
attributes in a typical XML element. For example, all of the following are
valid examples of XML declarations:

```
<?xml version="1.0"?>
<?xml version="1.0" encoding='US-ASCII'?>
<?xml version='1.0' standalone='no'?>
```

XML declarations normally are accessible through a special function
as part of the XML parser, which returns the XML declaration for the XML
document being processed.

WHAT'S NEXT?

XML is a language for describing data in a structured and formatted way
using normal ASCII text. It uses a format similar to the HTML and XHTML
standards but, unlike with HTML or XHTML, with XML you can define
your own tags, and those tag pairs contain the information in your XML
documents.

You can verify an XML document in a number of ways. You can use a
document type definition (DTD) or a schema document, which are formal
definitions of an XML document's structure. You also can use simpler
methods that check the validity of the tags to ensure that they match and
are not nested incorrectly.

Part V

APPENDICES

Appendix A

HTML and XHTML
Elements and Attributes

This is a comprehensive reference guide to all HTML and XHTML elements (often referred to as *tags*), including all standard elements and some other elements introduced by Netscape Navigator and Microsoft Internet Explorer. For each element, we provide sample code and indicate the following:

- **Standard/Usage:** The version of HTML in which the element was introduced

- **Widely Supported:** Whether browsers support the element widely

- **Empty:** Whether the element is an empty element

For each element, we also list the available attributes; then, for each attribute, we again describe its use with values, provide HTML version and browser-support information, and show some sample HTML or XHTML code.

Adapted from *Mastering HTML and XHTML*,
by Deborah S. Ray and Eric J. Ray
ISBN 0-7821-4141-2 $49.99

TIP

If an element or attribute says it was introduced in HTML 2, 3.2, or 4, you can use it in XHTML as well.

If elements and attributes were introduced in the HTML 4, HTML 3.2, or HTML 2 specification, that version number appears next to Standard/ Usage. For browser-specific elements and attributes, Standard/Usage tells you which browsers or browser versions support them.

You can safely use all HTML 2 elements and attributes—they provide basic functionality but few layout or design-oriented features.

HTML 3.2 remained backward compatible with HTML 2 but provided many new elements. Included in HTML 3.2 was support for tables, client-side imagemaps, embedded applets, and many new attributes that help control alignment of objects within documents. You can assume that all common browsers support all HTML 3.2 elements and attributes.

HTML 4 remained backward compatible with other versions of HTML and expanded the capabilities to better address multiple languages and browser technologies, such as speech or Braille. Additionally, most formatting elements and attributes were deprecated in HTML 4 and later in favor of style sheets, which provide better formatting capabilities.

NOTE

Deprecated means the element is no longer recommended for use and is likely to be removed in a future version of the specification. You should use alternatives if at all possible.

Because XHTML is a reformulation of HTML 4 as XML, the elements and attributes used are the same. Therefore, if an element or attribute can be used with HTML 4 or earlier, it can be used with XHTML. However, you should consider using style sheets instead of the deprecated elements or attributes.

NOTE

XHTML 1.0 is a reformulation of HTML 4.0 as an XML 1.0 application. XHTML 1.1, the first version of XHTML to implement modules, is a reformulation of XHTML 1.0 Strict into a module framework. XHTML 2.0 expands on the modules of XHTML 1.1. For more information on the varieties of XHTML, see Chapter 19, "XHTML: HTML Goes XML."

The current HTML 4 and XHTML 1.0 and 1.1 specifications provide three subtypes: Transitional, Frameset, and Strict. The Transitional DTD accepts the elements and attributes that are deprecated for use in HTML 4 and later and XHTML 1. For general-purpose web authoring, this continues to be the best choice. The XHTML Frameset DTD supports frames.

NOTE

XHTML 2.0 was released as a W3C Working Draft in August 2002. The DTD is still in development. It will not include a Frameset DTD. XFrames, an XML application to replace HTML and XHTML frames, was also released as a Working Draft in August 2002.

The XHTML Strict DTD focuses on document structure elements and leaves out all deprecated elements (shown in Table B.1) and attributes. This DTD is good if you're authoring for:

▶ Netscape Navigator 4 or later versions

▶ Internet Explorer 4 or later versions

▶ Opera 5 or later versions

We strongly emphasize using clean XHTML markup and style sheets. See Chapter 3, "Creating Your First HTML or XHTML Document," for details on the different specifications and when to use them.

If you want to comply with the XHTML 1.1 specification (released May 2001), you need to stay away from the deprecated elements shown in Table B.1.

TABLE B.1: Deprecated Elements in XHTML 1.0 and Above

DEPRECATED ELEMENT	DESCRIPTION	NOTES
applet	Java applet	Deprecated in favor of the object element
basefont	Base font size	Deprecated in favor of CSS
center	Shorthand for div align="center"	Deprecated in favor of CSS
dir	Directory list	Deprecated in favor of unordered lists
font	Local change to font	Deprecated in favor of CSS
isindex	Single-line prompt	Deprecated in favor of using input elements to create text-input controls

TABLE B.1 continued: Deprecated Elements in XHTML 1.0 and Above

DEPRECATED ELEMENT	DESCRIPTION	NOTES
menu	Menu list	Deprecated in favor of unordered lists
s	Strikethrough text	Deprecated in favor of CSS
strike	Strikethrough text	Deprecated in favor of CSS
u	Underlined text	Deprecated in favor of CSS

TIP

To see a table that shows which attributes are deprecated in which elements in HTML 4.01, visit www.w3.org/TR/html401/index/attributes.html and check out the Depr column.

Elements labeled as deprecated throughout this section are acceptable to the Transitional and Frameset DTDs but not to the Strict DTD. Elements labeled with earlier versions of HTML but not as deprecated are acceptable for all HTML DTDs, including Strict. Elements in the Frameset DTD are labeled as HTML 4 (Frames).

Specifying that an element or attribute is widely supported means that approximately 85 to 90 percent of browsers in common use accommodate the element. All commonly used versions of Internet Explorer (5.5 and later) and Netscape Navigator (6 and later), as well as alternative browsers like Opera (5 and later) and Mozilla (.9 and later), recognize all widely supported elements and attributes.

We indicate common variables as follows:

Variable	What You Substitute
n	A number (such as a size)
url	Some form of address (as in a hyperlink)
#rrggbb	A color value (in hex format) *or* a standard color name
...	Some other value, such as a title or a name

TIP

Where values are given as a comma-separated list, the values are variable. Where values are given as a pipe-separated list, they're fixed values, and you should choose one.

COMMON ATTRIBUTES

Some attributes apply to almost all elements. These are called *common attributes*, and they are as follows.

lang="..."

Specifies the language used within the section. This attribute is used most often within documents to override site-wide language specifications. Use standard codes for languages, such as DE for German, FR for French, IT for Italian, and HE for Hebrew. See ISO International Standard 639 at

```
http://www.oasis-open.org/cover/iso639a.html
```

for more information about language codes.

Although these codes aren't case sensitive as HTML or XHTML attribute values, the ISO requires them to be uppercase in other contexts, such as SGML, so it's better to use capital letters.

Standard/Usage: HTML 4   **Widely Supported:** No

Sample:

```
<p>The following quote is in German.
<q lang="DE">Guten tag!</q></p>
```

dir="ltr/rtl"

Specifies the direction (left-to-right or right-to-left) for the text used within the section. This attribute is used most often within documents to override site-wide language direction specifications.

Standard/Usage: HTML 4   **Widely Supported:** No

Sample:

```
<p>The following quote is in Hebrew; therefore, it's written
 right to left, not left to right. <q lang="HE" dir="rtl">
Hebrew text goes here and is presented right to left, not
left to right.</q></p>
```

EVENT HANDLERS

Each of the following event handlers helps link user actions to scripts.

onload="..."

Occurs when the browser finishes loading a window or all frames within a frameset. This handler works with body and frameset elements.

onunload="..."

Occurs when the browser removes a document from a window or frame. This handler works with body and frameset elements.

onclick="..."

Occurs when a user clicks the mouse over an element. This handler works with most elements.

ondblclick="..."

Occurs when a user double-clicks the mouse over an element. This handler works with most elements.

onmousedown="..."

Occurs when a user presses the mouse button over an element. This handler works with most elements.

onmouseup="..."

Occurs when a user releases the mouse button over an element. This handler works with most elements.

onmouseover="..."

Occurs when a user moves the mouse over an element. This handler works with most elements.

onmousemove="..."

Occurs when a user moves the mouse while still over an element. This handler works with most elements.

onmouseout="..."

Occurs when a user moves the mouse away from an element. This handler works with most elements.

onfocus="..."

Occurs when a user moves the focus to an element with either the mouse or the Tab key. This handler works with label, input, select, textarea, and button.

onblur="..."

Occurs when a user moves focus away from an element with either the mouse or the Tab key. This handler works with label, input, select, textarea, and button.

onkeypress="..."

Occurs when a user presses and releases a key over an element. This handler works with most elements.

onkeydown="..."

Occurs when a user presses a key over an element. This handler works with most elements.

onkeyup="..."

Occurs when a user releases a key over an element. This handler works with most elements.

onsubmit="..."

Occurs when a user submits a form. This handler works only with the form element.

onreset="..."

Occurs when a user resets a form. This handler works only with the form element.

onselect="..."

Occurs when a user selects text in a text field. This handler works with the input and textarea elements.

onchange="..."

Occurs when a user modifies a field and moves the input focus to a different control. This handler works with the input, select, and textarea elements.

<!-- -->

Inserts comments into a document. Browsers do not display comments, although comments are visible in the document source.

Standard/Usage: HTML 2   **Widely Supported:** Yes
Empty: No

Sample:

```
<!-- This paragraph was modified on 4-15-02 -->
<p>XML is the latest and greatest in markup languages.</p>
```

<!DOCTYPE>

Appears at the beginning of the document and indicates the version of the document.

Standard/Usage: HTML 2   **Widely Supported:** Yes

Samples:

The HTML Strict standard:

```
<!DOCTYPE HTML PUBLIC
 "-//W3C//DTD HTML 4.01//EN"
              "http://www.w3.org/TR/html401/strict.dtd">
```

The HTML Transitional standard:

```
<!DOCTYPE html PUBLIC
 "-//W3C//DTD HTML 4.01 Transitional//EN"
    "http://www.w3.org/TR/html401/loose.dtd">
```

The HTML Frameset standard:

```
<!DOCTYPE html PUBLIC
 "-//W3C//DTD HTML 4.01 Frameset//EN"
    "http://www.w3.org/TR/html401/frameset.dtd">
```

The XHTML Strict standard:

```
<!DOCTYPE html PUBLIC
"-//W3C//DTD XHTML 1.0 Strict//EN"
    "http://www.w3.org/TR/xhtml1/DTD/xhtml1-strict.dtd">
```

The XHTML Transitional standard:

```
<!DOCTYPE html PUBLIC
"-//W3C//DTD XHTML 1.0 Transitional//EN"
    "http://www.w3.org/TR/xhtml1/DTD/xhtml1-transitional.dtd">
```

The XHTML Frameset standard:

```
<!DOCTYPE html PUBLIC
"-//W3C//DTD XHTML 1.0 Frameset//EN"
    "http://www.w3.org/TR/xhtml1/DTD/xhtml1-frameset.dtd">
```

WARNING

DOCTYPE is not an element; therefore, it's not written with a closing tag or a trailing /. It's a document type definition and should be written as shown in this section.

A

Also called the *anchor* element; identifies a link to another document or a link to a location within a document. You commonly use this element to create a hyperlink, using the href attribute. You also can use the a element to identify sections within a document, using the name attribute.

Standard/Usage: HTML 2   **Widely Supported:** Yes
Empty: No

Sample:

```
<a href="http://www.sybex.com/">Visit Sybex
for the latest in quality computer books.</a>
```

accesskey="..."

Assigns a single keyboard key to the element.

Standard/Usage: HTML 4   **Widely Supported:** No

Sample:

```
<a href="help.html" accesskey="h">Help</a>
```

charset="..."

Specifies character encoding of the data designated by the link. Use the name of a character set defined in RFC2045. The default value for this attribute, appropriate for all Western languages, is ISO-8859-1.

Standard/Usage: HTML 4   **Widely Supported:** No

Sample:

```
<a href="help.html" charset="ISO-8859-1">Help</a>
```

class="..."

Indicates the style class to apply to the a element. Note that you must define the class in a style sheet. See Chapter 16, "Using Style Sheets," for more information on creating and using style classes.

Standard/Usage: HTML 4   **Widely Supported:** Yes

Sample:

```
<a href="next.html" class="casual">Next</a>
```

coords="x1,y1,x2,y2,..."

Identifies the coordinates that define a clickable area in a client-side imagemap. Measures coordinates, in pixels, from the top-left corner of the image.

Standard/Usage: HTML 4   **Widely Supported:** Yes

Sample:

```
<a shape="rect" coords="20,8,46,30" href="food.html">
Food</a>
```

href="url"

Specifies the relative or absolute location of a file to which you want to provide a hyperlink.

Standard/Usage: HTML 2   **Widely Supported:** Yes

Sample:

```
<a href="details.html">More Info</a>
```

hreflang="..."

Specifies the language used in the document linked to, which can be useful for aural browsers. Use standard codes for languages, such as DE for German, FR for French, IT for Italian, and HE for Hebrew. See ISO International Standard 639 at

www.oasis-open.org/cover/iso639a.html

for more information about language codes.

Standard/Usage: HTML 4   **Widely Supported:** No

Sample:

```
<a href="german.html" hreflang="DE">Read this in German!</a>
```

id="..."

Assigns a unique ID selector to an instance of the a element. When you then assign a style to that ID selector, it affects only that one instance of the a element.

Standard/Usage: HTML 4   **Widely Supported:** Yes

Sample:

```
<a href="next.html" id="123">Next</a>
```

name="..."

Marks a location within the current document with a name. The browser then can move quickly to specific information within a document. You can link to existing named locations in a document by using a partial URL, consisting of just a pound sign (#) and the name (from within that document), or by using a more complete URL with a pound sign and a name at the end (from other documents or sites). This attribute is deprecated; use the id attribute instead of or together with name.

Standard/Usage: HTML 2; deprecated   **Widely Supported:** Yes

Sample:

```
<a href="#ingredients">Ingredients</a>
...
<a name="ingredients" id="ingredients">
<h1>Ingredients</h1></a>
```

rel="..."

Specifies forward relationship hyperlinks.

Standard/Usage: HTML 3.2   **Widely Supported:** No

Sample:

```
<a rel="Next" href="otherdoc.html">Other Doc</a>
```

rev="..."

Specifies reverse relationship hyperlinks.

Standard/Usage: HTML 3.2   **Widely Supported:** No

Sample:

```
<a rev="Prev" href="http://www.sybex.com/">Link</a>
```

shape="rect/circle/poly"

Specifies the type of shape used to represent the clickable area in a client-side imagemap.

Value	Shape Indicated
rect	Rectangle
circle	Circle
poly	Polygon bounded by three or more sides

Standard/Usage: HTML 4   **Widely Supported:** Yes

Sample:

```
<a shape="rect" coords="20,8,46,30" href="food.html">...</a>
```

style="..."

Specifies style sheet commands that apply to the contents of the a element.

Standard/Usage: HTML 4   **Widely Supported:** Yes

Sample:

```
<a style="background: red" href="page2.html">Page 2</a>
```

tabindex="n"

Indicates where the element appears in the tabbing order of the document.

Standard/Usage: HTML 4   **Widely Supported:** No

Sample:

```
<a href="food.html" tabindex="4">Food</a>
```

target="..."

Indicates the name of a specific frame into which you load the linked document. You establish frame names within the frame element. The value of this attribute can be any word you specify.

Standard/Usage: HTML 4 (Frames)   **Widely Supported:** Yes

Sample:

```
<a href="/frames/frame2.html" target="pages">
Go to Page 2</a>
```

title="..."

Specifies text assigned to the element that you can use for context-sensitive help within the document. Browsers may use this to show tooltips over the hyperlink.

Standard/Usage: HTML 4   **Widely Supported:** Yes

Sample:

```
<a href="page2.html" title="Go to the next page">
Next page</a>
```

type="..."

Indicates the MIME type of the linked file or object. For example, specify text/html, image/jpeg, application/java, text/css, or text/javascript. For the full list of types, see

```
ftp://ftp.isi.edu/in-notes/iana/assignments/media-types/
    media-types
```

Standard/Usage: HTML 4   **Widely Supported:** No

Sample:

```
<a href="shocknew.dcr" type="application/x-director">
    Choose Shockwave</a>
```

Other Attributes

The a element also accepts the lang, dir, onclick, ondblclick, onmousedown, onmouseup, onmouseover, onmousemove, onmouseout, onkeypress, onkeydown, and onkeyup attributes.

ABBR

Indicates an abbreviation in a document.

Standard/Usage: HTML 4   **Widely Supported:** No
Empty: No

Sample:

```
<p><abbr>ABBR</abbr>
is an abbreviation for abbreviation.</p>
```

class="..."

Indicates which style class applies to the abbr element.

Standard/Usage: HTML 4   **Widely Supported:** Yes

Sample:

```
<p><abbr class="casual">ABBR</abbr>
is short for abbreviation.</p>
```

id="..."

Assigns a unique (within the document) ID selector to an instance of the abbr element. When you then assign a style to that ID selector, it affects only that one instance of the abbr element.

Standard/Usage: HTML 4   **Widely Supported:** Yes

Sample:

```
<p><abbr id="123">ABBR</abbr> is short for abbreviation.</p>
```

style="..."

Specifies style sheet commands that apply to the abbreviation.

Standard/Usage: HTML 4   **Widely Supported:** Yes

Sample:

```
<p><abbr style="background: blue; color: white">abbr</abbr>
is short for abbreviation.</p>
```

title="..."

Specifies text assigned to the element. For the abbr element, use this
to provide the expansion of the term. You also can use this attribute for
context-sensitive help within the document. Browsers may use this to show
tooltips over the text.

Standard/Usage: HTML 4   **Widely Supported:** No

Sample:

```
<p><abbr title="Abbreviation">ABBR</abbr>
is short for abbreviation.</p>
```

Other Attributes

The abbr element also accepts the lang, dir, onclick, ondblclick,
onmousedown, onmouseup, onmouseover, onmousemove, onmouseout,
onkeypress, onkeydown, and onkeyup attributes.

ACRONYM

Indicates an acronym in a document.

Standard/Usage: HTML 4   **Widely Supported:** No
Empty: No

Sample:

```
<p><acronym>HTTP</acronym>
stands for Hypertext Transfer Protocol.</p>
```

class="..."

Indicates which style class applies to the acronym element.

Standard/Usage: HTML 4   **Widely Supported:** Yes

Sample:

```
<p><acronym class="casual">HTTP</acronym> stands for
Hypertext Transfer Protocol.</p>
```

id="..."

Assigns a unique ID selector to an instance of the acronym element. When you then assign a style to that ID selector, it affects only that one instance of the acronym element.

Standard/Usage: HTML 4   **Widely Supported:** Yes

Sample:

```
<p><acronym id="123">HTTP</acronym>
stands for Hypertext Transfer Protocol.</p>
```

style="..."

Specifies style sheet commands that apply to the acronym.

Standard/Usage: HTML 4   **Widely Supported:** Yes

Sample:

```
<p><acronym style="background: blue; color: white">
ESP</acronym> stands for extra-sensory perception.</p>
```

title="..."

Specifies text assigned to the element. For the acronym element, use this to provide the expansion of the term. You also can use this attribute for context-sensitive help within the document. Browsers may use this to show tooltips over the text.

Standard/Usage: HTML 4   **Widely Supported:** No

Sample:

```
<p><acronym title="Hypertext Transfer Protocol">
HTTP</acronym> stands for Hypertext Transfer Protocol.</p>
```

Other Attributes

The acronym element also accepts the lang, dir, onclick, ondblclick, onmousedown, onmouseup, onmouseover, onmousemove, onmouseout, onkeypress, onkeydown, and onkeyup attributes.

ADDRESS

Used to provide contact information in a document. This element sometimes is used to contain footer information. The enclosed text usually is
rendered in italic.

> **Standard/Usage:** HTML 2   **Widely Supported:** Yes
> **Empty:** No
>
> **Sample:**
>
> ```
> <address>Sybex<br />
>     <a href="mailto:info@sybex.com">
>     Sybex Information</a><br />
> </address>
> ```

class="..."

Indicates the style class to apply to the address element.

> **Standard/Usage:** HTML 4   **Widely Supported:** Yes
>
> **Sample:**
>
> ```
> <address class="casual">Author info</address>
> ```

id="..."

Assigns a unique ID selector to an instance of the address element.
When you then assign a style to that ID selector, it affects only that one
instance of the address element.

> **Standard/Usage:** HTML 4   **Widely Supported:** Yes
>
> **Sample:**
>
> ```
> <address id="123">Author info</address>
> ```

style="..."

Specifies style sheet commands that apply to the contents of the address
element.

> **Standard/Usage:** HTML 4   **Widely Supported:** Yes
>
> **Sample:**
>
> ```
> <address style="background: red">Author info</address>
> ```

title="..."

Specifies text assigned to the element. You can use this attribute for context-sensitive help within the document. Browsers may use this to show tooltips over the address text.

Standard/Usage: HTML 4 **Widely Supported:** No

Sample:

```
<address title="My Address">Author info</address>
```

Other Attributes

The address element also accepts the lang, dir, onclick, ondblclick, onmousedown, onmouseup, onmouseover, onmousemove, onmouseout, onkeypress, onkeydown, and onkeyup attributes.

APPLET

Embeds a Java applet object into an HTML or XHTML document. Typically, items that appear inside the applet element enable browsers that do not support Java applets to view alternative text. Browsers that support Java ignore all information between the applet tags. This element is deprecated in HTML 4 and later in favor of the object element.

Standard/Usage: HTML 3.2; deprecated **Widely Supported:** Yes
Empty: No

Sample:

```
<applet code="game.class">It appears your browser does not
support Java. You're missing out on a whole world of neat
things!</applet>
```

align="left/center/right"

Specifies the relative horizontal alignment of the Java applet displayed. For example, a value of center tells the browser to place the applet evenly spaced between the left and right edges of the browser window. This attribute is deprecated in HTML 4 and later in favor of style sheets.

Standard/Usage: HTML 3.2; deprecated **Widely Supported:** No

Sample:

```
<applet align="center" code="hangman.class">
You lose. Would you like to play again?
Hit the RELOAD button.</applet>
```

alt="..."

Displays a textual description of a Java applet, if necessary.

Standard/Usage: HTML 3.2   **Widely Supported:** No

Sample:

```
<applet code="hangman.class" alt="A Game of Hangman">
We could have had a relaxing game of Hangman if your
browser supported Java applets.</applet>
```

archive="url, url"

Used to provide a comma-separated list of URLs of classes and other resources to be preloaded to improve applet performance.

Standard/Usage: HTML 4   **Widely Supported:** Yes

Sample:

```
<applet code="hangman.class" archive="hgman.htm,
hgman2.htm">Hangman</applet>
```

code="url"

Specifies the relative or absolute location of the Java bytecode file on the server.

Standard/Usage: HTML 3.2   **Widely Supported:** No

Sample:

```
<applet code="hangman.class">Hangman</applet>
```

codebase="url"

Specifies the directory where you can find all necessary Java class files on a web server. If you set this attribute, you don't need to use explicit URLs in other references to the class files. For example, you would not need an absolute reference in the code attribute.

Standard/Usage: HTML 3.2   **Widely Supported:** No

Sample:

```
<applet codebase="http://www.example.com/"
code="hangman.class">If your browser supported inline Java
applets, you'd be looking at a Hangman game right now.
</applet>
```

height="n"

Specifies the height (in pixels or percentage of available space) of the Java applet object within the document.

Standard/Usage: HTML 3.2　　**Widely Supported:** No

Sample:

```
<applet height="200" code="hangman.class">
Because your browser does not support inline Java applets,
we won't be playing Hangman today.</applet>
```

hspace="n"

Specifies an amount of blank space (in pixels) to the left and right of the Java applet within the document.

Standard/Usage: HTML 3.2　　**Widely Supported:** No

Sample:

```
<applet hspace="10" code="hangman.class">
Sorry. Because your browser does not support embedded Java
applets, you'll have to play Hangman the old way.</applet>
```

name="..."

Assigns the applet instance a name so that other elements can identify it within the document. This attribute is deprecated; use the id attribute instead of or together with name.

Standard/Usage: HTML 3.2; deprecated　　**Widely Supported:** No

Sample:

```
<applet code="hangman.class" name="Hangman" id="Hangman">
</applet>
```

object="url"

Specifies the relative or absolute location of the locally saved Java program.

Standard/Usage: HTML 4   **Widely Supported:** No

Sample:

```
<applet object="http://www.example.com/hangman.class">
Whoops! Your browser does not support serialized Java
applets. You may want to install a newer web browser.
</applet>
```

title="..."

Specifies text assigned to the element. You can use this attribute for context-sensitive help within the document. Browsers may use this to show tooltips over the embedded applet, and aural browsers or accessibility aids might read it aloud.

Standard/Usage: HTML 4   **Widely Supported:** No

Sample:

```
<applet code="/java/thing.class" title="Thing">
Thing</applet>
```

vspace="n"

Specifies the amount of vertical space (in pixels) above and below the Java applet.

Standard/Usage: HTML 3.2   **Widely Supported:** No

Sample:

```
<applet vspace="10" code="/hangman.class">
If you had a Java-capable browser, you could be
playing Hangman!</applet>
```

width="n"

Specifies the width (in pixels) of a Java applet within a document.

Standard/Usage: HTML 3.2   **Widely Supported:** No

Sample:

```
<applet width="350" code="/hangman.class">
Hangman can be a lot of fun, but it's more fun if your
browser supports Java. Sorry.</applet>
```

Other Attributes

The applet element also accepts the lang, dir, onclick, ondblclick, onmousedown, onmouseup, onmouseover, onmousemove, onmouseout, onkeypress, onkeydown, and onkeyup attributes.

AREA

Defines an active area within a client-side imagemap definition (see the map element). It indicates an area where audiences can choose to link to another document.

Standard/Usage: HTML 3.2 **Widely Supported:** Yes
Empty: Yes

Sample:

```
<area shape="rect" coords="20,8,46,30" href="food.html" />
```

alt="..."

Provides a textual description for users who have text-only browsers, and should be used (and is required by the specifications to be included) for all images.

Standard/Usage: HTML 4; required **Widely Supported:** Yes

Sample:

```
<area alt="This blue rectangle links to blue.html"
href="blue.html" />
```

accesskey="..."

Associates a single keyboard key with the area.

Standard/Usage: HTML 4 **Widely Supported:** No

Sample:

```
<area accesskey="b" />
```

class="..."

Indicates the style class you want to apply to the area element.

Standard/Usage: HTML 4 **Widely Supported:** Yes

Sample:

```
<area class="casual" shape="rect" coords="20,8,46,30"
href="food.html" />
```

coords="x1,y1,x2,y2..."

Identifies the coordinates within an imagemap that define the image-map area. Measure coordinates, in pixels, from the top-left corner of the image.

Standard/Usage: HTML 3.2   **Widely Supported:** Yes

Sample:

```
<area shape="rect" coords="20,8,46,30" href="food.html" />
```

href="url"

Identifies the location of the document you want to load when the indicated imagemap area is selected.

Standard/Usage: HTML 3.2   **Widely Supported:** Yes

Sample:

```
<area shape="rect" coords="20,8,46,30" href="food.html" />
```

id="..."

Assigns a unique ID selector to an instance of the area element. When you then assign a style to that ID selector, it affects this instance of the area element.

Standard/Usage: HTML 4   **Widely Supported:** Yes

Sample:

```
<area id="123" />
```

nohref="nohref"

Defines an imagemap area that does not link to another document.

Standard/Usage: HTML 3.2   **Widely Supported:** Yes

Sample:

```
<area shape="rect" coords="20,8,46,30" nohref="nohref" />
```

shape="default/rect/circle/poly"

Specifies the type of shape used to represent the imagemap area.

Value	Shape Indicated
rect	Rectangle
circle	Circle
poly	Polygon bounded by three or more sides
default	Any area not otherwise defined

Standard/Usage: HTML 3.2   **Widely Supported:** Yes

Sample:

```
<area shape="rect" coords="20,8,46,30" href="food.html" />
```

style="..."

Specifies style sheet commands that apply to the imagemap area.

Standard/Usage: HTML 4   **Widely Supported:** No

Sample:

```
<area shape="rect" coords="20,8,46,30" href="food.html"
    style="background: red" />
```

tabindex="n"

Indicates where the imagemap area appears in the tabbing order of the document.

Standard/Usage: HTML 4   **Widely Supported:** Yes

Sample:

```
<area shape="rect" coords="20,8,46,30" href="food.html"
tabindex="4" />
```

target="..."

Identifies the named frame in which the linked document should load. For example, when a user selects an area within an imagemap, the linked document may load in the same frame (the default if target is omitted) or in a different frame, specified by the value of target.

Standard/Usage: HTML 4 (Frames)   **Widely Supported:** Yes

Sample:

```
<area shape="rect" coords="20,8,46,30" href="food.html"
target="leftframe" />
```

title="..."

Specifies text assigned to the element. You can use this attribute for context-sensitive help within the document. Browsers may use this to show tooltips over the imagemap area.

Standard/Usage: HTML 4   **Widely Supported:** No

Sample:

```
<area shape="rect" coords="20,8,46,30" href="food.html"
title="food" id="food"/>
```

Other Attributes

The area element also accepts the lang, dir, onclick, ondblclick, onmousedown, onmouseup, onmouseover, onmousemove, onmouseout, onkeypress, onkeydown, and onkeyup attributes.

B

Indicates text that should appear in boldface.

Standard/Usage: HTML 2   **Widely Supported:** Yes
Empty: No

Sample:

```
The afternoon was <b>so</b> hot!
```

class="..."

Indicates which style class applies to the b element.

Standard/Usage: HTML 4   **Widely Supported:** Yes

Sample:

```
<b class="casual">Boom!</b>
```

id="..."

Assigns a unique ID selector to an instance of the b element. When you assign a style to that ID selector, it affects only that one instance of the b element.

Standard/Usage: HTML 4   **Widely Supported:** Yes

Sample:

```
I work for <b id="123">Widgets, Inc.</b>
```

style="..."

Specifies style sheet commands that apply to the contents of the b element.

Standard/Usage: HTML 4   **Widely Supported:** Yes

Sample:

```
<b style="background: red">text with red background</b>
```

title="..."

Specifies text assigned to the element. You can use this attribute for context-sensitive help within the document. Browsers may use this to show tooltips over the boldface text.

Standard/Usage: HTML 4   **Widely Supported:** No

Sample:

```
<b title="Species">Dog Species</b>
```

Other Attributes

The b element also accepts the lang, dir, onclick, ondblclick, onmousedown, onmouseup, onmouseover, onmousemove, onmouseout, onkeypress, onkeydown, and onkeyup attributes.

BASE

Identifies the location where all relative URLs in your document originate.

Standard/Usage: HTML 2   **Widely Supported:** Yes
Empty: Yes

Sample:

```
<base href="http://www.sybex.com/" />
```

href="url"

Indicates the relative or absolute location of the base document.

> **Standard/Usage:** HTML 2; required   **Widely Supported:** Yes
>
> **Sample:**
>
> ```
> <base href="http://www.sybex.com/" />
> ```

target="..."

Identifies the named frame in which you load a document (see the href attribute).

> **Standard/Usage:** HTML 4 (Frames)   **Widely Supported:** Yes
>
> **Sample:**
>
> ```
> <base href="http://www.example.com/frames/" target="main" />
> ```

BASEFONT

Provides a font setting for normal text within a document. Font settings (see the font element) within the document are relative to settings specified with this element. Use this element in the document header (between the head elements). The basefont element is deprecated in HTML 4 and later in favor of style sheets.

> **Standard/Usage:** HTML 3.2; deprecated   **Widely Supported:** Yes
> **Empty:** Yes
>
> **Sample:**
>
> ```
> <basefont size="5" />
> ```

color="#rrggbb" or "..."

Sets the font color of normal text within a document. Color names may substitute for the explicit RGB hexadecimal values. This attribute is deprecated in HTML 4 and later in favor of style sheets.

> **Standard/Usage:** HTML 3.2; deprecated   **Widely Supported:** Yes
>
> **Sample:**
>
> ```
> <basefont size="2" color="#ff00cc" />
> ```

face="..., ..."

Specifies the font face of normal text within a document. You can set this attribute to a comma-separated list of font names. The browser will select the first font from the list if the font is installed on the user's computer. This attribute is deprecated in HTML 4 and later in favor of style sheets.

Standard/Usage: HTML 3.2; deprecated   **Widely Supported:** Yes

Sample:

```
<basefont face="Verdana, Helvetica, Arial" />
```

id="..."

Assigns a unique ID selector to an instance of the basefont element. When you then assign a style to that ID selector, it affects only that one instance of the basefont element.

Standard/Usage: HTML 4   **Widely Supported:** Yes

Sample:

```
<basefont size="+2" id="d3e" />
```

size="n"

Specifies the default font size of normal text within a document. Valid values are integer numbers in the range 1 and 7, with 3 being the default setting. This attribute is deprecated in HTML 4 and later in favor of style sheets.

Standard/Usage: HTML 3.2; deprecated   **Widely Supported:** Yes

Sample:

```
<basefont size="5" />
```

Other Attributes

The basefont element also accepts the lang and dir attributes.

BDO

Indicates text that should appear with the direction specified (left-to-right or right-to-left), overriding other language-specific settings. The bdo element accepts the lang and dir attributes.

Standard/Usage: HTML 4   **Widely Supported:** No
Empty: No

Sample:

```
<p lang="HE" dir="rtl">This Hebrew text contains a number,
<bdo="ltr">29381</bdo>, that must appear left to right.</p>
```

BGSOUND

Embeds a background sound file within documents. Use in the document head of documents intended for users who use Internet Explorer.

Standard/Usage: Internet Explorer 2   **Widely Supported:** No
Empty: Yes

Sample:

```
<bgsound src="scream.wav" />
```

loop="n/infinite"

Specifies the number of times a background sound file repeats. The value infinite is the default.

Standard/Usage: Internet Explorer 2   **Widely Supported:** No

Sample:

```
<bgsound src="bugle.wav" loop="2" />
```

src="url"

Indicates the absolute or relative location of the sound file.

Standard/Usage: Internet Explorer 2   **Widely Supported:** No

Sample:

```
<bgsound src="wah.wav" />
```

BIG

Indicates that text appears in a larger font. Although this element is not deprecated, big is a presentational element, and its use is discouraged in favor of style sheets.

Standard/Usage: HTML 3.2   **Widely Supported:** Yes
Empty: No

Sample:

```
<big>Lunch</big>
<p>Lunch will be served at 2 P.M.</p>
```

class="..."

Indicates which style class applies to the big element.

Standard/Usage: HTML 4   **Widely Supported:** Yes

Sample:

```
<big class="casual">Instructions</big>
```

id="..."

Assigns a unique ID selector to an instance of the big element. When you then assign a style to that ID selector, it affects only that one instance of the big element.

Standard/Usage: HTML 4   **Widely Supported:** Yes

Sample:

```
<big id="123">REMINDER:</big>
Eat five servings of fruits and vegetables every day!
```

style="..."

Specifies style sheet commands that apply to the contents of the big element.

Standard/Usage: HTML 4   **Widely Supported:** Yes

Sample:

```
<big style="background: red">This text is red and big.</big>
```

title="..."

Specifies text assigned to the element. You can use this attribute for context-sensitive help within the document. Browsers may use this to show tooltips over the text inside the big element.

Standard/Usage: HTML 4   **Widely Supported:** No

Sample:

```
<big title="Bigger">This text is bigger.</big>
```

Other Attributes

The big element also accepts the lang, dir, onclick, ondblclick, onmousedown, onmouseup, onmouseover, onmousemove, onmouseout, onkeypress, onkeydown, and onkeyup attributes.

BLINK

A Netscape-specific element that makes text blink on and off. Style sheets offer the same functionality in a more widely recognized syntax (the text-decoration property with a value of blink).

Standard/Usage: Netscape Navigator   **Widely Supported:** No
Empty: No

Sample:

```
<p><blink>NEW INFO</blink>: We moved!</p>
```

class="..."

Indicates which style class applies to the blink element.

Standard/Usage: HTML 4   **Widely Supported:** Yes

Sample:

```
<blink class="casual">NEW INFORMATION</blink>
```

id="..."

Assigns a unique ID selector to an instance of the blink element. When you then assign a style to that ID selector, it affects only that one instance of the blink element.

Standard/Usage: HTML 4   **Widely Supported:** Yes

Sample:

```
<blink id="123">12-Hour Sale!</blink>
```

style="..."

Specifies style sheet commands that apply to the contents of the blink element.

Standard/Usage: HTML 4 **Widely Supported:** No

Sample:

```
<blink style="background: red">This text is blinking and
has a red background if you're using Netscape Navigator.
</blink>
```

BLOCKQUOTE

Useful for quoting a direct source within a document (a block quotation).

Standard/Usage: HTML 2 **Widely Supported:** Yes
Empty: No

Sample:

```
In So Long and Thanks for All the Fish, Douglas Adams wrote:
<blockquote>Man had always assumed that he was more
intelligent than dolphins because he had achieved so much...
 the wheel, New York, wars, and so on, whilst all the
dolphins had ever done was muck about in the water having
a good time. But conversely the dolphins believed
themselves to be more intelligent than man for precisely
the same reasons.</blockquote>
```

cite="..."

Specifies a reference URL for the quotation.

Standard/Usage: HTML 4 **Widely Supported:** No

Sample:

```
<blockquote cite="http://www.example.com/">Twas the
    night...</blockquote>
```

class="..."

Indicates which style class applies to the blockquote element.

Standard/Usage: HTML 4 **Widely Supported:** Yes

Sample:

```
<blockquote class="holiday">Twas the night before
Christmas... </blockquote>
```

id="..."

Assigns a unique ID selector to an instance of the blockquote element. When you then assign a style to that ID selector, it affects only that one instance of the blockquote element.

Standard/Usage: HTML 4 **Widely Supported:** Yes

Sample:

```
In So Long and Thanks for All the Fish, Douglas Adams wrote:
<blockquote id="DAq1">Man had always assumed that he was
more intelligent than dolphins because he had achieved so
   much...</blockquote>
```

style="..."

Specifies style sheet commands that apply to the contents of the blockquote element.

Standard/Usage: HTML 4 **Widely Supported:** Yes

Sample:

```
<blockquote style="background: red">This quote is red.
</blockquote>
```

title="..."

Specifies text assigned to the element. You can use this attribute for context-sensitive help within the document. Browsers may use this to show tooltips over the quoted text.

Standard/Usage: HTML 4 **Widely Supported:** No

Sample:

```
<blockquote title="Quotation">Quoted text goes here.
</blockquote>
```

Other Attributes

The blockquote element also accepts the lang, dir, onclick, ondblclick, onmousedown, onmouseup, onmouseover, onmousemove, onmouseout, onkeypress, onkeydown, and onkeyup attributes.

BODY

Acts as a container for the body of the document. It is a child of the html element and appears after the head element. In previous versions of HTML, the body element was used to set various color settings and background characteristics of the document; however, in HTML 4 and XHTML, those formatting attributes are deprecated in favor of style sheets.

Standard/Usage: HTML 2; required   **Widely Supported:** Yes
Empty: No

Sample:

```
<html xmlns="http://www.w3.org/1999/xhtml">
    <head>...</head>
    <body>
        <h1>hello!</h1>
    </body>
</html>
```

alink="#rrggbb" or "..."

Indicates the color of hyperlink text while the text is selected. Color names can substitute for the RGB hexadecimal values. This attribute is deprecated in HTML 4 and later in favor of style sheets.

Standard/Usage: HTML 3.2; deprecated   **Widely Supported:** Yes

Sample:

```
<body bgcolor="#000abc" text="#000000" link="#ffffff"
vlink="#999999" alink="#ff0000">
    The rest of your document
</body>
```

background="url"

Specifies the relative or absolute location of an image file that tiles across the document's background. This attribute is deprecated in HTML 4 and later in favor of style sheets.

Standard/Usage: HTML 3.2; deprecated   **Widely Supported:** Yes

Sample:

```
<body background="images/slimey.gif">
The rest of your document</body>
```

bgcolor="#rrggbb" or "..."

Indicates the color of a document's background. Color names can substitute for the RGB hexadecimal values. This attribute is deprecated in HTML 4 and later in favor of style sheets.

Standard/Usage: HTML 3.2; deprecated   **Widely Supported:** Yes

Sample:

```
<body bgcolor="#000abc" text="#000000" link="#ffffff"
vlink="#999999" alink="#ff0000">
   The rest of your document
</body>
```

bgproperties="fixed"

Specifies the behavior of the background image (see the `background` attribute). The only current value for this attribute is `fixed`, which indicates that the background image remains in place as you scroll the document, creating a watermark effect.

Standard/Usage: Internet Explorer 2   **Widely Supported:** No

Sample:

```
<body background="waves.jpg" bgproperties="fixed">
The rest of your document</body>
```

class="..."

Indicates which style class applies to the body element.

Standard/Usage: HTML 4   **Widely Supported:** Yes

Sample:

```
<body class="casual">The rest of your document</body>
```

id="..."

Assigns a unique ID selector to an instance of the body element. When you then assign a style to that ID selector, it affects only that one instance of the body element.

Standard/Usage: HTML 4   **Widely Supported:** Yes

Sample:

```
<body id="123">The rest of your document</body>
```

leftmargin="n"

Specifies the width (in pixels) of a margin of white space along the left edge of the entire document.

Standard/Usage: Internet Explorer 2   **Widely Supported:** No

Sample:

```
<body leftmargin="30">The rest of your document</body>
```

link="#rrggbb" or "..."

Indicates the color of hyperlink text within the document for documents not already visited by the browser. Color names can substitute for the RGB hexadecimal values. This attribute is deprecated in HTML 4 and later in favor of style sheets.

Standard/Usage: HTML 3.2; deprecated   **Widely Supported:** Yes

Sample:

```
<body bgcolor="#000abc" text="#000000" link="#ffffff"
vlink="#999999" alink="#ff0000">
    The rest of your document
</body>
```

scroll="yes/no"

Indicates whether scrolling is possible within the document body.

Standard/Usage: Internet Explorer 4   **Widely Supported:** No

Sample:

```
<body bgcolor="silver" scroll="no">
The rest of your document</body>
```

style="..."

Specifies style sheet commands that apply to the document body.

Standard/Usage: HTML 4   **Widely Supported:** Yes

Sample:

```
<body style="background: red">
The rest of your document</body>
```

text="#rrggbb" or "..."

Indicates the color of normal text within the document. Color names can substitute for the RGB hexadecimal values. This attribute is deprecated in HTML 4 and later in favor of style sheets.

Standard/Usage: HTML 3.2; deprecated   **Widely Supported:** Yes

Sample:

```
<body bgcolor="#000abc" text="#000000" link="#ffffff"
vlink="#999999" alink="#ff0000"> The rest of your document
</body>
```

title="..."

Specifies text assigned to the element. You can use this attribute for context-sensitive help within the document. Browsers may use this to show tooltips.

Standard/Usage: HTML 4   **Widely Supported:** No

Sample:

```
<body title="Document body">The rest of your document</body>
```

topmargin="n"

Specifies the size (in pixels) of a margin of white space along the top edge of the entire document.

Standard/Usage: Internet Explorer 2   **Widely Supported:** No

Sample:

```
<body topmargin="10">The rest of your document</body>
```

vlink="#rrggbb" or *"..."*

Indicates the color of hyperlink text within the document for documents
already visited by the browser. Color names can substitute for the RGB
hexadecimal values. This attribute is deprecated in HTML 4 and later in
favor of style sheets.

Standard/Usage: HTML 3.2; deprecated   **Widely Supported:** Yes

Sample:

```
<body bgcolor="#000abc" text="#000000" link="#ffffff"
vlink="#999999" alink="#ff0000">
    The rest of your document</body>
```

Other Attributes

The body element also accepts the lang, dir, onload, onunload, onclick,
ondblclick, onmousedown, onmouseup, onmouseover, onmousemove,
onmouseout, onkeypress, onkeydown, and onkeyup attributes.

BR

Breaks a line of continuous text and prevents text alignment around
images.

Standard/Usage: HTML 2   **Widely Supported:** Yes
Empty: Yes

Sample:

```
I live at: <p>123 Nowhere Ave.<br />New York, NY 12345</p>
```

class="..."

Indicates which style class applies to the element.

Standard/Usage: HTML 4   **Widely Supported:** Yes

Sample:

```
<br class="casual" />
```

clear="all/left/right/none"

Discontinues alignment of text to inline graphic images. The sample
demonstrates how you can force the text to appear after the image and
not alongside it.

Standard/Usage: HTML 3.2; deprecated   **Widely Supported:** Yes

Sample:

```
<img src="portrait.jpg" align="right" /><br clear="all" />
<p>The above photo was taken when I was in Florida.</p>
```

id="..."

Assigns a unique ID selector to an instance of the br element. When you then assign a style to that ID selector, it affects only that one instance of the br element.

Standard/Usage: HTML 4   **Widely Supported:** Yes

Sample:

```
<br id="123" />
```

style="..."

Specifies style sheet commands that apply to the br element, although applying a style to an element, like br, that is not visible is not likely to be effective most of the time.

Standard/Usage: HTML 4   **Widely Supported:** Yes

Sample:

```
<br style="background: red" />
```

title="..."

Specifies text assigned to the element. You can use this attribute for context-sensitive help within the document. Browsers may use this to show tooltips.

Standard/Usage: HTML 4   **Widely Supported:** No

Sample:

```
<br clear="all" title="stop image wrap" />
```

BUTTON

Sets up a button to submit or reset a form as well as to activate a script. Use the img element between the opening and closing button elements to specify a graphical button.

Standard/Usage: HTML 4   Widely Supported: Yes
Empty: No

Sample:

```
<button type="button" value="Run Program" onClick(doit)>
   <img src="button.gif" alt="Button" /></button>
```

accesskey="..."

Associates a single keyboard key with the button.

Standard/Usage: HTML 4   Widely Supported: Yes

Sample:

```
<button accesskey="B">Click Me! </button>
```

class="..."

Indicates which style class applies to the button element.

Standard/Usage: HTML 4   Widely Supported: Yes

Sample:

```
<button class="casual" type="submit" value="Submit">
   <img src="submit.gif" alt="submit" /></button>
```

disabled="disabled"

Denies access to the input method.

Standard/Usage: HTML 4   Widely Supported: No

Sample:

```
<button type="submit" disabled="disabled">
<img src="button.gif" alt="button" /></button>
```

id="..."

Assigns a unique ID selector to an instance of the input element. When you then assign a style to that ID selector, it affects only that one instance of the input element.

Standard/Usage: HTML 4   Widely Supported: Yes

Sample:

```
<button id="123" type="submit" value="Submit">
   <img src="button.gif" alt="Button" /></button>
```

name="..."

Gives a name for the value you pass to the form processor.

Standard/Usage: HTML 4   **Widely Supported:** Yes

Sample:

```
<button type="button" name="runprog" value="Click to run">
   <img src="button.gif" alt="Button" /></button>
```

style="..."

Specifies style sheet commands that apply to the element.

Standard/Usage: HTML 4   **Widely Supported:** Yes

Sample:

```
<button style="background: red" type="button"
name="runprog" value="Click to Run">
   <img src="button.gif" alt="Button" /></button>
```

tabindex="n"

Specifies where the input method appears in the tab order. For example, tabindex="3" places the cursor at the button element after the user presses the Tab key three times.

Standard/Usage: HTML 4   **Widely Supported:** No

Sample:

```
<button type="button" name="runprog" value="Click to run"
 tabindex="5">
   <img src="button.gif" alt="Button" /></button>
```

title="..."

Specifies text assigned to the element. You can use this attribute for context-sensitive help within the document. Browsers may use this to show tooltips over the input method.

Standard/Usage: HTML 4   **Widely Supported:** No

Sample:

```
<button type="submit" name="cc" value="visa"
 title="VisaCard">
   <img src="visacard.gif" alt="VisaCard button" /></button>
```

type="submit/button/reset"

Indicates the kind of button to create. submit produces a button that, when selected, submits all the name-value pairs to the form processor. reset sets all the input methods to empty or default settings (as specified when the page was loaded). button creates a button with no specific behavior that can interact with scripts.

Standard/Usage: HTML 4   **Widely Supported:** Yes

Sample:

```
<button type="button" value="Send Data" onClick(verify())>
Send Data<img src="button.gif" alt="Button" /></button>
```

value="..."

Sets the default value for the button face.

Standard/Usage: HTML 4   **Widely Supported:** No

Sample:

```
<button type="button" name="id" value="Press Me">
   <img src="button.gif" alt="Button" /></button>
```

Other Attributes

The button element also accepts the lang, dir, onfocus, onblur, onclick, ondblclick, onmousedown, onmouseup, onmouseover, onmousemove, onmouseout, onkeypress, onkeydown, and onkeyup attributes.

CAPTION

Used inside a table element to specify a description for the table.

Standard/Usage: HTML 3.2   **Widely Supported:** Yes
Empty: No

Sample:

```
<table>
   <caption valign="top" align="center">
   Test Grades for Cooking 101</caption>
   <tr><th>Student</th>  <th>Grade</th> </tr>
   <tr><td>B. Smith</td> <td>88</td>    </tr>
   <tr><td>J. Doe</td>   <td>45</td>    </tr>
</table>
```

align="top/bottom/left/right"

Indicates whether the caption appears at the top (default) or the bottom, left, or right of the table. The values left and right were added in HTML 4, but this attribute is deprecated in HTML 4 and later in favor of style sheets.

Standard/Usage: HTML 3.2; deprecated   **Widely Supported:** Yes

Sample:

```
<caption align="top">Seattle Staff Directory</caption>
```

class="..."

Indicates which style class applies to the caption element.

Standard/Usage: HTML 4   **Widely Supported:** Yes

Sample:

```
<caption class="chemical">Hydrogen vs. Oxygen</caption>
```

id="..."

Assigns a unique ID selector to an instance of the caption element. When you then assign a style to that ID selector, it affects only that one instance of the caption element.

Standard/Usage: HTML 4   **Widely Supported:** Yes

Sample:

```
<table>
   <caption id="123">Great Painters</caption>...
</table>
```

style="..."

Specifies style sheet commands that apply to the contents of the caption element.

Standard/Usage: HTML 4   **Widely Supported:** Yes

Sample:

```
<caption style="background: red">This title caption will
have a red background.</caption>
```

title="..."

Specifies text assigned to the element. You can use this attribute for context-sensitive help within the document. Browsers may use this to show tooltips over the caption.

Standard/Usage: HTML 4   **Widely Supported:** Yes

Sample:

```
<caption title="Table caption">Great Painters</caption>
```

Other Attributes

The caption element also accepts the lang, dir, onclick, ondblclick, onmousedown, onmouseup, onmouseover, onmousemove, onmouseout, onkeypress, onkeydown, and onkeyup attributes.

CENTER

Positions text an equal distance between the left and right edges of the document. This element, now officially replaced by <div align= "center">, was included in HTML 3.2 only because of its widespread use.

Standard/Usage: HTML 3.2; deprecated   **Widely Supported:** Yes
Empty: No

Sample:

```
<center><h1>ONE-DAY SALE!</h1></center>
```

CITE

Provides an in-text citation of a proper title such as the title of a book. Most browsers display the text inside the cite elements in italic.

Standard/Usage: HTML 2 **Widely Supported:** Yes
Empty: No

Sample:

```
<p>I've read <cite>The Hitchhiker's Guide to the Galaxy
</cite> by Douglas Adams.</p>
```

class="..."

Indicates which style class applies to the cite element.

Standard/Usage: HTML 4 **Widely Supported:** Yes

Sample:

```
This came from Homer's <cite class="classic">Odyssey</cite>.
```

id="..."

Assigns a unique ID selector to an instance of the cite element. When you then assign a style to that ID selector, it affects only that one instance of the cite element.

Standard/Usage: HTML 4 **Widely Supported:** Yes

Sample:

```
I read about this in <cite id="123">
World Weekly News</cite>.
```

style="..."

Specifies style sheet commands that apply to the contents of the cite element.

Standard/Usage: HTML 4 **Widely Supported:** Yes

Sample:

```
<cite style="background: red">...</cite>
```

title="..."

Specifies text assigned to the element. You can use this attribute for context-sensitive help within the document. Browsers may use this to show tooltips over the cited text.

Standard/Usage: HTML 4   **Widely Supported:** No

Sample:

```
<cite title="citation">FDA Vegetable Pamphlet</cite>
```

Other Attributes

The `cite` element also accepts the `lang`, `dir`, `onclick`, `ondblclick`, `onmousedown`, `onmouseup`, `onmouseover`, `onmousemove`, `onmouseout`, `onkeypress`, `onkeydown`, and `onkeyup` attributes.

CODE

Embeds excerpts of program source code into your document text. This is useful if you want to show program source code within a paragraph of normal text. For showing formatted segments of source code longer than one line, use the `pre` element.

Standard/Usage: HTML 2   **Widely Supported:** Yes
Empty: No

Sample:

```
To see the variable's value, use the
<code>printf("%0.2f\n",cost);</code> function call.
```

class="..."

Indicates which style class applies to the code element.

Standard/Usage: HTML 4   **Widely Supported:** Yes

Sample:

```
The <code class="casual">html</code> element is required.
```

id="..."

Assigns a unique ID selector to an instance of the code element. When you then assign a style to that ID selector, it affects only that one instance of the code element.

Standard/Usage: HTML 4   **Widely Supported:** Yes

Sample:

```
<code id="123">while(x) x--;</code>
```

style="..."

Specifies style sheet commands that apply to the contents of the code element.

Standard/Usage: HTML 4   **Widely Supported:** Yes

Sample:

```
<code style="background: red">while(x) x--;</code>
```

title="..."

Specifies text assigned to the element. You can use this attribute for context-sensitive help within the document. Browsers may use this to show tooltips over the code text.

Standard/Usage: HTML 4   **Widely Supported:** No

Sample:

```
<code title="c code">exit(1);</code>
```

Other Attributes

The code element also accepts the lang, dir, onclick, ondblclick, onmousedown, onmouseup, onmouseover, onmousemove, onmouseout, onkeypress, onkeydown, and onkeyup attributes.

COL

Specifies properties for table columns.

Standard/Usage: HTML 4   **Widely Supported:** No
Empty: Yes

Sample:

```
<table>
  <colgroup>
    <col align="right" />
    <col align="center" />
  </colgroup>
  <tr>
    <td>This cell is aligned right.</td>
    <td>This cell is centered.</td>
  </tr>
</table>
```

align="left/right/center/justify/char"

Specifies how text within the table columns will line up with the edges of the table cells or, if the value is char, on a specific character (the decimal point by default).

Standard/Usage: HTML 4   **Widely Supported:** No

Sample:

```
<col align="center" />
```

char="..."

Specifies the character on which cell contents will align if align="char". If you omit the char attribute, the default value is the decimal point in the specified language.

Standard/Usage: HTML 4   **Widely Supported:** No

Sample:

```
<col align="char" char="," />
```

charoff="n"

Specifies the number of characters from the left at which the alignment character appears.

Standard/Usage: HTML 4   **Widely Supported:** No

Sample:

```
<col align="char" char="," charoff="7" />
```

id="..."

Assigns a unique ID selector to an instance of the col element. When you assign a style to that ID selector, it affects only that one instance of the col element.

Standard/Usage: HTML 4   **Widely Supported:** Yes

Sample:

```
<col id="123" />
```

span="n"

Indicates the number of columns in the group.

Standard/Usage: HTML 4   **Widely Supported:** No

Sample:

```
<colgroup><col align="right" span="2" /></colgroup>
```

style="..."

Specifies style sheet commands that apply to the columns.

Standard/Usage: HTML 4   **Widely Supported:** Yes

Sample:

```
<col style="background: black" />
```

title="..."

Specifies text assigned to the element. You can use this attribute for context-sensitive help within the document. Browsers may use this to show tooltips over the table column.

Standard/Usage: HTML 4   **Widely Supported:** No

Sample:

```
<col title="Table column" />
```

width="n"

Specifies the horizontal dimension of a column (in pixels or as a percentage). Special value of "0*" forces the column to the minimum required width, and "2*" requires that the column receive proportionately twice as much space as it otherwise would.

Standard/Usage: HTML 4   **Widely Supported:** No

Sample:

```
<col width="100" />
```

valign="top/bottom/middle/baseline"

Positions the contents of the table column vertically.

Value	Effect
top	Positions the contents flush with the top of the column.
bottom	Positions the contents flush with the bottom of the column.
middle	Centers the contents between the top and bottom of the column.
baseline	Aligns the contents with the baseline of the current text font.

Standard/Usage: HTML 4   **Widely Supported:** No

Sample:

```
<col valign="top" />
```

Other Attributes

The col element also accepts the lang, dir, onclick, ondblclick, onmousedown, onmouseup, onmouseover, onmousemove, onmouseout, onkeypress, onkeydown, and onkeyup attributes.

COLGROUP

Specifies characteristics for a group of table columns.

Standard/Usage: HTML 4   **Widely Supported:** No
Empty: No

Sample:

```
<table>
  <colgroup valign="top">
    <col align="right" />
```

```
    <col align="center" />
  </colgroup>
  <tr>
    <td>This cell is aligned top and right.</td>
    <td>This cell is aligned top and centered.</td>
  </tr>
</table>
```

align="left/right/center/justify/char"

Specifies how text within the table columns lines up with the edges of the table cells or, if the value is char, on a specific character (the decimal point by default).

Standard/Usage: HTML 4   **Widely Supported:** No

Sample:

```
<colgroup align="center">...</colgroup>
```

char="..."

Specifies the character on which cell contents align if align="char". If you omit the char attribute, the default value is the decimal point in the specified language.

Standard/Usage: HTML 4   **Widely Supported:** No

Sample:

```
<colgroup align="char" char=",">...</colgroup>
```

charoff="n"

Specifies the number of characters from the left at which the alignment character appears.

Standard/Usage: HTML 4   **Widely Supported:** No

Sample:

```
<colgroup align="char" char="," charoff="7">...</colgroup>
```

id="..."

Assigns a unique ID selector to an instance of the element. When you then assign a style to that ID selector, it affects only that one instance of the element.

Standard/Usage: HTML 4   **Widely Supported:** Yes

Sample:

```
<colgroup id="123">...</colgroup>
```

span="n"

Indicates how many consecutive columns exist in the column group and to which columns the specified attributes apply.

Standard/Usage: HTML 4   **Widely Supported:** No

Sample:

```
<colgroup span="2" align="left">...</colgroup>
```

style="..."

Specifies style sheet commands that apply to the contents of the colgroup element.

Standard/Usage: HTML 4   **Widely Supported:** Yes

Sample:

```
<colgroup style="color: red">...</colgroup>
```

title="..."

Specifies text assigned to the element. You can use this attribute for context-sensitive help within the document. Browsers may use this to show tooltips over the column group.

Standard/Usage: HTML 4   **Widely Supported:** No

Sample:

```
<colgroup title="column group">...</colgroup>
```

width="n"

Specifies the horizontal dimension of columns within the column group (in pixels or as a percentage).

Standard/Usage: HTML 4   **Widely Supported:** No

Sample:

```
<colgroup width="100"><col align="right" />...</colgroup>
```

valign="top/bottom/middle/baseline"

Vertically positions the contents of the table column.

Value	Effect
top	Positions the contents flush with the top of the column group.
bottom	Positions the contents flush with the bottom of the column group.
middle	Centers the contents between the top and bottom of the column group.
baseline	Aligns the contents with the baseline of the current text font.

Standard/Usage: HTML 4   **Widely Supported:** No

Sample:

```
<colgroup valign="top">...</colgroup>
```

Other Attributes

The colgroup element also accepts the lang, dir, onclick, ondblclick, onmousedown, onmouseup, onmouseover, onmousemove, onmouseout, onkeypress, onkeydown, and onkeyup attributes.

DD

Contains a definition in a definition list (dl). Use this element inside the dl element. The dd element can contain block-level elements.

Standard/Usage: HTML 2   **Widely Supported:** Yes
Empty: No

Sample:

```
<dl>
   <dt>Butter</dt>
   <dd>Butter is a dairy product.</dd>
</dl>
```

class="..."

Indicates which style class applies to the dd element.

Standard/Usage: HTML 4   **Widely Supported:** Yes

Sample:

```
<dl>
    <dt>HTML</dt>
    <dd class="casual">Hypertext Markup Language</dd>
</dl>
```

id="..."

Assigns a unique ID selector to an instance of the dd element. When you then assign a style to that ID selector, it affects only that one instance of the dd element.

Standard/Usage: HTML 4   **Widely Supported:** Yes

Sample:

```
<dl>
    <dt>RS-232C</dt>
    <dd id="123">A standard for serial communication between
        computers.</dd>
</dl>
```

style="..."

Specifies style sheet commands that apply to the definition.

Standard/Usage: HTML 4   **Widely Supported:** Yes

Sample:

```
<dd style="background: blue; color: white">...</dd>
```

title="..."

Specifies text assigned to the element. You can use this attribute for context-sensitive help within the document. Browsers may use this to show tooltips over the definition.

Standard/Usage: HTML 4   **Widely Supported:** No

Sample:

```
<dd title="Definition">...</dd>
```

Other Attributes

The dd element also accepts the `lang`, `dir`, `onclick`, `ondblclick`, onmousedown, onmouseup, onmouseover, onmousemove, onmouseout, onkeypress, onkeydown, and onkeyup attributes.

DEL

Indicates text marked for deletion in the document. May be either block-level or inline, as necessary.

Standard/Usage: HTML 4   **Widely Supported:** No
Empty: No

Sample:

```
<p>HTTP stands for Hypertext Transfer
<del>Transport</del>Protocol.</p>
```

cite="url"

Indicates the address of the reference (a definitive source, for example) for the deletion.

Standard/Usage: HTML 4   **Widely Supported:** No

Sample:

```
<del cite="http://www.w3.org/">
HTML 3.0 was used for 10 years.</del>
```

class="..."

Indicates which style class applies to the del element.

Standard/Usage: HTML 4   **Widely Supported:** Yes

Sample:

```
<del class="casual">
POP stands for Post Office Protocol.</del>
```

datetime="..."

Indicates the date and time in precisely this format: YYYY-MM-DDThh:mm:ssTZD. For example, 2001-07-14T08:30:00-07:00 indicates July 14, 2001, at 8:30 A.M., in U.S. Mountain Time (7 hours from Greenwich time). This time also could be presented as 2001-07-14T08:30:00Z.

Standard/Usage: HTML 4   **Widely Supported:** No

Sample:

```
<del datetime="2001-07-14T08:30:00Z">
POP stands for Post Office Protocol.</del>
```

id="..."

Assigns a unique ID selector to an instance of the element. When you then assign a style to that ID selector, it affects only that one instance of the del element.

Standard/Usage: HTML 4   **Widely Supported:** Yes

Sample:

```
<del id="123">WWW stands for World Wide Web.</del>
```

style="..."

Specifies style sheet commands that apply to the deleted text.

Standard/Usage: HTML 4   **Widely Supported:** Yes

Sample:

```
<del style="background: blue; color: white">
ESP stands for extra-sensory perception.</del>
```

title="..."

Specifies text assigned to the element. You can use this attribute for context-sensitive help within the document. Browsers may use this to show tooltips over the text.

Standard/Usage: HTML 4   **Widely Supported:** No

Sample:

```
<del title="Definition">More deleted text.</del>
```

Other Attributes

The del element also accepts the lang, dir, onclick, ondblclick, onmousedown, onmouseup, onmouseover, onmousemove, onmouseout, onkeypress, onkeydown, and onkeyup attributes.

DFN

Indicates the definition of a term in the document.

> **Standard/Usage:** HTML 3.2   **Widely Supported:** No
> **Empty:** No
>
> **Sample:**
>
> ```
> <dfn>HTTP stands for Hypertext Transfer Protocol.</dfn>
> ```

class="..."

Indicates which style class applies to the dfn element.

> **Standard/Usage:** HTML 4   **Widely Supported:** Yes
>
> **Sample:**
>
> ```
> <dfn class="computer">
> POP stands for Post Office Protocol.</dfn>
> ```

id="..."

Assigns a unique ID selector to an instance of the dfn element. When you then assign a style to that ID selector, it affects only that one instance of the dfn element.

> **Standard/Usage:** HTML 4   **Widely Supported:** Yes
>
> **Sample:**
>
> ```
> <dfn id="123">WWW stands for World Wide Web.</dfn>
> ```

style="..."

Specifies style sheet commands that apply to the definition.

> **Standard/Usage:** HTML 4   **Widely Supported:** Yes

Sample:

```
<dfn style="background: blue; color: white">
ESP stands for extra-sensory perception.</dfn>
```

title="..."

Specifies text assigned to the element. You can use this attribute for context-sensitive help within the document. Browsers may use this to show tooltips over the definition text.

Standard/Usage: HTML 4   **Widely Supported:** No

Sample:

```
<dfn title="Definition">...</dfn>
```

Other Attributes

The dfn element also accepts the lang, dir, onclick, ondblclick, onmousedown, onmouseup, onmouseover, onmousemove, onmouseout, onkeypress, onkeydown, and onkeyup attributes.

DIR

Contains a directory list. Use the li element to indicate list items within the list. Use ul rather than this deprecated element.

Standard/Usage: HTML 2; deprecated   **Widely Supported:** Yes
Empty: No

Sample:

```
Choose a music genre:
<dir>
    <li><a href="rock/">Rock</a></li>
    <li><a href="country/">Country</a></li>
    <li><a href="newage/">New Age</a></li>
</dir>
```

class="..."

Indicates which style class applies to the dir element.

Standard/Usage: HTML 4   **Widely Supported:** Yes

Sample:

```
<dir class="food">
    <li>Apples</li>
    <li>Kiwis</li>
    <li>Mangos</li>
    <li>Oranges</li>
</dir>
```

compact="compact"

Causes the list to appear in a compact format. This attribute probably will not affect the appearance of the list because most browsers do not present lists in more than one format. It's deprecated in HTML 4 and later.

Standard/Usage: HTML 2; deprecated   **Widely Supported:** No

Sample:

```
<dir compact="compact">...</dir>
```

id="..."

Assigns a unique ID selector to an instance of the dir element. When you then assign a style to that ID selector, it affects only that one instance of the dir element.

Standard/Usage: HTML 4   **Widely Supported:** Yes

Sample:

```
<dir id="123">
    <li>Thingie 1</li>
    <li>Thingie 2</li>
</dir>
```

style="..."

Specifies style sheet commands that apply to the dir element.

Standard/Usage: HTML 4   **Widely Supported:** Yes

Sample:

```
<dir style="background: blue; color: white">
    <li>Thingie 1</li>
    <li>Thingie 2</li>
</dir>
```

title="..."

Specifies text assigned to the element. You can use this attribute for context-sensitive help within the document. Browsers may use this to show tooltips over the directory list.

Standard/Usage: HTML 4   **Widely Supported:** No

Sample:

```
<dir title="Directory List">...</dir>
```

Other Attributes

The dir element also accepts the lang, dir, onclick, ondblclick, onmousedown, onmouseup, onmouseover, onmousemove, onmouseout, onkeypress, onkeydown, and onkeyup attributes.

DIV

Indicates logical divisions within a document. You can use this element to apply alignment, line wrapping, and particular style sheet attributes to a section of your document. <div align="center"> is the official replacement for the center element—although it's also deprecated in favor of using style sheets.

Standard/Usage: HTML 3.2; deprecated   **Widely Supported:** No
Empty: No

Sample:

```
<div align="center" style="background: blue">
All About Formic Acid</div>
```

align="left/center/right/justify"

Specifies whether the content of the section aligns with the left or right margin (left, right), is evenly spaced between them (center), or stretches between the left and right margins (justify). This attribute is deprecated in HTML 4 and later in favor of style sheets.

Standard/Usage: HTML 3.2; deprecated   **Widely Supported:** No

Sample:

```
<div align="right">Look over here!</div>
<div align="left">Now, look over here!</div>
```

class="..."

Indicates which style class applies to the div element.

Standard/Usage: HTML 4   **Widely Supported:** Yes

Sample:

```
<div class="casual">...</div>
```

id="..."

Assigns a unique ID selector to an instance of the div element. When you then assign a style to that ID selector, it affects only that one instance of the div element.

Standard/Usage: HTML 4   **Widely Supported:** Yes

Sample:

```
<div id="123">...</div>
```

nowrap="nowrap"

Disables line wrapping for the section.

Standard/Usage: Internet Explorer 4   **Widely Supported:** No

Sample:

```
<div align="left" nowrap="nowrap">
The contents of this section will not automatically
wrap as you size the window.</div>
```

style="..."

Specifies style sheet commands that apply to the contents of the div element.

Standard/Usage: HTML 4   **Widely Supported:** Yes

Sample:

```
<div style="background: red">...</div>
```

title="..."

Specifies text assigned to the element. You can use this attribute for context-sensitive help within the document. Browsers may use this to show tooltips over the contents of the div element.

Standard/Usage: HTML 4   **Widely Supported:** No

Sample:

```
<div title="Title" class="casual">...</div>
```

Other Attributes

The div element also accepts the lang, dir, onclick, ondblclick, onmousedown, onmouseup, onmouseover, onmousemove, onmouseout, onkeypress, onkeydown, and onkeyup attributes.

DL

Contains the dt and dd elements that form the term and definition portions of a definition list.

Standard/Usage: HTML 2   **Widely Supported:** Yes
Empty: No

Sample:

```
<dl>
    <dt>Hygeine</dt>
    <dd>Being clean.</dd>
</dl>
```

class="..."

Indicates which style class applies to the dl element.

Standard/Usage: HTML 4   **Widely Supported:** Yes

Sample:

```
<dl class="computer">
    <dt>RAM</dt>
    <dd>Random Access Memory</dd>
</dl>
```

compact="compact"

Causes the definition list to appear in a compact format. This attribute probably will not affect the appearance of the list because most browsers do not present lists in more than one format. It's deprecated in HTML 4 and later.

Standard/Usage: HTML 2; deprecated   **Widely Supported:** No

Sample:

```
<dl compact="compact">...</dl>
```

id="..."

Assigns a unique ID selector to an instance of the dd element. When you then assign a style to that ID selector, it affects only that one instance of the dd element.

Standard/Usage: HTML 4   **Widely Supported:** Yes

Sample:

```
<dl id="123">
    <dt>food</dt>
    <dd>We will be eating three meals/day.</dd>
</dl>
```

style="..."

Specifies style sheet commands that apply to contents of the dl element.

Standard/Usage: HTML 4   **Widely Supported:** Yes

Sample:

```
<dl style="background: red">...</dl>
```

title="..."

Specifies text assigned to the element. You can use this attribute for context-sensitive help within the document. Browsers may use this to show tooltips over the definition list.

Standard/Usage: HTML 4   **Widely Supported:** No

Sample:

```
<dl title="Definition List">...</dl>
```

Other Attributes

The dl element also accepts the lang, dir, onclick, ondblclick, onmousedown, onmouseup, onmouseover, onmousemove, onmouseout, onkeypress, onkeydown, and onkeyup attributes.

DT

Contains the terms inside a definition list. Place the dt element inside dl elements.

Standard/Usage: HTML 2   **Widely Supported:** Yes
Empty: No

Sample:

```
<dl>
    <dt>Hygeine</dt>
    <dd>Being clean.</dd>
</dl>
```

class="..."

Indicates which style class applies to the dt element.

Standard/Usage: HTML 4   **Widely Supported:** Yes

Sample:

```
<dl>
    <dt class="casual">CUL8R</dt>
    <dd>See You Later</dd>
</dl>
```

id="..."

Assigns a unique ID selector to an instance of the dt element. When you then assign a style to that ID selector, it affects only that one instance of the dt element.

Standard/Usage: HTML 4   **Widely Supported:** Yes

Sample:

```
<dl>
    <dt id="123">Caffeine</dt>
    <dd>What most people need to start their days.</dd>
</dl>
```

style="..."

Specifies style sheet commands that apply to the contents of the dt element.

Standard/Usage: HTML 4   **Widely Supported:** Yes

Sample:

```
<dt style="background: red">...</dt>
```

title="..."

Specifies text assigned to the element. You can use this attribute for context-sensitive help within the document. Browsers may use this to show tooltips over the definition term.

Standard/Usage: HTML 4   **Widely Supported:** No

Sample:

```
<dt title="Term">XHTML</dt>
<dd>HTML reformulated as an XML application</dd>
```

Other Attributes

The dt element also accepts the lang, dir, onclick, ondblclick, onmousedown, onmouseup, onmouseover, onmousemove, onmouseout, onkeypress, onkeydown, and onkeyup attributes.

EM

Makes the text stand out. Browsers usually render the enclosed text in italic or boldface.

Standard/Usage: HTML 2   **Widely Supported:** Yes
Empty: No

Sample:

```
It's <em>very</em> important to read the instructions
before beginning.
```

class="..."

Indicates which style class applies to the em element.

Standard/Usage: HTML 4   **Widely Supported:** Yes

Sample:

```
Did you say my house was on <em class="urgent">FIRE?!</em>
```

id="..."

Assigns a unique ID selector to an instance of the em element. When you then assign a style to that ID selector, it affects only that one instance of the em element.

Standard/Usage: HTML 4   **Widely Supported:** Yes

Sample:

```
I have complained
<em id="123">ten</em> times about the leaking faucet.
```

style="..."

Specifies style sheet commands that apply to the contents of the em element.

Standard/Usage: HTML 4   **Widely Supported:** Yes

Sample:

```
You want this <em style="background: red">when</em>?
```

title="..."

Specifies text assigned to the element. You can use this attribute for context-sensitive help within the document. Browsers may use this to show tooltips over the emphasized text.

Standard/Usage: HTML 4   **Widely Supported:** No

Sample:

```
<em title="Emphasis">...</em>
```

Other Attributes

The em element also accepts the lang, dir, onclick, ondblclick, onmousedown, onmouseup, onmouseover, onmousemove, onmouseout, onkeypress, onkeydown, and onkeyup attributes.

EMBED

Places an embedded object into a document. Examples of embedded objects include MIDI files and digital video files. Because the embed element is not part of the HTML standard, you should use the object element instead. If the browser does not have built-in support for an object, users will need a plug-in to use the object within the document. This element was introduced in Netscape Navigator, but it's also supported by Internet Explorer.

Standard/Usage: Netscape Navigator, Internet Explorer 3
Widely Supported: No   **Empty:** Yes

Sample:

```
<embed src="fur_elise.midi" />
```

accesskey="..."

Specifies a single keyboard key that binds to the embedded object.

Standard/Usage: Internet Explorer 4   **Widely Supported:** No

Sample:

```
<embed src="st.ocx" accesskey="e" />
```

align="left/right/center/texttop/top/ absbottom/absmiddle/baseline/bottom"

Indicates how an embedded object is positioned relative to the document borders and surrounding contents.

Value	Effect
left	Floats the embedded object between the edges of the window, on the left side.
right	Floats the embedded object between the edges of the window, on the right side.
center	Floats the embedded object between the edges of the window, evenly between left and right.
texttop	Aligns the top of the embedded object with the top of the current text.
top	Aligns the top of the embedded object with the top of the current text.
absmiddle	Aligns the middle of the embedded object with the middle of the current text.

Value	Effect
absbottom	Aligns the bottom of the embedded object with the bottom of the current text.
baseline	Aligns the bottom of the embedded object with the baseline of the surrounding text.
bottom	Aligns the bottom of the embedded object with the baseline of the surrounding text.

Standard/Usage: Internet Explorer 4   **Widely Supported:** No

Sample:

```
<embed src="song.mid" align="center" />
```

height="n"

Specifies the vertical dimension of the embedded object.

Standard/Usage: Netscape Navigator, Internet Explorer 3; required
Widely Supported: No

Sample:

```
<embed src="rocket.avi" width="50" height="40" />
```

src="url"

Indicates the relative or absolute location of the file containing the object you want to embed.

Standard/Usage: Netscape Navigator, Internet Explorer 3; required
Widely Supported: No

Sample:

```
<embed src="beethoven_9.midi" />
```

title="..."

Specifies text assigned to the element. You can use this attribute for context-sensitive help within the document. Browsers may use this to show tooltips over the embedded object.

Standard/Usage: Internet Explorer 4   **Widely Supported:** No

Sample:

```
<embed src="explode.avi" title="movie" />
```

width="n"

Indicates the horizontal dimension of the embedded object.

Standard/Usage: Netscape Navigator, Internet Explorer 3; required
Widely Supported: No

Sample:

```
<embed src="cartoon.avi" width="50" />
```

Other Attributes

The embed element also accepts the lang, dir, onclick, ondblclick, onmousedown, onmouseup, onmouseover, onmousemove, onmouseout, onkeypress, onkeydown, and onkeyup attributes.

FIELDSET

Groups related form elements.

Standard/Usage: HTML 4   **Widely Supported:** No
Empty: No

Sample:

```
<form>
   <fieldset>
      ...Logically related field elements...
   </fieldset>...
</form>
```

class="..."

Indicates which style class applies to the fieldset element.

Standard/Usage: HTML 4   **Widely Supported:** Yes

Sample:

```
<fieldset class="casual">...</fieldset>
```

id="..."

Assigns a unique ID selector to an instance of the `fieldset` element. When you then assign a style to that ID selector, it affects only that one instance of the `fieldset` element.

Standard/Usage: HTML 4   **Widely Supported:** Yes

Sample:

```
<fieldset id="123">...</fieldset>
```

style="..."

Specifies style sheet commands that apply to the contents of the `fieldset` element.

Standard/Usage: HTML 4   **Widely Supported:** Yes

Sample:

```
<fieldset style="background: red">...</fieldset>
```

title="..."

Specifies text assigned to the element. You can use this attribute for context-sensitive help within the document. Browsers may use this to show tooltips over the text.

Standard/Usage: HTML 4   **Widely Supported:** No

Sample:

```
<fieldset title="Personal data fields">...</fieldset>
```

Other Attributes

The `fieldset` element also accepts the `lang`, `dir`, `onclick`, `ondblclick`, `onmousedown`, `onmouseup`, `onmouseover`, `onmousemove`, `onmouseout`, `onkeypress`, `onkeydown`, and `onkeyup` attributes.

FONT

Alters or sets font characteristics of the font the browser uses to display text. This element is deprecated in HTML 4 and later in favor of style sheets.

Standard/Usage: HTML 3.2; deprecated   **Widely Supported:** Yes

Empty: No

Sample:

```
That cat was really <font size="+3">BIG</font>!
```

color="#rrggbb" or "..."

Indicates the color the browser uses to display text. Color names can substitute for the RGB hexadecimal values. This attribute is deprecated in HTML 4 and later in favor of style sheets.

Standard/Usage: HTML 3.2; deprecated   **Widely Supported:** Yes

Sample:

```
<font color="#ff0000"><h2>Win A Trip!</h2></font>
<font color="lightblue"><p>That's right! A trip to Hawaii
can be yours if you scratch off the right number!</font>
```

face="..., ..."

Specifies a comma-separated list of font names the browser uses to render text. If the browser does not have access to the first named font, it tries the second, then the third, and so forth. This attribute is deprecated in favor of style sheets.

Standard/Usage: HTML 4; deprecated   **Widely Supported:** Yes

Sample:

```
<font size="+1"
face="AvantGarde, Helvetica, Lucida Sans, Arial">
This text will appear in AvantGarde
if it's available.</font>
```

size="n"

Specifies the size of the text affected by the font element. You can specify the size relative to the base font size (see the basefont element), which is normally 3. You also can specify the size as a digit in the range 1 through 7. This attribute is deprecated in HTML 4 and later in favor of style sheets.

Standard/Usage: HTML 3.2; deprecated   **Widely Supported:** Yes

Sample:

```
<basefont size="4" />
<font size="+2">This is a font of size 6.</font>
<font size="1">This is a font of size 1.</font>
```

FORM

Sets up a container for a form element. Within the form element, you can place form input elements such as fieldset, input, select, and textarea.

Standard/Usage: HTML 2   **Widely Supported:** Yes
Empty: No

Sample:

```
<form method="post" action="/cgi-bin/search.pl">
    Search: <input type=text name="name" size="20" /><br />
    <input type="submit" value="Start Search" />
    <input type="reset" />
</form>
```

accept-charset="..."

Specifies the character encodings for input data that the server processing the form must accept. The value is a list of character sets as defined in RFC2045, separated by commas or spaces.

Standard/Usage: HTML 4   **Widely Supported:** No

Sample:

```
<form method="post" accept-charset="ISO-8859-1"
action="/stat-collector.cgi">...</form>
```

accept="..."

Specifies a list of MIME types, separated by commas, that the server processing the form will handle correctly.

Standard/Usage: HTML 4   **Widely Supported:** No

Sample:

```
<form method="post" accept="image/gif, image/jpeg"
action="/image-collector.cgi">...</form>
```

action="url"

Specifies the absolute or relative location of the form-processing CGI application.

Standard/Usage: HTML 2; required   **Widely Supported:** Yes

Sample:

```
<form method="post" action="/stat-collector.cgi">...</form>
```

class="..."

Indicates which style class applies to the form.

Standard/Usage: HTML 4   **Widely Supported:** Yes

Sample:

```
<form method="post" class="casual"
action="/stat-collector.cgi">...</form>
```

enctype="..."

Specifies the MIME type used to submit (post) the form to the server. The default value is "application/x-www-form-urlencoded". Use the value "multipart/form-data" when the returned document includes files.

Standard/Usage: HTML 4   **Widely Supported:** No

Sample:

```
<form method="post"
enctype="application/x-www-form-urlencoded"
action="/stat-collector.cgi">...</form>
```

id="..."

Assigns a unique ID selector to an instance of the form element. When you then assign a style to that ID selector, it affects only that one instance of the form element.

Standard/Usage: HTML 4   **Widely Supported:** Yes

Sample:

```
<form action="/cgi-bin/ttt.pl" method="get" id="123">
...</form>
```

method="post/get"

Changes how form data is transmitted to the form processor. When you use get, the form data is given to the form processor in the form of an environment variable (query_string). When you use post, the form data is given to the form processor as the standard input to the program.

Standard/Usage: HTML 2   **Widely Supported:** Yes

Sample:

```
<form method="post" action="/cgi-bin/www-search">
    Enter search keywords:
    <input type="text" name="query" size="20" />
    <input type="submit" value="search" />
</form>
```

name="..."

Assigns the form a name accessible by bookmark, script, and applet resources. This attribute is deprecated; use the id attribute instead of or together with name.

Standard/Usage: HTML 4; deprecated   **Widely Supported:** No

Sample:

```
<form method="post" action="/cgi-bin/ff.pl" name="ff"
id="ff">...</form>
```

style="..."

Specifies style sheet commands that apply to the contents of the form element.

Standard/Usage: HTML 4   **Widely Supported:** Yes

Sample:

```
<form style="background: red">...</form>
```

target="..."

Identifies in which previously named frame the output from the form processor should appear.

Standard/Usage: HTML 4 (Frames)   **Widely Supported:** Yes

Sample:

```
<form target="output" method="get"
action="/cgi-bin/thingie.sh">...</form>
```

title="..."

Specifies text assigned to the element. You can use this attribute for context-sensitive help within the document. Browsers may use this to show tooltips over the fill-out form.

Standard/Usage: HTML 4   **Widely Supported:** No

Sample:

```
<form method="post" action="/cgi-bin/ff.pl"
title="Fill-out form">...</form>
```

Other Attributes

The form element also accepts the lang, dir, onsubmit, onreset, onclick, ondblclick, onmousedown, onmouseup, onmouseover, onmousemove, onmouseout, onkeypress, onkeydown, and onkeyup attributes.

FRAME

Defines a frame within a frame set (see the frameset element). The frame element specifies the source file and visual characteristics of a frame.

Standard/Usage: HTML 4 (Frames)   **Widely Supported:** Yes
Empty: Yes

Sample:

```
<frameset rows="*,70">
   <frame src="frames/body.html" name="body" />
   <frame src="frames/buttons.html" name="buttons"
   scrolling="no"        noresize="noresize" />
</frameset>
```

bordercolor="#rrggbb" or "..."

Specifies the color of the border around the frame. Use the color's hexadecimal RGB values or the color name.

Standard/Usage: Internet Explorer 4, Netscape Navigator 3
Widely Supported: Yes

Sample:

```
<frame src="hits.html" bordercolor="red" />
```

class="..."

Indicates which style class applies to the frame element.

Standard/Usage: HTML 4   **Widely Supported:** Yes

Sample:

```
<frame src="hits.html" class="casual" />
```

frameborder="1/0"

Indicates whether the frame's border is visible. A value of 1 (default) indicates that the border is visible; 0 indicates that it's invisible.

Standard/Usage: HTML 4 (Frames)   **Widely Supported:** Yes

Sample:

```
<frame src="weather.html" frameborder="0" />
```

id="..."

Assigns a unique ID selector to an instance of the frame element. When you then assign a style to that ID selector, it affects only that one instance of the frame element.

Standard/Usage: HTML 4   **Widely Supported:** Yes

Sample:

```
<frame src="weather.html" id="123" />
```

longdesc="url"

Specifies the URL of a long description of the frame.

Standard/Usage: HTML 4 (Frames)   **Widely Supported:** Yes

Sample:

```
<frame src="cats.html" longdesc="whycatsrcool.htm" />
```

marginheight="n"

Specifies the vertical dimension (in pixels) of the top and bottom margins in a frame.

> **Standard/Usage:** HTML 4 (Frames)   **Widely Supported:** Yes
>
> **Sample:**
>
> ```
> <frame src="cats.html" marginheight="10" />
> ```

marginwidth="n"

Specifies the horizontal dimension (in pixels) of the left and right margins in a frame.

> **Standard/Usage:** HTML 4 (Frames)   **Widely Supported:** Yes
>
> **Sample:**
>
> ```
> <frame src="dogs.html" marginwidth="10" />
> ```

name="..."

Gives the frame you're defining a name. You can use this name later to load new documents into the frame (see the target attribute) and within scripts to control attributes of the frame. Reserved names with special meaning include _blank, _parent, _self, and _top.

> **Standard/Usage:** HTML 4 (Frames)   **Widely Supported:** Yes
>
> **Sample:**
>
> ```
> <frame src="/cgi-bin/weather.cgi"
> name="weather" id="weather" />
> ```

noresize="noresize"

Makes a frame's dimensions unchangeable. Otherwise, if a frame's borders are visible, users can resize the frame by selecting a border and moving it with the mouse.

> **Standard/Usage:** HTML 4 (Frames)   **Widely Supported:** Yes
>
> **Sample:**
>
> ```
> <frame src="bottom.html" name="bottom" id="bottom"
>  noresize="noresize" scrolling="no" />
> ```

scrolling="yes/no/auto"

Indicates whether a scroll bar is present within a frame when text dimensions exceed the dimensions of the frame. Set `scrolling="no"` when using a frame to display only an image.

Standard/Usage: HTML 4 (Frames)   **Widely Supported:** Yes

Sample:

```
<frame name="titleimg" id="titleimg"
src="title.gif" scrolling="no" />
```

src="url"

Specifies the relative or absolute location of a document that you want to load within the defined frame.

Standard/Usage: HTML 4 (Frames)   **Widely Supported:** Yes

Sample:

```
<frame name="main" id="main" src="intro.html" />
```

style="..."

Specifies style sheet commands that apply to the frame.

Standard/Usage: HTML 4   **Widely Supported:** Yes

Sample:

```
<frame name="main" id="main" src="intro.html"
style="background: red" />
```

title="..."

Specifies text assigned to the element. You can use this attribute for context-sensitive help within the document. Browsers may use this to show tooltips over the fill-out form.

Standard/Usage: HTML 4   **Widely Supported:** No

Sample:

```
<frame name="main" id="main"
src="intro.html" title="Main Frame" />
```

FRAMESET

Contains frame definitions and specifies frame spacing, dimensions, and attributes. Place `frame` and `noframes` elements inside `frameset` elements.

Standard/Usage: HTML 4 (Frames)   **Widely Supported:** Yes
Empty: No

Sample:

```
<frameset cols="*,70">
    <frame src="frames/body.html" name="body" id="body" />
    <frame src="frames/side.html" name="side" id="side" />
</frameset>
```

border="n"

Specifies the thickness of borders (in pixels) around frames defined within the frameset. You also can control border thickness with the frame element.

Standard/Usage: Netscape Navigator 3, Internet Explorer 4
Widely Supported: No

Sample:

```
<frameset cols="*,150" border="5">
    <frame src="left.html" name="main" id="main" />
    <frame src="side.html" name="side" id="side" />
</frameset>
```

bordercolor="#rrggbb" or "..."

Sets the color of the frame borders. Color names can substitute for the hexadecimal RGB color values.

Standard/Usage: Netscape Navigator 3, Internet Explorer 4
Widely Supported: Yes

Sample:

```
<frameset bordercolor="red" rows="100,*">
    <frame src="top.html" name="title" id="title" />
    <frame src="story.html" name="story" id="story" />
</frameset>
```

class="..."

Indicates which style class applies to the frameset.

Standard/Usage: HTML 4   **Widely Supported:** Yes

Sample:

```
<frameset bordercolor="red" class="casual">
    <frame src="top.html" name="title" id="title" />
    <frame src="story.html" name="story" id="story" />
</frameset>
```

cols="..."

Specifies the number and dimensions of the vertical frames within the current frameset.

Set cols to a comma-separated list of numbers or percentages to indicate the width of each frame. Use the asterisk (*) to represent a variable width. A frame of variable width fills the space left over after the browser formats space for the other frames (<frameset cols="100,400,* ">).

Setting cols with percentage values controls the ratio of frame horizontal space relative to the amount of space available within the browser (<frameset cols="10%,*">).

You cannot use cols and rows in the same element.

Standard/Usage: HTML 4 (Frames)   **Widely Supported:** Yes

Sample:

```
<frameset cols="*,100,* ">
    <frame src="left.html" name="left" id="left" />
    <frame src="middle.html" name="middle" id="middle" />
    <frameset rows="2">
        <frame src="top.html" name="top" id="top" />
        <frame src="bottom.html" name="bottom" id="bottom" />
    </frameset>
</frameset>
```

framespacing="n"

Specifies the space (in pixels) between frames within the browser window.

Standard/Usage: Internet Explorer 3   **Widely Supported:** No

Sample:

```
<frameset rows="*,100" framespacing="10">
    <frame src="top.html" name="top" id="top" />
    <frame src="middle.html" name="middle" id="middle" />
</frameset>
```

id="..."

Assigns a unique ID selector to an instance of the frameset element. When you then assign a style to that ID selector, it affects only that one instance of the frameset element.

Standard/Usage: HTML 4   **Widely Supported:** Yes

Sample:

```
<frameset rows="*,100" framespacing="10" id="123" >
    <frame src="top.html" name="top" id="top" />
    <frame src="middle.html" name="middle" id="middle" />
</frameset>
```

rows="..."

Specifies the number and dimensions of the horizontal frames within the current frameset.

Set rows to a comma-separated list of numbers or percentages to indicate the height of each frame. Use the asterisk (*) to represent a variable height. A frame of variable height fills the space remaining after the browser formats space for the other frames (<frameset rows="100,400,* ">).

Setting rows to a comma-separated list of percentages enables you to control the ratio of frame vertical space relative to the space available within the browser (<frameset rows="10%,*">).

You cannot use rows and cols in the same element.

Standard/Usage: HTML 4 (Frames)   **Widely Supported:** Yes

Sample:

```
<frameset rows="*,100,* ">
    <frame src="top.html" name="top" id="top" />
    <frame src="middle.html" name="middle" id="middle" />
    <frameset cols="2">
        <frame src="bottom1.html" name="left" id="left" />
        <frame src="bottom2.html" name="right" id="right" />
    </frameset>
</frameset>
```

style="..."

Specifies style sheet commands that apply to the contents of the frameset element.

Standard/Usage: HTML 4   **Widely Supported:** No

Sample:
```
<frameset rows="100,* " style="background: red">
    <frame src="top.html" name="title" id="title" />
    <frame src="story.html" name="story" id="story" />
</frameset>
```

title="..."

Specifies text assigned to the element. You can use this attribute for context-sensitive help within the document. Browsers may use this to show tooltips over the frame.

Standard/Usage: HTML 4   **Widely Supported:** No

Sample:
```
<frameset rows="100,* " title="Stories">
    <frame src="top.html" name="title" id="title" />
    <frame src="story.html" name="story" id="story" />
</frameset>
```

Other Attributes

The frameset element also accepts the onload and onunload attributes.

HN

Specifies headings in a document. Headings are numbered 1–6, with h1 representing the heading for the main heading in the document and h3 representing a nested subtopic. Generally, text inside heading elements appears in boldface and may be larger than normal document text.

Standard/Usage: HTML 2   **Widely Supported:** Yes
Empty: No

Sample:

```
<h1>Caring for Your Canary</h1>
<p>This document explains how you should
take care of a canary.</p>
<h2>Feeding</h2>
<h2>Caging</h2>
```

align="left/center/right"

Positions the heading in the left, right, or center of a document. This attribute is deprecated in HTML 4 and later in favor of style sheets.

Standard/Usage: HTML 3.2; deprecated   **Widely Supported:** Yes

Sample:

```
<h3 align="center">History of the Platypus</h3>
```

class="..."

Indicates which style class applies to the h*n* element.

Standard/Usage: HTML 4   **Widely Supported:** Yes

Sample:

```
<h1 class="casual" align="left">River Tours</h1>
```

id="..."

Assigns a unique ID selector to an instance of the h*n* element. When you then assign a style to that ID selector, it affects only that one instance of the h*n* element.

Standard/Usage: HTML 4   **Widely Supported:** Yes

Sample:

```
<h2 id="123">Paper Products</h2>
```

style="..."

Specifies style sheet commands that apply to the heading.

Standard/Usage: HTML 4   **Widely Supported:** Yes

Sample:

```
<h1 style="background: red">Heading 1</h1>
```

title="..."

Specifies text assigned to the element. You can use this attribute for context-sensitive help within the document. Browsers may use this to show tooltips over the heading.

Standard/Usage: HTML 4   **Widely Supported:** No

Sample:

```
<h1 title="Headline">Meals On Wheels Gets New Truck</h1>
```

Other Attributes

The h*n* elements also accept the lang, dir, onclick, ondblclick, onmousedown, onmouseup, onmouseover, onmousemove, onmouseout, onkeypress, onkeydown, and onkeyup attributes.

HEAD

Contains document head information. The following elements can be used within the document head: link, meta, title, script, base, and style.

Standard/Usage: HTML 2; required   **Widely Supported:** Yes
Empty: No

Sample:

```
<html>
   <head>
      <title>Making a Peanut Butter and Jelly Sandwich
      </title>
      <link rel="parent" href="sandwiches.html" />
   </head>
...</html>
```

profile="url"

Specifies the address of metadata profiles. You can use this attribute to specify the location of meta element information, for example.

Standard/Usage: HTML 4   **Widely Supported:** No

Sample:

```
<head profile="http://www.sybex.com/">...</head>
```

Other Attributes

The head element also accepts the lang and dir attributes.

HR

Draws horizontal lines (rules) in your document. This is useful for visually separating document sections.

> **Standard/Usage:** HTML 2   **Widely Supported:** Yes
> **Empty:** Yes
>
> **Sample:**
> ```
> <h2>Birthday Colors</h2>
> <hr align="left" width="60%" />
> <p>Birthdays are usually joyous celebrations so we
>  recommend bright colors.</p>
> ```

align="left/center/right"

Positions the line flush left, flush right, or in the center of the document. These settings are irrelevant unless you use the width attribute to make the line shorter than the width of the document. This attribute is deprecated in HTML 4 and later in favor of style sheets.

> **Standard/Usage:** HTML 3.2; deprecated   **Widely Supported:** Yes
>
> **Sample:**
> ```
> <h2 align="left">Shopping List</h2>
> <hr width="40%" align="left" />
> <ul type="square">
>     <li>eggs</li> <li>butter</li>
>     <li>bread</li> <li>milk</li>
> </ul>
> ```

class="..."

Indicates which style class applies to the hr element.

> **Standard/Usage:** HTML 4   **Widely Supported:** Yes
>
> **Sample:**
> ```
> <hr class="casual" width="50%" />
> ```

color="#rrggbb" or "..."

Specifies the color of the line. A color name can be substituted for the hexadecimal RGB values. This attribute on the hr element is supported only by Internet Explorer; style sheets provide more functionality for a wider variety of browsers.

Standard/Usage: Internet Explorer 3   **Widely Supported:** No

Sample:

```
<hr color="#09334c" />
```

id="..."

Assigns a unique ID selector to an instance of the hr element. When you then assign a style to that ID selector, it affects only that one instance of the hr element.

Standard/Usage: HTML 4   **Widely Supported:** Yes

Sample:

```
<hr id="123" />
```

noshade="noshade"

Specifies that the browser should not shade the line.

Standard/Usage: HTML 3.2; deprecated   **Widely Supported:** Yes

Sample:

```
<hr noshade="noshade" align="center" width="50%" />
<img src="bobby.jpg" align="center"
border="0" alt="bobby" /><br clear="all" />
<hr noshade="noshade" align="center" width="50%" />
```

size="n"

Specifies the thickness of the line (in pixels). This attribute is deprecated in HTML 4 and later in favor of style sheets.

Standard/Usage: HTML 3.2; deprecated   **Widely Supported:** Yes

Sample:

```
<hr size="10" />
```

style="..."

Specifies style sheet commands that apply to the horizontal rule.

Standard/Usage: HTML 4 **Widely Supported:** Yes

Sample:

```
<hr width="50%" style="color: red" />
```

width="n"

Specifies the length of the line. You can specify the value with an absolute number of pixels or as a percentage to indicate how much of the total width available is used. This attribute is deprecated in HTML 4 and later in favor of style sheets.

Standard/Usage: HTML 3.2; deprecated **Widely Supported:** Yes

Sample:

```
<h2 align="center">The End!</h2>
<hr width="85%" />
```

title="..."

Specifies text assigned to the element. You can use this attribute for context-sensitive help within the document. Browsers may use this to show tooltips over the horizontal rule.

Standard/Usage: HTML 4 **Widely Supported:** No

Sample:

```
<hr title="A line" />
```

Other Attributes

The hr element also accepts the onclick, ondblclick, onmousedown, onmouseup, onmouseover, onmousemove, onmouseout, onkeypress, onkeydown, and onkeyup attributes.

HTML

Contains the entire document. Place the opening html tag at the top and the closing html tag at the bottom of all your HTML files. (The only code outside of the `html` tag should be the required DOCTYPE declaration and the optional XML declaration.) The `html` element is required. Remember the XHTML namespace for XHTML documents.

Standard/Usage: HTML 2; required   **Widely Supported:** Yes

Empty: No

Sample:

```
<?xml version="1.0" encoding="UTF-8" standalone="no"?>
<!DOCTYPE html PUBLIC
 "-//W3C//DTD XHTML 1.0 Transitional//EN"
   "http://www.w3.org/TR/xhtml1/DTD/xhtml1-transitional.dtd">
<html xmlns="http://www.w3.org/1999/xhtml">
   <head><title>Test Page</title></head>
   <body><h1>Is this working?</h1></body>
</html>
```

version="..."

Specifies the version of HTML used. This attribute is deprecated in XHTML because it contains the same information as the DOCTYPE declaration.

Standard/Usage: HTML 4; deprecated   **Widely Supported:** No

Sample:

```
<html version="-//W3C//DTD HTML 4.0 Transitional//EN">
This is an HTML 4.0 document. Not valid XHTML...</html>
```

xmlns="..."

Specifies the XHTML namespace. There's only one possible value for XHTML at this time: `xmlns="http://www.w3.org/1999/xhtml"`.

Standard/Usage: XHTML 1; required   **Widely Supported:** No

Sample:

```
<html xmlns="http://www.w3.org/1999/xhtml">...</html>
```

Other Attributes

The `html` element also accepts the `lang` and `dir` attributes.

I

Italicizes text.

Standard/Usage: HTML 2   **Widely Supported:** Yes
Empty: No

Sample:

```
Mary told me to read <i>Mostly Harmless</i>.
```

class="..."

Indicates which style class applies to the i element.

Standard/Usage: HTML 4   **Widely Supported:** Yes

Sample:

```
This mouse is <i class="casual">enhanced</i>.
```

id="..."

Assigns a unique ID selector to an instance of the i element. When you then assign a style to that ID selector, it affects only that one instance of the i element.

Standard/Usage: HTML 4   **Widely Supported:** Yes

Sample:

```
He called it a <i id="123">doohickie</i>!
```

style="..."

Specifies style sheet commands that apply to the italicized text.

Standard/Usage: HTML 4   **Widely Supported:** Yes

Sample:

```
<i style="color: green">green, italicized text</i>
```

title="..."

Specifies text assigned to the element. You can use this attribute for context-sensitive help within the document. Browsers may use this to show tooltips over the italicized text.

Standard/Usage: HTML 4   **Widely Supported:** No

Sample:

```
<i title="italicized">italicized text</i>
```

Other Attributes

The i element also accepts the lang, dir, onclick, ondblclick, onmousedown, onmouseup, onmouseover, onmousemove, onmouseout, onkeypress, onkeydown, and onkeyup attributes.

IFRAME

Creates floating frames within a document. Floating frames differ from normal frames because they can be manipulated independently within another HTML document.

Standard/Usage: HTML 4 (Frames)   **Widely Supported:** No
Empty: No

Sample:

```
<iframe name="new_win" id="new_win"
src="http://www.sybex.com">iframe>
```

align="left/center/right"

Specifies how the floating frame lines up with respect to the left and right sides of the browser window. This attribute is deprecated in favor of style sheets.

Standard/Usage: HTML 4; deprecated   **Widely Supported:** No

Sample:

```
<iframe align="left" src="goats.html"
name="g1" id="g1">...</iframe>
```

frameborder="1/0"

Indicates whether the floating frame has visible borders. A value of 1 (default) indicates that the border is visible, and a value of 0 indicates that it is not visible.

Standard/Usage: HTML 4 (Frames)   **Widely Supported:** No

Sample:

```
<iframe src="main.html" name="main"
id="main" frameborder="0">...</iframe>
```

height="n"

Specifies the vertical dimension (in pixels) of the floating frame.

Standard/Usage: HTML 4 (Frames)   **Widely Supported:** No

Sample:

```
<iframe src="joe.html" name="Joe" id="Joe" width="500"
  height="200">...</iframe>
```

hspace="n"

Indicates the size (in pixels) of left and right margins within the floating frame.

Standard/Usage: Internet Explorer 4   **Widely Supported:** No

Sample:

```
<iframe src="joe.html" name="Joe" id="Joe" hspace="10"
  vspace="10">...</iframe>
```

id="..."

Assigns a unique ID selector to an instance of the iframe element. When you then assign a style to that ID selector, it affects only that one instance of the iframe element.

Standard/Usage: HTML 4 (Frames)   **Widely Supported:** Yes

Sample:

```
<iframe src="joe.html" name="Joe" id="Joe">...</iframe>
```

marginheight="n"

Specifies the size of the top and bottom margins (in pixels) within the floating frame.

Standard/Usage: HTML 4 (Frames)   **Widely Supported:** No

Sample:

```
<iframe src="top.html" name="topbar" id="topbar"
    marginheight="50">...</iframe>
```

marginwidth="n"

Specifies the size of the left and right margins (in pixels) within the floating frame.

Standard/Usage: HTML 4 (Frames)   **Widely Supported:** No

Sample:

```
<iframe src="body.html" name="body" id="body"
    marginwidth="50">...</iframe>
```

name="..."

Assigns the frame a unique name. You can use this name within other frames to load new documents in the frame and to manipulate the attributes of the frame.

Standard/Usage: HTML 4 (Frames)   **Widely Supported:** No

Sample:

```
<iframe src="jane.html" name="Jane" id="Jane" width="500"
    height="200">...</iframe>
```

scrolling="yes/no/auto"

Indicates whether the floating frame has scroll bars. The default is auto.

Standard/Usage: HTML 4 (Frames)   **Widely Supported:** No

Sample:

```
<iframe src="top.html" scrolling="auto">...</iframe>
```

src="url"

Specifies the relative or absolute location of the document file to load in the floating frame.

Standard/Usage: HTML 4 (Frames)   **Widely Supported:** No

Sample:

```
<iframe name="pics" id="pics" src="pics.htm">...</iframe>
```

style="..."

Specifies style sheet commands that apply to the floating frame.

Standard/Usage: HTML 4 (Frames)   **Widely Supported:** No

Sample:

```
<iframe src="dots.html" name="dots" id="dots"
style="background: red">...</iframe>
```

width="n"

Specifies the horizontal dimension (in pixels) of the floating frame.

Standard/Usage: HTML 4 (Frames)   **Widely Supported:** No

Sample:

```
<iframe src="joe.html" name="Joe" id="Joe" width="500"
    height="200">...</iframe>
```

vspace="n"

Indicates the size (in pixels) of top and bottom margins within the floating frame.

Standard/Usage: Internet Explorer 4   **Widely Supported:** No

Sample:

```
<iframe src="joe.html" name="Joe" id="Joe" hspace="10"
    vspace="10">...</iframe>
```

Other Attributes

The iframe element also accepts the lang, dir, onclick, ondblclick, onmousedown, onmouseup, onmouseover, onmousemove, onmouseout, onkeypress, onkeydown, and onkeyup attributes.

IMG

Places an inline image in a document. You can use the attributes ismap and usemap with the img element to implement imagemaps.

Standard/Usage: HTML 2   **Widely Supported:** Yes
Empty: Yes

Sample:

```
<img src="images/left_arrow.gif" alt="&lt;- " />
```

align="left/right/top/middle/bottom"

Specifies the appearance of text that is near an inline graphic image. For example, if you use right, the image appears flush to the right edge of the document, and the text appears to its left. Using left produces the opposite effect.

HTML 2 mentions only attribute values of top, middle, and bottom. top aligns the top of the first line of text after the img element to the top of the image. bottom (the default) aligns the bottom of the image to the baseline of the text. middle aligns the baseline of the first line of text with the middle of the image.

HTML 3.2 added left and right to the list of attribute values.

You can use the br element to control specific points where text stops wrapping around an image and continues below the instance of the image.

The align attribute is deprecated in HTML 4 and later in favor of style sheets.

Standard/Usage: HTML 2; deprecated   **Widely Supported:** Yes

Sample:

```
<img src="red_icon.gif" align="left" />
It's about time for volunteers to pitch in.
<br clear="all" />
```

alt="..."

Provides a textual description of images, which is both useful for users who have text-only browsers and required by the specifications. Some browsers also may display the alt text as a tooltip when the user places the mouse pointer over the image.

Standard/Usage: HTML 2; required   **Widely Supported:** Yes

Sample:

```
<img src="smiley.gif" alt=":-)" />
```

border="n"

Specifies the width (in pixels) of a border around an image. The default value is usually 0 (no border). The border color is the color of normal text within your document. This attribute is deprecated in favor of style sheets.

Standard/Usage: HTML 3.2; deprecated   **Widely Supported:** Yes

Sample:

```
<img src="portrait.jpg" border="2" />
```

class="..."

Indicates which style class applies to the image.

Standard/Usage: HTML 4   **Widely Supported:** Yes

Sample:

```
<img class="casual" src="dots.gif" />
```

controls="controls"

If the image is a video file, indicates the playback controls that appear below the image.

Standard/Usage: Internet Explorer 2   **Widely Supported:** No

Sample:

```
<img dynsrc="foo.avi" controls="controls" />
```

dynsrc="url"

Specifies the relative or absolute location of a dynamic image (VRML, video file, and so on).

Standard/Usage: Internet Explorer 2   **Widely Supported:** No

Sample:

```
<img dynsrc="foo.avi" />
```

height="n"

Specifies the vertical dimension of the image (in pixels). If you don't use this attribute, the image appears at its default height. Use this attribute, along with the width attribute, to fit an image within a space. You can fit a large image into a smaller space, and you can spread a smaller image. Some web designers use the width and height attributes to spread a single pixel image over a large space to produce the effect of a larger solid-color image.

Standard/Usage: HTML 3.2   **Widely Supported:** Yes

Sample:

```
<img src="images/smiley.jpg" width="50" height="50" />
```

hspace="n"

Establishes a margin of white space (in pixels) to the left and right of a graphic image. (See the vspace attribute for how to control the top and bottom margins around an image.) This attribute is deprecated in favor of style sheets.

Standard/Usage: HTML 3.2; deprecated   **Widely Supported:** Yes

Sample:

```
<img src="pics/pinetree.jpg" hspace="20" vspace="15" />
```

id="..."

Assigns a unique ID selector to an instance of the img element. When you then assign a style to that ID selector, it affects only that one instance of the img element.

Standard/Usage: HTML 4   **Widely Supported:** Yes

Sample:

```
<img src="grapes.jpg" id="123" />
```

ismap="ismap"

Indicates that the graphic image functions as a clickable imagemap. The ismap attribute instructs the browser to send the pixel coordinates to the server imagemap CGI application when a user selects the image with the mouse pointer. When HTML 2 established the ismap attribute, imagemaps were implemented in a server-side fashion only. Now, client-side imagemaps are more popular (see the usemap attribute).

Standard/Usage: HTML 2   **Widely Supported:** Yes

Sample:

```
<a href="/cgi-bin/imagemap/mymap">
<img ismap="ismap" src="images/main.gif" /></a>
```

longdesc="..."

Provides a long textual description of images, which is useful for users who have text-only browsers or who cannot view images for other reasons.

Standard/Usage: HTML 4   **Widely Supported:** No

Sample:

```
<img src="smiley.gif" alt=":-)"
longdesc="This is a smiley face,
placed here for decoration. " />
```

loop="n/infinite"

Indicates the number of times a video file plays back.

Standard/Usage: Internet Explorer 2   **Widely Supported:** No

Sample:

```
<img dynsrc="bar.avi" loop="infinite" />
```

name="..."

Specifies a name by which bookmarks, scripts, and applets can reference the image. This attribute is deprecated; use the id attribute instead of or together with name.

Standard/Usage: HTML 2; deprecated   **Widely Supported:** No

Sample:

```
<img src="tweakie.jpg" name="img_1" id="img_1" />
```

src="url"

Specifies the relative or absolute location of a file that contains the graphic image you want to embed in a document.

Standard/Usage: HTML 2; required   **Widely Supported:** Yes

Sample:

```
<img src="images/left_arrow.gif" alt="&lt;- " />
```

style="..."

Specifies style sheet commands that apply to the inline image.

Standard/Usage: HTML 4   **Widely Supported:** Yes

Sample:

```
<img src="dots.gif" style="background: red" />
```

title="..."

Specifies text assigned to the element. You can use this attribute for context-sensitive help within the document. Browsers may use this to show tooltips over the image.

Standard/Usage: HTML 4   **Widely Supported:** No

Sample:

```
<img src="pics/jill.jpg" title="Image" />
```

usemap="url"

Specifies the location of the client-side imagemap data (see the map element). Because the map element gives the map data an anchor name, be sure to include the name with the URL of the document that contains the map data.

Standard/Usage: HTML 3.2   **Widely Supported:** Yes

Sample:

```
<img ismap="ismap" src="map1.gif" usemap="maps.html#map1" />
```

vrml="..."

Specifies the absolute or relative location of a VRML (Virtual Reality Markup Language) world to embed in a document.

Standard/Usage: Internet Explorer 2   **Widely Supported:** No

Sample:

```
<img vrml="vr/myroom.vrml" />
```

vspace="n"

Establishes a margin of white space (in pixels) above and below a graphic image. (See the hspace attribute for how to control the left and right margins of an image.) This attribute is deprecated in favor of style sheets.

Standard/Usage: HTML 3.2; deprecated   **Widely Supported:** Yes

Sample:

```
<img src="pics/pinetree.jpg" hspace="20" vspace="15" />
```

width="n"

Specifies the horizontal dimension of the image (in pixels). If you don't use this attribute, the image appears in the default width. Use this attribute, along with the height attribute, to fit an image within a space. You can fit a large image into a smaller space, and you can spread a smaller image. Some web designers use width and height to spread a single pixel image over a large space to produce the effect of a larger solid-color image.

Standard/Usage: HTML 3.2   **Widely Supported:** Yes

Sample:

```
<img src="images/smiley.jpg" width="50" height="50" />
```

Other Attributes

The img element also accepts the lang, dir, onclick, ondblclick, onmousedown, onmouseup, onmouseover, onmousemove, onmouseout, onkeypress, onkeydown, and onkeyup attributes.

INPUT

Identifies several input methods for forms. This element must appear between the opening and closing form tags.

Standard/Usage: HTML 2   **Widely Supported:** Yes
Empty: Yes

Sample:

```
<form action="/cgi-bin/order/" method="post">
   <input name="qty" type="text" size="5" />
   <input type="submit" value="order" />
</form>
```

align="left/center/right"

Lines up a graphical submit button (type="image"). The behavior of this element is identical to that of the align attribute of the img element. This attribute is deprecated in HTML 4 and later in favor of style sheets.

Standard/Usage: HTML 3.2; deprecated   **Widely Supported:** Yes

Sample:

```
<input type="image" src="picture.gif" align="right" />
```

accept="..."

Specifies a comma-separated list of acceptable MIME types for submitted files.

Standard/Usage: HTML 4   **Widely Supported:** No

Sample:

```
<input type="file" accept="image/gif, image/jpg" />
Please submit an image.
```

accesskey="..."

Specifies a single keyboard key that users can use to navigate to the input field.

Standard/Usage: HTML 4   **Widely Supported:** No

Sample:

```
<input type="checkbox" name="test"
value="unproven" accesskey="t" />
```

alt="..."

Provides a textual description of the input element, which is useful for users who have text-only browsers. Some browsers also may display the alt text as a floating message when the user places the mouse pointer over the image.

Standard/Usage: HTML 2 **Widely Supported:** Yes

Sample:

```
Age: <input type="text" name="age" alt="age" id="123" />
```

checked="checked"

Use with the type="radio" or type="checkbox" to set the default state of those input methods to true.

Standard/Usage: HTML 2 **Widely Supported:** Yes

Sample:

```
One <input type="checkbox" checked="checked"
name="foo" value="1" /><br />
Two <input type="checkbox" name="foo" value="2" /><br />
```

class="..."

Indicates which style class applies to the input element.

Standard/Usage: HTML 4 **Widely Supported:** Yes

Sample:

```
<input class="casual" type="text" name="age" />
```

disabled="disabled"

Disables an instance of the input method so that data cannot be accepted or submitted. Also removes this element from the tab sequence.

Standard/Usage: HTML 4 **Widely Supported:** No

Sample:

```
<input type="password" name="pass" disabled="disabled" />
```

id="..."

Assigns a unique ID selector to an instance of the input element. When you then assign a style to that ID selector, it affects only that one instance of the input element.

Standard/Usage: HTML 4   **Widely Supported:** Yes

Sample:

```
Age: <input type="text" name="age" id="123" />
```

ismap="ismap"

Indicates that the input element functions as a clickable imagemap. type must be equal to image.

Standard/Usage: HTML 2   **Widely Supported:** Yes

Sample:

```
<input src="mapimage.gif" type="image" ismap="ismap" />
```

maxlength="n"

Indicates the number of characters you can enter into a text input field; useful only to input methods of type text or password. Unlike the size attribute, maxlength does not affect the size of the input field shown on the screen.

Standard/Usage: HTML 2   **Widely Supported:** Yes

Sample:

```
Phone: <input type="text" name="phone" maxlength="11" />
```

name="..."

Gives a name to the value you pass to the form processor. For example, if you collect a person's last name with an input method of type text, you assign a value to the name attribute similar to lastname. This establishes a name-value pair for the form processor.

Standard/Usage: HTML 2   **Widely Supported:** Yes

Sample:

```
Enter your last name: <input type="text"
name="lastname" size="25" />
```

readonly="readonly"

Indicates that changes to the input method data cannot occur.

Standard/Usage: HTML 4   **Widely Supported:** No

Sample:

```
<input type="text" name="desc"
value="1/4 inch flange assembly" readonly="readonly" />
```

size="n"

Specifies the width of the input field, in characters for input fields of type text or password and in pixels for all other input methods.

Standard/Usage: HTML 2   **Widely Supported:** Yes

Sample:

```
Your Age: <input type="text" name="age" size="5" />
```

src="url"

Implements a graphic image for a submit button. For this to work, indicate type="image".

Standard/Usage: HTML 3.2   **Widely Supported:** Yes

Sample:

```
<input type="image" src="/images/push-button.gif" />
```

style="..."

Specifies style sheet commands that apply to this input element.

Standard/Usage: HTML 4   **Widely Supported:** Yes

Sample:

```
<input type="radio" name="food" value="1"
style="background: red" />
```

tabindex="n"

Specifies where the input method appears in the tab order.

Standard/Usage: HTML 4   **Widely Supported:** No

Sample:

```
Information:
<input type="text" name="first name" tabindex="1" />
<input type="text" name="middle name" tabindex="2" />
<input type="text" name="last name" tabindex="3" />
```

title="..."

Specifies text assigned to the element. You can use this attribute for context-sensitive help within the document. Browsers may use this to show tooltips over the input method.

Standard/Usage: HTML 4   **Widely Supported:** No

Sample:

```
<input type="radio" name="cc"
value="visa" title="visacard" />
```

type="button/checkbox/file/hidden/image/ password/radio/reset/submit/text"

Indicates the kind of input method to use:

Value	Effect
button	Creates a generic button that can interact with scripts.
checkbox	Produces a small check box that the user can check or uncheck, depending on the settings.
file	Allows the user to submit a file with the form.
hidden	Creates a hidden field that the user cannot interact with. This field typically is used to transmit data between the client and server.
image	Replaces the Submit button with an image. The behavior of this value is identical to that of the Submit button, except that the x,y coordinates of the mouse position over the image when selected also are sent to the form processor.
password	Gives the user a simple one-line text input field similar to the text type. However, when users enter data into the field, they do not see individual characters; rather, they see asterisks.
radio	Produces a small radio button that can be turned on and off (in groups of two or more). Use radio buttons when you want a user to select only one of several items. For multiple-value selections, see the checkbox type of input element or the select element.

Value	Effect
reset	Sets all the input methods to their empty or default settings.
submit	Produces a button that when selected submits all the name-value pairs to the form processor.
text	Produces a simple one-line text input field that is useful for obtaining simple data such as a person's name, a person's age, a dollar amount, and so on. To collect multiple lines of text, use the textarea element.

Standard/Usage: HTML 2   **Widely Supported:** Yes

Sample:

```
<form method="post" action="/cgi-bin/thingie">
   Name:       <input type="text" name="name" /><br />
   Password:   <input type="password" name="pass" /><br />
   Ice Cream: Vanilla<input type="radio" value="1"
    checked="checked" name="ice_cream" />Chocolate
   <input type="radio" value="2" name="ice_cream" /><br />
   <input type="submit" value="Send Data..." />
</form>
```

usemap="url"

Indicates the relative or absolute location of a client-side imagemap to use with the form.

Standard/Usage: HTML 4   **Widely Supported:** No

Sample:

```
<input src="mapimage.gif" usemap="maps.html#map1" />
```

value="..."

Sets the default value input method. Required when input is set to type="radio" or type="checkbox".

Standard/Usage: HTML 2   **Widely Supported:** Yes

Sample:

```
<input type="hidden" name="id" value="123" />
```

Other Attributes

The `input` element also accepts the `lang`, `dir`, `onfocus`, `onblur`, `onselect`, `onchange`, `onclick`, `ondblclick`, `onmousedown`, `onmouseup`, `onmouseover`, `onmousemove`, `onmouseout`, `onkeypress`, `onkeydown`, and `onkeyup` attributes.

INS

Indicates text to be inserted in the document. May be either block level or inline, as necessary.

Standard/Usage: HTML 4   **Widely Supported:** No
Empty: No

Sample:

```
<p>HTTP stands for Hypertext
<ins>Transfer</ins> Protocol.</p>
```

cite="url"

Indicates the address of the reference (a definitive source, for example) for the insertion.

Standard/Usage: HTML 4   **Widely Supported:** No

Sample:

```
<ins cite="http://www.w3.org/">
HTML 2 was used for two years.</ins>
```

class="..."

Indicates which style class applies to the `ins` element.

Standard/Usage: HTML 4   **Widely Supported:** Yes

Sample:

```
<ins class="joeadd">
POP stands for Post Office Protocol.</ins>
```

datetime="..."

Indicates the date and time in precisely this format: YYYY-MM-DDThh:mm:ssTZD. For example, 2001-07-14T08:30:00-07:00 indicates July 14, 2001, at 8:30 A.M., in U.S. Mountain Time (7 hours from Greenwich time). This time also could be presented as 2001-07-14T08:30:00Z.

Standard/Usage: HTML 4   **Widely Supported:** No

Sample:

```
<ins datetime="2001-07-14T08:30:00Z">
POP stands for Post Office Protocol.</ins>
```

id="..."

Assigns a unique ID selector to an instance of the ins element. When you then assign a style to that ID selector, it affects only that one instance of the ins element.

Standard/Usage: HTML 4   **Widely Supported:** Yes

Sample:

```
<ins id="123">WWW stands for World Wide Web.</ins>
```

style="..."

Specifies style sheet commands that apply to the inserted text.

Standard/Usage: HTML 4   **Widely Supported:** Yes

Sample:

```
<ins style="background: blue; color: white">
ESP stands for extra-sensory perception.</ins>
```

title="..."

Specifies text assigned to the element. You can use this attribute for context-sensitive help within the document. Browsers may use this to show tooltips over the inserted text.

Standard/Usage: HTML 4   **Widely Supported:** No

Sample:

```
<ins title="Definition">More inserted text.</ins>
```

Other Attributes

The ins element also accepts the lang, dir, onclick, ondblclick, onmousedown, onmouseup, onmouseover, onmousemove, onmouseout, onkeypress, onkeydown, and onkeyup attributes.

ISINDEX

Inserts an input field into the document so that users can enter search queries. The queries then go to a CGI application indicated by the `action` attribute. This element is deprecated in HTML 4 and later in favor of the `input` element.

Standard/Usage: HTML 2; deprecated   **Widely Supported:** Yes
Empty: Yes

Sample:

```
<isindex prompt="keyword search"
action="/cgi-bin/search.cgi" />
```

prompt="..."

Changes the input prompt for keyword index searches. If you don't specify prompt, the browser displays a default prompt.

Standard/Usage: HTML 3.2   **Widely Supported:** Yes

Sample:

```
<isindex prompt="Search for something" />
```

Other Attributes

The `isindex` element also accepts the `lang`, `dir`, `id`, `class`, `style`, and `title` attributes.

KBD

Specifies text to be entered at the keyboard or keystrokes to be entered by the user within a document.

Standard/Usage: HTML 2   **Widely Supported:** Yes
Empty: No

Sample:

```
Press <kbd>Ctrl+S</kbd> to save your document.
```

class="..."

Indicates which style class applies to the kbd element.

Standard/Usage: HTML 4   **Widely Supported:** Yes

Sample:

```
Now press the <kbd class="casual">F4</kbd> key!
```

id="..."

Assigns a unique ID selector to an instance of the kbd element. When you then assign a style to that ID selector, it affects only that one instance of the kbd element.

Standard/Usage: HTML 4   **Widely Supported:** Yes

Sample:

```
Press <kbd id="123">F1</kbd> for help.
```

style="..."

Specifies style sheet commands that apply to the text within the kbd element.

Standard/Usage: HTML 4   **Widely Supported:** Yes

Sample:

```
<kbd style="background: red">Type me</kbd>
```

title="..."

Specifies text assigned to the element. You can use this attribute for context-sensitive help within the document. Browsers may use this to show tooltips over the keyboard text.

Standard/Usage: HTML 4   **Widely Supported:** No

Sample:

```
Now press the <kbd title="Keyboard stuff">F4</kbd> key.
```

Other Attributes

The kbd element also accepts the lang, dir, onclick, ondblclick, onmousedown, onmouseup, onmouseover, onmousemove, onmouseout, onkeypress, onkeydown, and onkeyup attributes.

LABEL

Provides identifying text for a form widget.

Standard/Usage: HTML 4   **Widely Supported:** No

Empty: No

Sample:

```
<label for="idname">First Name</label>
<input type="text" id="idname" />
```

accesskey="..."

Assigns a keystroke to the element.

Standard/Usage: HTML 4   **Widely Supported:** No

Sample:

```
<label for="idname" accesskey="h">...</label>
```

class="..."

Indicates which style class applies to the label element.

Standard/Usage: HTML 4   **Widely Supported:** Yes

Sample:

```
<label for="idname" class="short">First Name</label>
<input type="text" id="idname" />
```

disabled="disabled"

Denies access to the label input method.

Standard/Usage: HTML 4   **Widely Supported:** No

Sample:

```
<label for="idname" accesskey="h" disabled="disabled">
...</label>
```

for="..."

Specifies the ID of the widget associated with the label.

Standard/Usage: HTML 4   **Widely Supported:** No

Sample:

```
<label for="idname">First Name</label>
<input type="text" id="idname" />
```

id="..."

Assigns a unique ID selector to an instance of the label element. When you then assign a style to that ID selector, it affects only that one instance of the label element.

Standard/Usage: HTML 4   **Widely Supported:** Yes

Sample:

```
<label for="idname" id="234">First Name</label>
<input type="text" id="idname" />
```

style="..."

Specifies style sheet commands that apply to this label element.

Standard/Usage: HTML 4   **Widely Supported:** Yes

Sample:

```
<label for="idname" style="background: red">
First Name</label><input type="text" id="idname" />
```

tabindex="n"

Specifies where the label input method appears in the tab order. For example, tabindex="3" places the cursor at the label element after the user presses the Tab key three times.

Standard/Usage: HTML 4   **Widely Supported:** No

Sample:

```
Credit card number: <label for="ccard" tabindex="5">
Credit Card</label><input type="text" name="ccard" />
```

title="..."

Specifies text assigned to the element. You can use this attribute for context-sensitive help within the document. Browsers may use this to show tooltips over the label.

Standard/Usage: HTML 4   **Widely Supported:** No

Sample:

```
<label for="ccard" title="credit card">Credit Card</label>
```

Other Attributes

The label element also accepts the lang, dir, onfocus, onblur, onselect, onchange, onclick, ondblclick, onmousedown, onmouseup, onmouseover, onmousemove, onmouseout, onkeypress, onkeydown, and onkeyup attributes.

LAYER

Defines a layer within a document, which you can then manipulate with JavaScript. You specify the layer's contents by placing markup between the layer elements or by using the src attribute. Netscape Navigator 6 or later, Internet Explorer 4 or later, and Opera 5 or later support the DOM, which allows comparable functionality in a more generally accessible form than Netscape's layer element. See Chapter 18, "Bringing Pages to Life with Dynamic HTML and XHTML," for more details on using the DOM.

Standard/Usage: Netscape Navigator 4   **Widely Supported:** No
Empty: No

Sample:

```
<layer src="top.html" height="100" width="100" z-index="4"
name="top" visibility="show">...</layer>
```

above="..."

Specifies the name of a layer above which the current layer should appear.

Standard/Usage: Netscape Navigator 4   **Widely Supported:** No

Sample:

```
<layer src="grass.gif" z-index="1"
 name="grass" visibility="show">
<layer src="dog.gif" above="grass" name="dog">...</layer>
</layer>
```

background="url"

Specifies the relative or absolute location of an image file that the browser tiles as the background of the layer.

Standard/Usage: Netscape Navigator 4   **Widely Supported:** No

Sample:

```
<layer z-index="5" name="info" background="goo.gif">
<h1>Hi there</h1></layer>
```

below="..."

Specifies the name of a layer below which the current layer should appear.

Standard/Usage: Netscape Navigator 4   **Widely Supported:** No

Sample:

```
<layer background="road.jpg" name="Road" below="Car">
...</layer>
```

bgcolor="#rrggbb" or "..."

Specifies the background color of the layer. Use either the hexadecimal RGB values or the color name.

Standard/Usage: Netscape Navigator 4   **Widely Supported:** No

Sample:

```
<layer bgcolor="#ff0011">
<div align="center"><h1><blink>EAT AT JOE'S!</blink>
</h1></div></layer>
```

clip="x1,y1,x2,y2"

Indicates the dimensions of a clipping rectangle that specifies which areas of the layer are visible. Areas outside this rectangle become transparent.

You can give the x and y coordinates in pixels or as percentages to indicate relative portions of the layer. You can omit *x1* and *y1* if you want to clip from the top-left corner of the layer.

Standard/Usage: Netscape Navigator 4   **Widely Supported:** No

Sample:

```
<layer src="hawk.jpg" clip="20%,20%">...</layer>
```

height="n"

Specifies the vertical dimension of the layer (in pixels or as a percentage of the browser window height).

Standard/Usage: Netscape Navigator 4   **Widely Supported:** No

Sample:

```
<layer src="frame.gif" above="bg" name="frame" width="200"
    height="200">...</layer>
```

left="n"

Specifies the layer's horizontal position (in pixels) relative to the left edge of the parent layer. Use the top attribute for vertical positioning.

Standard/Usage: Netscape Navigator 4   **Widely Supported:** No

Sample:

```
<layer left="100" top="150">
This layer is at {100,150}.</layer>
```

name="..."

Gives the layer a name by which other layer definitions and JavaScript code can reference it.

Standard/Usage: Netscape Navigator 4   **Widely Supported:** No

Sample:

```
<layer src="car.gif" name="carpic" above="road">...</layer>
```

src="url"

Specifies the relative or absolute location of the file containing the contents of the layer.

Standard/Usage: Netscape Navigator 4   **Widely Supported:** No

Sample:

```
<layer src="ocean.jpg">...</layer>
```

top="n"

Specifies the layer's vertical position (in pixels) relative to the top edge of the parent layer. Use the left attribute for horizontal positioning.

Standard/Usage: Netscape Navigator 4   **Widely Supported:** No

Sample:

```
<layer left="100" top="150">
This layer is at {100,150}.</layer>
```

visibility="show/hide/inherit"

Indicates whether the layer is visible initially. A show value indicates the layer is initially visible, hide indicates the layer is not initially visible, and inherit indicates the layer has the same initial visibility attributes as its parent layer.

Standard/Usage: Netscape Navigator 4   **Widely Supported:** No

Sample:

```
<layer src="grass.gif" z-index="1" name="grass"
   visibility="show">...</layer>
```

width="n"

Specifies the horizontal dimension of the layer (in pixels or as a percentage of the browser window width).

Standard/Usage: Netscape Navigator 4   **Widely Supported:** No

Sample:

```
<layer src="frame.gif" above="bg" name="frame" width="200"
   height="200">...</layer>
```

z-index="n"

Specifies where the layer appears in the stack of layers. A higher value indicates a position closer to the top of the stack.

Standard/Usage: Netscape Navigator 4   **Widely Supported:** No

Sample:

```
<layer z-index="0" name="bottom">You may never see this
text if other layers are above it.</layer>
```

Other Attributes

The layer element also accepts the onfocus, onblur, onselect, onchange, onclick, ondblclick, onmousedown, onmouseup, onmouseover, onmousemove, onmouseout, onkeypress, onkeydown, and onkeyup attributes.

LEGEND

Specifies a description for a fieldset. Use inside the fieldset element.

Standard/Usage: HTML 4   **Widely Supported:** No
Empty: No

Sample:

```
<fieldset><legend valign="top" align="center">
Grades for Cooking 101</legend>...</fieldset>
```

align="top/bottom/left/right"

Indicates whether the legend appears at the top or bottom and left or right of the fieldset element. This attribute is deprecated in favor of style sheets.

Standard/Usage: HTML 4; deprecated   **Widely Supported:** No

Sample:

```
<legend align="top">Seattle Staff Directory</legend>
```

accesskey="..."

Specifies a single keyboard key that users can use to navigate to the legend.

Standard/Usage: HTML 4   **Widely Supported:** No

Sample:

```
<legend accesskey="c">Criteria for Judging</legend>
```

class="..."

Indicates which style class applies to the legend element.

Standard/Usage: HTML 4   **Widely Supported:** Yes

Sample:

```
<legend class="chemical">Hydrogen vs. Oxygen</legend>
```

id="..."

Assigns a unique ID selector to an instance of the legend element. When you then assign a style to that ID selector, it affects only that one instance of the legend element.

Standard/Usage: HTML 4   **Widely Supported:** Yes

Sample:

```
<legend id="123">Great Painters</legend>
```

style="..."

Specifies style sheet commands that apply to the contents of the legend element.

Standard/Usage: HTML 4   **Widely Supported:** Yes

Sample:

```
<legend style="background: red">...</legend>
```

title="..."

Specifies text assigned to the element. You can use this attribute for context-sensitive help within the document. Browsers may use this to show tooltips over the legend.

Standard/Usage: HTML 4   **Widely Supported:** Yes

Sample:

```
<legend title="sleepy hollow">...</legend>
```

Other Attributes

The legend element also accepts the lang, dir, onclick, ondblclick, onmousedown, onmouseup, onmouseover, onmousemove, onmouseout, onkeypress, onkeydown, and onkeyup attributes.

LI

Identifies items in ordered (see the ol element), menu (see the menu element), directory (see the dir element), and unordered (see the ul element) lists.

Standard/Usage: HTML 2   **Widely Supported:** Yes
Empty: No

Sample:

```
<p>My favorite foods are:
<ul>
    <li>Pepperoni pizza</li>
    <li>Lasagna</li>
    <li>Taco salad</li>
    <li>Bananas</li>
</ul></p>
```

class="..."

Indicates which style class applies to the li element.

Standard/Usage: HTML 4   **Widely Supported:** Yes

Sample:

```
<li class="casual">Dogs</li>
```

compact="compact"

Specifies that the list item appears in a space-saving form. This attribute may not affect the appearance of the list because most browsers do not present lists in more than one format. The attribute is deprecated in HTML 4 and later.

Standard/Usage: HTML 2; deprecated   **Widely Supported:** Yes

Sample:

```
<ul>
    <li>Cola</li>
    <li>Fruit drink</li>
    <li compact="compact">Orange juice</li>
    <li>Water</li>
</ul>
```

id="..."

Assigns a unique ID selector to an instance of the li element. When you then assign a style to that ID selector, it affects only that one instance of the li element.

Standard/Usage: HTML 4 **Widely Supported:** Yes

Sample:

```
<li id="123">Bees</li>
```

style="..."

Specifies style sheet commands that apply to the list item.

Standard/Usage: HTML 4 **Widely Supported:** Yes

Sample:

```
<li style="background: red">Fruit drink</li>
```

title="..."

Specifies text assigned to the element. You can use this attribute for context-sensitive help within the document. Browsers may use this to show tooltips over the list item.

Standard/Usage: HTML 4 **Widely Supported:** No

Sample:

```
<li title="List Item">Thingie</li>
```

type="..."

Specifies the bullets for each unordered list item (see the ul element) or the numbering for each ordered list item (see the ol element). If you omit the type attribute, the browser chooses a default type.

Valid type values for unordered lists are disc, square, and circle.

Valid type values for ordered lists are 1 for Arabic numbers, a for lowercase letters, A for uppercase letters, i for lowercase Roman numerals, and I for uppercase Roman numerals.

The type attribute is deprecated in favor of style sheets.

Standard/Usage: HTML 3.2; deprecated **Widely Supported:** Yes

Sample:

```
<ul>
    <li type="square">Food</li>
    <ol>
        <li type="1">Spaghetti</li>
        <li type="1">Tossed salad</li>
    </ol>
</ul>
```

value="..."

Sets a number in an ordered list. Use this attribute to continue a list after interrupting it with something else in your document. You also can set a number in an ordered list with the start attribute of the ol element.

Because unordered lists do not increment, the value attribute is meaningless when used with them. This attribute is deprecated in favor of style sheets.

Standard/Usage: HTML 3.2; deprecated   **Widely Supported:** Yes

Sample:

```
<ol type="1">
    <li value="5">Watch</li>
    <li>Compass</li>
</ol>
```

Other Attributes

The li element also accepts the lang, dir, onclick, ondblclick, onmousedown, onmouseup, onmouseover, onmousemove, onmouseout, onkeypress, onkeydown, and onkeyup attributes.

LINK

An empty element that establishes relationships between the current document and other documents. Use this element within the head section. For example, if you access the current document by choosing a hyperlink from the site's home page, you can establish a relationship between the current document and the site's home page (see the rel attribute). At this time, however, most browsers don't use most of those relationships; only rel="stylesheet" is widely supported. You can place several link elements within the head section of your document to define multiple relationships.

With newer implementations of HTML, you use the `link` element to establish information about Cascading Style Sheets (CSS). Some other relationships (link types) that the `link` element defines with either the `rel` or `rev` attribute include the following:

Value of `rel` or `rev`	References
alternate	A different version of the same document. When used with `lang`, `alternate` implies a translated document; when used with `media`, it implies a version for a different medium.
appendix	An appendix.
bookmark	A bookmark, which links to an important entry point within a longer document.
chapter	A chapter.
contents	A table of contents.
copyright	A copyright notice.
glossary	A glossary of terms.
help	A document offering help or more information.
index	An index.
next	The next document in a series (use with `rel`).
prev	The previous document in a series (use with `rev`).
section	A section.
start	The first document in a series.
stylesheet	An external style sheet.
subsection	A subsection.

Standard/Usage: HTML 2   **Widely Supported:** Yes
Empty: Yes

Sample:

```
<head>
   <title>Prices</title>
   <link rel="top" href="http://www.example.com/" />
   <link rel="stylesheet"
    href="http://www.example.com/styles.css" />
</head>
```

charset="..."

Specifies character encoding of the data designated by the link. Uses the name of a character set defined in RFC2045. The default value for this attribute, appropriate for all Western languages, is ISO-8859-1.

Standard/Usage: HTML 4   **Widely Supported:** No

Sample:

```
<link rel="top" href="http://www.example.com/"
charset="ISO-8859-1" />
```

href="url"

Indicates the relative or absolute location of the resource you're establishing a relationship to/from.

Standard/Usage: HTML 2   **Widely Supported:** Yes

Sample:

```
<link rel="prev" href="page1.html" />
```

hreflang="..."

Specifies the language used in the document linked to. Use standard codes for languages, such as DE for German, FR for French, IT for Italian, and HE for Hebrew. See ISO International Standard 639 at

```
www.oasis-open.org/cover/iso639a.html
```

for more information about language codes.

Standard/Usage: HTML 4   **Widely Supported:** No

Sample:

```
<link href="german.html" hreflang="DE" />
```

media="..."

Specifies the destination medium for style information. It may be a single type or a comma-separated list. Media types include the following:

Value	Description
all	Applies to all devices.
braille	For Braille tactile feedback devices.

Value	Description
print	For traditional printed material and for documents on-screen viewed in print preview mode.
projection	For projectors.
screen	For online viewing (default setting).
speech	For a speech synthesizer.

Standard/Usage: HTML 4   **Widely Supported:** No

Sample:

```
<link media="screen" rel="stylesheet" href="/global.css" />
```

rel="..."

Defines the relationship you're establishing between the current document and another resource. The values for this attribute are the link types provided in the element definition section.

Standard/Usage: HTML 2   **Widely Supported:** Yes

Sample:

```
<head>
    <link rel="help" href="/help/index.html" />
    <link rel="stylesheet" href="sitehead.css" />
</head>
```

rev="..."

Establishes reverse relationships between the current document and other resources. The values for this attribute are the link types provided in the element definition section.

Standard/Usage: HTML 2   **Widely Supported:** Yes

Sample:

```
<link rev="stylesheet" href="/global.css" />
```

target="..."

Specifies the name of a frame in which the referenced link appears.

Standard/Usage: HTML 4   **Widely Supported:** No

Sample:

```
<link target="_blank" rel="home"
href="http://www.sybex.com/" />
```

title="..."

Specifies text assigned to the element that can be used for context-sensitive help within the document. Browsers may use this to show tooltips.

Standard/Usage: HTML 4   **Widely Supported:** Yes

Sample:

```
<link rel="top" href="/index.html" title="Home Page" />
```

type="..."

Specifies the MIME type of a style sheet to import with the link element.

Standard/Usage: HTML 4   **Widely Supported:** No

Sample:

```
<link rel="stylesheet" type="text/css"
href="/style/main.css" />
```

Other Attributes

The link element also accepts the lang, dir, onfocus, onblur, onchange, onselect, onclick, ondblclick, onmousedown, onmouseup, onmouseover, onmousemove, onmouseout, onkeypress, onkeydown, and onkeyup attributes.

MAP

Specifies a container for client-side imagemap data. You use the area element inside the map element.

Standard/Usage: HTML 3.2   **Widely Supported:** Yes
Empty: No

Sample:

```
<map name="mainmap" id="mainmap">
   <area nohref="nohref"    alt="home"    shape="rect"
   coords="0,0,100,100" />
   <area href="yellow.html" alt="yellow" shape="rect"
   coords="100,0,200,100" />
   <area href="blue.html"    alt="blue"    shape="rect"
   coords="0,100,100,200" />
   <area href="red.html"    alt="red"    shape="rect"
   coords="100,100,200,200" />
</map>
```

class="..."

Indicates which style class applies to the element.

Standard/Usage: HTML 4   Widely Supported: Yes

Sample:

```
<map class="casual" name="simba" id="simba">...</map>
```

id="..."

Indicates an identifier to associate with the map. You also can use this to apply styles to the object.

Standard/Usage: HTML 4   Widely Supported: Yes

Sample:

```
<map id="123" name="simba" id="simba">...</map>
```

name="..."

Establishes a name for the map information you can reference later using the usemap attribute of the img element.

Standard/Usage: HTML 3.2   Widely Supported: Yes

Sample:

```
<map name="housemap" id="housemap">
   <img src="house.gif" usemap="#housemap"
   alt="map of house" />...</map>
```

style="..."

Specifies style sheet commands that apply to the contents of the map element.

Standard/Usage: HTML 4   **Widely Supported:** Yes

Sample:

```
<map style="background: black">...</map>
```

title="..."

Specifies text assigned to the element. You can use this attribute for context-sensitive help within the document. Browsers may use this to show tooltips.

Standard/Usage: HTML 4   **Widely Supported:** No

Sample:

```
<map title="imagemap spec">...</map>
```

MARQUEE

Displays a scrolling text message within a document. Only Internet Explorer recognizes this element. Use the more widely supported Java, JavaScript, or Flash to achieve the same effect for a broader audience.

Standard/Usage: Internet Explorer 2   **Widely Supported:** No
Empty: No

Sample:

```
<marquee direction="left" behavior="scroll"
  scrolldelay="250" scrollamount="10">
  Big sale today on fuzzy-wuzzy widgets!</marquee>
```

behavior="scroll/slide/alternate"

Indicates the type of scrolling. A value of scroll scrolls text from one side of the marquee, across, and off the opposite side; slide scrolls text from one side of the marquee, across, and stops when the text reaches the opposite side; alternate bounces the marquee text from one side to the other.

Standard/Usage: Internet Explorer 2   **Widely Supported:** No

Sample:

```
<marquee direction="left" behavior="alternate">
 Go Bears! Win Win Win!</marquee>
```

bgcolor="#rrggbb" or "..."

Specifies the background color of the marquee. You use a hexadecimal
RGB color value or a color name.

Standard/Usage: Internet Explorer 2   **Widely Supported:** No

Sample:

```
<marquee bgcolor="red" direction="left">
Order opera tickets here!</marquee>
```

direction="left/right"

Indicates the direction in which the marquee text scrolls.

Standard/Usage: Internet Explorer 2   **Widely Supported:** No

Sample:

```
<marquee direction="left">
Order opera tickets here!</marquee>
```

height="n"

Specifies the vertical dimension of the marquee (in pixels).

Standard/Usage: Internet Explorer 2   **Widely Supported:** No

Sample:

```
<marquee width="300" height="50">Go Bears!</marquee>
```

hspace="n"

Specifies the size of the margins (in pixels) to the left and right of the
marquee.

Standard/Usage: Internet Explorer 2   **Widely Supported:** No

Sample:

```
<marquee direction="left" hspace="25">
Check out our detailed product specs!</marquee>
```

id="..."

Assigns a unique ID selector to an instance of the marquee element. When you then assign a style to that ID selector, it affects only that one instance of the marquee element.

Standard/Usage: Internet Explorer 4   **Widely Supported:** No

Sample:

```
<marquee id="3d4">...</marquee>
```

loop="n/infinite"

Controls the appearance of the marquee text.

Standard/Usage: Internet Explorer 2   **Widely Supported:** No

Sample:

```
<marquee loop="5">
December 12 is our big, all-day sale!</marquee>
```

scrollamount="n"

Indicates how far (in pixels) the marquee text shifts between is redrawn. Decrease this value for a smoother (but slower) scroll; increase it for a faster (but bumpier) scroll.

Standard/Usage: Internet Explorer 2   **Widely Supported:** No

Sample:

```
<marquee scrollamount="10" scrolldelay="40">
 Plant a tree for Arbor Day!</marquee>
```

scrolldelay="n"

Indicates how often (in milliseconds) the marquee text is redrawn. Increase this value to slow the scrolling action; decrease it to speed the scrolling action.

Standard/Usage: Internet Explorer 2   **Widely Supported:** No

Sample:

```
<marquee direction="right" scrolldelay="30">
Eat at Joe's!</marquee>
```

style="..."

Specifies style sheet commands that apply to the text within the marquee element.

Standard/Usage: Internet Explorer 4   **Widely Supported:** No

Sample:

```
<marquee style="background: red">...</marquee>
```

title="..."

Specifies text assigned to the element. You can use this attribute for context-sensitive help within the document. Browsers may use this to show tooltips over the marquee.

Standard/Usage: Internet Explorer 4   **Widely Supported:** No

Sample:

```
<marquee title="scrolling marquee">...</marquee>
```

truespeed="truespeed"

A stand-alone attribute that specifies that the scrolldelay values should be maintained. If this attribute is not used, scrolldelay values under 59 are rounded up to 60 milliseconds.

Standard/Usage: Internet Explorer 2   **Widely Supported:** No

Sample:

```
<marquee direction="right" scrolldelay="30"
truespeed="truespeed">Eat at Joe's!</marquee>
```

vspace="n"

Specifies the size of the margins (in pixels) at the top and bottom of the marquee.

Standard/Usage: Internet Explorer 2   **Widely Supported:** No

Sample:

```
<marquee direction="left" vspace="25">
 Check out our detailed product specs!</marquee>
```

width="n"

Specifies the horizontal dimension (in pixels) of the marquee.

Standard/Usage: Internet Explorer 2   **Widely Supported:** No

Sample:

```
<marquee width="300">Go Bears!</marquee>
```

MENU

Defines a menu list. Uses the li element to indicate list items. However, use ul instead of this deprecated element.

Standard/Usage: HTML 2; deprecated   **Widely Supported:** No
Empty: No

Sample:

```
Now you can:<menu>
    <li>Eat the sandwich.</li>
    <li>Place the sandwich in the fridge.</li>
    <li>Feed the sandwich to the dog.</li>
</menu>
```

class="..."

Indicates which style class applies to the menu element.

Standard/Usage: HTML 4   **Widely Supported:** Yes

Sample:

```
<menu class="casual">
    <li>Information</li>
    <li>Members</li>
    <li>Guests</li>
</menu>
```

compact="compact"

Specifies that the menu list appears in a space-saving form. This attribute may not affect the appearance of the list because most browsers do not present lists in more than one format. This attribute is deprecated in HTML 4 and later.

Standard/Usage: HTML 2; deprecated **Widely Supported:** Yes

Sample:

```
<h2>Drinks Available</h2>
<menu compact="compact">
    <li>Cola</li>
    <li>Fruit drink</li>
    <li>Orange juice</li>
    <li>Water</li>
</menu>
```

id="..."

Assigns a unique ID selector to an instance of the menu element. When you then assign a style to that ID selector, it affects only that one instance of the menu element.

Standard/Usage: HTML 4 **Widely Supported:** Yes

Sample:

```
You'll need the following:<menu id="123">
    <li>Extra socks</li>
    <li>Snack crackers</li>
    <li>Towel</li>
</menu>
```

style="..."

Specifies style sheet commands that apply to the menu list.

Standard/Usage: HTML 4 **Widely Supported:** Yes

Sample:

```
<menu style="background: black; color: white">...</menu>
```

title="..."

Specifies text assigned to the element. You can use this attribute for context-sensitive help within the document. Browsers may use this to show tooltips over the menu list.

Standard/Usage: HTML 4 **Widely Supported:** No

Sample:

```
<menu title="menu list">...</menu>
```

Other Attributes

The menu element also accepts the lang, dir, onclick, ondblclick, onmousedown, onmouseup, onmouseover, onmousemove, onmouseout, onkeypress, onkeydown, and onkeyup attributes.

META

This empty element specifies information about the document to browsers, applications, and search engines. Place the meta element within the document head. For example, you can use the meta element to instruct the browser to load a new document after 10 seconds (client-pull), or you can specify keywords for search engines to associate with your document.

Standard/Usage: HTML 2   **Widely Supported:** Yes
Empty: Yes

Sample:

```
<head>
    <title>Igneous Rocks in North America</title>
    <meta http-equiv="keywords"
      content="geology, igneous, volcanoes" />
</head>
```

content="..."

Assigns values to the HTTP header field. For example, when using the refresh HTTP header, assign a number along with a URL to the content attribute; the browser then loads the specified URL after the specified number of seconds.

Standard/Usage: HTML 2; required   **Widely Supported:** Yes

Sample:

```
<meta http-equiv="refresh" content="2;url=nextpage.html" />
```

http-equiv="..."

Indicates the HTTP header value you want to define, such as refresh, expires, or content-language. Other header values are listed in RFC2068.

Standard/Usage: HTML 2   **Widely Supported:** Yes

Sample:

```
<meta http-equiv="expires"
 content="Tue, 04 Aug 2002 22:39:22 GMT" />
```

name="..."

Specifies the name of the association you are defining, such as keywords or description.

Standard/Usage: HTML 2   **Widely Supported:** Yes

Sample:

```
<meta name="keywords" content="travel,automobile" />
<meta name="description" content="The Nash Metro moves fast
 and goes beep beep. " />
```

scheme="..."

Specifies additional information about the association you're defining.

Standard/Usage: HTML 4   **Widely Supported:** No

Sample:

```
<meta name="number" scheme="priority" content="1" />
```

Other Attributes

The meta element also accepts the lang and dir attributes.

MULTICOL

Formats text into newspaper-style columns.

Standard/Usage: Netscape Navigator 4   **Widely Supported:** No
Empty: No

Sample:

```
<multicol cols="2" gutter="10">...</multicol>
```

cols="n"

Indicates the number of columns.

Standard/Usage: Netscape Navigator 4   **Widely Supported:** No

Sample:

```
<multicol cols="4">...</multicol>
```

gutter="n"

Indicates the width of the space (in pixels) between multiple columns.

Standard/Usage: Netscape Navigator 4   **Widely Supported:** No

Sample:

```
<multicol cols="3" gutter="15">...</multicol>
```

width="n"

Indicates the horizontal dimension (in pixels or as a percentage of the total width available) of each column.

Standard/Usage: Netscape Navigator 4   **Widely Supported:** No

Sample:

```
<multicol cols="2" width="30%">...</multicol>
```

NOBR

Disables line wrapping for a section of text. To force a word break within a nobr clause, use the wbr empty element. The nobr element is a proprietary Internet Explorer element that is also supported by Netscape but not the XHTML or HTML specification.

Standard/Usage: Internet Explorer, Netscape Navigator
Widely Supported: Yes   **Empty:** No

Sample:

```
<nobr>All this text will
remain on one single line in the
browser window, no matter how wide the
window is, until the closing
tag appears. That doesn't happen
until right now.</nobr>
```

class="..."

Indicates which style class applies to the element.

Standard/Usage: Internet Explorer 3, Netscape Navigator 4
Widely Supported: Yes

Sample:

```
<nobr class="casual">...</nobr>
```

id="..."

Assigns a unique ID selector to an instance of the nobr element. When you then assign a style to that ID selector, it affects only that one instance of the nobr element.

Standard/Usage: Internet Explorer 3, Netscape Navigator 4
Widely Supported: No

Sample:

```
You'll need the following:<nobr id="123">...</nobr>
```

style="..."

Specifies style sheet commands that apply to the nonbreaking text.

Standard/Usage: Internet Explorer 4, Netscape Navigator 3
Widely Supported: Yes

Sample:

```
<nobr style="background: black">...</nobr>
```

NOFRAMES

Provides content for browsers that do not support frames or are configured not to present frames. The body element is required within the noframes section. It provides additional formatting and style sheet features.

Standard/Usage: HTML 4 (Frames)   **Widely Supported:** Yes
Empty: No

Sample:

```
<frameset cols="*,70">...
    <noframes>
```

```
<body>
    <p>Your browser doesn't support frames.
        Please follow the links below for
        the rest of the story.</p>
    <p><a href="prices.html">Prices</a> |
        <a href="about.html">About Us</a> |
        <a href="contact.html">Contact Us</a></p>
</body>
</noframes>
</frameset>
```

class="..."

Indicates which style class applies to the noframes element.

Standard/Usage: HTML 4   **Widely Supported:** Yes

Sample:

```
<noframes class="short"><body>...</body></noframes>
```

id="..."

Assigns a unique ID selector to an instance of the noframes element. When you then assign a style to that ID selector, it affects only that one instance of the noframes element.

Standard/Usage: HTML 4   **Widely Supported:** Yes

Sample:

```
<noframes id="234"><body>...</body></noframes>
```

style="..."

Specifies style sheet commands that apply to the noframes element.

Standard/Usage: HTML 4   **Widely Supported:** No

Sample:

```
<noframes style="background: red"><body>...</body></noframes>
```

title="..."

Specifies text assigned to the element. You can use this attribute for context-sensitive help within the document. Browsers may use this to show tooltips.

Standard/Usage: HTML 4   **Widely Supported:** No

Sample:

```
<noframes title="XHTML for nonframed browsers">
<body>...</body></noframes>
```

Other Attributes

The noframes element also accepts the lang, dir, onclick, ondblclick, onmousedown, onmouseup, onmouseover, onmousemove, onmouseout, onkeypress, onkeydown, and onkeyup attributes.

NOSCRIPT

Provides alternative content for browsers that do not support scripts. Use the noscript element inside a script definition.

Standard/Usage: HTML 4   **Widely Supported:** No   **Empty:** No

Sample:

```
<noscript>Because you can see this, you can tell that your
browser will not run (or is set not to run) scripts.
</noscript>
```

class="..."

Indicates which style class applies to the noscript element.

Standard/Usage: HTML 4   **Widely Supported:** Yes

Sample:

```
<noscript class="short">...</noscript>
```

id="..."

Assigns a unique ID selector to an instance of the noscript element. When you then assign a style to that ID selector, it affects only that one instance of the noscript element.

Standard/Usage: HTML 4   **Widely Supported:** Yes

Sample:

```
<noscript id="234">...</noscript>
```

style="..."

Specifies style sheet commands that apply to the noscript element.

Standard/Usage: HTML 4   **Widely Supported:** Yes

Sample:

```
<noscript style="background: red">...</noscript>
```

title="..."

Specifies text assigned to the element. You can use this attribute for context-sensitive help within the document. Browsers may use this to show tooltips.

Standard/Usage: HTML 4   **Widely Supported:** No

Sample:

```
<noscript title="XHTML for nonscript browsers">...</noscript>
```

Other Attributes

The noscript element also accepts the lang, dir, onclick, ondblclick, onmousedown, onmouseup, onmouseover, onmousemove, onmouseout, onkeypress, onkeydown, and onkeyup attributes.

OBJECT

Embeds a software object into a document. The object can be an ActiveX object, a QuickTime movie, a Flash animation, or any other object or data that a browser supports.

Use the param element to supply parameters to the embedded object. You can place messages and other elements between the object elements for browsers that do not support embedded objects.

Standard/Usage: HTML 4   **Widely Supported:** No
Empty: No

Sample:

```
<object classid="/thingie.py">
   <param name="thing" value="1" />
```

```
<param name="autostart" value="true" />
Sorry. Your browser does not support embedded objects.
If it supported these objects, you would not see
this message.
</object>
```

align="left/center/right/texttop/middle/textmiddle/baseline/textbottom"

Indicates how the embedded object lines up relative to the edges of the browser windows and/or other elements within the browser window. This attribute is deprecated in favor of style sheets.

Value	Effect
left	Floats the embedded object between the edges of the window, on the left side.
right	Floats the embedded object between the edges of the window, on the right side.
center	Floats the embedded object between the edges of the window, evenly between left and right.
texttop	Aligns the top of the embedded object with the top of the surrounding text.
textmiddle	Aligns the middle of the embedded object with the middle of the surrounding text.
textbottom	Aligns the bottom of the embedded object with the bottom of the surrounding text.
baseline	Aligns the bottom of the embedded object with the baseline of the surrounding text.
middle	Aligns the middle of the embedded object with the baseline of the surrounding text.

Standard/Usage: HTML 4; deprecated   **Widely Supported:** No

Sample:

```
<object data="shocknew.dcr" type="application/director"
 width="288" height="200" align="right">...</object>
```

archive="url url url"

Specifies a *space-separated* list of URLs for archives containing resources relevant to the object, which may include the resources specified by the classid and data attributes. Preloading archives generally results in reduced load times for objects.

Standard/Usage: HTML 4   **Widely Supported:** No

Sample:

```
<object archive="bear.htm lion.htm">...</object>
```

border="n"

Indicates the width (in pixels) of a border around the embedded object. border="0" indicates no border. This attribute is deprecated in favor of style sheets.

Standard/Usage: HTML 4; deprecated   **Widely Supported:** No

Sample:

```
<object data="shocknew.dcr" type="application/director"
 width="288" height="200" border="10">...</object>
```

classid="url"

Specifies the location of an object resource, such as a Java applet. Use classid="java:appletname.class" for Java applets.

Standard/Usage: HTML 4   **Widely Supported:** No

Sample:

```
<object classid="java:appletname.class">...</object>
```

codebase="url"

Specifies the absolute or relative location of the base directory in which the browser will look for data and other implementation files.

Standard/Usage: HTML 4   **Widely Supported:** No

Sample:

```
<object codebase="/fgm/code/">...</object>
```

codetype="..."

Specifies the MIME type for the embedded object's code.

Standard/Usage: HTML 4   **Widely Supported:** No

Sample:

```
<object codetype="application/x-msword">...</object>
```

class="..."

Indicates which style class applies to the element.

Standard/Usage: HTML 4   **Widely Supported:** Yes

Sample:

```
<object class="casual" codetype="application/x-msword">
...</object>
```

classid="url"

Specifies the URL of an object resource.

Standard/Usage: HTML 4   **Widely Supported:** No

Sample:

```
<object classid="http://www.example.com/bogus.class">...
</object>
```

data="url"

Specifies the absolute or relative location of the embedded object's data.

Standard/Usage: HTML 4   **Widely Supported:** No

Sample:

```
<object data="/fgm/goo.avi">...</object>
```

declare="declare"

Defines the embedded object without actually loading it into the document.

Standard/Usage: HTML 4   **Widely Supported:** No

Sample:

```
<object classid="clsid:99B42120-6EC7-11CF-A6C7-00AA00A47DD3"
declare="declare">...</object>
```

height="n"

Specifies the vertical dimension (in pixels) of the embedded object.

Standard/Usage: HTML 4   **Widely Supported:** No

Sample:

```
<object data="shocknew.dcr" type="application/director"
 width="288" height="200">...</object>
```

hspace="n"

Specifies the size of the margins (in pixels) to the left and right of the embedded object.

Standard/Usage: HTML 4   **Widely Supported:** No

Sample:

```
<object data="shocknew.dcr" width="288" height="200"
    hspace="10">...</object>
```

id="..."

Indicates an identifier to associate with the embedded object. You also can use this to apply styles to the object.

Standard/Usage: HTML 4   **Widely Supported:** Yes

Sample:

```
<object data="shocknew.dcr" width="288" height="200"
    id="swave2">...</object>
```

name="..."

Specifies the name of the embedded object.

Standard/Usage: HTML 4   **Widely Supported:** No

Sample:

```
<object data="shocknew.dcr" name="Very Cool Thingie">
...</object>
```

standby="..."

Specifies a message that the browser displays while the object is loading.

Standard/Usage: HTML 4   **Widely Supported:** No

Sample:

```
<object standby="Please wait. Movie loading. " width="100"
    height="250">...</object>
```

tabindex="n"

Indicates the place of the embedded object in the tabbing order.

Standard/Usage: HTML 4   **Widely Supported:** No

Sample:

```
<object classid="clsid:99b42120-6ec7-11cf-a6c7-00aa00a47dd3"
    tabindex="3">...</object>
```

title="..."

Specifies text assigned to the element. You can use this attribute for context-sensitive help within the document. Browsers may use this to show tooltips over the embedded object.

Standard/Usage: HTML 4   **Widely Supported:** No

Sample:

```
<object title="Earth Movie" width="100" height="250">
...</object>
```

type="..."

Indicates the MIME type of the embedded object.

Standard/Usage: HTML 4   **Widely Supported:** No

Sample:

```
<object data="shock.dcr" type="application/x-director"
 width="288" height="200">...</object>
```

usemap="url"

Indicates the relative or absolute location of a client-side imagemap to use with the embedded object.

Standard/Usage: HTML 4   **Widely Supported:** No

Sample:

```
<object usemap="maps.html#map1">...</object>
```

vspace="n"

Specifies the size of the margins (in pixels) at the top and bottom of the embedded object.

Standard/Usage: HTML 4   **Widely Supported:** No

Sample:

```
<object data="shocknew.dcr" width="288" height="200"
    vspace="10">...</object>
```

width="n"

Indicates the horizontal dimension (in pixels) of the embedded object.

Standard/Usage: HTML 4   **Widely Supported:** No

Sample:

```
<object data="shock.dcr" type="application/director"
 width="288" height="200">...</object>
```

Other Attributes

The object element also accepts the lang, dir, onclick, ondblclick, onmousedown, onmouseup, onmouseover, onmousemove, onmouseout, onkeypress, onkeydown, and onkeyup attributes.

OL

Contains a numbered (ordered) list.

Standard/Usage: HTML 2   **Widely Supported:** Yes
Empty: No

Sample:

```
<ol>
    <li>Introduction</li>
    <li>Part One</li>
    <ol type="A">
        <li>Chapter 1</li>
        <li>Chapter 2</li>
    </ol>
</ol>
```

class="..."

Indicates which style class applies to the ol element.

Standard/Usage: HTML 4   **Widely Supported:** Yes

Sample:

```
<ol class="car">
    <li>Check engine oil</li>
    <li>Check tire pressures</li>
    <li>Fill with gasoline</li>
</ol>
```

compact="compact"

Indicates that the ordered list appears in a compact format. This attribute may not affect the appearance of the list because most browsers do not present lists in more than one format. This attribute is deprecated in HTML 4 and later.

Standard/Usage: HTML 2; deprecated   **Widely Supported:** No

Sample:

```
<ol compact="compact">...</ol>
```

id="..."

Assigns a unique ID selector to an instance of the ol element. When you then assign a style to that ID selector, it affects only that one instance of the ol element.

Standard/Usage: HTML 4   **Widely Supported:** Yes

Sample:

```
<ol id="123">...</ol>
```

start="..."

Specifies the value at which the ordered list should start. This attribute is deprecated in HTML 4 and later.

Standard/Usage: HTML 2; deprecated   **Widely Supported:** Yes

Sample:

```
<ol type="a" start="f">...</ol>
```

style="..."

Specifies style sheet commands that apply to the ordered list.

Standard/Usage: HTML 4   **Widely Supported:** Yes

Sample:

```
<ol style="background: black; color: white">...</ol>
```

title="..."

Specifies text assigned to the element. You can use this attribute for context-sensitive help within the document. Browsers may use this to show tooltips over the ordered list.

Standard/Usage: HTML 4   **Widely Supported:** No

Sample:

```
<ol title="ordered list">...</ol>
```

type="..."

Specifies the numbering style of the ordered list. Possible values are 1 for Arabic numbers, i for lowercase Roman numerals, I for uppercase Roman numerals, a for lowercase letters, and A for uppercase letters. This attribute is deprecated in HTML 4 and later in favor of style sheets.

Standard/Usage: HTML 2; deprecated   **Widely Supported:** Yes

Sample:

```
<ol type="a">
    <li>is for apple.</li>
    <li>is for bird.</li>
    <li>is for cat.</li>
    <li>is for dog.</li>
</ol>
```

Other Attributes

The ol element also accepts the lang, dir, onclick, ondblclick, onmousedown, onmouseup, onmouseover, onmousemove, onmouseout, onkeypress, onkeydown, and onkeyup attributes.

OPTGROUP

Specifies a description for a group of options. Use inside `select` elements, and use the `option` element within the `optgroup` element.

Standard/Usage: HTML 4   **Widely Supported:** No
Empty: No

Sample:

```
<select name="dinner">
  <optgroup label="choices">
    <option>Vegan</option>
    <option>Vegetarian</option>
    <option>Traditional</option>
  </optgroup>
</select>
```

class="..."

Indicates which style class applies to the `optgroup` element.

Standard/Usage: HTML 4   **Widely Supported:** Yes

Sample:

```
<optgroup label="Fake or False" class="casual">
  <option>Fake</option>
  <option>False</option>
</optgroup>
```

disabled="disabled"

Denies access to the group of options.

Standard/Usage: HTML 4   **Widely Supported:** No

Sample:

```
<optgroup label="food" disabled="disabled">
  <option>Prime Rib</option>
  <option>Lobster</option>
</optgroup>
```

id="..."

Assigns a unique ID selector to an instance of the optgroup element. When you then assign a style to that ID selector, it affects only that one instance of the optgroup element.

Standard/Usage: HTML 4   **Widely Supported:** Yes

Sample:

```
<optgroup label="Fake or False" id="123">
    <option>Fake</option>
    <option>False</option>
</optgroup>
```

label="..."

Specifies alternative text assigned to the element. You can use this attribute for context-sensitive help within the document.

Standard/Usage: HTML 4; required   **Widely Supported:** Yes

Sample:

```
<optgroup label="Dinner selections">
    <option>Prime Rib</option>
    <option>Lobster</option>
</optgroup>
```

style="..."

Specifies style sheet commands that apply to the contents of the optgroup element.

Standard/Usage: HTML 4   **Widely Supported:** No

Sample:

```
<optgroup label="dinner" style="background: red">
...</optgroup>
```

title="..."

Specifies text assigned to the element. You can use this attribute for context-sensitive help within the document.

Standard/Usage: HTML 4   **Widely Supported:** No

Sample:

```
<optgroup label="party" title="Select a political party">
...</optgroup>
```

Other Attributes

The optgroup element also accepts the lang, dir, onfocus, onblur, onchange, onselect, onclick, ondblclick, onmousedown, onmouseup, onmouseover, onmousemove, onmouseout, onkeypress, onkeydown, and onkeyup attributes.

OPTION

Indicates items in a fill-out form selection list (see the select element).

Standard/Usage: HTML 2   **Widely Supported:** Yes
Empty: No

Sample:

```
Select an artist from the 1970s:<select name="artists">
   <option>Simon and Garfunkel</option>
   <option selected="selected">Pink Floyd</option>
   <option>Boston</option>
</select>
```

class="..."

Indicate which style class applies to the element.

Standard/Usage: HTML 4   **Widely Supported:** Yes

Sample:

```
<option name="color" class="casual">...</option>
```

disabled="disabled"

Denies access to the input method.

Standard/Usage: HTML 4   **Widely Supported:** No

Sample:

```
<option value="Bogus" disabled="disabled">
Nothing here.</option>
```

id="..."

Assigns a unique ID selector to an instance of the `option` element. When you then assign a style to that ID selector, it affects only that one instance of the `option` element.

Standard/Usage: HTML 4   **Widely Supported:** Yes

Sample:

```
<option id="123">Mastercard</option>
```

label="..."

Specifies shorter, alternative text assigned to the `option` element. You can use this attribute for context-sensitive help within the document. Browsers may use this to show tooltips over the group.

Standard/Usage: HTML 4   **Widely Supported:** Yes

Sample:

```
<option label="Trad">Traditional Dinner Menu</option>
```

selected="selected"

Marks a selection list item as preselected.

Standard/Usage: HTML 2   **Widely Supported:** Yes

Sample:

```
<option selected="selected" value="1">Ice Cream</option>
```

title="..."

Specifies text assigned to the element. You can use this attribute for context-sensitive help within the document. Browsers may use this to show tooltips over the selection list option.

Standard/Usage: HTML 4   **Widely Supported:** No

Sample:

```
<option title="Option">Thingie</option>
```

value="..."

Indicates which data is sent to the form processor if you choose the selection list item. If the value attribute is not present within the option element, the text between the option elements is sent instead.

Standard/Usage: HTML 2   **Widely Supported:** Yes

Sample:

```
<option value="2">Sandwiches</option>
```

Other Attributes

The option element also accepts the lang, dir, onfocus, onblur, onchange, onselect, onclick, ondblclick, onmousedown, onmouseup, onmouseover, onmousemove, onmouseout, onkeypress, onkeydown, and onkeyup attributes.

P

Indicates a paragraph in a document.

Standard/Usage: HTML 2   **Widely Supported:** Yes
Empty: No

Sample:

```
<p>I'm a paragraph.</p>
<p>I'm another paragraph.</p>
```

align="left/center/right"

Aligns paragraph text flush left, flush right, or in the center of the document. This attribute is deprecated in HTML 4 and later in favor of style sheets.

Standard/Usage: HTML 3.2; deprecated   **Widely Supported:** Yes

Sample:

```
<p align="center">
There will be fun and games for everyone!</p>
```

class="..."

Indicates which style class applies to the p element.

Standard/Usage: HTML 4   **Widely Supported:** Yes

Sample:

```
<p class="casual">
Tom turned at the next street and stopped.</p>
```

id="..."

Assigns a unique ID selector to an instance of the p element. When you then assign a style to that ID selector, it affects only that one instance of the p element.

Standard/Usage: HTML 4   **Widely Supported:** Yes

Sample:

```
<p id="123">This paragraph is yellow on black!</p>
```

style="..."

Specifies style sheet commands that apply to the contents of the paragraph.

Standard/Usage: HTML 4   **Widely Supported:** Yes

Sample:

```
<p style="background: red; color: white">...</p>
```

title="..."

Specifies text assigned to the element. You can use this attribute for context-sensitive help within the document. Browsers may use this to show tooltips over the paragraph.

Standard/Usage: HTML 4   **Widely Supported:** No

Sample:

```
<p title="paragraph">...</p>
```

Other Attributes

The p element also accepts the lang, dir, onclick, ondblclick, onmousedown, onmouseup, onmouseover, onmousemove, onmouseout, onkeypress, onkeydown, and onkeyup attributes.

PARAM

Specifies parameters passed to an embedded object. Use the `param` element within the `object` and `applet` elements.

Standard/Usage: HTML 3.2   **Widely Supported:** No
Empty: Yes

Sample:

```
<object classid="/thingie.py">
    <param name="thing" value="1" />
    Sorry. Your browser does not support embedded objects.
</object>
```

name="..."

Indicates the name of the parameter passed to the embedded object.

Standard/Usage: HTML 3.2; required   **Widely Supported:** No

Sample:

```
<param name="startyear" value="1920" />
```

type="..."

Specifies the MIME type of the data found at the specified URL. Use this attribute with the `valuetype="ref"` attribute.

Standard/Usage: HTML 4   **Widely Supported:** No

Sample:

```
<param name="data" value="/data/sim1.zip" valuetype="ref"
    type="application/x-zip-compressed" />
```

value="..."

Specifies the value associated with the parameter passed to the embedded object.

Standard/Usage: HTML 3.2   **Widely Supported:** No

Sample:

```
<param name="startyear" value="1920" />
```

valuetype="ref/object/data"

Indicates the kind of value passed to the embedded object. A value of ref indicates that the value of value is a URL passed to the embedded object; object indicates that the value attribute specifies the location of object data; and data indicates that the value attribute is set to a plain-text string. Use this for passing alphanumeric data to the embedded object.

Standard/Usage: Internet Explorer 3, HTML 4
Widely Supported: No

Sample:
```
<param name="length" value="9" valuetype="data" />
```

PRE

Contains preformatted plain text (including line breaks and spaces). This is useful for including computer program output or source code within your document.

Standard/Usage: HTML 2   **Widely Supported:** Yes
Empty: No

Sample:
```
Here's the source code:
<pre>
#include <stdio.h>
void main()
{
 printf("Hello World!\n");
}
</pre>
```

class="..."

Indicates which style class applies to the pre element.

Standard/Usage: HTML 4   **Widely Supported:** Yes

Sample:
```
<pre class="food">BBQ Info</pre>
```

id="..."

Assigns a unique ID selector to an instance of the pre element. When you then assign a style to that ID selector, it affects only that one instance of the pre element.

Standard/Usage: HTML 4   **Widely Supported:** Yes

Sample:

```
An example of an emoticon:<pre id="123"> :-) </pre>
```

style="..."

Specifies style sheet commands that apply to the contents of the pre element.

Standard/Usage: HTML 4   **Widely Supported:** Yes

Sample:

```
<pre style="background: red">...</pre>
```

title="..."

Specifies text assigned to the element. You can use this attribute for context-sensitive help within the document. Browsers may use this to show tooltips over the preformatted text.

Standard/Usage: HTML 4   **Widely Supported:** No

Sample:

```
<pre title="preformatted text">...</pre>
```

width="n"

Specifies the horizontal dimension of the preformatted text (in pixels). This attribute is deprecated in favor of style sheets.

Standard/Usage: HTML 4; deprecated   **Widely Supported:** No

Sample:

```
<pre width="80">...</pre>
```

Other Attributes

The pre element also accepts the lang, dir, onclick, ondblclick, onmousedown, onmouseup, onmouseover, onmousemove, onmouseout, onkeypress, onkeydown, and onkeyup attributes.

Q

Quotes a direct source within a paragraph. Use blockquote to signify a longer or block quotation.

Standard/Usage: HTML 4   **Widely Supported:** No
Empty: No

Sample:

```
Dr. Bob said <q>I really like the procedure.</q>
```

cite="url"

Specifies a reference URL for a quotation.

Standard/Usage: HTML 4   **Widely Supported:** No

Sample:

```
<q cite="http://www.example.com/url.html">
The book was good.</q>
```

class="..."

Indicates which style class applies to the q element.

Standard/Usage: HTML 4   **Widely Supported:** Yes

Sample:

```
<q class="holiday">Twas the night before Christmas</q>
```

id="..."

Assigns a unique ID selector to an instance of the q element. When you then assign a style to that ID selector, it affects only that one instance of the q element.

Standard/Usage: HTML 4   **Widely Supported:** Yes

Sample:

```
On July 12, John wrote a profound sentence in his diary:
<q id="123">I woke up this morning, and it was raining.</q>
```

style="..."

Specifies style sheet commands that apply to the contents of the q element.

Standard/Usage: HTML 4   **Widely Supported:** Yes

Sample:

```
<q style="background: red">...</q>
```

title="..."

Specifies text assigned to the element. You can use this attribute for context-sensitive help within the document. Browsers may use this to show tooltips over the quoted text.

Standard/Usage: HTML 4   **Widely Supported:** No

Sample:

```
<q title="quotation">Quoted text goes here.</q>
```

Other Attributes

The q element also accepts the `lang`, `dir`, `onclick`, `ondblclick`, `onmousedown`, `onmouseup`, `onmouseover`, `onmousemove`, `onmouseout`, `onkeypress`, `onkeydown`, and `onkeyup` attributes.

S

Deprecated. See `strike`.

SAMP

Indicates a sequence of literal characters.

Standard/Usage: HTML 2   **Widely Supported:** Yes
Empty: No

Sample:

```
An example of a palindrome is the word <samp>MOM</samp>.
```

class="..."

Indicates which style class applies to the samp element.

Standard/Usage: HTML 4   **Widely Supported:** Yes

Sample:

```
The PC screen read: <samp class="casual">
Command Not Found</samp>.
```

id="..."

Assigns a unique ID selector to an instance of the samp element. When you then assign a style to that ID selector, it affects only that one instance of the samp element.

Standard/Usage: HTML 4   **Widely Supported:** Yes

Sample:

```
Just for fun, think of how many words end with the letters
<samp id="123">ing</samp>.
```

style="..."

Specifies style sheet commands that apply to the contents of the samp element.

Standard/Usage: HTML 4   **Widely Supported:** Yes

Sample:

```
<samp style="background: red">...</samp>
```

title="..."

Specifies text assigned to the element. You can use this attribute for context-sensitive help within the document. Browsers may use this to show tooltips.

Standard/Usage: HTML 4   **Widely Supported:** No

Sample:

```
<samp title="Sample">...</samp>
```

Other Attributes

The samp element also accepts the lang, dir, onclick, ondblclick, onmousedown, onmouseup, onmouseover, onmousemove, onmouseout, onkeypress, onkeydown, and onkeyup attributes.

SCRIPT

Places a script within a document. Examples include JavaScript and VBScript.

Standard/Usage: HTML 3.2   **Widely Supported:** Yes
Empty: No

Sample:

```
<script type="text/javascript">...</script>
```

charset="..."

Specifies character encoding of the data designated by the script. Use the name of a character set defined in RFC2045. The default value for this attribute, appropriate for all Western languages, is ISO-8859-1.

Standard/Usage: HTML 4   **Widely Supported:** No

Sample:

```
<script type="text/javascript" charset="ISO-8859-1">
...</script>
```

defer="defer"

Indicates to the browser that the script does not affect the initial document display, so the script can be processed after the page loads.

Standard/Usage: HTML 4   **Widely Supported:** No

Sample:

```
<script type="text/javascript" defer="defer">...</script>
```

language="..."

Indicates the type of script; deprecated in favor of type="...".

Standard/Usage: HTML 4; deprecated   **Widely Supported:** Yes

Sample:

```
<script language="JavaScript">...</script>
```

‌src="url"

Specifies the relative or absolute location of a script to include in the document.

Standard/Usage: HTML 4   **Widely Supported:** Yes

Sample:

```
<script type="text/javascript"
    src="http://www.example.com/sc/script.js">...</script>
```

type="..."

Indicates the MIME type of the script. This is a preferred alternative to the language element for declaring the type of scripting.

Standard/Usage: HTML 3.2; required   **Widely Supported:** Yes

Sample:

```
<script type="text/javascript">document.write
    ("<em>Great!</em>")</script>
```

SELECT

Specifies a selection list within a form. Use the option element to specify items in the selection list.

Standard/Usage: HTML 2   **Widely Supported:** Yes
Empty: No

Sample:

```
What do you use our product for?<br />
<select multiple="multiple" name="use">
    <option value="1">Pest control</option>
    <option selected="selected" value="2">
     Automotive lubricant</option>
    <option value="3">Preparing pastries</option>
    <option value="4">Other</option>
</select>
```

accesskey="..."

Indicates a keystroke sequence associated with the selection list.

Standard/Usage: Internet Explorer 4   **Widely Supported:** No

Sample:

```
<select name="size" accesskey="s">...</select>
```

class="..."

Indicates which style class applies to the element.

Standard/Usage: HTML 4   **Widely Supported:** Yes

Sample:

```
<select name="color" class="casual">...</select>
```

disabled="disabled"

Denies access to the selection list.

Standard/Usage: HTML 4   **Widely Supported:** No

Sample:

```
<select name="color" disabled="disabled">...</select>
```

id="..."

Assigns a unique ID selector to an instance of the `select` element. When you then assign a style to that ID selector, it affects only that one instance of the `select` element.

Standard/Usage: HTML 3   **Widely Supported:** Yes

Sample:

```
<select id="123" name="salary">...</select>
```

multiple="multiple"

Indicates that a user can select more than one selection list item at the same time.

Standard/Usage: HTML 2   **Widely Supported:** Yes

Sample:

```
<select multiple="multiple">...</select>
```

name="..."

Gives a name to the value you are passing to the form processor. This establishes a name-value pair with which the form processor application can work.

Standard/Usage: HTML 2   **Widely Supported:** Yes

Sample:

```
What is your shoe size?
<select size="4" name="size">
    <option>5</option>
    <option>6</option>
    <option>7</option>
    <option>8</option>
    <option>9</option>
    <option>10</option>
</select>
```

size="n"

Specifies the number of visible items in the selection list. If there are more items in the selection list than are visible, a scroll bar provides access to the other items.

Standard/Usage: HTML 2   **Widely Supported:** Yes

Sample:

```
<select size="3">...</select>
```

style="..."

Specifies style sheet commands that apply to the contents of the select element.

Standard/Usage: HTML 4   **Widely Supported:** Yes

Sample:

```
<select style="background: red" name="color">...</select>
```

tabindex="n"

Indicates where in the tabbing order the selection list is placed.

Standard/Usage: HTML 4   **Widely Supported:** No

Sample:

```
<select name="salary" tabindex="3">...</select>
```

title="..."

Specifies text assigned to the element. You can use this attribute for context-sensitive help within the document. Browsers may use this to show tooltips over the selection list.

Standard/Usage: HTML 4   **Widely Supported:** No

Sample:

```
<select title="select list" name="car">...</select>
```

Other Attributes

The select element also accepts the lang, dir, onfocus, onblur, onchange, onselect, onclick, ondblclick, onmousedown, onmouseup, onmouseover, onmousemove, onmouseout, onkeypress, onkeydown, and onkeyup attributes.

SMALL

Specifies text that should appear in a small font.

Standard/Usage: HTML 3.2   **Widely Supported:** Yes
Empty: No

Sample:

```
<p>Our lawyers said we need to include some fine print:</p>
<p><small>By reading this document, you're breaking the
 rules and will be assessed a $2000 fine.</small></p>
```

class="..."

Indicates which style class applies to the small element.

Standard/Usage: HTML 4   **Widely Supported:** Yes

Sample:

```
<small class="casual">Void where prohibited.</small>
```

id="..."

Assigns a unique ID selector to an instance of the small element. When you then assign a style to that ID selector, it affects only that one instance of the small element.

Standard/Usage: HTML 4   **Widely Supported:** Yes

Sample:

```
<p>Most insects are <small id="123">small</small>.</p>
```

style="..."

Specifies style sheet commands that apply to the contents of the small element.

Standard/Usage: HTML 4   **Widely Supported:** Yes

Sample:

```
<small style="background: red">...</small>
```

title="..."

Specifies text assigned to the element. You can use this attribute for context-sensitive help within the document. Browsers may use this to show tooltips over the text inside the small element.

Standard/Usage: HTML 4   **Widely Supported:** No

Sample:

```
<small title="Legalese">This will subject you to risk of
criminal prosecution.</small>
```

Other Attributes

The small element also accepts the lang, dir, onclick, ondblclick, onmousedown, onmouseup, onmouseover, onmousemove, onmouseout, onkeypress, onkeydown, and onkeyup attributes.

SPACER

A Netscape-specific element that specifies a blank space within the document. We strongly recommend using style sheets or other formatting techniques.

Standard/Usage: Netscape Navigator 3   **Widely Supported:** No
Empty: Yes

Sample:

```
<spacer type="horizontal" size="150" />
Doctors Prefer MediWidget 4 to 1
```

align="left/right/top/texttop/middle/absmib/baseline/bottom/absbottom"

Specifies the alignment of text around the spacer. Used only when
type="block".

> **Standard/Usage:** Netscape Navigator 3   **Widely Supported:** No
>
> **Sample:**

```
<spacer type="block" align="left" />
```

height="n"

Specifies the height of the spacer (in pixels). Used only when type=
"block".

> **Standard/Usage:** Netscape Navigator 3   **Widely Supported:** No
>
> **Sample:**

```
<spacer type="block" height="50" />
<img src="rosebush.jpg" />
```

size="n"

Specifies the dimension of the spacer (in pixels).

> **Standard/Usage:** Netscape Navigator 3   **Widely Supported:** No
>
> **Sample:**

```
<spacer type="horizontal" size="50" />
<img src="rosebush.jpg" />
```

type="horizontal/vertical/block"

Indicates whether the spacer measures from left to right, from top to
bottom, or as a block (acts like a transparent image).

Standard/Usage: Netscape Navigator 3 **Widely Supported:** No

Sample:

```
<p>After you've done this, take a moment to review
your work.<spacer type="vertical" size="400" /></p>
<p>Now, isn't that better?</p>
```

SPAN

Defines an inline section of a document affected by style sheet attributes. Use div to apply styles at the block element level.

Standard/Usage: HTML 4 **Widely Supported:** Yes
Empty: No

Sample:

```
<span style="background: red">...</span>
```

class="..."

Indicates which style class applies to the span element.

Standard/Usage: HTML 4 **Widely Supported:** Yes

Sample:

```
<span class="casual">...</span>
```

id="..."

Assigns a unique ID selector to an instance of the span element. When you then assign a style to that ID selector, it affects only that one instance of the span element.

Standard/Usage: HTML 4 **Widely Supported:** Yes

Sample:

```
<span id="123">...</span>
```

style="..."

Specifies style sheet commands that apply to the contents of the span element.

Standard/Usage: HTML 4   **Widely Supported:** Yes

Sample:

```
<span style="background: red">...</span>
```

title="..."

Specifies text assigned to the element. You can use this attribute for context-sensitive help within the document. Browsers may use this to show tooltips.

Standard/Usage: HTML 4   **Widely Supported:** No

Sample:

```
<span title="section" style="background: red">...</span>
```

Other Attributes

The span element also accepts the lang, dir, onclick, ondblclick, onmousedown, onmouseup, onmouseover, onmousemove, onmouseout, onkeypress, onkeydown, and onkeyup attributes.

STRIKE

Indicates strikethrough text. This element is deprecated in HTML 4 and later in favor of style sheets.

Standard/Usage: HTML 3.2; deprecated   **Widely Supported:** Yes
Empty: No

Sample:

```
My junior high biology teacher was
<strike>sort of</strike> really smart.
```

class="..."

Indicates which style class applies to the strike element.

Standard/Usage: HTML 4   **Widely Supported:** Yes

Sample:

```
<strike class="casual">Truman</strike> lost.
```

id="..."

Assigns a unique ID selector to an instance of the strike element. When you then assign a style to that ID selector, it affects only that one instance of the strike element.

Standard/Usage: HTML 4   **Widely Supported:** Yes

Sample:

```
Don <strike id="123">ain't</strike> isn't coming tonight.
```

style="..."

Specifies style sheet commands that apply to the contents of the strike element.

Standard/Usage: HTML 4   **Widely Supported:** Yes

Sample:

```
<strike style="background: red">...</strike>
```

title="..."

Specifies text assigned to the element. You can use this attribute for context-sensitive help within the document. Browsers may use this to show tooltips over the text.

Standard/Usage: HTML 4   **Widely Supported:** No

Sample:

```
<p>He was <strike title="omit">
ambitious</strike>enthusiastic.</p>
```

Other Attributes

The strike element also accepts the lang, dir, onclick, ondblclick, onmousedown, onmouseup, onmouseover, onmousemove, onmouseout, onkeypress, onkeydown, and onkeyup attributes.

STRONG

Indicates strong emphasis. The browser will probably display the text in a boldface font.

Standard/Usage: HTML 2   **Widely Supported:** Yes
Empty: No

Sample:

```
If you see a poisonous spider in the room then
<strong>get out of there!</strong>
```

class="..."

Indicates which style class applies to the strong element.

Standard/Usage: HTML 4   **Widely Supported:** Yes

Sample:

```
Did you say my dog is
<strong class="urgent">missing?!</strong>
```

id="..."

Assigns a unique ID selector to an instance of the strong element. When you then assign a style to that ID selector, it affects only that one instance of the strong element.

Standard/Usage: HTML 4   **Widely Supported:** Yes

Sample:

```
Sure, you can win at gambling.
But you'll probably <strong id="123">lose</strong>.
```

style="..."

Specifies style sheet commands that apply to the contents of the strong element.

Standard/Usage: HTML 4   **Widely Supported:** Yes

Sample:

```
<strong style="background: red">...</strong>
```

title="..."

Specifies text assigned to the element. You can use this attribute for context-sensitive help within the document. Browsers may use this to show tooltips over the emphasized text.

Standard/Usage: HTML 4   **Widely Supported:** No

Sample:

```
I mean it was <strong title="emphasis">HOT!</strong>
```

Other Attributes

The strong element also accepts the lang, dir, onclick, ondblclick, onmousedown, onmouseup, onmouseover, onmousemove, onmouseout, onkeypress, onkeydown, and onkeyup attributes.

STYLE

Contains style sheet definitions and appears in the document head (see the head element). Place style sheet data within comment markup (<!--...-->) to accommodate browsers that do not support the style element.

Standard/Usage: HTML 3.2   **Widely Supported:** Yes   **Empty:** No

Sample:

```
<html xmlns="http://www.w3.org/1999/xhtml">
   <head>
      <title>Edible Socks: Good or Bad?</title>
      <style type="text/css">
         <!--
            h1    { background: black; color: yellow }
            li dd { background: silver; color: black }
         -->
      </style>
   </head>
```

media="..."

Specifies the destination medium for style information. It may be a single type or a comma-separated list. Media types include the following:

Value	Media Type
all	Applies to all devices.
aural	Speech synthesizer.
braille	Braille tactile feedback devices.
handheld	Handheld devices.

Value	Media Type
print	Traditional printed material and documents on-screen viewed in print preview mode.
projection	Projectors.
screen	Online viewing (default setting).
tty	Teletypes, terminals, or portable devices with limited display capabilities.
tv	Television-type devices.

Standard/Usage: HTML 4   **Widely Supported:** No

Sample:

```
<style type="text/css" media="all">
   <!--
      h1    { background: black; color: white }
      li dd { background: silver; color: darkgreen }
   -->
</style>
```

title="..."

Specifies text assigned to the element. You can use this attribute for context-sensitive help within the document. Browsers may use this to show tooltips, although there's really nothing for them to show the tooltips over.

Standard/Usage: HTML 4   **Widely Supported:** No

Sample:

```
<style title="Stylesheet 1" type="text/css">
   <!--
      h1 { background: black; color: yellow }
      li dd { background: silver; color: black }
   -->
</style>
```

type="..."

Specifies the MIME type of the style sheet specification standard used.

Standard/Usage: HTML 4; required   **Widely Supported:** No

Sample:

```
<style type="text/css">
   <!--
      h1 { background: black; color: white }
      li dd { background: silver; color: darkgreen }
   -->
</style>
```

Other Attributes

The style element also accepts the lang and dir attributes.

SUB

Indicates subscripted text.

Standard/Usage: HTML 3.2   **Widely Supported:** Yes
Empty: No

Sample:

```
<p>Chemists refer to water as H<sub>2</sub>O.</p>
```

class="..."

Indicates which style class applies to the sub element.

Standard/Usage: HTML 4   **Widely Supported:** Yes

Sample:

```
H<sub class="chemical">2</sub>O
```

id="..."

Assigns a unique ID selector to an instance of the sub element. When you then assign a style to that ID selector, it affects only that one instance of the sub element.

Standard/Usage: HTML 4   **Widely Supported:** Yes

Sample:

```
At the dentist I ask for lots of NO<sub id="123">2</sub>.
```

style="..."

Specifies style sheet commands that apply to the contents of the sub element.

> **Standard/Usage:** HTML 4   **Widely Supported:** Yes
>
> **Sample:**
>
> ```
> <sub style="background: red">...</sub>
> ```

title="..."

Specifies text assigned to the element. You can use this attribute for context-sensitive help within the document. Browsers may use this to show tooltips over the subscripted text.

> **Standard/Usage:** HTML 4   **Widely Supported:** No
>
> **Sample:**
>
> ```
> Before he fell asleep, he uttered, "Groovy. "<sub
>     title="Footnote">2</sub>
> ```

Other Attributes

The sub element also accepts the lang, dir, onclick, ondblclick, onmousedown, onmouseup, onmouseover, onmousemove, onmouseout, onkeypress, onkeydown, and onkeyup attributes.

SUP

Indicates superscripted text.

> **Standard/Usage:** HTML 3.2   **Widely Supported:** Yes
> **Empty:** No
>
> **Sample:**
>
> ```
> <p>Einstein's most famous equation is E=mc<sup>2</sup>.</p>
> ```

class="..."

Indicates which style class applies to the sup element.

Standard/Usage: HTML 4   **Widely Supported:** Yes

Sample:

```
z<sup class="exp">2</sup> = x<sup class="exp">2</sup> +
y<sup class="exp">2</sup>
```

id="..."

Assigns a unique ID selector to an instance of the sup element. When you then assign a style to that ID selector, it affects only that one instance of the sup element.

Standard/Usage: HTML 4   **Widely Supported:** Yes

Sample:

```
The Pythagorean theorem says z
<sup id="123">2</sup> = 4 + 16.
```

style="..."

Specifies style sheet commands that apply to the contents of the sup element.

Standard/Usage: HTML 4   **Widely Supported:** Yes

Sample:

```
<sup style="background: red">...</sup>
```

title="..."

Specifies text assigned to the element. You can use this attribute for context-sensitive help within the document. Browsers may use this to show tooltips over the superscripted text.

Standard/Usage: HTML 4   **Widely Supported:** No

Sample:

```
x<sup title="Exponent">2</sup>
```

Other Attributes

The sup element also accepts the lang, dir, onclick, ondblclick, onmousedown, onmouseup, onmouseover, onmousemove, onmouseout, onkeypress, onkeydown, and onkeyup attributes.

TABLE

Specifies a container for a table within your document. Inside these elements you can place tr, td, th, caption, and other table elements.

Standard/Usage: HTML 3.2   **Widely Supported:** Yes
Empty: No

Sample:

```
<table border="0">
    <tr>
        <td><img src="pine.jpg" border="0" alt="pine" /></td>
        <td valign="middle">Pine trees naturally grow at
        higher elevations. They require less water and do
        not shed leaves in the fall.</td>
    </tr>
</table>
```

align="left/right/center"

Positions the table flush left, flush right, or in the center of the window. This attribute is deprecated in favor of style sheets.

Standard/Usage: HTML 3.2; deprecated   **Widely Supported:** Yes

Sample:

```
<table align="center">...</table>
```

background="url"

Specifies the relative or absolute location of an image file loaded as a background image for the entire table.

Standard/Usage: Internet Explorer 3, Netscape Navigator 4; deprecated   **Widely Supported:** No

Sample:

```
<table background="paper.jpg">...</table>
```

bgcolor="#rrggbb" or "..."

Specifies the background color within all table cells in the table. You can substitute color names for the hexadecimal RGB values. This attribute is deprecated in favor of style sheets.

Standard/Usage: HTML 4; deprecated   **Widely Supported:** No

Sample:

```
<table bgcolor="peach">...</table>
```

border="n"

Specifies the thickness (in pixels) of borders around each table cell. Use a value of 0 to produce a table with no visible borders.

Standard/Usage: HTML 3.2   **Widely Supported:** Yes

Sample:

```
<table border="0">...</table>
```

bordercolor="#rrggbb" or "..."

Specifies the color of the borders of all the table cells in the table. You can substitute color names for the hexadecimal RGB values.

Standard/Usage: Internet Explorer 2, Netscape Navigator 4
Widely Supported: No

Sample:

```
<table bordercolor="#3f9a11">...</table>
```

bordercolordark="#rrggbb" or "..."

Specifies the darker color used to draw 3D borders around the table cells. You can substitute color names for the hexadecimal RGB values.

Standard/Usage: Internet Explorer 2   **Widely Supported:** No

Sample:

```
<table bordercolordark="silver">...</table>
```

bordercolorlight="#rrggbb" or "..."

Specifies the lighter color used to draw 3D borders around the table cells. You can substitute color names for the hexadecimal RGB values.

Standard/Usage: Internet Explorer 2   **Widely Supported:** No

Sample:

```
<table bordercolorlight="white">...</table>
```

cellpadding="n"

Specifies the space (in pixels) between the edges of table cells and their contents.

> **Standard/Usage:** HTML 3.2   **Widely Supported:** Yes
>
> **Sample:**
>
> `<table cellpadding="5">...</table>`

cellspacing="n"

Specifies the space (in pixels) between the borders of table cells and the borders of adjacent cells.

> **Standard/Usage:** HTML 3.2   **Widely Supported:** Yes
>
> **Sample:**
>
> `<table border="2" cellspacing="5">...</table>`

class="..."

Indicates which style class applies to the `table` element.

> **Standard/Usage:** HTML 4   **Widely Supported:** Yes
>
> **Sample:**
>
> `<table class="table" border="2">...</table>`

cols="n"

Specifies the number of columns in the table.

> **Standard/Usage:** Internet Explorer 3, Netscape Navigator 4
> **Widely Supported:** No
>
> **Sample:**
>
> `<table border="2" cols="5">...</table>`

frame="void/border/above/below/ hsides/lhs/rhs/vsides/box"

Specifies the external borderlines around the table. For the `frame` attribute to work, set the `border` attribute to a nonzero value.

Value	Specifies
void	No borderlines.
box or border	Borderlines around the entire table (the default).
above	A borderline along the top edge.
below	A borderline along the bottom edge.
hsides	Borderlines along the top and bottom edges.
lhs	A borderline along the left edge.
rhs	A borderline along the right edge.
vsides	Borderlines along the left and right edges.

Standard/Usage: HTML 4   **Widely Supported:** No

Sample:

```
<table border="2" rules="all" frame="vsides">...</table>
```

id="..."

Assigns a unique ID selector to an instance of the table element. When you then assign a style to that ID selector, it affects only that one instance of the table element.

Standard/Usage: HTML 4   **Widely Supported:** Yes

Sample:

```
<table id="123">...</table>
```

rules="none/rows/cols/all/groups"

Specifies where rule lines appear *inside* the table. For the rules attribute to work, set the border attribute to a nonzero value.

Value	Specifies
none	No rule lines.
rows	Rule lines between rows.
cols	Rule lines between columns.
all	All possible rule lines.
groups	Rule lines between the groups defined by the tfoot, thead, tbody, and colgroup elements.

Standard/Usage: HTML 4   **Widely Supported:** No

Sample:

```
<table border="2" rules="all">...</table>
```

style="..."

Specifies style sheet commands that apply to the contents of cells in the table.

Standard/Usage: HTML 4   **Widely Supported:** Yes

Sample:

```
<table style="background: red">...</table>
```

summary="..."

Specifies descriptive text for the table. It's recommended that you use this attribute to summarize or describe the table for use by browsers that do not display tables visually (for example, Braille or text-only browsers).

Standard/Usage: HTML 4   **Widely Supported:** No

Sample:

```
<table summary="This table shows that 50% of sick days are
taken on Mondays. ">...</table>
```

title="..."

Specifies text assigned to the element. You can use this attribute for context-sensitive help within the document. Browsers may use this to show tooltips over the table.

Standard/Usage: HTML 4   **Widely Supported:** No

Sample:

```
<table title="table">...</table>
```

width="n"

Specifies the width of the table. You can set this value to an absolute number of pixels or to a percentage amount so that the table is proportionally as wide as the available space.

Standard/Usage: HTML 3.2   **Widely Supported:** Yes

Sample:

```
<table align="center" width="60%">...</table>
```

Other Attributes

The `table` element also accepts the `lang`, `dir`, `onclick`, `ondblclick`, `onmousedown`, `onmouseup`, `onmouseover`, `onmousemove`, `onmouseout`, `onkeypress`, `onkeydown`, and `onkeyup` attributes.

TBODY

Defines the table body within a table. This element must follow the tfoot element.

> **Standard/Usage:** HTML 4   **Widely Supported:** No
> **Empty:** No

> **Sample:**

```
<table>
    <thead>...</thead>
    <tfoot>...</tfoot>
    <tbody>...</tbody>
</table>
```

align="left/right/center/justify/char"

Specifies how text within the table footer will line up with the edges of the table cells or, if `align="char"`, on a specific character (the decimal point by default).

> **Standard/Usage:** HTML 4   **Widely Supported:** Yes

> **Sample:**

```
<tbody align="left">...</tbody>
```

char="..."

Specifies the character on which cell contents will align if `align="char"`. If you omit the char attribute, the default value is the decimal point in the specified language.

> **Standard/Usage:** HTML 4   **Widely Supported:** No

> **Sample:**

```
<tbody align="left" char="a">...</tbody>
```

charoff="n"

Specifies the number of characters from the left at which the alignment character appears.

> **Standard/Usage:** HTML 4   **Widely Supported:** No
>
> **Sample:**
>
> ```
> <tbody align="char" char="," charoff="7">...</tbody>
> ```

class="..."

Indicates which style class applies to the tbody element.

> **Standard/Usage:** HTML 4   **Widely Supported:** Yes
>
> **Sample:**
>
> ```
> <tbody class="casual">...</tbody>
> ```

id="..."

Assigns a unique ID selector to an instance of the tbody element. When you then assign a style to that ID selector, it affects only that one instance of the tbody element.

> **Standard/Usage:** HTML 4   **Widely Supported:** Yes
>
> **Sample:**
>
> ```
> <tbody id="123"></tbody>
> ```

style="..."

Specifies style sheet commands that apply to the contents of the tbody element.

> **Standard/Usage:** HTML 4   **Widely Supported:** Yes
>
> **Sample:**
>
> ```
> <tbody style="background: red">...</tbody>
> ```

title="..."

Specifies text assigned to the element. You can use this attribute for context-sensitive help within the document. Browsers may use this to show tooltips over the table body.

Standard/Usage: HTML 4   **Widely Supported:** No

Sample:

```
<tbody title="Table Body">...</tbody>
```

valign="top/bottom/middle/baseline"

Specifies the vertical alignment of the contents of the table body.

Standard/Usage: Internet Explorer 4   **Widely Supported:** No

Sample:

```
<tbody valign="middle">...</tbody>
```

Other Attributes

The tbody element also accepts the lang, dir, onclick, ondblclick, onmousedown, onmouseup, onmouseover, onmousemove, onmouseout, onkeypress, onkeydown, and onkeyup attributes.

TD

Contains a table cell. These elements go inside tr elements.

Standard/Usage: HTML 3.2   **Widely Supported:** Yes
Empty: No

Sample:

```
<tr>
   <td>Bob Jones</td>
   <td>555-1212</td> <td>Democrat</td>
</tr>
```

abbr="..."

Specifies short replacement text associated with the element contents. When appropriate, browsers may use this text in place of the actual contents.

Standard/Usage: HTML 4   **Widely Supported:** No

Sample:

```
<td title="Year to Date Summary" abbr="ytd">
Year to Date</td>
```

axis="..."

Specifies cell categories. The values can be a comma-separated list of category names.

> **Standard/Usage:** HTML 4   **Widely Supported:** No
>
> **Sample:**
>
> ```
> <td axis="TV">Television</td>
> ```

align="left/right/center/justify/char"

Specifies how text within the table header will line up with the edges of the table cells or, if align="char", on a specific character (the decimal point by default).

> **Standard/Usage:** HTML 4   **Widely Supported:** Yes
>
> **Sample:**
>
> ```
> <tr>
>     <td align="center">Television</td>
>     <td><img src="tv.gif" alt="TV" border="0" /></td>
> </tr>
> ```

background="url"

Specifies the relative or absolute location of an image file for the browser to load as a background graphic for the table cell.

> **Standard/Usage:** Internet Explorer 4, Netscape Navigator 3
> **Widely Supported:** No
>
> **Sample:**
>
> ```
> <td background="waves.gif">Oceanography</td>
> ```

bgcolor="#rrggbb" or "..."

Specifies the background color inside a table cell. You can substitute the hexadecimal RGB values for the appropriate color names. This attribute is deprecated in favor of style sheets.

> **Standard/Usage:** HTML 4; deprecated   **Widely Supported:** No
>
> **Sample:**
>
> ```
> <td bgcolor="pink">Course Number</td>
> ```

bordercolor="#rrggbb" or "..."

Indicates the color of the border of the table cell. You can specify the color with hexadecimal RGB values or by the color name.

Standard/Usage: Internet Explorer 2   **Widely Supported:** No

Sample:

```
<td bordercolor="blue">Time Taught</td>
```

bordercolordark="#rrggbb" or "..."

Indicates the darker color used to form 3D borders around the table cell. You can specify the color with its hexadecimal RGB values or with its color name.

Standard/Usage: Internet Explorer 2   **Widely Supported:** No

Sample:

```
<td bordercolorlight="#ffffff" bordercolordark="#88aa2c">
...</td>
```

bordercolorlight="#rrggbb" or "..."

Indicates the lighter color used to form 3D borders around the table cell. You can specify the color with its hexadecimal RGB values or with its color name.

Standard/Usage: Internet Explorer 2   **Widely Supported:** No

Sample:

```
<td bordercolorlight="#ffffff" bordercolordark="#88aa2c">
...</td>
```

char="..."

Specifies the character on which cell contents will align if `align="char"`. If you omit the `char` attribute, the default value is the decimal point in the specified language.

Standard/Usage: HTML 4   **Widely Supported:** No

Sample:

```
<td align="char" char=",">...</td>
```

charoff="n"

Specifies the number of characters from the left at which the alignment character appears.

Standard/Usage: HTML 4   **Widely Supported:** No

Sample:

```
<td align="char" char="," charoff="7">...</td>
```

class="..."

Indicates which style class applies to the td element.

Standard/Usage: HTML 4   **Widely Supported:** Yes

Sample:

```
<td class="casual">Jobs Produced</td>
```

colspan="n"

Specifies that a table cell occupies more columns than the default of 1. This is useful when you have a category name that applies to multiple columns of data.

Standard/Usage: HTML 3.2   **Widely Supported:** Yes

Sample:

```
<tr>
   <td colspan="2">Students</td>
</tr>
<tr>
   <td>Bob Smith</td>
   <td>Jane Doe</td>
</tr>
```

id="..."

Assigns a unique ID selector to an instance of the td element. When you then assign a style to that ID selector, it affects only that one instance of the td element.

Standard/Usage: HTML 4   **Widely Supported:** Yes

Sample:

```
<td id="123">...</td>
```

headers="..."

Specifies the ID names of table header cells associated with the current cell for use by browsers in presenting the table contents.

Standard/Usage: HTML 4   **Widely Supported:** No

Sample:

```
<td title="Year to Date Summary" headers="th1,th4">
Year to Date</td>
```

height="n"

Specifies the vertical dimension (in pixels) of the cell. This attribute is deprecated in favor of style sheets.

Standard/Usage: HTML 3.2; deprecated   **Widely Supported:** No

Sample:

```
<td title="Year to Date Summary" height="200">
Year to Date</td>
```

nowrap="nowrap"

Disables the default word-wrapping within a table cell, thus maximizing the amount of the cell's horizontal space. This attribute is deprecated in favor of style sheets.

Standard/Usage: HTML 3; deprecated   **Widely Supported:** No

Sample:

```
<td nowrap="nowrap">
The contents of this cell will not wrap at all.</td>
```

rowspan="n"

Specifies that a table cell occupies more rows than the default of 1. This is useful when several rows of information are related to one category.

Standard/Usage: HTML 3.2   **Widely Supported:** Yes

Sample:

```
<tr>
   <td valign="middle" align="right" rowspan="3">
   Pie Entries</td>
```

```
    <td>Banana Cream</td>
    <td>Mrs. Robinson</td></tr>
<tr>
    <td>Strawberry Cheesecake</td>
    <td>Mr. Barton</td></tr>
<tr>
    <td>German Chocolate</td>
    <td>Ms. Larson</td></tr>
```

scope="row/col/rowgroup/colgroup"

Specifies the row, row group, column, or column group to which the specific header information contained in the current cell applies. When appropriate, browsers may use this information to help present the table.

Standard/Usage: HTML 4   **Widely Supported:** No

Sample:

```
<td title="Year to Date Summary" scope="rowgroup">
Year to Date</td>
```

style="..."

Specifies style sheet commands that apply to the contents of the table cell.

Standard/Usage: HTML 4   **Widely Supported:** Yes

Sample:

```
<td style="background: red">...</td>
```

title="..."

Specifies text assigned to the element. You can use this attribute for context-sensitive help within the document. Browsers may use this to show tooltips over the table header.

Standard/Usage: HTML 4   **Widely Supported:** No

Sample:

```
<td title="table cell heading">...</td>
```

valign="top/middle/bottom/baseline"

Aligns the contents of a cell within the cell.

Standard/Usage: HTML 3.2   **Widely Supported:** Yes

Sample:

```
<td valign="top"><img src="images/bud.gif"
alt="bud.gif" border="0" /></td>
```

width="n"

Specifies the horizontal dimension of the cell in pixels or as a percentage of the table width. This attribute is deprecated in favor of style sheets.

Standard/Usage: HTML 3.2; deprecated   **Widely Supported:** Yes

Sample:

```
<td width="200" align="left">African Species</td>
```

Other Attributes

The td element also accepts the lang, dir, onclick, ondblclick, onmousedown, onmouseup, onmouseover, onmousemove, onmouseout, onkeypress, onkeydown, and onkeyup attributes.

TEXTAREA

Defines a multiple-line text input field within a form. Place the textarea elements inside the form elements. To specify a default value in a textarea field, place the text between the textarea elements.

Standard/Usage: HTML 2   **Widely Supported:** Yes   **Empty:** No

Sample:

```
Enter any comments here:
<textarea name="comments" cols="40" rows="5">
No Comments.</textarea>
```

accesskey="..."

Assigns a keystroke sequence to the textarea element.

Standard/Usage: HTML 4   **Widely Supported:** No

Sample:

```
<textarea cols="40" rows="10" name="story" accesskey="s">
...</textarea>
```

class="..."

Indicates which style class applies to the textarea element.

Standard/Usage: HTML 4   **Widely Supported:** Yes

Sample:

```
<textarea cols="50" rows="3" class="casual">...</textarea>
```

cols="n"

Indicates the width (in characters) of the text input field.

Standard/Usage: HTML 2; required   **Widely Supported:** Yes

Sample:

```
<textarea name="desc" cols="50" rows="3">...</textarea>
```

disabled="disabled"

Denies access to the text input field.

Standard/Usage: HTML 4   **Widely Supported:** No

Sample:

```
<textarea rows="10" cols="10" name="comments"
disabled="disabled">...</textarea>
```

id="..."

Assigns a unique ID selector to an instance of the textarea element. When you then assign a style to that ID selector, it affects only that one instance of the textarea element.

Standard/Usage: HTML 4   **Widely Supported:** Yes

Sample:

```
<textarea rows="10" cols="10" id="123">...</textarea>
```

name="..."

Names the value you pass to the form processor. For example, if you collect personal feedback, assign the name attribute something like comments. This establishes a name-value pair with which the form processor can work.

Standard/Usage: HTML 2   **Widely Supported:** Yes

Sample:

```
<textarea cols="30" rows="10" name="comments">...</textarea>
```

readonly="readonly"

Specifies that the user cannot change the contents of the text input field.

Standard/Usage: HTML 4   **Widely Supported:** No

Sample:

```
<textarea rows="10" cols="10" name="notes"
    readonly="readonly">...</textarea>
```

rows="n"

Indicates the height (in lines of text) of the text input field.

Standard/Usage: HTML 2; required   **Widely Supported:** Yes

Sample:

```
<textarea name="desc" cols="50" rows="3">...</textarea>
```

style="..."

Specifies style sheet commands that apply to the textarea element.

Standard/Usage: HTML 4   **Widely Supported:** Yes

Sample:

```
<textarea rows="5" cols="40" style="background: red">
...</textarea>
```

tabindex="n"

Indicates where textarea appears in the tabbing order.

Standard/Usage: HTML 4   **Widely Supported:** No

Sample:

```
<textarea rows="5" cols="40" name="story" tabindex="2">
...</textarea>
```

title="..."

Specifies text assigned to the element. You can use this attribute for context-sensitive help within the document. Browsers may use this to show tooltips over the text entry input method.

Standard/Usage: HTML 4   **Widely Supported:** No

Sample:

```
<textarea cols="10" rows="2" name="tt"
 title="text entry box">...</textarea>
```

Other Attributes

The `textarea` element also accepts the `lang`, `dir`, `onfocus`, `onblur`, `onchange`, `onselect`, `onclick`, `ondblclick`, `onmousedown`, `onmouseup`, `onmouseover`, `onmousemove`, `onmouseout`, `onkeypress`, `onkeydown`, and `onkeyup` attributes.

TFOOT

Defines a table footer within a table. It must *precede* the tbody element.

Standard/Usage: HTML 4   **Widely Supported:** No   **Empty:** No

Sample:

```
<table>
    <thead>...</thead>
    <tfoot>
        <tr><td>Totals</td><td>$100.25</td></tr>
    </tfoot>
    <tbody>...</tbody>
</table>
```

align="left/right/center/justify/char"

Specifies how text within the table footer will line up with the edges of the table cells or, if `align="char"`, on a specific character.

Standard/Usage: HTML 4   **Widely Supported:** Yes

Sample:

```
<tfoot align="center">...</tfoot>
```

char="..."

Specifies the character on which cell contents will align if align="char". If you omit the char attribute, the default value is the decimal point in the specified language.

Standard/Usage: HTML 4   **Widely Supported:** No

Sample:

```
<tfoot align="char" char=",">...</tfoot>
```

charoff="n"

Specifies the number of characters from the left at which the alignment character appears.

Standard/Usage: HTML 4   **Widely Supported:** No

Sample:

```
<tfoot align="char" char="," charoff="7">...</tfoot>
```

class="..."

Indicates which style class applies to the tfoot element.

Standard/Usage: HTML 4   **Widely Supported:** Yes

Sample:

```
<tfoot class="casual">...</tfoot>
```

id="..."

Assigns a unique ID selector to an instance of the tfoot element. When you then assign a style to that ID selector, it affects only that one instance of the tfoot element.

Standard/Usage: HTML 4   **Widely Supported:** Yes

Sample:

```
<tfoot id="123">...</tfoot>
```

style="..."

Specifies style sheet commands that apply to the contents of the tfoot element.

Standard/Usage: HTML 4   **Widely Supported:** Yes

Sample:

```
<tfoot style="background: red">...</tfoot>
```

title="..."

Specifies text assigned to the element. You can use this attribute for context-sensitive help within the document. Browsers may use this to show tooltips over the table footer.

Standard/Usage: HTML 4   **Widely Supported:** No

Sample:

```
<tfoot title="Table Footer">...</tfoot>
```

valign="top/bottom/middle/baseline"

Aligns the contents of the table footer with the top, bottom, or middle of the footer container.

Standard/Usage: HTML 4   **Widely Supported:** No

Sample:

```
<tfoot align="center" valign="top">...</tfoot>
```

Other Attributes

The tfoot element also accepts the lang, dir, onclick, ondblclick, onmousedown, onmouseup, onmouseover, onmousemove, onmouseout, onkeypress, onkeydown, and onkeyup attributes.

TH

Contains table cell headings. The th element is identical to the td element except that text inside th usually is emphasized with boldface font, centered within the cell, and represents a table heading instead of table data.

Standard/Usage: HTML 3.2   **Widely Supported:** Yes
Empty: No

Sample:

```
<table>
    <tr>
        <th>Name</th>
        <th>Phone No.</th>
    </tr>
```

```
    <tr>
        <td>Jane Doe</td>
        <td>555-1212</td>
    </tr>
    <tr>
        <td>Bob Smith</td>
        <td>555-2121</td>
    </tr>
</table>
```

abbr="..."

Specifies short replacement text associated with the element contents. When appropriate, browsers may use this text in place of the actual contents.

Standard/Usage: HTML 4   **Widely Supported:** No

Sample:

```
<th title="Year to Date Summary" abbr="ytd">
Year to Date</th>
```

align="left/right/center/justify/char"

Specifies how text within the table header will line up with the edges of the table cells or, if align="char", on a specific character (by default, the decimal point).

Standard/Usage: HTML 4   **Widely Supported:** Yes

Sample:

```
<th align="right">Television</th>
<th align="left">
<img src="tv.gif" alt="tv" border="0" /></th>
```

axis="..."

Specifies cell categories. The value can be a comma-separated list of category names.

Standard/Usage: HTML 4   **Widely Supported:** No

Sample:

```
<th axis="TV">Television</th>
```

background="url"

Specifies the relative or absolute location of an image file for the browser to load as a background graphic for the table cell.

Standard/Usage: Internet Explorer 4, Netscape Navigator 3
Widely Supported: Yes

Sample:

```
<th background="waves.gif">Oceanography</th>
```

bgcolor="#rrggbb" or "..."

Specifies the background color inside a table cell. You can substitute the hexadecimal RGB values for the appropriate color names. This attribute is deprecated in favor of style sheets.

Standard/Usage: HTML 4; deprecated   **Widely Supported:** Yes

Sample:

```
<th bgcolor="pink">Course Number</th>
```

bordercolor="#rrggbb" or "..."

Indicates the color of the border of the table cell. You can specify the color with hexadecimal RGB values or by the color name.

Standard/Usage: Internet Explorer 2   **Widely Supported:** Yes

Sample:

```
<th bordercolor="blue">Time Taught</th>
```

bordercolordark="#rrggbb" or "..."

Indicates the darker color used to form 3D borders around the table cell. You can specify the color with its hexadecimal RGB values or with its color name.

Standard/Usage: Internet Explorer 2   **Widely Supported:** No

Sample:

```
<th bordercolorlight="#ffffff" bordercolordark="#88aa2c">
...</th>
```

bordercolorlight="#rrggbb" or "..."

Indicates the lighter color used to form 3D borders around the table cell. You can specify the color with its hexadecimal RGB values or with its color name.

Standard/Usage: Internet Explorer 2   **Widely Supported:** No

Sample:

```
<th bordercolorlight="#ffffff" bordercolordark="#88aa2c">
...</th>
```

char="..."

Specifies the character on which cell contents align if align="char". If you omit the char attribute, the default value is the decimal point in the specified language.

Standard/Usage: HTML 4   **Widely Supported:** No

Sample:

```
<th align="char" char=",">...</th>
```

charoff="n"

Specifies the number of characters from the left at which the alignment character appears.

Standard/Usage: HTML 4   **Widely Supported:** No

Sample:

```
<th align="char" char="," charoff="7">...</th>
```

class="..."

Indicates which style class applies to the th element.

Standard/Usage: HTML 4   **Widely Supported:** Yes

Sample:

```
<th class="casual">Jobs Produced</th>
```

colspan="n"

Specifies that a table header cell occupies more columns than the default of 1. Use this, for example, if a category name applies to more than one column of data.

Standard/Usage: HTML 3.2   **Widely Supported:** Yes

Sample:

```
<tr>
    <th colspan="2">Students</th>
</tr>
<tr>
    <td>Bob Smith</td>
    <td>Jane Doe</td>
</tr>
```

height="n"

Specifies the vertical dimension (in pixels) of the cell. This attribute is deprecated in favor of style sheets.

Standard/Usage: HTML 3.2; deprecated   **Widely Supported:** No

Sample:

```
<th title="Year to Date Summary" height="200">
Year to Date</th>
```

id="..."

Assigns a unique ID selector to an instance of the th element. When you then assign a style to that ID selector, it affects only that one instance of the th element.

Standard/Usage: HTML 4   **Widely Supported:** Yes

Sample:

```
<th id="123">...</th>
```

headers="..."

Specifies the ID names of table header cells associated with the current cell for use by browsers in presenting the table contents.

Standard/Usage: HTML 4   **Widely Supported:** No

Sample:

```
<th title="Year to Date Summary" headers="th1,th4">
Year to Date</th>
```

nowrap="nowrap"

Disables default word wrapping within a table cell, maximizing the cell's horizontal space. This attribute is deprecated in favor of style sheets.

Standard/Usage: HTML 4; deprecated   **Widely Supported:** No

Sample:

```
<th nowrap="nowrap">
The contents of this cell will not wrap at all.</th>
```

rowspan="n"

Specifies that a table header cell occupies more rows than the default of 1. This is useful if several rows of information relate to one category.

Standard/Usage: HTML 3.2   **Widely Supported:** Yes

Sample:

```
<tr>
    <th valign="middle" align="right" rowspan="3">
     Pie Entries</th>
    <td>Banana Cream</td>
    <td>Mrs. Robinson</td></tr>
<tr>
    <td>Strawberry Cheesecake</td>
    <td>Mr. Barton</td></tr>
<tr>
    <td>German Chocolate</td>
    <td>Ms. Larson</td></tr>
```

scope="row/col/rowgroup/colgroup"

Specifies the row, row group, column, or column group to which the specific header information contained in the current cell applies. When appropriate, browsers may use this information to help present the table.

Standard/Usage: HTML 4   **Widely Supported:** No

Sample:

```
<th title="Year to Date Summary" scope="rowgroup">
Year to Date</th>
```

style="..."

Specifies style sheet commands that apply to the contents of the table header.

> **Standard/Usage:** HTML 4   **Widely Supported:** Yes
>
> **Sample:**
>
> ```
> <th style="background: red">...</th>
> ```

title="..."

Specifies text assigned to the element. You can use this attribute for context-sensitive help within the document. Browsers may use this to show tooltips over the table header.

> **Standard/Usage:** HTML 4   **Widely Supported:** No
>
> **Sample:**
>
> ```
> <th title="Table Cell Heading">...</th>
> ```

valign="top/middle/bottom/baseline"

Aligns the contents of a cell within the cell.

> **Standard/Usage:** HTML 3.2   **Widely Supported:** Yes
>
> **Sample:**
>
> ```
> <th valign="top">
> <img src="images/bud.gif alt="bud.gif" border="0" /></th>
> ```

width="n"

Specifies the horizontal dimension of the cell in pixels or as a percentage of the table width. This attribute is deprecated in favor of style sheets.

> **Standard/Usage:** HTML 3.2; deprecated   **Widely Supported:** Yes
>
> **Sample:**
>
> ```
> <th width="200" align="left">African Species</th>
> ```

Other Attributes

The th element also accepts the lang, dir, onclick, ondblclick, onmousedown, onmouseup, onmouseover, onmousemove, onmouseout, onkeypress, onkeydown, and onkeyup attributes.

THEAD

Defines a table header section. At least one table row must go within thead.

Standard/Usage: HTML 4   **Widely Supported:** No
Empty: No

Sample:

```
<table rules="rows">
   <thead>
      <tr><td>Column 1</td><td>Column 2</td></tr>
   </thead>
</table>
```

align="left/right/center/justify/char"

Specifies how text within the table header will line up with the edges of the table cells or, if align="char", on a specific character (by default, the decimal point).

Standard/Usage: HTML 4   **Widely Supported:** Yes

Sample:

```
<thead align="center">
   <tr>
      <th>Television</th>
      <th>Radio</th>
   </tr>
</thead>
```

char="..."

Specifies the character on which cell contents align if align="char". If you omit the char attribute, the default value is the decimal point in the specified language.

Standard/Usage: HTML 4   **Widely Supported:** No

Sample:

```
<thead align="char" char=",">...</thead>
```

charoff="n"

Specifies the number of characters from the left at which the alignment character appears.

Standard/Usage: HTML 4   **Widely Supported:** No

Sample:

```
<thead align="char" char="," charoff="7">...</thead>
```

class="..."

Indicates which style class applies to the thead element.

Standard/Usage: HTML 4   **Widely Supported:** Yes

Sample:

```
<thead class="casual">...</thead>
```

id="..."

Assigns a unique ID selector to an instance of the thead element. When you then assign a style to that ID selector, it affects only that one instance of the thead element.

Standard/Usage: HTML 4   **Widely Supported:** No

Sample:

```
<thead id="123">...</thead>
```

style="..."

Specifies style sheet commands that apply to the contents of the thead element.

Standard/Usage: HTML 4   **Widely Supported:** Yes

Sample:

```
<thead style="background: red">...</thead>
```

title="..."

Specifies text assigned to the element. You can use this attribute for context-sensitive help within the document. Browsers may use this to show tooltips over the table head.

Standard/Usage: HTML 4   **Widely Supported:** No

Sample:

```
<thead title="table heading">...</thead>
```

valign="top/middle/bottom/baseline"

Aligns the contents of the table header with respect to the top and bottom edges of the header container.

Standard/Usage: HTML 4   **Widely Supported:** No

Sample:

```
<thead align="left" valign="top">...</thead>
```

Other Attributes

The thead element also accepts the lang, dir, onclick, ondblclick, onmousedown, onmouseup, onmouseover, onmousemove, onmouseout, onkeypress, onkeydown, and onkeyup attributes.

TITLE

Gives the document an official title. The title element appears in the document header inside the head element and is required for valid XHTML.

Standard/Usage: HTML 2; required   **Widely Supported:** Yes
Empty: No

Sample:

```
<head><title>How To Build a Go-Cart</title>...</head>
```

Other Attributes

This element accepts the lang and dir attributes.

TR

Contains a row of cells in a table. You must place the `tr` elements inside the `table` container, which can contain `th` and `td` elements.

Standard/Usage: HTML 3.2   **Widely Supported:** Yes
Empty: No

Sample:

```
<table>
   <tr>
      <th colspan="3">Test Scores</th></tr>
   <tr>
      <td>Bob Smith</td>
      <td>78</td>
      <td>85</td></tr>
   <tr>
      <td>Jane Doe</td>
      <td>87</td>
      <td>75</td></tr>
</table>
```

align="left/right/center/justify/char"

Specifies how text within the table row will line up with the edges of the table cells or, if `align="char"`, on a specific character (by default, the decimal point).

Standard/Usage: HTML 4   **Widely Supported:** Yes

Sample:

```
<tr align="center">
   <td>Television</td>
   <td>Internet</td>
</tr>
```

bgcolor="#rrggbb" or "..."

Specifies the background color of table cells in the row. You can substitute the color names for the hexadecimal RGB values. This attribute is deprecated in favor of style sheets.

Standard/Usage: HTML 4; deprecated   **Widely Supported:** No

Sample:

```
<tr bgcolor="yellow">
   <td><img src="bette.jpg" alt="bette" border="0" /></td>
   <td align="left" valign="middle">
    Bette Smith sitting at her desk.</td>
</tr>
```

bordercolor="#rrggbb" or "…"

Specifies the color of cell borders within the row. Only Internet Explorer supports this attribute. You can substitute color names for the hexadecimal RGB values.

Standard/Usage: Internet Explorer 2   **Widely Supported:** No

Sample:

```
<tr bordercolor="#3F2A55">
   <td align="right" valign="middle">Computers</td>
   <td><img src="computers.jpg" /></td>
</tr>
```

bordercolordark="#rrggbb" or "…"

Indicates the darker color for the 3D borders around the table row. You can specify the color with its hexadecimal RGB values or with its color name.

Standard/Usage: Internet Explorer 2   **Widely Supported:** No

Sample:

```
<tr bordercolorlight="silver" bordercolordark="black">...</tr>
```

bordercolorlight="#rrggbb" or "…"

Indicates the lighter color for 3D borders around the table row. You can specify the color with its hexadecimal RGB values or with its color name.

Standard/Usage: Internet Explorer 2   **Widely Supported:** No

Sample:

```
<tr bordercolorlight="silver" bordercolordark="black">...</tr>
```

char="..."

Specifies the character on which cell contents align if align="char". If you omit the char attribute, the default value is the decimal point in the specified language.

> **Standard/Usage:** HTML 4   **Widely Supported:** No
>
> **Sample:**
>
> ```
> <tr align="char" char=",">...</tr>
> ```

charoff="n"

Specifies the number of characters from the left at which the alignment character appears.

> **Standard/Usage:** HTML 4   **Widely Supported:** No
>
> **Sample:**
>
> ```
> <tr align="char" char="," charoff="7">...</tr>
> ```

class="..."

Indicates which style class applies to the tr element.

> **Standard/Usage:** HTML 4   **Widely Supported:** Yes
>
> **Sample:**
>
> ```
> <tr class="elementary">
>    <td>Uranium</td>
>    <td>Plutonium</td>
>    <td>Radon</td>
> </tr>
> ```

id="..."

Assigns a unique ID selector to an instance of the tr element. When you then assign a style to that ID selector, it affects only that one instance of the tr element.

> **Standard/Usage:** HTML 4   **Widely Supported:** Yes
>
> **Sample:**
>
> ```
> <tr id="123">...</tr>
> ```

style="..."

Specifies style sheet commands that apply to all cells in the table row.

Standard/Usage: HTML 4   **Widely Supported:** Yes

Sample:

```
<tr style="background: red">...</tr>
```

title="..."

Specifies text assigned to the element. You can use this attribute for context-sensitive help within the document. Browsers may use this to show tooltips.

Standard/Usage: HTML 4   **Widely Supported:** No

Sample:

```
<tr title="table row">...</tr>
```

valign="top/middle/bottom/baseline"

Specifies the vertical alignment of the contents of all cells within the row.

Standard/Usage: HTML 3.2   **Widely Supported:** Yes

Sample:

```
<tr valign="top">
    <td align="center">Jane Smith</td>
    <td align="center">Bob Doe</td>
</tr>
```

Other Attributes

The tr element also accepts the lang, dir, onclick, ondblclick, onmousedown, onmouseup, onmouseover, onmousemove, onmouseout, onkeypress, onkeydown, and onkeyup attributes.

TT

Displays text in a monospace font.

Standard/Usage: HTML 2   **Widely Supported:** Yes
Empty: No

Sample:

```
After I typed help, the words
<tt>help: not found</tt> appeared on my screen.
```

class="..."

Indicates which style class applies to the tt element.

Standard/Usage: HTML 4   **Widely Supported:** Yes

Sample:

```
<p>I began to type.
<tt class="casual">It was a dark and stormy night.</tt></p>
```

id="..."

Assigns a unique ID selector to an instance of the tt element. When you then assign a style to that ID selector, it affects only that one instance of the tt element.

Standard/Usage: HTML 4   **Widely Supported:** Yes

Sample:

```
<tt id="123">...</tt>
```

style="..."

Specifies style sheet commands that apply to the contents of the tt elements.

Standard/Usage: HTML 4   **Widely Supported:** Yes

Sample:

```
<tt style="background: red">...</tt>
```

title="..."

Specifies text assigned to the element. You can use this attribute for context-sensitive help within the document. Browsers may use this to show tooltips over the text within the tt elements.

Standard/Usage: HTML 4   **Widely Supported:** No

Sample:

```
<p>Now, type <tt title="user typing">mail</tt>
and hit the <kbd>Enter</kbd> key.</p>
```

Other Attributes

The tt element also accepts the lang, dir, onclick, ondblclick, onmousedown, onmouseup, onmouseover, onmousemove, onmouseout, onkeypress, onkeydown, and onkeyup attributes.

U

Underlines text in a document. Use this element in moderation; underlined text can confuse users because they're accustomed to seeing hyperlinks underlined. This element is deprecated in HTML 4 and later in favor of style sheets.

Standard/Usage: HTML 2; deprecated   **Widely Supported:** Yes
Empty: No

Sample:

```
After waterskiing, I was <u>really</u> tired.
```

class="..."

Indicates which style class applies to the u element.

Standard/Usage: HTML 4   **Widely Supported:** Yes

Sample:

```
Have you seen <u class="casual">Tomb Raider</u> yet?
```

id="..."

Assigns a unique ID selector to an instance of the u element. When you then assign a style to that ID selector, it affects only that one instance of the u element.

Standard/Usage: HTML 4   **Widely Supported:** Yes

Sample:

```
<u id="123">...</u>
```

style="..."

Specifies style sheet commands that apply to the contents of the u element.

Standard/Usage: HTML 4   **Widely Supported:** Yes

Sample:

```
<u style="background: red">...</u>
```

title="..."

Specifies text assigned to the element. You can use this attribute for context-sensitive help within the document. Browsers may use this to show tooltips over the underlined text.

Standard/Usage: HTML 4   **Widely Supported:** No

Sample:

```
<p>Read the book <u title="BookTitle">Walden</u>
and you'll be enlightened.</p>
```

Other Attributes

The u element also accepts the lang, dir, onclick, ondblclick, onmousedown, onmouseup, onmouseover, onmousemove, onmouseout, onkeypress, onkeydown, and onkeyup attributes.

UL

Contains a bulleted (unordered) list. You then use the li (list item) element to add bulleted items to the list.

Standard/Usage: HTML 2   **Widely Supported:** Yes
Empty: No

Sample:

```
Before you can begin, you need:
<ul>
   <li>Circular saw</li>
   <li>Drill with Phillips bit</li>
   <li>Wood screws</li>
</ul>
```

class="..."

Indicates which style class applies to the ul element. Use li elements within the ul element.

Standard/Usage: HTML 4   **Widely Supported:** Yes

Sample:

```
<ul class="casual">...</ul>
```

compact="compact"

Indicates that the unordered list appears in a compact format. This attribute may not affect the appearance of the list because most browsers do not present lists in more than one format. This attribute is deprecated in HTML 4 and later.

Standard/Usage: HTML 2; deprecated   **Widely Supported:** No

Sample:

```
<ul compact="compact">...</ul>
```

id="..."

Assigns a unique ID selector to an instance of the ul element. When you then assign a style to that ID selector, it affects only that one instance of the ul element.

Standard/Usage: HTML 4   **Widely Supported:** Yes

Sample:

```
<ul id="123">...</ul>
```

style="..."

Specifies style sheet commands that apply to the contents of the unordered list.

Standard/Usage: HTML 4   **Widely Supported:** Yes

Sample:

```
<ul style="background: red">...</ul>
```

title="..."

Specifies text assigned to the element. You can use this attribute for context-sensitive help within the document. Browsers may use this to show tooltips over the unordered list.

Standard/Usage: HTML 4   **Widely Supported:** No

Sample:

```
<ul title="Food List">
   <li>Spaghetti</li>
   <li>Pizza</li>
   <li>Fettuccini Alfredo</li>
</ul>
```

type="square/circle/disc"

Specifies the bullet type for each unordered list item. If you omit the type attribute, the browser chooses a default type.

Standard/Usage: HTML 2; deprecated   **Widely Supported:** Yes

Sample:

```
<ul type="disc">
   <li>Spaghetti</li>
   <ul type="square">
      <li>Noodles</li>
      <li>Sauce</li>
      <li>Cheese</li>
   </ul>
</ul>
```

Other Attributes

The ul element also accepts the lang, dir, onclick, ondblclick, onmousedown, onmouseup, onmouseover, onmousemove, onmouseout, onkeypress, onkeydown, and onkeyup attributes.

VAR

Indicates a placeholder variable in document text. This is useful when describing commands for which the user must supply a parameter.

Standard/Usage: HTML 2   **Widely Supported:** Yes
Empty: No

Sample:

```
To copy a file in DOS, type <samp>COPY <var>file1</var>
   <var>file2</var></samp>
   and press the Enter key.
```

class="..."

Indicates which style class applies to the var element.

Standard/Usage: HTML 4   **Widely Supported:** Yes

Sample:

```
<p>I, <var class="casual">your name</var>, solemnly swear
to tell the truth.</p>
```

id="..."

Assigns a unique ID selector to an instance of the var element. When you then assign a style to that ID selector, it affects only that one instance of the var element.

Standard/Usage: HTML 4   **Widely Supported:** Yes

Sample:

```
<var id="123">...</var>
```

style="..."

Specifies style sheet commands that apply to the contents of the var element.

Standard/Usage: HTML 4   **Widely Supported:** Yes

Sample:

```
<var style="background: red">...</var>
```

title="..."

Specifies text assigned to the element. You can use this attribute for context-sensitive help within the document. Browsers may use this to show tooltips over the text within the var elements.

Standard/Usage: HTML 4   **Widely Supported:** No

Sample:

```
Use an <code>h</code>
<var title="Heading level number">n</var> element.
```

Other Attributes

The var element also accepts the lang, dir, onclick, ondblclick, onmousedown, onmouseup, onmouseover, onmousemove, onmouseout, onkeypress, onkeydown, and onkeyup attributes.

WBR

Forces a word break. This is useful in combination with the nobr element to permit line breaks where they would otherwise not occur. This element has no attributes.

Standard/Usage: Netscape Navigator   **Widely Supported:** No
Empty: Yes

Sample:

```
<nobr>This line would go on
forever, except that I have
this neat tag called wbr
that does <wbr />this!</nobr>
```

Appendix B
CASCADING STYLE SHEETS REFERENCE

This appendix lists properties that you can use to set up style sheets or to introduce styles into a document. For a thorough introduction to style sheets and their capabilities, including an introduction to some of the specialized terminology used in this reference section, see Chapter 16, "Using Style Sheets."

This appendix includes a complete discussion of Cascading Style Sheets level 1 (traditionally noted as CSS1) as well as introductions to some of the Cascading Style Sheets level 2 (noted as CSS2) features that might be of value to you as you're developing your HTML or XHTML documents. At the time of this writing, most commonly available browsers support CSS1 completely, and the newest browsers (Netscape Navigator 6 and later and Internet Explorer 6) support most CSS2 features. As always, test your documents thoroughly on as many browsers and computers as possible before you use new features.

Adapted from *Mastering HTML and XHTML*, by Deborah S. Ray and Eric J. Ray

ISBN 0-7821-4141-2 $49.99

NOTE

As described in Chapter 16, CSS3 is currently being developed, but as of the time of this writing, it does not yet have any browser support. You can keep up with the latest CSS3 developments at the W3C website at www.w3.org/TR/css3-roadmap/.

You might refer to the following chapters as you're reading this section:

▶ Chapter 6, "Planning for a Usable, Maintainable Website," for information on implementing a coherent website

▶ Chapter 12, "Web Typography," to learn about web typography

▶ Chapter 16, if you're getting started with style sheets

NOTE

The Sybex website includes an expanded version of this appendix, including coverage of the property categories omitted from this print version because of space limitations: classification properties, aural style sheet properties, and autogenerated content properties, along with examples of all properties. To find the appendix, go to the *HTML Complete* page on www.sybex.com and click the Appendix link.

GENERAL INFORMATION

The CSS properties are organized into the following categories:

▶ Selectors, which summarize the combinations of selectors you can use

▶ Colors, which describe the many ways to specify colors in style sheets

▶ Universal properties and values, which apply in many or most cases through style sheets

▶ Font properties, which affect the style of the typeface

▶ Text properties, which control paragraph and line values

▶ Box padding, border, margin, and position properties, which place the box contents within its boundaries on a page

▶ Color and background properties, which specify background colors and images, not just for the whole page, but for each element

- Classification properties, which control the presentation of standard elements, such as display and lists. (Omitted from the print version of this appendix; see www.sybex.com as described above.)

- Aural style sheet properties, which control the aural presentation of HTML and XHTML documents. (Omitted from the print version of this appendix; see www.sybex.com as described above.)

- Printed style sheet properties, which add features specifically to control the printed output of HTML and XHTML documents

- Autogenerated content properties, which add features that help automatically insert content or automatically number parts of HTML and XHTML documents. (Omitted from the print version of this appendix; see www.sybex.com as described above.)

WARNING

We don't cover the CSS2 table properties in this appendix because they currently are not widely supported, and the traditional HTML and XHTML table elements are still widely supported. If you're feeling brave and lucky (or if you know you're writing for browsers that implement CSS2) and want to check out the CSS2 tables for yourself, visit the CSS2 tables section at www.w3.org/TR/REC-CSS2/tables.html. If not, use the HTML and XHTML table elements discussed in Chapter 11, "Presenting Information in Tables," to develop your tables.

In this appendix, you'll generally find a description of the property, a list of the property's values, and notes about the use of the property. Note that in the "Values" sections, if the value is a keyword, it's in program font (like this), and you use it as written. If it's a category of value, such as Length or Percentage, it appears in normal font, and you use the appropriate values as discussed in the description.

WARNING

At the time of this writing, the newest versions of Internet Explorer 6 and Netscape 6 and 7 support CSS1 almost completely (but not always consistently), and they support most features of CSS2. Be sure to test extensively on a variety of browsers before relying on any of the properties listed in this appendix. See Chapter 16 for additional information about tailoring your style sheets to specific browser capabilities. See www.webreview.com/style/css1/charts/mastergrid.shtml for a good reference of browser support for various features.

Throughout this appendix, you also will see references to various element types. The common element types are defined as follows:

Inline Element   Does not start and stop on its own line, but is included in the flow of another element. A standard inline element is em, for emphasis; you also can include an image in the stream of text as an inline element.

Block Element   Starts on its own line and ends with another line break.

List Item   A subset of block elements but contained within a larger block element.

Comments

Comments in CSS begin with the characters /* and end with the characters */. Don't use the traditional HTML and XHTML comment markup `<!-- -->` within your CSS markup. Additionally, don't nest comments inside each other.

```
/* this is a comment in a CSS file */
```

Selectors

You use selectors to indicate to which HTML or XHTML elements a style statement applies. You can assemble selectors in several combinations, each of which will have a different meaning. Table B.1 shows selectors, examples, and descriptions. The first five selectors come from CSS1 and work for all CSS implementations; the remaining selectors come from CSS2 and work only in CSS2-compliant browsers. You can use these selectors individually or together.

TABLE B.1: Selectors

SELECTOR PATTERN	EXAMPLE	DESCRIPTION
element	p {color: black}	Sets all p elements to black. (CSS1)
element element	p em {color: black}	Sets all em elements contained in p elements to black. This contextual selector does not affect em elements contained in other elements (such as h1, for example). (CSS1)

TABLE B.1 continued: Selectors

SELECTOR PATTERN	EXAMPLE	DESCRIPTION
`element.classname`	`p.newclass {color: black}`	Sets all p elements that have `class="newclass"` to black. (CSS1)
`.classname`	`.newclass {color: black}`	Sets all elements that have `class="newclass"` to black. (CSS1)
`#idvalue`	`#uniqueid {color: black}`	Sets the element with `id="uniqueid"` to black. (CSS1)
`*`	`* {color: black}`	Sets all elements to black. (CSS2)
`element > element`	`p > em {color: black}`	Sets any em element that is contained in a p element to black. (CSS2)
`element + element`	`p + blockquote {color: black}`	Sets any blockquote element that immediately follows a p element to black. (CSS2)
`element[attribute]`	`a[href] {color: black}`	Sets any a element that includes an href attribute to black. (CSS2)
`element [attribute ="value"]`	`a[href="http:// www.example.com/"] {color: black}`	Sets any a element that includes an href attribute with the value `"http://www.example.com/"` to black (the value must be exact). (CSS2)
`element [attribute~ ="value"]`	`a[href~="index"] {color: black}`	Sets any a element that includes an href attribute with a value of a space-separated list of words containing `"index"` to black. (CSS2)
`element [attribute| ="value"]`	`a[lang|="en"] {color: black}`	Sets any a element that includes a language attribute beginning with the value `"en"` in a hyphen-separated list of words to black. (CSS2)

Pseudoclasses

Pseudoclasses, which are closely related to selectors, refer to elements that do not explicitly exist in HTML and XHTML documents but that can be inferred from location. For example, CSS1 offers the pseudoclasses `:first-letter` and `:first-line` (supported in Internet Explorer 5.5 and later, and Netscape Navigator 6.0 and later). Table B.2 summarizes CSS1 and CSS2 pseudoclasses.

TABLE B.2: Pseudoclasses

PSEUDOCLASS	EXAMPLE	DESCRIPTION
:first-line	p:first-line {color: red} p {color: black}	Sets the first line of all p elements to red, with the remaining lines black. (CSS1)
:first-letter	p:first-letter {color: red} p {color: black}	Sets the first letter of all p elements to red, with the remaining letters and lines black. (CSS1)
:first-child	h1:first-child {color: red}	Sets the first child element under a h1 element to red. (CSS2)
:hover	p:hover {color: red}	Sets all p elements to red when the mouse cursor hovers over them. (CSS2)
:lang	p:lang(en) {color: red}	Sets all p elements set to language "en" (English) to red. (CSS2)
:first	@page:first {page-break-before: left}	Specifies that the first printed page start on the left. (CSS2)
:left	@page:left {margin: 2in}	Specifies 2-inch margins on all left printed pages. (CSS2)
:right	@page:right {margin: 2in}	Specifies 2-inch margins on all right printed pages. (CSS2)
:before	p:before {content: "para: "}	Specifies content to insert before an element.
:hover:after	p:after {content: "\""}	Places " after all paragraph elements (the \ escapes the " in the statement). (CSS2)
:focus	button:focus {color: red}	Sets properties for a form element when the element has the focus. This example sets button elements to red when they have the cursor focus. (CSS2)
:active	button:active {color: red}	Sets properties for a form element when the element is active. This example sets button elements to red when they are active. (CSS2)

See also the outline-color, outline-style, outline-width, and outline properties, which can be used with the :focus pseudoclass.

inherit Values

The inherit value can apply for any property in a style sheet. It explicitly indicates that the value of that property must be inherited from the parent element's value. This value is new (and available only) in CSS2. For example:

```
p {font-family: inherit}
```

means that every p element should inherit its font-family from its immediate parent.

Colors

You can set color values for many CSS properties. In all CSS properties that accommodate color specifications, you can use either color keywords or RGB values to specify border colors. If you name a color, the browser must be able to recognize the keyword. Because all browsers recognize the RGB colors, they're generally a safe choice.

Table B.3 lists the keyword, hexadecimal, integer, and percentage values for all colors that have generally recognized keywords (these colors are taken from the Windows VGA palette). You can include many more colors in a style sheet.

WARNING

Even though browsers recognize the RGB colors, and you can use more than the ones listed here, they may not render some of the more obscure colors the way you expect. Therefore, always test your pages on as many browsers as you can.

TABLE B.3: Equivalent Color Specifications in Various Systems

COLOR KEYWORD	RGB HEX	RGB INTEGER	RGB PERCENTAGE
aqua	#00ffff	rgb(0,255,255)	rgb(0%,100%,100%)
black	#000000	rgb(0,0,0)	rgb(0%,0%,0%)
blue	#0000ff	rgb(0,0,255)	rgb(0%,0%,100%)
fuchsia	#ff00ff	rgb(255,0,255)	rgb(100%,0%,100%)

TABLE B.3 continued: Equivalent Color Specifications in Various Systems

COLOR KEYWORD	RGB HEX	RGB INTEGER	RGB PERCENTAGE
gray	#808080	rgb(128,128,128)	rgb(50%,50%,50%)
green	#008000	rgb(0,128,0)	rgb(0%,50%,0%)
lime	#00ff00	rgb(0,255,0)	rgb(0%,100%,0%)
maroon	#800000	rgb(128,0,0)	rgb(50%,0%,0%)
navy	#000080	rgb(0,0,128)	rgb(0%,0%,50%)
olive	#808000	rgb(128,128,0)	rgb(50%,50%,0%)
purple	#800080	rgb(128,0,128)	rgb(50%,0%,50%)
red	#ff0000	rgb(255,0,0)	rgb(100%,0%,0%)
silver	#c0c0c0	rgb(192,192,192)	rgb(75%,75%,75%)
teal	#008080	rgb(0,128,128)	rgb(0%,50%,50%)
white	#ffffff	rgb(255,255,255)	rgb(100%,100%,100%)
yellow	#ffff00	rgb(255,255,0)	rgb(100%,100%,0%)

When specifying colors with RGB numbers in any system, it's helpful (and good code form) to include a comment that indicates what color you expect. For example, as you read this line:

```
p {border-color: #000080 #00008b blue #0000cd}
```

it's a little difficult to tell what the outcome should look like. But this code:

```
p {border-color: #000080 #00008b blue #0000cd}
    /* TOP navy blue, R dark blue, BOT blue, L med. blue */
```

is much easier to picture.

TIP

For more information about choosing colors, visit Chapter 10, "Adding Graphics."

CSS2 Color Features

The following additional CSS2 color values let your HTML and XHTML documents use the user's operating system colors:

ActiveBorder	InfoBackground
ActiveCaption	InfoText
AppWorkspace	Menu
Background	MenuText
ButtonFace	Scrollbar
ButtonHighlight	ThreeDDarkShadow
ButtonText	ThreeDFace
CaptionText	ThreeDHighlight
GrayText	ThreeDLightshadow
Highlight	ThreeDShadow
HighlightText	Window
InactiveBorder	WindowFrame
InactiveCaption	WindowText

For example, this code:

```
p {color: MenuText}
```

makes paragraph text the same color as the menu text on the user's computer.

Lengths

Many properties can be defined as a length. Length values set a property as a number plus a unit abbreviation. Some standard units of measurement are described in Table B.4.

TABLE B.4: Standard Units of Measurement

ABBREVIATION	UNIT	EXAMPLE	NOTES
cm	Centimeters	2.5cm	
em	Ems	3em	1 em equals the font's point size.
in	Inches	1in	

TABLE B.4 continued: Standard Units of Measurement

ABBREVIATION	UNIT	EXAMPLE	NOTES
mm	Millimeters	25mm	
pc	Picas	6pc	1 inch = 6 picas
px	Pixels	96px	
pt	Points	72pt	1 inch = 72 points
ex	X-heights	2ex	1 x-height usually equals the height of the lowercase letter *x*.

When you specify a length, relative units set up the property in relation to other font and size properties. Use relative units wherever you can because they scale more easily from situation to situation (for example, in different browsers and displays, or in the transition from display to printer). Relative units include em (in CSS, 1 em is equal to the font's point size), ex (usually the height of the lowercase letters that have no ascenders or descenders: *x* or *e*), and px (screen pixels). The em and ex settings usually generate a font size relative to the parent font.

Absolute lengths are useful when the properties of the browser are well known or when you want to set a particular value to conform to a specification. Absolute units include inches, millimeters, centimeters, points (1 point = 1/72 inch), and picas (1 pica = 12 points = 1/6 inch).

Percentages

You can set many properties as a percentage of something else—a percentage of the parent element's value for the property, or a percentage of another property of the current element. Specify this type of value simply by including a % symbol after the number, as in font-size: 90%.

FONT PROPERTIES

The font properties control the display of text elements, such as headings and paragraphs. This is the most common type of formatting you'll use in style sheets. Those properties—particularly the font-family property—also are the most problematic because no standard exists for fonts. Therefore, what works on one system or one platform might not work on another. Fortunately, you can specify alternative font families, as well as a generic font family.

The six font properties cover the font family (typeface), weight, and effects such as small caps or italics. The first property, font, is a *shorthand* property, as explained next.

font

Use this property as a shortcut to incorporate any or all of the other font properties. If you use the font shorthand property, you also can set the line spacing using the line-height property (listed later in the "Text Properties" section of this appendix). You can include one, many, or all of the font properties in this one property.

If you do not set font-style, font-variant, font-weight, or font-family in this statement, essentially you're accepting the document default values for those properties. Shorthand properties do not have default settings; refer to entries for the individual properties for their default values.

If you set the font properties for an element, those settings are used by inline elements (such as em) that are nested within such an element and by all elements of that type unless a class definition overwrites the settings.

Values

The possible values for the font property are the set of all possible values listed in the individual property entries, which must be set in this order (though optional properties can be omitted altogether):

Property	Effect
font-style	Sets the font to an oblique or italic face (optional) or back to normal face.
font-weight	Sets the font to lighter or bolder (optional).
font-variant	Sets the font to small caps (optional).
font-size	Sets the size of the font (required).
line-height	Sets the line spacing for the font (optional).
font-family	Sets the font face or type used (required).

See the entries for the individual properties for more details about these values. (Note that the sections for the individual properties are arranged alphabetically, whereas this table is arranged in the order in which the properties should occur.)

Notes

If you do not include a setting for a particular property (such as font-variant), the browser uses the parent value of that property.

CSS2 Font Features

CSS2 adds values for caption, icon, menu, messagebox, smallcaption, and statusbar. Each of these should set the font characteristics to the values in the user's system. For example, if you want text in your HTML and XHTML document to look like the text displayed in your user's status bar, use a statement such as this:

```
p {font: statusbar}
```

font-family

Use this property when you want to change just the font family for an HTML or XHTML element. This sets the font to a particular or a generic font family. You can set a comma-separated list of font families and include a generic family at the end of the list. The browser works through the list until it finds a matching font family on the user's system.

The font-family property defaults to the browser settings, which may be the browser preferences, the browser default style sheet, or the user's default style sheet. If the setting is the browser preferences or style sheet, your settings take precedence, but if it's the user's style sheet, your settings are overridden by the user's style sheet.

Inline elements (such as em) use this property, as do child elements and all elements of the specified type (in other words, the elements this property applies to—for example, if the font-family property is declared for p elements, *all* p elements will use this property) unless the settings are overwritten by a class definition.

TIP

A paragraph (p) or heading (h1, h2, and so on) element is the child of the body element; list items (li) are the children of a list element (ol and ul). Class definitions allow you to have more than one type or version of an element for formatting. For example, a warning note could have its own class of paragraph element, as discussed in Chapter 16.

Values

Here are the values you can use with the font-family property.

Family Name   Use any specific font family name. For font names, check the list of fonts on your system.

Generic Family   Use one of the following generic family names:

- ► serif for fonts such as Times or Palatino
- ► sans-serif for fonts such as Helvetica
- ► cursive for fonts such as Zapf Chancery
- ► fantasy for fonts such as Western or Circus
- ► monospace for fonts such as System or Courier

You can list several choices for the font family, specific or generic; it's best at least to conclude your list with one choice for a generic family. Separate the list members with a comma, and put single quotes around font names with white space, such as the 'Times New Roman' face.

Notes

With this property, you have the option of listing a series of alternatives separated by commas. You should *end* each list with a generic family name; the browser then can substitute an available font of the correct generic type when none of your specific family types are available. The browser works through the list from left to right until it finds a match on the user's system.

If a font family name contains spaces, place that name in quotation marks.

TIP

Apply the properties you want as defaults for the page to the body element.

font-size

Use this property when you want to control the size of text. font-size lets you set the size using a variety of measurements. It's more flexible than the font element in the HTML and XHTML specifications, which scales text only by reference to the default size.

Values

font-size takes the following values:

Absolute Size   This defines font-size using a table of computed font sizes. These values can be xx-small, x-small, small, medium (the default), large, x-large, or xx-large. Different font families may have different table values; thus, a small in one family might not be exactly the same size as a small in another family.

Relative Size   Defines font-size by increasing it (larger) or decreasing it (smaller) relative to the parent container font size rather than to the base browser font size.

Length   This sets font-size as a number plus a unit abbreviation as a measurement. See the "Lengths" section earlier in this appendix.

Percentage   This sets the font-size as a percentage of the parent element's font-size.

Notes

You can assign a single value for this property. If you use a keyword such as x-large or larger, the browser recognizes the keyword and acts accordingly. If you use a numeric value, be sure to follow it with the appropriate measurement indicator, such as pt to indicate a point size or % to indicate a percentage.

When you use the absolute size value, the browser adjusts the font size according to the user's preferences. For example, if the default font size for the browser is 10 points, this corresponds to the medium value. The adjustment from medium is a multiplier of 1.5 for each increment in the list. If medium is 10 points, then small is 6.7 points and large is 15 points. Relative size is the best choice for sizing fonts because if the user changes the base font from 10 points to 14 points, your document scales with the change.

In terms of absolute size and relative size, the default is expressed as medium.

Length and percentage values do not use the absolute or relative table of values. The font sizes are interpreted, so they may appear differently in different situations.

For length values, the default is taken from the browser or user's settings. The em and ex values are interpreted as references to the parent font size. For example, 1.5em is equivalent to large, larger, and 150% for absolute, relative, and percentage font sizes.

If the size is expressed as a percentage, the default is 100%. Any value less than 100 percent is smaller than the parent, and any value more than 100 percent is larger than the parent. For example, if the parent font is 12 points and this property is set to 110%, the font size for this element is 13.2 points. If the font size is set to 80% of the 12-point parent, the element appears as 9.6 points.

font-style

Use this property to add emphasis with an oblique or italic version of the font. If the default setting inherited for a particular element is an italic-style font, you can use the font-style property to set the current element to normal, sometimes called roman (or upright).

When you set font-style for an element, inline elements (such as em) and included block elements use this style. Also, if you set font-style for a body or list container, all the elements within it use the setting.

Values

Value	Effect
normal	Chooses the roman or upright style in a font family.
italic	Chooses the italic style in a font family. Fonts with *italic*, *cursive*, or *kursiv* in their names are usually listed as italic in the browser's database.
oblique	Chooses the oblique style in a font family. Fonts with *oblique*, *slanted*, or *incline* in their names usually are listed in the browser's database as oblique fonts. The browser also may generate an oblique font from a family that does not have an oblique or italic style.

Notes

The browser maintains a list of the fonts available on the system, with the font name, font family, and values of the font, such as oblique or italic.

font-variant

Use this property to switch between normal and small-caps fonts. Similar to the `font-style` property, `font-variant` handles one piece of font information. If you assign this property to an element, all included blocks and inline elements use the setting.

Values

A value of `small-caps` sets the lowercase letters to appear as uppercase letters in a smaller font size. If the element has inherited a small-caps setting from its parent, a value of `normal` sets `font-variant` to the usual uppercase and lowercase; this is the default value.

Notes

In some cases, when a small-caps version of the font is not available to the browser, the browser creates small caps by using scaled uppercase letters.

font-weight

Use this property to set the weight of a font, creating darker or lighter versions of the normal font. You can set the `font-weight` property as a relative weight or as a specific numeric value that represents a degree of darkness (or heaviness) or lightness for the font.

Values

Use only one of the following values.

Relative Weight   This sets `font-weight` relative to the weight inherited by the element. In this method, the value can be either `bolder` or `lighter`; these increase (`bolder`) or decrease (`lighter`) the `font-weight` by one setting from its current weight (but not beyond the limits of 100 and 900).

Absolute Weight   This sets the `font-weight` as a degree of heaviness on a 9-point scale. The value can be one of the following: 100, 200, 300, 400 or `normal` (these two values are equivalent), 500, 600, 700 or `bold` (these two values are equivalent), 800, or 900. The default is `normal`.

Notes

When you set a `font-weight` value for an element, its child elements inherit the weight of the font. This weight becomes their default weight, and you can increase or decrease the weight based on the inherited weight. When you then set a child element's weight using a relative weight (for example, `bolder` or `lighter`), it's relative to the weight of the parent element's font. However, the weight will never exceed 900 or go below 100; if you set `bolder` on an element that is already inheriting 900, it stays at 900.

The numeric, gradient weight values give you greater control over the weight of the font. These values must be stated exactly; an intermediate value such as 250 is not acceptable.

There are no guarantees that the font family will include the full range of weight values. The browser will map the values you assign to those available for the font it uses. Fonts that have a weight lighter than normal are usually listed in the browser's database as *thinner*, *light*, or *extra-light*.

TEXT PROPERTIES

Text properties control the layout or display of lines and words on a page and within a text element. These properties include the familiar values for spacing and aligning text within an area, as well as values for controlling text capitalization and effects (such as underlining and blinking). Combined with the font properties, the text properties give you almost complete control over the appearance of the text on your page. The font properties control the typeface; the text properties control the paragraph settings.

letter-spacing

Use this property to control the spacing between characters in words in a text element. The distance you set applies across the elements; you cannot insert larger or smaller spaces between characters. This property is useful if you want to add space between characters for an open-looking presentation.

This property defaults to the spacing set in the parent element, or in the browser if no style is set. Inline and included block elements use the value set with the `letter-spacing` property.

Values

`letter-spacing` sets standard spacing length between characters with a number plus a unit abbreviation. (See the "Lengths" section earlier in this appendix.) The value adds to the normal length inherited by the element from its parent or reduces the normal length if you use a negative value.

To reset the distance between characters to whatever is common for the font and font size in use, use a value of `normal`. This is the default.

Notes

When you use a length unit, you can use a positive or negative number or a decimal number (for example, `0.4em` or `1.2em`). If you use a negative value, be sure that you don't make your text illegible with spacing too small between characters.

line-height

Use this property to set the distance (leading or spacing) between lines of text within an element. Elements inherit the settings for this property; if you change the settings in the child element, you change the inherited results. For example, if you set an unordered list (`ul`) to 2 (for double-spaced) and then set list items (`li`) to `1.5`, you've effectively triple-spaced list items (2×1.5). In other words, the inheritance is cumulative, rather than a setting for a child element replacing the parent's setting.

Values

To set the spacing value to default to the browser-specific setting, which is usually 1 to 1.2 times the font size, use the default value of `normal`. To change the spacing, use one of the following techniques.

Number   This sets the distance between the baselines of each line of text in the element to the font size multiplied by the specified number. For example, if the font size is 10 points and you set `line-height` to 2, the spacing will be 20 points.

Length   This sets the spacing using one of the standard relative or absolute measurements. See the "Lengths" section earlier in this appendix.

Percentage   This sets the spacing to a percentage of the line's font size.

Notes

When you use a length unit, you can use a positive or negative number. If you use a negative number, you'll create overlapping text, which may make it illegible.

Using a percentage for the `line-height` property is a flexible way to set line spacing because it adapts to the font and display of the browser. Child elements will inherit the result of this setting.

outline

Using this CSS2 shorthand property, you can outline individual elements such as buttons, fields, or emphasized text. Outlines do not take space—they fit just outside the border (if any) and do not affect the layout of any elements. Additionally, they enclose the text precisely, even if the lines result in irregular shapes, rather than forming a rectangle.

The `outline` property is a shorthand property and sets any of the `outline-color`, `outline-style`, and `outline-width` properties.

Values

The possible values for the `outline` property are the set of all possible values listed in the individual property entries:

Property	Effect
`outline-color`	Sets the color for all sides of the outline.
`outline-style`	Sets the pattern used for the outline.
`outline-width`	Sets the outline width.

See other properties in this appendix, including the `border-color` for `outline-color` values, `border-style` for `outline-style` values, and `border-width` for `outline-width` values. Possible values for `outline-style` are the same as for the `border-style` property, except that `hidden` is not permitted for `outline-style`.

The `outline-color` property accepts all colors, as well as the keyword `invert`, which is expected to perform a color inversion on the pixels on the screen. This is a trick you can use to ensure that the focus border is visible regardless of color background.

Notes

This property is a CSS2 property and, therefore, won't work in browsers that don't support CSS2.

See the "Notes" sections for the `border-width`, `border-style`, and `border-color` properties under "Box Border Properties," later in this appendix.

text-align

Use this property to arrange the text horizontally within the element box. This is useful for centering headings or creating effects with justification. You can set the alignment on any block-level element such as p, h1, and ul. The browser sets the property default (from the browser properties, browser style sheet, or user's style sheet). Inline and included block elements use the settings. For example, if you justify an unordered list (ul), the list items (which are included block elements) are justified.

Values

Here are the values you can use with the text-align property:

Value	Effect
left	Aligns text along the left margin, for a "ragged-right" layout.
right	Aligns text along the right margin, for a "ragged-left" layout.
center	Places the text an equal distance from the left and right margins.
justify	Creates uniform line lengths. The browser will use word and letter spacing to create lines of text that touch both the left and right margins of the element box.

text-decoration

Use this property to control the effects used on text elements. This property is particularly useful for drawing attention to text elements such as notes and warnings.

The default is no text decoration, and the property is not inherited, although some properties do continue throughout sections. For example, a p with underlining will be underlined throughout, even through sections with other formatting, such as boldface. The decoration uses the settings from the color property (listed in the "Background and Color Properties" section, later in this appendix).

Values

Here are the values you can use with the `text-decoration` property:

Value	Effect
none	Leaves the text plain (unadorned). This is the default.
underline	Draws a single thin line under the text.
overline	Draws a single thin line above the text.
line-through	Draws a single thin line through the text, similar to strikethrough text.
blink	Makes the text blink.

You can combine `underline`, `overline`, `line-through`, and `blink` in a single statement—though that would be pretty ugly.

Notes

If you apply `text-decoration` to an empty element (such as `br`) or an element that has no text, the property has no effect.

Be careful using underlined text in your web pages. Users are accustomed to underlined text representing hyperlinks and may get confused if you use it for other reasons.

The `blink` element will get readers' attention, but it also will make pages look amateurish. Think carefully before you use it.

text-indent

Use this property to create paragraphs with the first line indented. Traditionally, indented first lines compensate for a lack of space between paragraphs and act as a visual cue for the reader. You can set the indent as an absolute or relative measurement.

Elements use whatever setting the parent has, so if you set `text-indent` for body, all block elements, such as `h1` and `p`, default to first-line indentation. The default value is 0, for no indentation. Negative values can be used to "outdent" the element to the left from the rest of the block.

Values

text-indent takes the following values.

Length   This sets the size of the first-line indent to the specified measurement. Some measurements are relative, and some are absolute. See the "Lengths" section earlier in this appendix.

Percentage   This sets the first-line indent to a percentage of the line length.

Notes

For most browsers, you can use negative values to create a hanging-indent format.

An indent is not added to the first line of the second text stream if the text within the element is separated by an inline element that breaks the line (such as br).

text-shadow

Use this CSS2 property to control shadow effects on text elements. We recommend using this effect sparingly, because too much text shadow can make text difficult to read.

Values

To restore an element to no text shadow, use the default value none.

To set a text shadow, you *must* provide the horizontal and vertical shadow offsets, but the blur radius and color are optional. You also can specify separate groups of settings for multiple shadows under the same text.

Horizontal Shadow Offset   This value specifies the horizontal distance to the right where the shadow appears. Use negative numbers to move the shadow to the left from the text. Specify a unit of measurement.

Vertical Shadow Offset   This value specifies the vertical distance down where the shadow appears. Use negative numbers to move the shadow above the text. Specify a unit of measurement.

Blur Radius   This value specifies the fuzziness of the shadow. Specify a unit of measurement.

Color   This value specifies the shadow color. See the "Colors" section earlier in this appendix for more about colors.

Notes

This property is new in CSS2 and is not yet supported by browsers.

If you apply the text shadow to an empty element (such as br) or an element that has no text, the property has no effect.

text-transform

Use this property to set the capitalization standard for one or more elements. For example, if you want all uppercase letters for a warning or title case for all headings, you can set this property in one place and allow the browser to adjust the text. Child elements, including both block and inline elements, use the parent's setting for this property.

Values

Here are the values you can use with `text-transform`:

Value	Effect
none	Does not change the case for any of the text. This is the default.
capitalize	Creates a title-cased element, capitalizing the first letter of each word in the element.
lowercase	Sets all text to lowercase, eliminating any uppercase letters from the element text.
uppercase	Sets all text to uppercase.

vertical-align

Use this property to set inline text elements within a parent element to have different vertical alignment from the parent. The `vertical-align` property is an important layout tool for document designers. For example, you could define a class for superscript or subscript text and apply it where required. This property typically is used to set the alignment between inline graphics (such as keycaps or toolbar icons) and the surrounding text. The default value is to align along the baselines of the elements. These settings are not used by any other elements.

Values

Here are the values you can use with the vertical-align property:

Value	Effect
baseline	Aligns the bottom of lowercase letters in the two elements (the default setting).
bottom	Aligns the inline element with the lowest part of the parent element on the same line. Use with caution—may produce unexpected results.
middle	Centers the inline text and the parent element text, aligning the midpoints of the two elements. May be required when the two elements are of different sizes or when the inline element is an image.
sub	Moves the inline element below the baseline of the parent element.
super	Moves the inline element up from the baseline of the parent element.
text-bottom	Aligns the bottom of the inline element with the bottom of the parent font's descender. This is the preferred method for aligning inline elements with the bottom of a textual parent element.
text-top	Aligns the inline element with the top of the ascender in the parent element.
top	Aligns the inline element with the highest part of the parent element, similar to superscript. Works line by line—for example, if the line has no ascenders, top moves the inline text to the top of the x-height for the parent element.

The vertical-align property also can be set as a percentage, raising or lowering (with negative values) the baseline of the inline element the given percentage above or below the baseline of the parent element. Use this in combination with the line-height property of the element.

Notes

If you use subscript (sub) or superscript (super) alignment, decrease the font size in relation to the parent element.

If you want to include inline images that replace words or letters in your text (such as toolbar buttons or keycaps), use a percentage value with the vertical-align property. This enables you to obtain precision in the placement of inline elements that do not have true baselines, such as images.

word-spacing

Use this property to control the spacing between words in a text element. As with the letter-spacing property, the distance you set applies across the elements; you cannot insert larger and smaller spaces between words, as in typesetting. This property is useful if you want to add space between words for an open-looking presentation.

This property assumes the settings for its parent element or the browser, and inline or included block elements use any changes you make in the word-spacing property.

Values

This sets standard spacing between words with a length value. (See the "Lengths" section earlier in this appendix.) The value adds to the length inherited by the element from its parent or reduces the length if you use a negative value. For example, if body sets the font size to 10pt and the word spacing to 1em, the child elements will use a 10-point word spacing (1em = the point size). If you then add 0.4em to the word spacing, the child element has a wider word spacing than the parent.

To reset the distance between words to whatever is normal for the font and font size in use, use a value of normal (which is the default).

Notes

When you use a length unit, you can use a positive or negative number, as well as a decimal number (such as 0.4em). If you use a negative value, be careful that you do not eliminate the spaces between words, making your text unreadable.

Box Padding Properties

In the element box, the padding provides the distance between the element contents and the border. You can use the padding shorthand property to set the padding on all sides of the element or use the individual properties to set the padding on each side separately.

TIP

With box properties, you can manipulate the layers around the element. These layers, from the element out, are padding, border, margin, and position. Each of these layers has its own set of properties, which are included in this appendix in the order listed, beginning with box padding.

padding

Use this shorthand property to set the distance for all four padding directions (top, right, bottom, and left). This area uses the element's settings for background (such as color and image).

Padding is not inherited, so included and inline elements use the default of zero rather than the settings from the parent element.

Values

The padding property accepts the following values:

Length   This sets an absolute or relative distance between the element contents and the inside of the box border. See the "Lengths" section earlier in this appendix.

Percentage   This sets the distance between the element contents and the inside of the box border as a percentage of the parent element.

Use a single value to make the padding on each side equidistant. If you use two values, the browser uses the first one for the top and bottom padding and the second one for the left and right padding. If you provide three values, the browser assigns them to the top padding, the left and right padding, and the bottom padding. If you provide all four values, the browser assigns them, in order, to the top, right, bottom, and left padding. You can mix value types—specifying padding in percentage for some and absolute measurements for other values.

Notes

You cannot have negative padding values; however, you can use decimal numbers, such as 0.4 or 1.2.

padding-bottom

Use this property to add space between the bottom of the contents and the border below. Padding is not inherited, so included and inline elements use the default of zero rather than the settings from the parent element.

Values

`padding-bottom` accepts two values:

Length   This sets an absolute or relative distance between the bottom of the contents and the border below. See the "Lengths" section earlier in this appendix.

Percentage   This sets the bottom padding size to a percentage of the parent element.

Notes

You cannot have negative padding values; however, you can use decimal numbers, such as 0.4 or 1.2.

padding-left

Use this property to add space between the left edge of the contents and the border location. Padding is not inherited, so included and inline elements use the default of zero rather than the settings from the parent element.

Values

The `padding-left` property accepts two values:

Length   This sets an absolute or relative distance between the left edge of the contents and the border. See the "Lengths" section earlier in this appendix.

Percentage   This sets the left padding size to a percentage of the parent element.

Notes

You cannot have negative padding values; however, you can use decimal numbers, such as 0.4 or 1.2.

padding-right

Use this property to add space between the right edge of the contents and the border location. Padding is not inherited, so included and inline elements use the default of zero rather than the settings from the parent element.

Values

padding-right accepts two values:

Length   This sets an absolute or relative distance between the right edge of the contents and the border. See the "Lengths" section earlier in this appendix.

Percentage   This sets the right padding size to a percentage of the parent element.

Notes

You cannot have negative padding values; however, you can use decimal numbers, such as 0.4 or 1.2.

padding-top

Use this property to add space between the top of the contents and the border location. Padding is not inherited, so included and inline elements use the default of zero rather than the settings from the parent element.

Values

padding-top accepts two values:

Length   This sets an absolute or relative distance between the top of the contents and the border. See the "Lengths" section earlier in this appendix.

Percentage   This sets the top padding size to a percentage of the parent element.

Notes

You cannot have negative padding values; however, you can use decimal numbers, such as 0.4 or 1.2.

BOX BORDER PROPERTIES

Every container has a border. Element borders reside between the padding and margin in the element container. By default, borders have no style set (and are not visible), regardless of color or width.

The default for the border is a medium-width line with no pattern that inherits the color (foreground) setting for the parent element.

You can use the border shorthand property to set any of the border properties, or you can use the individual properties.

border

Use this shorthand property to set some or all of the border properties. You can set a single value for all four sides of the border.

See the sections on the border-color, border-style, and border-width properties for their values and notes on each.

Values

The possible values for the border property are all possible values listed in the individual property entries:

Property	Effect
border-color	Sets the color for all sides of the border.
border-style	Sets the pattern used to fill the border.
border-width	Sets the border width for the border.

Notes

Unlike other shorthand properties, you can use only one setting for each value you include (as opposed to separate settings for top, bottom, and so on). The property is applied evenly to all sides of the box border. To set borders differently on various sides, use the more specific shorthand properties such as border-bottom.

border-bottom

Use this shorthand property to set some or all of the border properties for the bottom border of the element container.

See the sections on the `border-color`, `border-style`, and `border-width` properties for their values and notes on each.

Values

The possible values for the `border-bottom` property are all possible values listed in the individual property entries:

Property	Effect
`border-color`	Sets the color for the bottom border.
`border-style`	Sets the pattern used to fill the bottom border.
`border-width`	Sets the width for the bottom border.

border-bottom-width

Use this property to set the thickness of the bottom border for an element. The border width, by default, is a medium thickness and is unaffected by any border settings for the parent element.

Values

This sets the bottom border width, using an absolute or a relative measurement. For valid absolute value measurements, see the "Lengths" section earlier in this appendix. Possible relative values are `thin`, `medium` (the default), and `thick`; the specific interpretation of thickness is up to the browser.

Notes

See the "Notes" section for the `border-width` property.

border-color

Use this property to create a border using different colors than the foreground color for the element. The border color uses the foreground color of the element as a default setting. This shorthand property sets the visible border to the selected color(s).

Values

The values for `border-color` can be predefined color names or RGB values. See the "Colors" section earlier in this appendix.

Notes

If you specify a single color, all four borders will appear in that color. If you include two colors, the top and bottom borders use the first color and the left and right borders use the second color. If you include three colors, the top border uses the first color, the left and right borders use the second color, and the bottom border uses the third color. To give each border a unique color, list four colors; the browser will use them in the following order: top, right, bottom, left.

border-left

Use this shorthand property to set some or all of the border properties for the border on the left side of the element container.

See the sections on the border-color, border-style, and border-width properties for values and notes on each.

Values

The possible values for the border-left property are all possible values listed in the individual property entries:

Property	Effect
border-color	Sets the color for the left border.
border-style	Sets the pattern used to fill the left border.
border-width	Sets the width for the left border.

border-left-width

Use this property to set the thickness of the border on the left side of an element. The border width, by default, is a medium thickness and is unaffected by any border settings for the parent element.

Values

This sets the left border width, using an absolute or a relative measurement. Possible relative values are thin, medium (the default), and thick; the specific interpretation of thickness is up to the browser. For absolute values and other valid relative measurements, see the "Lengths" section earlier in this appendix.

Notes

See the "Notes" section for the border-width property.

border-right

Use this shorthand property to set some or all of the border properties for the border to the right of the element contents.

See the sections on the border-color, border-style, and border-width properties for values and notes on each.

Values

The possible values for the border-right property are all possible values listed in the individual property entries:

Property	Effect
border-color	Sets the color for the right border.
border-style	Sets the pattern used to fill the right border.
border-width	Sets the width for the right border.

border-right-width

Use this property to set the thickness of the border on the right side of an element. The border width, by default, is a medium thickness and is unaffected by any border settings for the parent element.

Values

This sets the right border width, using an absolute or a relative measurement. Possible relative values are thin, medium (the default), and thick; the specific interpretation of thickness is up to the browser. For absolute values and other valid relative measurements, see the "Lengths" section earlier in this appendix.

Notes

See the "Notes" section for the border-width property.

border-style

Use this property to display a border and specify a border style. You can create different effects by combining line styles with color and width. This property uses none as the default, which doesn't display the border at all, regardless of the color or width settings.

Values

Here are the values you can use with border-style:

Value	Effect
none	Prevents the display of one or more borders. This is the default.
dashed	Sets the border as a series of dashes, alternating the element background and the border color.
dotted	Sets the border as a dotted line, with spaces where the element background shows through.
double	Sets the border as two solid lines in the border color or element foreground color.
groove	Sets the border as a 3D rendering of a grooved line drawn in the border color.
hidden	Identical to none except in reference to table element border conflict resolution.
inset	Sets the border as a 3D rendering, creating the illusion that the inside of the element is sunken into the page.
outset	Sets the border as a 3D rendering, creating the illusion that the inside of the element is raised above the page.
ridge	Sets the border as a raised 3D rendering, peaking in the middle of the line, drawn in the border color.
solid	Sets the border as a single solid line in the border color or element foreground color.

Use up to four values from the preceding list to stylize the borders around an element. Because the initial setting for the border-style property is none, no borders are visible unless you set them up with a style and width.

Notes

Not all browsers are capable of displaying the more esoteric styles, such as ridge, inset, and outset. If the browser cannot interpret the style, it substitutes a solid line. Some browsers may simply render all borders as solid lines.

border-top

Use this shorthand property to set some or all of the border properties for the top border of the element container.

See the sections on the `border-color`, `border-style`, and `border-width` properties for their values and notes on each.

Values

The possible values for the `border-top` property are all possible values listed in the individual property entries:

Property	Effect
`border-color`	Sets the color for the top border.
`border-style`	Sets the pattern used to fill the top border.
`border-width`	Sets the width for the top border.

border-top-width

Use this property to set the thickness of the border along the top of an element. The border width, by default, is a medium thickness and is unaffected by any border settings for the parent element.

Values

This sets the top border width, using an absolute or a relative measurement. Possible relative values are `thin`, `medium` (the default), and `thick`; the specific interpretation of thickness is up to the browser. For absolute values and other valid relative measurements, see the "Lengths" section earlier in this appendix.

Notes

See the "Notes" section for the `border-width` property.

border-width

Use this shorthand property to set the thickness of all the borders for an element. You can give the borders unique widths, or you can use a single width for all the borders.

Values

This sets the width of the border on all sides, using an absolute or a relative measurement. Possible relative values are thin, medium (the default), and thick; the specific interpretation of thickness is up to the browser. For absolute values and other valid relative measurements, see the "Lengths" section earlier in this appendix.

If you use one value, it applies evenly to the borders on the four sides of the element. If you use two values, the browser applies the first to the top and bottom borders of the element and the second to the left and right borders. If you include three values, the browser uses the first for the top border, the second for the left and right borders, and the last for the bottom border. If you use four values, the browser applies them in the following order: top, right, bottom, and left.

Notes

The thin setting always will be less than or equal to the medium setting, which always will be less than or equal to the thick setting. The border widths do not depend on the element font or other settings. The thick setting, for example, is rendered in the same size wherever it occurs in a document. You can use the relative length values to produce variable (font-dependent) widths.

With a length setting, you cannot have a border with a negative width. However, you can use a decimal number, for example, 0.4 or 1.2.

CSS2 Border Properties

CSS2 also provides border properties that offer you even more control over border appearance. Choose from these:

- border-bottom-color
- border-bottom-style
- border-left-color
- border-left-style
- border-right-color
- border-right-style
- border-top-color
- border-top-style

For example:

```
h1, h2, h3 {font-size: 15pt; font-style: Futura, sans-serif;
            border-left-style: solid;
            border-left-color: blue}
```

applies to the three levels of headings, giving each heading a solid blue line on the left. See the corresponding CSS1 properties for valid values and notes.

Box Margin Properties

Margins set the size of the box around an element. You measure margins from the border area to the edge of the box.

margin

This property is shorthand to set up all the margins for an element's box. This measurement gives the browser the distance between the element border and the edge of the box. This area is always transparent, so you can view the underlying page background.

Values

The value auto sets the margin to the browser's default.

Length   This sets an absolute or relative distance between the border and the box edge. See the "Lengths" section earlier in this appendix.

Percentage   This sets the margin size as a percentage of the parent element's width.

Use one of the preceding values. For length and percentage, you can use one, two, three, or four numbers. If you use one number, the browser applies it to all four margins (top, right, bottom, and left). If you use two numbers, the first number sets the top and bottom margins, and the second number sets the left and right margins. If you use three numbers, you set the top margin with the first, the right and left margins with the second, and the bottom margin with the third. You can mix length and percentage values.

Notes

You can use negative values for margins, but not all browsers will handle the settings correctly, and some may ignore the setting and substitute the default of zero or use their own algorithm.

margin-bottom

Use this property to set just the bottom margin of an element's box. The bottom margin is the distance between the bottom border and the bottom edge of the box. This generally defaults to zero and is not used by included block or inline elements.

Values

The value auto sets the bottom margin to the browser's default.

Length   This sets an absolute or relative distance between the border and the box's bottom edge. See the "Lengths" section earlier in this appendix.

Percentage   This sets the bottom margin size as a percentage of the parent element's width.

Notes

You can use negative values for margins, but not all browsers will handle the settings correctly, and some may ignore the setting and substitute the default of zero or use their own algorithm.

margin-left

Use this property to set just the left margin of an element's box. The left margin is the distance between the border and the left edge of the box. You can use this to create indented text or other element placements. The default for the left margin is zero, or no space. The settings in one element are not used by its included or inline elements.

Values

The value auto sets the left margin to the browser's default.

Length   This sets an absolute or relative distance between the border and the box's left edge. See the "Lengths" section earlier in this appendix.

Percentage   This sets the left margin size as a percentage of the parent element's width.

Notes

You can use negative values for margins, but not all browsers will handle the settings correctly, and some may ignore the setting and substitute the default of zero or use their own algorithm.

margin-right

Use this property to set just the right margin of an element's box. The right margin is the distance between the border and the right edge of the box. You can use this to force the element away from the right edge of the page. This generally defaults to zero and is not used by included block or inline elements.

Values

The value auto sets the right margin to the browser's default.

Length   This sets an absolute or relative distance between the border and the box's right edge. See the "Lengths" section earlier in this appendix.

Percentage   This sets the right margin size as a percentage of the parent element's width.

Notes

You can use negative values for margins, but not all browsers will handle the settings correctly, and some may ignore the setting and substitute the default of zero or use their own algorithm.

margin-top

Use this property to set just the top margin of an element's box. The top margin is the distance between the border and the top of the box. You can use this to insert space above an element, perhaps to reinforce its visual relationship with the elements around it. This generally defaults to zero and is not used by included block or inline elements.

Values

The value auto sets the top margin to the browser's default.

Length   This sets an absolute or relative distance between the border and the box's top edge. See the "Lengths" section earlier in this appendix.

Percentage   This sets the top margin size as a percentage of the parent element's width.

Notes

You can use negative values for margins, but not all browsers will handle the settings correctly, and some may ignore the setting and substitute the default of zero or use their own algorithm.

Box Position Properties

The box position properties control the arrangement of elements in relation to each other and the page, rather than within themselves. The float and clear properties control which elements can sit next to each other. The width and height properties set dimensions for elements, giving you more control of the page layout.

clear

Use this property to allow or disallow other elements, usually inline images, to float beside the element specified. You can allow floating elements on either side, both sides, or neither side. The default is to allow floating elements on both sides of the element (the none setting). This property is not used by inline and included elements.

Values

Use one of these values to designate the position for floating elements in relation to a particular element.

Value	Effect
none	Allows floating elements on either side of the element. This is the default.
both	Does not allow floating elements on either side of the element.

Value	Effect
left	Not on the left; moves the element below any floating elements on the left.
right	Not on the right; moves the element below any floating elements on the right.

Notes

This property indicates where floating elements are not allowed.

float

Use this property to set an element in a position outside the rules of placement for the normal flow of elements. For example, the float property can raise an element from an inline element to a block element. This is usually used to place an image. The default, which is not an inherited value, is to display the element where it appears in the flow of the document (none).

Values

Here are the values you can use with the float property.

Value	Effect
none	Displays the element where it appears in the flow of the parent element. This is the default.
left	Wraps other element contents to the right of the floating element.
right	Wraps other element contents to the left of the floating element.

Notes

A floating element cannot overlap the margin in the parent element used for positioning. For example, an illustration that is a left-floating element (pushes other contents to the right of itself) cannot overlap the left margin of its parent container.

height

Use this property to set the height of an element on a page. Browsers will enforce the height, scaling the image to fit. This property will be familiar to anyone who has used the height and width attributes of an image (img) element in HTML or XHTML.

Values

The value auto allows the browser either to set height to the actual image height or, if the width is set, to preserve the aspect ratio of images. You can use absolute or relative length measurements instead, as described in the "Lengths" section earlier in this appendix. Use a percentage to set the image size as a percentage of the parent element's height.

Notes

Some browsers may not handle the height (or width) property if the element is not a replaced element (one that uses a pointer in the HTML or XHTML source to indicate the file with the actual content, such as an img element).

Generally, a replaced element has its own intrinsic measurements. If you want to replace those dimensions with a height (and/or width) property setting, the browser tries to resize the replaced element to fit. To maintain the aspect ratio, you need to set one of the height or width properties to auto. To preserve the aspect ratio of images positioned with height, include the width property in the statement and set width to auto. If you position an image with the width property, include the height property in the statement and set height to auto.

If you need to set the size of an image, it's usually best to set it in proportion to the container element (using a relative setting); otherwise, leave those settings at auto, which allows the browser to use the image's original size.

You cannot use a negative value for the height or width property of an element.

width

Use this property to set the width of an element on a page. Browsers will enforce the width, scaling the image to fit. This property will be familiar to anyone who has used the height and width attributes of an image (img) element in HTML or XHTML.

Values

The value auto allows the browser to either set width to the actual image height or, if height is set, to preserve the aspect ratio of images.

Length   This sets an absolute or relative width for images in a particular element or class. See the "Lengths" section earlier in this appendix.

Percentage   This sets the image size as a percentage of the parent element's width.

Notes

See the "Notes" section for the `height` property.

BACKGROUND AND COLOR PROPERTIES

Color affects the foreground elements, such as text and borders, and background properties affect the surface on which the document elements appear. You can set these globally and locally for individual elements. When you paint the background for an element, you're layering on top of the document's background. If you do not set a background for an element, it defaults to transparent, allowing the document background to show. The `color` property inherits from the document body.

You can control a wide variety of properties for backgrounds, including position, repetition, and scrolling. You can use the `background` shorthand property to set all the background properties or use the individual properties. The background is set relative to the element's box properties.

background

This is a shorthand property used to include the full collection of background values. The `background` property will be familiar to anyone who has changed the page color of a web page or added a graphic as wallpaper. This property now extends to individual elements, allowing you to have a variety of backgrounds. It also allows more functionality in the background, including scrolling and repetitions.

Values

The possible values for `background` are all possible values listed in the individual property entries:

Property	Effect
background-attachment	Sets up a background that scrolls with the element.

Property	Effect
`background-color`	Sets a background color for the page or elements on the page.
`background-image`	Sets an image behind the element.
`background-position`	Positions the background within the element's box.
`background-repeat`	Sets the number of times and direction that a background repeats.

See the sections for the individual properties for details about these values.

Notes

If you do not include a property (such as `background-repeat`), the browser uses the default.

The order of the properties in a statement is not important.

background-attachment

Use this property to specify whether an image used for the background of an element will scroll with the element or remain at a fixed location on the page. If the image is larger than the element box, when users scroll down the screen, they see either different parts of the background image (a fixed attachment) or a single part of the image (a scrolling attachment) that moves with the display of the element down the page.

Inline and included block elements do not inherit this property.

Values

A value of `scroll` moves the image with the element on the page, so the same part is visible when users scroll down the screen. This is the default, and it applies only to the element in the statement. A value of `fixed` keeps the image fixed in relation to the page so that different parts are visible when users scroll down the screen.

Notes

Use this property in conjunction with the `background-image` property.

background-color

Use this property to set the background color for the page or elements on the page. If you set the background for the base class body, your other elements will appear to inherit that color unless you change their background colors from transparent.

Values

This sets the color for the background. This value can be one of the color names or RGB values. See the "Colors" section earlier in this appendix. The keyword value `transparent` makes the page background the default for viewing.

Notes

This value sets the background color only. To set the background as an image, you need to use either the `background` property or the `background-image` property.

This property affects the box area owned by the element. This is set using the margin and padding properties, listed in the "Box Margin Properties" and "Box Padding Properties" sections.

When you set an element's background to transparent or don't set it at all, the page's background color or image appears in its place.

background-image

Use this property to define an image for the background. The browser will look for additional information about the image's position, repetition, and attachment (or association). If you accept the defaults for those properties, your background image will not repeat, will be attached to the page (not the element), and will have a starting position at the upper-left corner of the element's box.

Values

The default value, none, does not use an image for the background. A value of `url(...)` cues the browser that you're going to provide a filename. You must include the file with the page.

Notes

The images you use should be `gif` or `jpg` image files to ensure that all graphical browsers can read them.

You also should include a `background-color` property in case the image you have selected is not available.

background-position

Use this property to position the element background within its space, using the initial position as a mark. Every element has a box that describes the area it controls. The `background-position` property is useful when your image is not the same size as the element it provides a background for. With this property, you can indicate the position of the image relative to the element box.

Values

Here are the values you can use with the `background-position` property:

Length   This sets the starting point on the element's box edge in an absolute or a relative measurement and also gives the coordinates as measurements. See the "Lengths" section earlier in this appendix.

Percentage   Indicates, as a percentage, where on the box edge the browser begins placing the image. You can repeat this value to give a vertical and horizontal starting point.

Vertical Position   This sets the vertical starting position. Use the keyword `top`, `center`, or `bottom`. The browser determines the size of the element box and works from there.

Horizontal Position   This sets the horizontal starting position. Use the keyword `left`, `center`, or `right`. The browser determines the width of the element box and works from there.

With the length and percentage settings, you can use two numbers to indicate the vertical and horizontal starting point. Unlike percentage, however, the length measurement does not apply to both the image and the element box in the same way. The length measurement indicates the coordinates inside the element box where the top-left corner of the image appears.

Notes

Using 0% 0% is synonymous with using `top left`. In the first case, the initial position of the image is determined this way: The upper-left corner of the image is considered to be 0% horizontal and 0% vertical, and the same is done with the element box. You could position an image using 50% 50%, and the browser would then begin at the middle of the element and the image. If the image is larger than the element box, you lose the edges that extend beyond the element box. Similarly, if your image is smaller than the element box, you will have an edge inside your element box with no image.

You can combine the percentage and length measurements. It's legal to set the property using 25% 2cm. This would start rendering the image at one-fourth the way into the image and one-fourth the distance across the element box. The image would begin to appear 2 centimeters below the top of the element box.

The length measurements indicate the distance from the box border where the browser starts to render the image.

When you use a length unit, you can use a positive or negative number. In some cases, you can use a decimal number. Whichever system of measurement you choose to use must be communicated with the short form for the system (for example, cm or in).

You also can use keywords to position the image within the element's box. Table B.5 gives you some corresponding values to work with.

TABLE B.5:   Background Position Keywords

KEYWORD	PERCENTAGE	DESCRIPTION
top left, left top	0% 0%	The top-left corner of the image starts at the top-left corner of the element box.
top, top center, center top	50% 0%	The horizontal middle of the image appears in the horizontal middle of the element box. The top of the image begins at the top of the element box.
right top, top right	100% 0%	The top-right corner of the image starts at the top-right corner of the element box.
left, left center, center left	0% 50%	The vertical middle of the image appears in the vertical middle of the element box. The left side of the image is flush against the left side of the element box.
center, center center	50% 50%	The absolute middle of the image is positioned over the absolute middle of the element box.

TABLE B.5 continued: Background Position Keywords

KEYWORD	PERCENTAGE	DESCRIPTION
`right, right center, center right`	100% 50%	The vertical middle of the image is positioned over the vertical middle of the element box. The right edge of the image is flush against the right side of the element box.
`bottom left, left bottom`	0% 100%	The bottom-left corner of the image is positioned at the bottom-left corner of the element box.
`bottom center, center bottom`	50% 100%	The horizontal centers of the image and element box appear together, and the bottom edges of each remain together.
`bottom right, right bottom`	100% 100%	The lower-right corner of the image positions in the lower-right corner of the element box.

background-repeat

Use this property to control whether an image repeats horizontally, vertically, both, or neither. Images normally repeat both horizontally and vertically, filling in the area within the element's margins. By default, backgrounds repeat both horizontally and vertically.

Values

Here are the values you can use with the background-repeat property:

Value	Effect
`repeat`	Sets horizontal and vertical repetitions of the image. This is the default.
`repeat-x`	Sets horizontal repetitions only.
`repeat-y`	Sets vertical repetitions only.
`no-repeat`	Prevents repeated copies of the image from being displayed.

Notes

This property works in conjunction with the background-image and background-position properties. Combining these properties into a single statement enables you to create a pattern of background images that enhances the presentation of information.

color

Use this property to set the foreground, or element, color. If the element is text, you can set the color of the text with this property. Both inline (such as a) and included block elements (such as p) use this property.

Values

This sets the color using color names or RGB values. See the "Colors" section earlier in this appendix.

Notes

You can set this property using one of the three RGB systems or by using a color keyword. Although most browsers should recognize the color keyword, individual browser/system configurations may display the same color differently.

POSITIONING

Using positioning, one of the first CSS2 features to be supported by browsers, you can add properties to style rules to control the positioning of the element. For example, you can identify specific locations for elements, as well as specify locations that are relative to other elements. You can use other box properties to control the layout as well, in conjunction with the positioning features. Furthermore, these features, used with scripting features, enable you to create dynamic HTML or XHTML documents.

bottom

Use this property to specify how far a box's bottom content edge is offset above the bottom of the box's containing block.

Values

The value auto specifies automatic offset, based on related settings.

Length   Specifies offset as a distance from the edge of the containing element. See the "Lengths" section earlier in this appendix.

Percentage   Specifies offset as a percentage of the containing element's size (vertical or horizontal, as appropriate).

clear

Use this property to indicate which sides of an element's box(es) may not be adjacent to an earlier floating box.

Values

Here are the values you can use with the `clear` property:

Value	Effect
left	Specifies that the element start below any left-floating elements above the current element.
right	Specifies that the element start below any right-floating elements above the current element.
both	Specifies that the element start below all floating boxes of earlier elements.
none	Specifies no constraints on element placement.

clip

A clipping region defines which portion of an element's rendered content is visible. By default, the clipping region has the same size and shape as the element's box(es). However, the clipping region may be modified by the `clip` property.

Values

Specifies `rect` (for rectangle, which is the only valid shape in CSS2). Use code `rect (top, right, bottom, left)` with each value specifying the length offset from the respective sides of the box. Substitute an absolute or relative length or `auto` for each of `top`, `right`, `bottom`, and `left`. The keyword `auto` specifies that the clipping region has the same size and location as the element's box(es).

float

Use this property to specify that a box may shift to the left or right on the current line. The HTML and XHTML `img` elements with `clear` and `align` attributes are similar to `float`.

Values

Here are the values you can use with the float property:

Value	Effect
left	Specifies a box that is floated to the left with other content flowing around the right.
right	Specifies a box that is floated to the right with other content flowing around the left.
none	Specifies that the box does not float.

left

Use this property to specify how far a box's left content edge is offset to the right of the left edge of the box's containing block.

Values

The value auto specifies automatic offset, based on related settings.

Length   Specifies offset as a distance from the edge of the containing element. See the "Lengths" section earlier in this appendix.

Percentage   Specifies offset as a percentage of the containing element's size (vertical or horizontal, as appropriate).

overflow

Use this property to specify what happens to the extra content when a box is too small for the content it includes. In that case, the box is often called "clipped."

Values

Here are the values you can use with the overflow property:

Value	Effect
auto	Specifies that a scrolling mechanism is to be provided when necessary, but not always.
hidden	Specifies that content is clipped and that users should be unable to access the hidden region.

Value	Effect
scroll	Specifies that the content is clipped and that scroll bars (if applicable) should always be shown to allow access to the content.
visible	Specifies that content not be clipped to box boundaries.

position

Use this property to control the positioning of elements.

Values

Here are the values you can use with the position property:

Value	Effect
absolute	Specifies the element position and, optionally, size with respect to the containing element.
fixed	Specifies the element position and, optionally, size as with the absolute value, but with respect to a specific reference point (in the browser window or on a printed sheet, for example).
relative	Specifies that the position be calculated relative to the position in the normal flow, with no effect on other elements. Relatively positioned elements can overlap.
static	Specifies that the element belongs to the normal document flow with no specific positioning requirements.

right

Use this property to specify how far a box's right content edge is offset to the left of the right edge of the box's containing block.

Values

The value auto specifies automatic offset, based on related settings.

Length   Specifies offset as a distance from the edge of the containing element. See the "Lengths" section earlier in this appendix.

Percentage   Specifies offset as a percentage of the containing element's size (vertical or horizontal, as appropriate).

top

Use this property to specify the vertical offset for an element in relation to the containing block.

Values

The value auto specifies automatic offset, based on related settings.

Length   Specifies offset as a distance from the edge of the containing element. See the "Lengths" section earlier in this appendix.

Percentage   Specifies offset as a percentage of the containing element's size (vertical or horizontal, as appropriate).

visibility

Use the visibility property to specify whether the boxes generated by an element are rendered. Invisible boxes still affect layout; set the display property to none to suppress box generation altogether.

Values

Here are the values you can use with the visibility property:

Value	Effect
collapse	Specifies a collapsed (hidden) display for table rows and columns, or the same as hidden for other elements.
hidden	Specifies that the box is invisible but present for layout purposes.
visible	Specifies that the box is visible.

z-index

Using CSS2, you can *layer* box elements. Each box element has a position in three dimensions, including the normal horizontal and vertical positions and a depth dimension, which is described on a z-axis. Each box belongs to one *stacking context* and has a number that indicates its position relative to other elements in the stack—the higher the number, the closer to the top (revealed) portion of the stack.

Use this property to specify the stack level of the box in the current stacking context. This property also specifies implicitly that new context is started.

Values

A numeric value specifies the stack level of the current element using an integer. The keyword auto specifies that the stack level is the same as the parent.

PRINTED MEDIA STYLE SHEETS

Your users will view many of your documents online and scroll up or down to access page content. In some cases, however, your users might print your documents rather than read them online. You can use printed (or paged) media style sheets to set up documents to accommodate printing needs. These CSS2 properties let you set values for the page box, which you can think of as the area of your printout. For example, in hard copy, your page box might be the 8.5 × 11 piece of paper; the page box is the content, margins, and edges. Remember that these are available only to users with CSS2-compliant browsers.

@page

Use this special element to specify the dimensions, orientation, and margins of a page box. Use @page, which selects a page. For example:

```
@page {size: 8.5in 11in}
```

sets a standard North American paper size.

You also can use optional pseudoclasses, :first, :left, and :right, to specify styles for the first, left, and right pages of a document, respectively. For example:

```
@page :first {margin-top: 2em}
```

You also can use the names of specific pages and any properties and declarations you want. For example:

```
@page squirrel {margin-bottom: 1in}
```

margin

Use this property to set up all the margins for a page. This shorthand measurement specifies the distance between the page box and the edge of the media.

Values

margin takes the following values:

Length   This sets the border width using an absolute or a relative measurement. See the "Lengths" section earlier in this appendix.

Percentage   This sets the margin size as a percentage of the page width.

Browser Default   The value auto sets the margin to the browser's default on all four sides.

For length and percentage, you can use one, two, three, or four numbers. If you use one number, the browser applies it to all four margins (top, right, bottom, and left). If you use two numbers, the first number sets the top and bottom margins, and the second number sets the left and right margins. If you use three numbers, you're setting the top margin with the first, the right and left margins with the second, and the bottom margin with the third. You can mix length and percentage values.

margin-bottom

Use this property to set only the bottom margin of a page box. The bottom margin is the distance between the bottom border and the bottom edge of the box. This generally defaults to zero and is not used by included block or inline elements.

Values

margin-bottom takes the following values:

Length   This sets an absolute or relative distance between the border and the box's bottom edge. See the "Lengths" section earlier in this appendix.

Percentage   This sets the bottom margin size as a percentage of the parent element's width.

Browser Default   The value auto sets the bottom margin to the browser's default.

margin-left

Use this property to set only the left margin of a page box. The left margin is the distance between the border and the left edge of the box.

Values

margin-left takes the following values:

Length   This sets an absolute or relative distance between the border and the box's left edge. See the "Lengths" section earlier in this appendix.

Percentage   This sets the left margin size as a percentage of the parent element's width.

Browser Default   The value auto sets the left margin to the browser's default.

margin-right

Use this property to set only the right margin of a page. The right margin is the distance between the border and the right edge of the page. You can use this to force the element away from the right edge of the page.

Values

margin-right accepts the following values:

Length   This sets an absolute or relative distance between the border and the box's right edge. See the "Lengths" section earlier in this appendix.

Percentage   This sets the right margin size as a percentage of the parent element's width.

Browser Default   The value auto sets the right margin to the browser's default.

margin-top

Use this property to set only the top margin of a page box. The top margin is the distance between the page and the top of the physical page.

Values

margin-top accepts the following values:

Length   This sets an absolute or relative distance between the border and the box's top edge. See the "Lengths" section earlier in this appendix.

Percentage This sets the top margin size as a percentage of the parent element's width.

Browser default The value auto sets the top margin to the browser's default.

marks

You use this property to specify whether crop or cross marks should be printed outside the page box (if the output device can do so) to help with alignment of physical media for binding.

Values

The value crop specifies to print crop marks. The value cross specifies to print cross marks. The default value is none.

orphans

Use this property to specify the minimum number of lines of a paragraph that must be left at the bottom of a page. By using the orphans property, you can avoid a single line dangling at the bottom of a page.

Values

orphans accepts an integer that sets the minimum number of lines of a paragraph that must appear at the bottom of a page.

page

Using the page property, you can specify the specific page on which an element should appear.

Values

The value specifies the name or identification of a page.

page-break-after

Use this property to control page breaks after elements.

Values

Here are the values you can use with the `page-break-after` property:

Value	Effect
always	Specifies a page break after the element.
auto	Specifies default action for page breaks (this is the default value).
avoid	Specifies no page break after the element.
left	Specifies a page break after the element to make sure the element starts on a left-side page.
right	Specifies a page break after the element to make sure the element starts on a right-side page.

page-break-before

Use this property to control page breaks before elements.

Values

Value	Effect
always	Specifies a page break before the element.
auto	Specifies default action for page breaks (this is the default value).
avoid	Specifies no page break before the element.
left	Specifies a page break before the element to make sure the element starts on a left-side page.
right	Specifies a page break before the element to make sure the element starts on a right-side page.

page-break-inside

Use this property to control page breaks within elements.

Values

The (default) value `auto` specifies a default action for page breaks. The value `avoid` specifies no page break within the element.

size

Use this property to specify the size of the page box.

Values

Use a keyword value or a number. Numeric values specify the dimensions (horizontal and vertical) of the box, using an absolute or (in the case of pixels) a relative measurement. This type of sizing forces a particular measurement to be used for the element, ignoring any browser settings. Specify the measurement after the number as in for inches, mm for millimeters, cm for centimeters, pt for points, px for pixels, or pc for picas. If you provide one measurement, the box will be square. If you provide two, you specify the width and length of the box.

Possible keyword values are as follows:

Value	Effect
auto	Specifies that the page box be set to the size and orientation of the target sheet. This is the default.
landscape	Specifies that the long sides of the page box are horizontal.
portrait	Specifies that the long sides of the page box are vertical.

If you use auto, you can follow it with landscape or portrait to override the default orientation while maintain the auto setting for size.

widows

Use this property to set the minimum number of lines of a paragraph that must appear at the top of a page. Similar to the orphans property, widows will prevent a single line dangling at the top of a new page.

Values

The widows property takes an integer that sets the minimum number of lines of a paragraph that must appear at the top of a page.

INDEX

Note to the reader: Throughout this index **boldfaced** page numbers indicate primary discussions of a topic. *Italicized* page numbers indicate illustrations.

H

ABOUT THE CONTRIBUTORS

Some of the best—and best-selling—Sybex authors have contributed chapters from their books to *HTML Complete*, Third Edition.

Martin C. Brown has written books on Perl, as well as books on Python programming, the iMac, and the BeOS operating system. He has more than 15 years of multi-platform programming experience in Perl, C/C++, Java, JavaScript, VBScript, and others. He writes regular columns for Linux-Programming.com and ApacheToday.com and helped start one of the U.K.'s largest ISPs.

Linda Burman is Vice President of Kinecta Corporation. A respected XML industry consultant and analyst, she chairs the PRISM Working Group, teaches XML at the University of Toronto, and helps companies develop their XML strategies.

James Jaworski is an independent consultant specializing in JavaScript, Java, and information security. He has written nine books on these topics. He also writes the security column for O'Reilly's OnJava website and the Superscripter column for CNET's Builder.com website.

Liam Quin is an XML, open source, and digital typography consultant in Toronto. *Mastering XML Premium Edition* is Liam's third book on XML. He has been using SGML since 1987 and was involved in the original development of XML.

Deborah S. Ray and **Eric J. Ray**, authors of many books on web-related topics, are recipients of several awards from the Society for Technical Communication, including an International Distinguished Technical Communication award. Deborah publishes TECHWR-L (www.techwr-1.com), a high-profile, high-traffic website for technical writers. Eric is a technical writer for Sun Microsystems.

Ethan Watrall is the author of *Dreamweaver 4/Fireworks 4 Visual Jump-Start* and *Flash MX Savvy*, both from Sybex. He is an adjunct instructor in the department of Visual Communications at Ivy Tech State College in Columbus, IN, where he teaches several web design classes. He is also a trained archaeologist, working on his Ph.D. at Indiana University.

Chuck White is a communications professional who has done extensive work for numerous Fortune 500 companies. He is president and chief executive officer of the Tumeric Partnership, an integrated marketing communications company, and author of several Web development books.

MASTERING™ JAVASCRIPT® PREMIUM EDITION™

JAMES JAWORSKI
ISBN: 0-7821-2819-X   1,136 pages   US $49.99

JavaScript is the most widely used scripting language for the Web and continues to grow in popularity. With this Premium Edition of *Mastering JavaScript* and its companion CD, savvy HTML users can learn to write JavaScript programs that will make their websites come alive! This is the most comprehensive tutorial and reference available, with information on both Netscape and Microsoft's enhancements of JavaScript. The book starts with advanced topics, such as scripting ActiveX components, working with plug-ins, building a multimedia application, and interfacing with CGI programs. The author is a well-known Internet programming expert and writes C/net's JavaScript column, SuperScripter.

MASTERING™ XML PREMIUM EDITION

CHUCK WHITE, LIAM QUIN, AND LINDA BURMAN
ISBN: 0-7821-2847-5   1,200 pages   US $49.99

Perhaps no other web standard is having as great an impact as XML. The reason? XML is all about structuring data so that you can use it the way you need—getting it into and out of databases and displaying it on any browser, including wireless devices. *Mastering XML Premium Edition* gives you everything you need to leverage the power of XML: structure data for seamless multi-platform processing, create links that point to multiple documents, and dynamically incorporate data in the linking page. You will also learn about the evolving standards, new vocabularies for vertical markets, and the way XML is being used in real enterprises.

XML PROCESSING WITH PERL™, PYTHON, AND PHP

MARTIN C. BROWN
ISBN: 0-7821-4021-1   448 pages   US $49.99

As programmers look for ways to build applications that work across the Web, XML is the leading standard for enabling business-to-business e-commerce, as well as any application that needs to communicate across different platforms. This book focuses on the usage of XML with the most popular scripting languages, including Perl, Python, PHP, Ruby, Rebol, TCL, and MacOS X's AppleScript. It provides complete coverage of the core XML processing issues, including the basics of parsing XML documents, converting XML to and from different formats (including HTML), and translating objects for use with databases. Martin Brown goes beyond the basics into advanced topics, such as using the SAX API for Perl, and using SOAP and XML-RPC to share XML formatted information over a network connection.

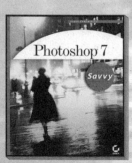

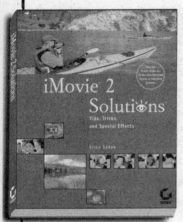